Chapter 8: *Comparing Two Repeated Group Means:* The Paired Samples t Test		
Statistical Concept	**Plain English Description**	
Paired samples t test statistic (t)	Mean of the difference scores divided by the standard error of the difference scores	$t = \frac{\text{Mean of the difference scores}}{\text{Standard error of the difference scores}}$
Standard error of the difference scores	Standard deviation of the difference scores divided by the square root of the sample size	$S_D = \frac{\text{Standard deviation of the difference scores}}{\text{Square root of the sample size}}$
Degrees of freedom (dfs)	Total sample size – 1	Degrees of freedom = Sample size – 1
Effect size (Cohen's d)	Mean difference score divided by the standard deviation of the difference scores	$d = \frac{\text{Mean difference score}}{\text{Standard deviation of the difference scores}}$
Confidence interval	Mean difference, ± the critical value multiplied by the standard error of the difference scores	95% CI = Mean difference ± critical value for t × (standard error of the difference scores)

Chapter 9: Comparing Three or More Group Means: The One-Way Between Subjects Analysis of Variance (ANOVA)		
Statistical Concept	**Plain English Description**	**Mathematical Formula**
Sums of squares	Sum of the squared deviations from the group mean	$\Sigma(x - M)^2$
Total sums of squares	Sum of the squared deviation of each score in the entire dataset from the grand mean in a dataset	$\Sigma(\text{x – grand mean})^2$
Within-groups sums of squares	Sum of the squared deviation of each score within a group from its group mean	$\Sigma(\text{x – group mean})^2$
Between-groups sums of squares	Sum of the squared deviation of each group mean from the grand mean	$\Sigma(\text{group mean – grand mean})^2$
Total degrees of freedom	Total sample size minus 1	df_{total} = sample size – 1
Within-groups degrees of freedom	Total sample size minus the number of groups being compared	$df_{within\text{-}groups}$ = sample size – number of groups in the ANOVA
Between-groups sums of squares	Number of groups being compared minus 1	$df_{between}$-groups = number of groups in the ANOVA – 1
Mean Square (MS)	Sums of squares divided by degrees of freedom	$MS = \frac{\text{Sums of squares}(SS)}{df}$
Mean Square within-group	Within-groups sums of squares divided by within-groups degrees of freedom	$SS_{within\text{-}groups}/df_{within\text{-}groups}$
Mean Square between-groups	Between-groups sums of squares divided by between-groups sums of squares	$SS_{between\text{-}groups}/df_{between\text{-}groups}$
F ratio test statistic	Mean Square between-groups divided by mean square within-groups	$MS_{between\text{-}groups}/MS_{within\text{-}groups}$
Effect size (partial eta squared)	Between-groups sums of squares divided by between-groups sums of squares plus within-groups sums of squares	$\eta_p^2 = \frac{SS_{\text{between-groups}}}{SS_{\text{between-groups}} + SS_{\text{within-groups}}}$
Honestly Significant Difference (HSD)	Square root of mean square within-groups divided by the number of participants in each group, all multiplied by a constant (Q)	$\text{HSD} = Q \times \sqrt{\frac{MS_{\text{within groups}}}{\text{number of participants in each group}}}$

Interpreting and Using Statistics in Psychological Research

SAGE was founded in 1965 by Sara Miller McCune to support the dissemination of usable knowledge by publishing innovative and high-quality research and teaching content. Today, we publish over 900 journals, including those of more than 400 learned societies, more than 800 new books per year, and a growing range of library products including archives, data, case studies, reports, and video. SAGE remains majority-owned by our founder, and after Sara's lifetime will become owned by a charitable trust that secures our continued independence.

Los Angeles | London | New Delhi | Singapore | Washington DC | Melbourne

Interpreting and Using Statistics in Psychological Research

Andrew N. Christopher

Los Angeles | London | New Delhi
Singapore | Washington DC | Melbourne

FOR INFORMATION:

SAGE Publications, Inc.
2455 Teller Road
Thousand Oaks, California 91320
E-mail: order@sagepub.com

SAGE Publications Ltd.
1 Oliver's Yard
55 City Road
London EC1Y 1SP
United Kingdom

SAGE Publications India Pvt. Ltd.
B 1/I 1 Mohan Cooperative Industrial Area
Mathura Road, New Delhi 110 044
India

SAGE Publications Asia-Pacific Pte. Ltd.
3 Church Street
#10-04 Samsung Hub
Singapore 049483

Acquisitions Editor: Lara Parra
eLearning Editor: Morgan Shannon
Editorial Assistant: Zachary Valladon
Production Editor: David C. Felts
Copy Editor: Sheree Van Vreede
Typesetter: C&M Digitals (P) Ltd.
Proofreader: Scott Oney
Indexer: Amy Murphy
Cover Designer: Anupama Krishnan
Marketing Manager: Katherine Hepburn

Printed in the United States of America

Library of Congress Cataloging-in-Publication Data

Names: Christopher, Andrew N., author.

Title: Interpreting and using statistics in psychological research / Andrew N. Christopher.

Description: Los Angeles : SAGE Publications, [2017] | Includes bibliographical references and index.

Identifiers: LCCN 2016013368 | ISBN 978-1-5063-0416-8 (pbk. : alk. paper)

Subjects: LCSH: Psychology—Statistical methods. | Psychometrics. | Psychology—Research—Methodology.

Classification: LCC BF39 .C48855 2017 | DDC 150.1/5195—dc23
LC record available at https://lccn.loc.gov/2016013368

This book is printed on acid-free paper.

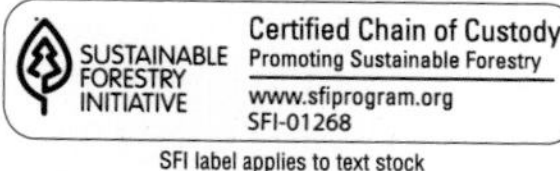

SFI label applies to text stock

16 17 18 19 20 10 9 8 7 6 5 4 3 2 1

Brief Contents

Detailed Contents

Chapter 3 Describing Data With Frequency Distributions and Visual Displays 53

Chapter 4 Making Sense of Data: Measures of Central Tendency and Variability 89

Chapter 5 Determining "High" and "Low" Scores: The Normal Curve, *z* Scores, and Probability 125

Chapter 6 Drawing Conclusions From Data: Descriptive Statistics, Inferential Statistics, and Hypothesis Testing 145

Chapter 9 Comparing Three or More Group Means: The One-Way, Between-Subjects Analysis of Variance (ANOVA) 243

Chapter 14 When We Have Exceptions to the Rules: Nonparametric Tests 450

Preface

In almost any class at my college, there is a natural gap between the teacher's enthusiasm for the subject matter and the students' level of enthusiasm for that same material. This makes sense. The teacher has made a career of that subject matter, whereas students are still learning to appreciate it. Perhaps in no class within psychology is this enthusiasm gap wider than it is in statistics classes. This is unfortunate, as statistics are useful not only for interpreting and conducting research but also in navigating many of life's everyday situations. I make no qualms about my love for statistics. They can be, once understood, powerful tools not only in research but also in many life situations more generally. Most of my students come into this class with dread and apprehension about what's to come. Most of these same students leave the class with reactions such as "It wasn't that bad," and some even admit "It was pretty interesting." Indeed, I want all students to see statistics as at least "pretty interesting," and I am hoping this book can help you not only learn statistics but also see the practical value they hold.

GUIDING PHILOSOPHY OF THIS BOOK

Teachers in the social sciences are fortunate to have inherently interesting material to discuss with students. However, the research process used to systematically investigate our subject matter is of lesser interest to many students. I can understand why. To paraphrase from a conversation with a colleague at another college, when learning about various statistics, students get lost in a myriad of symbols, numbers, and formulas, and when they finish calculating a statistic, they often have no idea what it means or how to use it. Indeed, to many students, statistics courses tend to be an evil necessity. Therefore, this book attempts to use the inherently interesting content of the discipline as the basis for teaching the statistical techniques we use to learn about the subject matter. In a sense, this book starts its discussions of statistical tools with what people often find interesting and then discusses the statistical tools needed to discern such information.

This book is written in the same tone as I teach in the classroom. I mention this because there are attempts at humor throughout (notice I said "*attempts* at humor"). Indeed, statistical information does not come naturally to many of us (yes, that does include me, as you'll see in Chapter 1). Anything to add some lightheartedness to a potentially intimidating subject matter, I firmly believe, can only hold your attention. I know when I read books as an undergraduate student, I never appreciated that there was a person on the other end trying to teach me. I hope you will be able to have that appreciation reading this book.

Most psychology and social science majors will not go into research-specific careers. You may or may not pursue this career path. Regardless of your eventual career route, this book allows you to become skilled at using and interpreting statistical information with which you are presented. Being able to competently interpret statistical information is a skill needed in almost any career and is essential to being a liberally educated citizen. For those who do go into research-related careers, this book will show you how to conduct and interpret statistical analyses as they are conducted when one engages in research. If you are thinking about a research-oriented career, you will want to gain research experience outside the classroom. Indeed, after reading this book, you will be able to make valuable contributions to a faculty member's research lab with respect to both conceptual understanding of tools and the ability to conduct and interpret the statistical tools presented in this book.

CONTENT ORGANIZATION

Chapter 1 begins with an overview of why learning about statistics is important, not so much in research, but in life more generally. As human beings, we are remarkably efficient at navigating the world around us. However, such efficiency comes with certain drawbacks that are rooted in our difficultly processing quantitative information. In Chapter 1, you will learn about your efficient mind, how it naturally makes inferences about the world, where it can lead you astray, and how competence at interpreting statistical information can help you compensate for the drawbacks that come with being the efficient thinker that you are. In addition, basic statistical concepts that will recur throughout the book will be introduced in this opening chapter.

Chapter 2 through Chapter 5 contain information about *descriptive statistics*. The statistical tools in these chapters form the foundation for understanding large amounts of data, something you will likely need to do at some point in your career. Chapter 2 uses a study on gender differences in aggression to describe basic considerations in defining and measuring variables in research. Chapter 3 uses a study on academic burnout to help us learn how to interpret and construct frequency distributions and visual displays of large sets of data. Chapter 4 begins our discussion of quantitative information. By using the same study as we used in the previous chapter, we will learn about summarizing large sets of data in ways that are easy to understand. We will learn the pros and cons of various statistical tools that serve the purpose of summarizing data. Finally, Chapter 5 will introduce the notion of data distributions and locating individual scores within a large dataset. Each of these chapters will help you develop your ability to use a statistical software package commonly used in psychological and social science research.

Chapter 6 through Chapter 14 contain information about *inferential statistics*. Chapter 6 introduces the notion of inferential statistics and how they are related to descriptive statistics covered in the previous four chapters. Each of the next eight chapters presents one or more inferential statistical tools. Each chapter is divided into two major themes. The first major theme will be *Conceptual Understanding of the Tool*. Within this major theme will be three subthemes. The first is called "The Study." Each chapter opens with a description of a fairly mundane situation. For instance, Chapter 11 opens with a discussion of making pizza for dinner. That situation leads into a description of a research study that is used to begin discussion of a statistical tool. As a study is introduced, basic methodological information is presented in an effort to bridge the gap between research methods and the resulting statistical analyses. The second subtheme is called "The Tool," and it introduces the statistical tool used to answer the research question. The conceptual logic of the statistic and associated formula are presented in detail. As appropriate for a given chapter, information regarding the hypothesis/ses being tested will be provided in this subsection. Finally, the third subtheme is called "Interpreting the Tool," and it presents pertinent portion(s) of the results sections of published articles. Explanations of these results presentations allow you to connect what has been learned in the first two subsections of the chapter to a published research study. You do not have to read entire primary source journal articles to understand the statistical information presented in a given chapter.

The second major theme in each chapter will be *Using Your New Statistical Tool* and will contain two subthemes. The first subtheme will be "Hand-Calculating the Statistical Tool Under Consideration," where there will be guidance on how to do just that. Although not always the case, efforts will be made to use a hand-calculation example that is related to the study that was used to open the chapter. For instance, in Chapter 7, when hand-calculating the independent samples t test, a dependent variable related to but not used in the actual research study will be introduced. Only a limited number of datapoints will be used in hand-calculations to make doing so manageable. After each hand-calculation subsection, there will be opportunities to practice calculating the statistical tool being presented. The second subtheme will be "Statistical Tool Under Consideration and SPSS." Here, you will learn how to set up a spreadsheet using the software program IBM® SPSS® Statistics* for the statistical tool in that chapter. Then, you will read step-by-step instructions of how to do the appropriate statistical analysis in SPSS with screenshots to point out precisely what should be done at each step. Given that SPSS is often how data are analyzed in "real" research (as opposed to computing statistics by hand), this feature will be one that you can refer to in any situation in which you have to analyze data, even after this class is over. Finally, you will learn how to interpret the SPSS output, with call-out bubbles to highlight what the relevant numbers mean on the SPSS printout and how they relate to the statistic under consideration in that chapter.

Chapter 15, the last chapter of the book, does not present new statistical information. Rather, it focuses on published research studies and the role of statistics in those studies. It starts with a flowchart that helps you decide what inferential statistical tool to use, given the research hypothesis presented and type of research design used. You can use your kit of statistical tools to help determine the appropriate analysis(ses) to use in a given situation. There are descriptions of six published research studies that used various statistical tools covered in the earlier chapters. These descriptions will include a research hypothesis and a description of the methodology. For each of these six studies, we will walk through the flowchart and determine which tool(s) should be used to answer the research question given the stated hypothesis and methodology used. After we finish discussing these six studies, you will read about three additional published studies and answer a series of questions after each one. This series of questions, in conjunction with the flowchart provided, will help you determine the appropriate statistical tool(s) to use to analyze the data in each study.

HELPFUL FEATURES

1. Each chapter begins with a series of learning objectives, that is, what you should be able to do after reading and thinking about that chapter. I know as a student I typically never looked at, much less thought about, such learning objectives; however, they are helpful in previewing and organizing what you are about to read. Please read and think about them (i.e., don't do what I did).

2. Each chapter contains technical terminology that is highlighted in marginal definitions. As a general rule, don't simply memorize these definitions but try to think about how they relate to other information in the chapter. Doing so will help you accomplish the learning objectives at the beginning of each chapter.

3. Throughout each of the first 14 chapters are periodic Learning Checks to help assure you're understanding the material up to that point in the chapter. The answers to these questions appear in each Learning Check, so you don't need to flip around the book to locate the answers. Please don't just look at the answers and say "Yeah, I get it." Test yourself because if you don't get the correct answer, that is a signal to go back and reread that section.

4. At the end of each of these chapters are Chapter Application Questions that help you integrate the information in that chapter. This feature is like a massive Learning Check that we just discussed. These end-of-chapter questions provide a good way to make sure you "get it" after reading each chapter. They contain a variety of short-answer and multiple-choice questions.

5. After the Chapter Application Questions are Questions for Class Discussion. Try to answer these questions, as your teacher can use them to help you make sure you understand the material and work with you in case there is any confusion that needs to be ironed out.

* SPSS is a registered trademark of International Business Machines Corporation.

SUGGESTIONS WELCOMED!

If you have any comments or suggestions that could improve this book, I would very much like to hear them. Please feel free to email me at achristopher@albion.edu with any ideas and observations that you have. I look forward to hearing from you. Have a great course!

Acknowledgments

A couple of years ago, I went to a Kansas City Royals baseball game at Kaufman Stadium. A young Royals fan was wearing a shirt that read something to the effect of, "Play for the name on the front of the uniform, not the name on the back of the uniform." That there is only one name on the cover of this book is misleading. Any of the people mentioned here could claim a piece of this work. Indeed, there are many people who played a role of some sort in this product, and I am sorry I cannot detail all of them here.

Working with the people at SAGE has been such a pleasure in all phases of this project. Reid Hester, Morgan Shannon, and Nathan Davidson have each helped throughout this undertaking, from the initial idea through the product we have now. Their efforts to mentor me as a first-time book author have greatly enhanced the quality of this product. Indeed, teaching through writing a book is different than teaching in a classroom, and working with Reid, Morgan, and Nathan has made me a better all-around teacher.

My department colleagues, Barbara Keyes, Jeff Wilson, Mareike Wieth, Holger Elichberger, Tammy Jechura, Eric Hill, Andrea Francis, Schara Swan, and Ben Beirmeier-Hanson, are great sources of support, ideas, and laughs on everything from teaching to research to campus life. I particularly want to thank Barbara not only for hiring me when she was department chair but also for her perpetual support on this project. Her gentle check-ins and encouragement kept me going when I was "hitting the wall." In addition, Mareike has been a great office suitemate over the years, enduring my random thoughts and ideas on almost any topic imaginable. I've lost track of all the situations she's helped me think through during the past 11 years. Finally, Eric has been a constant source of ideas and advice on this project and on teaching research-based classes more generally.

I would not be able to enjoy such a great job and place to work if not for many people who guided me to this point. Most obviously, many thanks and much love to my parents, Margaret and Raymond Christopher. My younger brother, Jim Christopher, deserves thanks for simply putting up with me as his big brother while growing up. Professionally, Dan Hale, my undergraduate mentor, showed me that people really need to make their careers out of something "cool," which for me was psychology. In graduate school, Barry Schlenker and Richard Griggs provided me with the best role models a graduate student could ask for, although I know I did not appreciate their efforts as much as I should have at that time. Since coming to Albion, I've relied not only on Barbara Keyes but also on Emeritus Professor David Hogberg for counsel on what now feels like countless situations. Outside of my department, I have benefitted from excellent mentoring from other campus colleagues, including Lynne Chytillo, Geoffrey Cocks, Lisa Lewis, Bindu Madhok, and Ruth Schmitter.

Of course, without my students, this book and my professional life in general would be of little value. I first want to thank Jordan Troisi, Ori Shewach, Ryan Walker, Laura Wendt, and Kevin Zabel, each of whom provided me with valuable ideas and feedback on this project before I wrote a single word of it. These five former students continued to provide perspectives and ideas as the book evolved. Great colleagues bring out the best in those around them, and these five people certainly attest to that fact. Indeed, I have had the pleasure of teaching so many excellent students over the years, and those listed here are only a small sample from this population: Kristen Abraham, Alexis Ahee, Jeremy Benton, Travis Boyd, Casey Dexter, Darcy Crain, Kris Gauthier, Liz Haas, Jess Hauser, Heather Holleman, Jason Jones, Maggie Keller, Zach Kribs, Adam Kudirka, Vicki Kuo, Kendra Malcomnson, Dave Mendrygal, Kim Mutch, David Nelson, Ross O'Hara, Lindsey Peterson, Katie Pickworth, Andrew Rush, Sarah Storbeck, Danielle Wesolowicz, Dan Westerhof, Mark Wojda, Keith Zabel, and Lauren Zabel.

Finally, I want to thank the following reviewers who provided a wealth of helpful suggestions throughout the developmental process. Many of their ideas I have already integrated into my classes.

Melanie S. Anderson, Argosy University–Phoenix
Steve Bounds, Arkansas State University
Lillian Campbell, Humber College Institute of Technology
Mary Jo Carnot, Chadron State College
Linda R. Cote, Marymount University
Andy Dattel, Embry-Riddle Aeronautical University
Catherine Diaz-Asper, Marymont University
Jimmeka Guillory, Spelman College
Karl N. Kelley, North Central College
Larry Maucieri, Governors State University
Courtney McManus, Colby-Sawyer College
Robert Sheehan, Costal Carolina University
Royce Simpson, Spring Hill College
Jeanette Stein, University of Michigan–Flint
Patricia Tomich, Kent State University–Trumbell Region

About the Author

Andrew (Drew) N. Christopher grew up in Plano, Texas. He received his undergraduate degree from Stetson University in 1992 with a major in economics and finance and a minor in psychology. He holds an MBA from Southern Methodist University and his Ph.D. from the University of Florida. Drew has taught at Albion College since 2001. In addition to teaching courses in research design and analysis, he also teaches "Introductory Psychology," "Industrial/Organizational Psychology," "Senior Research Seminar," and an honor's college course called "Black Swans and Everyday Life," and is developing a new first-year seminar titled "Football and American Society." He has published more than 30 peer-reviewed papers with 28 undergraduate authors since arriving at Albion. Many more undergraduate collaborators have presented their work at venues such as the International Society for the Scientific Study of Individual Differences (ISSID), Association for Psychological Science (APS), Michigan Undergraduate Psychology Research Conference (MUPRC), and Albion College's Elkin Isaac Research Symposium. Drew has twice been named Albion College's Phi Beta Kappa Scholar of the Year. In recognition of his work with students, he was awarded the Robert S. Daniel Excellence in Teaching Award at a 4-year college or university in 2013 and named his College's Teacher of the Year in 2014. He has been editor-in-chief of the Society for the Teaching of Psychology's journal, *Teaching of Psychology*, since 2009.

Away from academic responsibilities, Drew works out regularly, not because he enjoys doing so (in fact, he hates it) but because it allows him to eat foods that he probably otherwise should not eat so much of. Toward that end, he enjoys cooking and is particularly adept at making various types of pizza and a wide range of unhealthy desserts. Any leftovers from his creations are gladly consumed by his two beagles, Sybil and Hans. Drew enjoys almost all sports, particularly college football and professional hockey. As a University of Florida graduate, Drew maintains his loyalty to the Southeastern Conference despite living in Big Ten territory. As a Tampa Bay Lightning fan living in south central Michigan, he is a regular recipient of dirty looks from Detroit Red Wings and Chicago Blackhawks fans who populate the area.

CHAPTER 1

Why Do I Have to Learn Statistics?

The Value of Statistical Thinking in Life

After reading this chapter, you will be able to

- Identify reasons why people tend to ignore information about probability in everyday life
- Identify reasons why people tend to misunderstand connections between events in everyday life
- Differentiate research methods for each of the four goals of research
- Differentiate basic concepts in statistical thinking

> "Statistical thinking will one day be as necessary a qualification for efficient citizenship as the ability to read and write."
>
> —H. G. Wells

When I was in high school and college, I took a math-based class (e.g., algebra, geometry, statistics, and calculus) every semester. I did fairly well in these classes because I worked hard and usually earned decent grades, never spectacular but not bad either. Playing around with numbers was a fun intellectual exercise for me back then. During that same time, I took writing-based classes (e.g., composition, creative writing, business communications, and literature). At the risk of being arrogant, I usually earned solid "A"s in those classes (and even some "A+"s because we could get those at my high school). Candidly, I did not work nearly as hard in my writing classes as I did in my math classes. I was by no means a gifted writer, but thanks in large part to my parents, I always understood the importance of writing and communication abilities even when I was in middle school. Indeed, how can good writing and other communication skills do anything but help a person in a job or many other life situations, such as developing personal relationships? I took more writing classes than my high school and college required just because they were so much fun and easy for me. Math classes? Not so much. Until I was in graduate school, I never saw the relevance of math classes outside of the classroom. Then, in my third

"Now, keep in mind that these numbers are only as accurate as the fictitious data, ludicrous assumptions and wishful thinking they're based upon!"

Photo 1.1 Statistical information is everywhere. Understanding it is essential for success not just in school, but also in life more generally.

Source: ©Bradford Veley/CartoonStock

graduate-level statistics class (yes, you read that correctly, my *third graduate-level statistics class*), something clicked. Even now, 19 years later, I don't know what it was that clicked. But something clicked, and I began understanding the relevance of the numbers I was using. When I began to see the logic of each statistic that I was calculating, all I wanted to do was learn more about statistics. And as I did so, I understood the logic of statistics, even fairly high-level statistics, more quickly and became much better able to use such logic not only in research but in "real-life" situations as well.

Maybe I was not very smart in high school or college, but I look back at that time and cannot understand what took me so long to see the logic behind statistics. When I started teaching statistics more than 15 years ago, I swore that my students would leave the class understanding the logic of statistics. Some have gone on and used statistics in research careers; most have not. Those who are not using technical statistics in their work are still dealing with situations that require the same logical thinking that statistics requires. If you are interested in doing research or are already enthusiastic about dealing with quantitative information, you probably don't need to be sold on the idea that statistics will be important to you. However, before we dive into specific statistical information, I want to take some time to discuss the general importance of statistics, both to researchers and to alike. For those of you taking this class solely because you have to take it, I hope it will give you some idea of why you are here and the benefits you should expect to gain while you are here. It is my hope that by the time you complete this class, you will understand the importance of statistics in making sense of research, in addition to using the logic of statistical thinking in more everyday situations.

In the first part of this chapter, we will discuss why a lot of people are not good at using statistical logic in their daily lives. I do not want you to be like a lot of people in this regard as it can be costly in many ways. We will highlight the reasons most people are not good at dealing with statistical information in daily life and, in doing so, detail some of these everyday situations, describing how statistical logic is (or should be) used in each one. The second section will discuss some basic goals of research and the role that statistics play in achieving each of these goals. Finally, we will introduce some basic statistical information we will see throughout this course and, in doing so, highlight how such information can improve our ability to think about the world.

STATISTICAL THINKING AND EVERYDAY LIFE

We easily can get our hands on information via the Internet for any situation we may be in. However, we need to know how to interpret and make use of such information, especially as not all of it is objective or even correct. The world is full of statistical information, much of it we hardly ever notice or pay much attention to (until now). In addition to potential value in the workplace, learning about statistics and the logic behind them will help you navigate everyday situations you will encounter, some of which we'll discuss in this section.

Before we begin this section in detail, let me say that, in general, the human mind works magnificently well. We rarely notice how well it works until something goes wrong. I say this because as you read this section of the chapter, you might think people are generally stupid, but that is just not the case. But here, I want to draw your attention to some flaws in our ability to process information as they relate to statistical thinking. By learning about statistics in subsequent chapters, I hope that you will be able to spot these shortcomings in your thinking and in the thinking of other people.

I have classified these flaws in human thinking loosely into two categories: failing to use information about probability and misunderstanding connections between events. However, in practice, they are more interrelated than I will present them here.

> "What has been very successful for me through my whole life is to not be arrogant about knowing, but to embrace the fact that I have weaknesses, that I don't know a lot about this, that and the other thing. The more you learn, the more you realize you don't know."
>
> —**Ray Dalio,** *Founder and Co-Chief Investment Officer, Bridgewater Associates, the world's largest hedge fund*

Failing to Use Information About Probability

Last night, I put my life in great jeopardy. I did so voluntarily. What did I do, you ask? I carried dirty clothes downstairs and did laundry.

If you are wondering what the risk was, more than 8 million visits to the emergency room each year are due to falls at home, and more than 17,000 people in the United States die each year from such falls and resulting complications (National Safety Council, 2015). Now, I said I put my life in "great jeopardy." Almost anything we do (e.g., walking, exercising, or eating) carries some risk. While walking, we could trip and fall. While exercising, we could dislocate a joint. While eating, we could choke or ingest something poisonous. So, I need to clarify what I meant by "great jeopardy." I am guessing the risks associated with these everyday behaviors have not crossed your mind unless, of course, they have happened to you. However, other risks may well have crossed your mind. Terrorism is in the news a lot. There is a chance you could be a victim of terrorism. However, how great is that risk? The U.S. Department of State (2014) reported that worldwide, 16 Americans died from terrorist-related activity worldwide in 2013. Another 12 Americans were kidnapped and another 7 were injured from terrorism. Compare that total (35 Americans) with the 17,000 Americans who die from falling each year. I have a 485 times greater chance of dying trying to do my laundry than I do of dying in a terrorist attack. Based on these statistics, should we be more concerned about falling at home or about terrorism?

Even with this statistical information, you may not be convinced that terrorism is less of a threat than is falling at home, and that is understandable. We tend to ignore probabilities for a very good reason. We need to make a lot of decisions in our lives. We make decisions all of the time. What class to study for first? Go running or go to yoga (or, in my case, what TV show to watch)? What to eat for a snack? What to wear today? We make many of our decisions using **heuristics**, which are mental shortcuts, based on prior experience, that allow us to make decisions quickly. Let's take a simple example. Suppose you are at the grocery store needing to buy toothpaste;

Photos 1.2a and 1.2b Stairs to the basement. A killer in plain sight?

Source: ©iStockphoto.com/danhowl

you probably would not look in the fresh produce section. Likewise, if you want to buy fresh strawberries, you probably would not look on the baking supplies isle. Did you ever notice those signs above the various isles in the grocery store (and many other types of stores)? Those signs are heuristics in that they give shoppers a general idea of the products contained on that isle. They do not guarantee that the product you are looking for will be there, but in all likelihood (i.e., probability), it will be. We can contrast heuristics with **algorithms**, which are step-by-step procedures that guarantee, eventually, that we will solve a problem correctly. In the grocery store example, you could walk up and down each isle looking for the toothpaste, and eventually, you would indeed find it. However, who wants to spend their time that way? Most people prefer to navigate the world as quickly and efficiently as possible, and heuristics, not algorithms, make that possible.

Heuristic: mental shortcut that allows us to make decisions quickly.

Algorithm: step-by-step procedure that guarantees a correct solution to a problem.

So it is with making many, if not most, of our decisions in life. Last night, I made a decision to go downstairs and do laundry, and no, the risk I was taking never crossed my mind. I bet that the notion of being a victim of terrorism scares people more than being the victim of a fall despite the overwhelming odds of dying from a fall. Let's examine why this is the case.

Availability heuristic

Which of these two headlines do you think will capture people's attention more? First, "Statistics Teacher Dies Carrying Laundry Downstairs." Or second, "Civilian Killed in Terrorist Attack." I am betting more people will read the story that accompanies the second headline. In fact, would the first headline even make the news? I doubt it would. The **availability heuristic** involves estimating the frequency of some event happening, based on how easily we can think of examples of that event (Tversky & Kahneman, 1974). When there is an act of terrorism, it is much more likely to be on the news than when a person dies falling in his or her home. Perhaps the local news would make mention of a person dying in a fall, but even if that is the case, hearing about a terrorist act is more frightening to people and more likely to stick in their minds. Let's discuss one reason we rely on the availability heuristic, and then we'll discuss a couple of applications of it.[1]

At some point, I bet you have had to do a group project. One characteristic of a functional work group is that each member has an assigned role and responsibilities (West, Borrill, & Unsworth, 1998). Even if this task was done in your groups, did you ever get the feeling that as the project moved along, you were doing more than other members of your group? If so, there is a reason why we, at least in Western cultures, tend to think this way. How does the availability heuristic work in this situation? Because we are **egocentric**, we have difficulty seeing the world from other people's perspectives. We are each fully aware of the work we are doing, how challenging that work is, the time we invested in that work, and so on. However, that information about the work other people have done is not so readily available to us; hence, it is why most people in this culture tend to overestimate their individual contribution to a group project.

Availability heuristic: estimating the frequency of some event happening, based on how easily we can think of examples of that event.

Egocentrism: tendency to perceive the world from our individual, unique perspective.

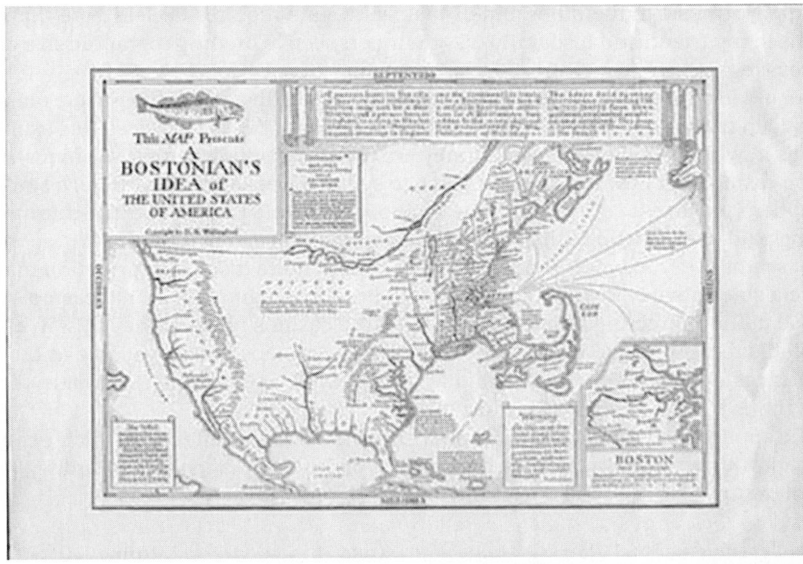

Photo 1.3 An example of egocentrism, Boston style.

Photo 1.4 Winning at the casino seems so easy on TV.

Source: ©iStockphoto.com/DarrenMower

Indeed, egocentrism is an important reason why we rely on the availability heuristic. It takes a lot of time and effort to perceive the world from a perspective other than our own. Take another example. In this culture, we often say, "The run rises in the morning," and "The sun sets in the evening." In reality, the sun does not go anywhere; we on Earth are moving, but we cannot see or feel that motion. Therefore, what is available to us is whether we can see the sun. Thanks to our egocentrism, it appears thesun is moving, but it is not. Although being egocentric is normally not a problem to our daily functioning, it can require some altering of our thinking when presented with information, especially quantitative information that may feel impersonal and that counters our perspectives. For instance, one of my best friends from high school grew up in Massachusetts before moving to Plano, Texas, where we met. A few months after he moved, his family decided to vacation in the Rio Grande Valley in South Texas. They were shocked at how long a drive it would be from Plano (about 9 hours). After all, it was all in the same state. However, states in the northeastern United States are geographically smaller than they are in the southwestern United States. So to get from one end of a state in the Northeast to the other end of that same state requires far less time than it does in Texas. What was available to my friend and his family was their perspective on the geographic size of a "state," which varies greatly across regions of the country.

So now that we understand why we rely on availability, let's see it in action. Advertisers make good use of the availability heuristic in trying to persuade people to buy their products and services. For example, casinos will create commercials in which people who won money are proudly displaying their winnings, saying how much fun they had at the casino, and how it is the best place to spend a weekend, all with huge smiles on their faces.

If someone happens to win a lot of money at the casino, why would they not be in a commercial (which they are perhaps getting paid to do on top of their gambling winnings)? If it is that easy to win money, we should all go the casino, as it seems everybody is a winner there. Of course, there is some information that is missing. That is, those commercials never show the people who lost their money gambling at that casino. And, in fact, most people have to lose money gambling as it is one way that the casinos make money to stay in business! But by only making available to viewers the people who won money, casinos make available in our minds that they exist just to hand us cash. So naturally, why would we not go there and gamble? Of course, the casinos neglect to make available the reality of gambling for most people.

Another specific application of the availability heuristic is the **framing effect**, in which people are persuaded by the way information is presented rather than by the value of the information itself (Hardisty, Johnson, & Weber, 2010). Let's take an example from a food that I tend to eat too much of: potato chips.

Photo 1.5a and 1.5b Are baked chips really better for you?

Let's look at RUFFLES® Original Potato Chips (hereafter, "Original Ruffles") and RUFFLES® Oven Baked Original Potato Chips (hereafter, "Baked Ruffles"), made by Frito-Lay® (Purchase, NY). As you might have guessed, Baked Ruffles are baked. The Original Ruffles are fried. So if one type is called "Baked" Ruffles, why not call the other type "Fried" Ruffles to signify how the chips were made? What image does "fried" make available in your mind? It is likely not one of health food. "Baked," on the other hand, sounds like it might be healthy, so therefore it is included on that package. This is an example of the framing effect. Health-conscious consumers might not buy Original Ruffles because there is no real health value in them. However, by baking the chips instead of frying them, it does reduce the fat content, so this benefit gets advertised on the package. Original Ruffles do not advertise that they were fried on the package because most people perceive fried foods to be unhealthy.

Framing effect: tendency to be persuaded by the way information is presented.

You might be asking at this point whether Baked Ruffles are healthier than Original Ruffles. Let's look at the nutritional information to see whether that is the case.

In looking at the nutritional labels for each type of Ruffles, indeed, the Baked Ruffles have more than 50% less fat than Original Ruffles. However, the Original Ruffles have more potassium than do Baked Ruffles. Examining the protein, vitamin, and mineral contents of each bag, they are both low on all dimensions. When we look at the data regarding nutritional content of both types of Ruffles, we see that in terms of vitamins and minerals, there is no big health advantage to Baked Ruffles (maybe less of a "health disadvantage"), no matter how healthy an image such a label may create in our minds. If I want to eat something healthy, data suggest eating snacks such as peppers, bananas, and apples.

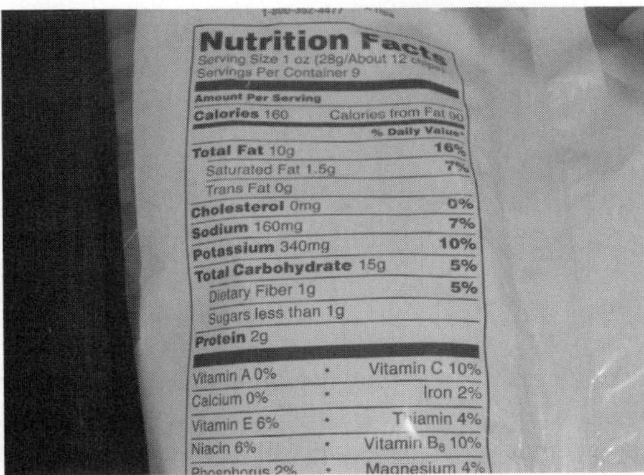

Photo 1.6a and 1.6b Are baked chips really better for you?

Representativeness heuristic

The availability heuristic is one barrier to using statistical information. There is another heuristic we use that also makes it difficult to use statistical information. To start this discussion, let me to tell you about my cousin Adam. When he was a toddler, he lived in a house with two dogs. So when Adam saw any four-legged, furry creature, he called it "doggie." One day when we were at a petting zoo, he saw what I, as a teenager, knew was a horse. But to him, it was a "big doggie." And indeed, dogs and horses do share some outward similarities (e.g., four legs, fur, and a tail). One difference between dogs and horses is that whereas dogs bark, horses neigh.

So when this "big doggie" neighed, Adam looked most perplexed. That sound did not fit in his mental notion of "dog." He was forced to change his mental picture of what a dog was, and in addition, he needed to create a new, distinct mental category for this creature he had encountered called a "horse." In this example, Adam was using the **representativeness heuristic** (Gilovich & Savitsky, 2002). That is, he had created a mental category of "dog" that included all animals with four legs, fur, and a tail.

Representativeness heuristic: judging how likely something or someone is to the typical instance of a mental category that we hold; can lead us to ignore other relevant information.

So what's the problem that representativeness plays in our thinking? Those mental categories had to come from somewhere, and indeed, they are often correct or else we would stop using them. In Adam's situation, the sound that the horse made forced him to redefine his mental category of "dog." This may not be too difficult to

Photo 1.7 They look similar, don't they?

Source: ©iStockphoto.com/GlobalP; ©iStockphoto.com/fotojagodka

do at least in theory. But remember, I want you to be aware of when our thinking goes awry and how such missteps are rooted in statistical thinking.

There are two potentially problematic results of using representativeness that we will discuss. First, the **base-rate fallacy** is the tendency to ignore information that describes (i.e., represents) most people or situations. Rather, we rely on information that fits a mental category we have formed (Bar-Hillel, 1980). To take a simple example, approximately 90% of the students at my college are from Michigan, Indiana, and Ohio. At first-year orientation this fall, I talked with a tall, athletic-looking, suntanned student who had long blond hair and was wearing a Ron Jon Surf Shop® (Cocoa Beach, FL) T-shirt. Where was he from? California? Florida? Perhaps. But without knowing any additional information, you have a 90% chance of being correct (assuming you say "Michigan," "Indiana," or "Ohio"). Even though the description seems to fit someone from California or Florida, those states are sparsely represented in our student body. Thus, there was minimal chance he was from one of those places despite fitting our mental category of "Californian" or "Floridian." Let's explore the base-rate fallacy in a little more detail.

Base-rate fallacy: tendency to prefer information derived from one's experience and ignore information that is representative of most people or situations.

When we started this chapter, I lamented that we as humans often have difficulty thinking statistically. Again, 90% of the student population at my college is from three states. Therefore, the probability of a student being from any of the other 47 states or another country is low. That probability is even lower for any one specific state of those 47. However, in this instance, the only thing I "saw" was that one student I talked with at orientation. He was a sample of the entire student body at my college. The entire study body at my college consists of people primarily from three states. Therefore, even though he fit my mental representation of "Californian" or "Floridian," the odds are that he was from Michigan, Indiana, or Ohio.

One danger, in terms of statistical thinking, of our everyday experiences is that rarely, if ever, do we have all of the information about a given situation (we are egocentric, remember). Much as we can rarely, if ever, be familiar with everyone in a large group of people, we rely on our personal experiences to draw conclusions about the world. An extension of the base-rate fallacy is the **law of small numbers**, which is the second potential problem with using representativeness. The law of small numbers holds that results based on a small number of observations are less likely to be accurate than are results based on a larger number of observations (Asparouhova, Hertzel, & Lemmon, 2009; Taleb, 2004). We assume that our experiences are representative of the larger world around us when, in fact, that is not always the case. For instance, when you toss a coin, there is a 50% chance the coin will land on heads and a 50% chance it will lands on tails. If you flip that coin four times, you would expect it to land on heads twice and on tails twice. That would be 50/50, just the way coin tosses should turn out. However, with only four flips of the coin, weird things might happen. You might flip three tails but only one heads. Or maybe all four flips will be heads. Does this mean the coin is "fixed"? No. Rather, with such a small number of flips (i.e., a small sample), you might get outcomes that are markedly different than what you would expect to find (i.e., all coin flips in history). Flip a coin 20 times. I bet you will not get exactly 10 heads and 10 tails, but overall, it should be closer to 50/50 than 75/25. Now flip the coin 40 times, and again, you are likely to be closer to 50/50 than you were with 20 flips.[2]

Law of small numbers: results based on small amounts of data are likely to be a fluke and not representative of the true state of affairs in the world.

Let's take another, more mundane example of the law of small numbers. You are thinking about where to go for dinner tonight. Your roommate said a friend of hers really liked the local pizza place. Based on this information, you decide to have dinner at the local pizza place. How is this instance an example of the law of small numbers? Let me ask you, how much information did you gather to make your decision? You have a suggestion from one friend of your roommate; that is all. So, with one piece of data, you drew your conclusion of where to eat dinner. Let's hope your food preferences are similar to those of your roommate's friend. Had you read reviews of this restaurant, you would have had more data on which to base your decision of where to eat.

As one real-world example of the law of small numbers, many people are afraid to invest their money in stocks because they think bonds are a safer investment. However, a great deal of research (e.g., Index Fund Advisors, 2014) has demonstrated that over the long term, investing in stocks is the best way to grow one's money. Since 1928, the U.S. stock market's average annual return has been about 9.6%. During that same time span, U.S. government long-term bonds have grown on average by only about 5.4% each year. So, when deciding where to invest our money, clearly it should go into the stock market, right? Maybe. Keep in mind that 1928 was a long, long time ago. Over a long period of time, then yes, the stock market has indeed been the best investment available. However, you know enough about history to know what happened in October 1929, again in October 1987, and in the fall of 2008. There are comparatively small pockets of time during which stocks do poorly, sometimes disastrously so. These time periods are the exceptions, but if it is your money being lost when stocks decline in value, you probably will not take comfort in this knowledge. Therefore, money you need in the near future probably should not be invested too heavily in stocks because during brief (i.e., small) periods of time, the value of stocks can decline, sometimes precipitously. However, money you do not need for a longer period of time probably is better invested in stocks than in bonds.

Now that we have learned some reasons why we tend not to incorporate statistical information into our thinking, let's distinguish among three concepts that we've already implicitly touched on and that are foundational for statistical thinking: a population, a variable, and a sample. These are not complicated distinctions, but they are critical in this course and in being better consumers of statistical information. A **population** is the entire group of people you want to draw conclusions about. In our example of stock market and bond market gains, the population would be every year since 1928. In our example of where to eat on Friday night, the population would be every person who's eaten at that restaurant. All members of a population must have some characteristic in common. In research, such a characteristic is called a **variable.** A variable is a quality that has different values or changes in the population. For instance, qualities such as height, age, personality, happiness, and

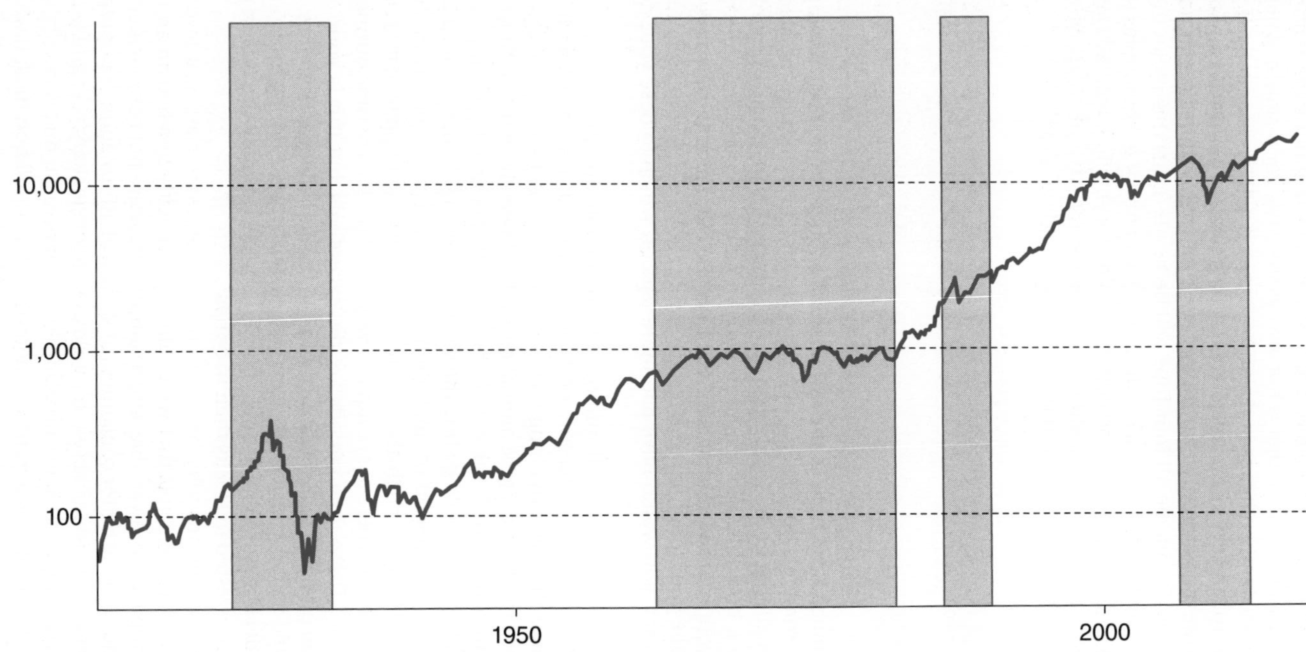

Photo 1.8 Stocks generally rise in value. The highlighted pockets of time note the exceptions to this historical trend.

Source: ©Macrotrends LLC/"Down Jones – 100 Year Historical Chart" intelligence each differ among people; hence, each is a variable. Variables can also be environmental features, such as classroom wall color or investment returns.

For most research studies, and for most situations in life more generally, it is impossible to examine or be familiar with each and every member of the population. Therefore, we make particular observations from the population, and based on that **sample**, we draw conclusions about the population (see Figure 1.1). One year could be a sample of stock market and bond market gains (or depending on the one year in question, losses). Your roommate's friend is the sample in that example. Had you read reviews of the restaurant, doing so would have provided a larger sample of data on which to base your decision on where to eat dinner.

Figure 1.1 Relationship Between and Purposes of a Population and a Sample

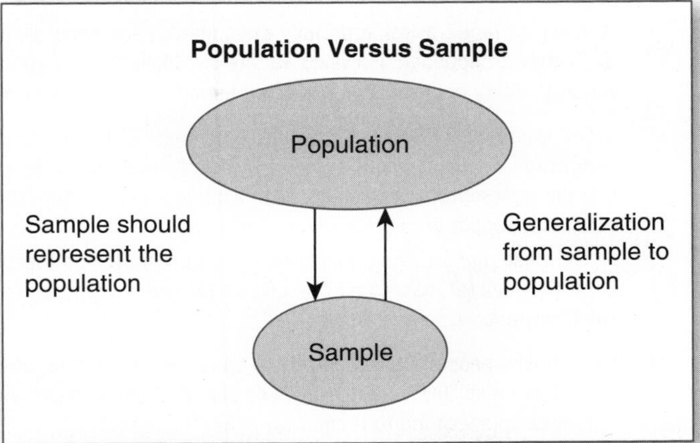

Population: entire group of people you want to draw conclusions about.

Variable: characteristic that has different values or changes among individuals.

Sample: subset of people from the population that is intended to represent the characteristics of the larger population.

Let's return to two other previous examples. Regarding casinos advertising the people who won money gambling at their facilities, the population would be all people who gamble in casinos. The sample would be the winners that are in the advertisements. Based only on this sample, it appears that winning money in casinos is normal (which of course it is not; it is just the opposite, actually). In our example of the base-rate fallacy and the "surfer-looking" student at my college, the population would be all students at my college, 90% of whom are from either Michigan, Ohio, or Indiana. The sample is the one student who looks like he is a surfer, which is something we associate with people from California or Florida more than with people from these other three states. He was one of about 1,500 students in the population. Given his appearance, it would be easy to assume he was from somewhere other than what is indicative of the population he was a member of.[3]

LEARNING CHECK

1. Because algorithms guarantee a correct solution to a problem, why do people tend to prefer heuristics in their thinking?

   A: Heuristics provide us with answers to our problems more quickly than do algorithms. In addition, heuristics are not necessarily going to lead us astray (despite the tone of much of what you're reading). So, we keep using them because they are efficient and sometimes correct.

(Continued)

(Continued)

2. We are far more likely to die in a car accident than in an airplane accident. Yet, people tend to fear flying more than driving. Explain why people fear flying more than driving even though driving is more dangerous.

   A: When a plane crashes, especially a commercial passenger plane, we hear about it on the news perhaps for several days after it happened. However, we are less likely to hear about car accidents on the news. Therefore, because of the availability heuristic, flying is often feared more than is driving even though driving is far more dangerous.

3. Vicks® VapoRub™ (Procter & Gamble, Cincinnati, OH) is medicine you can spread on your chest to help break up congestion. To me, it smells a lot like menthol cough drops. So as a kid when I had a cold, I ate the Vicks VapoRub. Use the representativeness heuristic to explain why I ate the VapoRub instead of spreading it across my chest as the product is supposed to be used.

   A: We make mental categories of things that seem to "go together." Here, both cough drops and VapoRub have a menthol smell (at least to me), so given that one is supposed to eat cough drops, I figured anything with a similar smell is supposed to be eaten as well.

4. Explain why people are more likely to carry their umbrellas when they hear there is a "20% chance of rain" than when there is an "80% chance it will be dry." Both phrases contain the same information, so why is there a difference in how people respond to them?

   A: This is an example of the framing effect. By hearing the word "rain," people think about getting wet. By hearing the word "dry," people do not think about getting wet. Therefore, the image of being wet prompts people to carry their umbrellas.

5. LeBron James, one of the best players in professional basketball, has challenged me to a game of one-on-one basketball. By using information about the law of small numbers, explain how I could maximize the likelihood that I beat James at his sport.

   A: Even the best basketball players will sometimes miss a shot. Even the worst basketball players will sometimes make a shot. Therefore, to maximize my chances of winning, which on the surface seem nonexistent, I would want to play just one shot against LeBron James. This is an application of the law of small numbers. Perhaps he'll miss his shot and I will make mine and, thus, win. The longer the game goes, the more likely I am to lose because he is the better basketball player.

6. Suppose I made you the following offer: You pay me $4, and I will flip a legitimate coin for which you call "heads" or "tails." If you call the flip correctly, I'll pay you $10. If you call it incorrectly, you get nothing. How many times, if any, would you play this game with me? Explain your reasoning.

   A: If you want to make a lot of money, you should play this game as often as possible. On average, you will call the flip correctly 50% of the time. When you do, you win $10. When you don't, you lose $4. Suppose you played this game twice, winning once and losing once. To play twice costs $8 ($4 each time). If you win only once, you walk away with $10, so you made $2. The more you play this game, the more money you will make. However, we know from the law of small numbers that you want to play it more than once or twice because it is possible you could end up losing money with a small number of flips. But over the course of many flips, you will win money.

7. What is the difference between a population and a sample?

   A: The population is larger than the sample. The sample is used to draw conclusions about the population, which is the entire group you want to learn about in a research study.

8. Why is blood pressure a variable?

   A: A variable is a characteristic that differs among members of a population. People have different blood pressure levels, so therefore it is a variable (and one of great interest to medical researchers).

Misunderstanding Connections Between Events

In addition to not using information about probability, we as human beings also have a need to perceive order in the world. Think about being at a party, and you suddenly find yourself around people you do not know. You know almost nothing about them (other than they are at the same party you are), so what do you say to them? You have almost no idea where to begin to strike up a conversation. Maybe you look at their clothes for some hint of what they are like. If someone is wearing a University of Florida T-shirt, you might ask them if they are from the state of Florida and perhaps mention you visited there (assuming that you did). You look for something, anything, to break the uneasiness of that situation. Even for the most socially outgoing among us, it is an awkward situation. So, you start looking to make connections with these people.

Our need to make connections is powerful. The world is much less stressful when it is predictable. Therefore, our minds seek to make connections between events in the world. We will highlight two of these tendencies now. The first tendency concerns perceiving connections that in fact do not exist. The second of these tendencies is a result of the first and concerns the misinterpretation of future events based on prior events.

Figure 1.2 Two Equally Likely Outcomes

Illusory correlations

To start a discussion of the first of these two tendencies, take a look at these two poker hands of cards in Figure 1.2. Which one is a player more likely to be dealt? A hand of 10 through ace, all of the same suit, feels highly unlikely. However, in reality, the odds of getting that hand are no lower than the odds of getting the other, seemingly random, hand of cards. We are wired as human beings to detect patterns in the world, and so it is here. We feel as though the 10 through ace is a more unusual hand than the other hand of cards. Statistically, however, the odds of getting either one are the same. This is an example of an **illusory correlation**. By "illusory," we mean "not real" or an "illusion." By correlation, we mean an "association" or "connection" between two behaviors or events. Much as an optical illusion is seeing something that is not present, an illusory correlation is perceiving a relationship when no relationship exists (Fiedler, 2000). We want the world to be a predictable, orderly place. So our minds impose order and logic even when order and logic do not exist.

Illusory correlation: tendency to perceive a relationship when no relationship really exists.

Let's discuss some additional examples of illusory correlations. In college, I had a roommate, Alex, who was not only a nice guy, but smart, too. Alex worked hard and never took his natural intellectual ability for granted. He did well in all of his classes, and he went on to become an immigration lawyer in South Florida. We were roommates for our entire college careers, and he is still a good friend to this day. I am sure this information does not impress you. But here is what might impress you. Take a guess as to why Alex did so well in college and beyond. His intelligence? His hard work? Those would be reasonable guesses. Ask Alex, however, and he will tell you something different. Let me explain. In our first year of college, we had our first round of tests

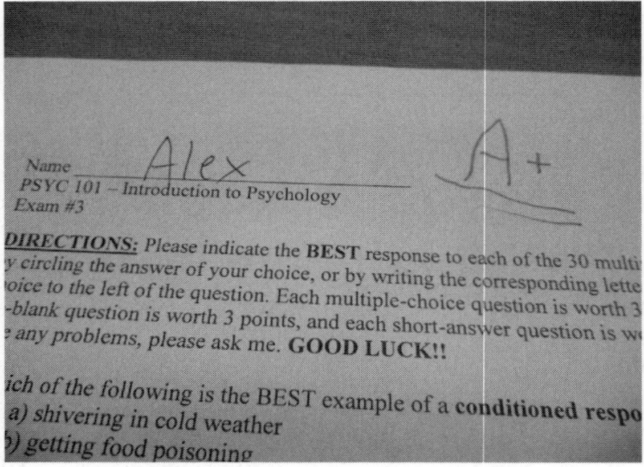

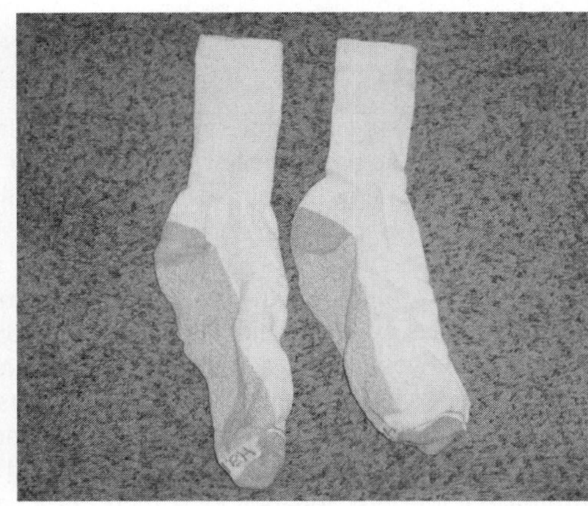

Photo 1.9a and 1.9b Does a "lucky" charm really help us get good grades?

about five weeks into the semester. We both had two or three tests that week. Of course, as would become the norm, Alex did well on these assessments. About five weeks later, we had our second round of tests and papers coming due. Because Alex had done so well on tests and papers earlier in the semester, I asked him for some study tips. Here is what he told me: *He told me that I could not wear his pair of "lucky socks."* They were his lucky socks, and no one else could wear them. He had worn them every day during the week of our first round of tests and papers, and because he did so well, he was going to wear them again when tests and papers came due. Of course, I thought he was joking, but no, it quickly became clear that in his mind, the reason he did well on tests was because of his lucky pair of socks. By believing, albeit erroneously, that his pair of socks aided his performance on his tests, Alex was able to feel as though he had gained some control over his environment. The next time he had a test, he just needed to wear that same pair of socks again, and he would do well.[4]

If you have ever played a sport or been involved in the performing arts, did you ever have some sort of pre-performance routine that you felt you had to follow? Just like my college roommate and his belief that wearing a certain pair of socks contributed to his academic success, some highly accomplished professional athletes have pre-performance routines that they follow. For instance, three-time Ironman champion Chrissie Wellington wrote the Rudyard Kipling poem "If" on her water bottles before each event. Similarly, professional baseball player Justin Verlander reportedly used to eat Taco Bell® (Yum! Brands Inc., Louisville, KY) the night before the games in which he was the starting pitcher. Is there really a relationship between writing a poem on a water bottle and performance in an Ironman event? How about between eating Taco Bell and pitching a baseball? I doubt it; however, for these athletes, they have come to make these connections in their minds.

Illusory correlations arise in part, as we said previously, from our need to detect order in the world. To satisfy this need, we tend to pay attention to instances that confirm this connection and disregard those instances that disconfirm that connection. Did my roommate ever do poorly on a test? Yes, actually, a few times he did. But in his mind, those exceptions had nothing to do with his socks. Did Chrissie Wellington win every race she competed in? No, but in her mind, she likely would have done even worse had she not written that poem on her water bottles. Indeed, once we establish relationships between events in our mind, they are difficult to dislodge.

Gambler's fallacy

Our second obstacle in understanding connections between events is closely related to the illusory correlation. The **gambler's fallacy** is a thinking tendency that involves making a connection between prior outcomes and future outcomes when those outcomes are independent of each other (Nickerson, 2002). Let's discuss some examples of the gambler's fallacy.

Gambler's fallacy: tendency to think that two mutually exclusive outcomes are somehow related.

After graduating from high school in Texas, I went to college in a small town in Florida. At that time, Texas did not have a lottery, but Florida did have one. So, a few weeks after starting college, I decided to buy a lottery ticket for the weekly drawing on Saturday nights. I did so each week during my first year in college. By late April of that school year, I had won nothing. I figured I was overdue to win something, so instead of buying one ticket that week, I bought five tickets. After all, with such a long losing streak, I was bound to win something at some point, right? If you are shaking your head at my logic, good for you. My logic is an example of the gambler's fallacy. That is, I thought that a previous outcome (not winning lottery money) was somehow connected to a future event (likelihood of winning lottery money) when in fact there was no connection between the prior outcome and the future outcome.

To take another example of the gambler's fallacy, consider the game of roulette. The dealer spins the wheel and a ball lands in one of the slots, each of which has a number and color associated with it. Players can bet on what color the ball lands on (red, black, or green), which specific number or set of numbers (e.g., evens or odds) the ball lands on, and so on. I have this game, and I decided to spin the wheel 50 times. Here are the outcomes of those spins. The color of the number represents whether it is a "red" or "black" number (or a "gray" number in a few outcomes). The first column is the first 10 spins, the second column is the second 10 spins, and so on.

8	20	24	34	18
26	2	19	14	0
16	0	21	6	22
26	31	18	23	16
13	3	9	13	21
10	30	15	34	21
24	8	21	5	35
20	33	16	29	26
0	12	21	13	17
20	28	6	34	14

"Red number outcomes appear in blue font"

Look at the first 10 spins. There were 8 black numbers that came up. So, on the 11th spin, it would just seem I was overdue for a red number. But of course, the 11th outcome had nothing to do with the first 10 outcomes, and indeed, the 11th outcome was another black number. The odds of the ball landing on a red number or a black number are the same for the 12th spin as they were for each of the first 11 spins.

You might be thinking at this point that these examples of the gambler's fallacy involve small numbers of observations (e.g., one spin of the roulette wheel). And indeed, you are correct. As we said at the outset of this section of the chapter, these issues in statistical thinking are closely related. With the gambler's fallacy, it is more likely to manifest itself in our thinking when we have only a limited number of observations available. Take a look back at the outcomes of my 50 spins of the roulette wheel. If you take only my first 10 spins, it looks like the wheel

Photo 1.10 A roulette table and a roulette wheel.

Source: ©iStockphoto.com/macrovector

is somehow "fixed" because so many black numbers emerged. But then consider the middle 10 spins; here, we have disproportionately more red numbers emerge. However, on average across the 50 spins, the emergence of red and black numbers is close to 50% each (24 black numbers and 23 red numbers).

Let's consider a nongambling example of the gambler's fallacy. In well-known research, Thomas Gilovich and his colleagues (Gilovich, Vallone, & Tversky, 1985) examined the belief that basketball players have "hot streaks" when shooting the ball. That is, if basketball players have made a few shots consecutively, are they more likely to make their next shot than if they had missed their previous shot? In other words, is there a connection between the prior outcome (i.e., making a previous shot) and a future outcome (i.e., making one's next shot)? Gilovich and his colleagues examined shooting statistics for the Philadelphia 76ers and the Boston Celtics for the 1980–1981 season. For the 76ers, it was found that players were slightly *less likely* to make a shot after making their previous shot (51%) than after missing their previous shot (54%). Furthermore, the odds of making a shot after making the previous three or four shots (50%) were slightly lower than the odds of making a shot after missing the previous three or four shots (57%). For the Celtics, it was found that players are no more likely to make a second free throw attempt after making the previous free throw attempt or missing that first attempt. In fact, the team as a whole made 75% of its second free throw attempts after making the first free throw, and it made 75% of its second free throws after missing the first one. Taken together, these data strongly suggest that there is no "hot hand" in shooting a basketball even though it may feel that way when playing or watching a game.

LEARNING CHECK

1. In college, it sometimes seemed as though the harder I studied for a test, the worse I did on it. Explain how my thinking could be an example of an illusory correlation.

   A: If I study hard, I should do well on tests. If I don't study hard, I should do poorly on tests. Those are normal states of affairs. What I recall, though, are the "weird" instances in which I studied hard but did poorly on a test. Because such instances are rare, they stand out and are easier to recall. Thus, I've made a false (illusory) connection between my study habits and test scores.

2. If a couple has had three children who were all girls, they might assume their fourth child is likely to be a boy. Explain why the couple might think their fourth child is likely to be a boy.

   A: There should be an "evening out" that occurs eventually (or so it feels to this couple). Of course, the sex of their fourth child has nothing to do with the sex of their first three children. This is an example of the gambler's fallacy.

3. Explain why some people have a "lucky charm" that they like to carry with them wherever they go.

   A: People have established a connection in their mind between an object and desirable outcomes that resulted from that object. That's how it became a "lucky charm" to them. For instance, some students have a "lucky pen" that they like to write with. For whatever reason, they have developed an illusory correlation that the pen is associated with good things, so they keep it with them. Likewise, some people may have a "lucky coin" that they keep in their possession at all times, figuring it will bring them good luck (or at least avoid bad luck). Indeed, illusory correlations are pervasive!

GOALS OF RESEARCH

As we have discussed, we as humans tend to have "efficient flaws" in our thinking. They are efficient because they allow us to navigate the world quickly and prevent us from exhausting our cognitive capacities. They are flaws, though, because they allow for mistakes in how we think about the world. When conducting scientific research, we want to do what we can to minimize mistakes. This is where statistics can help. I find it helps students to approach classes in statistics with the mind-set that statistics are tools we need to understand research. Just as we need a screwdriver to tighten a loose screw or scissors to cut paper, we need statistics to understand scientific research. The goal of a research study will guide the type of statistic (or tool) that the researcher needs to use. We now examine four goals of scientific research.

Scientific research in psychology has four overriding goals: (1) to describe, (2) to predict, (3) to explain, and (4) to apply behavioral and cognitive phenomena. The first three goals have different statistical tools associated with them, which we will discuss as we present each goal in turn now.

Goal: To Describe

Descriptive research aims to communicate variables as they exist in the world. To conduct descriptive research, we need to make observations and measurements of the phenomena we want to study. If you want to know the temperature outside, a thermometer located outside can provide this information. The temperature is descriptive information. If we want to describe the health-related behaviors of college students, we can take measurements of how much sleep they get each night, how many times per week they exercise, and their daily fruit and vegetable consumption. We could then describe the health-related behaviors of college students along these dimensions.

How might we go about collecting data to describe the health behaviors of college students? First, we can conduct **observational studies**. By using *naturalistic observation*, we could sit in the student cafeteria and record what students eat. Likewise, we can go to the student recreational facility and see how many students work out there, including the types of exercises that they perform. Naturalistic observation will be more difficult to use to record sleep habits; however, we might use *laboratory observations*, in which we observe behavior in a more controlled setting, such as a research laboratory. In this case, we could have a bed available and record how long students sleep.

In addition to observational research, we can use **case studies** to describe behavior. A case study involves studying one or more people in great depth. We could examine the health behaviors of a small number, perhaps three or four, college students. An advantage of using the case study method over observational studies is that we can go into great detail on the behaviors of this small sample. In addition, case studies are particularly useful when studying rare phenomena, such as certain diseases that occur in only a few people. The disadvantage, though, is that it is extremely time-consuming to conduct a large number of case studies, especially if we want the research to be representative of the college student population.

Finally, **surveys** can be used to describe behavior. In our case, we would ask questions of college students about their health-related behaviors. Surveys can be administered through *questionnaires* via campus mail, over the Internet, or in a research lab setting. Likewise, surveys can be administered as *interviews* either in person or over the phone. Questionnaires are advantageous because the researcher asks respondents to provide the same information. Interviews are advantageous because the researchers can ask follow-up questions depending on a respondent's answers. Surveys are particularly helpful because it is easier to collect more data than with case studies or most observational research. However, researchers must pay close attention to the wording of the questions to make sure respondents are interpreting them correctly. We must also be sure that the sample of survey respondents is representative of the population we want to study. In this case, it might only be the more health-conscious students who complete a survey. If that happens, our sample data will not reflect the population of college students.

Descriptive research: depicts variables as they exist in the world.

Observational studies: consist of watching behaviors in naturalistic and laboratory settings.

Case studies: examine in depth one or more people with a certain characteristic.

Surveys: series of questions to which people respond via a questionnaire or an interview.

Description is typically the first step in conducting predictive and explanatory research. In the next section of this chapter, we will preview what are called descriptive statistics. In Chapters 2 through 5, we will look extensively at these types of statistics. Their overriding purpose is to help researchers describe data from a sample.

Goal: To Predict

Predictive research aims to make forecasts about future events. In the case of the weather, if we know the time of year it is, wind flow patterns, and barometric pressure, we can predict the temperature and likelihood of precipitation. Returning to our health-behaviors research, if we have data on college students' health behaviors, we can use those data to predict outcomes such as grade-point average and satisfaction with college, both of which most colleges are keenly interested in. There are two methods of conducting predictive research. First, using the **correlational method**, researchers measure the extent to which two or more variables are related to each other (i.e., co-related). In our example, if we know how much sleep a college student gets each night, how many times per week he or she exercises, and his or her daily fruit and vegetable consumption, we can predict, to some extent, outcomes such as GPA and satisfaction with college.

We will explore correlational research in more detail in Chapters 12 and 13. For now, understand that there are **positive correlations**, in which increases (or decreases) in the frequency of one behavior tend to be accompanied by increases (or decreases) in the frequency of a second behavior. To illustrate what a positive correlation looks like, consider Figure 1.3, which displays the nature of the

Figure 1.3 What a Positive Correlation Looks Like

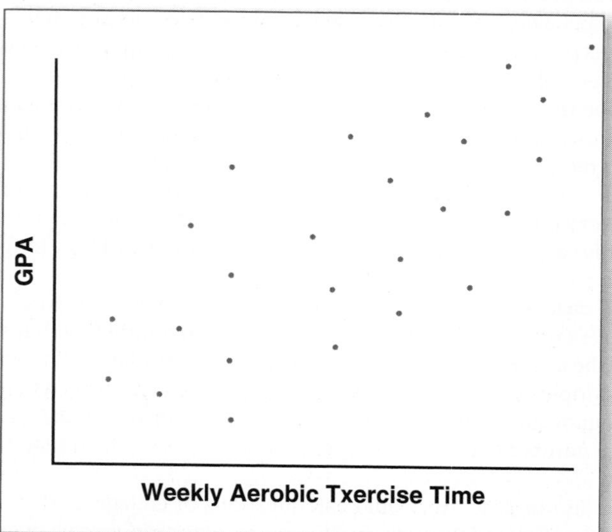

relationship between weekly exercise habits and GPA (Bass, Brown, Laurson, & Coleman, 2013). Each dot on this scatterplot represents one student's weekly aerobic exercise time (x-axis) and the student's corresponding GPA (y-axis). In general, as weekly aerobic exercise time increases, GPA increases. This does not happen for every student, but *in general*, this is the case. Therefore, weekly aerobic exercise and GPA are positively correlated.

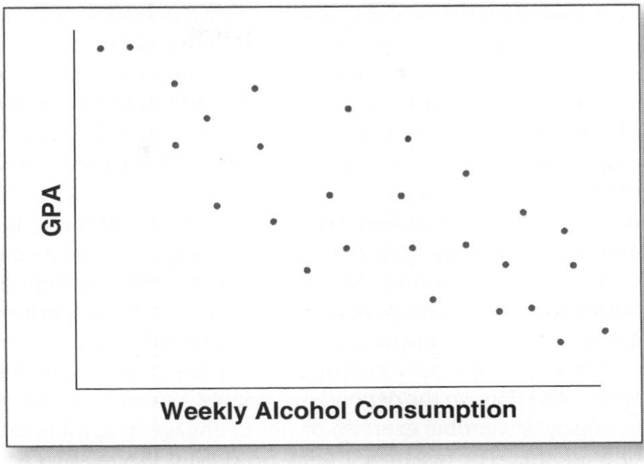

In addition, the second type of correlation is a **negative correlation**, which results when increases in the frequency of one behavior tend to be accompanied by decreases in the frequency of a second behavior. To illustrate what a negative correlation looks like, consider Figure 1.4, which displays the hypothetical relationship between weekly alcohol consumption and GPA. In general, as weekly alcohol consumption increases, GPA decreases (Singleton & Wolfson, 2009).

Figure 1.4 What a Negative Correlation Looks Like

GPA

Weekly Alcohol Consumption

Finally, the third type of correlation is a **zero correlation**. As you might have guessed, a zero correlation exists when there is no pattern between the frequency of one behavior and the frequency of a second behavior. I am aware of no research that suggests any relationship between physical height and frequency of flossing one's teeth. I doubt that taller people floss more often than shorter people (which would have been a positive correlation) or that shorter people floss more often than taller people (which would have been a negative correlation).

In addition to the correlational method, predictive research makes use of **quasi-experiments**. A quasi-experiment compares naturally occurring groups of people. We could compare whether first-years, sophomores, juniors, or seniors have higher GPAs and higher levels of college satisfaction. Here, year-in-school is a *quasi-independent variable* in the sense that people tend to fall into one of these four types of students. Realize, as with correlational methods, we cannot conclude that being a senior causes students to do better or worse in school (or anything else) than being a first-year. However, such data could still be of interest. For instance, suppose we find the somewhat counterintuitive result that first-years earn higher GPAs and are more satisfied with college than are sophomores. College faculty and administrators would likely want to do more research to understand this relationship (and perhaps do something to facilitate the sophomore experience on their campuses).

Prediction is more powerful than description. Although prediction is never perfect (just think about weather forecasts), it does provide insights into the world around us. Chapters 12 and 13 will provide us with tools that allow us to make predictions from our data.

Predictive research: makes forecasts about future events.

Correlational method: examines how and the extent to which two variables are related to each other.

Positive correlation: increases (or decreases) in one variable tend to be accompanied by increases (or decreases) in a second variable. In other words, the two variables tend to relate in the same direction.

Negative correlation: increases in one variable tend to be accompanied by decreases in a second variable. In other words, the two variables tend to relate in the opposite direction.

Zero correlation: no relationship exists between two variables.

Quasi-experiment: compares naturally existing groups, such as socioeconomic groups.

Goal: To Explain

Explanatory research takes descriptive and predictive research one step further; that is, explanatory research (also called *experimental research*) allows researchers to draw cause-and-effect conclusions between phenomena of interest. The researcher uses "control" to establish cause-and-effect conclusions. By "control" in the context of explanatory research, a researcher must manipulate (i.e., control) some aspect of behavior. The behavior that is controlled is called the **independent variable**. In this example, the independent variable is level of aerobic exercise. It is "independent" because the researchers can decide, within ethical boundaries, what to expose participants to in the experiment. It is called "variable" because some participants engaged in aerobic exercise, and others did not. Had all participants engaged in aerobic exercise, there would be nothing that varied. There must be at least two groups created by manipulating (controlling) an independent variable. Without at least two groups, you would have no way to make a comparison on how people's behavior was affected.[5]

Of course, we want to know an outcome of the independent variable. That outcome is called the **dependent variable**. That is, are there differences in academic performance based on whether people engaged in aerobic exercise? Such potential differences "depend" on the independent variable.

You might well be wondering at this point how we can draw cause-and-effect conclusions from the independent variable's effect on the dependent variable. Researchers use **random assignment** of participants in the sample either to engage in aerobic exercise or not to engage in aerobic exercise. Think about the many ways people differ from one another. For instance, I grew up during the relative economic boom years of the 1980s in the North Dallas suburbs, raised by parents from the northeastern United States. Such an upbringing may well differ from yours, likely in more than one way. And that's just a couple of ways we might differ from each other. Not that such differences are unimportant, but in this context, they are not of interest to the researchers. Therefore, we want to control for their influence on how people in the sample behave, so that we can isolate the effect of the independent variable. *Through the process of random assignment, we can minimize the influences of variables (e.g., where people grew up, when people grew up, and socioeconomic status) other than the independent variable. In doing so, any effects we find can be linked to the independent variable.*

Suppose we find that students who engaged in aerobic exercise throughout the semester had higher grades at the end of that semester. By using experimentation, which involves manipulating at least one variable, and by using random assignment of participants to groups created by that manipulation, we can draw cause-and-effect conclusions between behaviors. We will explore statistical tools that are often used with experimental data in Chapters 7 through 11.

Explanatory research: draws cause-and-effect relationships between variables.

Independent variable: variable that a researcher manipulates (changes) to create experimental groups (conditions). It should affect subsequent behavior or mental processes.

Dependent variable: behavior that results from the independent variable.

Random assignment: uses a random process, such as flipping a coin, to put members of a sample in one of the groups (conditions) in an experiment. Its purpose is to minimize preexisting differences among members of the sample so that researchers can be confident of the effects of the independent variable.

Goal: To Apply

Finally, **applied research** does not have specific research methods associated with it. Rather, it makes use of the findings from the methods described previously and uses them in specific contexts. For instance, when you listen to the weather forecast (a prediction) for the next day, you will apply that information by dressing accordingly. Likewise, we already know that the manner in which information is presented influences how people respond to that information (called the framing effect). The makers of Ruffles potato chips were clearly aware of the framing effect when they labeled the cooking method of "baked" on those bags of chips, but they did not label the cooking method of the "fried" chips.

To continue our example of health-related behaviors in college students, many colleges and universities are keenly interested in promoting physical and psychological well-being in their student populations. Like all organizations, these schools face budgetary constraints. Therefore, they want to maximize the desired outcomes (well-being in their student populations) within those financial limitations. To do so, many schools rely on the sorts of research studies we have described in this part of the chapter. For instance, one college wanted to update its aerobic exercise machines. It first conducted a survey of its students and faculty by asking these people to complete a questionnaire. Based on the results of this survey, the college invested a portion of available funds and updated some of the aerobic exercise equipment. Then, after this new equipment was available for use, it conducted naturalistic observation to learn if in fact the equipment was being used as indicated it would be used on the questionnaire. When those naturalistic observations suggested heavy use of the new equipment, the college immediately invested the remaining portion of its funds for this purpose.

Applied research: uses descriptive, predictive, and explanatory research methods to answer specific research questions in specific contexts.

LEARNING CHECK

1. What is the difference between naturalistic and laboratory observations?

   A: Naturalistic observations occur in the normal environment in which a behavior occurs. Laboratory observations occur in a more controlled setting. For instance, if we want to study driving behaviors, we could conduct naturalistic observation by watching and recoding driving behaviors on the interstate. We could conduct laboratory observation by using a driving simulator in a research lab.

2. Case studies are not used as much as other descriptive research methods. Why is this the case?

   A: Case studies tend to be used to study rare phenomena. For instance, much of what we know about the effects of strokes we gained through case studies of people who have actually experienced a stroke. Depending on where precisely in the brain a stroke occurred, a case study allows us to learn what happens when that part of the brain is damaged.

3. Explain the difference between a positive correlation and a negative correlation.

   A: A positive correlation exists when two variables tend to "move in the same direction." A negative correlation exists when two variables tend to "move in opposite directions." For example, there is a positive correlation between the number of hours that students study for tests and their scores on those tests. There is a negative correlation between the amount of alcohol consumed the night before a test and scores on that test.

4. I do a study in which I compare students' political beliefs at the start of their first year of college and again when they graduate from college. Explain why this study is a quasi-experiment.

   A: As year-in-school is a participant variable, I cannot randomly assign people to be first-years or seniors. These are naturally occurring groups to which people belong.

(Continued)

(Continued)

5. How does random assignment allow an experimenter to claim that an independent variable influenced a dependent variable?

   A: Random assignment minimizes preexisting differences between people who are in an experiment. Therefore, with these differences minimized, researchers can isolate the effects of the independent variable on the dependent variable.

6. A college registrar did a research project and found the typical 18- to 22-year-old college student is mentally more alert later in the morning than earlier in the morning. Therefore, her college decides not to schedule any classes before 11 a.m. How is this an example of applied research?

   A: The college is taking a research finding (that students aren't as mentally alert early in the morning) and then using it to implement a policy in a specific situation.

STATISTICAL THINKING: SOME BASIC CONCEPTS

One commonalty in the flaws in our thinking is that they all, to varying extents, rely on our personal experiences to learn about the world. Personal experiences can sometimes be helpful. For instance, when I was three years old, I touched a hot stove burner. I learned right then and there never to do it again. However, just because our experiences may provide us with information, it does not mean that such information is necessarily correct or true of people in general. We use statistics not to learn about any one person but to learn about people (and animals, chemicals, and many other topics of study) in general. Let's discuss, and in some cases, reinforce, some extremely important statistical concepts that will appear throughout this class.

Parameters Versus Statistics

We discussed the notions of population and sample previously in this chapter. We will expand on them here. Recall that a population is the entire group of people we want to learn about, and a sample is a subset of people drawn from that population that is intended to represent the characteristics of its population. In research, the purpose of the sample is to learn about characteristics of the population. As we said, when we say "characteristics of the population," we are talking about variables, which again, are qualities that have different values or change among individuals.

P for Population, **P** for Parameter
S for Sample, **S** for Statistic
A nice heuristic to remember these concepts

As we discussed in this chapter, in most walks of life, we must operate with information about a sample from our personal experiences, and that can be problematic when drawing conclusions about the world. Variables, typically expressed quantitatively, that describe a population are called **parameters**. An example of a parameter would be the odds of dying in a terrorist attack and the odds of dying from a fall at home. However, we rarely, if ever, know and use parameters in our daily thinking. Rather, we rely on samples. This can be a problem when our goal is to be objective. When we want to be objective, we need some help. Therefore, we make use of **statistics**, which are accepted quantitative procedures that allow us to organize, summarize, and interpret information (called data) to draw conclusions about the world (i.e., the population). At this point and throughout the remainder of the book, we want to learn how to interpret and use statistics correctly.

Parameter: number that expresses a value in the population.

Statistic: number that expresses a value in the sample.

Descriptive Statistics Versus Inferential Statistics

There are two different broad categories of statistics, and each one has a specific purpose. With **descriptive statistics**, we are organizing and summarizing a body of information. We will discuss descriptive statistical tools at length in Chapters 2 through 5. Descriptive statistics are useful for learning about the characteristics of our sample. For instance, Pam Mueller and Daniel Oppenheimer (2014) conducted a study to learn whether college students (the population) retain more information when taking notes in class with a computer or with a pen and paper. They sampled college students and measured their performance on test questions based on which note-taking method they used. They calculated certain statistics, such as those we will encounter in the next four chapters, to compare the performance of students using the two different note-taking methods in their sample.

Although descriptive statistics are vital to research, we tend to be more interested in drawing conclusions about a population based on information from our sample. And, again, most always we cannot collect information from everyone in our population, so we rely on our sample to make inferences about the population. In that situation, we use **inferential statistics**. The purpose of inferential statistics is to draw an inference about conditions that exist in a population by studying a sample drawn from the population. We will learn about different inferential statistical tools in Chapters 6 through 14. Mueller and Oppenheimer (2014) were interested in learning about how note-taking was related to academic performance in a population of college students. Not being able to test all college students, they sampled students from Princeton University and UCLA. From this sample, they drew conclusions about college students and the effects of how they take notes on test performance.

Descriptive statistics: quantitative procedures that are used to organize and summarize (describe) information about a sample.

Inferential statistics: quantitative procedures that are used to learn if we can draw conclusions (inferences) about a population based on a sample.

Sampling Error

Of course, samples are not always (and hardly ever are) perfect representations of populations. The extent to which a sample doesn't reflect the population is called **sampling error**. Sampling error occurs when there is a difference between the characteristics of the population and the characteristics of the sample. Let's consider an example of sampling error. Let's again consider Mueller and Oppenheimer's (2014) research. They drew their sample of college students from two schools, Princeton and UCLA. From this sample, they wanted to learn about the population of college students. Let's list some parameters for the population of college students in the United States (National Center for Education Statistics, 2014). These parameters for three variables appear in the top portion of Figure 1.5. How well does the sample that Mueller and Oppenheimer (2014) used map onto the population? The statistics for the same variables appear in the lower portion of Figure 1.5.

Sampling error: discrepancy between characteristics of the population and characteristics of the sample.

As you can see, there are some discrepancies between the population parameters and the sample statistics. For example, the sample did not contain any students from two-year schools. Does such sample error make Mueller and Oppenheimer's (2014) work pointless? Absolutely not. We just need to remember the sample characteristics when drawing conclusions from this research. For instance, it might be a worthwhile idea to conduct this study again using a sample of students from two-year colleges, as no such students were included in this sample.

Figure 1.5 Population Parameter and Sample Statistics in Mueller and Oppenheimer's (2014) Research

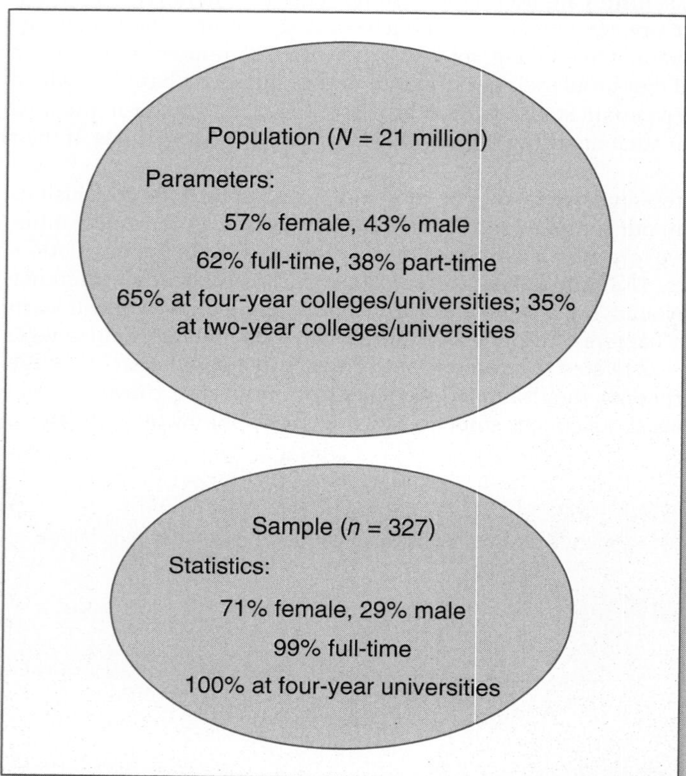

Indeed, learning about the world around us through research is a process that can never be accomplished in a single research study. Indeed, one could argue correctly that the population in this research was in fact college students at four-year universities. Would the results of this research apply to my school, which is a four-year liberal arts college that serves only undergraduate students? Would the results apply to your school? Without conducting the research with a sample of students from my school and a sample of students from your school, we cannot know.

To take another example of sampling error, suppose the average SAT score at your college or university is 1700 (if your college or university required the ACT, suppose that the average ACT score is 22). The population in this instance is students at your school. Now, if you take two samples of 10 students each, do you think each sample will have an average SAT of 1700 (or average ACT of 22)? Probably not; in fact, I bet neither sample will have precisely that average. One sample may have an average SAT of 1684 (20 ACT), and the second sample may have an average SAT of 1733 (23 ACT). The discrepancy is the sampling error.

You may often hear on the news about public opinion surveys that various polling groups (e.g., the *Wall Street Journal* or CNN) conduct on different topics (e.g., feelings about the economy or Congressional approval ratings). To conduct such surveys, the polling agencies do not (and realistically cannot) ask every member of the population for their input. So, they sample the population of interest. As you know, we now have to consider sampling error. That is what is meant when you hear about this "margin of error" the news is (or should be) reporting. If the president has a 54% approval rating, there should be a margin of error reported. That 54% is based on the sample, so there will be some variability around that number in the larger population. A 54% approval rating with a "plus or minus 3% margin of error" means that the presidential approval rating in the population is between 51% and 57%.

LEARNING CHECK

1. Explain the difference between a parameter and a statistic.

   A: A parameter is a population value, whereas a statistic is a sample value.

2. Explain the difference between descriptive statistics and inferential statistics.

A: Descriptive statistics organize and summarize information about a sample. They are the first step toward using inferential statistics, which are procedures used to learn whether we can make conclusions about a population based on data from a sample.

3. Why is it the case that in almost any research study, there will be some degree of sampling error?

   A: Unless everyone in the population is included in the sample, there will be some discrepancy between the population characteristics and the sample characteristics.

NOTES

1. If you've ever suffered a serious fall in your home, you may well fear this event more than a terrorist attack. However, if you are basing this relative fear on your experience and not on statistical information, you are still making use of the availability heuristic.
2. The expression "A broken clock is correct twice each day" is making use of the law of small numbers. At two times out of the 1,440 possible times (60 minutes × 24 hours) each day, the broken clock will tell the correct time. Of course, the other 1,438 times, the clock is incorrect, but if you looked at it those 2 other times, it would appear to be functioning correctly.
3. This student was indeed from Michigan.
4. If you are interested, Alex continued to keep that same pair of socks and wear them every time he had a test as an undergraduate. Again, he isn't a dumb person. It is not a lack of intelligence that makes one susceptible to illusory correlations.
5. The difference between an independent variable and a quasi-independent variable is that an independent variable is controlled by the researcher. A quasi-independent variable is not controlled by the researcher. In our example of a quasi-independent variable, the researchers cannot assign people to be first-years, sophomores, juniors, or seniors. These are naturally occurring groups.

CHAPTER APPLICATION QUESTIONS

1. Holly resisted changing her answer on a test question because she reminded herself that "it's always best to stick with your first answer." Holly's decision best illustrates:

   a) an algorithm.
   b) a heuristic.
   c) egocentrism.
   d) the gambler's fallacy.

2. Reliance on the representativeness heuristic is ***beneficial/helpful*** when it:

   a) simplifies a complex social world.
   b) is selectively applied.
   c) is reserved for ambiguous situations.
   d) minimizes differences within a group of people.

3. The law of small numbers states that:
   a) we are more influenced by information that contradicts our beliefs than by information that supports our beliefs.
   b) we like to categorize people, places, and events to simplify a complex world.
   c) conclusions drawn from a limited number of observations are likely to be a fluke.
   d) we pay conscious attention to a limited amount of information at any given point in time.

4. Which of the following set of outcomes is **MOST** probable?
   a) flipping 6 or more heads in 10 coin flips.
   b) flipping 60 or more heads in 100 coin flips.
   c) flipping 600 or more heads in 1,000 coin flips.
   d) All of the above are equally probable.

5. In an experiment, the behavior being measured as a *result* of the manipulated/changed variable is called the ______ variable.
   a) independent
   b) dependent
   c) spurious
   d) illusory

6. You would probably find **NO correlation** between:
   a) height and weight.
   b) shoe size and scores on an intelligence test.
   c) ACT scores and SAT scores.
   d) distance from the equator and average daily high temperature.

Answers

1. b
2. a
3. c
4. a
5. b
6. b

QUESTIONS FOR CLASS DISCUSSION

1. The use of phrases such as "federal revenue enhancement" when the government announces a "tax increase" is making use of:
   a) the framing effect.
   b) the representativeness heuristic.
   c) illusory correlation.
   d) spurious correlation.

2. The tendency to conclude that a person who is athletic is more likely to be a cross-country runner than a master piano player illustrates use of:

   a) the law of small numbers.
   b) egocentrism.
   c) the availability heuristic.
   d) the representativeness heuristic.

3. Which of the following is **NOT** an example of the gambler's fallacy?

   a) A number will not be drawn in the lottery on a particular day because it was drawn on the two preceding days.
   b) A fifth child in a family will be a boy because the first four children were girls.
   c) Carl is more likely to carry his umbrella to work when there is a "20% chance of rain" than when there is an "80% chance of dry weather."
   d) All of the above are examples of the gambler's fallacy.

4. Drew erroneously believes that his test grades are **NEGATIVELY** correlated with the amount of time he studies for tests. Research on illusory correlation suggests that he is most likely to notice instances in which:

   a) poor grades follow either brief or lengthy study.
   b) either poor grades or good grades follow lengthy study.
   c) good grades follow lengthy study and poor grades follow brief study.
   d) poor grades follow lengthy study and good grades follow brief study.

5. The purpose of random assignment in an experiment is to:

   a) reduce the likelihood that participants within any group know each other.
   b) increase the likelihood that research participants are representative of the population being studied.
   c) reduce the influence of any preexisting differences between people assigned to the conditions of the experiment.
   d) ensure that the independent variable will have a strong influence on the dependent variable.

CHAPTER 2

Basics of Quantitative Research

Variables, Scales of Measurement, and an Introduction to the Statistical Package for the Social Sciences (SPSS)

After reading this chapter, you will be able to

- Identify and differentiate among independent variables, quasi-independent variables, and dependent variables
- Present operational definitions for constructs
- Summarize the notions and forms of reliability and validity
- Classify data into appropriate scales of measurement
- Establish a basic SPSS spreadsheet

As we discussed in the previous chapter, we as humans tend to have what I call "efficient flaws" in our thinking. They are efficient because they allow us to navigate the world quickly and prevent us from exhausting our cognitive capacities. They are flaws, though, because they allow for mistakes in how we think about the world. When conducting scientific research, we want to do what we can to minimize mistakes. Here is where statistics come in. I find it helps to approach classes in statistics with the mind-set that statistics are tools we need to understand research. Just as we need a spoon to eat soup, we need statistics to understand scientific research and to understand the world in as objective a manner as is possible.

In the first section of this chapter, we will summarize a research study that we will use to refresh certain information from Chapter 1 and illustrate new information in this chapter. Then, we will discuss the notion of research variables and begin discussion of how to measure them. The third section will provide more details on the measurement of variables and on how such measurements are related to statistical tools we will encounter throughout this class. In the final section, we will introduce a computer software package that will help us manage and analyze variables when we conduct research. As we will use the software package in later chapters, we will stick to the basics in this chapter so that you are comfortable navigating your way through it in later chapters when we consider various statistical tools.

THE STUDY

We will begin by discussing a research study titled "Gender differences in aggression: The role of status and personality in competitive interactions," which was conducted by Heather Terrell, Eric Hill, and Craig Nagoshi (2008). In this study, there were 150 undergraduate students (78 women and 72 men) at a large southwestern U.S. university. Upon arriving at the research lab, each participant completed measures of his or her personality.

Each participant then answered six questions about his or her hobbies, interests, and accomplishments. These questions are contained in Table 2.1. The researchers told each participant that his or her responses to these six questions would be exchanged with the "other participant," who was located in a room down the hallway. However, there was no other participant. The supposed other participant was a confederate; that is, he or she was part of the experiment and pretended to be a participant in this study. The answers that the real participant received were "staged" to make the supposed other participant appear to be either "high status" or "low status." Recall from Chapter 1 the notion of *random assignment*. Each of the 150 participants was randomly assigned to receive feedback that made the (not real) other participant appear to be "high status" or "low status."

Table 2.1 Questions Used to Establish "Status" in Terrell et al.'s (2008) Research

The responses to establish high status are in all caps; the responses to establish low status are in lower-case.

1. What three words would you use to describe yourself?
   "AMBITIOUS, INDEPENDENT, OUTGOING"
   "Laid back, shy, nice"
2. Do you hold, or have you held, any special positions related to extracurricular activities, i.e., president, treasurer, team captain, etc.?
   "TEAM CAPTAIN FOR INTRAMURAL TENNIS TEAM, I WAS STUDENT BODY PRESIDENT DURING MY SENIOR YEAR IN HIGH SCHOOL"
   "not really"
3. If you work outside of school, do you hold any special positions, i.e., manager, trainer, key-holder, etc.?
   "SHIFT MANAGER"
   "I have a job but no special positions"
4. Please list any honors/awards you have received recently.
   "DEAN'S LIST SCHOLARSHIP FOR LEADERSHIP"
   "none really"
5. Do you consider yourself to be someone who likes to lead, or would you rather stay in the background?
   "DEFINITELY LIKE TO LEAD"
   "I'd rather stay in the background"
6. Do you consider yourself to be someone who likes to have control over your life, or do you just go with the flow?
   "I REALLY LIKE TO BE IN CHARGE"
   "Just go with the flow"

Figure 2.1 Sample Screen Displays in Terrell et al.'s (2008) Research

Sample trial #1:

Target Letter: P

G Y P X

Sample trial #2:

Target Letter: U

J Q C R

After learning the status of the other supposed participant, the real participant was then informed that he or she would be competing with this person on an upcoming task that involved learning and reaction time. Here are the directions that the researchers gave the participant:

> The task (in the experiment) is to find a target letter among four letters on the computer screen. As soon as you press the response key, the screen will change. If there is no response, the screen will change approximately every 2 seconds. If the target letter is in the layout of letters, you will press 1. If the target letter is not in the layout of letters, you will press 2. (Terrell et al., 2008, p. 819)

You can see an example of one of these computer screen displays in Figure 2.1.

After practicing the task for two minutes, participants were informed:

> [F]or the competitive trials, both of you (the actual participant and the supposed participant down the hallway) will be wearing headphones, and you will have the option of administering noise blasts to your competitor in order to distract (him/her). Pressing the space bar produces the noise blasts. These noise blasts are very unpleasant, and will disrupt performance, causing errors in the competitive task. (Terrell et al., 2008, p. 819)

Of course, the real participant was told that the other (bogus) participant could also give noise blasts. Indeed, each real participant received 30 randomly spaced noise blasts while performing the task, which lasted 10 minutes. The real participant could administer noise blasts, too, which again, would impair the performance of his or her supposed high- or low-status competitor. Terrell and her colleagues (2008) wanted to see how aggressive the real participant would be toward his or her supposed competitorbased on the real participant's sex and personality and the competitor's supposed status.

LEARNING CHECK

We will take some of our knowledge from the third section of Chapter 1 and apply it to Terrell et al.'s (2008) research. It may help to keep in mind the title of Terrell et al.'s research, "Gender Differences in Aggression: The Role of Status and Personality in Competitive Interactions," as you answer these questions.

1. What is (are) the independent variable(s) in this study?

   A: Status of the other (nonexistent) participant.

2. What is (are) the quasi-independent variable(s) in this study?

   A: Participant's sex and participant's personality. Remember that people cannot be randomly assigned to have a sex or a particular type of personality. That's why these are quasi-independent variables. The status of the other participant is a "real" independent variable because random assignment was used to determine whether a participant thought he or she was competing with a low- or high-status other participant.

3. What is (are) the dependent variable(s) in this study?

   A: Aggression is the dependent variable. It is the outcome of the status of the other participant, as well as the participant's sex and personality; that is, aggression depends on these factors.

VARIABLES

Let's dissect this research study and introduce some basic statistical considerations that are critical for any research study to consider. First, there are, as you saw in the last Learning Check, several variables in Terrell et al.'s (2008) study. As mentioned briefly in the previous chapter, a variable is a quality that has different values or changes among individuals. For instance, qualities such as height, age, personality, happiness, and intelligence differ among people; hence, each is a variable. Variables can also be environmental features, such as noise level in the room. We all probably have some idea of what is meant by variables such as height and age. However, research in psychology specifically and social sciences more broadly needs to be able to measure variables that are not as readily apparent. In Terrell et al.'s research, they measured personality. What exactly does "personality" mean? I bet we all have an idea of what it means, but those ideas may not be the same for all of us. We need to know precisely what "personality" means in this example. Three aspects of personality were examined: tendency to act aggressively (Buss & Perry, 1992), narcissism (Raskin & Terry, 1988), and venturesomeness (Eysenck, Pearson, Easting, & Allsopp, 1985).

These sorts of "internal" variables, such as personality, are called **constructs**; they cannot be observed directly but instead must be inferred in some way. We know what specific aspects of "personality" Terrell and her colleagues (2008) measured, and I bet you have an idea of what a "tendency to act aggressively," "narcissism," and "venturesomeness" each mean. For instance, when we say someone is a "narcissist," we might think of someone who is self-absorbed and thinks highly of his or her abilities. But this is not good enough in research. We need to know precisely how each one of these aspects of personality was measured.

Constructs: variables that cannot be directly assessed but must be inferred in some way.

Operational Definitions

Researchers must state explicitly not only what variables and constructs they examined, but also precisely how they measured them. An **operational definition** specifies the process used to measure a variable quantitatively in a research study. For instance, in Terrell and colleagues' (2008) research, they measured narcissism using a 40-item survey that was constructed in prior research (Raskin & Terry, 1988). Table 2.2 contains four sample items from this survey. For each item that a person answers "TRUE," he or she gets a point toward his or her total narcissism score. Scores could range from 0 to 40, with higher scores indicating higher levels of narcissism. This is the operational definition of narcissism in Terrell et al.'s (2008) research.

Table 2.2 Example Items That Operationally Defined "Narcissism" in Terrell et al.'s (2008) Research

I think I am a special person.	TRUE	FALSE
I would do almost anything on a dare.	TRUE	FALSE
Everybody likes to hear my stories.	TRUE	FALSE
I want to amount to something in the eyes of the world.	TRUE	FALSE

Each item to which a person answers "TRUE" earns them one point toward their overall narcissism score. Each item to which a person answers "FALSE" earns them nothing toward their overall narcissism score.

To get a score for the variable of "narcissism," we sum the scores for each individual item (1 for TRUE; 0 for FALSE).

Operational definition: specification of precisely how a variable is measured in a research study.

Operational definitions should be perfectly clear in any research study. They allow readers to understand precisely what was done in the study, and they allow other researchers to conduct additional research to build on prior research. Let's take another, potentially more difficult variable to operationalize in Terrell et al.'s (2008) study. Specifically, the variable of aggressive behavior is one that could be operationalized in many ways. When psychologists discuss aggressive behavior, they focus on a person's intention of trying to harm someone else (Baron & Richardson, 1994). Here, *aggressive behavior was operationalized as the numbers of noise blasts that the participant gave an unmet other participant to harm his or her task performance.* How else could aggressive behavior be operationalized? Hitting another person could qualify as aggressive behavior if the intent is to harm the person being hit. However, in this research, such an operationalization was not possible because there was no actual other participant.[1] Alternatively, aggressive behavior could have been operationalized by asking participants how much they would like to harm the other participant. Doing so would get around the fact that there was no other participant. Regardless, the important point to remember here is that however a variable is operationally defined, it must be made explicitly clear. People reading about the research study must be able to judge how good or poor the operational definition was, and other researchers need to be able to use it in their research.

Measurement Reliability and Validity

Let's take a fairly simple variable to operationalize: foot size. It is a variable because people have various foot sizes. Suppose you measured your foot size right now. If you measured your foot size again tomorrow, I bet the two measurements would give you close to, if not precisely, the same number. It is unlikely that your foot size would change much between now and tomorrow. This is the essence of measurement reliability. The measurement of a variable is **reliable** to the extent that the measurement provides consistent scores. Think about a friend of yours whom you consider to be "reliable." That means you can count on him or her to behave consistently over time. If she says she will meet you at 11 a.m., she will be there by that time or even several minutes before that time. It is the same notion with measurement reliability. If the same person completes a measure of a personality construct (e.g., venturesomeness), his or her score on that measure should be consistent.

Reliability: extent to which a measure produces consistent results.

There are several forms of measurement reliability. We will briefly discuss two of them here. A measurement has **test–retest reliability** when people complete a measurement twice and they tend to have similar scores on that measurement each time they take it. For instance, in psychology, personality traits are understood to be stable (consistent) behavioral patterns that a person displays across situations. So, we would expect if people completed a measure of a personality trait today, they should score similarly when they complete that measure at another time.

Test–retest reliability: extent to which people tend to score similarly on a measurement that is completed at two different points in time.

It is important to realize that measurement reliability is established by examining a large sample of data, not scores from one or two people. For instance, I took the Scholastic Aptitude Test (SAT®; College Board, New York, NY) twice and earned very different scores on the two testing occasions. However, when we examine a large group of students taking the SAT, we will see that, *in general*, people who scored low the first time *tend to* score low when they take the test again. Similarly, people who scored well the first time *tend to* score well when they take the test again. Remember that the law of small numbers, that is, results based on a small sample of data (such as only my SAT scores), is not enough to draw conclusions about the world.

To establish test–retest reliability, people must complete a measure twice. By definition, this is a problem. Not every student will take the SAT twice. In Terrell et al.'s (2008) research, I doubt participants would have wanted to complete the measures a second time. Therefore, there is a second type of reliability called **internal reliability**. Take a look at Figure 2.2. This figure contains an instrument to measure a construct called grit. Grit is a construct of task persistence and tenacity (Duckworth, Peterson, Matthews, & Kelly, 2007). As you look at each item on the Grit Scale, it should be reasonable to assume that each person would tend to respond to these items fairly consistently; after all, they are all supposed to tap into a person's grit. To get an idea of how reliable this measure is, researchers can divide it in half, and then see whether scores on one half of the measure (6 items) are consistent with scores on the other half of the measure (the other 6 items).[2] This is why it is called "internal" reliability; we are looking for consistency between halves of the measure.

Internal reliability: extent to which people tend to score similarly on different parts of a measurement that is completed only once.

Now suppose we took a measure of foot size and used it to predict performance as a counselor. Foot size is reliable; however, to use it to predict job performance is not a valid use of this measurement. We say a measurement of a variable is **valid** when that measurement is used as it was intended to be used. I do not think that foot

Figure 2.2 Duckworth et al.'s (2007) Grit Scale

Respondents complete each item using the following response range:

5 = Very much like me
4 = Mostly like me
3 = Somewhat like me
2 = Not much like me
1 = Not like me at all

1. I have overcome setbacks to conquer an important challenge.
2. New ideas and projects sometimes distract me from previous ones.
3. My interests change from year to year.
4. Setbacks don't discourage me.
5. I have been obsessed with a certain idea or project for a short time but later lost interest.
6. I am a hard worker.
7. I often set a goal but later chose to pursue a different one.
8. I have difficulty maintaining my focus on projects that take more than a few months to complete.
9. I finish whatever I begin.
10. I have achieved a goal that took years of work.
11. I become interested in new pursuits every few months.
12. I am diligent.

Source: Copyright © 2007 American Psychological Association. Reproduced [or Adapted] with permission. The official citation that should be used in referencing this material is [list the original APA bibliographic citation]. No further reproduction or distribution is permitted without written permission from the American Psychological Association.

size would in any way be related to job performance as a counselor. However, a measure of knowledge about appropriate counseling techniques probably is a valid indicator of job performance as a counselor.

Valid: extent to which a measure is appropriate to use in a given context.

As there are different types of reliability, there are different types of validity. We will focus on two forms of validity here. First, **construct validity** refers to how well a variable, such as a person's level of narcissism, is operationalized. It is generally not the case that a measure has construct validity or it does not have construct validity. Rather, it is the degree to which that measure has construct validity. To assess the extent to which a measure has construct validity, we can see how well it is associated with measures of closely related constructs. For instance, what constructs might be related to being narcissistic? Perhaps self-esteem? If we find our measure of narcissism is related to measures of self-esteem, we can be confident that it possesses some degree of construct validity.

Construct validity: degree to which a variable is operationalized appropriately.

We also have **criterion validity**, which refers to the extent to which a measure is related to some outcome of interest. For instance, when evaluating the job performance of counselors, we can see whether our measure of knowledge of counseling techniques predicted such performance. If our measure did predict performance, it would be high in criterion validity. Likewise, to the extent that the SAT predicts academic performance in college, we can say that the SAT possesses criterion validity.

Criterion validity: how well a measure predicts an outcome.

Researchers take great care in ensuring that their measurements are both reliable and valid. It requires a great deal of work to provide evidence of reliability and validity of measurements in published scientific research. Indeed, it generally requires large samples of data, often involving thousands of respondents, to establish both reliability and validity. That is why when conducting their research, investigators often use measurements that have already been published because they can be more confident in the reliability and validity of those measurements. For these reasons, Terrell and her colleagues (2008) used measurements that other researchers had demonstrated were both reliable and valid.

LEARNING CHECK

1. How might we operationally define each of the following constructs? Realize that for each construct, there are many possible ways to operationalize it, more than I've provided in the answers.
   a) Hostility

      A: blood pressure while interacting with another person; self-report measure of the tendency to experience hostility toward others

b) Helping behavior

A: number of times people hold the door open to a building for other people over a period of time; number of hours a person volunteers in his or her community each week

c) Intelligence

A: Grade-point average (GPA); scores on a standardized test such as the Weschsler Adult Intelligence Scale (WAIS)

d) Investment returns

A: interest earned on a savings account this past year; stock market gains or losses in the past year

e) Exercise behavior

A: number of miles walked each day; number of pull-ups a person does each week

f) Diet

A: daily sodium intake; number of servings of fruits and vegetables each day

g) Stress

A: cortisol levels; blood pressure

h) Job burnout

A: number of cynical comments a person makes at work each day; scores on a self-report measure of burnout (e.g., Maslach & Jackson, 1981)

2. In Terrell et al.'s (2008) research, how was the dependent variable operationally defined?

   A: The dependent variable of aggression was operationalized as the number of noise blasts delivered during the 10-minute experimental task.

3. In Terrell et al.'s (2008) research, how was the variable of "status of the other participant" operationally defined?

   A: It was operationalized with the answers to the six questions that appear in Table 2.1.

4. What is the difference between the reliability and the validity of a measurement?

   A: Reliability refers to consistency of the measurement, whereas validity refers to the appropriateness of the measurement.

5. Explain why a measurement can be reliable but not valid.

   A: We can consistently measure a variable (e.g., an adult person's height) that is irrelevant to a given situation (e.g., parenting ability). An adult's height won't change much, if at all, so it is reliable. But I doubt physical height has anything to do with one's effectiveness as a parent, so it is not valid.

6. Explain why a measurement cannot be valid if it is not also reliable.

   A: If a measurement is not providing consistent (reliable) scores, then we have no way of knowing what it is measuring (if it is valid). For instance, if we have a measure that is supposed to assess academic ability, but people don't score reliably on it, then we cannot conclude it measures academic ability or anything else.

SCALES OF MEASUREMENT: HOW WE MEASURE VARIABLES

Even before you started this course, you probably knew you would be dealing with numbers. In this section, we will discuss different ways that we quantify variables. The previous section already gave you some insight into the process. Here, we will make explicit the types of data we can collect when we operationally define a variable.

"Uh oh. I measured the drywall in feet, but you measured it in metric."

Photo 2.1 One reason why scales of measurement are critical!

Source: ©Theresa McCracken/CartoonStock

When we talk about scales of measurement, we are simply talking about assigning numbers to events or objects using rules. *The rules you use to assign numbers determines the kinds of statistical tools you can use to understand the data.* In this section, we distinguish four types of measurement scales according to the rules by which numbers are assigned to objects or events. In the Learning Check following this section, we will identify the scales of measurement that Terrell and her colleagues (2008) used to measure the variables in their research.

Nominal Data

A **nominal scale** is a measurement that divides people, objects, or events into categories according to their similarities or differences. It identifies which category an entity falls into. A nominal scale is the simplest kind of measurement scale because people, objects, or events of the same category are assigned the same number, and those of a different category get different numbers. For example, if we did a nationwide survey of college students, you might ask them what college or university they attend, whether they attend that school full time or part time, their political affiliation, and their class standing. These would be examples of nominal data. A student generally attends only one college or university and can be only a first-year, sophomore, junior, or senior.

> **Nominal scale**: categorical data.

Photo 2.2 Is the player on the right better than the player on the left?

Source: ©iStockphoto.com/cstewart

We can assign numbers to the different categories (which are often called "levels") of a nominal variable. For example, for the variable of enrollment status (full time or part time), we can label students attending full time as "0" and those attending part time as "1." Realize, though, that these numbers carry no meaning and are arbitrary. Obviously, students attending college full time are not somehow "less than" students attending part time. To take another example, I wore the number 44 on my jersey when I played football in high school. That does not mean I was twice as good a player as the person who wore number 22 on my team. In reality, jersey numbers identified positions that people played on their teams.

With nominal data, we can form what are called *frequency distributions*; calculate certain statistics, such as the mode; and perform what is called a *chi-squared test* to help us make sense of this type of data. Chapters 3, 4, and 15 will help us use nominal data.

Ordinal Data

An **ordinal scale** is a measurement that identifies people, objects, or events in categories, and the categories are *ranked in order of their magnitude* (e.g., from best to worst). For instance, here are five different vegetables: broccoli, asparagus, green beans, carrots, and red peppers.

You ask me to put them in the order of my preference, with "5" for my most preferred and "1" for my least preferred. Here is my order of preference:

5 = red peppers
4 = asparagus
3 = carrots
2 = green beans
1 = broccoli

Each vegetable is identified by a number, which conveys magnitude, that is, how many vegetables are preferred to a specified other vegetable (e.g., relative to green beans, I like carrots, asparagus, and red peppers more, but I don't like broccoli as much).

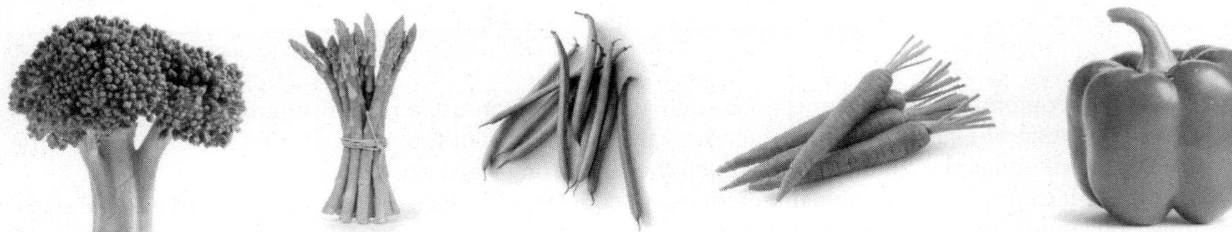

Photo 2.3 Putting these vegetables in "order" gives you "ordinal" data.

Source: ©iStockphoto.com/subjug; ©iStockphoto.com/GooDween123; ©iStockphoto.com/Floortje; ©iStockphoto.com/dionisvero; ©iStockphoto.com/suslik83

Ordinal scale: ranked-ordered data.

The rule for assigning numbers on an ordinal scale is that the position (rank order) of numbers on the scale must represent the rank order of the psychological attributes of the objects or events. Here, those psychological attributes are my liking of each vegetable. Notice that the scale does not tell us how much more I prefer red peppers to asparagus. It gives only the order of preference, not the difference in degree of preference. This is a major limitation of ordinal data. My preference for carrots over green beans may be fairly small, but my preference for green beans over broccoli may be quite large.

With ordinal data, we can calculate certain statistics, such as the mode or median, and perform what is called the Spearman rank-order correlation and the Mann–Whitney *U* test to help us make sense of this type of data. We will learn how to use such tools in Chapters 3, 4, and 15.

Interval and Ratio (Scale) Data

An **interval scale** is a measurement in which the differences between numbers are meaningful. It includes the same information as do nominal and ordinal scales; however, with interval data, the differences between the numbers are of equal size. For example, you have probably at some point been asked to complete a customer satisfaction survey, such as those in Figure 2.3. For these items, we can easily assign numeric values to each response. We can give a 1 to a mark of "Highly Satisfied," a 2 for "Satisfied," and so on, with a 5 for "Highly Dissatisfied."

Interval scale: distance (interval) between each number is of the same magnitude.

Figure 2.3 Example Items From a Grocery Store Customer Satisfaction Survey

Please rate your satisfaction with:

	Highly Satisfied	Satisfied	Neither Satisfied nor Dissatisfied	Dissatisfied	Highly Dissatisfied
1. The friendliness of the cashier.	______	______	______	______	______
2. The availability of the products you needed.	______	______	______	______	______
3. The price you paid.	______	______	______	______	______

When we ask people to respond to questions such as these, which use a response range, this is an interval scale. The rule for assigning numbers on an interval scale is that equal differences between the numbers on the scale must represent equal psychological differences between the events or objects.

Returning to our example of vegetable preferences, we could have collected such data using an interval scale. Here is how. You could have asked me how much I liked each one of the five vegetables, perhaps using an interval scale such as this one:

1	2	3	4	5	6	7
Do not like it at all			Like it somewhat			Like it very much

If I gave red peppers a 7, asparagus a 4, and carrots a 3, it would mean my liking of red peppers is quite a bit stronger than my liking of asparagus even though asparagus is my second favorite vegetable. My liking of carrots is closer to my liking of asparagus more than my liking of asparagus is to my liking of red peppers. The interval scale gives us more details than does an ordinal scale.

It is important to note that the interval scale does not contain a meaningful zero point. That is, a score of zero, when using an interval scale, does not indicate the absence of a variable being measured. Temperature is an example of an interval scale. A temperature of 0 degrees Fahrenheit does not mean that there is no temperature outside. Without a meaningful zero point, we cannot form ratios using interval data. So when it is 80 degrees Fahrenheit outside, we cannot say it is twice as warm as when it is 40 degrees Fahrenheit outside.

Just as with nominal and ordinal data, there are different statistical tools we can calculate and statistical tests we can perform on interval data. We can calculate all measures of central tendency and all measures of variability (Chapter 4). We can also use *t* tests (Chapters 7 and 8), analyses of variance (ANOVAs; Chapters 9–11), and correlational analyses (Chapters 12 and 13). As you can see, there are a lot more statistical tools available for interval data than there are for nominal and ordinal data.

Unlike an interval scale, a **ratio scale** has a meaningful zero point, as well as all of the characteristics of nominal, ordinal, and interval scales. The rule for assigning numbers on a ratio scale is that the ratios between the numbers on the scale must represent the psychological ratios between the events or objects. Examples of ratio data include many physical measures, such as time or weight. With a ratio scale and its meaningful zero point, it is possible to form ratios to make comparisons. For instance, the two minutes it takes someone to solve a statistics problem is half the time it took the person needing four minutes to solve the problem. So, we can conclude that the second person took twice as long. Someone who weighs 150 pounds is twice as heavy as someone who weighs 75 pounds.

Ratio scale: interval data that has a meaningful zero point.

The same sort of statistical tools can be used with ratio data as are used on interval data. That is why you might encounter a type of data called **scale data**. In practice, th e distinction between interval and ratio data is not nearly as important as the differences they have with nominal and ordinal data. The reason we care about scales of measurement is that some statistical techniques can only be used on interval or ratio scales. If all of your data are measured at a nominal level, then you are limited in what you can do with your data. This will be clear as we talk about how to present data in various parts of the book. Table 2.3 contains a summary of our scales of measurement.

Scale data: refers to interval and ratio data without making a distinction between them.

Table 2.3 Summary of the Scales of Measurement

	Nominal	Ordinal	Scale (interval and ratio)
Examples	Religious affiliation	Ranking of favorite movies	Most psychological tests
	College attended	College rankings	College tuition cost
	Favorite hockey team	Sports divisional standings	Number of wins a sports team has
Available Mathematical Operations	None	Rankings	Add, subtract, multiply, divide
Types of Statistics Used	Frequency distributions	Mode	Mode
	Mode	Median	Median
	Chi-square tests	Spearman correlation	Mean
		Mann–Whitney *U* test	*t* tests
			ANOVAs
			Pearson correlations
			Regression

Discrete Versus Continuous Variables

In addition to classifying variables by their scale of measurement, there is another way that researchers classify variables. This second classification system is not as closely tied to statistical analyses as are the scales of measurement, but as you will observe these terms used in research, I want you to be aware of them.

A **discrete variable** typically takes a whole-number value. For example, the number of children in a family is a discrete variable because only whole numbers are possible. A change in the value of a discrete value occurs one whole number at a time. If a family with three children has another child, it now has four children. No single value can occur between three and four in this example. Table 2.4 contains some examples of discrete variables in Terrell et al.'s (2008) research. We see that the variables of sex, class standing, and ethnicity are discrete variables. For each one, a respondent takes on one value or category. Most of the time, discrete variables will be measured on a nominal or an ordinal scale.

A **continuous variable** is one whose measurement can take on fractional values. For example, time is a continuous variable. The passage of time may be broken into an infinite number of units. When running a 40-yard dash, one person may run it in five seconds and another person may run it in six seconds. A third person could run that distance between those two times, for instance, in 5.4 seconds. The term "continuous" means that numbers continue between the whole numbers. In Terrell et al.'s (2008) research, GPA, height, and weight are continuous variables. In addition, the three personality measures are also continuous variables. At first glance, this may seem confusing. Let's examine the tendency to act aggressively by examining some sample items that appear at the bottom of Table 2.4. Respondents used a 1–5 response range to indicate how much each statement describes them. If we average the responses across all items on this survey, then indeed, we can obtain fractional

Table 2.4 Examples of Discrete and Continuous Variables in Terrell et al.'s (2008) Research

Discrete Variables:

Sex (circle one):	male	female	transgendered	
Class standing (circle one):	first-year	sophomore	junior	senior

Ethnicity (check one):

____ African-American
____ Caucasian
____ Hispanic
____ Native American
____ Asian
____ other ______________________

Continuous Variables:

Last year's grade-point average (GPA) (0.0–4.0): ______________________

Height (feet and inches): ______________________

Weight (pounds): __________

Tendency to Act aggressively

For each of the following items, indicate the number that corresponds to how that statement describes you in general, using the following scale:

1 = very much like me
2 = much like me
3 = somewhat like me
4 = slightly like me
5 = not at all like me

_____ 1. If I have to resort to violence to protect my rights, I will.
_____ 2. My friends say that I'm somewhat argumentative.
_____ 3. When frustrated, I let my irritation show.
_____ 4. I wonder why sometimes I feel so bitter about things.

values, which is why this is a continuous variable. Most of the time, continuous variables will be quantified by using a scale (interval or ratio) measurement.

Discrete variable: variable that can have only a whole number value.

Continuous variable: variable that can have a fractional value.

LEARNING CHECK

Refer back to Table 2.4, which contains some of the materials from Terrell and colleagues' (2008) research study described at the start of this chapter. Use it to answer the following questions:

1. What, if any, are the nominal variables in this study?

   A: sex, class standing, ethnicity

2. What, if any, are the ordinal variables in this study?

   A: none

3. What, if any, are the scale variables in this study?

   A: tendency to act aggressively, grade-point average, height, weight

4. Why is it that data collected using an interval or ratio measurement can be considered simply "scale" data?

   A: Both interval and ratio measurement scales can use the same statistical tools, so such a differentiation is not as important as it is for nominal and ordinal data.

5. For each variable, identify the scale of measurement (nominal, ordinal, interval, or ratio) and whether it is discrete or continuous:

Variable	Scale of Measurement?	Discrete or Continuous?
Letter grades (e.g., A, A–, B+)		
The number of miles between two locations		
A person's wireless provider		
Time to run a 5-kilometer (5K) race		
Place finished in a 5K race		
Number of whole cookies in the cookie jar		
Amount of money in a person's savings account		
Total score on the SAT		
Postal zip code		
High school class standings		
Ranking of restaurant preferences		

(Continued)

(Continued)

A:

Variable	**Scale of Measurement?**	**Discrete or Continuous?**
Letter grades (e.g., A, A−, B+)	ordinal	discrete
The number of miles between two locations	ratio	continuous
A person's wireless provider	nominal	discrete
Time to run a 5-kilometer (5K) race	ratio	continuous
Place finished in a 5K race	ordinal	discrete
Number of whole cookies in the cookie jar	ratio	continuous
Amount of money in a person's savings account	ratio	continuous
Total score on the SAT	interval	discrete
Postal zip code	nominal	discrete
High school class standings	ordinal	discrete
Ranking of restaurant preferences	ordinal	discrete

THE BASICS OF SPSS

In any sort of statistics class, numerical information is going to be important and, really, the centerpiece of the class. We will encounter many different statistics and statistical tools throughout this class. As I said in the previous chapter, above all else, I want you to understand the information that statistics provides you. Toward that end, as we move along, there will be some opportunities to do some calculations, as doing calculations will help you understand what information various statistics are giving you. In addition, it is important to note that most researchers do not calculate statistics themselves; rather, they have software that helps them do this task. One particularly popular software program for statistical analyses is the Statistical Package for the Social Sciences (SPSS). It can do a lot of great statistical work for us. That's a good thing; however, we must understand what exactly it is that SPSS is doing for us. The software can "spit out" a lot of statistical information that we need to be able to interpret correctly, or else we will misuse the statistical tools we are learning about in this class. Each chapter, with the exception of the last one, will contain at least one opportunity to use this software.

Let us start to familiarize ourselves with SPSS right now. It would be helpful if, as you read this section, you have access to a computer with SPSS loaded on it. That way, you can work along in SPSS as you read this information. If you cannot access SPSS right now, that's fine. There will be screenshots, as there will be in all subsequent SPSS sections of this book, to help you see what's going on as you use this software.

First, let's open SPSS. To do so, click on the name of the program from the Start menu as we do for any Microsoft Windows–based program (Microsoft Corporation, Redmond, WA). Here is the dialogue box you will see:

Simply click "Cancel" because we want to create a new spreadsheet.

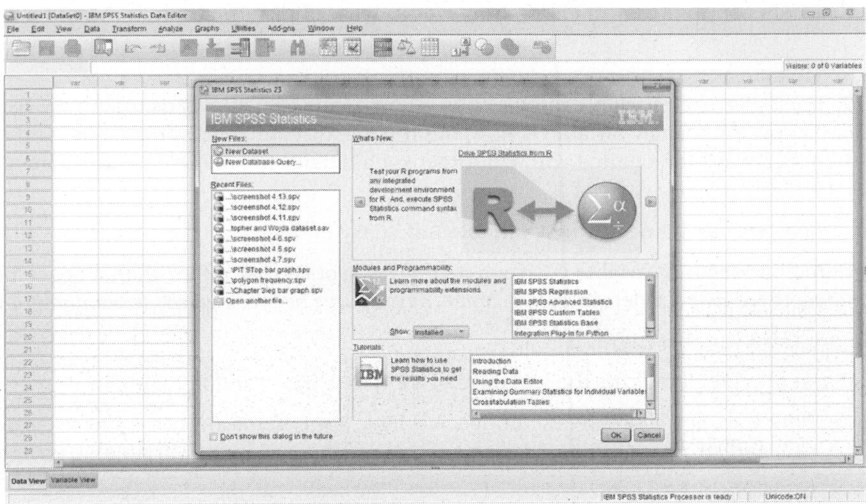

SPSS has two main screens that we will navigate: *Data View* and *Variable View*. In the lower left-hand corner of the screen, you will see two tabs, one for *Data View* (which is the one SPSS normally opens into) and one for *Variable View*. The *Data View* is where we enter data into SPSS; the *Variable View* is where we manage our data and is the place we should start when using SPSS. So at this point, select *Variable View* and let's set up our first SPSS spreadsheet.

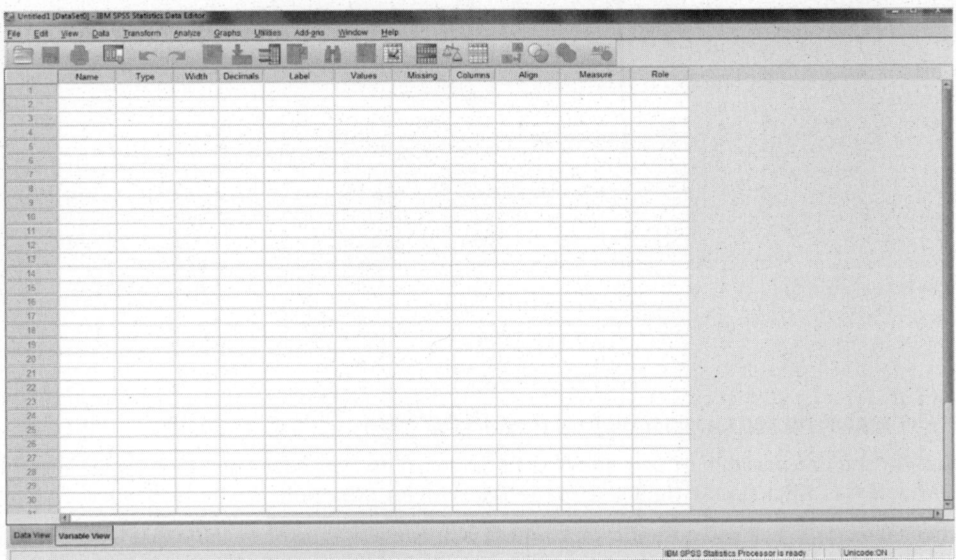

Variable View

What we will do is set up a spreadsheet in *Variable View*, and then we will get some practice entering data into *Data View*. We will use some of the variables measured in Terrell et al.'s (2008) research, specifically those in Table 2.4. Let's make sense of the *Variable View* of SPSS. There are 11 columns in *Variable View*; some are vitally important, whereas others are much less important. We will discuss them in the order in which they appear in SPSS.

1. ***Name.*** We must give each variable in our study a name, one that allows us to know what the variable is. You may know what each variable is now, but if you exit your SPSS spreadsheet and come back to it later, there is always the chance you will forget such details. So, name each variable as precisely as possible.

   In our example, we can name our first variable `Sex`. Easy enough.

   We can name our second variable `Class_Standing`. Notice that rather than a space between *Class* and *Standing*, there is an underscore. *We cannot have spaces between words when naming variables*.

   Let's call our third variable `Ethnicity`.

   Go ahead and provide names for the variables of `GPA`, `Height`, and `Weight`.

   For the tendency to act aggressively, notice we have four items (`Aggressive1`, `Aggressive2`, `Aggressive3`, and `Aggressive4`). Each one at this point is a separate variable, so each needs its own name.

   Once you have provided a name to each of our 10 variables, here is what the *Variable View* will look like:

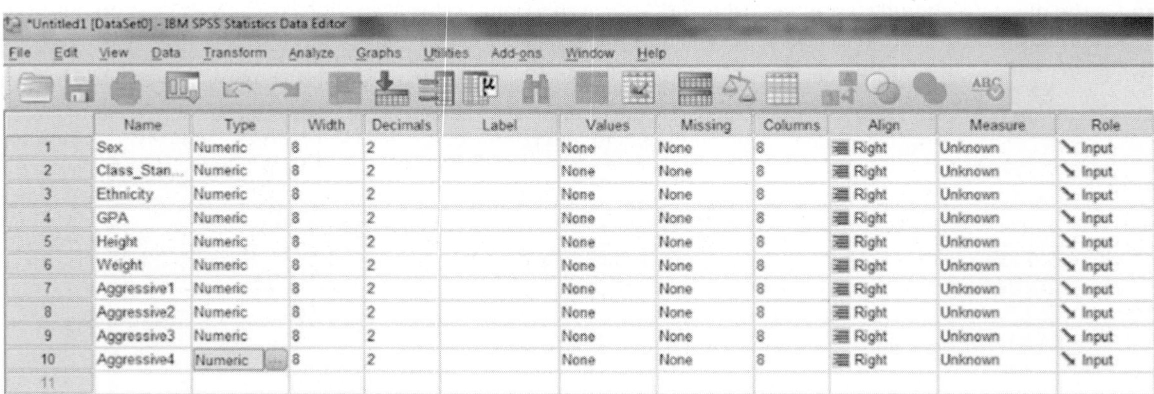

*Untitled1 [DataSet0] - IBM SPSS Statistics Data Editor

File Edit View Data Transform Analyze Graphs Utilities Add-ons Window Help

	Name	Type	Width	Decimals	Label	Values	Missing	Columns	Align	Measure	Role
1	Sex	Numeric	8	2		None	None	8	Right	Unknown	Input
2	Class_Stan...	Numeric	8	2		None	None	8	Right	Unknown	Input
3	Ethnicity	Numeric	8	2		None	None	8	Right	Unknown	Input
4	GPA	Numeric	8	2		None	None	8	Right	Unknown	Input
5	Height	Numeric	8	2		None	None	8	Right	Unknown	Input
6	Weight	Numeric	8	2		None	None	8	Right	Unknown	Input
7	Aggressive1	Numeric	8	2		None	None	8	Right	Unknown	Input
8	Aggressive2	Numeric	8	2		None	None	8	Right	Unknown	Input
9	Aggressive3	Numeric	8	2		None	None	8	Right	Unknown	Input
10	Aggressive4	Numeric	8	2		None	None	8	Right	Unknown	Input
11											

   Now let's move on and consider more of the *Variable View*.

2. ***Type.*** For the first variable of `Sex`, move your cursor to its *Type* box. This is where we specify the type of variable it is. Click on the right side of the *Type* box for `Sex`. Here is what you will see:

   Almost always we will use numeric data, which is the default type of variable that SPSS provides. There will be some exceptions, and when they arise, we will deal them at that time. As you can see on the right side of the Variable Type dialogue box, you can format the width and number of decimal places for that variable as well. The width of eight characters and two decimal places are the SPSS defaults.

3. ***Width.*** Of course, you can set the width here, as well as in the previous dialogue box. To do so here, just click on the *Width* box for the variable you want to adjust the width for, and then click the "up" or "down" arrow to set your desired width.

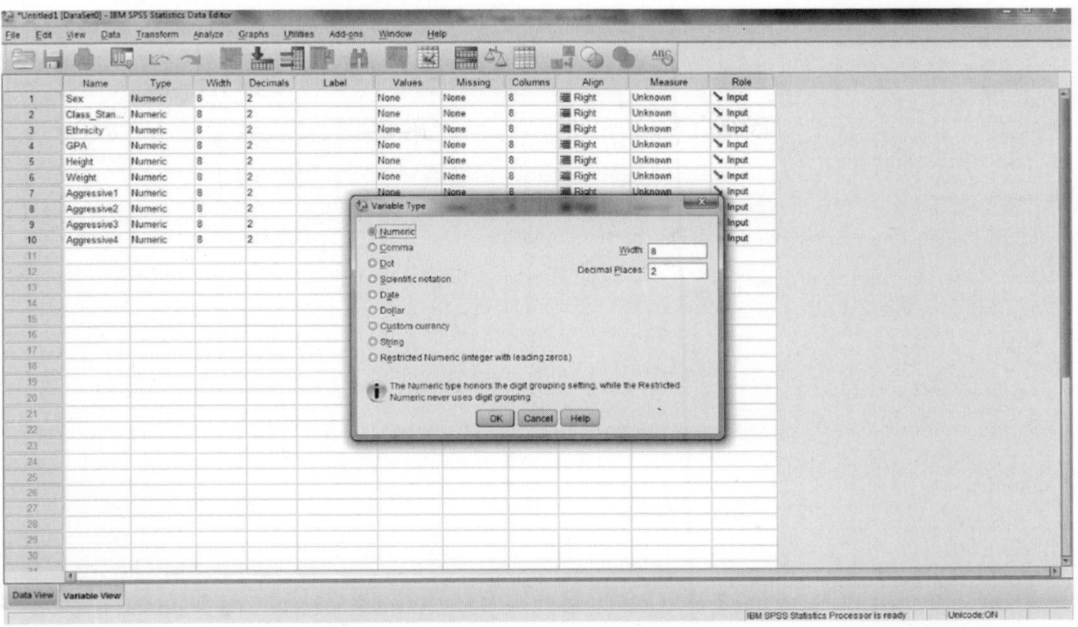

4. ***Decimals.*** Similar to setting the width, you can click on the *Decimals* box for the variable you want to adjust the number of decimal places for; then you can click the arrows accordingly. In this example, only the variable of `GPA` needs to have decimals as GPAs can take on at least two decimal places. However, even if a variable cannot take on any decimal value, it is fine to leave the default of two decimal places intact.

5. ***Label.*** Here, you can give a variable a more precise name that will appear on the statistical output we generate. It can be the same as the name designation we gave that variable previously, but it does not have to be. In fact, it is easier to be more descriptive with labels because you can leave spaces between words here. For example, for the variable named `Class_Standing`, we can give it a label such as `Class Standing of the Participant`. When we ask SPSS to provide us with statistical information, it will use the labels we provide in making its output for us to interpret.

6. ***Values.*** SPSS needs numbers to do its work for us. For nominal variables, we need to provide SPSS with numbers. For example, SPSS won't understand input such as `male`, `female`, or `transgendered`. However, it does understand `1`, `2`, and `3`. So, in the *Values* box, this is where we assign numbers to certain data. For the variable of `Sex`, click on the right side of its *Values* box. Here is what you will see:

   For *Value*, enter a `1`. For *Label*, enter `male`. Then click on *Add*. When we begin entering our data in SPSS, for a male participant, we will enter a `1` for the `Sex` variable. Now for *Value*, enter a `2`. For *Label*, enter `female`. Then click on *Add*. Finally, for *Value*, enter a `3`. For *Label*, enter `transgendered` and then click on *OK*.

   We have two other variables for which we need to provide values to SPSS, specifically, `Class_Standing` and `Ethnicity`. For `Class_Standing`, let's give a value of `1` for `first-year`; a value of `2` for `sophomore`; a value of `3` for `junior`; and a value of `4` for `senior`. For `Ethnicity`, let's give a value of `1` to `African American`; a value of `2` to `Caucasian`, and so on, with a value of `6` to `other`.

   As these are all nominal (categorical) data, remember that the number value we give each category means nothing in terms of relative standing of the categories. For instance, for `Sex`, a `2` for `female` does not mean women are twice as much of anything as men, who are coded as a `1`.

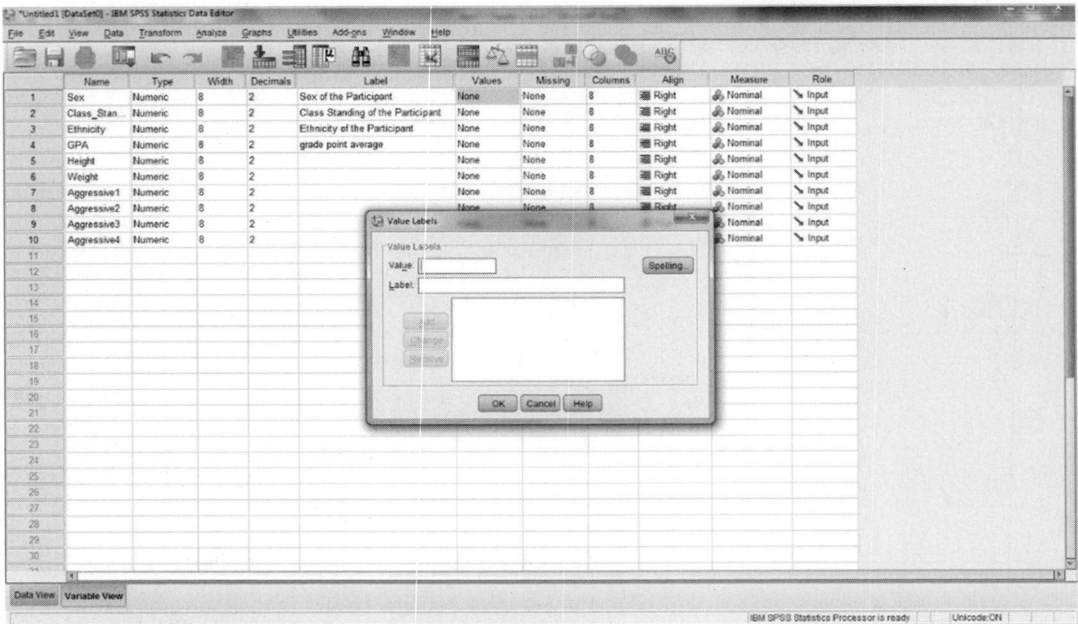

We do not need to enter a value for scale variables (in this case, for `GPA`, `Height`, `Weight`, or the four aggression items) because such measurements are numeric to start with. We can simply enter the raw data that each respondent provided us. However, you can always do so; it will never hurt to include a value for each and every variable in your SPSS spreadsheets.

7. ***Missing.*** Sometimes a researcher cannot collect data on every variable from every participant in a study. In such cases, this column allows us to specify how to tell SPSS when there is missing data for a variable. For our purposes in this class, we will use examples in which all participants supplied data for each variable we are dealing with. However, should you collect data in your class, here is how you can handle any missing data you might have. Click on the right side of the *Missing* column for one of the variables. Select *Discrete Missing Values*, and enter a number that makes no sense given how the variable was measured. For instance, a grade-point average can be from 0 to 4.00. So if a GPA is missing for a participant, we can just enter it as `99999`. Clearly, that value is nonsense given how GPA is measured, and now SPSS knows to treat it as missing data.

8. ***Columns.*** If you've changed the width of a variable in the third column, you will need to change this number as well to match the width.
9. ***Align.*** Here we tell SPSS how we want our data to appear, either right-justified, left-justified, or centered. For our statistical purposes, it makes no difference what you select here. I typically use the right-justified default.
10. ***Measure.*** We need to specify each variable as being a nominal, an ordinal, or a scale variable. Go ahead and see whether you can identify the scale of measurement for each of our 10 variables. You can check yourself with this screenshot (or the answers to the previous Learning Check).
11. ***Role.*** We should keep the default of *Input* here. The other choices are beyond the scope of what we need to do in this class.

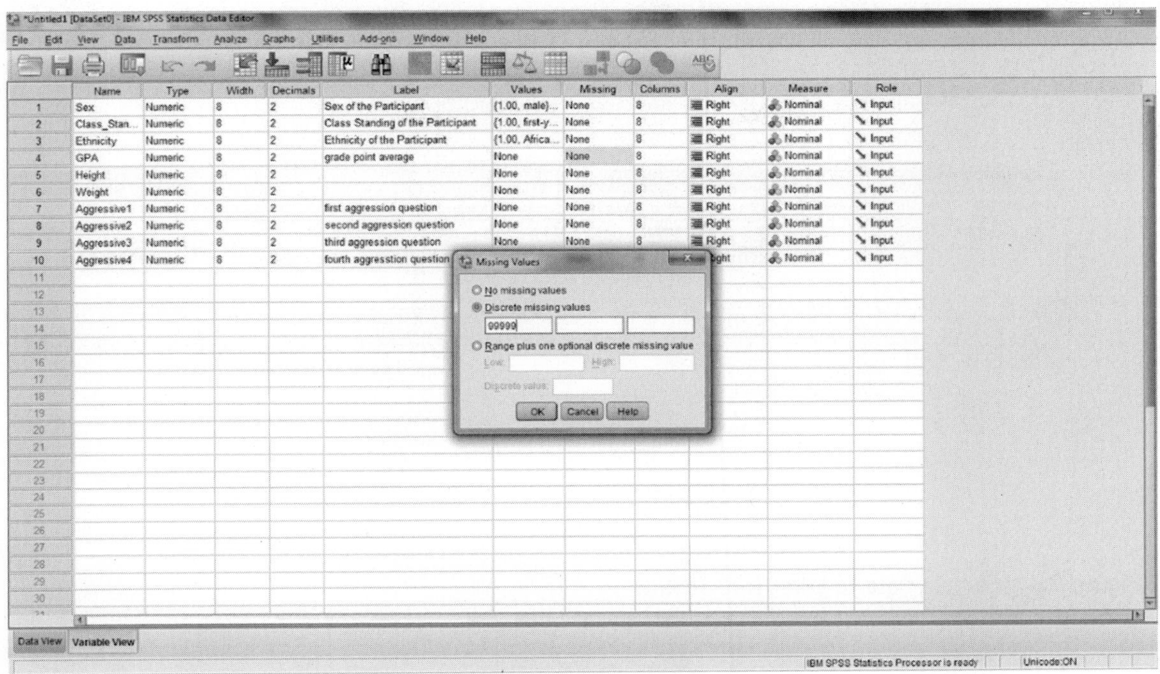

*Untitled1 [DataSet0] - IBM SPSS Statistics Data Editor

File Edit View Data Transform Analyze Graphs Utilities Add-ons Window Help

	Name	Type	Width	Decimals	Label	Values	Missing	Columns	Align	Measure	Role
1	Sex	Numeric	8	2	Sex of the Participant	{1.00, male}...	None	8	Right	Nominal	Input
2	Class_Stan...	Numeric	8	2	Class Standing of the Participant	{1.00, first-y...	None	8	Right	Nominal	Input
3	Ethnicity	Numeric	8	2	Ethnicity of the Participant	{1.00, Africa...	None	8	Right	Nominal	Input
4	GPA	Numeric	8	2	grade point average	None	None	8	Right	Nominal	Input
5	Height	Numeric	8	2		None	None	8	Right	Nominal	Input
6	Weight	Numeric	8	2		None	None	8	Right	Nominal	Input
7	Aggressive1	Numeric	8	2	first aggression question	None	None	8	Right	Nominal	Input
8	Aggressive2	Numeric	8	2	second aggression question	None	None	8	Right	Nominal	Input
9	Aggressive3	Numeric	8	2	third aggression question	None	None	8	Right	Nominal	Input
10	Aggressive4	Numeric	8	2	fourth aggresstion question				ght	Nominal	Input

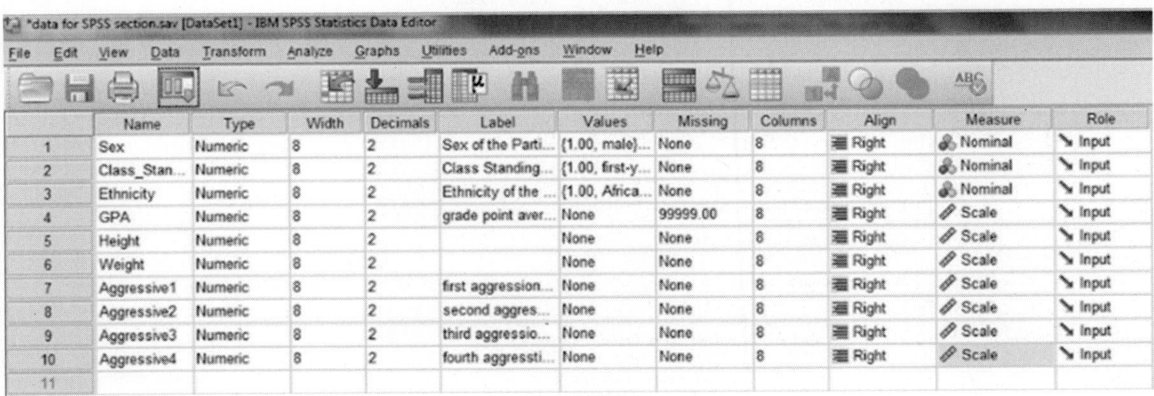

*data for SPSS section.sav [DataSet1] - IBM SPSS Statistics Data Editor

File Edit View Data Transform Analyze Graphs Utilities Add-ons Window Help

	Name	Type	Width	Decimals	Label	Values	Missing	Columns	Align	Measure	Role
1	Sex	Numeric	8	2	Sex of the Parti...	{1.00, male}...	None	8	Right	Nominal	Input
2	Class_Stan...	Numeric	8	2	Class Standing...	{1.00, first-y...	None	8	Right	Nominal	Input
3	Ethnicity	Numeric	8	2	Ethnicity of the ...	{1.00, Africa...	None	8	Right	Nominal	Input
4	GPA	Numeric	8	2	grade point aver...	None	99999.00	8	Right	Scale	Input
5	Height	Numeric	8	2		None	None	8	Right	Scale	Input
6	Weight	Numeric	8	2		None	None	8	Right	Scale	Input
7	Aggressive1	Numeric	8	2	first aggression...	None	None	8	Right	Scale	Input
8	Aggressive2	Numeric	8	2	second aggres...	None	None	8	Right	Scale	Input
9	Aggressive3	Numeric	8	2	third aggressio...	None	None	8	Right	Scale	Input
10	Aggressive4	Numeric	8	2	fourth aggressti...	None	None	8	Right	Scale	Input
11											

Data View

Now that we have set up our *Variable View*, we click on *Data View* (bottom left corner of the screen) to begin entering our data. Notice that *across the top of the spreadsheet, each column is one of our variables. Each row will contain the data for one participant.*

Figure 2.4 contains the (hypothetical) data from two people on the 10 variables we have established in our SPSS spreadsheet. Now that we are in *Data View*, let's enter those data into SPSS and get some practice in this important detail.

As you begin to enter your data, it is critically important that you recall the numerical values you gave for your nominal variables. Remember, for instance, that we will give male respondents a 1, female respondents

*data for SPSS section.sav [DataSet1] - IBM SPSS Statistics Data Editor

File Edit View Data Transform Analyze Graphs Utilities Add-ons Window Help

1 : Sex

	Sex	Class_Standing	Ethnicity	GPA	Height	Weight	Aggressive1	Aggressive2	Aggressive3	Aggressive4	var
1											
2											
3											
4											

Figure 2.4 Sample Data to Enter Into SPSS

Participant #1

Sex (**circle one**): male (female) transgendered

Class standing (**circle one**): first-year (sophomore) junior senior

Ethnicity (**check one**):
____ African-American
____ Caucasian
____ Hispanic
____ Native American
X Asian
____ other ________

Last year's grade point average (GPA) (0.0-4.0): 3.45

Height (feet and inches): 5' 5"

Weight (pounds): 112

For each of the following items, indicate the number that corresponds to how that statement describes you in general, using the following scale:

1 = very much like me
2 = much like me
3 = somewhat like me
4 = slightly like me
5 = not at all like me

5 1. If I have to resort to violence to protect my rights, I will.

3 2. My friends say that I'm somewhat argumentative.

2 3. When frustrated, I let my irritation show.

3 4. I wonder why sometimes I feel so bitter about things.

Participant #2

Sex (**circle one**): (male) female transgendered

Class standing (**circle one**): first-year sophomore junior (senior)

Ethnicity (**check one**):
X African-American
____ Caucasian
____ Hispanic
____ Native American
____ Asian
____ other ____________

Last year's grade point average (GPA) (0.0-4.0): 3.65

Height (feet and inches): 6 feet 2 inches

Weight (pounds): 188 pounds

For each of the following items, indicate the number that corresponds to how that statement describes you in general, using the following scale:

1 = very much like me
2 = much like me
3 = somewhat like me
4 = slightly like me
5 = not at all like me

4 1. If I have to resort to violence to protect my rights, I will.

2 2. My friends say that I'm somewhat argumentative.

3 3. When frustrated, I let my irritation show.

3 4. I wonder why sometimes I feel so bitter about things.

*data for SPSS section.sav [DataSet1] - IBM SPSS Statistics Data Editor

File Edit View Data Transform Analyze Graphs Utilities Add-ons Window Help

Visible: 10 of 10 Variables

	Sex	Class_Standing	Ethnicity	GPA	Height	Weight	Aggressive1	Aggressive2	Aggressive3	Aggressive4
1	2.00	2.00	5.00	3.45	65.00	112.00	5.00	3.00	2.00	3.00
2	1.00	4.00	1.00	3.65	74.00	188.00	4.00	2.00	3.00	3.00

Data View Variable View

IBM SPSS Statistics Processor is ready Unicode:ON

a `2`, and transgendered respondents a `3` when entering data for the variable of `Sex` into SPSS. If you ever have any doubts about the values you provided in the *Variable View*, go back and look. Incorrectly entering data into SPSS renders worthless all the statistical tools we will learn in this class. *SPSS is only as good as the data we enter into it.*

Let's start entering participant 1's data into SPSS. This person reported being a female who is a sophomore and is Asian. As I just preached, we must code these nominal data correctly into SPSS or else we might as well just enter garbage into the spreadsheet. For the variable of `Sex`, we give participant 1 a `2`. For the variable of `Class_Standing`, we give this participant a `2`. For the variable of `Ethnicity`, we give her a `5`.

The good news now is that scale variables tend to be easier to enter into SPSS than are nominal variables. As mentioned, we can normally just enter the value that the participant provided. So for the variable of `GPA`, enter `3.45`. The variable of `Height` is a little trickier only because we cannot enter"5 feet, 5 inches" into the spreadsheet. Rather, we need to convert this height into inches (or whatever scale you want to use so that we have a single number). "5 feet, 5 inches" converts to 65 inches, so I entered `65` for this variable. Go ahead and enter the remaining data for the first participant. Then, enter the data for participant 2 (this is not an exercise in converting measurements of feet into inches, participant 2 is 74 inches tall). Here is what your *Data View* will look like:

The main menu runs across the top of the *Data View*, starting with *File* on the left across to *Help* on the right. At this point in the class, we do not have any statistical tools in our toolkit to use with these data, but know that for our purposes, we will be primarily using the *Analyze* tab and the *Graphs* tab in this class.[3]

NOTES

1. All research involving human participants must be approved by what's called an institutional review board (IRB) or other committee that reviews the ethics of research studies. In this example, a research study in which participants would be allowed to hit each other probably would not be approved by such a committee.
2. There are of course many ways to divide a 12-item scale into halves (e.g., even- and odd-numbered items or first six items and last six items). Typically, researchers use computer software, such as the program we will begin learning later in this chapter, to assess internal reliability. We'll discuss more about internal reliability in Chapter 12.
3. In case you are interested in Terrell et al.'s (2008) results, they found that men who were more narcissistic gave more noise blasts (that is, acted more aggressively) than men who were less narcissistic. Women did not differ in their aggressive behavior based on their level of narcissism. In addition, women with a tendency to act aggressively were more likely to display aggression against a low-status competitor, whereas males with a tendency to act aggressively were more likely to display aggression against a high-status competitor.

CHAPTER APPLICATION QUESTIONS

1. How does a measurement's reliability differ from validity?
2. What is the difference between construct validity and criterion validity?
3. What information does scale data (interval and ratio data) provide in addition to what an ordinal scale provides?
4. For each variable, identify the scale of measurement (nominal, ordinal, interval, or ratio) and whether it is discrete or continuous:

Variable	Scale of Measurement?	Discrete or Continuous?
Numbers used to identify political affiliation: Republican, Democrat, or Independent		
Social security number		
Amount of time it takes a pain reliever to work		
Length or width of a room		

5. When your "intelligence" is defined as your score on the Wechsler Adult Intelligence Scale, you are:
   a) testing the validity of this measure.
   b) testing the reliability of this measure.
   c) operationalizing the term intelligence.
   d) determining the correlation between two variables.
6. Which of the following **BEST** represents a *nominal scale* of measurement?
   a) scores on a personality measure
   b) the number of inches of rain in Detroit on September 15, 2015
   c) letter grades in school
   d) a person's membership in one particular Greek organization
7. Which of the following is **NOT** a continuous variable?
   a) number of siblings
   b) temperature
   c) height
   d) time needed to solve a problem

Answers

1. Reliability refers to a measurement's consistent scores, whereas validity refers to how appropriate a measure is to use in a given context.
2. Construct validity concerns how well a variable is operationalized. Criterion validity concerns how well a measurement tool predicts some outcome.
3. Scale data are meaningful numeric data; with nominal and ordinal data, the numbers are identifiers. With scale data, the differences between numbers are meaningful and allow us to use a wide range of statistical tools to understand them.
4.

Variable	Scale of Measurement?	Discrete or Continuous?
Numbers used to identify U.S. political affiliation: Republican, Democrat, or Independent	nominal	discrete
Social security number	nominal	discrete
Amount of time it takes a pain reliever to work	ratio	continuous
Length or width of a room	ratio	continuous

5. c

6. d
7. a

QUESTIONS FOR CLASS DISCUSSION

1. What is the difference between test–retest reliability and internal reliability?
2. What information does an ordinal scale of measurement provide in addition to the information that a nominal scale provides?
3. Why would a researcher likely NOT record a participant's religious affiliation on a scale (i.e., interval or ratio) measurement?
4. A study was conducted to determine whether physically fit persons sleep more hours than those who are not physically fit. Two groups of people were selected. One group consisted of people who work out at least three times a week. The other group consisted of people that do not work out at all. For one week, participants slept in a sleep lab and an experimenter recorded the number of hours each person slept.
   a) Is there an independent variable or a quasi-independent variable being examined in this research? What is this independent or quasi-independent variable?
   b) What is the dependent variable?
   c) Is the dependent variable discrete or continuous?
   d) What scale of measurement is the dependent variable measured on (nominal, ordinal, or scale)?
5. Graduate Record Exam (GRE) scores are very weakly related to performance in graduate school. Therefore, there is controversy about what consideration, if any, GRE scores should have in admissions decisions. This controversy centers on:
   a) construct validity.
   b) criterion validity.
   c) test–retest reliability.
   d) internal reliability.
6. Ranking a group of cities in terms of "quality of life" would be an example of measurement of a(n) _______________ scale of measurement.
   a) nominal
   b) ordinal
   c) interval
   d) ratio

CHAPTER 3

Describing Data With Frequency Distributions and Visual Displays

After reading this chapter, you will be able to

- Differentiate between a frequency distribution table and a grouped frequency distribution table
- Discuss how bar graphs, histograms, and frequency polygons are used to communicate frequency distributions visually
- Interpret frequency distribution information conveyed in bar graphs, histograms, and frequency polygons
- Discuss how bar graphs, scatterplots, and line graphs are used to communicate relationships between variables visually
- Interpret relationships between variables that are displayed using bar graphs, scatterplots, and line graphs
- Construct visual displays of frequency data and relationships between variables using SPSS

In the previous chapter, we learned about basic considerations in conducting quantitative research. With these basic concepts in hand, we can now begin discussing what to do once we have collected data from a sample. In this chapter, we will discuss a study by Laura Wendt (2013) that examined predictors of academic burnout in first-year and senior-year college students. We will continue to use this same study and its data in the next three chapters as we extend our discussions of descriptive statistical tools in those chapters. In this chapter, we will first discuss this study, the constructs it examined, and how the constructs were operationalized. In subsequent sections of this chapter, we will discuss ways that researchers can summarize large amounts of data, both with tables and with visual displays. After learning about three commonly used tools researchers use to visually display data and relationships between variables, we will conclude this chapter by using the software program Statistical Package for the Social Sciences (SPSS) to construct these commonly used tools. Be aware that you have access to Wendt's (2013) data in the file titled "Wendt's data.sav". We will use these data later in this chapter and in the next chapter.

THE STUDY

In her research, Wendt (2013) had 46 college first-years and 62 college seniors complete a packet of surveys. In this packet were measures of demographic variables, including participant sex, age, and year in college. In addition, the packet contained three additional measures. First, there was a 15-item measure of academic burnout (Schaufeli, Martinez, Marques Pinto, Salanova, & Bakker, 2002). By "burnout," we mean prolonged stress that causes people to feel exhausted, cynical, and as if they cannot accomplish their responsibilities effectively. Burnout tends to result not from working too hard per se but from feeling that one does not reap the benefits associated with one's efforts. For example, if you study a lot and make good grades, you're not likely to burn out because despite working hard, you're reaping the rewards of your hard work. The burnout questionnaire contained items such as "I have become less enthusiastic about my studies" and "Studying is really a strain for me."

Second, there was a 13-item measure of role overload (Reilly, 1982). By "role overload," we mean the extent to which a person feels he or she can manage the demands with the different roles that must be played. For instance, in your role as a student, certain types of behaviors (e.g., attending class, studying, and making presentations) are expected. Likewise, in your role as a friend to other people, different types of behavior are expected (e.g., returning texts, talking, and providing advice as needed). Role overload occurs when people believe they are having a difficult time meeting all of these demands. This questionnaire contained items such as "There are times when I cannot meet everyone's expectations" and "I can't ever seem to get caught up."

Finally, there was an 11-item measure of dysfunctional perfectionism (Khawaja & Armstrong, 2005). Being a perfectionist can of course be a good thing as it often drives people to do well at work and in school. However, perfectionism becomes dysfunctional when it creates an obsession with avoiding failure and mistakes, setting unattainable goals, and being unable to learn from feedback. For instance, it is good to proofread a paper, but if you spend so much time proofreading that you don't study for a test the next day, that's dysfunctional perfectionism. This measure contained items such as "Even when I do something very carefully, I often feel that it is not quite right" and "I set higher standards than most people."

Students responded to the burnout, role overload, and perfectionism items using a 1 (*strongly disagree*) to 5 (*strongly agree*) response range. Thus, burnout scores could range from 15 to 75; role overload scores could range from 13 to 65; and dysfunctional perfectionism scores could range from 11 to 55.

Before we begin using Wendt's (2013) research to illustrate basic ideas in this chapter, let's make sure we're thinking the same way about *why* we are discussing these ideas. In this chapter and the two chapters that immediately follow it, we are going to discuss ideas about how to use *descriptive statistics*. Recall from Chapter 1 the notion of descriptive statistics. Specifically, we want to make sense of (i.e., describe) large amounts of data so that people can understand them easily. The purpose of frequency distributions, visual depictions, and SPSS is to help us make sense of large amounts of data. I think of the tools we are about to discuss as being to a psychologist what clay and a kiln are to a ceramicist. Without clay and a kiln, there can be no pottery. Without understanding descriptive statistics, there can be no quantitative psychological research.

FREQUENCY DISTRIBUTIONS

In Wendt's (2013) research, there were a total of 108 respondents. Each respondent had a score on each variable in this study, which means that there were a lot of data that she needed to organize. In this section, we will focus on the scores from the measure of burnout. Table 3.1 contains the burnout score for each respondent. Recall that scores on the burnout measure could fall between 15 and 75. If you can meaningfully summarize Table 3.1, you're more insightful than I am. What we need to do here is somehow organize these 108 burnout scores so that people can make sense of them. The purpose of a frequency distribution is to organize a large amount of data in a format that people can understand quickly. There are two formats that a frequency distribution can take: a *frequency distribution table* and a *frequency distribution graph*. Let's use the 108 burnout scores from Wendt's research to illustrate both formats.

Frequency Distribution Tables

Again, if you can make sense of the burnout scores in Table 3.1, I am happy for you. However, most of us need some tools to organize these data better than they are currently presented. We can do this in three ways by using tables of the scores. We will discuss each of these three types of tables in the order of increasing organization of our scores.

First, let's organize our 108 burnout scores from highest to lowest. We've done this in Table 3.2. Now we can now get a sense of what constitutes "high" and "low" burnout scores. For instance, although scores could go as high as 75, the highest score in this sample is 55. This means that there weren't any "completely burned out" students in this sample. This table is somewhat informative, but we are left to figure out how frequently each score occurred. Furthermore, we don't know with much precision what "high" and "low" scores are at this point.

So let's now consider Table 3.3, which contains a second type of table to organize data for a variable. This table contains a **frequency distribution** in which all of the burnout scores are listed along with how often (frequently) each score appears in the dataset. Importantly, we can discern the relative frequency (percentage of the sample that had a particular score on that variable) of a given score, allowing us to be more precise in what we mean by "high" and "low" scores on this variable. As you can see in Table 3.3, the score of 41 occurred three times, representing 2.78% of the total scores. Likewise, the scores of 28 and 31 both occurred more than any other score in this dataset.

Frequency distribution: table that contains all scores in a dataset, along with each score's frequency of occurrence.

Of course, similar to Table 3.2, the presentation in Table 3.3 is perhaps a bit much to understand, at least easily. Therefore, we have a third type of frequency table, what's called a **grouped frequency distribution table**. You can see a grouped frequency distribution in Table 3.4. What we've done is combine scores into *categories*. We present these categories of scores and the frequency with which a score falls into each category. A grouped frequency distribution does not tell us about every score in the dataset, but in research, the reality is that we need to be parsimonious in how we present data. That is, we need to simplify our presentations, and a grouped frequency distribution allows us to do this.

Grouped frequency distribution table: table that contains all scores in a dataset, clustering the scores into categories, and presents the frequency of occurrence for each category rather than for individual scores.

Before we interpret the information in Table 3.4, let's discuss two guidelines for making a grouped frequency distribution table.

1. We should have approximately 10 categories of scores (Hinkle, Wiersma, & Jurs, 1988). Although more categories are not necessarily "wrong," remember we want to be parsimonious in our presentation. For most people, 10 categories are enough to be informative without being overwhelming.
2. The range of possible scores for each category should be the same. To determine the range of possible scores for the categories, locate the highest and lowest score in the dataset. Take the difference between these two scores, and then divide that difference by the number of categories you want to have. For example, in Wendt's (2013) data, the lowest score was 16 and the highest score was 55. This means that, including the scores of 16 and 55, we have a range of 40 scores. With 10 categories, we have four possible scores that can fall into each of the categories.

Now let's interpret the information in Table 3.4. Perhaps as you might expect, most of the scores fall in the middle of the distribution. For example, approximately 66% of the burnout scores fall in the middle four

Table 3.1 Burnout Scores for Wendt's (2013) 108 Participants

36	37	51	42
38	40	41	40
48	36	44	34
30	30	36	28
31	32	34	37
16	42	50	39
34	40	25	28
25	28	41	28
42	35	43	52
35	35	31	39
37	49	47	46
45	38	34	50
27	34	55	40
54	20	53	36
20	28	38	23
32	16	37	32
34	22	43	24
35	25	41	47
33	19	46	25
33	32	53	45
31	42	38	40
49	49	31	45
20	39	40	37
31	31	35	42
28	40	45	28
31	49	45	38
35	31	39	28

Table 3.2 Burnout Scores Presented from Highest to Lowest

55	42	36	31
54	42	36	31
53	42	36	31
53	41	36	30
52	41	35	30
51	41	35	28
50	40	35	28
50	40	35	28
49	40	35	28
49	40	35	28
49	40	34	28
49	40	34	28
48	40	34	28
47	39	34	27
47	39	34	25
46	39	34	25
46	39	33	25
45	38	33	25
45	38	32	24
45	38	32	23
45	38	32	22
45	38	32	20
44	37	31	20
43	37	31	20
43	37	31	19
42	37	31	16
42	37	31	16

Table 3.3 Absolute and Relative Frequencies of Burnout Scores

Score	*f* (frequency)	*rf* (relative frequency)
55	1	.0093
54	1	.0093
53	2	.0185
52	1	.0093
51	1	.0093
50	2	.0185
49	4	.0370
48	1	.0093
47	2	.0185
46	2	.0185
45	5	.0463
44	1	.0093
43	2	.0185
42	5	.0463
41	3	.0278
40	7	.0648
39	4	.0370
38	5	.0463
37	5	.0463
36	4	.0370
35	6	.0556
34	6	.0556
33	2	.0185
32	4	.0370
31	8	.0740
30	2	.0185
28	8	.0740

Score	*f* (frequency)	*rf* (relative frequency)
27	1	.0093
25	4	.0370
24	1	.0093
23	1	.0093
22	1	.0093
20	3	.0278
19	1	.0093
16	2	.0185
	108	1.0000

Table 3.4 A Grouped Frequency Distribution of Burnout Scores

Class interval	*f* (frequency)	*rf* (relative frequency)
52–55	5	.0463
48–51	8	.0741
44–47	10	.0926
40–43	17	.1574
36–39	18	.1667
32–35	18	.1667
28–31	18	.1667
24–27	6	.0556
20–23	5	.0463
16–19	3	.0278
	108	1.0000

categories (that is, scores between 28 and 31, between 32 and 35, between 36 and 39, and between 40 and 43). As we move away from those four middle categories, what do you notice? Indeed, the further away from the middle we go, the progressively fewer scores we see. As noted earlier, the possible range of scores on this measure was 15 to 75. With no scores greater than 55 in this sample, it appears that we have a sample that is not terribly burned out when it comes to school. This kind of information that a frequency distribution provides is helpful in understanding the sample that we are studying.

Frequency Distribution Graphs

Frequency distribution tables, as I am sure you will agree, are great tools to organize data. But, of course, a picture is worth 1,000 words. So in addition to frequency distribution tables, frequency distribution graphs can be helpful in understanding a dataset. In fact, in psychological research, it is more common to see a frequency distribution graph than a similar type of table. Let's now discuss the three major types of frequency distribution graphs.

A critical consideration in selecting a frequency distribution graph is the scale of measurement for a variable. In the previous chapter, we discussed nominal, ordinal, and scale measurements. If our data are nominal, we use what's called a *bar graph*. If our data are ordinal or scale, we use what are called *histograms* and *frequency polygons*.

A **bar graph** uses vertical bars above each category listed on the x-axis to display the frequency for a category. There is a space between the bars because each category is distinctly different from the other categories. For example, Figure 3.1 contains a bar graph for a nominal variable in Wendt's (2013) research, students' year in college. This is a nominal variable because each participant was either a first-year or a senior. No person could be in both categories.

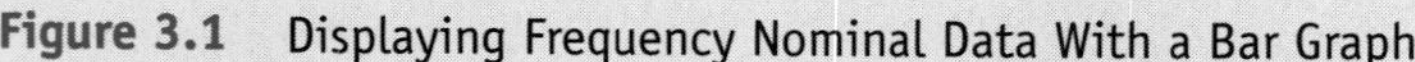

Bar graph: graphical representation of the frequency of nominal data in which each category appears on the x-axis and the frequency of occurrence for a given score appears on the y-axis.

Looking closely at Figure 3.1, notice that each category is listed on the x-axis, with the name of the variable beneath the category names. Each bar is centered above its category name. There is a space between the two

Figure 3.1 Displaying Frequency Nominal Data With a Bar Graph

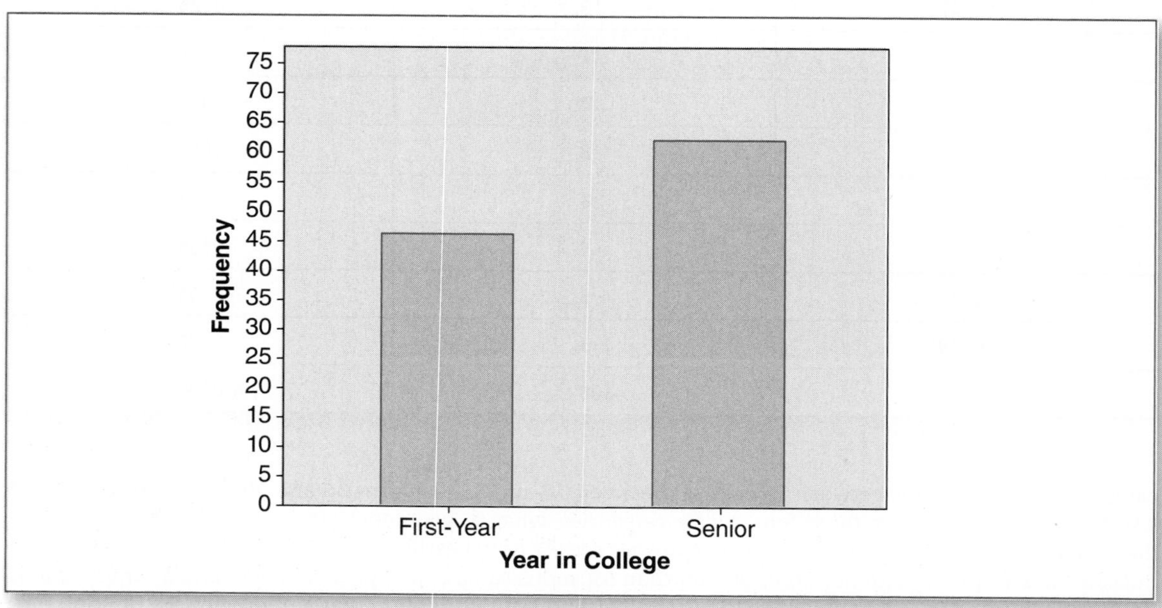

bars because there can be no overlap between the categories; that is, a first-year cannot be a senior, and a senior cannot be a first-year. Finally, the *y*-axis provides the frequency numbers.

Whereas a bar graph is used for nominal data, we use a **histogram** for ordinal and scale data. Once again we have the values of a variable on the *x*-axis and the frequencies on the *y*-axis. A histogram for Wendt's (2013) burnout scores appears in Figure 3.2. Notice here how there is no space between the values along the *x*-axis as there was for a bar graph. Because we are dealing with scale data, we have values that inherently increase as we move from the left to the right side of the axis (the same would be true of ordinal data). If you look back at the bar graph in Figure 3.1, there is no reason that the category of "senior" could not appear before the category of "first-year."[1]

Figure 3.2 Displaying Frequency Scale Data With a Histogram

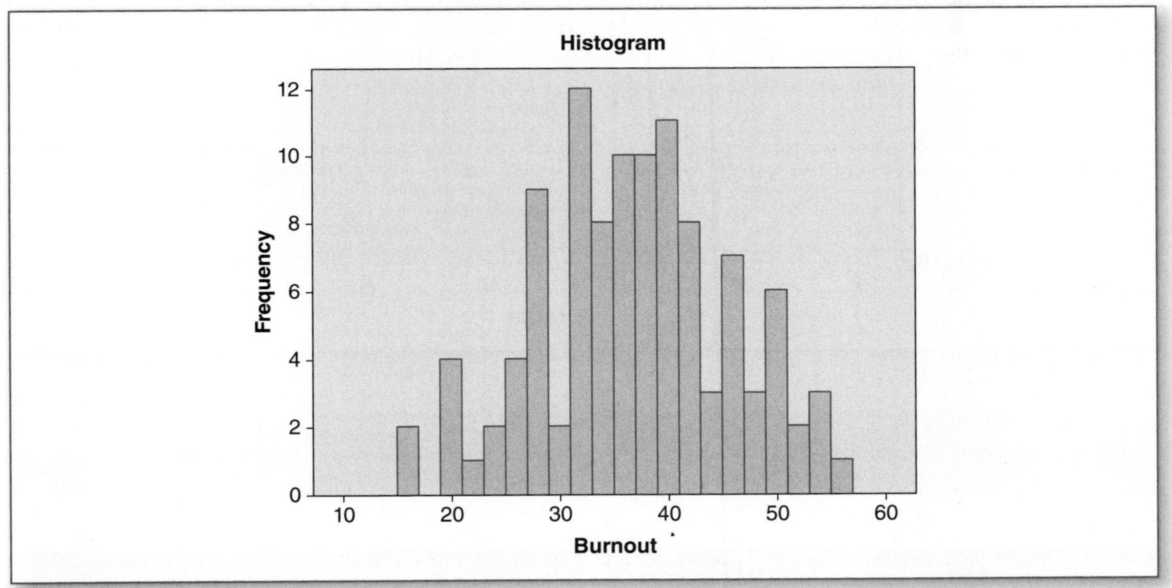

Histogram: similar to a bar graph, except used for ordinal and scale data that are discrete; that is, each score is different from all other scores.

Similar to histograms, **frequency polygons** are used for ordinal and scale data. Rather than bars, a polygon uses a line graph to display the frequency of scores or categories of scores. We again have scores or categories of scores on the *x*-axis and frequencies on the *y*-axis. With each frequency plotted, we place a dot centered above each category score. We then connect the dots to form a polygon, such as the one in Figure 3.3. Frequency polygons are particularly helpful in displaying frequencies for continuous data, which, as you'll recall from the previous chapter, can take on any fractional value along the *x*-axis (such as time, which can be measured in seconds or fractions of seconds). Histograms are better to use with discrete data, such as the burnout scores, which could take on only a whole-number value in Wendt's (2013) research.

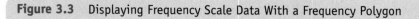

Figure 3.3 Displaying Frequency Scale Data With a Frequency Polygon

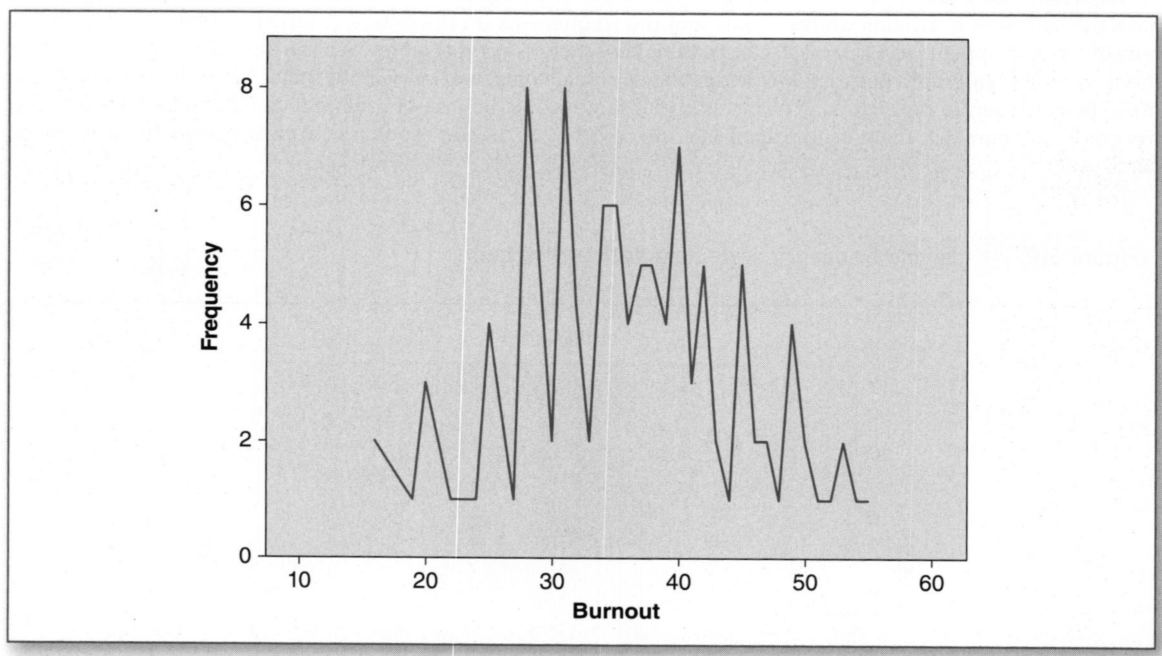

Frequency polygon: line graph that displays frequency of occurrence of scores; used for continuous data.

LEARNING CHECK

1. Table 3.5 is a frequency distribution table for the ages of participants in Wendt's (2013) research. Use it to answer the following questions:
   a) What was the range of participant ages in this research?
      A: 15 years old to 23 years old
   b) How many 20-year-olds were there in this research?
      A: 6
   c) What percentage of the participants were 18 years old?
      A: 30.6%

Table 3.5 Absolute and Relative Frequencies of Participant Ages

Age (years)	*f* (frequency)	*rf* (relative frequency)
23	4	.037
22	3	.028
21	49	.454
20	6	.056
19	4	.037
18	33	.306
17	8	.074
15	1	.009
	108	1.000

2. What is the difference between a histogram and a frequency polygon?

   A: A histogram is more appropriate for discrete data, whereas a frequency polygon is more appropriate for continuous data.

3. Why might frequency distribution graphs be preferable to tables as a way to display data?

   A: Visual information is typically easier for people to understand quickly. Tables convey the same information, but it is often more difficult for people to digest information in tabular format than in pictorial format.

4. Figure 3.4 contains a histogram that displays the frequency of occurrence for scores on a class midterm exam (these data are for illustrative purposes only). Use this histogram to answer the following questions:

   a) How many students took this midterm exam?

      A: To get this number, add the frequency for each exam score. Doing so reveals that 40 students took the midterm exam.

   b) What was the most frequently occurring score on the midterm?

      A: Look for the highest point on the histogram; then see what score along the *x*-axis it corresponds to. Here, the most frequently occurring score is 85.

   c) How many students scored 91% on the midterm?

      A: 3

(Continued)

(Continued)

Figure 3.4 Histogram of Class Scores on a Midterm Exam

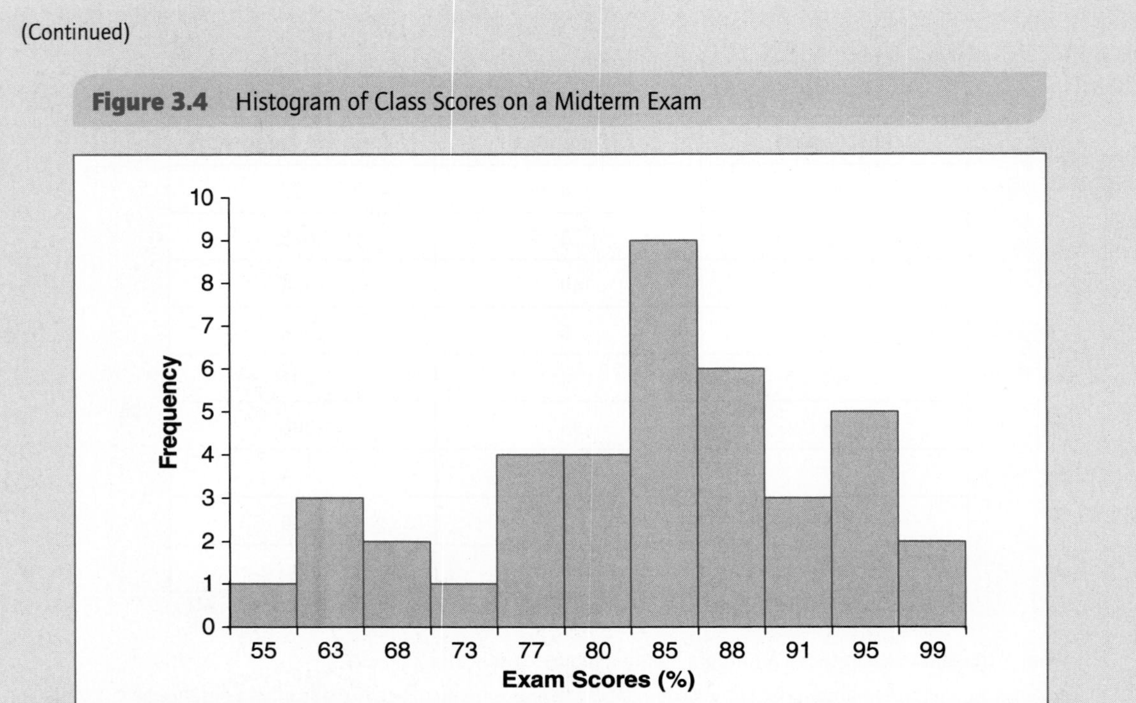

5. In Wendt's (2013) research, she recorded respondent's sex. What sort of frequency distribution graph would be used for these data? Explain your response.

   A: A bar graph is the best choice because a person's sex, similar to a person's year in college, is measured on a nominal scale.

COMMON VISUAL DISPLAYS OF DATA IN RESEARCH

Frequency tables and graphs are helpful in understanding large quantities of data. To get a sense of how variables are related to each other, researchers often present visual displays of relationships. In this section, we will discuss three types of visual displays that are frequently used in psychological research. In doing so, we will highlight the appropriate uses for each one and how to interpret them. In the next section of this chapter, we will learn how to make each of these types of displays using SPSS.

Bar Graphs

As we discussed in the previous section, bar graphs are used to display categorical (i.e., nominal) data. For example, suppose we want to know which group of students, first-years or seniors, scored higher on the measure of burnout. To find out, we can make a bar graph with the variable of year in school on the x-axis and average burnout score on the y-axis. As you can see in Figure 3.5, seniors did have a higher score on the burnout

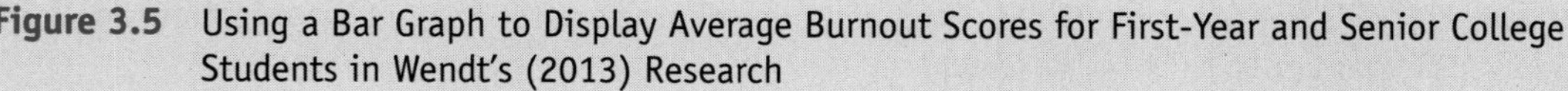

Figure 3.5 Using a Bar Graph to Display Average Burnout Scores for First-Year and Senior College Students in Wendt's (2013) Research

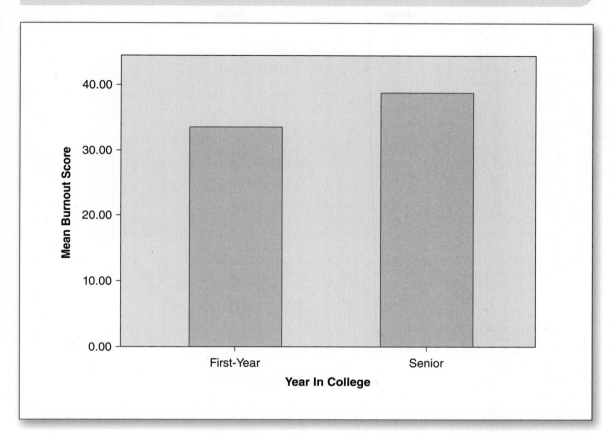

measure than did first-year students. In Chapters 7 and 8, we will learn to use tools that will allow us to determine whether in fact this is a meaningful difference between the two groups of students.

Let's examine another example of a bar graph. In a research study that we will detail in more depth in Chapter 10, Donte Bernard and his colleagues (Bernard, McManus, & Saucier, 2014) asked students to allocate a fixed amount of money to various campus student organizations. Some of their results are displayed in a bar graph that you can see in Figure 3.6. Along the x-axis is the name of each student organization. The y-axis contains the average amount of money that participants allocated to each organization. Again, notice that there is a space between each bar because student organization is a nominal variable.

Scatterplots

Scatterplots are used to display the relationship between two variables operationalized using a scale measurement. For example, in Wendt's (2013) research, she constructed a scatterplot between two of her variables, specifically, a scatterplot of the relationship between role overload and burnout. This scatterplot

Figure 3.6 Using a Bar Graph to Display Average Dollar Allocations for Student Organizations in Bernard et al.'s (2014) Research

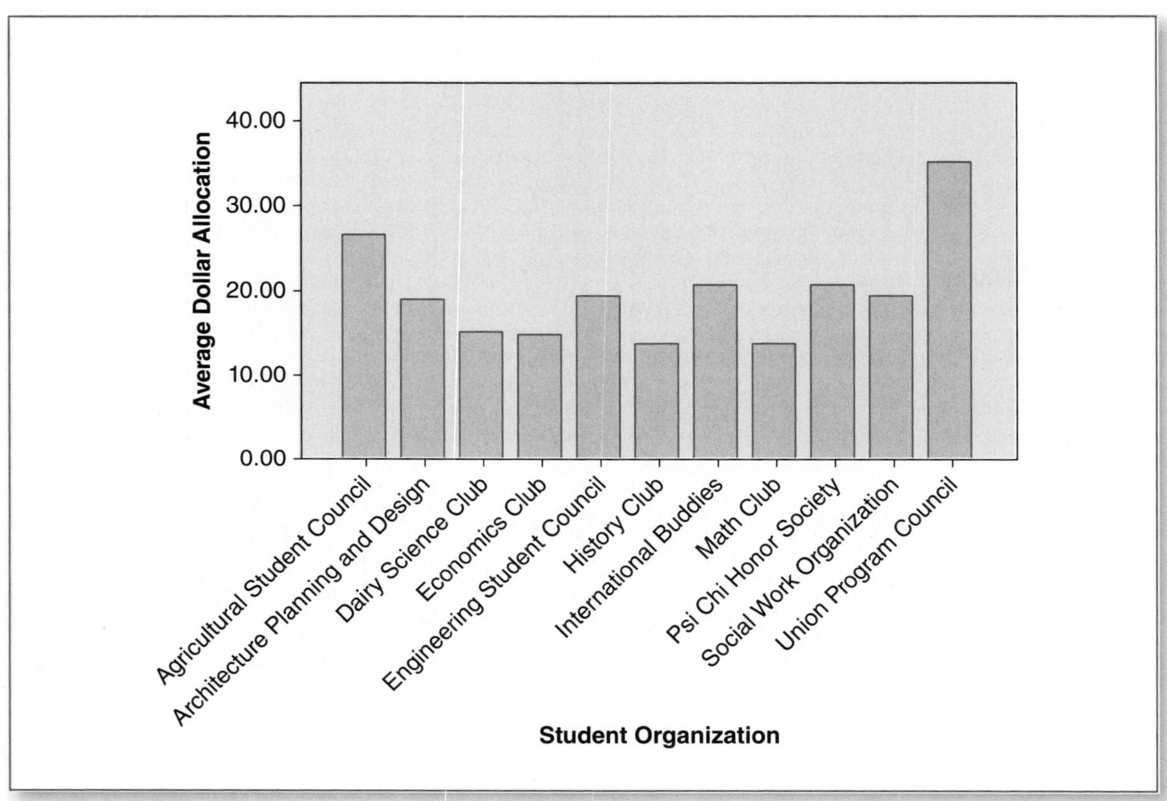

appears in Figure 3.7. Each dot in the scatterplot represents the score of one respondent on the role overload measure (along the x-axis) and the burnout measure (along the y-axis). We examine the trend that these dots display and see that, in general, as people score toward the high end of the role overload measure, they tend to score toward the high end of the burnout measure. Of course, there are exceptions to this general trend, but that's the overall picture that is painted in this scatterplot.

Scatterplot: graph that visually displays the relationship between two scale variables.

In Chapters 12 and 13, we will learn statistical tools that quantify the strength of the relationship between two scale variables displayed in a scatterplot. For now, understand that there are three types of relationships between scale variables that a scatterplot can reveal. First, there is a **linear relationship**; that is, the relationship can be displayed with a straight line. The relationship between role overload and burnout in Wendt's (2013)

Figure 3.7 Using a Scatterplot to Display a Positive Linear Relationship Between Role Overload and Burnout in Wendt's (2013) Research

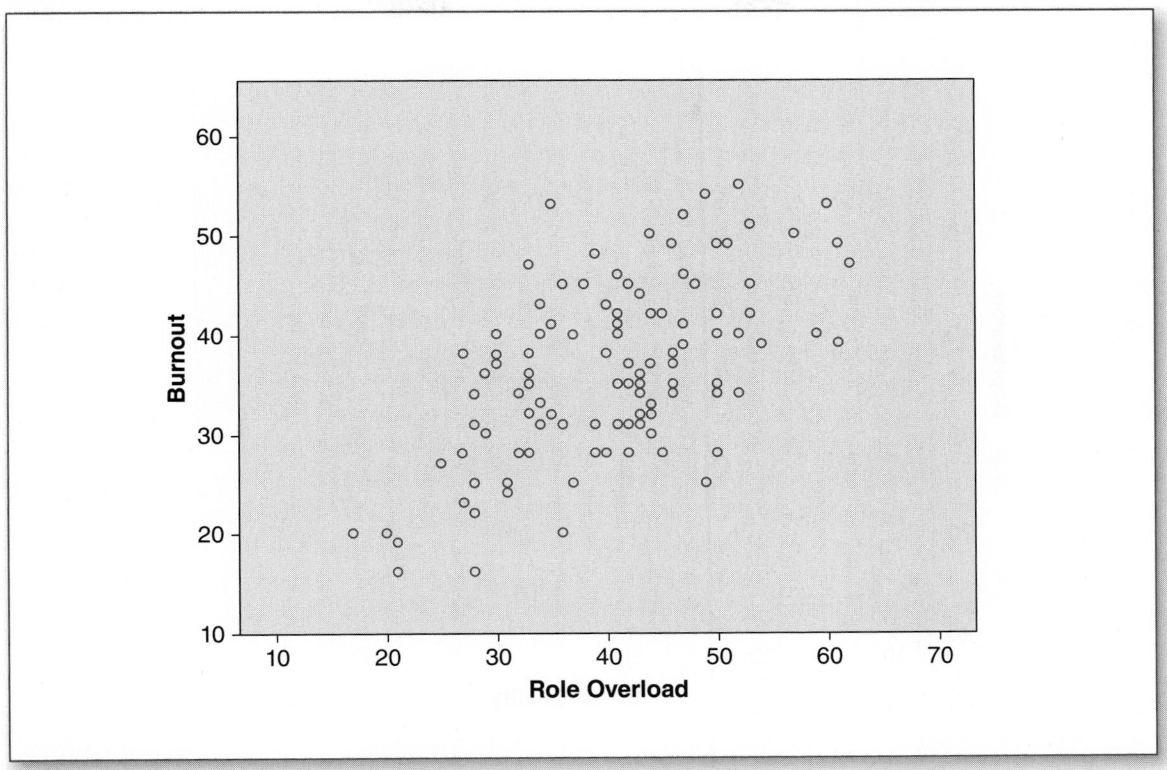

research is an example of a linear relationship because the general pattern of data points flows from the lower left to the upper right (what is called a "positive" linear relationship, which we touched on quickly in Chapter 1 and will discuss in detail in Chapter 12). Another example of a linear relationship would be the relationship between sleep quality and depression (Davidson, Babson, Bonn-Miller, Soutter, & Vannoy, 2013). You can see an example of this linear relationship in Figure 3.8. Here, the data points flow from the upper left corner to the lower right corner (what is called a "negative" linear relationship).

Linear relationship: relationship between two variables that is displayed with a straight line.

If one type of relationship is called linear, it will come as no surprise that another type of relationship between scale variables is called a **nonlinear relationship**. That is, the relationship is displayed by a curve rather than by a straight line. Let's take an example that you are likely familiar with. Have you ever been so

Figure 3.8 Using a Scatterplot to Display a Negative Linear Relationship Between Sleep Quality and Depression

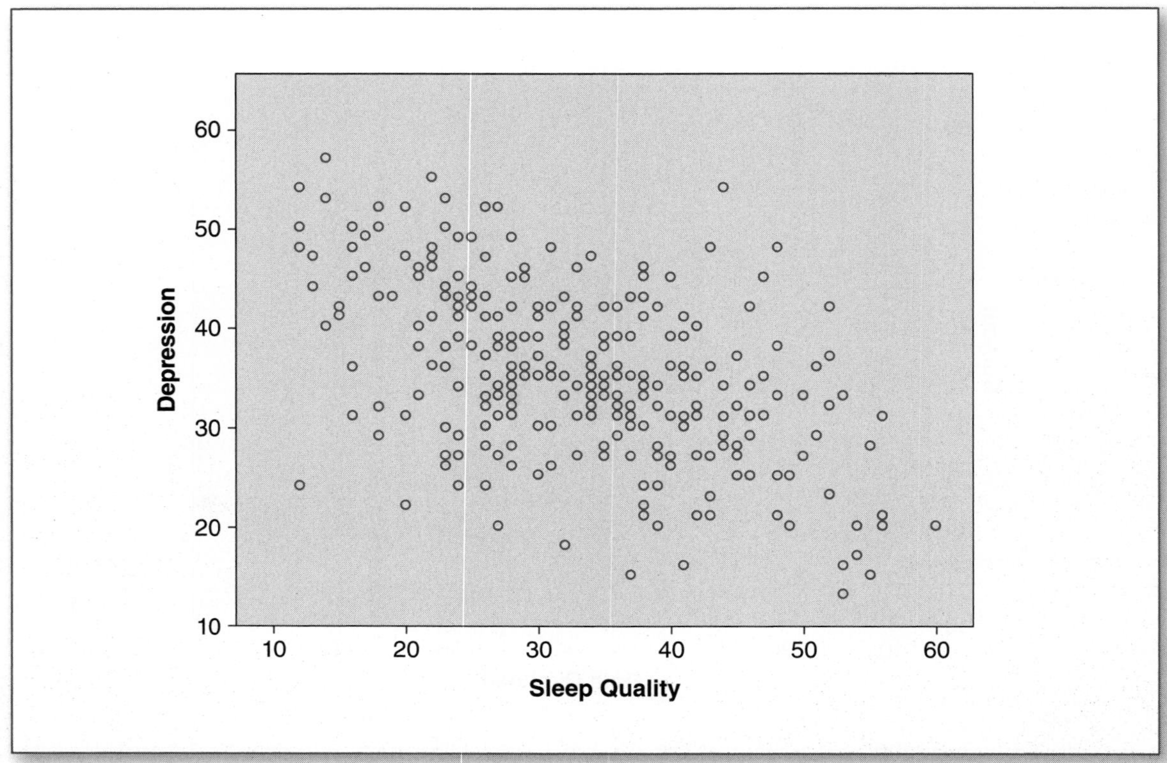

excited or nervous about a test or some sort of performance (e.g., sports or music) that you couldn't concentrate on doing what you needed to do to succeed at the task? Conversely, have you ever been so unmotivated in a situation that you simply did not care that your performance would be bad? According to Yerkes–Dodson's Law (1908), our performance on a task is at its best not when we are highly motivated or lacking motivation but at some optimal (midlevel) point of arousal. This nonlinear relationship is displayed in Figure 3.9. As you can see, too much motivation can lead to a decrement in performance because at those overly motivated levels, it becomes difficult to focus on the task itself.

The final type of relationship that a scatterplot can reveal is no relationship between the two variables. That is, the dots on the scatterplot look like they were randomly thrown onto it with no linear or nonlinear relationship. I know of no research suggesting any sort of relationship between shoe size and intelligence. You can see such this relationship in Figure 3.10.

Nonlinear relationship: relationship between two variables that is displayed by a curved line.

Figure 3.9 Yerkes–Dodson's Law: A Nonlinear Relationship

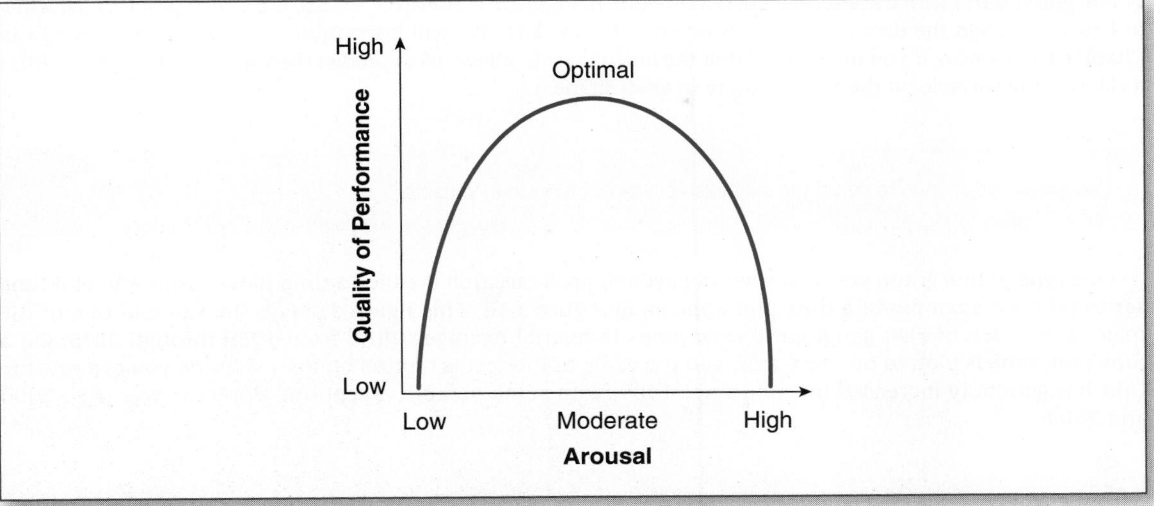

Figure 3.10 Scatterplot That Displays What "No Relationship" Between Shoe Size and Intelligence Would Look Like

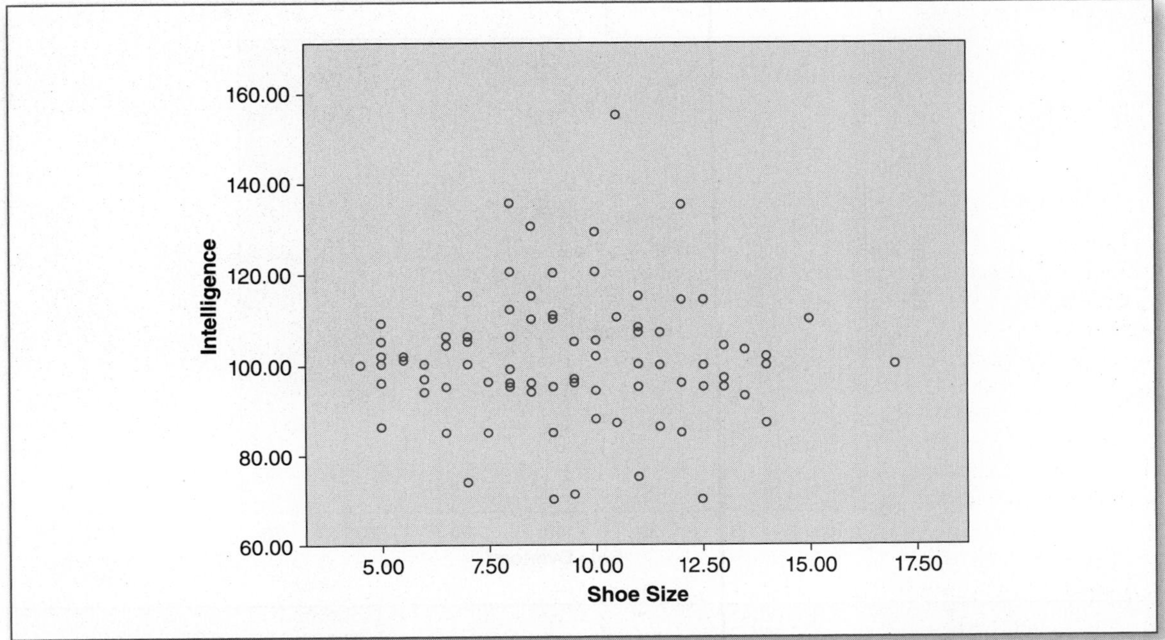

Line Graphs

Similar to scatterplots, **line graphs** are used to depict how two scale variables are related. Typically in psychology, many line graphs are used to predict the variable on the *y*-axis from the variable on the *x*-axis. In fact, this type of line graph starts with a scatterplot such as the one in Figure 3.7. However, we use the scatterplot to draw a line of best fit through the data points, as observed in Figure 3.11. We will learn more about the line of best fit in Chapter 13. For now, if you understand that the line of best fit allows us to predict the variable on the *y*-axis from a value of the variable on the *x*-axis, you're in great shape.

Line graph: graph used to depict the relationship between two scales variables.

One type of line graph we encounter in psychological research is called a **time plot**, or sometimes a time series plot. An example of a time plot appears in Figure 3.12. This figure displays the value of one of the major U.S. stock market gauges, the Dow Jones Industrial Average (DJIA), from 1989 through 2015. On a time plot, time is plotted on the *x*-axis, and the value of interest is plotted on the *y*-axis. As you can see, the DJIA has generally increased in value since 1989, with some notable exceptions along the way (e.g., 2000 and 2008).

Figure 3.11 "Line of Best Fit" That Allows Us to Predict Burnout (on the y-axis) from Role Overload (on the x-axis)

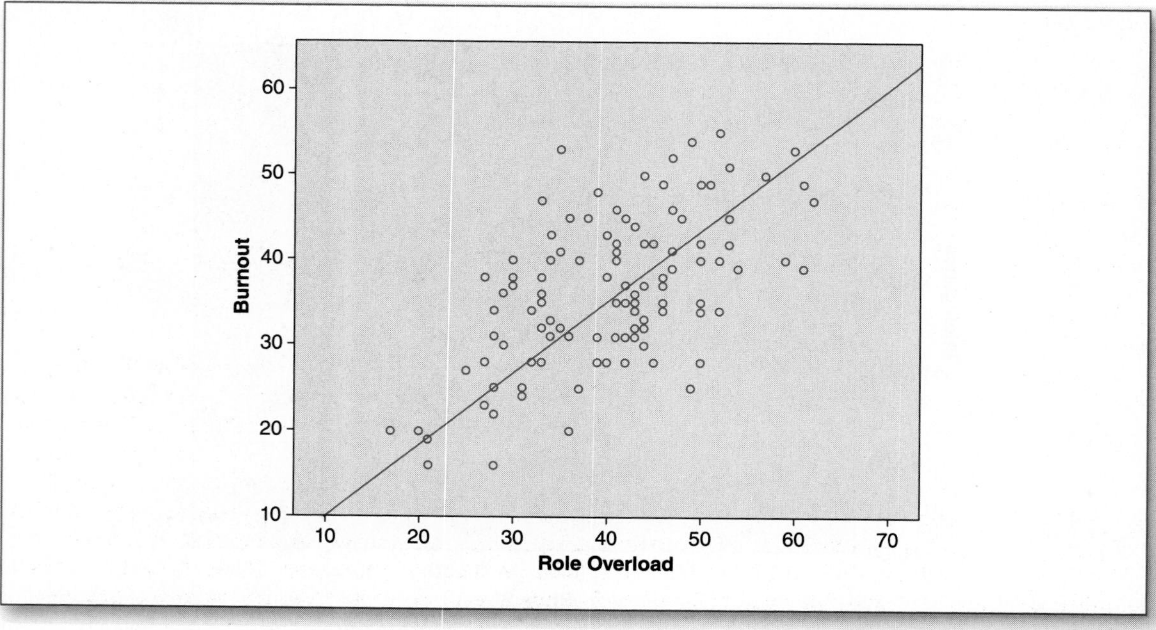

Figure 3.12 Time Plot of The Dow Jones Industrial Average Since 1989

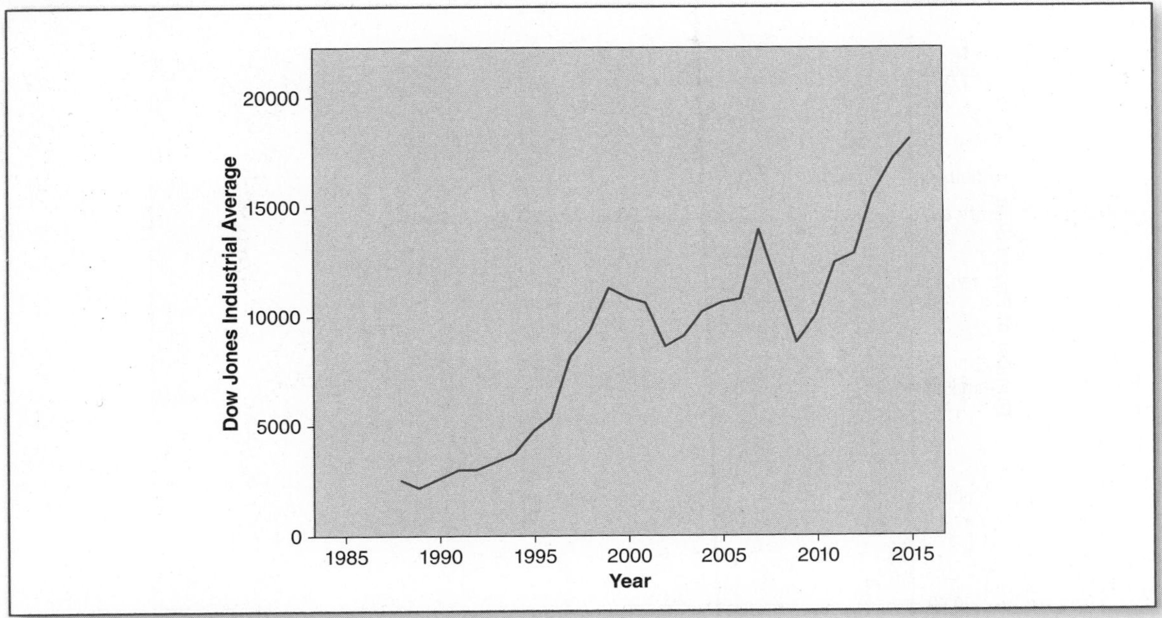

Time plot: type of line graph that plots the value of a variable on the *y*-axis as it changes over time, which is displayed on the *x*-axis.

How might a time plot be useful in making decisions? Let's discuss an example. There is a local pizza place in the small town in which my college is located. They asked me to help predict how much pizza people order so that they can have enough fresh ingredients on hand to meet customers' demands. To start this process, we plotted how many pizzas the restaurant sold each day for two months. These data are displayed in Figure 3.13. As we can see in this time plot, we know a lot of pizza is ordered on Sundays, with not many ordered on Mondays, Tuesdays, or Wednesdays, but then sales progressively pick up again Thursday, Friday, and Saturday. Armed with this time plot, the restaurant is now in a better position to predict when it will need to have fresh ingredients on hand to meet customer orders.[2]

Let's consider another use of line graphs. In their research, Caroline Campbell and Katherine White (2015) had undergraduate students complete a mood scale (Mayer & Gaschke, 1988) before and after engaging in moderately strenuous exercise. Half of the students listened to music while exercising, whereas the other half of the students did not listen to music while exercising. Their results are presented in a line graph in Figure 3.14. Along the *x*-axis is time, which was preexercise and postexercise. Along the *y*-axis is the average mood rating. There are two lines, one for the group of students who listened to music and one for the group of students who did not listen to music (the control group). As you can see in this line graph, both groups of students were in a better mood after exercising than before exercising. However, the mood of the group of students who listened to music while exercising improved even more than did the mood of the control group, who did not listen to music while exercising.

Figure 3.13 How Can This Time Plot Help a Restaurant Manage Its Pizza Business?

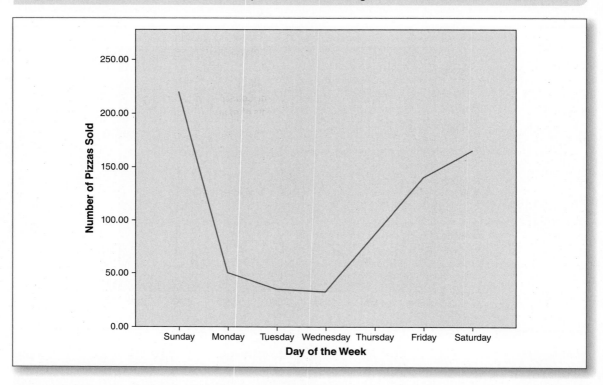

Figure 3.14 Results of Campbell and White's (2015) Experiment

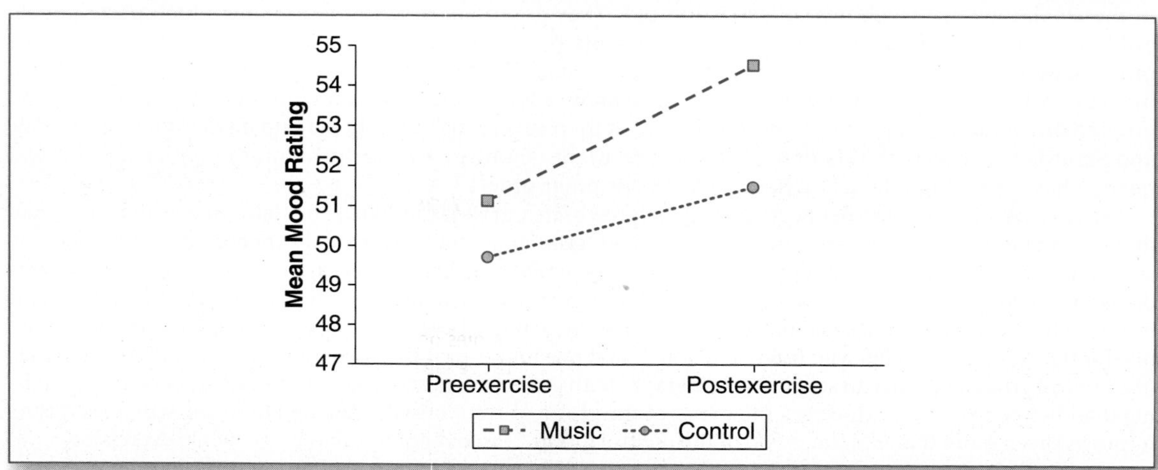

Source: Campbell, C. R., & White, K. R. G. (2015). Working it out: Examining the psychological effects of music on moderate-intensity exercise. *Psi Chi Journal of Psychological Research, 20,* 73–79.

LEARNING CHECK

1. Look back at Figure 3.6. Interpret what information this visual display is communicating by using as simple language as possible.

   A: The Union Program Council was awarded more money (more than \$30/respondent) than any other student organization was awarded, followed by the Agricultural Student Council (slightly less than \$30/respondent). The History Club and the Math Club were awarded the least amounts of money of any student organization.

2. Interpret the bar graph in Figure 3.15 by using as simple language as possible:

Figure 3.15

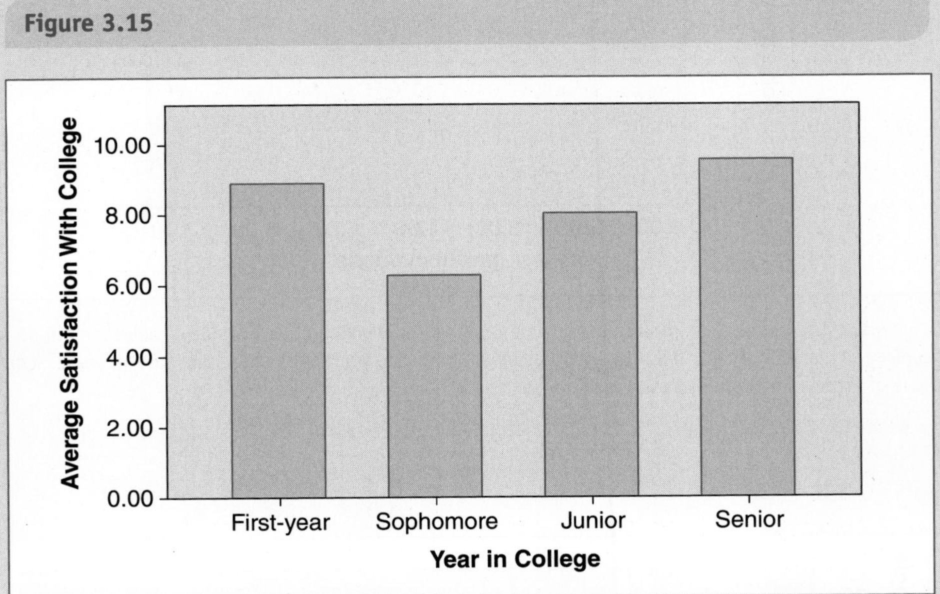

   A: Satisfaction with college tends to be particularly high among first-years and seniors, with sophomores having the lowest level of satisfaction with college.

3. Look back at Figure 3.7. Interpret what information this visual display is communicating by using as simple language as possible.

   A: As scores on the measure of role overload increase in value, scores on the burnout measure tend to increase in value as well. Stated differently, as scores on the measure of role overload decrease in value, scores on the burnout measure tend to decrease in value.

(Continued)

(Continued)

4. Interpret the scatterplot in Figure 3.16 by using as simple language as possible.

Figure 3.16

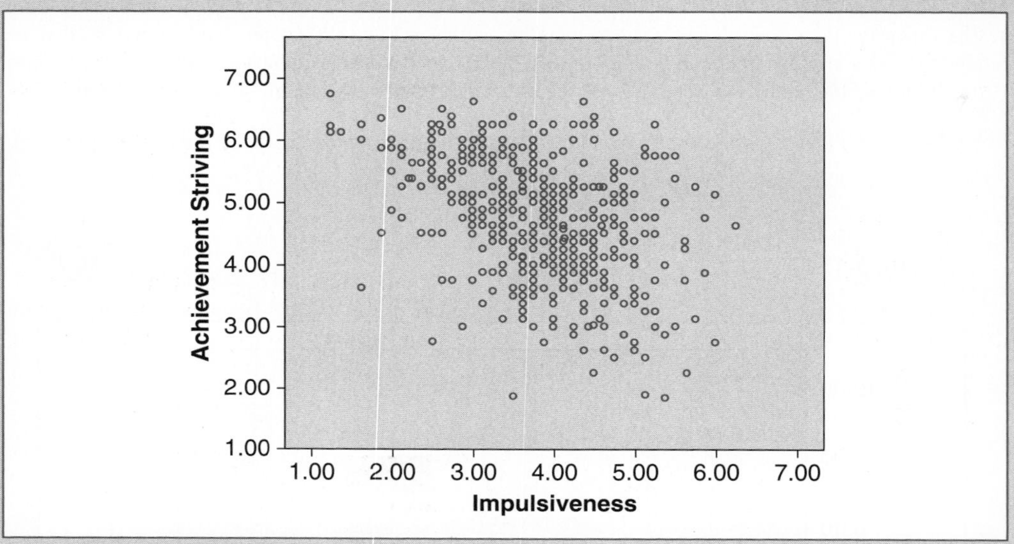

A: As scores on the measure of impulsiveness increase in value, scores on the measure of achievement striving tend to decrease in value. Stated differently, as scores on the measure of impulsiveness decrease in value, scores on the measure of achievement striving tend to increase in value.

5. Interpret the time plot in Figure 3.17 by using as simple language as possible.

Figure 3.17

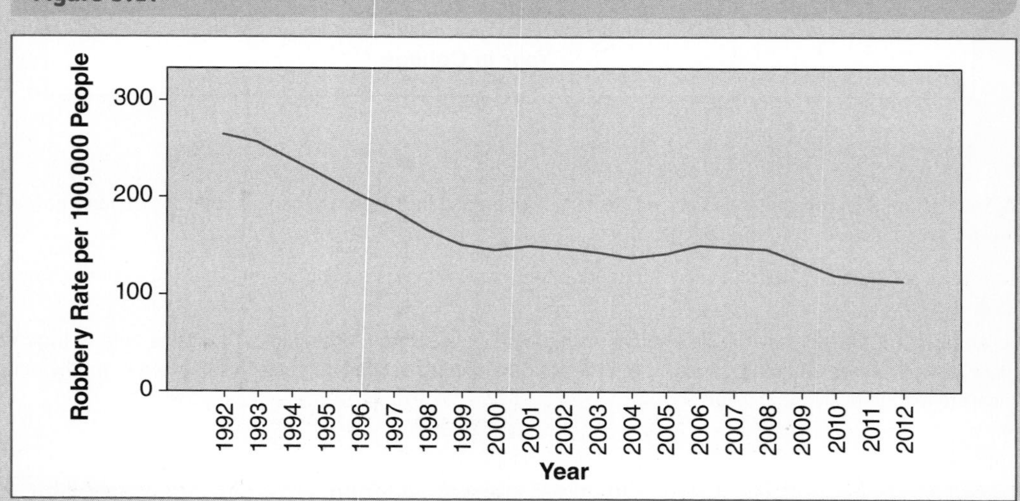

A: In 1992, there were close to 300 robberies per 100,000 people. That rate declined steadily until 2000, to about 150 robberies per 100,000 people. It remained at about that level until 2008 when it began to decline again.

USING SPSS TO MAKE VISUAL DISPLAYS OF DATA

In addition to being able to make sense of these three common visual displays, you might need to construct them at some point, particularly if you need to collect and present data in your class. In this section, we will learn how to make each type of display using SPSS.

We will use Wendt's (2013) data in the SPSS spreadsheet file titled "Wendt's data.sav". Let's open that spreadsheet and get to work on our visual displays.

Making a Bar Graph

Let's first make the bar graph that appears in Figure 3.5. This figure shows the average burnout scores of first-year and senior-year students. Remember that we make a bar graph when we have a nominal (categorical) variable for which we want information. In this example, we want to see burnout scores for first-year and senior students. Let's make this bar graph with SPSS.

1. Click on *Graphs* and then on *Chart Builder*.

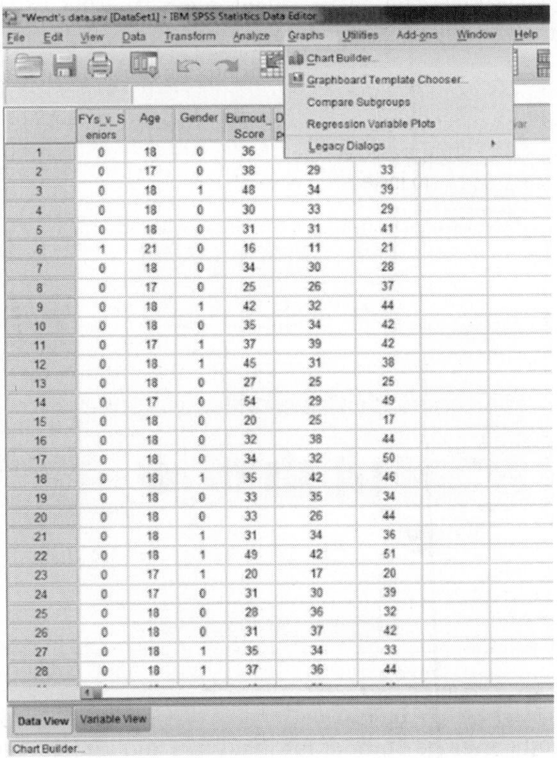

*Wendt's data.sav [DataSet1] - IBM SPSS Statistics Data Editor

File Edit View Data Transform Analyze Graphs Utilities Add-ons Window Help

Chart Builder...
Graphboard Template Chooser...
Compare Subgroups
Regression Variable Plots
Legacy Dialogs

	FYs_v_Seniors	Age	Gender	Burnout_Score	D...		var
1	0	18	0	36			
2	0	17	0	38	29	33	
3	0	18	1	48	34	39	
4	0	18	0	30	33	29	
5	0	18	0	31	31	41	
6	1	21	0	16	11	21	
7	0	18	0	34	30	28	
8	0	17	0	25	26	37	
9	0	18	1	42	32	44	
10	0	18	0	35	34	42	
11	0	17	1	37	39	42	
12	0	18	1	45	31	38	
13	0	18	0	27	25	25	
14	0	17	0	54	29	49	
15	0	18	0	20	25	17	
16	0	18	0	32	38	44	
17	0	18	0	34	32	50	
18	0	18	1	35	42	46	
19	0	18	0	33	35	34	
20	0	18	0	33	26	44	
21	0	18	1	31	34	36	
22	0	18	1	49	42	51	
23	0	17	1	20	17	20	
24	0	17	0	31	30	39	
25	0	18	0	28	36	32	
26	0	18	0	31	37	42	
27	0	18	1	35	34	33	
28	0	18	1	37	36	44	

Data View Variable View

Chart Builder...

2. At the bottom of the *Chart Builder* window, choose *Bar*, and from the visual options to the right, select (by double-clicking) the *Simple Bar* graph option.

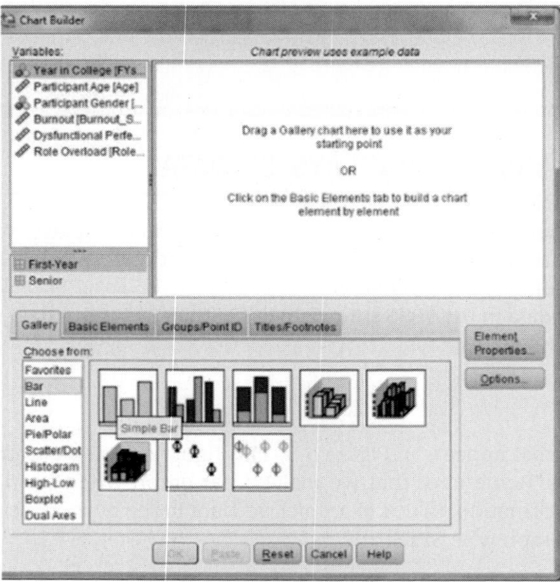

3. At the top of the *Chart Builder* window will be a blank graph. Drag the variable `Year in College` onto the x-axis. Then drag the variable `Burnout` onto the y-axis.

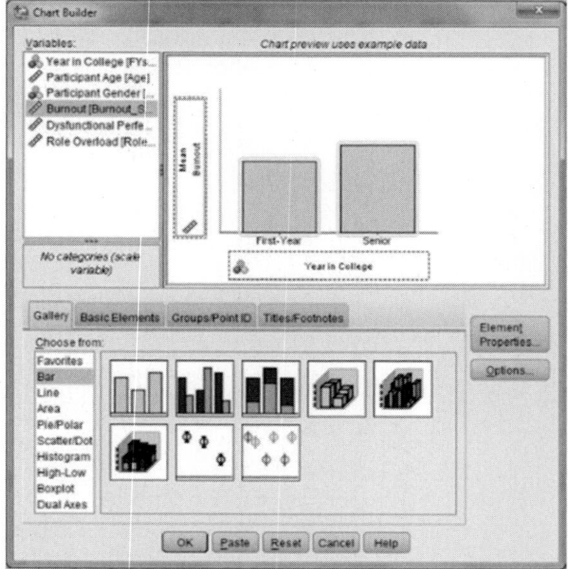

4. Click *OK*, and your bar graph will appear.

Our first bar graph displayed the average burnout for first-years and seniors. Let's make another bar graph, with this one displaying the total number of first-years and seniors in Wendt's (2013) research. We saw this frequency distribution graph in Figure 3.1, and now we will make it ourselves.

1. Click on *Graphs* and then on *Chart Builder*.
2. As in the previous example, choose *Bar* and then *Simple Bar*.
3. Once again, put the variable `Year in College` on the *x*-axis and `Burnout` on the *y*-axis.

Here's where things get a little different.

4. In the *Element Properties* window, click on the *Statistic:* dropdown menu in the middle of that window. Choose *Valid N*. By selecting *Valid N*, we are getting frequency counts for the number of first-years and the number of seniors in this research.

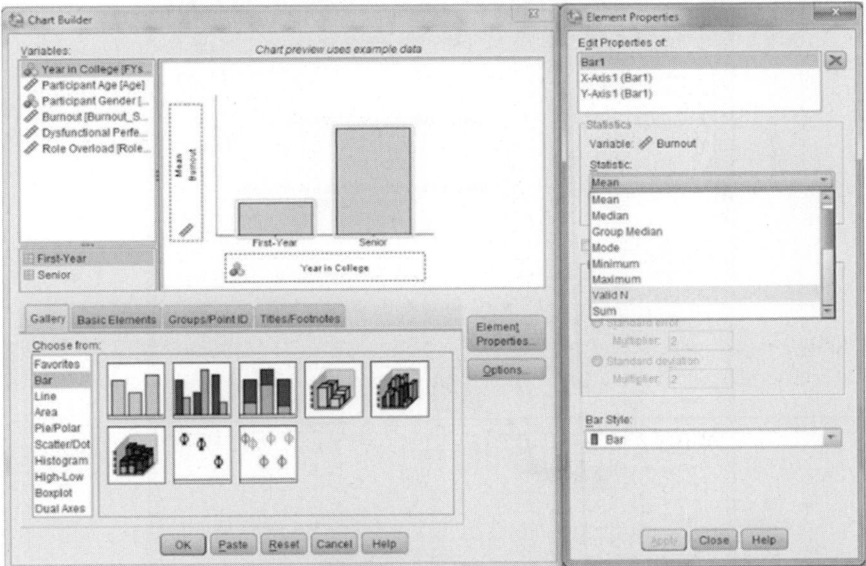

5. Click *Apply* at the bottom of the *Element Properties* window.

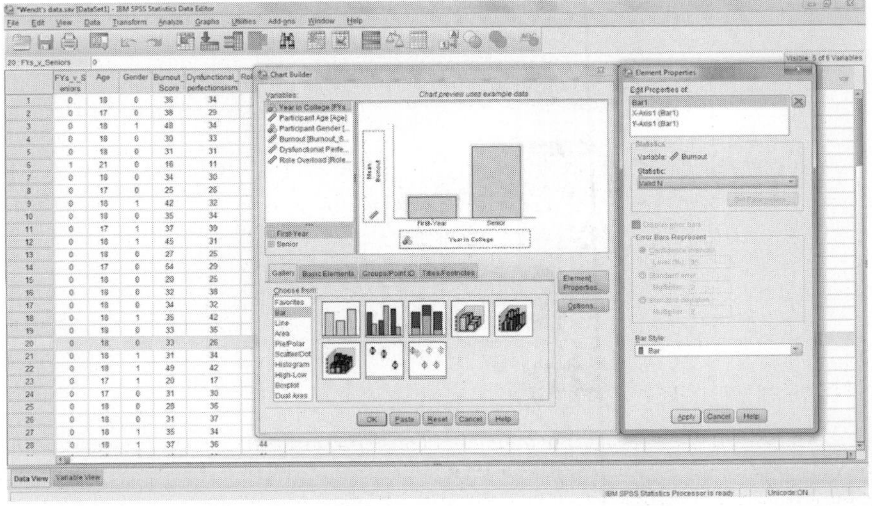

6. Click *OK*, and your frequency distribution bar graph will soon appear.

Making a Scatterplot

Let's make the scatterplot that appears in Figure 3.7. This scatterplot displayed the relationship between role overload and burnout in Wendt's (2013) research. Here is how we use SPSS to make a scatterplot:

1. Click on *Graphs* and then on *Chart Builder*.
2. Choose *Scatter/Dot*, and then double-click on *Simple Scatter*.

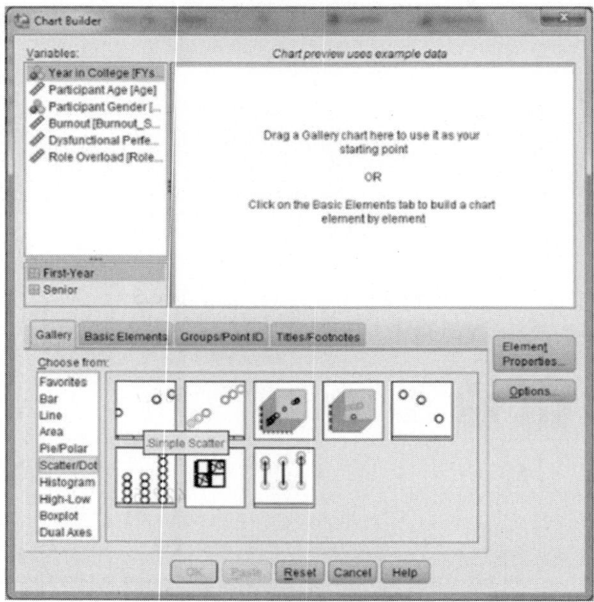

3. Drag `Role Overload` onto the x-axis and `Burnout` onto the y-axis.

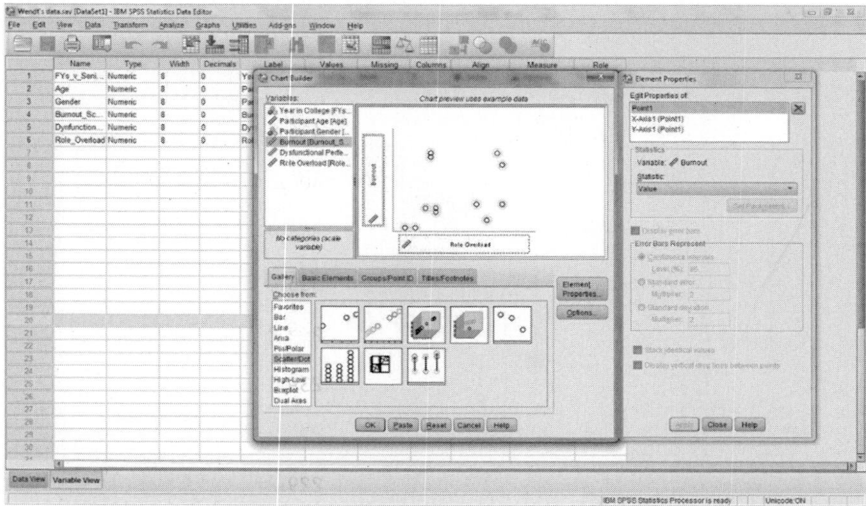

4. Click *OK*, and your scatterplot will soon appear.

Making a Line Graph

To give you some experience creating an SPSS spreadsheet and entering data into a spreadsheet, we'll use some new data and create a time plot. Table 3.6 contains the number of motor vehicle thefts per 100,000 people in United States between 1995 and 2012 (Federal Bureau of Investigation, 2015). Let's enter these data into SPSS and create a time plot.

You will need to start a new SPSS spreadsheet. To enter these data into SPSS, we need to first go into *Variable View* (in the bottom left corner of the spreadsheet). Here, we create two variables: (1) year and (2) motor vehicle thefts per 100,000 people.

Table 3.6 Yearly Motor Vehicle Theft Rate, 1995–2012

Year	Motor vehicle thefts per 100,000 people
1995	560.3
1996	525.7
1997	505.7
1998	459.9
1999	422.5
2000	412.5
2001	430.5
2002	432.9
2003	433.7
2004	421.5
2005	416.8
2006	400.2
2007	364.9
2008	315.4
2009	259.2
2010	239.1
2011	230.0
2012	229.7

In the first column, titled *Name*, you need to give each variable a name. I called the first variable `Year` and the second variable `Motor_vehicle_thefts`. Notice the underscores to connect the words in this second variable. SPSS does not allow you to have spaces between words in the *Name* column.

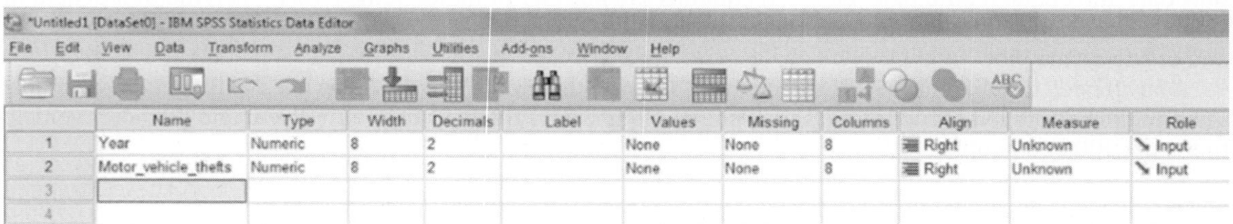

In the second column, make sure your type is *Numeric*. Although arbitrary, the *Width* column can be left at its default for our purposes. For the variable `Year`, change *Decimals* to zero (0). It makes no sense to have decimal places in the year. For the variable `Motor_vehicle_thefts`, Table 3.6 reveals they are reported to one decimal place, so for this variable, change *Decimals* to one (1).

In the *Label* column, we are allowed to call our variables anything we want. Given the constraints in the *Name* column, it is a good idea to provide some sort of label to each variable, as I have done here:

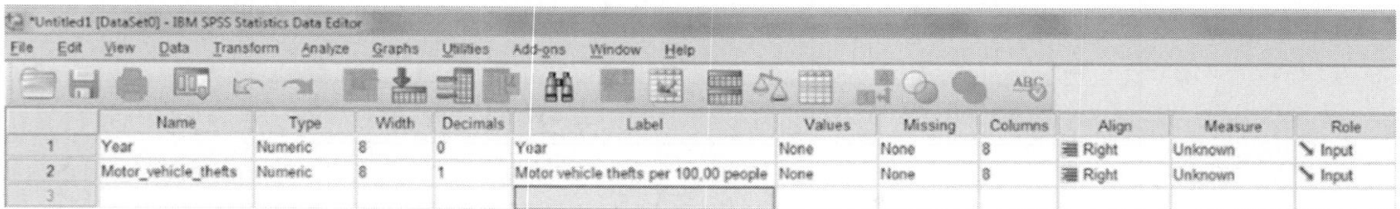

When you have a large dataset with many variables, providing a label for each variable is helpful in staying organized, which is something that will become even more important in later chapters.

Finally, move over to your *Measure* column. Here is where we tell SPSS how the data were measured. Test yourself here. Is the `Year` variable nominal, ordinal, or scale? How about the `Motor_vehicle_thefts` variable? Here's the screenshot to answer these two questions:

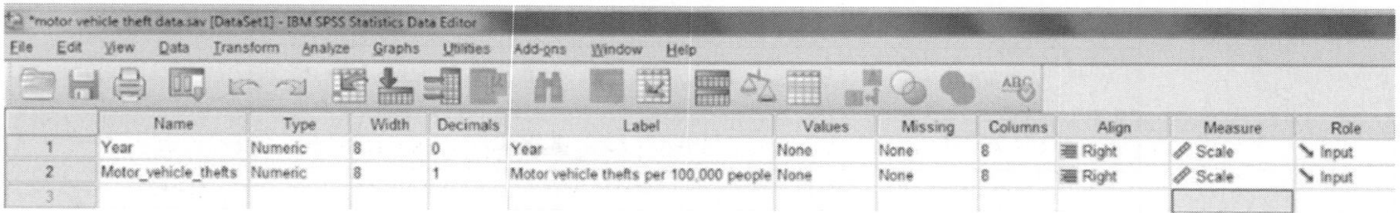

In the lower left corner of the screen, switch to *Data View*, and here's what you will see:

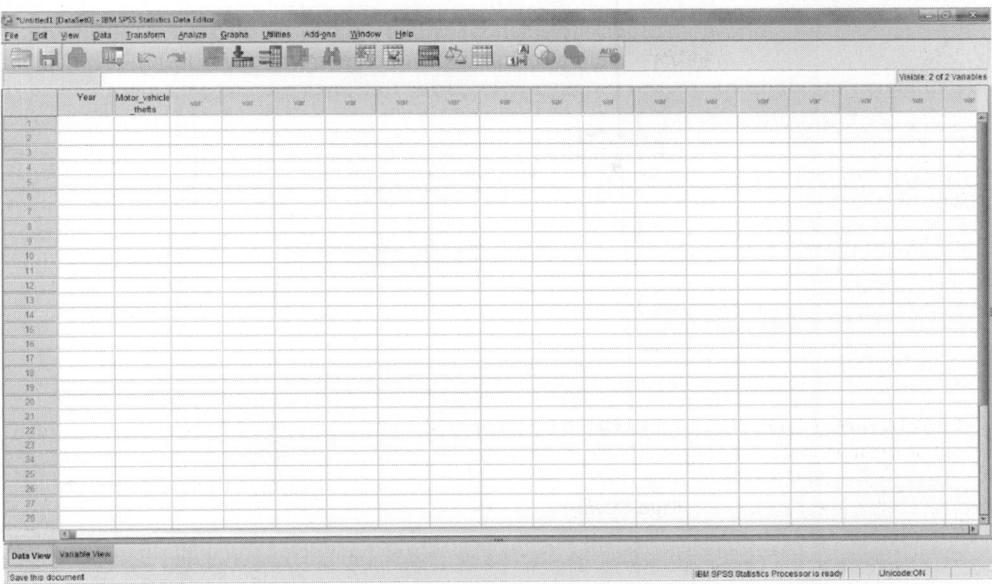

Now, enter your data from Table 3.6 into your spreadsheet. When you get done, here's what you will see:

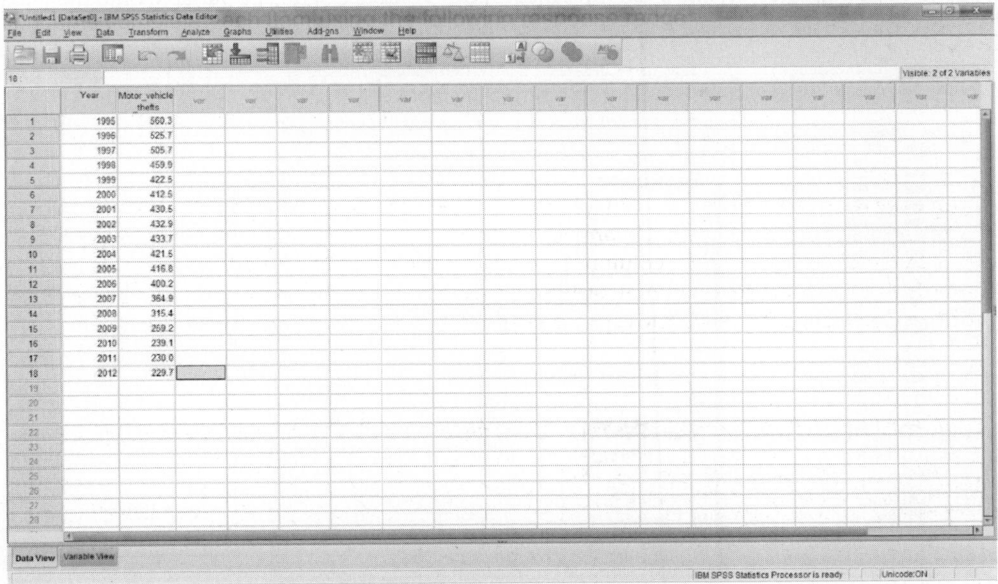

	Year	Motor_vehicle_thefts
1	1995	560.3
2	1996	525.7
3	1997	505.7
4	1998	459.9
5	1999	422.5
6	2000	412.5
7	2001	430.5
8	2002	432.9
9	2003	433.7
10	2004	421.5
11	2005	416.8
12	2006	400.2
13	2007	364.9
14	2008	315.4
15	2009	259.2
16	2010	239.1
17	2011	230.0
18	2012	229.7

1. Click on *Graphs* and then on *Chart Builder*.
2. Choose *Line*, and then double-click on *Simple Line*.

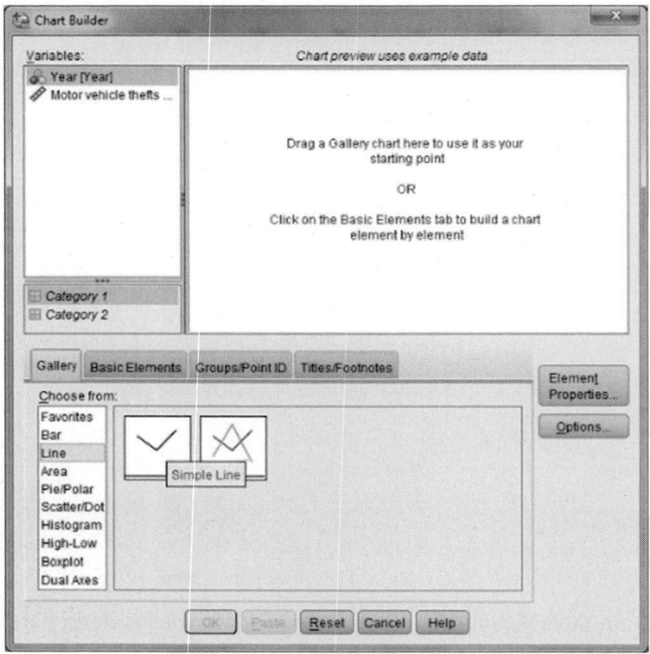

3. Drag the `Year` variable onto the x-axis and the `Motor_vehicle_thefts` variable onto the y-axis.

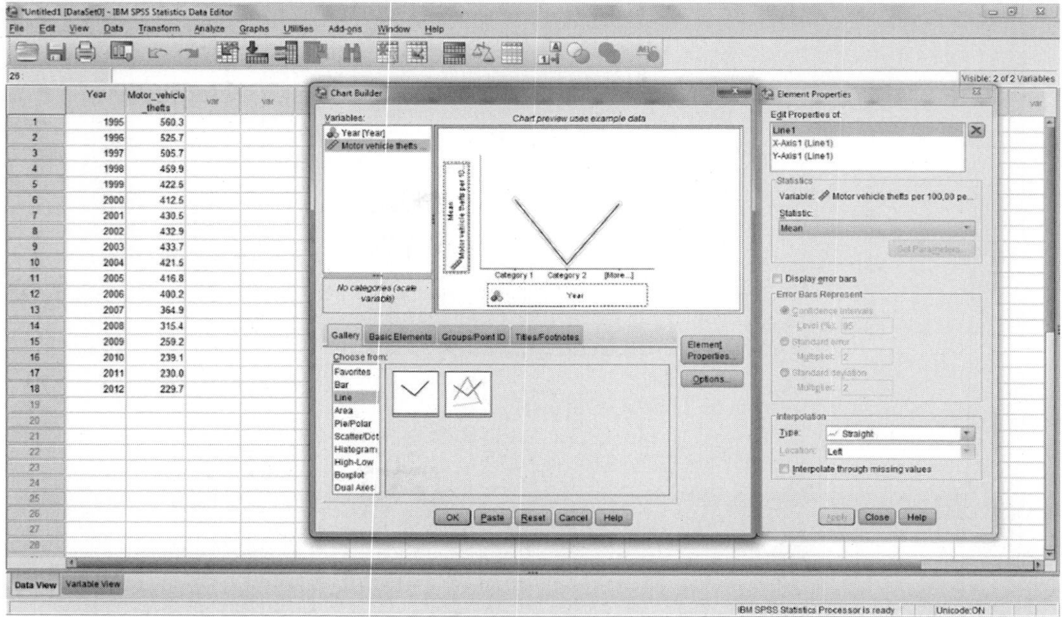

4. Now move over to the *Element Properties* window. In the *Statistic* box, click on the dropdown menu, and choose *Value*. Doing so will allow your *y*-axis to be labeled correctly.

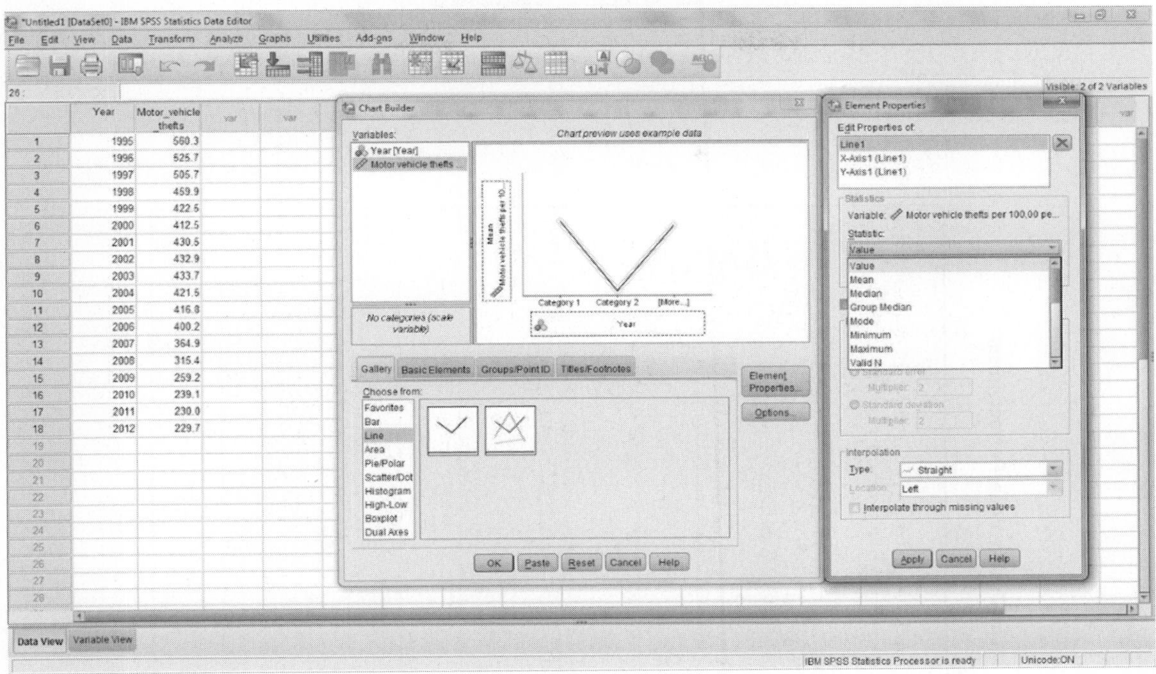

5. Hit *Apply* at the bottom of the *Element Properties* box.

6. Then hit *OK* in the *Chart Builder* box, and prepare to be impressed.

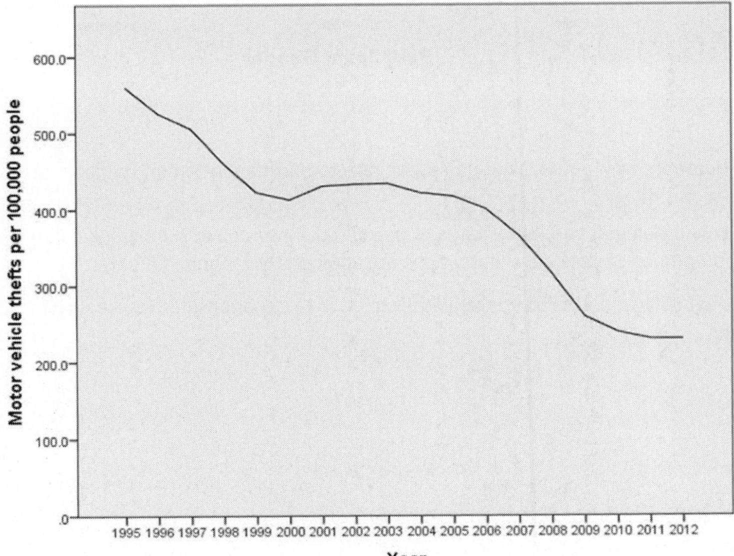

LEARNING CHECK

1. Use Wendt's (2013) data and in SPSS, make a bar graph to illustrate sex differences in dysfunctional perfectionism.

   A:

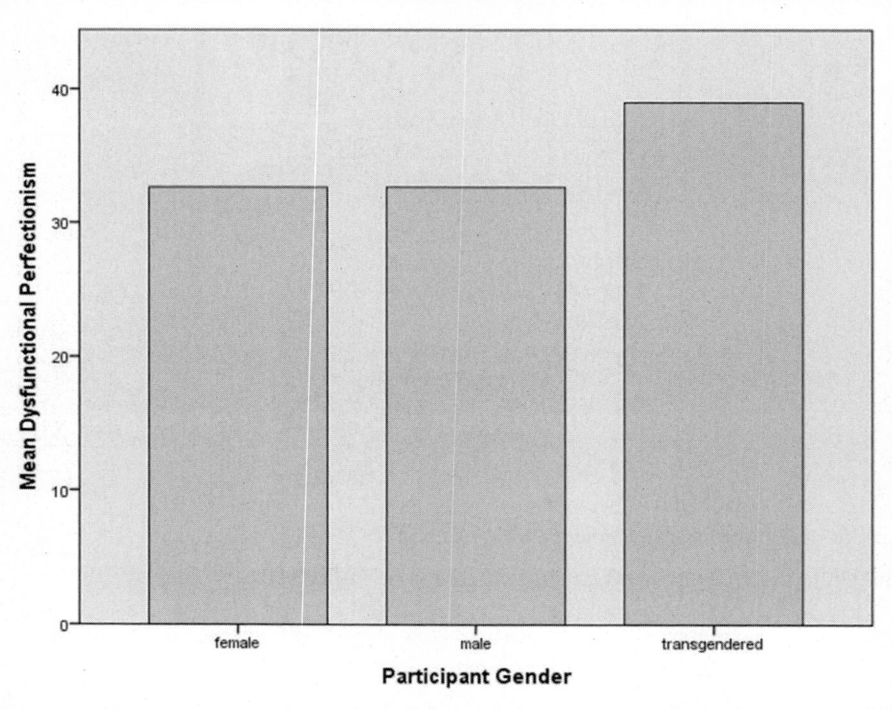

2. In the previous question, why would it not be appropriate to make a scatterplot to illustrate sex differences in dysfunctional perfectionism?

   A: A person's sex is a nominal variable. That is, a person falls into one and only one category on this variable. A scatterplot is appropriate for scale data; bar graphs are appropriate for nominal data.

3. Use Wendt's (2013) data and in SPSS, make a scatterplot of the relationship between dysfunctional perfectionism and role overload.

   A:

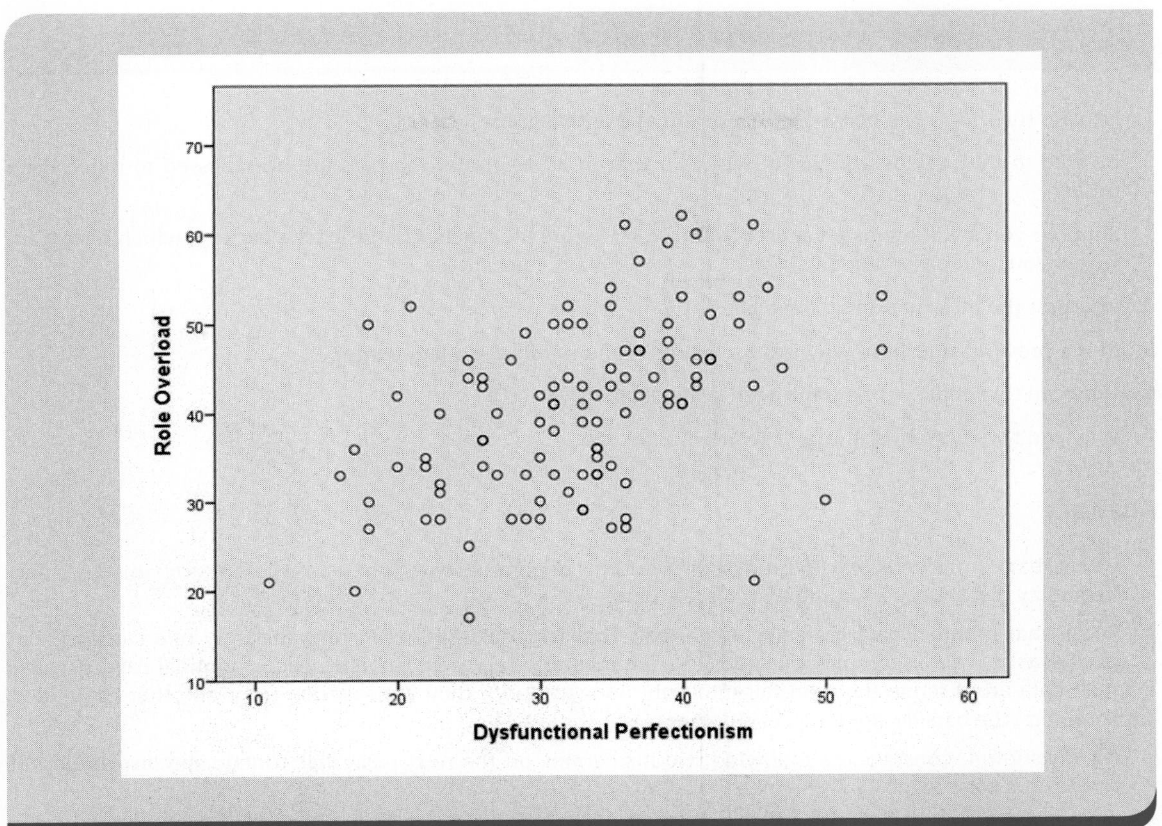

NOTES

1. It certainly does make logical sense to place "first-years" before "seniors" on the x-axis because students have to be first-year college students before they can become college seniors.

2. Of course, there are other pieces of data that the restaurant wanted to know, such as the types of pizzas ordered and whether customers dined in or ordered take-away. However, for the purposes of illustrating time plots, I presented only daily sales of pizzas.

CHAPTER APPLICATION QUESTIONS

1. Explain the difference between a bar graph and a histogram.
2. Related to the previous question, why is it that in a bar graph, the bars are not allowed to touch each other?
3. Suppose you are about to get a test back in class. Before the teacher hands back your test, which histogram would you (and other students) prefer to see? Explain your choice.
4. Interpret the information it conveys.
5. In the previous question, why is it an example of a nonlinear relationship?
6. Why can't we make a bar graph with scale data?
7. Why can't we make a scatterplot with nominal data?

Answers

1. We use bar graphs to display frequency distributions of nominal data, whereas we use histograms to display frequency distributions of ordinal and scale data.
2. Recall that nominal data are categorical data. That is, a datapoint is in one and only one category. Bar graphs, as we said in the previous question, are meant to represent frequencies for nominal data. Because such data are discrete (i.e., can fall into only one category), they are separate from all other categories. Therefore, the bars do not touch each other.

   For question 4, consider the following two histograms on the next page that contain the distribution of scores on a class exam.
3. The histogram in Figure 3.18a shows that many students tended to score toward the high end of the distribution on the test, whereas the histogram in Figure 3.18b shows more students toward the low end of the distribution on the test. So before knowing your own score, the top distribution would make you feel better about your chances of scoring well on the test.

   For question 5, consider the line graph in Figure 3.19.
4. This line graph shows that life satisfaction tends to decline in people's late teenage years, continuing through their 20s and 30s, but then it starts to increase once people reach their 40s and increases as people continue to age from that point in their lives.
5. This is a nonlinear relationship because the relationship between age and life satisfaction is different across different age levels. That is, it tends to decline in our teenage years until our 40s (a negative linear relationship), but then it tends to increase starting in our 40s as we age from that point (a positive linear relationship).
6. A bar graph displays categories. Scale data do not contain categories, so there is no practical way to make a bar graph with scale data.
7. Nominal data contain categories. But scatterplots are useful only when the two variables being plotted are both scale data. There is no practical way to make a scatterplot with nominal data because categories cannot be plotted on a scatterplot.

Figure 3.18a

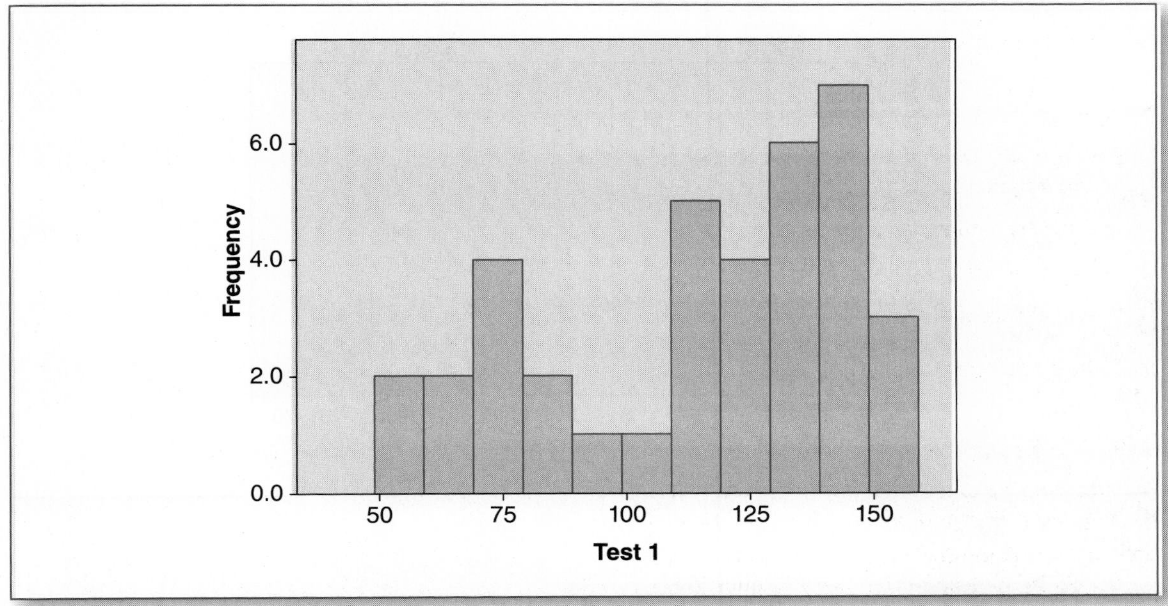

Figure 3.18b

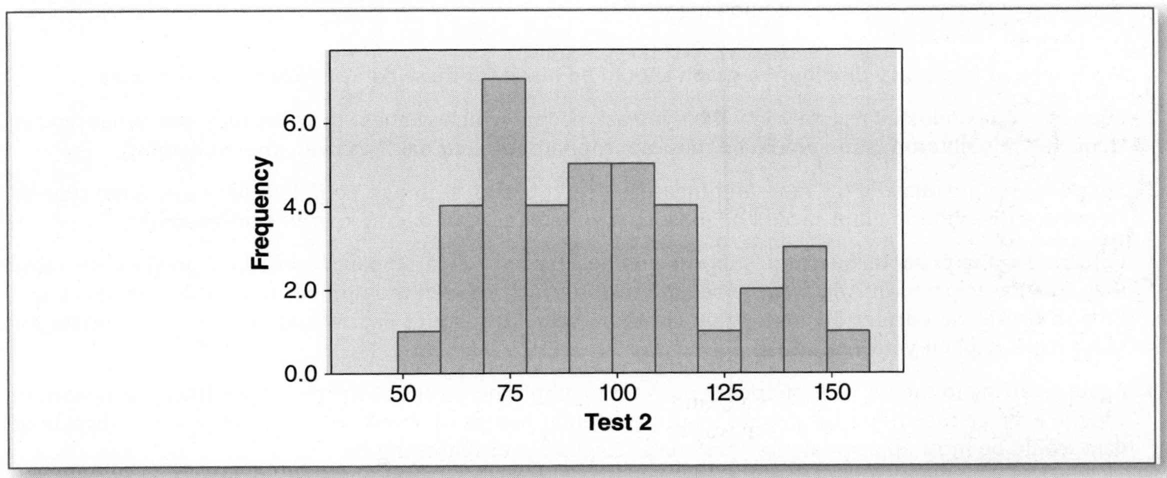

Figure 3.19

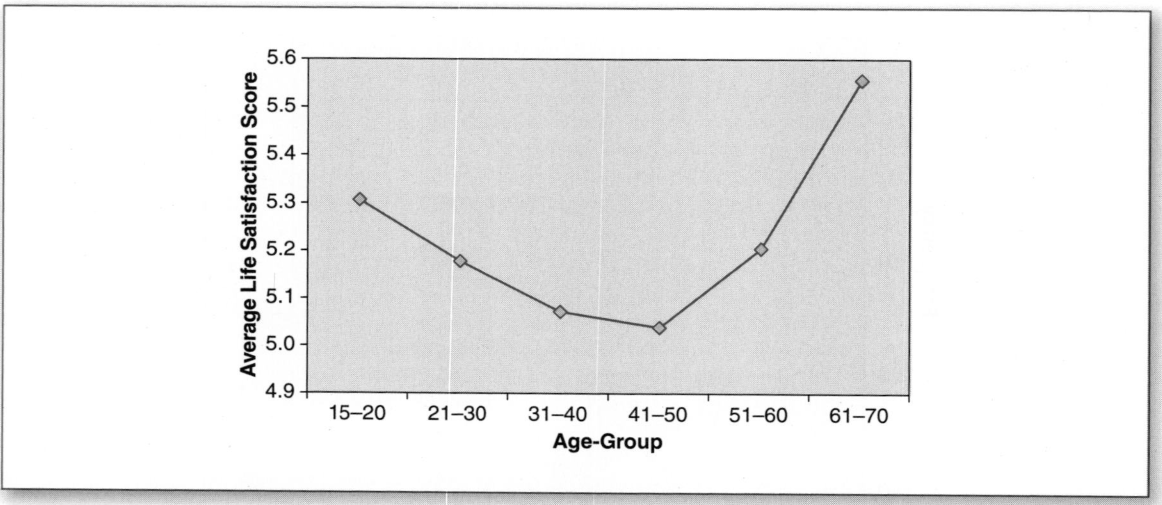

QUESTIONS FOR CLASS DISCUSSION

1. A researcher surveyed 10 undergraduate psychology majors about their study behaviors. The following is a list of the number of hours they spent studying on the weekend:

6	5	3	4	9
7	3	7	8	3

   What type of frequency distribution graph should be made for these data? Explain your response.

2. Suppose you conducted a survey in which you ask people which wireless provider they use. What type of frequency distribution graph would be most appropriate for your data? Explain your reasoning.
3. Suppose you organized a 5K race. You measured each person's time to complete the race. What type of frequency distribution graph would be most appropriate for your data? Explain your reasoning.
4. Referring to the previous question, suppose you had asked race participants how many previous 5K races they had participated in. You want to see the relationship between the number of previous 5K races and time to finish the current 5K race. What common visual display of data would be most appropriate for these data? Explain your reasoning.
5. Again referring to the 5K race, suppose you want to graph the results of the race. Specifically, you want to see the average race times for people wearing different brands of shoes. What common visual display of data would be most appropriate for these data? Explain your reasoning.

CHAPTER 4

Making Sense of Data

Measures of Central Tendency and Variability

After reading this chapter, you will be able to

- Calculate the three measures of central tendency and the three measures of variability
- Interpret the information conveyed by each measure of central tendency and variability
- Report the three measures of central tendency and variability in APA style
- Identify considerations when selecting a measure of central tendency
- Describe why variability is an essential part of research
- Generate the three measures of central tendency and variability using SPSS
- Interpret SPSS output with respect to the three measures of central tendency and variability

In the previous chapter, we discussed ways to organize and help us make sense of large quantities of data. Indeed, this is the essence of descriptive statistics. In this chapter, we will continue to add to our collection of descriptive statistical tools. Whereas the previous chapter emphasized tabular and graphical displays of data, this chapter and the next one will emphasize quantitative summaries of data. In this chapter, we will learn about what are called *measures of central tendency* and *measures of variability*. Much like an artist needs paint to paint a picture, a researcher needs measures of central tendency and variability to describe a dataset concisely.

In this chapter, we will begin by introducing the three measures of central tendency, how to calculate each one, and how they are reported in research studies. Next, we will discuss four considerations in choosing a measure of central tendency to describe a dataset. We will then discuss how to use the software program Statistical Package for the Social Sciences (SPSS) to generate these measures and interpret the output that SPSS gives us. After completing our discussion of the measures of central tendency, we will turn to three measures of variability. We will begin this discussion by explaining what is meant by "variability" and why it is an essential part of any research study. After learning how to calculate and interpret each measure of variability, we will use SPSS to generate them and interpret the corresponding output.

When learning about frequency tables and graphs in the previous chapter, we used a research study that Laura Wendt (2013) conducted. We will continue to use her study and data throughout most of this chapter. When we learn how to use SPSS, we will introduce a new study and use its data.

MEASURES OF CENTRAL TENDENCY

Three Measures of Central Tendency

As you saw in the previous chapter, research studies tend to contain a lot of data, and we need to make sense of it all somehow. You also know from the previous chapter that we could make a frequency distribution table or a frequency distribution graph of these data, and in doing so, it would help us understand what these data "look like" so that we can describe them quickly and understandably to other people. Now we are going to add to our collection of tools to describe data. In the first half of this chapter, we will examine measures of central tendency. In the second half, we will examine measures of variability.

I bet that when you first saw Table 4.1, which again contains the burnout score for each participant in Wendt's (2013) research, you wanted to throw your hands up in the air and walk away. At first glance, this table is a mess of random numbers between 15 and 75, the response range used on Wendt's measure of academic burnout. However, we can assign one number to describe all 108 datapoints. Of course, any one number used to describe so much data will have its limitations, but let's examine three ways we can assign one number to these data.

The purpose of a measure of central tendency is to provide one number that describes a large set of data. There are three measures of central tendency: mean, median, and mode. Let's discuss each one, including an examination of how they are calculated, by using a much smaller set of data than what Wendt (2013) used.

Mean

The **mean** is the arithmetic average of a set of numbers. It is the most commonly reported measure of central tendency in published research. To calculate a mean, we add together all of the scores in the dataset; then we divide by the number of scores in the dataset. Let's use the following (small) dataset to calculate its mean:

$$6, 5, 4, 6, 7, 8, 3, 5, 9, 2$$

To calculate the mean, sum these numbers (to get 55) and divide the sum by the number of scores (10). Formulaically, we have:

$$\frac{\Sigma x}{N}$$

where

Σ means "summation"

x is an individual score

N is the total number of scores in the dataset

The mean is thus:

$$\frac{6+5+4+6+7+8+3+5+9+2}{10}$$

$$\frac{55}{10} = 5.50$$

Table 4.1 Burnout Scores for Wendt's (2013) 108 Participants

36	37	51	42
38	40	41	40
48	36	44	34
30	30	36	28
31	32	34	37
16	42	50	39
34	40	25	28
25	28	41	28
42	35	43	52
35	35	31	39
37	49	47	46
45	38	34	50
27	34	55	40
54	20	53	36
20	28	38	23
32	16	37	32
34	22	43	24
35	25	41	47
33	19	46	25
33	32	53	45
31	42	38	40
49	49	31	45
20	39	40	37
31	31	35	42
28	40	45	28
31	49	45	38
35	31	39	28

Mean: arithmetic average of a dataset.

Recall from Chapter 1 the difference between parameters and statistics. Parameters are numbers based on the population characteristics; statistics are numbers derived from a sample that was drawn from a population. We are currently discussing statistics, but starting in Chapter 6, we need to incorporate certain parameters into our discussion. In this case, we need to distinguish some symbols you will see in psychological research (which almost always involves statistics) and how they correspond to certain parameters.

In psychological research, you will see a mean reported as an italicized capital *M*. Sometimes the mean will be reported as $\overline{x}$. These are sample statistics. However, when we begin to incorporate population parameters into our discussions, the symbol for the population mean is the Greek letter μ (pronounced *mew*). We will reiterate this distinction when the time comes, but as you will soon be seeing symbols for the mean in psychological research, I wanted to make sure you know what you are reading.

Median

The **median** is the "middle" number in a dataset. It is the number that divides a dataset in half so that 50% of the scores are greater than that number and 50% of the scores are less than that number. The median is often reported in research when the mean does not do a good job of describing a dataset. This occurs when the scores in the dataset tend to be toward the high end or toward the low end of the distribution of scores. In such cases, a few "extreme" scores would distort the mean because the mean uses all data points in its calculation. We will discuss a real-life example of such a situation in the next section of this chapter.

Median: middle score in a dataset that divides the dataset in half so that an equal number of scores fall above and below that score.

For now, to calculate a median, let's return to the small dataset we used to calculate the mean:

6, 5, 4, 6, 7, 8, 3, 5, 9, 2

To determine the median, we need to arrange the scores in a dataset from lowest to highest. We then find the score that divides the distribution of scores in half. Here are the scores arranged in order from lowest to highest:

2, 3, 4, 5, 5, 6, 6, 7, 8, 9

We now need to find the score that divides the dataset in half so that 50% of the scores are greater than that number and 50% of the scores are less than that number. With an odd number of scores (and a small dataset), this is easy to do. However, when we have an even number of scores as we do here, there is not a readily available score that divides the dataset in half. In this case, we take the two middle scores and find the mean of these two numbers. These two numbers are highlighted here:

2, 3, 4, 5, **5**, **6**, 6, 7, 8, 9

The mean of 5 and 6 is 5.5. Thus, our median is 5.5.

Source: Yeh, Sarah. "Median." Cartoon. Original Work. (July 21, 2016)

We said that the median is a "better" measure of central tendency when the mean does not do a good job of describing its dataset. Let's add an 11th score to our dataset to illustrate this point:

2, 3, 4, 5, 5, 6, 6, 7, 8, 9, 45

With this additional score of 45, our mean becomes 100 / 11 = 9.09.

What is our median? It is now 6 (the first 6 in the distribution). Which measure of central tendency does a better job of describing the dataset? The mean of 9.09 is misleading as only one score is greater than 9.09. When there are a few extreme scores, called **outliers**, the median is preferred to the mean as a measure of central tendency because the median is less affected by these extreme scores.

Outlier: score that is extremely high or extremely low compared with most other scores in a dataset.

Mode

The **mode** is the most frequently occurring score in a dataset. If you are looking at a frequency distribution graph, the mode will be the highest point on such a graph. When we have nominal data, the mode is the only measure of central tendency that can be used. It does not make sense to calculate a mean for a variable such as respondent's sex or religious affiliation. We don't see the mode reported often in research studies. There are two reasons why this is the case. First, the mean and median tend to do a better job of describing large sets of data because they both use all scores in their calculations. Second, although the mode is used with nominal data, as we discussed in Chapter 2, researchers generally prefer data quantified with a scale measurement because there are more statistical tools that can be used with such data, which we will see later on in this class.

Mode: most frequently occurring score in a dataset.

In our dataset, what is the mode? Realize that this is a bit of a trick question:

6, 5, 4, 6, 7, 8, 3, 5, 9, 2

The scores of 5 and 6 both occur most frequently (each occurs two times). Thus, the mode is 5 and 6. In this case, we have a *bimodal* distribution, meaning that there are two modes. A dataset with one mode is called a *unimodal* distribution, and a dataset with three or more modes is called a *multimodal* distribution.

Be aware that the mode is the score(s) that occurs most frequently, not the frequency of that score(s). If you said the mode was 2, that is indeed how often the most frequently occurring scores of 5 and 6 occurred, but it is not the mode.

Table 4.2 contains a summary of the three measures of central tendency.

Reporting the measures of central tendency in research

When reporting measures of central tendency, researchers will do so either in the text of an article or in a table that presents such statistics. For instance, returning to Wendt's (2013) research on burnout, she could have reported scores on the burnout measure in the text using these symbols:

For the mean, it would be reported as "$M = 36.50$"

Table 4.2 Summary of the Three Measures of Central Tendency

	Measure of Central Tendency		
	Mean	**Median**	**Mode**
Definition	Average number	Middle number	Most frequent number(s)
Appropriate for	Scale data	Ordinal and scale data	Nominal, ordinal, and scale data
Weakness	Influenced by extreme scores		Uses only two numbers in its calculation

Table 4.3 Descriptive Statistics for Variables in Wendt's (2013) Research

Variable	*M*	*Mdn*	Mode
Participant Age	19.7 years	21.0 years	21.0 years
Burnout	36.5	36.5	28.0 and 31.0
Dysfunctional Perfectionism	32.8	33.0	33.0
Role Overload	40.4	41.0	33.0, 34.0, and 36.0

Notes. For burnout, scores could range from 15 to 75. For dysfunctional perfectionism, scores could range from 11 to 55. For role overload, scores could range from 13 to 65.

Abbreviations. M = mean; Mdn = median.

For the median, it would reported as "$Mdn = 36.50$"

For the mode, it would be reported as "mode = 28.0 and 31.0"

Notice that the symbols for mean and median are italicized. It is general practice to italicize statistical symbols. We do not have a symbol for the mode; thus, it is not italicized.

In Wendt's (2013) research, she reported her measures of central tendency in a table, which you can see in Table 4.3. Notice the *Notes* at the bottom of the table. These are important because they give you information that is needed to interpret the numbers in the table. For example, knowing the possible range of scores on each variable is important because, as was the case here, those possible ranges were different for each variable. Thus, we cannot say, at this point in the class, that participants' scores were higher on role overload than on burnout even though each measure of central tendency is greater for role overload than it is for burnout.

Let's check our understanding of the three measures of central tendency before moving on to consider issues in selecting which one is the "best" way to summarize a dataset.

LEARNING CHECK

1. A researcher surveyed 10 undergraduate psychology majors about their study behaviors. The following is a list of the number of hours they spent studying on the weekend:

6	5	3	4	9
7	3	7	8	3

Calculate the mean.

$$A: \frac{\Sigma x}{N}$$

$$\text{Mean} = \frac{55}{10}$$

$$\text{Mean} = 5.50$$

Calculate the median.
Remember to arrange the scores from lowest to highest:

3, 3, 3, 4, 5, 6, 7, 7, 8, 9

A: 5.50 (which is the mean of the middle two numbers of 5 and 6)

Calculate the mode.

A: 3

2. In the previous chapter, you saw this frequency graph, which displays the distribution of scores on a midterm exam. Use the graph in Figure 4.1 on the next page to calculate each measure of central tendency.

A: mean = 83.0

median = 85.0

mode = 85.0

3. What is an "outlier?" Why do outliers tend to affect the mean more than the median?

A: An outlier is a score that is extremely high or extremely low compared with most other scores in a dataset. The mean uses all numbers in its calculation, so an outlier will pull the mean up or drag it down. The median needs only the middle number or middle two numbers in a dataset, so an outlier will not be as likely to affect the median as it is to affect the mean.

4. The value of one score in a dataset is changed from 20 to 30. Which measure(s) of central tendency is (are) certain to change?

   a) the mean
   b) the median
   c) the mean and the median
   d) the mode

   A: a

(Continued)

(Continued)

Figure 4.1

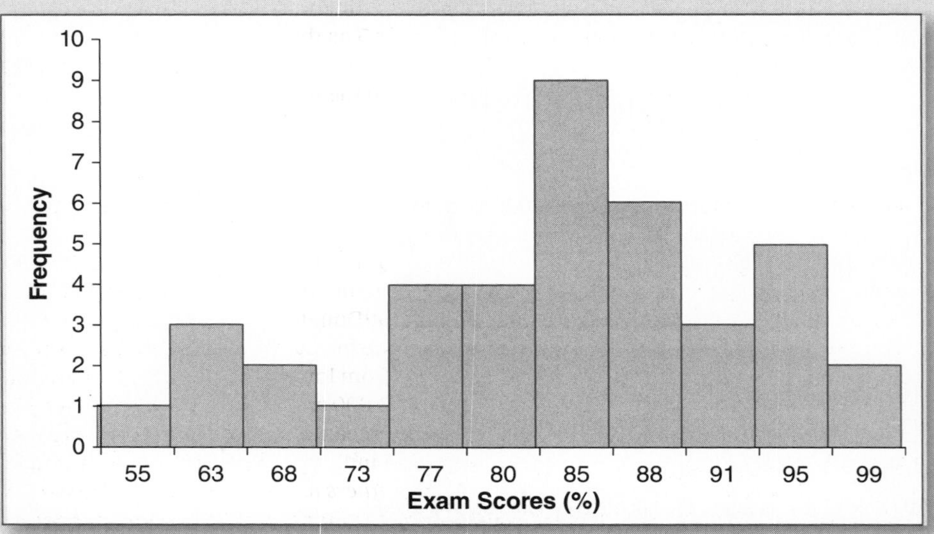

5. Explain why "the mean" is the correct answer to the previous question.

   A: The mean must use each and every score in its calculation, so it has to change when one score is added to the dataset. The median does not necessarily change because the middle number (or middle two numbers) are not guaranteed to change by adding one score to the dataset. The mode does not change unless its addition makes that score the most frequently occurring score in the dataset.

6. You read a research article that reports the following information: "Scores on the sexism measure (M = 5.5, Mdn = 5.0, mode = 5.0) were higher than scores on the measure of racial prejudice (M = 4.8, Mdn = 4.5, mode = 5.0)."

Use this information to answer the following questions:

a) What is the mean of the sexism measure?

   A: 5.5

b) What is the mean of the racial prejudice measure?

   A: 4.8

c) What is the median of the sexism measure?

   A: 5.0

d) What is the median of the racial prejudice measure?

   A: 4.5

e) What is the mode of the sexism measure?

   A: 5.0

f) What is the mode of the racial prejudice measure?

   A: 5.0

Choosing a Measure of Central Tendency

In this section, we will discuss four considerations in deciding which measure of central tendency is the best one to report for a given dataset. In general, researchers tend to prefer the mean as the measure of central tendency to report. There are reasons why this is the case, one of which is that it does require all scores in a dataset to be used in its calculation. Another will become evident in Chapter 5 as the mean, in combination with a measure of variability we'll learn about later in this chapter, can provide us with a great deal of information. In this section, however, we will discuss four considerations before defaulting to the mean as our measure of central tendency.

Consideration 1: Outliers in the data

The town I live in has a population of about 8,000 people, and the mean per capita (per person) income is $15,000. Now, suppose that Donald Trump moves to my town.

Although it is difficult to pinpoint precisely, let's say that Trump's income in 2014 was $380 million (Snyder, 2015). With 8,001 people now living my town, what is the mean income of my town? $62,492. Does this information indicate that the 8,000 people in my town who are not Donald Trump suddenly made $47,492 more this year? Of course not; in this example, we need to calculate the median because Trump's income is an outlier. I know it will take a lot of time to arrange 8,001 income scores from lowest to highest, so let's assume that 2,000 people in my town earn $5,000 annually, 4,000 people earn $12,000 annually, 2,000 people earn $31,000 annually, and Trump earns $380,000,000 annually. That gives us a mean of $62,492. However, the median will be $12,000, which is obviously quite a bit lower and a more valid indicator of incomes than the mean.

Unlike the mean, the median is not as influenced by a few outliers (extreme scores) in a dataset. If you really want a valid picture of incomes (in my town or throughout the United States), the median tends to be a better measure of central tendency to report than the mean because one extreme income (outlier), such as Donald Trump's, won't blur what is the case for the majority of the dataset.

Consideration 2: Skewed data distributions

You may have noticed in the previous section that in our example data, the mean, median, and mode were almost identical. Indeed, when we have a large dataset, this will normally be the case. In fact, because it is "normally" the case, we say that such distributions of data are **normally distributed**. That is, the three measures of central tendency are all approximately equal. This is important because when we have a normal distribution of data, there is a great deal of information available to us. We will reveal that information in the next chapter.

> **Normal distribution**: dataset in which the measures of central tendency are approximately equal to each other, thus creating a symmetrical, bell-shaped distribution of scores.

Figure 4.2 contains a normal distribution. The mode should be pretty easy to figure out as it is the highest point of the curve, which is where most scores cluster. As we move farther away from the highest point of the curve, we see that there are progressively fewer scores. Knowing that the measures of central tendency are approximately equal, it becomes easy to locate the mean and median.

Of course, as we just discussed in our example with the variable of income, not all distributions are normal. In the case of the distribution of income, the distribution is skewed. By "skewed," we mean that the distribution of scores is not symmetrical as it is in a normal distribution. That is, outliers affect the shape of the distribution and make it non-normal. Income distribution is a powerful example of a **positively skewed distribution**. Take a look at Figure 4.3, which contains a positively skewed distribution. Let's walk through Figure 4.3. The mode tends to be toward the low end of the distribution. If most scores are low, then why is it called a positively skewed distribution? That's because a few high (positive) scores are skewing the distribution. The high scores are "weird" or unusual in the distribution, hence, the term *positively skewed*.

Positively skewed distribution: data distribution in which there are a few unusually high (skewed) scores; most scores tend to be toward the low end of the distribution.

In a positively skewed distribution, as we saw with the example of incomes in my town, the mean will tend be higher than the mode, with median falling between these two statistics.

Figure 4.2 A Normal Distribution of Scores

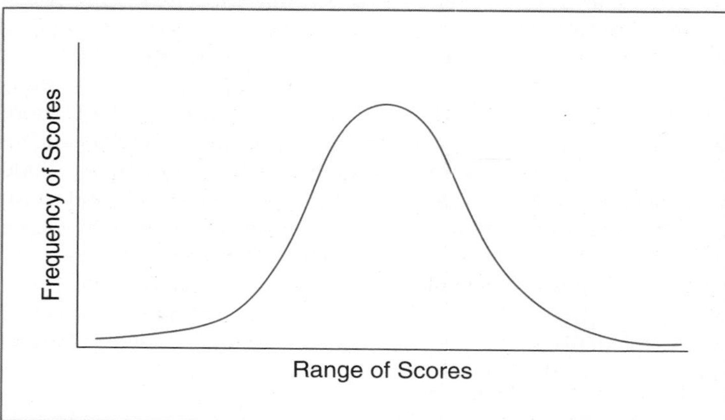

Figure 4.3 A Positively Skewed Distribution of Scores

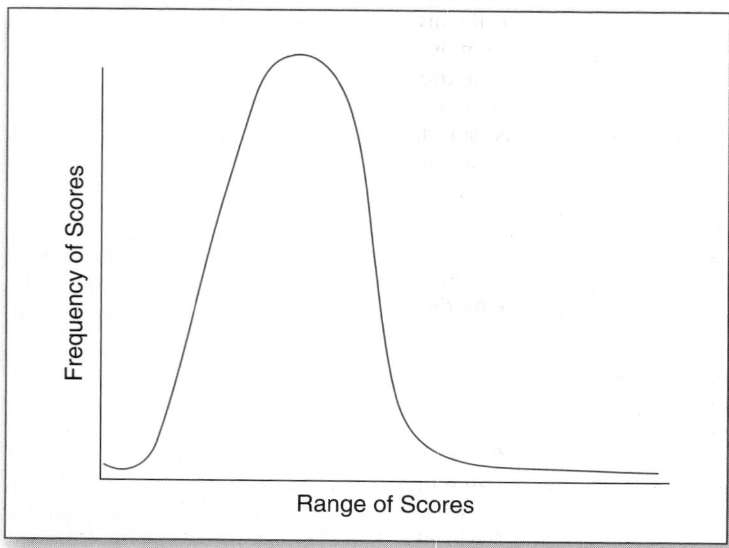

If we have positively skewed distributions, we must of course have **negatively skewed distributions**. Recall that in a positively skewed distribution, the mean is greater than the mode. So in a negatively skewed distribution, guess which is greater, the mean or the mode? If you don't know or don't feel like guessing, take a look at Figure 4.4. Here, the mode is toward the high end of the range of scores. However, the mean is less than the mode because a few low scores are dragging it down from the mode. The low scores are "weird" or skewed, so that's why it is called a negatively skewed distribution. For example, most college seniors apply for a lot of jobs during their last year of school. That's a normal behavior to engage in when looking for your first "post-college-degree" job. Therefore, the mode is fairly high. A few seniors may complete only a few or no job applications. These few seniors are outliers that drag down the value of the mean of this distribution. Therefore, it is negatively skewed.

Negatively skewed distribution: data distribution in which there are a few unusually low (skewed) scores; most scores tend to be toward the high end of the distribution.

When looking at a skewed distribution, you should "follow the tail." That is, look for the end of the distribution that contains very few scores. If there are few scores on the high

Figure 4.4 A Negatively Skewed Distribution of Scores

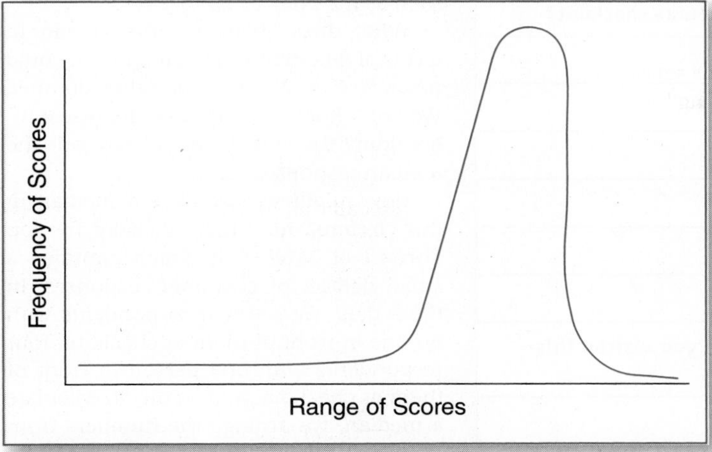

end of the distribution, it is positively skewed. If there are few scores on the low end of the distribution, it is negatively skewed.

Consideration 3: A variable's scale of measurement

To calculate a mean, we need all scores in a dataset. That's one critical reason why researchers tend to report the mean more than the other two measures of central tendency. *To calculate a mean, data need to be measured with a scale measurement*. Suppose, for instance, we had ordinal (rank-ordered) data. If we have data that are rankings, there is no way to calculate an interpretable mean. Likewise, with nominal (categorical) data, such as a person's sex, the mean is an impossible statistic to calculate.

For scale data, it is not a crime to report all three measures of central tendency as Wendt (2013) did. Again, researchers tend to prefer the mean and often report it without mentioning a median or mode. In reading published research studies, this is generally not a problem. However, be careful when you read or hear news stories that report a "mean" or "average." Always think about what these stories are telling you and whether outliers in the data may have skewed the results in the story being reported.

As we discussed in the two previous considerations, the median is a good alternative to the mean when we have outliers that may skew the picture of the data that the mean will paint for us. To calculate a median, we need scale data or ordinal data. In fact, *for ordinal data, the median is typically the most preferred measure of central tendency*. For example, suppose we look at the *U.S. News & World Reports* rankings of colleges and various graduate programs of study. These data are, of course, ordinal. We learned in Chapter 2 that we cannot tell how much one ranked score differs from the next ranked score. If University A is ranked 23rd and University B is ranked 24th, how much better, according to this ranking system, is University A than University B? We have no idea. Therefore, calculating a mean is meaningless. We use the median for ordinal data because it gives us an idea, albeit an imperfect one, of an entity's standing in relation to some standard.

What college or university do you attend? What is your class standing at your college? Data collected from these sorts of questions are all measured with a nominal measurement scale. *When using a nominal scale of measurement, we have to report the mode for that variable*. It would make no sense to report a mean or median. For instance, suppose we collected data on class standing (first-year, sophomore, junior, or senior). There is no practical way to calculate a mean or median on such data. However, we can calculate a mode simply by seeing how many students of each class participated in our research. If there were more sophomores than any other class standing, the mode would be sophomores. The mode is also a good choice to report when the data are bimodal or multimodal, especially in a large dataset.

Consideration 4: Open-ended response ranges

In many psychological studies, there are predetermined upper and lower limits on a response range. For instance, in question 2 in the previous Learning Check, scores on a midterm could fall only between 0% and 100%. But what happens when there is no limit on scores in a distribution? For example, I like to complete customer satisfaction surveys not only because I get a chance to win stuff, but also because as a social scientist,

Table 4.4 Typical Items on Customer Satisfaction Surveys

How many people were in line ahead of you at checkout?
_____ None
_____ One person
_____ Two people
_____ Three people
_____ Four people
_____ Five or more people
Including this visit, how many times have you visited this store in the past 30 days?
_____ Once
_____ Twice
_____ Three times
_____ Four times
_____ Five or more times

I think I can provide useful feedback that other researchers can make use of. On these sorts of surveys, we might see items such as the ones in Table 4.4.

What does "five or more" mean in terms of quantitative information? It could mean 5, 6, 9, 27, or some other number. We don't know. In this case, the researchers doing the survey should rely on the median response.

How might we calculate a median in this circumstance? Let's consider the top portion of Table 4.5, which contains a small dataset of customer responses. In these data, we see four respondents with no one in front of them at checkout, four respondents with one person in front of them at checkout, and so on. To calculate a median, we arrange the numbers from lowest to highest. Doing so gives us the following:

0, 0, 0, 0, 1, 1, 1, 1, 2, 2, 3, 3, 4, 5, 5

To find a median with an odd number of scores, we take the two numbers in the middle of the distribution and find the mean of those two numbers:

0, 0, 0, 0, 1, 1, 1, 1, 2, 2, 3, 3, 4, 5, 5

The mean of 1 and 1, is, of course 1. Thus, our median is 1. Although not a perfect representation of the dataset, using the median with an open-ended response range paints as valid of a picture the data as possible.

Table 4.5 Frequencies on Typical Items on Customer Satisfaction Surveys

How many people were in line ahead of you at checkout?	
	***f* (frequency)**
_____ None	4
_____ One person	4
_____ Two people	2
_____ Three people	2
_____ Four people	1
_____ Five or more people	2

Including this visit, how many times have you visited this store in the past 30 days?	
	f (frequency)
_____ Once	6
_____ Twice	2
_____ Three times	1
_____ Four times	3
_____ Five or more times	2

LEARNING CHECK

1. A distribution of scores has a mean = 30, median = 20, and mode = 10. The distribution
   a) has a positive skew.
   b) has a negative skew.
   c) is normal.
   d) is bimodal.

   A: a

2. Explain your response to the previous question.

   A: The mean is greater than the other two measures of central tendency because of a few high scores. These high scores are the unusual scores in the dataset, which makes the distribution *positively* skewed.

3. Seven friends have a mean income of $300/week, and their median income is $270/week. Rich, the lowest paid, gets fired from his $200/week job and now has an income of $0/week. What is the median weekly income of the seven friends after Rich lost his job?

   A: The median is still $270/week.

4. Explain your response to question 3.

   A: Let's arrange these data (before Rich got fired) so that we have a mean of $300 and a median of $270. Here is one way to do so (but if you can do it another way, go for it; it won't change the logic behind this question):

   $500, $350, $300, $270, $240, $240, $200

   The $270 is the median because it divides the dataset in half, with three incomes above it and three incomes below it.
   Now, with Rich being fired, here are the new incomes:

   $500, $350, $300, $270, $240, $240, $0

Here, the median is $270 because it still divides the dataset in half.

(Continued)

(Continued)

5. A survey asks whether people think a politician is innocent or guilty of embezzlement. Which would be the best measure of central tendency to describe this dataset?
   a) mean
   b) median
   c) mode

   A: c
6. Explain your response to the previous question.

   A: The data are nominal; that is, people believe the politician is innocent or guilty. Thus, with categorical data as in this example, the mode is the best measure of central tendency to report.
7. Look again at Table 4.5. Look at the second question, in the lower portion of that table.
   a) What is the correct measure of central tendency to report?

   A: median
   b) Why is it the correct measure of central tendency to report?

   A: It has an open-ended response range; that is, "five or more times" is an unknown quantity.
   c) What is the value of this measure of central tendency?

   A: 2

Measures of Central Tendency and SPSS

As we learn to generate measures of central tendency using SPSS, we will discuss a new study and use its data. Then in the Learning Check, we'll return to Wendt's (2013) data and test our understanding of using SPSS with the measures of central tendency.

We will use data from a study by Andrew Christopher and Mark Wojda (2008), who examined sources of sexist attitudes toward women. In their research, Christopher and Wojda studied two types of sexist attitudes toward women: hostile sexism and benevolent sexism. Hostile sexism is a type of sexism/prejudice in which people view women in a blatantly negative and mean way. For example, hiring a less qualified man over a more qualified woman or making openly disparaging comments about women would be two instances of hostile sexism. Benevolent sexism is a type of sexism/prejudice in which people view women with subjectively positive feelings (e.g., more sensitive to other people's feelings) but that place women in roles restrictive relative to men. Let's take an example of benevolent sexism. If a person thinks women are indeed more sensitive to other people's feelings, then that person might believe that women won't make good corporate leaders because they cannot make tough decisions for fear of upsetting other people.

In their research, Christopher and Wojda (2008) used an online survey to collect data from 349 U.S. citizens. The sample consisted of 182 women and 167 men, some as young as 18, some as old as 82. Included in a set of questionnaires were measures of hostile and benevolent sexism (Glick & Fiske, 1996). The measure of hostile sexism contained 11 items, such as "Most women fail to appreciate fully all that men do for them" and "When women lose to men in a fair competition, they typically complain about being discriminated against." The measure of benevolent sexism contained 11 items, such as "Women should be protected and cherished by men" and "Women, when compared to men, tend to have a superior moral sensibility." Participants used a 0 (*strongly disagree*) to 5 (*strongly agree*) response range to indicate the extent to which they agreed with each statement.

You have access to Christopher and Wojda's (2008) data in the SPSS file "Christopher and Wojda dataset.sav". Open that SPSS file now so that we can learn how to use SPSS to generate the measures of central tendency.

Before we generate our measures of central tendency, please humor me and click on the *Variable View* in the bottom left portion of the spreadsheet. Before we deal with our data, we must understand the nature of our data, and that is what *Variable View* does for us. For instance, notice the variable `Participant Sex`. Why do we need values for this variable? Why is its measure nominal? Why are benevolent and hostile sexism both scale measures? Understanding these sorts of issues is essential to generating output and to making sense of that output.

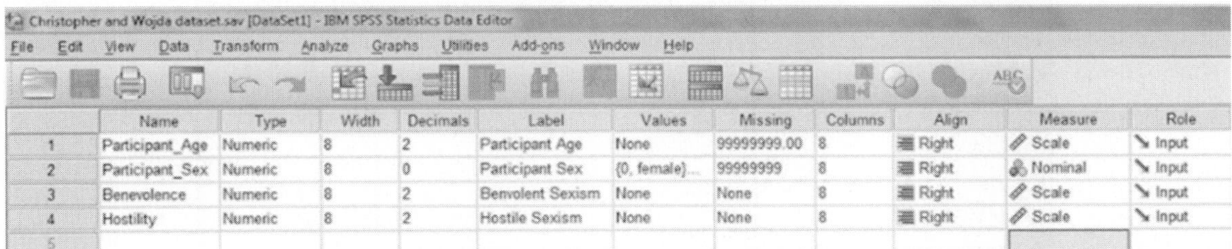

Christopher and Wojda dataset.sav [DataSet1] - IBM SPSS Statistics Data Editor

File Edit View Data Transform Analyze Graphs Utilities Add-ons Window Help

	Name	Type	Width	Decimals	Label	Values	Missing	Columns	Align	Measure	Role
1	Participant_Age	Numeric	8	2	Participant Age	None	99999999.00	8	Right	Scale	Input
2	Participant_Sex	Numeric	8	0	Participant Sex	{0, female}...	99999999	8	Right	Nominal	Input
3	Benevolence	Numeric	8	2	Benvolent Sexism	None	None	8	Right	Scale	Input
4	Hostility	Numeric	8	2	Hostile Sexism	None	None	8	Right	Scale	Input
5											

Click on *Data View* to see the data we are working with. To generate the measures of central tendency, here's what you do:

1. Click on *Analyze* → *Descriptive Statistics* → *Frequencies*.

Christopher and Wojda dataset.sav [DataSet1] - IBM SPSS Statistics Data Editor

File Edit View Data Transform Analyze Graphs Utilities Add-ons Window Help

Reports
Descriptive Statistics
Tables
Compare Means
General Linear Model
Generalized Linear Models
Mixed Models
Correlate
Regression
Loglinear
Classify
Dimension Reduction
Scale
Nonparametric Tests
Forecasting
Survival
Multiple Response
Simulation...
Quality Control
ROC Curve...

Frequencies...
Descriptives...
Explore...
Crosstabs...
TURF Analysis
Ratio...
P-P Plots...
Q-Q Plots...

	Participant_Age	Participant_Sex		
1	43.00	0		
2	28.00	0		
3	27.00	0		
4	24.00	1		
5	35.00	1		
6	26.00	0		
7	64.00	1		
8	36.00	0		
9	50.00	1		
10	30.00	1		
11	39.00	1		
12	25.00	1		
13	51.00	0		
14	60.00	1		
15	34.00	1		
16	32.00	1		
17	38.00	0	2.91	1.36
18	54.00	1	1.91	1.64
19	70.00	1	2.55	3.09
20	57.00	1	3.18	2.45
21	30.00	0	3.09	2.55
22	45.00	1	2.55	3.55
23	59.00	0	1.64	3.00
24	50.00	1	2.27	2.73
25	31.00	0	3.45	1.36
26	41.00	1	2.82	2.45
27	33.00	0	3.45	1.45
28	48.00	1	1.91	2.09

Data View | Variable View

Frequencies...

2. In the *Frequencies* window, we click into the *Variable(s)* box to find the variables we want descriptive statistics for. Here, let's get them for the variable `Benevolent Sexism`.

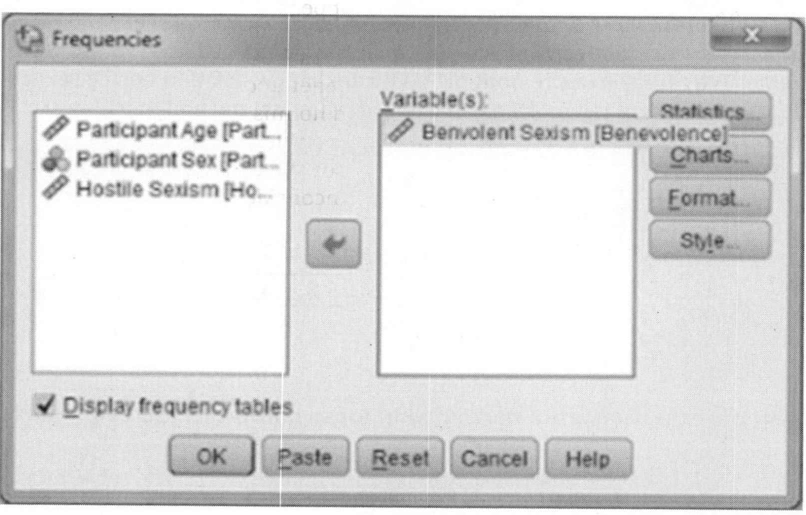

3. Now click on the *Statistics* box in the upper right part of the *Frequencies* window. Here is where we tell SPSS what information to give us. Right now, we're after the three measures of central tendency. These appear in the upper right part of the *Frequencies: Statistics* box.
4. Click *Continue* to return to the *Frequencies* window.

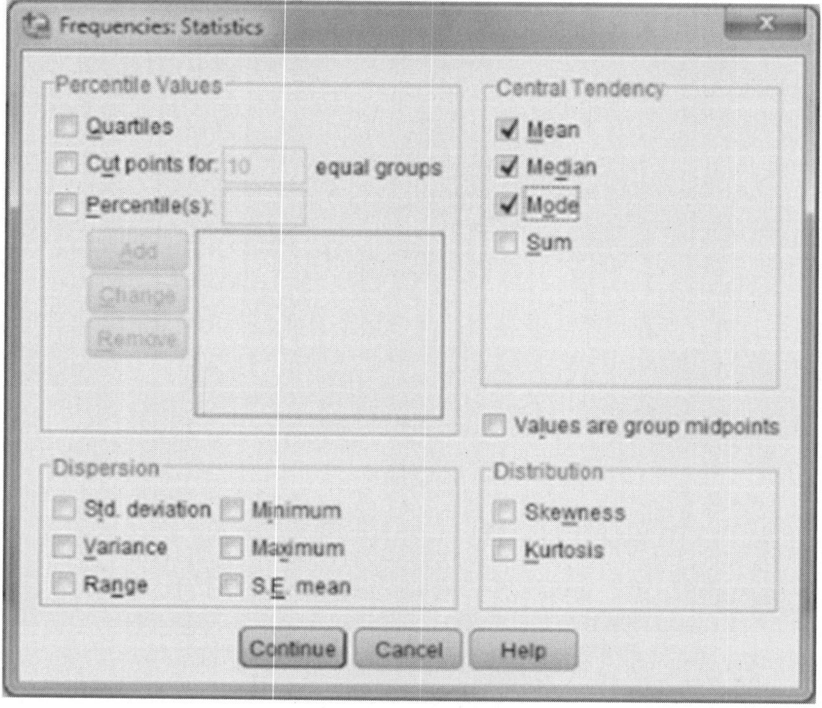

5. Notice how the *Display frequencies table* box is checked in the lower left corner of the window? Please keep that checked as it might come in handy in a moment.
6. Click *OK*, and your measures of central tendency will appear.

Let's start at the top of the SPSS output with the *Statistics* box. First, notice at the top of the box is `Benevolent Sexism`. This is our variable for which we generated this output. In the box is information about our sample size (*N*). We have 349 valid responses, and no missing data for this variable.

Next, we have listed each one of our three measures of central tendency. As we can see, our mean is 2.47; our median is 2.45; and our mode is 2.45. However, do you see the footnote after the mode? Multiple modes exist, but SPSS gives us only the smallest of the modes (how inconsiderate, I know).

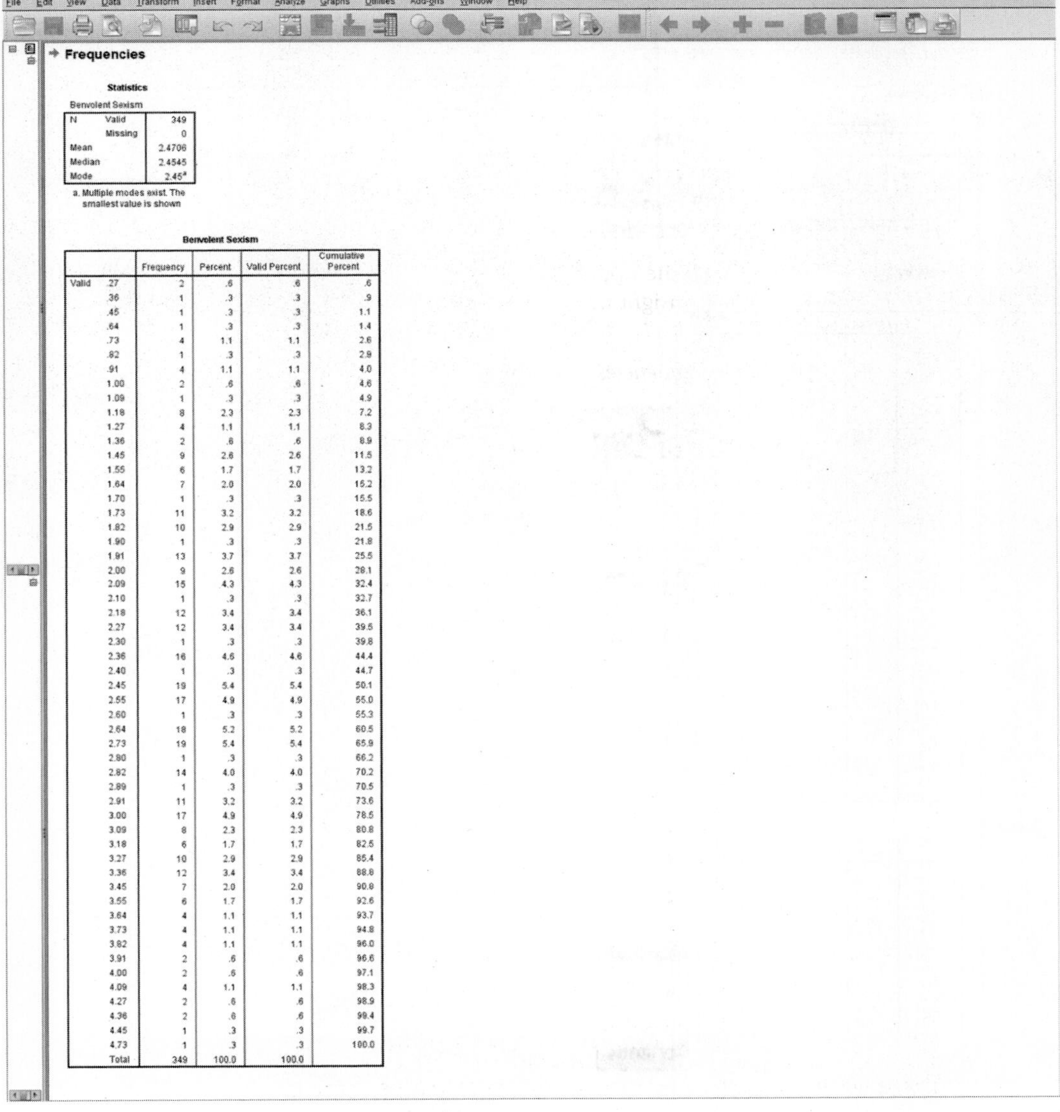

Statistics

Benvolent Sexism

N	Valid	349
	Missing	0
Mean		2.4706
Median		2.4545
Mode		2.45[a]

a. Multiple modes exist. The smallest value is shown

Benvolent Sexism

		Frequency	Percent	Valid Percent	Cumulative Percent
Valid	.27	2	.6	.6	.6
	.36	1	.3	.3	.9
	.45	1	.3	.3	1.1
	.64	1	.3	.3	1.4
	.73	4	1.1	1.1	2.6
	.82	1	.3	.3	2.9
	.91	4	1.1	1.1	4.0
	1.00	2	.6	.6	4.6
	1.09	1	.3	.3	4.9
	1.18	8	2.3	2.3	7.2
	1.27	4	1.1	1.1	8.3
	1.36	2	.6	.6	8.9
	1.45	9	2.6	2.6	11.5
	1.55	6	1.7	1.7	13.2
	1.64	7	2.0	2.0	15.2
	1.70	1	.3	.3	15.5
	1.73	11	3.2	3.2	18.6
	1.82	10	2.9	2.9	21.5
	1.90	1	.3	.3	21.8
	1.91	13	3.7	3.7	25.5
	2.00	9	2.6	2.6	28.1
	2.09	15	4.3	4.3	32.4
	2.10	1	.3	.3	32.7
	2.18	12	3.4	3.4	36.1
	2.27	12	3.4	3.4	39.5
	2.30	1	.3	.3	39.8
	2.36	16	4.6	4.6	44.4
	2.40	1	.3	.3	44.7
	2.45	19	5.4	5.4	50.1
	2.55	17	4.9	4.9	55.0
	2.60	1	.3	.3	55.3
	2.64	18	5.2	5.2	60.5
	2.73	19	5.4	5.4	65.9
	2.80	1	.3	.3	66.2
	2.82	14	4.0	4.0	70.2
	2.89	1	.3	.3	70.5
	2.91	11	3.2	3.2	73.6
	3.00	17	4.9	4.9	78.5
	3.09	8	2.3	2.3	80.8
	3.18	6	1.7	1.7	82.5
	3.27	10	2.9	2.9	85.4
	3.36	12	3.4	3.4	88.8
	3.45	7	2.0	2.0	90.8
	3.55	6	1.7	1.7	92.6
	3.64	4	1.1	1.1	93.7
	3.73	4	1.1	1.1	94.8
	3.82	4	1.1	1.1	96.0
	3.91	2	.6	.6	96.6
	4.00	2	.6	.6	97.1
	4.09	4	1.1	1.1	98.3
	4.27	2	.6	.6	98.9
	4.36	2	.6	.6	99.4
	4.45	1	.3	.3	99.7
	4.73	1	.3	.3	100.0
	Total	349	100.0	100.0	

So, to determine all of the modes, we need our frequency table that appears next. Let's look at the mode we do know, which is 2.45. We see that its frequency is 19, meaning the score of 2.45 occurred 19 times in the dataset. So, to determine all of the modes, we need to find that other score or scores that occurred 19 times. When we look carefully at the frequency of each score, we see that the score of 2.73 also occurred 19 times. Therefore, our modes are 2.45 and 2.73.

LEARNING CHECK

1. From the previous chapter, return to the file "Wendt's data.sav". From this file, use SPSS to generate the measures of central tendency for the variables of `Burnout` and `Role Overload`.

   A: Here is what your output should look like:

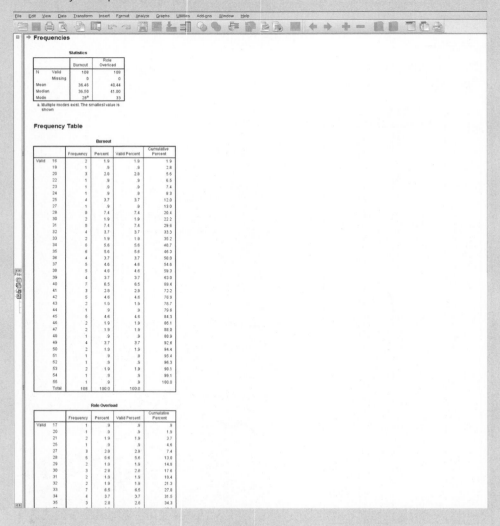

File Edit View Data Transform Insert Format Analyze Graphs Utilities Add-ons Window Help

Frequencies

Statistics

		Burnout	Role Overload
N	Valid	108	108
	Missing	0	0
Mean		36.46	40.44
Median		36.50	41.00
Mode		28[a]	33

a. Multiple modes exist. The smallest value is shown

Frequency Table

Burnout

		Frequency	Percent	Valid Percent	Cumulative Percent
Valid	16	2	1.9	1.9	1.9
	19	1	.9	.9	2.8
	20	3	2.8	2.8	5.6
	22	1	.9	.9	6.5
	23	1	.9	.9	7.4
	24	1	.9	.9	8.3
	25	4	3.7	3.7	12.0
	27	1	.9	.9	13.0
	28	8	7.4	7.4	20.4
	30	2	1.9	1.9	22.2
	31	8	7.4	7.4	29.6
	32	4	3.7	3.7	33.3
	33	2	1.9	1.9	35.2
	34	6	5.6	5.6	40.7
	35	6	5.6	5.6	46.3
	36	4	3.7	3.7	50.0
	37	5	4.6	4.6	54.6
	38	5	4.6	4.6	59.3
	39	4	3.7	3.7	63.0
	40	7	6.5	6.5	69.4
	41	3	2.8	2.8	72.2
	42	5	4.6	4.6	76.9
	43	2	1.9	1.9	78.7
	44	1	.9	.9	79.6
	45	5	4.6	4.6	84.3
	46	2	1.9	1.9	86.1
	47	2	1.9	1.9	88.0
	48	1	.9	.9	88.9
	49	4	3.7	3.7	92.6
	50	2	1.9	1.9	94.4
	51	1	.9	.9	95.4
	52	1	.9	.9	96.3
	53	2	1.9	1.9	98.1
	54	1	.9	.9	99.1
	55	1	.9	.9	100.0
	Total	108	100.0	100.0	

Role Overload

		Frequency	Percent	Valid Percent	Cumulative Percent
Valid	17	1	.9	.9	.9
	20	1	.9	.9	1.9
	21	2	1.9	1.9	3.7
	25	1	.9	.9	4.6
	27	3	2.8	2.8	7.4
	28	6	5.6	5.6	13.0
	29	2	1.9	1.9	14.8
	30	3	2.8	2.8	17.6
	31	2	1.9	1.9	19.4
	32	2	1.9	1.9	21.3
	33	7	6.5	6.5	27.8
	34	4	3.7	3.7	31.5
	35	3	2.8	2.8	34.3

36	3	2.8	2.8	37.0
37	2	1.9	1.9	38.9
38	1	.9	.9	39.8
39	3	2.8	2.8	42.6
40	3	2.8	2.8	45.4
41	6	5.6	5.6	50.9
42	5	4.6	4.6	55.6
43	6	5.6	5.6	61.1
44	6	5.6	5.6	66.7
45	2	1.9	1.9	68.5
46	6	5.6	5.6	74.1
47	4	3.7	3.7	77.8
48	1	.9	.9	78.7
49	2	1.9	1.9	80.6
50	6	5.6	5.6	86.1
51	1	.9	.9	87.0
52	3	2.8	2.8	89.8
53	3	2.8	2.8	92.6
54	2	1.9	1.9	94.4
57	1	.9	.9	95.4
59	1	.9	.9	96.3
60	1	.9	.9	97.2
61	2	1.9	1.9	99.1
62	1	.9	.9	100.0
Total	108	100.0	100.0	

2. Now use this output and answer the following questions about it:
   a) What was the mean `Burnout` score?

      A: 36.46

   b) What was the mode for the `Burnout` variable?

      A: 28 and 31

   c) Interpret what the number(s) in response to question 2b mean(s) in plain English.

      A: The most frequently occurring scores on the `Burnout` variable were 28 and 31.

   d) What was the sample size for the `Role Overload` variable?

      A: 108 respondents

   e) What was the median `Role Overload` score?

      A: 41.0

   f) Interpret what the number in question 2e means in plain English.

      A: 50% of the scores on the `Role Overload` variable were greater than 41.0, and 50% of the scores on the `Role Overload` variable were less than 41.0.

3. Use Christopher and Wojda's (2008) dataset to generate the measures of central tendency for the variable of hostile sexism. After doing so, present them in a table (see Table 4.3 for an example of such a table).

   A: Here is what your output should look like:

Frequencies

Statistics

Hostile Sexism

N	Valid	349
	Missing	0
Mean		2.1994
Median		2.2727
Mode		2.55

(Continued)

(Continued)

Hostile Sexism

		Frequency	Percent	Valid Percent	Cumulative Percent
Valid	.00	1	.3	.3	.3
	.09	2	.6	.6	.9
	.18	1	.3	.3	1.1
	.20	1	.3	.3	1.4
	.27	3	.9	.9	2.3
	.36	1	.3	.3	2.6
	.45	2	.6	.6	3.2
	.50	1	.3	.3	3.4
	.55	1	.3	.3	3.7
	.73	4	1.1	1.1	4.9
	.82	7	2.0	2.0	6.9
	.90	1	.3	.3	7.2
	.91	8	2.3	2.3	9.5
	1.00	7	2.0	2.0	11.5
	1.09	9	2.6	2.6	14.0
	1.18	10	2.9	2.9	16.9
	1.27	5	1.4	1.4	18.3
	1.36	7	2.0	2.0	20.3
	1.40	1	.3	.3	20.6
	1.45	7	2.0	2.0	22.6
	1.50	1	.3	.3	22.9
	1.55	10	2.9	2.9	25.8
	1.60	1	.3	.3	26.1
	1.64	15	4.3	4.3	30.4
	1.73	8	2.3	2.3	32.7
	1.82	7	2.0	2.0	34.7
	1.91	13	3.7	3.7	38.4
	2.00	15	4.3	4.3	42.7
	2.09	14	4.0	4.0	46.7
	2.18	9	2.6	2.6	49.3
	2.27	10	2.9	2.9	52.1
	2.30	1	.3	.3	52.4
	2.36	14	4.0	4.0	56.4
	2.40	1	.3	.3	56.7
	2.45	16	4.6	4.6	61.3
	2.55	17	4.9	4.9	66.2
	2.64	13	3.7	3.7	69.9
	2.73	11	3.2	3.2	73.1
	2.82	10	2.9	2.9	75.9
	2.91	16	4.6	4.6	80.5
	3.00	7	2.0	2.0	82.5
	3.09	9	2.6	2.6	85.1
	3.13	1	.3	.3	85.4
	3.18	6	1.7	1.7	87.1
	3.20	1	.3	.3	87.4
	3.27	7	2.0	2.0	89.4
	3.36	7	2.0	2.0	91.4
	3.45	3	.9	.9	92.3
	3.55	7	2.0	2.0	94.3
	3.64	8	2.3	2.3	96.6
	3.73	1	.3	.3	96.8
	3.82	1	.3	.3	97.1
	4.00	1	.3	.3	97.4
	4.09	1	.3	.3	97.7
	4.18	4	1.1	1.1	98.9
	4.27	1	.3	.3	99.1
	4.36	1	.3	.3	99.4
	4.64	1	.3	.3	99.7
	4.91	1	.3	.3	100.0
	Total	349	100.0	100.0	

Table 4.6 shows what your table should look like.

Table 4.6 Descriptive Statistics for Hostile Sexism

Variable	*M*	*Mdn*	Mode
Hostile Sexism	2.20	2.27	2.55

Note. Scores on hostile sexism could range from 0 to 5.

Abbreviations. M = mean; *Mdn* = median.

MEASURES OF VARIABILITY

In the first half of this chapter, we explored the three measures of central tendency. Although the mean, median, and mode are essential in helping describe a dataset concisely, they do not provide certain information that is often essential in learning about a dataset. In this section, we begin by examining what we mean by "variability" and why it is critical to any research study. We then examine three specific measures of variability and how to calculate and interpret each one. We conclude this chapter by learning how to generate the three measures of variability using SPSS and interpreting the output SPSS provides us. Throughout this half of the chapter, we will, as needed, use the two datasets we used when discussing the measures of central tendency.

What Is Variability? Why Should We Care About Variability?

On average in the United States, people eat 6,000 pieces of pizza during their lifetimes (Reiter, 2015). In addition, the average person uses 90 gallons of water in his or her daily routine (U.S. Geological Survey, 2015). Finally, the average American spends 40 minutes each day checking Facebook feeds (Brustein, 2014). These are interesting (perhaps) pieces of trivia about the typical American. Notice that each one involves the "average" American. In other words, we are talking the mean number of pieces of pizza, the mean number of gallons of water consumed, and the mean amount of time checking Facebook feeds.

You no doubt know people who will eat far less (or more) pizza than the mean of 6,000 pieces in a lifetime. In addition, some people use more or less than 90 gallons of water each day. Some Americans seem to spend all their time on Facebook, whereas others never or rarely check their accounts. In other words, there is a great deal of variability in the extent to which people engage in different behaviors. By **variability**, we are talking about the extent to which scores in a dataset tend to be similar (clustered together) or different (spread out).

Variability: extent to which scores are similar (or different) in a dataset.

In any research study, it is essential that scores on the variables contain variability. For example, suppose in Wendt's (2013) research, each of her 108 participants had the same score on the academic burnout measure. Why would this be a problem? If we want to learn about relationships between variables (such as year in college and academic burnout), there need to be differences among the scores on each measure. Let's look back at a scatterplot that we created in Chapter 3. You can see this scatterplot again in Figure 4.5 here.

It is a scatterplot between role overload and burnout. As you saw in Chapter 3 and can see again, as role overload scores increase, burnout scores tend to increase. Now, let's change it up a bit, and make the scatterplot that Wendt (2013) would have obtained had all 108 of her participants had the same score on the burnout measure. For the sake of

Figure 4.5 Scatterplot of the Positive Linear Relationship Between Role Overload and Burnout

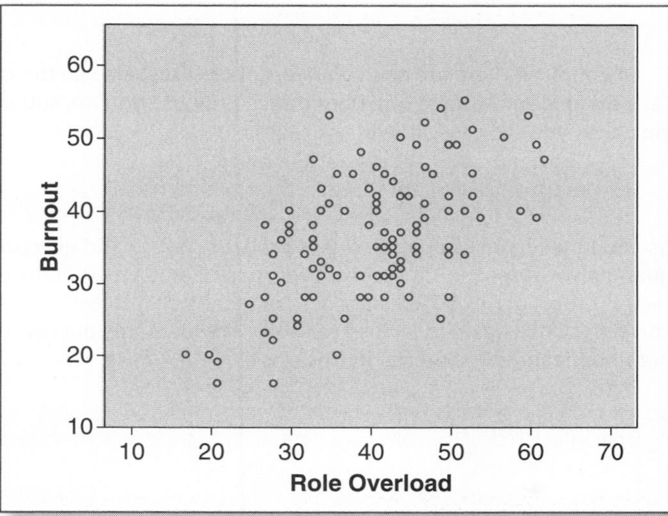

Figure 4.6 Scatterplot With Variability in Role Overload Scores but No Variability in Burnout Scores

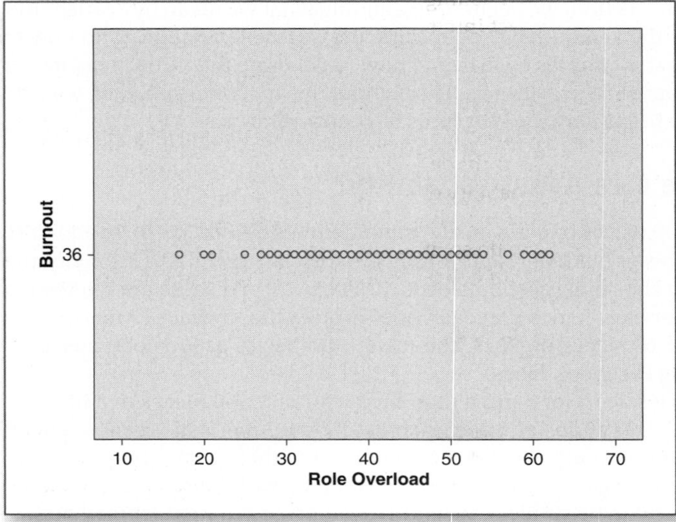

example, we'll set the burnout score to be 36.5. Now let's examine Figure 4.6 and compare it with Figure 4.5.

Which figure is more informative? I am not sure what we can learn from Figure 4.6 because there is no way to see how burnout is related to role overload. All burnout scores are the same. Because they are all the same, there is no way to learn anything from this research.

Researchers generally recognize the importance of variability in their work. However, there can be occasions when a study lacks variability in one or more of the variables it is studying. For instance, suppose you are taking an advanced college calculus class. Suppose your teacher asks you the following question on a test in this class:

$$1 + 1 = ?$$

I bet you don't need to have taken an advanced calculus class to answer this question correctly. As students, we all enjoy an easy question once in a while. However, if the purpose of a test is to determine who understands the material and who needs help, such a question is not good because everyone is going to get it correct. This is an example of a **ceiling effect**. That is, if everyone is getting 100% correct on such questions, there is no variability to determine mastery of course content. All scores are toward (or, in this case, at) the high end of the possible distribution of scores.

Ceiling effect: lack of variability in a dataset that occurs because scores are clustered together at the top end of the range of possible scores.

Of course, if there are ceiling effects, there must also be the opposite, which indeed are called **floor effects**. Let's discuss an example of a floor effect. Suppose you are still in your advanced college calculus class, and on your test, you see the following question:

How many counties are there in the state of Texas?

As you know from Chapter 2, this is probably not a valid question for a calculus class even though it asks for a quantitative response. Of course, I bet most, if not all, students in this class would answer this question incorrectly. If most or all of the responses are incorrect, it is just as big a problem as questions that everyone answers correctly. Once again, a lack of variability renders this question worthless in determining who does and does not understand the material in this class.

Floor effect: lack of variability in a dataset that occurs because scores are clustered together at the low end of the range of possible scores.

The bottom line is that when measuring behavior and cognition, whether with a test, survey, behavioral observation, or any other method, it is important that such behaviors and cognitions be given a chance to vary. That does not guarantee that they will vary; however, the researcher must not do things that introduce potential ceiling and floor effects into the dataset. The next time you are taking a test and encounter a particularly difficult question, just remember your teacher is trying to avoid ceiling effects. Of course, if the question is too difficult, your teacher runs the risk of introducing a floor effect into the test results.

Three Measures of Variability

Recall from the first half of this chapter that the purpose of the measures of central tendency was to describe a large set of data with one number (realizing that in the case of mode, there could be more than one number). Researchers also need to give readers an idea of how much variability there is in a dataset. Just as there were three measures of central tendency, we have three ways to measure variability. In this section, we will discuss these measures of variability and learn how to calculate each one. To do so, we will return to the small dataset we used in the first half of this chapter to calculate the three measures of central tendency. Here again is this dataset:

6, 5, 4, 6, 7, 8, 3, 5, 9, 2

Range

The simplest measure of variability is the **range**. To calculate the range, we simply take the highest score in a dataset and subtract from it the lowest score in a dataset. Stated differently, we subtract the minimum score from the maximum score. In our dataset, we have the highest scoring being 9 and the lowest score being 2. Thus, the range is $9 - 2 = 7$.

Range: the difference between the highest and the lowest score in a dataset.

The range is a nice first step in painting a picture of the variability in a dataset. However, how many numbers are involved in its calculation? Two: the highest score and the lowest score. With only two numbers being used, the range may not be terribly informative, especially if there is an outlier in the dataset. Instead, wouldn't it be great if we could paint a picture of variability based on all numbers in a dataset? As luck would have it, we can do so.

Recall that we said the mean is the most commonly reported measure of central tendency. In part this is because the mean is calculated using all numbers in a dataset. Another reason is because we need the mean to calculate the other two measures of variability, which we will discuss now.

Variance

The second measure of variability is called the **variance**. It is the average squared deviation from the dataset's mean. That definition probably makes little sense right now. It will make sense after we calculate a variance. Formulaically, we have

$$\frac{\Sigma(x - M)^2}{N - 1}$$

where

Σ means "summation"

x is an individual score

M is the sample mean

N is the total number of scores in the dataset

Here again is our small dataset:

6, 5, 4, 6, 7, 8, 3, 5, 9, 2

Variance: average squared deviation from the mean.

We know from earlier in this chapter that the mean (*M*) of this dataset is 5.50. This is the starting point for calculating a variance (and the third measure of variability that we'll discuss a little later). Indeed, to say there is variability, it must be in reference to some benchmark. That benchmark is the mean.

Therefore, we need to take each score and subtract from it the mean. Here are those calculations:

Score	Score – Mean
6	0.5
5	–0.5
4	–1.50
6	0.50
7	1.50
8	2.50
3	–2.50
5	–0.50
9	3.50
2	–3.50

To get a number that represents the variability in this dataset, it might be tempting to sum the differences between the scores and the mean. Go ahead and do so now. What did you get? If you got zero, you added correctly. Congratulations. However, there is a problem. There is not zero variability in this dataset. Just look at the numbers in the dataset; obviously, these are not all the same. When we sum the differences between individual scores and their mean, the answer will always be zero. So, we are not done calculating the variance.

What we need to do is get rid of those negative numbers. To do so, we will multiply each difference score by itself. That is, we square each difference score and, thus, eliminate the negative numbers. Let's do that now:

Score	Score – Mean	(Score – Mean)^2
6	0.5	0.25
5	–0.5	0.25
4	–1.50	2.25
6	0.50	0.25
7	1.50	2.25
8	2.50	6.25
3	–2.50	6.25
5	–0.50	0.25
9	3.50	12.25
2	–3.50	12.25
		42.50

Now we sum the squared difference scores. This will give us something called the **sum of squares**, the sum of each score's squared deviation from the mean. In this example, the sum of squares is 42.50.

With our sum of squares calculated, we can now finish computing the variance. To do so, we need the mean sum of squares but with one qualification. Specifically, rather than divide the sum of squares by the sample size of 10, we need to subtract 1 from the sample size. Why do we need to subtract 1 from the sample size? There is likely less variability in a sample than in that sample's corresponding population. Therefore, we try to obtain an "unbiased estimate" of the population variance based on our sample data. By making the variability greater (by decreasing the denominator), we are "correcting" for the fact that there is more variability in a population than in a sample because the population is larger than the sample.

As an expert on the mean from the previous chapter, you know what to do at this point. Take the sum of squares and divide it by the number of scores in the dataset minus 1.[1] Doing so gives us

$$\text{Variance} = \frac{42.50}{10-1}$$

$$\text{Variance} = \frac{42.50}{9}$$

$$\text{Variance} = 4.72$$

At this point, I have some good news and some bad news. Let's get the bad news out of the way. Variance is typically not reported in research. Frankly, it is difficult to interpret in any meaningful way. This 4.72 we just calculated does not have any useful meaning to us. You might be asking why we bothered to calculate it. That leads to the good news. We need the variance to calculate the standard deviation, our last measure of variability. It is the standard deviation that researchers use most often to describe the variability of a dataset.

Sum of squares: sum of each score's squared deviation from the mean.

Standard deviation

Conceptually, the **standard deviation** is the average amount by which scores in a dataset tend to vary around the mean. You might be thinking that it sounds a lot like the variance, and it is. Recall that when computing the variance, we needed to square the difference scores to remove the negative difference scores. Now we need to "undo" this procedure. To do so, we take the square root of the variance. Thus, we have

$$\begin{aligned}\text{Standard deviation} &= \sqrt{4.72} \\ &= 2.17\end{aligned}$$

That's it. Formulaically, we have

$$\sqrt{\frac{\Sigma(x-M)^2}{N-1}}$$

Standard deviation: measure of the extent to which scores in a dataset tend to vary around the mean.

Source: Yeh, Sarah. "Standard Deviation." Cartoon. Original Work. (July 21, 2016)

Now, we said that the variance is not useful to us (other than as a step to calculate the standard deviation) because it cannot be meaningfully interpreted. How then do we interpret our standard deviation of 2.17? We first need to consider the possible range of scores. Here again is our small dataset:

6, 5, 4, 6, 7, 8, 3, 5, 9, 2

We can see there is no score higher than 9 and no score lower than 2. Given these are only "example data," we don't know the possible range of scores. However, with a given range of 7, 2.17 would be a fairly large standard deviation compared with a dataset with a range of 14. A small value indicates there is little variability among scores in the dataset, whereas a large value indicates there is a great deal of variability among scores in the dataset. In the next chapter, we will learn how to take the descriptive statistics we are learning about now to uncover particular information about almost any dataset in psychology. At that time, we will learn how to use and interpret the standard deviation more precisely.

Reporting variability in research

When reporting measures of variability, like reporting the measures of variability, researchers tend to do so either in the text of an article or in a table. Typically, researchers do not report a variance for two reasons. First, as we said, it is difficult to interpret because we had to square all of the difference scores to calculate it. Second, we can take the standard deviation, which is typically reported, and square it to obtain the variance.

By using scores on her burnout measure, Wendt (2013) could have reported the measure of variability in the text as such:

For the range, there are no symbols. It would simply be "The range was 39."

For the standard deviation, it would be reported as "*SD* = 8.75."

Table 4.7 contains the range and standard deviation for the burnout measure in Wendt's (2013) research.

Table 4.7 Descriptive Statistics for Variables in Wendt's (2013) Researczh

Variable	Range	*SD*
Participant Age	23 − 15 = 8 years	1.73 years
Burnout	55 − 16 = 39	8.75
Dysfunctional Perfectionism	54 − 11 = 43	8.24
Role Overload	62 − 17 = 45	9.68

Notes. For burnout, scores could range from 15 to 75. For dysfunctional perfectionism, scores could range from 11 to 55. For role overload, scores could range from 13 to 65.

Abbreviation. *SD* = standard deviation.

LEARNING CHECK

1. In this chapter's first Learning Check, we used data in which a researcher surveyed 10 undergraduate psychology majors about their study behaviors. Here again is that list of the number of hours they spent studying on the weekend:

6	5	3	4	9
7	3	7	8	3

   a) Calculate the range.

      A: Highest score − lowest score = 9 − 3 = 6

   b) Calculate the variance.

      A: 4.94

   c) Calculate the standard deviation.

      A: 2.22

2. Why is "sample size − 1" used when calculating the sample standard deviation?

   A: We almost always work with sample data. Because a sample is smaller than its population, the sample will have less variability than its population. When calculating a sample standard deviation, we must correct for this state of affairs by "inflating" our calculation to try and reflect the population. With sample data, we subtract 1 from the sample size, thus, decreasing the denominator of the calculation. With a smaller denominator, we are increasing the quotient (increasing variability in describing the dataset).

3. The value of one score in a dataset is changed from 20 to 30. Which measure(s) of variability is (are) certain to be changed?

   a) the range.
   b) the variance.
   c) the range and standard deviation.
   d) the variance and standard deviation.

   A: d

4. Explain your answer to question 3.

   A: The range needs only the highest and lowest scores in the dataset for its calculation. Therefore, it may not change if that one score being changed isn't the highest or lowest one. However, the variance uses all numbers in a dataset in its calculation. Therefore, it is bound to change when one score is changed. The standard deviation is the square root of the variance, so it too must change when one score is changed.

5. Which measure of variability would be more affected by an outlier: the range or the standard deviation?

   A: the range

(Continued)

(Continued)

6. Explain your response to question 5.

   A: Because of how the range is calculated, an outlier will affect it more than the outlier would affect the standard deviation. An extreme score will affect the standard deviation but just not as much it will affect the range because the standard deviation uses all numbers in a dataset in its calculation.

7. You are reading a research article and you see Table 4.8.

Table 4.8 Descriptive Statistics for Variables in This Research

Variable	Range	*SD*
Participant Age	67 − 25 = 42 years	11.73 years
Benevolent Sexism	4.96 − 0.97 = 3.99	1.09
Hostile Sexism	4.79 − 0.50 = 4.29	1.89

Note. For both benevolent sexism and hostile sexism, scores could range from 0 to 5.

Abbreviation. SD = standard deviation.

Use this table to answer the following questions:

a) What was the range of participant ages in this research?

   A: 25 years old to 67 years old, for a range of 42 years

b) What is the standard deviation for the measure of benevolent sexism?

   A: 1.09

c) Interpret the difference in standard deviations for the measures of benevolent sexism and hostile sexism.

   A: The standard deviation for the measure of hostile sexism is higher than it is for benevolent sexism. This difference indicates more variability in hostile sexism scores than in benevolent sexism scores.

Measures of Variability and SPSS

Earlier in this chapter, we used a dataset that Christopher and Wojda (2008) gathered in which they examined hostile sexism and benevolent sexism toward women. We are going to use their data again here to learn how to generate and interpret the measure of variability using SPSS. If you want to refresh yourself on this research study, please reread the "Measures of Central Tendency and SPSS" section.

Once again, use the dataset titled "Christopher and Wojda dataset.sav". Open that SPSS file now, and let's get to work. To generate the measures of variability we have discussed,

1. Click on *Analyze* → *Descriptive Statistics* → *Frequencies*.

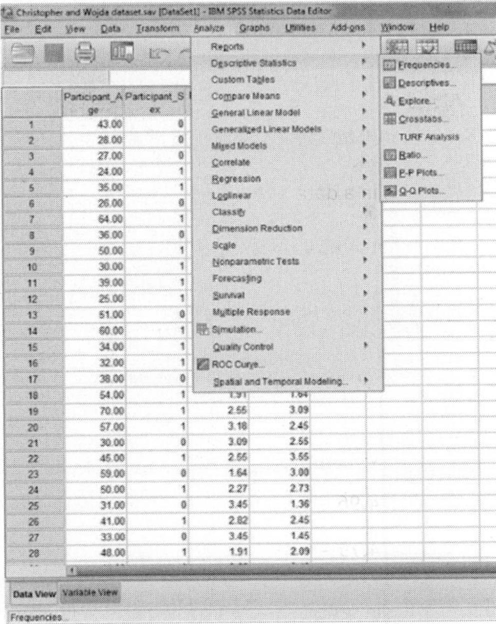

2. In the *Frequencies* window, we click on the variable in the *Variable(s)* box for which we want statistics (in this case, measures of variability). Let's get them for the variable `Benevolent Sexism`.

3. Now click on the *Statistics* box in the upper right part of the *Frequencies* window. Here is where we tell SPSS what information to give us. Right now, we're concentrating on the measures of variability, which SPSS calls measures of "dispersion" in the lower left corner of this window. There you will find the range, variance, and standard deviation. Select these measures, and for the sake of completeness, select *Minimum* and *Maximum* as well.

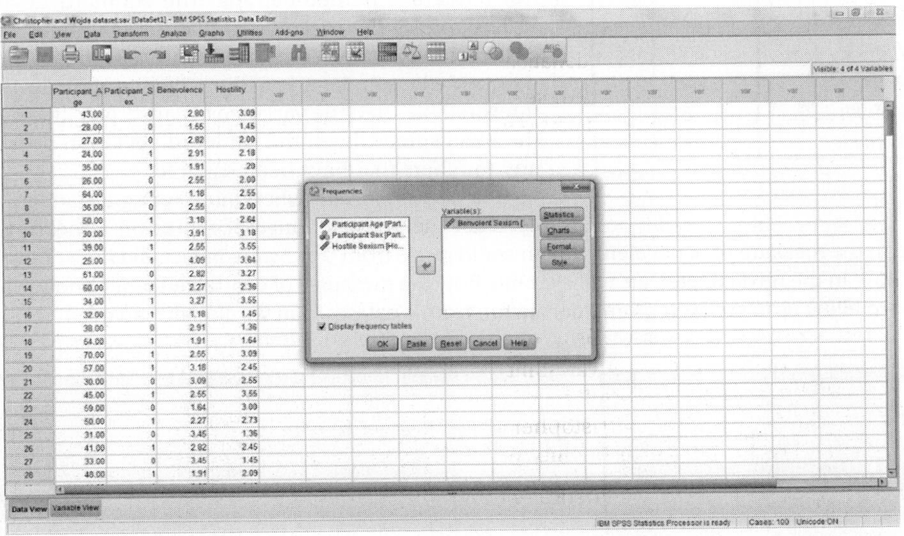

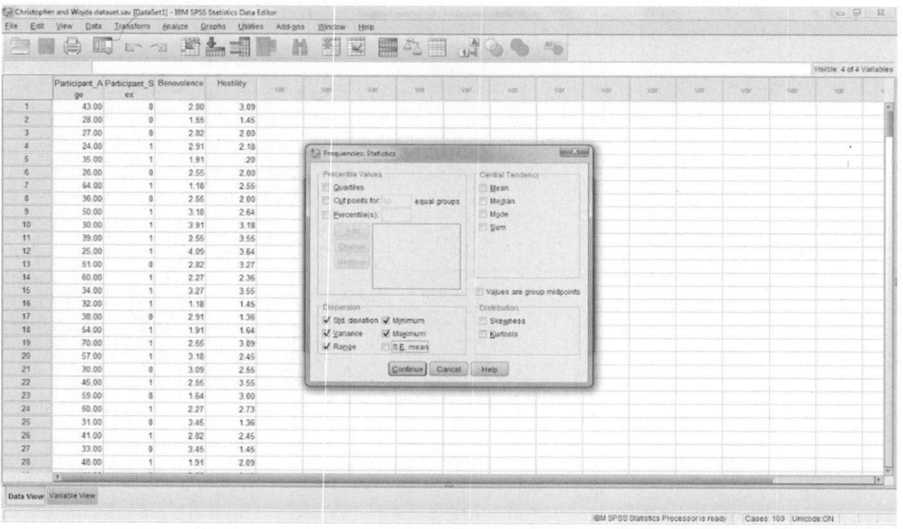

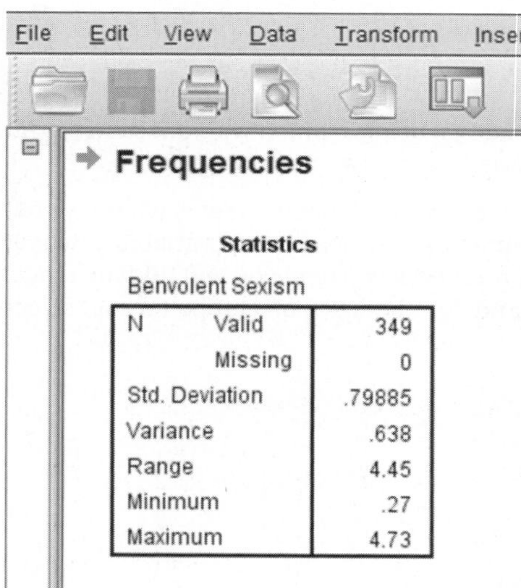

Statistics

Benvolent Sexism

N	Valid	349
	Missing	0
Std. Deviation		.79885
Variance		.638
Range		4.45
Minimum		.27
Maximum		4.73

4. Click *Continue* to return to the *Frequencies* window.
5. Click *OK*, and your output will soon appear.

(In the output displayed in this screenshot, I deleted the frequency distribution table.)

As we did when learning to interpret SPSS output for the measures of central tendency, let's start with the *Statistics* box, which contains the measures of variability statistics. First, we have our *N* (sample size), which is 349 with no missing data.

Next are the statistics for each of the three measures of central tendency. Remember that the standard deviation is the square root of the variance, and as we said previously, the variance is rarely reported in research because it is almost redundant with the standard deviation. The standard deviation is more interpretable than the variance because, just like the raw data in the SPSS spreadsheet, the standard deviation does not contain any numbers that have been squared.

It is also important when interpreting a standard deviation to consider the possible range of scores on a measure. Recall that mean scores on the measure of benevolent sexism could range from 0 to 5 and, in fact, did range from 0.27 to 4.73 (a range of 4.45).[2] In the next chapter, we will examine how the measures of central tendency and variability can be used together to allow us to get even more information from a dataset than we already can get.

LEARNING CHECK

1. Return to the SPSS file "Wendt's data.sav". From this file, use SPSS to generate the measures of variability for the variables `Burnout` and `Role Overload`.

A: Here is what your SPSS output should look like:

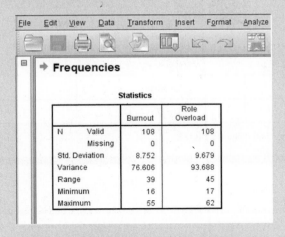

File Edit View Data Transform Insert Format Analyze

Frequencies

Statistics

		Burnout	Role Overload
N	Valid	108	108
	Missing	0	0
Std. Deviation		8.752	9.679
Variance		76.606	93.688
Range		39	45
Minimum		16	17
Maximum		55	62

Now, use this output and answer the following questions about it:

a) What was the range of scores for the `Burnout` measure?

A: 55 − 16 = 39

b) For the `Burnout` measure, explain how the standard deviation was calculated.

A: It is the square root of the variance; that is, $8.752 = \sqrt{76.606}$.

c) What was the sample size for the `Burnout` measure?

A: 108 participants

d) What was the standard deviation for the `Role Overload` measure?

A: 9.68

2. Use Christopher and Wojda's (2008) dataset to generate the measures of variability for the variable `Hostile Sexism`. After doing so, present them in a table (see Table 4.8 for an example of such a table).

A: Here is what your output should look like:

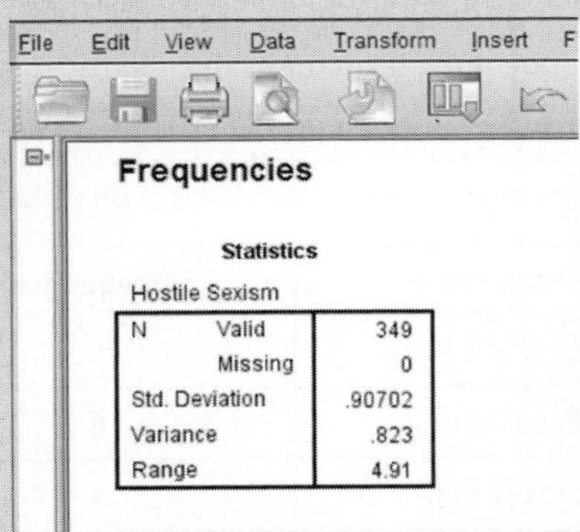

File Edit View Data Transform Insert F

Frequencies

Statistics

Hostile Sexism

N	Valid	349
	Missing	0
Std. Deviation		.90702
Variance		.823
Range		4.91

(Continued)

(Continued)

Table 4.9 shows what your table should look like:

Table 4.9 Descriptive Statistics for Hostile Sexism

Variable	Range	*SD*
Hostile Sexism	4.91 – 0 = 4.91	0.91

Notes. Scores on hostile sexism could range from 0 to 5.

NOTES

1. Recalculate the variance by taking 42.50 and dividing by 10 instead of 10 – 1. Do you see how the variance is now smaller than without subtracting 1 from the sample size? Without subtracting 1, we are likely underestimating how much variability is in the population because of the fact we are, necessarily, using sample data. There is more variability in the population than in a sample from that population because, as you already know, populations are larger than any of their corresponding samples.
2. The 4.45 on the output was a result of an SPSS rounding error, as 4.73 – .27 = 4.46.

CHAPTER APPLICATION QUESTIONS

1. Why can't we calculate a mean when we have nominal data?
2. The only measure of central tendency we are certain to observe as a value in our dataset is:
   a) the mean.
   b) the median.
   c) the mode.
   d) all measures of central tendency must be actual values in the distribution.
3. Explain why "c" is the correct answer to question 3.
4. A survey asked students which pizza place they preferred. The results are as follows:

Pizza Place	*f* (frequency)
Late Night Pizza®	5
Papa John's®	6
Pizza Hut®	3
Little Caesars®	5

a) What is the best measure of central tendency for these data?

b) Explain your answer to the previous question.

c) What is the mode of this distribution?

5. Not everything naturally follows a normal distribution, such as incomes in the United States. The distribution of salaries in the United States is:

   a) negatively skewed because poor people represent outliers who earn significantly less than most people.
   b) positively skewed because poor people represent outliers who earn significantly less than most people.
   c) negatively skewed because rich people represent outliers who earn significantly more than most people.
   d) positively skewed because rich people represent outliers who earn significantly more than most people.

6. In a positively skewed distribution, Betty scored the mean, Barney scored the median, and Fred scored the mode. Who had the highest score?

   a) Betty
   b) Barney
   c) Fred
   d) They all scored approximately the same.

7. Explain your response to the previous question.

8. Explain the difference between a ceiling effect and a floor effect.

9. Explain the relationship between the variance and the standard deviation.

10. Use the following sample data for questions a–e:

    7, 8, 0, 2, 6, 4, 5, 7, 6

    a) Calculate the range.
    b) Calculate the mean.
    c) Calculate the sum of squares.
    d) Calculate the variance.
    e) Calculate the standard deviation.

11. Which measure of variability is **MOST** affected by extreme scores (i.e., by outliers)?

    a) the range
    b) the median
    c) the standard deviation
    d) the mean

12. Dr. Hill noticed that the distribution of students' scores on his last math test had an extremely large standard deviation. This fact indicates that the:

    a) test was a good measure of students' knowledge.
    b) students' scores tended to vary quite a bit.
    c) students generally performed well on the test.
    d) test was given to a large number of students.

13. Gunnar wants to know how consistent his bowling scores have been during the past seasons. Which of the following measures would provide the most appropriate answer to his question?

    a) the mean
    b) the median
    c) the standard deviation
    d) the range

14. Explain why choice "c" is the best answer to the previous question.

15. In a set of five scores, suppose all scores are 8. What is the value of (a) the median, (b) the mode, and (c) the standard deviation?

Answers

1. Nominal data are categorical data. Therefore, any numerical value we place on these categories is arbitrary and has no interpretable meaning. Without scale data, we cannot calculate a mean.

2. c

3. The mean does not need to lie in our dataset. Suppose we have the following dataset:

   5, 5, 5, 5, 7, 7, 7, 7

   The mean is 6, and the median is 6. However, the number 6 is not in the dataset. The only measure of central tendency guaranteed to be in the dataset is the mode (which, in this example, is 5 and 7).

4. a) Mode

   b) These are nominal data, so the only appropriate measure of central tendency is the mode. It would make no sense to calculate a mean or median in this example.

   c) Papa John's® is the mode because it has the greatest frequency of student preference.

5. d

6. a

7. In a positively skewed distribution, a few unusually high scores "drag up" the mean so that it is higher than most of the other scores. In a positively skewed distribution, most scores are toward the low end of the distribution; the mean is larger than the median or mode in a positively skewed distribution.

8. A ceiling effect occurs when a dataset has a lack of variability because scores tend to cluster together at the high end of the possible range of scores. A floor effect also involves a lack of variability in a dataset; however, with a floor effect, scores tend to cluster together at the low end of the possible range of scores.

9. We need to calculate the variance as the preliminary step in calculating the standard deviation. Once we calculate the variance, we take the square root of it and we have our standard deviation.

10. a) 8

    b) 5.0

    c) 54

    d) 6.75

    e) 2.60

11. a
12. b
13. c
14. The mean and median are measures of central tendency and do not provide information about consistency (variability). The range tends to be affected by outliers in the data and requires only two datapoints in its calculation. Because the standard deviation uses all datapoints in its calculation, it is the best measure of consistency (variability) for Gunnar to calculate.
15. (a) median = 8; (b) mode = 8; (c) standard deviation = 0

QUESTIONS FOR CLASS DISCUSSION

1. Why can't we calculate a mean when we have ordinal data?
2. Use the following distribution to answer the three questions that follow it:

Score	*f* (frequency)
12	7
11	7
10	6
9	4
8	0
7	0
6	0
5	1

a) The above distribution:
   a) has a positive skew.
   b) has a negative skew.
   c) is normal.

b) The mode for the above distribution is:
   a) 7.
   b) 0 and 7.
   c) 11 and 12.
   d) 6, 7, and 8.

c) Which of the following numbers would be considered an outlier in the above distribution?
   a) 0
   b) 1
   c) 5
   d) 7

3. How does it affect the mean when you add a constant to every score? That is, if an instructor adds 5 points to everyone's test score, how will the mean change?
   a) The new mean and the old mean will be the same.
   b) The new mean will be 5 points higher than the old mean.
   c) The new mean will be 5 points less than the old mean.
   d) There is not enough information to answer this question.

4. Let's return to an example from a prior Learning Check. Seven friends have a mean income of $300/week, and their median income is $270/week. Rich, the lowest paid, gets fired from his $200/week job and now has an income of $0/week.

   What is the mean weekly income of the seven friends after Rich lost his job?

5. Students voted for their preferred professors by ranking them. To describe this dataset, which measure(s) of central tendency should be reported? Explain your response.

6. A sample of scores on a stress questionnaire is 2, 3, 5, 1, 6, 4, and 77. Which measure of central tendency is the most appropriate to describe this distribution?

7. Explain your response to the previous question.

8. Why is variability an absolute necessity in a research study?

9. Here are two sets of data with the same means:

   Dataset A: 14, 15, 15, 16, 16, 16, 17, 17

   Dataset B: 0, 2, 9, 15, 18, 22, 27, 33

   Without doing any calculations, explain which dataset has a larger standard deviation.

10. Why can't we calculate any of the measures of variability for nominal data?

CHAPTER 5

Determining "High" and "Low" Scores

The Normal Curve, z Scores, and Probability

After reading this chapter, you will be able to

- Distinguish among normal distributions, positively skewed distributions, and negatively skewed distributions
- Calculate a *z* score
- Interpret the information a *z* score conveys
- Use *z* scores to make decisions
- Use *z* scores to identify percentile ranks of raw scores
- Generate *z* scores using SPSS

In the previous chapter, we learned about three measures of central tendency (mean, median, and mode) and three measures of variability (range, variance, and standard deviation). In this chapter, we conclude our discussion of descriptive statistics by presenting distributions of data. We touched on the topic of data distributions in the previous chapter when we briefly discussed normal and skewed distributions. In this chapter, we explore these topics in more depth. In doing so, it will give us a chance to integrate some of the information we learned in the previous two chapters. In addition, we will add a powerful statistical tool to our kit, one that is used not only in psychological research but also in many situations that require making decisions based on data.

TYPES OF DISTRIBUTIONS

Normal Distributions

In Chapter 4, we encountered what are called *normal data distributions* and *skewed data distributions*. To refresh these concepts, a normal distribution occurs when all three measures of central tendency are approximately equal. Figure 5.1 illustrates what a normal distribution looks like. As you can see, it is bell-shaped and symmetrical; that is, if you could fold the normal distribution in half, it would be a perfect fit. In addition, most scores cluster around the middle of the distribution, with fewer and fewer scores appearing as we move away from the middle of the distribution. There is only one mode. Because the mode is approximately the same as the mean and median, these latter two statistics should be simple to locate. Finally, as we will discuss in great detail in the third section of this chapter, when we know the mean and standard deviation for a set of data that is normally distributed, we can determine precisely how "low" or "high" a specific score is. In addition, we can determine the percentage of scores that fall between any two given scores.

Figure 5.1 A Mesokurtic Normal Distribution

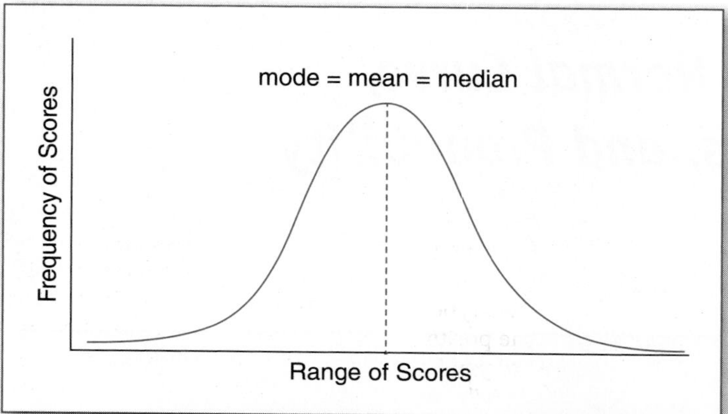

Figure 5.2 A Leptokurtic Normal Distribution

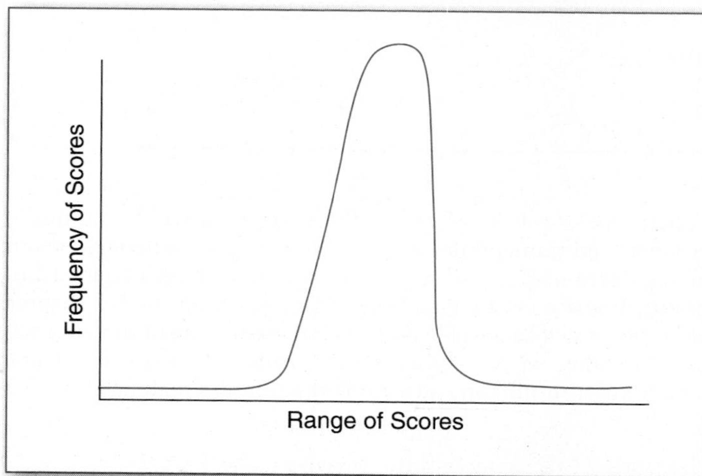

Figure 5.1 is a "normal" normal distribution. Its technical name is a *mesokurtic* normal distribution. "Meso" means "middle." I called it a "normal" normal distribution because there are a couple of other forms (or shapes) that a normal distribution can take on. For example, take a look at Figure 5.2. This is a normal distribution; however, notice how "tall" is it? There are a lot of scores clustered in the middle of this distribution with the frequency of a score dropping dramatically as we move away from the middle. This type of normal distribution is called a *leptokurtic* distribution. "Lepto" means "thin." Now look at Figure 5.3. This normal distribution is rather flat; that means scores are spread out across the range of possible scores. This type of normal distribution is called a *platykurtic* distribution. "Platy" means "flat." Compared with mesokurtic or leptokurtic normal distributions, scores in a platykurtic distribution cluster less in the middle of the distribution.

The concept of **kurtosis** is how "tall" or "short" the peak of a normal distribution is. In addition, it indicates how "crunched" or "spread out" scores in a normal distribution are. Think back to our measures of variability in the previous chapter. In which of the three types of normal distributions would you see the largest amount of variability? What about the least amount of variability? Think about these questions, and we'll discuss the answers to them in the next Learning Check.

Figure 5.3 A Platykurtic Normal Distribution

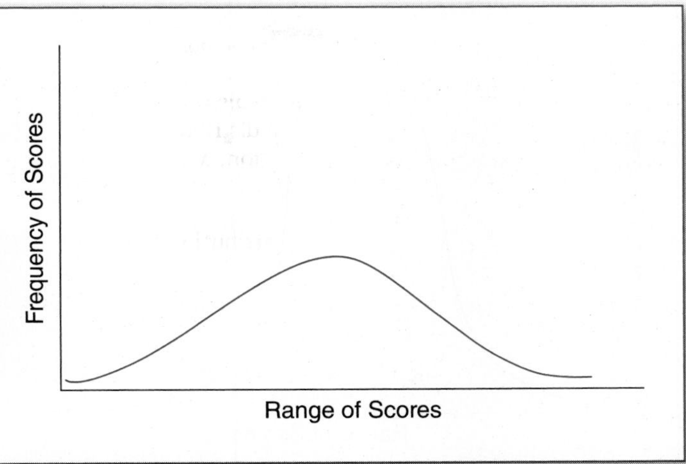

Kurtosis: how "flat" or "peaked" a normal distribution is; indicates how much variability there is in the distribution of scores.

Skewed Distributions

In addition to normal data distributions, we can have skewed data distributions. By "skewed," we mean that measures of central tendency are not approximately equal. That is, we have some particularly high scores or some particularly low scores in our data, called *outliers*. Figures 5.4 and 5.5 present examples of the two types of skewed distributions that we highlighted in Chapter 4. Can you identify which figure contains the positively skewed distribution and which one contains the negatively skewed distribution? Don't read on until you have tried to answer this question.

Figure 5.4 is an example of a *negatively skewed distribution*. Why is it negatively skewed? Before I tell you, think about this question, both in terms of how the distribution looks and in terms of the measures of central tendency. Visually, look where most scores tend to fall. The mode is toward the high end of the distribution; that is, the mode is greater than the median or the mean. Did you notice how there are only a few scores at the low end of the distribution? That's what makes this a "negatively" skewed distribution, a few low scores.

Figure 5.4 A Negatively Skewed Distribution

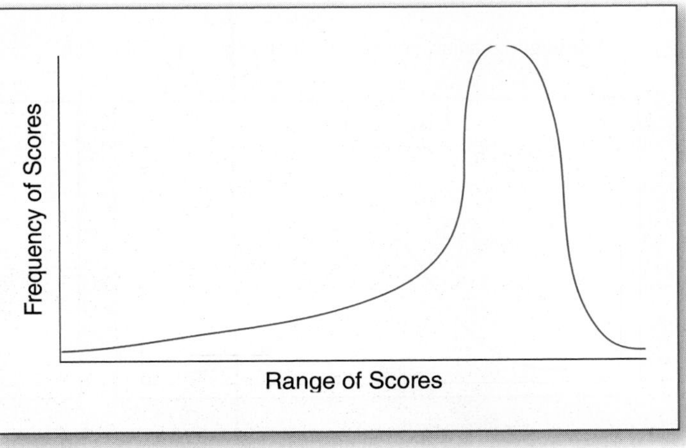

Figure 5.5 is a *positively skewed distribution*. Given what you know about negatively skewed distributions, think about why Figure 5.5 is positively skewed. We have only a few scores at the high end of the distribution. That's why this is a "positively" skewed distribution, because of a few high scores. And as a result of these few high scores, the mean is greater than the median or the mode.

When trying to remember the difference between a positively skewed distribution and a negatively skewed distribution, look at the tail of the distribution. That is, look to see where the few "weird" or "skewed" scores are located. If

Figure 5.5 A Positively Skewed Distribution

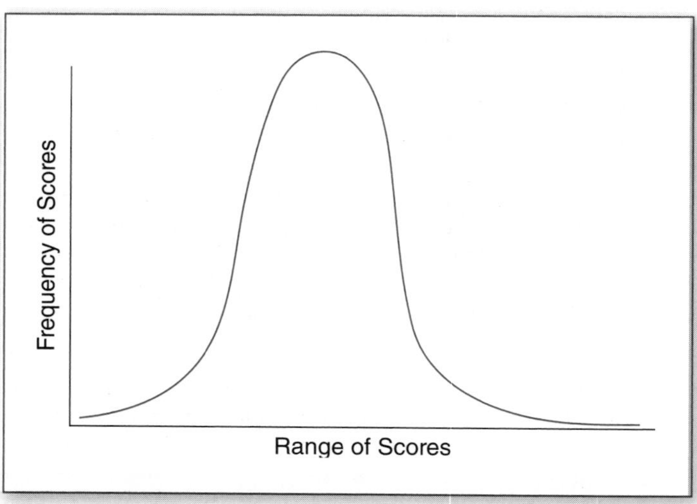

those weird or skewed scores are on the low end of the distribution, it is a negatively skewed distribution (Figure 5.4). If the weird or skewed scores are on the high end of the distribution, it is a positively skewed distribution (Figure 5.5).

Up to this point in the book, we have used the term *outlier* as a given. That is, we "just know" whether a score qualifies as an outlier. In reality, we need to have some sort of criteria for making the decision of whether a score is an outlier. In Chapter 3, we learned about frequency distribution tables and graphs. Such tools can provide insights into "extreme" scores. A more common and systematic way to identify outliers is to examine how many standard deviation units a score is from the mean. For example, suppose we have a dataset with a mean of 50 and a standard deviation of 10. We have a score of 75. Is that score an outlier?

Frankly, there is no definitive answer to this question. However, let me share a couple of heuristics that researchers use to determine outliers. Generally, if a given score is 2, 2.5, or 3 standard deviation units above or below the mean, it could be considered an outlier in the dataset. In this example, the score of 75 is 2.5 standard deviation units above the mean. It could qualify as an outlier. But, in practice, there is subjectivity on the part of the researcher in making this decision. So long as the researcher is candid and tells readers how such decisions were made, any of these heuristics is an acceptable cut-off for establishing the presence of outliers in a dataset.

LEARNING CHECK

1. Consider the following two normal distributions of data:

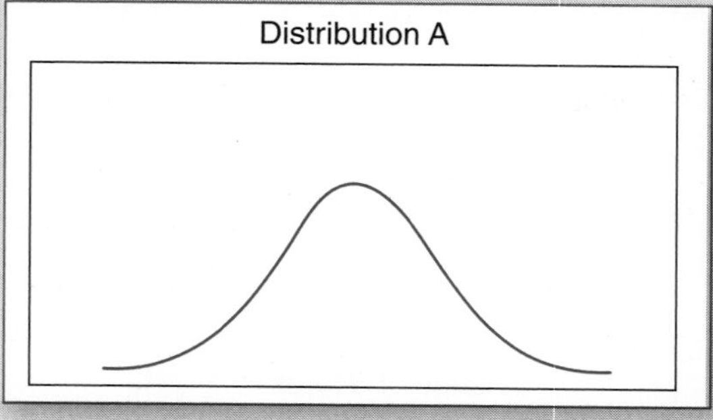

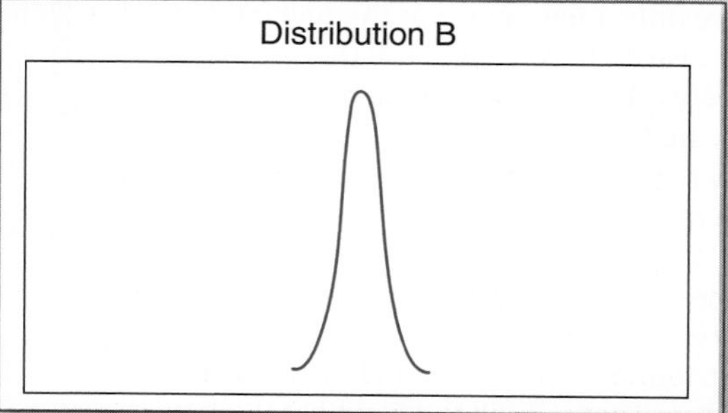

Which distribution has a larger standard deviation, distribution "a" or distribution "b?" Explain your response.

A: Distribution "a" has a larger standard deviation. The standard deviation is a measure of variability; that is, it provides an idea of how spread out scores are in a distribution. Clearly, scores are more spread out in distribution "a."

2. Suppose you take a test in a class. From your standpoint, and assuming you want to have a good test grade, would you want to hear that scores on your test were normally distributed, positively skewed, or negatively skewed? Explain your reasoning.

   A: From a student perspective, a negatively skewed distribution is preferable to a positively skewed or a normal distribution of scores. That's because in a negatively skewed distribution, there are a few low scores dragging down the mean. However, most people scored quite high, which is a good thing for most students. Obviously, if you're one of the students with an unusually negative score, this is not a good thing for you. But in general, negatively skewed distributions of test scores are good news for most students.

3. Explain the role that the standard deviation plays in identifying outliers in a dataset.

   A: Researchers identify outliers by seeing how many standard deviations a score is from the mean of the dataset. There are no definite rules about how many standard deviations a score needs to be from the mean to qualify as an outlier. The most critical consideration is that researchers disclose the number of standard deviation units used to identify outliers in their research.

STANDARDIZED SCORES (*Z* SCORES)

At some colleges and universities, students serve on the admissions staff and may even help review applications for admission to the school. Suppose you are fortunate enough to work in your school's admissions office. Although criteria for admitting students varies from school to school, most colleges and universities consider high school grades [grade-point average (GPA)] and standardized test performance [such as the Scholastic Aptitude Test (SAT®; College Board, New York, NY) or the American College Testing (ACT®; ACT, Inc., Iowa City, IA) exam]. There are likely other factors, but for our purposes, these will be the only two factors we will consider. In addition, there are a few assumptions we need to consider in this section of the chapter. The first assumption is that each factor counts equally toward admission. The second assumption is that the quality of each applicant's high school is the same. Finally, for the sake of example, the rigor of each applicant's high school coursework is the same, so we don't need to weigh GPA.[1]

Table 5.1 contains the admissions data for two applicants. You can only admit one of these two applicants. As you consider these data, realize that GPA at Ori's high school could range from 0 to 10.0, and at Katie's high

Table 5.1 Information for Two Applicants to Your School

	Candidate	
Data source	**Ori**	**Katie**
High School GPA	7.0	3.5
ACT Score	29	—
SAT Score	—	1,650

school, it could range from 0.0 to 4.0. Ori took the ACT, whereas Katie took the SAT. ACT scores can range from 1 to 36, whereas SAT scores can range from 300 to 2,400. Your job working in admissions is to take these data and decide which candidate is better. How might you do this?

If we look at GPA, it appears that Ori has a better GPA than Katie. After all, a 7.0 is greater than a 3.5. However, remember that GPA was measured differently at the two high schools. So how do we determine who had the better grade-point average? Enter the notion of *standardized scores*, also called *z* scores. A ***z* score** is a measure of how many standard deviation units a score falls from the mean of its distribution. Armed with a distribution's mean and standard deviation, we are in a position to determine whether Ori or Katie has the better GPA.

***z* score**: number that indicates how many standard deviations away from the mean a given score is.

Let's think through the definition of a *z* score because by doing so, I bet we can figure out how to calculate it. First, we need an individual score, such as an applicant's GPA. Table 5.1 has this information. Second, we also need the mean from which that individual score came. Here, that would be the mean GPA at the applicant's high school. Finally, we need the standard deviation from which the individual score came. Thus, in addition to the mean GPA for the high school, we need the standard deviation of the GPA for that high school. Information about our applicants' high schools appears in Table 5.2.

Here is the *z* score formula:

$$z = \frac{\text{individual score} - \text{group mean}}{\text{standard deviation}}$$

Let's plug in the information from Table 5.2 to see who has the better GPA. Let's take Ori's GPA first:

$$z = \frac{7.0 - 6.0}{1.5}$$
$$z = \frac{1.0}{1.5}$$
$$z = +0.67$$

Interpreting this *z* of + 0.67, Ori's GPA is 0.67 standard deviation units above his high school's mean GPA. It is important to have the plus sign. If Ori's GPA had been below the mean for his high school, there would have been a negative (–) sign before the value of the *z* score.

Now let's convert Katie's GPA to a *z* score:

$$z = \frac{3.5 - 3.0}{0.5}$$
$$z = \frac{0.5}{0.5}$$
$$z = +1.0$$

How do we interpret this *z* of + 1.0? Katie's GPA is 1 standard deviation unit above her high school's mean GPA. To reiterate, it is customary and informative (and, thus, necessary) to include the sign (positive or negative) before the actual value of the *z* score.

From our *z* score calculations, Katie has the higher GPA. But what about their test scores? Given that Ori took the ACT and Katie took the SAT, we need a way to compare who scored higher on their test. Thank goodness we have *z* scores that allow us to make these types of comparisons! That is, we can compare performance on tests that have vastly different scoring schemes, as is the case here. Go ahead and use Table 5.2 to determine who scored higher on their admissions test. Then, read on and make sure your calculations are correct.

Table 5.2 Group Means and Standard Deviations for Two Applicants to Your School

	Candidate	
Data source	**Ori**	**Katie**
High School GPA	7.0	3.5
High school's mean	6.0	3.0
High school's standard deviation	1.5	0.5
ACT Score	29	—
National mean	21	
National standard deviation	4	
SAT Score	—	1,650
National mean		1,500
National standard deviation		300

Don't read on until you attempt these calculations.

Assuming you have tried to calculate the z scores for Ori's ACT score and Katie's SAT score, let's make sure we understand this process. We'll start with Ori's ACT score:

$$z = \frac{29 - 21}{4}$$

$$z = \frac{8}{4}$$

$$z = +2.00$$

A z score of $+2.00$ means that Ori's admissions test score was 2 standard deviations above the mean for that test.

For Katie's SAT score,

$$z = \frac{1650 - 1500}{300}$$

$$z = \frac{150}{300}$$

$$z = +0.50$$

A z score of $+0.50$ means that Katie's admissions test score was one half of a standard deviation above the mean for that test. Thus, Ori scored higher on his admissions test than Katie scored on her admissions test.

Table 5.3 summarizes our z score data up to this point. As you read this table carefully, remember that the numbers in it are all z scores. So, where do all these z scores leave us with respect to which one of these two applicants to admit to your school? Actually, we can easily make a decision with just two more quick-and-easy calculations. The beauty of z scores is that by definition, they are all measured the same way. Recall the definition of a z score; it is a measure of how many standard deviation units a score falls from the mean of its distribution. Means and standard deviations are calculated the same way for any dataset, no matter how that dataset is measured. Therefore, in Table 5.3, high school GPA and admissions test (regardless of whether it was the ACT or the SAT) measure the data in the same way.

Table 5.3 *z* Score Information for Two Applicants to Your School

	Candidate	
Data source	**Ori**	**Katie**
High School GPA	+0.67	+1.00
Admissions Test Score	+2.00	+0.50

Because our data are all measured the same way, we can combine them and make an admissions decision. For example, we could simply take the mean *z* score for Ori and the mean *z* score for Katie and admit the student with the higher mean. This assumes we want to weight high school GPA and admissions test scores equally.[2] If so, Ori's mean *z* score is + 1.335, and Katie's mean *z* score is + 0.75. Therefore, we would admit Ori based strictly on these data.

As you might have inferred by this point, *z* scores are also called *standardized scores* because they allow us to compare scores across different measurements designed to accomplish the same or a similar purpose. Here, we can combine and compare GPAs measured on different ranges, SAT scores, and ACT scores, all thanks to *z* scores.

LEARNING CHECK

1. In a research study, a researcher gives a self-report measure of extraversion that asks respondents to indicate the extent to which each in a series of statements describes them (e.g., "I am a cheerful, high-spirited person") using a 1 (*not at all descriptive of me*) to 5 (*extremely descriptive of me*) response range. This researcher also includes a self-report measure of need for cognition, to which respondents used a 1 (*not at all descriptive of me*) to 9 (*extremely descriptive of me*) range to respond to items such as "I like to have the responsibility of handling a situation that requires a lot of thinking." If the same person completed both measures, how can you tell if a person scored higher on extraversion or on need for cognition?

   A: Because the extraversion measure and the need for cognition measure used different response ranges, it would make no sense to compare raw scores on these two measures. A score of 3 on the extraversion measure falls in the middle of the possible response range, whereas a score of 3 on the need for cognition measure falls toward the low end of the possible response range. Thus, we need to convert a person's score on the extraversion measure and his or her score on the need for cognition measure to get the respective *z* scores. Then, both measures will be the same scale of measurement, allowing to us to compare a person's scores on both measures.

Table 5.4 Information for Two Job Applicants for an RA position

	Candidate	
Data source	**Barbara**	**Mareike**
Interpersonal Skills	8.0	6.0
College GPA	3.25	3.85
Quality of Reference Letters	8.5	11.5

Notes. Interpersonal skills are measured on a 1 (*low*) to 9 (*high*) scale as judged by the Dean of Students. GPA is measured on a 0.0-to-4.0 range. Quality of reference letters is measured using a 1 (*poor*) to 15 (*outstanding*) range as judged by current RAs, and a mean is provided in the table.

2. Table 5.4 contains application data for two candidates, Barbara and Mareike, for a job as a resident assistant (RA) in the dorm. Table 5.5 contains the group means and standard deviations for each of the three sources of data used to decide which candidate to hire as an RA. Assume only one of these two people can be hired. First, perform the needed calculations to determine whom to hire. Second, assume that each source of data is weighed equally in making this hiring decision. Which candidate should be hired?

Table 5.5 Group Means and Standard Deviations for the Two RA Applicants

	Candidate	
Data source	**Barbara**	**Mareike**
Interpersonal Skills	8.0	6.0
Mean	5.0	5.0
Standard deviation	2.0	2.0
College GPA	3.25	3.85
Mean	3.00	3.00
Standard deviation	1.00	1.00
Quality of Reference Letters	8.5	11.5
Mean	8.0	8.0
Standard deviation	3.5	3.5

Notes. Interpersonal skills are measured on a 1 (*low*) to 9 (*high*) scale as judged by the Dean of Students. GPA is measured on a 0.0-to-4.0 range. Quality of reference letters is measured using a 1 (*poor*) to 15 (*outstanding*) range as judged by current RAs, and a mean is provided in the table.

Table 5.6 *z* Score Calculations for Measures Used to Select an RA

	Candidate	
Data source	**Barbara**	**Mareike**
Interpersonal Skills	$\frac{8-5}{2}$ $z = +1.50$	$\frac{6-5}{2}$ $z = +0.50$
College GPA	$\frac{3.25-3.00}{1.00}$ $z = +0.25$	$\frac{3.85-3.00}{1.00}$ $z = +0.85$
Quality of Reference Letters	$\frac{8.5-8.0}{3.5}$ $z = +0.14$	$\frac{11.5-8.0}{3.5}$ $z = +1.00$

(Continued)

(Continued)

A: First, Table 5.6 contains the *z* scores for Barbara's and Mareike's scores on each of the three variables being used to make this decision. If we calculate a mean *z* score for each candidate, Barbara has a mean *z* score of +0.63 and Mareike has a mean *z* score of +0.78. Therefore, we should hire Mareike.

Z SCORES, THE NORMAL DISTRIBUTION, AND PERCENTILE RANKS

In the previous chapter, I teased you that when certain assumptions about a dataset are met, there is some valuable information that you can get from such data. Specifically, when a dataset is normally distributed and you know the standard deviation of that dataset, you can locate precisely how high or low a score is in that distribution.

Locating Scores Under the Normal Distribution

For example, suppose you take a test in this class and get an 80% on it. Is that a good score or a not-so-good score? If the test scores are normally distributed, you can tell just how good your score is relative to the rest of the class.

With your score of 80%, let's assume the class mean was 70% with a standard deviation of 10%. You can see your score was above the mean, but how far above the mean is not yet known. Let's figure it out now.

The first thing we need to do is find the *z* score for your score of 80% on this exam. To calculate that *z* score, in addition to your raw score of 80%, we need the group mean and standard deviation. Conveniently, we have that information; the mean was 70%, and the standard deviation was 10%. Here is the *z* score calculation:

$$z = \frac{80\% - 70\%}{10\%}$$

$$z = \frac{10\%}{10\%}$$

$$z = +1.0$$

Armed with the *z* score, we consult Appendix A. This appendix contains the percentages of scores that fall between any two *z* scores. The columns are labeled "*z*," "Area Between Mean and *z*," and "Area Beyond *z* in Tail." The first column, labeled "*z*," contains *z* scores that you could be working with. The second column, labeled "Area Between Mean and *z*," contains the percentage of scores that fall between the mean and the *z* score in the previous column. The third column, labeled "Area Beyond *z* in Tail," is the percentage of scores from that *z* score through the tail end of the distribution.

Let's see just how good your test score, with its *z* score of + 1.0, is, using Appendix A. We want to know what percentage of the class scored better on the test than you did; once we know that information, we can tell how well you did relative to your classmates. Look at the first column, labeled "*z*," in the appendix. Find $z = 1.00$. We want to know how many of your classmates did better than you did. To find out, look at the third column for $z = 1.00$. You see it is 0.1587. That means 15.87% of the class did better on the test than you did. Or in other words, you did better than 100% − 15.87%, or 84.13%, of your classmates. Nice job!

Let's stick with this same example, in which the class mean was 70% and the standard deviation was 10%. Suppose your best friend in the class scored 67%. What proportion of the class scored better and worse than your friend did? First, calculate the *z* score for a raw score of 67%:

$$z = \frac{67\% - 70\%}{10\%}$$

$$z = \frac{-3\%}{10\%}$$

$$z = -0.30$$

Your friend scored 0.30 standard deviation units below the class mean. Our question was as follows: What proportion of the class scored better and worse than your friend did? Consult Appendix A. Find the z of 0.30. Here, your friend has a negative z score because he scored below the mean. However, we use Appendix A the same way for negative z scores as we do for positive z scores. Because scores in a normal distribution are symmetrical, the areas between the mean and a z score and the area beyond a z score are the same on either side of the mean. We see that with a z score of −0.30, 38.21% of the class did worse on the test than your friend did. Stated differently, 100% − 38.21%, or 61.79%, of the class did better on the test than your friend did.

Let's take one more example. With a class mean of 70% and a standard deviation of 10%, what percentage of students scored between 55 and 75 on this test? Before we dive into z score calculations, let's step back and make sure we know what we need to calculate to answer this question. First, we need the percentage of scores greater than 55%. However, we only need those scores greater than 55% up to 75%, not those scores above 75%. So, we need to find the percentage of scores above 55. Let's do that first:

$$z = \frac{55\% - 70\%}{10\%}$$

$$z = \frac{15\%}{10\%}$$

$$z = -1.50$$

By consulting Appendix A, we see that 6.68% of the scores are less than a z score of 1.50. Or, 100% − 6.68% = 93.32% of the scores are greater than a z score of −1.50.

Remember, we want the percentage of scores between 55% and 75%. So now, we need to "remove" those scores above 75%. To do so, let's calculate the z score for a test score of 75%:

$$z = \frac{75\% - 70\%}{10\%}$$

$$z = \frac{5\%}{10\%}$$

$$z = 0.5$$

Returning to Appendix A, we see now that 30.85% of the scores are greater than a z score of 0.5. To calculate the percentage of scores on the test between 55% and 75%, we need to subtract the proportion of scores greater than 75% from the proportion of scores greater than 55%. Therefore, 93.32% (percentage of scores greater than 55% on the test) − 30.85% (percentage of scores greater than 75% on the test) = 62.47%.

In summary, 62.47% of the raw scores (i.e., scores on the test in your class) fell between 55% and 75%.

Percentile Ranks

Now that we have some experience with z scores, how to interpret them, and how to use them, let's conclude this section by examining percentile ranks of scores. **A percentile rank** is the percentage of raw scores equal to or below a certain raw score. To determine a percentile rank for a raw score, we need to know that raw score's corresponding z score, a process with which you are now well acquainted.

Percentile rank: percentage of scores that are at or below a particular score in a normal distribution.

Let's return to Laura Wendt's (2013) research on academic burnout that we discussed in the previous two chapters. The following scores on the measure of burnout are from four participants in her research; the names I have given them are hypothetical as it would be unethical to tie a participant's data to that individual:

Person	Burnout Score
Sybil	50
Hans	25
Gracie	34
Sigmund	43

Now, we need to compute each person's *z* score. To do so, we need the group mean and standard deviation. Luckily, we calculated these statistics in Chapter 4. The mean was 36.50, and the standard deviation was 8.75. Let's now compute the *z* scores; we will do Sybil's *z* score together, and then you can calculate the other three *z* scores with a chance to check your work:

$$z \text{ score for Sybil} = \frac{50 - 36.5}{8.75}$$

$$z = \frac{13.5}{8.75}$$

$$z = +1.54$$

To refresh our understanding of what $z = +1.54$ means, it means that this burnout score of 50 is 1.54 standard deviations above the mean. Go ahead and calculate the other three *z* scores, and then check your work!

Person	Burnout Score	*z* Score
Sybil	50	+1.54
Hans	25	−1.31
Gracie	34	−0.29
Sigmund	43	+0.74

We are now ready to find the percentile rank for each burnout score. Remember the definition of percentile rank; it is the percentage of raw scores equal to or below a certain raw score. To find each percentile rank, we again need Appendix A. For each *z* score, we need to determine the percentage of scores at or less than that *z* score's position in the distribution of scores. Let's look at Sybil. Her z score is + 1.54. Locate 1.54 in the "*z*" column of Appendix A. In the third column of this appendix, we see that 6.18% of the scores are above Sybil's score. Of course, given the definition of percentile rank, we need the percentage of scores below Sybil's score. There must be 100% of the scores in the entire distribution. Therefore, we can subtract the percentage of scores above Sybil's score from 100, and that will give us her percentile rank. In short, 100% − 6.18% = 93.82%. Sybil scored at the 93.82nd percentile on the burnout measure.

Let's do Hans's percentile rank together; then you can calculate the percentile ranks for Gracie and Sigmund, and check your work after doing so. Hans has a *z* score of −1.31. We locate this "*z*" in the first column of Appendix A. We can see that with this *z* score, there are 9.51% of the scores in the tail of the distribution. Remember the definition of percentile rank; we are done! Overall, 9.51% of the scores were below Hans's score; therefore, his percentile rank is 9.51st.

Your turn: Calculate the percentile ranks for Gracie and Sigmund, and then check yourself. In the next Learning Check, the first two questions will ask you to explain how you obtained Gracie's and Sigmund's *z* scores.

Person	Burnout Score	*z* Score	Percentile Rank
Sybil	50	+1.54	93.82nd
Hans	25	−1.31	9.51st
Gracie	34	−0.29	38.59th
Sigmund	43	+0.74	77.04th

Source: Yeh, Sarah. "Normal Distributions." Cartoon. Original Work. (July 21, 2016)

LEARNING CHECK

1. Explain how you calculated Gracie's percentile rank.

   A: We took her burnout score of 34 and subtracted the mean (36.5). This gave us −2.5. We divided −2.5 by the standard deviation of the burnout measure (8.75), which gave us the *z* score of −0.29. From Appendix A, we see that with this *z* score, 38.59% of the scores in the distribution fall below this point. Therefore, she scored at the 38.59th percentile.

2. Explain how you calculated Sigmund's percentile rank.

   A: We took his burnout score of 43 and subtracted the mean (36.5). This gave us 6.5. We divided 6.5 by the standard deviation of the burnout measure (8.75), which gave us the *z* score of +0.74. From Appendix A, we see that with this *z* score, 22.96% of the scores in the distribution fall above this point. But remember that a percentile rank is the percentage of scores at or below a certain score. Therefore, we must subtract 22.96% from 100%, which leaves us with 77.04%. Therefore, Sigmund scored at the 77.04th percentile.

3. Use Appendix A to answer the following questions:

   a) What percentage of scores would fall between a *z* score of −1.35 and a *z* score of −0.21?

      A: We first need to find the percentage of the distribution that falls below a *z* score of −0.21. We see that the percentage is 41.68%. However, the question asks for the percentage of scores between a *z* score of −1.35 and −0.21. Thus, we need to know the percentage of the distribution below the *z* score of −1.35 and subtract this number from 41.68%. We see it is 8.85%. So, we have 41.68% − 8.85% = 32.83%. Therefore, 32.83% of the scores fall between these two *z* scores.

   b) What percentage of scores would fall below a *z* score of +0.89?

      A: 18.67% of the scores fall above this *z* score. To find the percentage of scores below this *z* score, take 100% and subtract 18.67% from it. That means 81.33% of the scores fall below a *z* score of +0.89.

   c) If we know that 90.99% of the scores fall above a specific point in a distribution, what is the *z* score of that specific point?

      A: We must look for a *z* score below which 100% − 90.99% = 9.01% of the scores fall. That *z* score is −1.34.

4. Look back at Table 5.2, and using Appendix A, answer the following questions:

   a) What percentage of students at Ori's high school had a higher GPA than he had?

      A: 25.14% of students had a higher GPA than Ori.

   b) What percentage of students scored lower on the SAT than Katie did?

      A: 69.15% of students scored lower on the SAT than Katie.

   c) What percentage of students scored between 19 and 23 on the ACT?

      A: 38.3% of students scored between 19 and 23.

   d) What percentage of students scored 1,400 or greater on the SAT?

      A: 62.93% of students scored 1,400 or better.

Z SCORES AND SPSS

In the previous two chapters, we used a dataset from Laura Wendt's (2013) research on academic burnout. We will use it here to illustrate how to generate *z* scores with data in the software program Statistical Package for the Social Sciences (SPSS).

Go ahead and open the SPSS file titled "Wendt data.sav". Your data view should look like this:

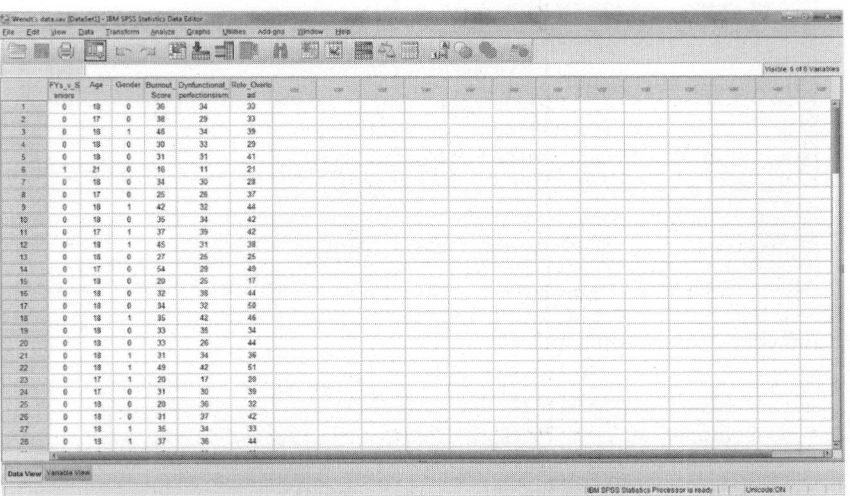

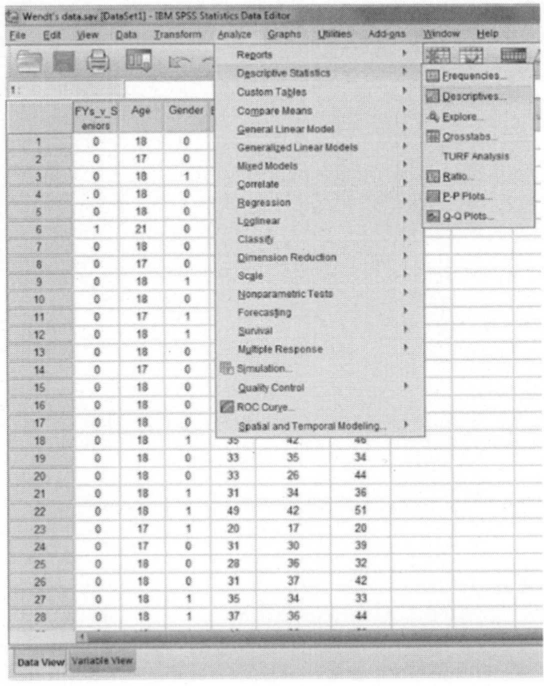

Here are the steps to derive *z* scores using SPSS:

1. Click on *Analyze* → *Descriptive Statistics* → *Descriptives*.
2. In the *Descriptives* dialogue box, click over the variable(s) for which you want *z* scores. In this example, I clicked over only the `Burnout` scores.
3. In the lower left corner of the dialogue box, click on *Save standardized values as variables*. Doing so tells SPSS to "Give me the *z* scores for the variables I requested."

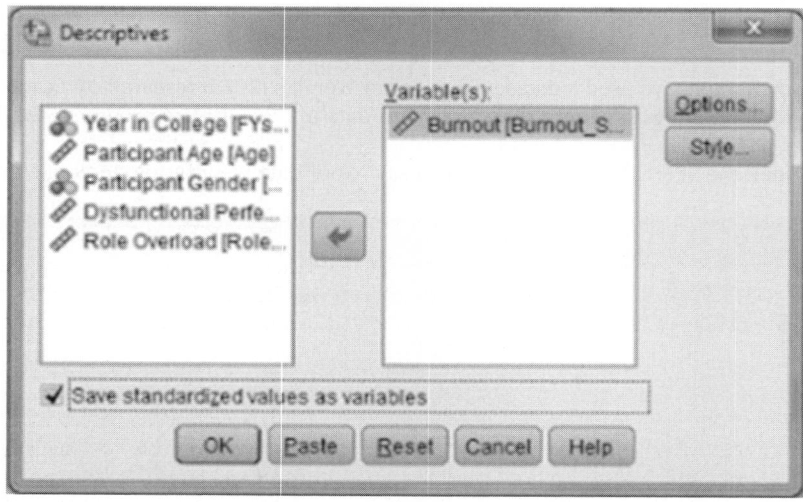

4. Click *OK*, and your *z* scores will appear.

*Wendt's data.sav [DataSet1] - IBM SPSS Statistics Data Editor

File Edit View Data Transform Analyze Graphs Utilities Add-ons Window Help

1 : ZBurnout_Score -.0528949967503

	FYs_v_Seniors	Age	Gender	Burnout_Score	Dynfunctional_perfectionsism	Role_Overload	ZBurnout_Score
1	0	18	0	36	34	33	-.05289
2	0	17	0	38	29	33	.17561
3	0	18	1	48	34	39	1.31814
4	0	18	0	30	33	29	-.73841
5	0	18	0	31	31	41	-.62416
6	1	21	0	16	11	21	-2.33796
7	0	18	0	34	30	28	-.28140
8	0	17	0	25	26	37	-1.30968
9	0	18	1	42	32	44	.63262
10	0	18	0	35	34	42	-.16715
11	0	17	1	37	39	42	.06136
12	0	18	1	45	31	38	.97538
13	0	18	0	27	25	25	-1.08117
14	0	17	0	54	29	49	2.00366
15	0	18	0	20	25	17	-1.88095
16	0	18	0	32	38	44	-.50991
17	0	18	0	34	32	50	-.28140
18	0	18	1	35	42	46	-.16715
19	0	18	0	33	35	34	-.39565
20	0	18	0	33	26	44	-.39565
21	0	18	1	31	34	36	-.62416
22	0	18	1	49	42	51	1.43240
23	0	17	1	20	17	20	-1.88095
24	0	17	0	31	30	39	-.62416
25	0	18	0	28	36	32	-.96692
26	0	18	0	31	37	42	-.62416
27	0	18	1	35	34	33	-.16715
28	0	18	1	37	36	44	.06136

Data View Variable View

The column that I highlighted in the last screenshot contains the z score for each participant on the burnout score. Remember what you are looking at. Each z score is the number of standard deviation units a person's score on the burnout measure is from the mean of that measure.

NOTES

1. Of course, in any "real" admissions decision, there are other factors we should consider, such as extracurricular involvement and demonstrated leadership skills and abilities. Please bear with my assumptions and shortcuts that are meant to help us learn about z scores, not about being an admissions counselor.
2. And remember another assumption, that the quality of their high schools was the same. If this assumption is not the case, the admissions office would have to account for that factor as well. And, of course, you can make a valid argument that GPA matters more than admissions test scores because GPA is earned over a long period of time but an admissions test is earned in one test sitting. We should also consider (I think) more than GPA and test scores when admitting applicants. Indeed, working in a college admissions office is a challenging job with a lot of factors to consider in making decisions that affect students' lives. Fortunately, a knowledge of z scores can make the admissions process slightly less complicated.

CHAPTER APPLICATION QUESTIONS

1. Take a look at the final SPSS screenshot in the last section of this chapter. For the third participant, interpret that person's score on the variable `ZBurnout_Score`.
2. Scores on the Wechsler Adult Intelligence Test tend to be normally distributed with a mean of 100 and a standard deviation of 15. Use this information to answer the following questions:
   a) What score on the intelligence test corresponds to the 35th percentile?
   b) What score on the intelligence test marks the top 20% of the distribution of scores?
   c) What is the median of this distribution?
   d) What percentage of scores fell between 86 and 108?
   e) What is the percentile rank of someone who scored 104?
3. In any normal distribution, what is the percentage area between a z score of +0.43 and a z score of +1.33?
4. If a normal distribution has a mean of 40 and a standard deviation of 4, between which two scores do about 95% of all the scores fall?

Answers

1. This is a z score of +1.31814 (with rounding, +1.32). This means the person's score was 1.32 standard deviation units above the mean burnout score in this dataset.

2. a) Remember the formula for calculating a z score:

$$z = \frac{\text{individual score} - \text{group mean}}{\text{standard deviation}}$$

We need to plug in information to this formula to determine the score on the intelligence test that corresponds to the 35th percentile. We know the mean (100) and standard deviation (15). We also know that we are looking for the 35th percentile, that is, the percentage of scores at or below that point on the distribution. We can consult Appendix A and find the z score that corresponds to 35% in the tail of the distribution. There is not a z score that precisely corresponds to 35%, but 0.39 comes the closest, so we can use it. Remember, the 35th percentile is below the mean, so we really have $z = -0.39$.

Now we can plug in three of the four ingredients to the z score formula and then solve for the missing ingredient, the individual score:

$$-0.39 = \frac{\text{individual score} - 100}{15}$$

To remove the denominator of the fraction, multiply both sides of the equal sign by the value of that denominator. Doing so gives us

$$-5.85 = \text{individual score} - 100$$

To get the individual score that answers this question, add 100 to both sides of the equal sign:

$$94.15 = \text{individual score}$$

In short, the score on the intelligence test that comes closest to the 35th percentile is a score of 94.15.

b) Look in Appendix A for the z score that denotes 20% in the tail. We see that it is approximately 0.84. Once again, let's plug in numbers to the z score formula and then solve for the missing number:

$$+0.84 = \frac{\text{individual score} - 100}{15}$$

$$12.6 = \text{individual score} - 100$$

$$112.6 = \text{the individual score that marks the top 20\% of the distribution of scores}$$

c) This is a trick question. Remember, we are dealing with a normal distribution, meaning that the measures of central tendency are the same. With a mean of 100, the median must also be 100.

d) We need to get the z scores that correspond to scores of 86 and 108. Once we do that, we can calculate the percentage of scores between these two points.

For a score of 86, the z score would be

$$z = \frac{86 - 100}{15}$$

$$z = -0.93$$

For a score of 108, the z score would be

$$z = \frac{108 - 100}{15}$$
$$z = +0.53$$

Now let's find the percentage of scores that fall above a z score of −0.93. That would be about 82.38% of the scores. However, we need to remove (subtract) those scores above a z score of +0.53. There are 29.81% of the scores above this z score. So, we take 82.38% and subtract 29.81% of the scores from it. That leaves us with 52.57% of the scores between 86 and 108.

d) Because we are dealing with a normal distribution, we know that half (50%) of the scores are below the mean. We need to add to that 50% the number of scores between 100 and 104. So, let's find the z score for a raw score of 104:

$$z = \frac{104 - 100}{15}$$
$$z = +0.27$$

There are 10.64% of the scores between 100 and 104, so therefore, we have 50% + 10.64% = 60.64% of the scores at or below 104. Therefore, a score of 104 is at the 60.64th percentile.

3. 24.18%

4. 32 and 48

QUESTIONS FOR CLASS DISCUSSION

1. If the 40th percentile on an examination is 70, then:
   a) 40% of the people got a score of 70.
   b) less than 40% of the people got a score higher than 70.
   c) 40% of the people got a score of 70 or less.
   d) 60% of the people got a score lower than 70.

2. Scores on a class test averaged 70% with a standard deviation of 8%. The following table has some information missing. Use your knowledge of z scores and percentile ranks to complete it:

Student	Score	*z* Score	Percentile Rank
Keith	55%		
Lauren			84.13th
Schara		+2.00	
Lori	98%		

3. In any normal distribution, what is the percentage area between a z score of -1.25 and a z score of $+0.36$?

4. The average man in an industrialized country lives 75 years with a standard deviation of 7 years. Use this information to answer the following questions:
   a) What percentage of men live 75 years or longer?
   b) What percentage of men live between 65 and 75 years?
   c) What percentage of men live 65 years or less?
   d) What percentage of men live between 55 and 60 years?

CHAPTER 6

Drawing Conclusions From Data

Descriptive Statistics, Inferential Statistics, and Hypothesis Testing

After reading this chapter, you will be able to

- Differentiate between null and research hypotheses
- Contrast directional (one-tailed) and nondirectional (two-tailed) research hypotheses
- Relate the notion of alpha level to directional and nondirectional hypothesis tests
- Describe the difference between Type I and Type II errors in hypothesis testing
- Apply basics of hypothesis testing to the *z* test
- Apply basics of hypothesis testing to the one-sample *t* test
- Apply the notion of statistical power to the basics of hypothesis testing

Up to this point, our discussion has focused on descriptive statistics. As we said in Chapter 1 and have reiterated since then, descriptive statistics provide information about a sample. In most research, though, we are interested in learning about a population. Indeed, the reason we conduct research on a sample is that we usually have a hypothesis about how variables are related to each other in the population. A **hypothesis** is a specific, formal prediction about how variables will be related in a research study. Obtaining descriptive statistics with a sample is important, but we need additional tools to draw conclusions about our population. These additional tools are called inferential statistics. When we say we want to draw conclusions about a population, we are making inferences about that population, based on a sample's worth of data.

Hypothesis: specific, formal prediction about the outcome of a research study.

In this chapter, we will first discuss the basic principles of hypothesis testing. Next, we will take an example of hypothesis testing using an inferential statistical tool when certain information about the population is available to us. We will then present a second inferential statistical tool when we do not have access to certain information about the population. We conclude this chapter with a discussion of statistical power, which will allow us to review some of the ideas presented throughout this chapter.

BASICS OF NULL HYPOTHESIS TESTING

When starting a research study, most researchers want to support their hypothesis about the world. Statistically, however, it is impossible to conclude something is 100% true without any chance of it being incorrect. For instance, suppose I told you that I had eggs for breakfast this morning. How might I prove to you that this claim is true? Perhaps there are dirty dishes with egg remnants on them in my kitchen. Perhaps there are egg shells in the trash. If you wanted more concrete evidence, you could have a medical expert somehow examine the contents of my stomach. However, there could be other explanations for each of these three pieces of evidence. Perhaps the dirty dishes with egg remnants were from my dinner last night; perhaps the egg shells ended up in the trash after I used the eggs to bake a cake; and finally, even if somehow there were egg contents in my stomach, perhaps they were from my eating some of the cake I made. But taken together, these three pieces of evidence would allow us to be *fairly confident* that I ate eggs for breakfast, but they would not prove with 100% certainty that I did so. The moral of the story is that when testing a hypothesis to draw conclusions about a population, we are always dealing with some degree of uncertainty. There is never 100% certainty.

Null Hypotheses and Research Hypotheses

So if we cannot use statistics to prove that a claim is true, what good are they? We use statistics to suggest that something is not true. What I am about to say may sound strange, but when using statistics, researchers must try to *disprove* what they think is the relationship between variables in the population. In other words, *researchers use statistics to test for a lack of relationship between variables*. If they cannot disprove what they think is the case in the population, then by default, their hypothesis about the population is supported. If you think about this carefully, there are essentially two types of hypotheses. One type of hypothesis is what is tested with statistics; the other type of hypothesis is what the researcher thinks is true of the population. From this point onward, we will use the term **null hypothesis** to refer to the hypothesis that is tested with statistics; we will use the term **research hypothesis** to refer to the hypothesis that the researcher holds about the population.

Null hypothesis: hypothesis that there is no relationship between variables in the population that are being studied in a sample.

Research hypothesis: hypothesis that there is a relationship between variables in the population that are being studied in a sample.

Let's take an example of a null hypothesis and a research hypothesis. Mentoring programs such as Big Brothers-Big Sisters pair successful high school and college students with younger children and adolescents who need positive role models. Do these programs have an effect on these younger children and adolescents? This is the question that Carla Herrera and her colleagues (Herrera, Grossman, Kauh, & McMaken, 2011) attempted to answer with their research. For instance, we might hypothesize that indeed, children and adolescents who have a Big Brother-Big Sister mentor might do better in school than children who do not have such a mentor (Herrera, Grossman, Kauh, & McMaken, 2011). That is our research hypothesis. What would the null hypothesis be? Understand that "null" means "nothing." Now it may be easier to answer this question. The null hypothesis is that there is no difference in school performance between children and adolescents who have a Big Brother-Big Sister mentor and those who do not have such a mentor. In most research you read, you will see a research hypothesis stated, and the null hypothesis is only implied. But with statistics, it is the null hypothesis that is being tested. Let's see how our null and research hypotheses can be expressed with symbols:

$$H_o: \mu_1 = \mu_2$$

where

H_o means "null hypothesis,"

μ_1 is the population mean for one group (having a mentor), and

μ_2 is the population mean for the second group (not having a mentor).

In plain English, the null hypothesis says that in the population, there is no difference in school performance between children and adolescents who have a Big Brother-Big Sister mentor and children and adolescents without such a mentor. It does not matter which population mean is 1 and which is 2. All that matters with these symbols is that we express that there is no difference between the means in the population.

Regarding the research hypothesis, there are two types of research hypotheses. When a researcher has a specific idea of the nature of the relationship between variables in the population, the research hypothesis is called a **directional hypothesis**. Another name for a directional hypothesis is a *one-tailed hypothesis*. Here is how we can express a one-tailed research hypothesis with symbols:

$$H_r: \mu_1 > \mu_2$$

where

H_r means "research hypothesis,"

μ_1 is the population mean for one group (having a mentor), and

μ_2 is the population mean for the second group (not having a mentor).

This one-tailed hypothesis says that in the population, children and adolescents who have a Big Brother-Big Sister mentor perform better in school than children and adolescents without such a mentor.

As you might have guessed, the other type of research hypothesis is called a **nondirectional hypothesis**, which is also known as a *two-tailed hypothesis*. With a two-tailed hypothesis, the researcher does not specify in advance the direction of the difference between the means in the population. Here is how we can express our two-tailed research hypothesis with symbols:

$$H_r: \mu_1 \neq \mu_2$$

where

H_r means "research hypothesis,"

μ_1 is the population mean for one group (having a mentor), and

μ_2 is the population mean for the second group (not having a mentor).

This two-tailed test says that we expect a difference in academic performance between children with a mentor and children without a mentor. You might be wondering why we need the nondirectional research hypothesis. After all, it seems reasonable to think that a researcher will have a specific idea of the relationship between variables in the population before doing a research study. For example, do we really expect children with a Big Brother-Big Sister mentor to do worse in school than children without such a mentor? In research, we must allow for counterintuitive outcomes. In addition to allowing for unanticipated outcomes, there is another excellent reason why we need nondirectional research hypotheses, which I hope to make clear in a just a moment when we discuss the importance of selecting what is called an alpha level and the region of null hypothesis rejection.

You may have noticed that when we expressed our hypotheses symbolically, we did so with the population mean symbol (μ). We do this by convention because it is the population we want to draw inferences about; the sample is merely the tool we use to do so.

Directional (one-tailed) hypothesis: research hypothesis that states the nature (i.e., direction) of the relationship between variables in the population.

Nondirectional (two-tailed) hypothesis: research hypothesis that does not state the nature (i.e., does not state the direction) of the relationship between variables in the population.

Alpha Level and the Region of Null Hypothesis Rejection

We will take a sample of students in the Big Brother-Big Sister program to learn if we can draw conclusions about the population of students in such programs. Given that samples are smaller than their corresponding populations, there is always some degree of *sampling error*, as we discussed in Chapter 1. To refresh, sampling error occurs when there is a difference between the characteristics of the population and the characteristics of the sample we are using to make inferences about the population. To generalize results from a sample to the population, we want to be reasonably sure that our results were not a function of sampling error. To do so, once we have stated our hypothesis, we need to decide on our **alpha level (or significance level)**. That is, we need to decide on the extent to which we are willing to say that our results were a result of random variation in the sample.

Alpha level (or significance level): probability value that states the likelihood that a statistical result occurred by chance.

Most social scientists use an alpha level of no higher than 5% (or .05). That is, researchers want the likelihood of a result occurring by chance to be less than 5%. If this is the case, then the result can be generalized from the sample to the population. In other words, when the likelihood of a sample result occurring by chance is less than 5%, we can make inferences about the population from the sample data. Some researchers use an alpha level of 1% (.01) or even .1% (.001). *The smaller the alpha level used, the more difficult it will be for the researcher to draw conclusions about the population from the sample data because the lower the alpha level, the less willing a researcher is to say his or her results are a function of sampling error.* Because alpha levels are percentages that cannot exceed 100%, we do not typically put a zero before the decimal.

So why might we want to make it difficult to make inferences about the population? If we "stack the deck" against making inferences about the population, but our sample data still suggest we can do so (by using a smaller alpha level), we can be more assured that the sample data are valid indicators of the population. Throughout the book, we will use an alpha of .05 in our examples.

The alpha level designates what is called a critical region or, as we will call it, **the region of null hypothesis rejection.** In our sample, there will almost certainly be a difference in academic performance between children with a Big Brother-Big Sister mentor and those without such a mentor. The question is whether that difference is generalizable from the sample to the population. That is, do our sample data provide convincing evidence to make inferences about the population? Only extreme differences in our sample will be inconsistent with the null hypothesis, which is that there is no difference in academic performance based on having a mentor.

Region of null hypothesis rejection: extreme sample results that are unlikely (depending on alpha level) to be obtained if the null hypothesis is true in the population. When a sample result lies in the region of null hypothesis rejection, we "reject" the null hypothesis.

We need to specify precisely the boundaries for the region of null hypothesis rejection. When testing a null hypothesis, using an alpha level of .05, we need to separate these extreme possible sample results (i.e., that occur less than 5% of the time by random variation) from the other 95% of possible sample results. Remember when we discussed the distinction between directional (one-tailed) and nondirectional (two-tailed) research hypotheses? Here is where that distinction becomes critical.

We are using an alpha level of .05. In addition, let's take our directional (one-tailed) research hypothesis, which is that children with a Big Brother-Big Sister mentor will perform better in school than children without such a mentor. Indeed, this is what Herrera and colleagues (2011) expected to find. The phrase "one-tailed" means that we focus on one direction or tail of the distribution of possible outcomes. Specifically, as seen in the top portion of Figure 6.1, we designate 5% of one tail of the distribution as the region of null hypothesis rejection. Our sample result must fall in this region of null hypothesis rejection for us to reject the null hypothesis.

Now let's consider the nondirectional (two-tailed) research hypothesis, which is that there will be a difference in school performance between children with a Big Brother-Big Sister mentor and children without such a mentor. Recall that with a nondirectional hypothesis, we do not specify which group will perform better than the other; we only state that a difference is expected. The phrase "two-tailed" means that we focus on both tails of the distribution. Specifically, as seen in the bottom portion of Figure 6.1,we designate 2.5% of each tail as the region of null hypothesis rejection (and 2.5% + 2.5% = 5%, which is our alpha level). By using a two-tailed hypothesis, we are

Figure 6.1 Region of Null Hypothesis Rejection for a (Top) Directional (One-Tailed) and for a (Bottom) Nondirectional (Two-Tailed) Hypothesis

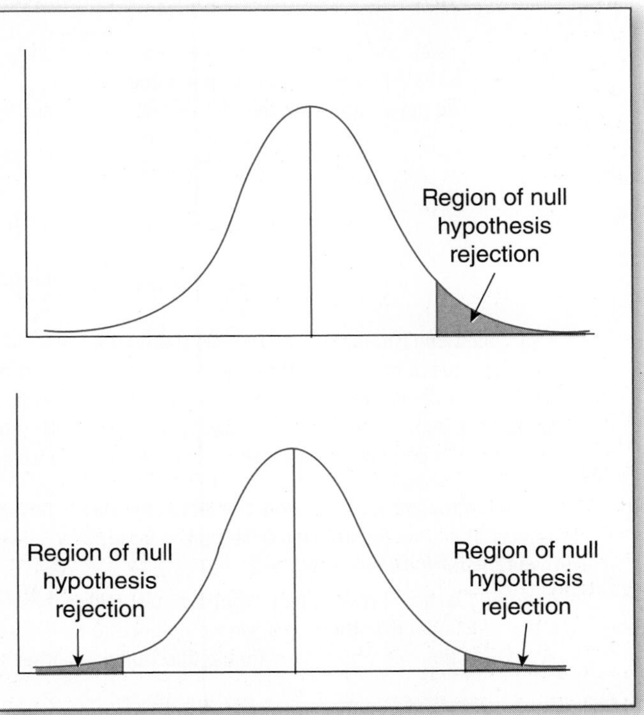

allowing for *two* types of differences between the groups. That is, we are allowing for the possibility that children without a mentor perform better in school than children with a mentor. Our one-tailed test does not allow us to test for this possibility.

I realize that it seems strange to think that children with a mentor could do worse in school than children without a mentor, but as researchers, we cannot allow our predispositions to influence our work. In addition to examining two outcomes instead of only one outcome, there is another reason to use two-tailed hypothesis tests. It is true that Herrera and colleagues (2011) hypothesized that children with a mentor would do better in school than children without a mentor. That is indeed a one-tailed hypothesis. However, by designating only 2.5% of the possible sample data outcomes in the direction we expect to find our results, we are "stacking the deck" against being able to reject the null hypothesis. Therefore, if our sample data do suggest an extreme outcome that falls in this region of null hypothesis rejection, we can be more assured that the sample data are valid indicators of the population.[1]

We have covered a lot of information, so let's take a break and make sure we have a good understanding of it before moving on.

LEARNING CHECK

1. What is the difference between the null hypothesis and the research hypothesis?

   A: A null hypothesis is what we test with inferential statistics and is a statement of no relationship between variables in the population. The research hypothesis is a statement that there is a relationship between variables in the population. A research hypothesis either states the nature of this relationship (a directional research hypothesis) or only states that a relationship will exist (a nondirectional research hypothesis).

2. Suppose a researcher wants to test the effects of pet therapy on children's anxiety levels about going to the doctor. She expects that children who get to pet a dog in the doctor's waiting room will be less anxious than children who do not get to pet a dog. State the null and research hypotheses, both symbolically and in plain English.

   A: $H_o: \mu_{pet\ therapy} = \mu_{no\ pet\ therapy}$

   $H_r: \mu_{pet\ therapy} < \mu_{no\ pet\ therapy}$ (directional research hypothesis)

   $\mu_{pet\ therapy} \neq \mu_{no\ pet\ therapy}$ (nondirectional research hypothesis)

   In plain English, the null hypothesis states that there will be no difference in children's anxiety about going to the doctor based on whether they got to pet a dog in the doctor's waiting room. The research hypothesis (directional) states that children who got to pet a dog in the doctor's waiting room will be less anxious than children who did not get to pet a dog. The research hypothesis (nondirectional) states that children who got to pet a dog and children who did not get to pet a dog in the waiting room will experience different levels of anxiety.

3. Related to the previous question, the researcher clearly has an expectation of what her research will find, and thus, a directional (one-tailed) hypothesis makes sense. Why, however, might it be better for her to use a nondirectional (two-tailed) hypothesis test?

   A: A nondirectional (two-tailed) hypothesis test makes it more difficult to reject the null hypothesis. Therefore, with a nondirectional hypothesis test, we would need to have stronger evidence from the sample data to reject the null hypothesis than we would need from a directional hypothesis test.

4. Why might a researcher use an alpha level of .01 instead of .05?

   A: A lower alpha level makes it more difficult to reject the null hypothesis because we are accepting less possibility that the sample result was a result of chance (i.e., random) factors.

5. Why is it more difficult to reject the null hypothesis with a nondirectional hypothesis test than with a directional hypothesis, assuming you are using the same alpha level for both types of tests?

   A: With a nondirectional hypothesis test, the alpha level is split between the two tails of the distribution of sample outcomes. Therefore, if we expect an outcome to fall in one tail of that distribution, it must be more extreme in a nondirectional test than in a directional test.

GATHERING DATA AND TESTING THE NULL HYPOTHESIS

Making a Decision About the Null Hypothesis

Recall in our example that the null hypothesis was that there is no difference in school performance between children and adolescents who have a Big Brother-Big Sister mentor and children and adolescents without such a mentor. To begin testing our null hypothesis, we take a sample of children and adolescents: 25 participated in this mentoring program, and 25 did not participate in it. We compare these two groups of students on their grades in school. Assuming grades are measured on a 0 (*letter grade of "F"*) to 4.0 (*letter grade of "A"*) scale, here are the mean grade-point averages (GPAs) for our two groups:

Have a mentor (n = 25)	Do not have a mentor (n = 25)
3.25	2.75

Clearly, a GPA of 3.25 is higher than a GPA of 2.75. But again, we must recall the notion of sampling error. These two mean GPAs are from a total sample of 50 students. It is possible that the difference in these mean GPAs is solely a result of something specific about our sample of students and does not exist in the larger population. In any study, there are two conclusions we can draw from our data:

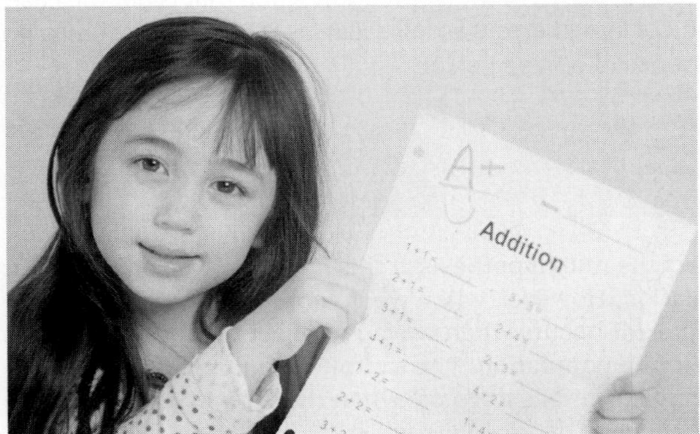

Photo 6.1 The benefits of a Big Brother-Big Sister mentor?

Source: ©iStockphoto.com/JonathanCohen

1. We reject the null hypothesis because the sample data fall in the region of null hypothesis rejection.
2. We fail to reject the null hypothesis because the sample data fall outside the region of null hypothesis rejection.

The inferential statistical tools we will learn about later in this chapter and in subsequent chapters will lead us to make one of these two decisions. If we reject the null hypothesis, we say that our statistical result is **statistically significant**. That is, our result is unlikely to have occurred by chance and likely exists in the population. In our example, we have a GPA difference of 0.5 grade points. Is that difference extreme enough to conclude that, in the population, having a Big Brother-Big Sister mentor is associated with better academic performance? When we select our alpha level, we are deciding how likely we are to tolerate a result that occurred by chance. Recall that we generally pick an alpha level of .05, which means we are willing to accept a 5% possibility that our results could be statistically significant because of random variation and not a real relationship in the population. If we reject the null hypothesis, we are rejecting the notion that there is no relationship in the population; therefore, the research hypothesis is *supported, but not proven,* to be correct.

Statistical significance: occurs when an inferential statistical tool suggests that the null hypothesis should be rejected.

Notice that when introducing the notion of statistical significance, we said a result is "unlikely" to have occurred by chance and "likely" exists in the population. Our conclusions about the population based on our sample data never guarantee we are drawing correct inferences. As mentioned at the start of this chapter, we are always dealing with probabilities (and, therefore, uncertainty) when making our inferences, so it is always possible our sample data lead us to make incorrect inferences about the population.

Type I Errors, Type II Errors, and Uncertainty in Hypothesis Testing

When you meet a person for the first time, you have a limited amount of information about that person. For instance, if you meet someone who is 6 feet, 8 inches tall, you might infer that he or she plays basketball. Indeed, basketball tends to be a "tall person's" sport. Perhaps that person does play basketball, but maybe not. Sometimes our inferences are wrong. Therefore, just like when meeting a new person, we never have all of the data about the population when drawing conclusions about it. Sometimes a sample is not representative of the population, and if that happens, we draw incorrect inferences about the population. Two types of errors can occur when testing a null hypothesis.

First, it is possible to reject the null hypothesis because of extreme results in our sample. In such cases, we conclude that there is a relationship between the variables we are studying. For instance, in Herrera et al.'s (2011) research, they rejected the null hypothesis that there is no difference in academic performance between children with a Big Brother-Big Sister mentor and children without such a mentor after the school year was complete. Take a look back at the bottom half of Figure 6.1. Their result fell in the region of null hypothesis rejection on the right side of the normal distribution of sample results. However, there is still a chance that the null hypothesis is true. Much as we assumed our new, tall acquaintance played basketball, researchers sometimes make the inference, based on sample data, that variables are related in the population when that is not the case. Such a mistaken inference is called a **Type I error**. Think of Type I errors as false alarms. The fire alarm may go off when there is no fire in the building. That is the essence of a Type I error.

Type I error: rejecting a null hypothesis when it is true.

Of course, our sample data may lead us to fail to reject the null hypothesis. If this happens, we conclude that there is no relationship between variables in the population. However, when we do not reject the null hypothesis, we still risk making an error. Specifically, a **Type II error** occurs when we fail to reject the null hypothesis when in fact there is a relationship between variables in the population. The sample data missed the relationship that the researcher was expecting to find. If the fire alarm fails to go off when there really is a fire in the building, it has missed a real occurrence. That is the essence of a Type II error.

Type II error: failing to reject the null hypothesis when it is false.

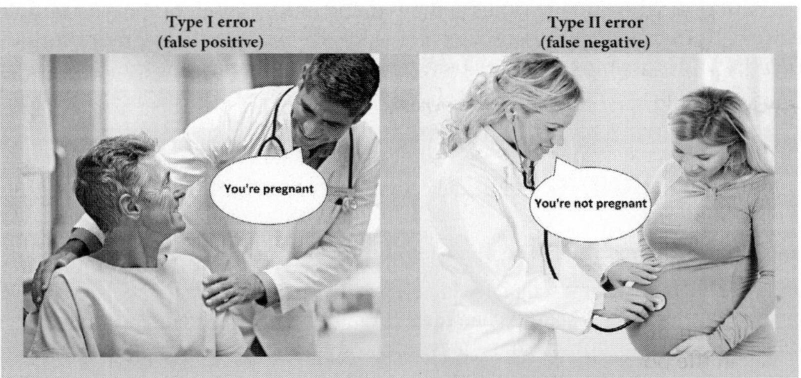

Photo 6.2 Examples of a Type I error and a Type II error.

Sources: ©iStockphoto.com/kristian sekulic; ©iStockphoto.com/kupicoo

How do we know if we made an error in hypothesis testing? If we get sample data that is statistically significant, we will make the decision to reject the null hypothesis. This decision will be correct or incorrect. Recall that for a result to be statistically significant, there must be less than a 5% possibility (our alpha level) that it occurred by chance. In 5% of such samples, we will obtain a statistically significant result that is not a valid indicator of the population. By professional convention, most researchers are willing to tolerate a 5% chance of making a Type I error. In published studies, researchers should report what is called a ***p* value (or significance level)** for each inferential statistical test. The *p* value provides the likelihood of a Type I error in an inferential statistical result. Because a *p* value is a percentage that cannot exceed 1.0, we typically do not put a zero before the decimal place when communicating *p* values.

***p* value (or significance level)**: probability that a statistical outcome was obtained by chance and is a Type I error.

Assume researchers want to minimize the chance of a Type I error. How might they do this? If they use an alpha level of 1% (.01) instead of 5% (.05), that would indeed reduce the Type I error rate. However, this introduces a new problem. Specifically, a lower alpha level means we are making it more difficult to reject the null hypothesis and, in doing so, increasing the chances of making a Type II error. Whereas we can specify the precise likelihood of making a Type I error through our alpha level that we select, the likelihood of making a Type II error depends on a variety of factors, including the selected alpha level. Therefore, unlike the Type I error rate, there is no statistic reported in research that specifies the probability of a Type II error.

As you might see, there is a trade-off that needs to be considered between making a Type I error and making a Type II error. Which would be a worse mistake to make? Most researchers, if they have to make an error, would prefer to make a Type II error. They would rather miss a result than conclude that something is present in the population when it really is not. As we said previously, researchers like to "stack the deck" against rejecting the

Table 6.1 Four Possible Outcomes When Testing a Hypothesis

		Reality in the population	
		Null hypothesis (H_o) is false	**Null hypothesis (H_o) is true**
Your decision based on your sample data	**Reject null hypothesis (Ho)**	Correct decision	Type I error
	Fail to reject null hypothesis (H_o)	Type II error	Correct decision

null hypothesis. If they do so and can still reject the null hypothesis, they can be more confident that the sample result does reflect the larger population. Therefore, most researchers consider the Type I error the more serious error to make. Table 6.1 summarizes the four possible outcomes using inferential statistics.

LEARNING CHECK

1. Why is it that we can never "prove" a research hypothesis to be true?

   A: There will always some possibility, no matter how small, that our sample results were a function of random variation. We can only "suggest" the research hypothesis is correct when there is sufficient evidence from the sample to reject the null hypothesis.

2. A statistically significant outcome is defined as an outcome that has a _____ probability of occurring if the _____ hypothesis is true.

   a) small; null
   b) large; null
   c) small; research
   d) large; research

   A: a

3. If we change our alpha level from .05 to .06, then the Type I error rate will:

   a) decrease.
   b) increase.
   c) remain the same.
   d) it is impossible to tell without additional information.

   A: b

4. You conduct an experiment, analyze the results, and obtain statistically significant effects at an alpha level of .01. Which one of the following statements is true?

   a) You've made a Type I error.
   b) You've made a Type II error.
   c) The probability that the statistical result is due to chance is 1% or less.
   d) The probability that the difference between the groups is due to a true effect in the population is 1% or less.

   A: c

5. Although we said that most researchers think a Type I error is more serious than a Type II error, provide an argument why Type II errors could be considered more serious than Type I errors.

   A: To commit a Type II error, we fail to reject the null hypothesis when in fact it should have been rejected. If this happens, future researchers might not conduct additional research because it appears that "nothing is there" from our research. With a Type I error, it appears there is some relationship between variables in the population, which might stimulate additional research.

Now that we understand the basic principles of hypothesis testing, let's start our discussion of specific inferential statistical tools, the topic that will take us through Chapter 14. Each inferential statistical tool is used with a specific research design. For each one we discuss, we will highlight a research design with an actual research question that makes use of that tool to test the null hypothesis. We will now begin discussion of two inferential statistical tools: the z test and the one-sample t test.

THE *Z* TEST

A Real-World Example of the *z* Test

For better or for worse, many primary and secondary schools are judged by how well their students do on standardized tests. One such test that is widely used is the Scholastic Aptitude Test (SAT®; College Board, New York, NY). The SAT is used by many colleges and universities to make admissions decisions. Of course, students from some high schools tend to do better on the SAT than do students from other high schools. It may be of interest to researchers, policy makers, and the public at large to learn which high schools tend to have students who score particularly high and particularly low on the SAT.

Suppose we want to know whether the average SAT score for students from your high school is different from the national average SAT score. In this instance, we have a sample of SAT scores (those from students at your high school), and we know the population parameters for SAT math scores. The mean SAT score in the United States is approximately 1,500 with a standard deviation of approximately 300 (College Board, 2015). These are the population parameters. For this example, let's suppose the mean SAT math score at your school is 1,560. A score of 1,560 is obviously higher than a score of 1,500. However, is that difference between the sample (scores at your school) and the population large enough to infer that your school is in fact different from the larger population of high school SAT scores? That is the question we want to answer here.

Enter the ***z* test**. The *z* test is a parametric statistical tool that allows us to determine whether a sample is in fact different from the population from which it is drawn. Recall from the previous chapter that a *z* score allows us to pinpoint a score relative to all other scores in the distribution of those scores. Specifically, a *z* score is a measure of how many standard deviations an individual score falls from the group mean. The *z* test, as we will see soon, is an application of *z* score logic. To refresh, the formula for the *z* score is

$$z = \frac{\text{individual score} - \text{mean}}{\text{standard deviation}}$$

To be able to use the *z* test, we must know the population parameters (if such population data are not available, we will use the statistical tool presented later in this chapter). In our example, the *z* test will allow us to learn whether SAT scores at your high school, assuming an average score of 1,560, are in fact really different from the population mean SAT score, which is 1,500, with a standard deviation of 300.

***z* test**: parametric statistical tool that allows us to compare a sample to the population from which it was drawn when the population parameters are known.

Ingredients for the *z* Test

Before we explore the heart of the *z* test, there are two concepts we need to know about: the sampling distribution and the standard error of the mean. Once we understand these two concepts, we will then have all of the ingredients necessary to conduct a *z* test and answer our research question.

Keep in mind that students from your high school comprise only one sample drawn from the population of high school students taking the SAT. For the sake of example, suppose there are 80 students taking the SAT in a given year at your high school. We could have examined many different samples of 80 students drawn from the population. The **sampling distribution** is the distribution of sample means based on random samples of a particular size drawn from a population. Most sample means will be near the population mean. In our example, most sample means will be close to 1,500. Indeed, *the mean for the sampling distribution is in fact the mean of the scores in the population*, in this example, 1,500. Only a few of the sample means will be extremely different from the population mean. The distribution of sample means will be normally distributed around the population mean, allowing us to identify these extreme samples by using the z test.

Just as there is a standard deviation for each sample drawn from the population, there is a standard deviation for the sampling distribution. It is called the **standard error of the mean**. The standard error of the mean is always going to be smaller than the standard deviation for an individual sample drawn from that population. Why is this so? A few people in any sample will have extreme scores, but in just one sample, it is more likely we will have a larger proportion of extreme scores than will be present in all possible samples. Thus, for an individual sample, it is more likely to see a higher level of variability in scores than will be found in the entire sample distribution. In the sampling distribution, which is obviously larger than a single sample, extreme scores will tend to average out around the population mean.

Sampling distribution: distribution of sample means for a fixed sample size drawn from a population.

Standard error of the mean: standard deviation of the sampling distribution.

We know our population mean is 1,500, but how do we calculate the standard error of the mean? Theoretically, we need to draw numerous samples from the population and determine the standard deviation for the distribution of our sample means. Obviously, this is not practical to do. Fortunately, we can make use of the **Central Limit Theorem**. This theorem states that

(a) for a given sample size, the distribution of sample means will have a mean equal to the population mean;

(b) the distribution will have a standard deviation calculated by taking the population standard deviation and dividing it by the square root of the sample size; and

(c) as the sample size increases, the distribution will be a normal distribution.

Central Limit Theorem: (a) for a given sample size, the distribution of sample means will have a mean equal to the population mean; (b) the distribution will have a standard deviation calculated by taking the population standard deviation and dividing it by the square root of the sample size; and (c) as the sample size increases, the distribution will be a normal distribution.

Thus, to calculate the standard error of the mean (abbreviated as $\sigma_{\text{x-bar}}$), we take the population standard deviation and divide it by the square root of the sample size. Recall from Chapter 4 that "σ" is the symbol for the population standard deviation. For the standard error of the mean, symbolically, we have

$$\sigma_{\text{x-bar}} = \frac{\sigma}{\sqrt{\text{sample size } (N)}}$$

We now have all of the ingredients needed for the z test.

The formula for the z test is

$$z = \frac{\overline{x} - \mu}{\sigma_{\text{x-bar}}}$$

where

$\bar{x}$ is the mean for our sample,

μ is the population mean, and

$\sigma_{x\text{-bar}}$ is the standard error of the mean.

This formula looks similar to the *z* score formula. What we have done with the *z* test is (a) replace an individual score with a group mean; (b) replace a sample mean with a population mean; and (c) replace the sample standard deviation with the standard error of the mean.

LEARNING CHECK

1. Random samples, each with 50 scores, are selected from a normal population with a population mean of 85 and a standard deviation of 18. The mean is calculated for each sample. What would be the average of all the sample means? Why?

   A: The average for all sample means would be about 85. This is because the mean of the sampling distribution will be equal to the population mean, which in this example is 85.

2. A distribution has $\mu = 50$ and $\sigma = 20$. How does the standard error of the mean ($\sigma_{x\text{-bar}}$) change as your sample size increases from $n = 1$ to $n = 4$, to $n = 9$, to $n = 16$, to $n = 64$?

   A: The larger the sample size, the smaller the standard error of the mean will be. Larger samples tend to represent the populations from which they were drawn better. This is because as the sample size increases, the denominator of the standard error formula will also increase. When the denominator of any fraction is increased, the quotient is smaller.

3. Which of the following samples would have the largest standard error of the mean?

   a) $n = 25$ scores from a population with $\sigma = 10$

   b) $n = 25$ scores from a population with $\sigma = 20$

   c) $n = 100$ scores from a population with $\sigma = 10$

   d) $n = 100$ scores from a population with $\sigma = 20$

   A: b

Using the *z* Test for a Directional (One-Tailed) Hypothesis

Now that we have the ingredients for the *z* test, let's put them to use. I know that earlier in this chapter I said researchers generally prefer nondirectional (two-tailed) hypothesis tests instead of directional (one-tailed) hypothesis tests. But for the purposes of illustration and to help you understand the general principles of hypothesis testing, let's do both directional and nondirectional hypothesis tests here.

Let's first state our hypotheses. Remember that we always statistically test the null hypothesis even though what researchers are interested in and report in articles is a research hypothesis. For a directional hypothesis test, what would be our null and research hypotheses? In symbols, we have

$$H_o: \mu_{\text{your high school}} = \mu_{\text{national}}$$

$$H_r: \mu_{\text{your high school}} > \mu_{\text{national}}$$

Figure 6.2 Region of Null Hypothesis Rejection for a Directional *z* Test (Region Is 5% of All Possible Statistical Outcomes)

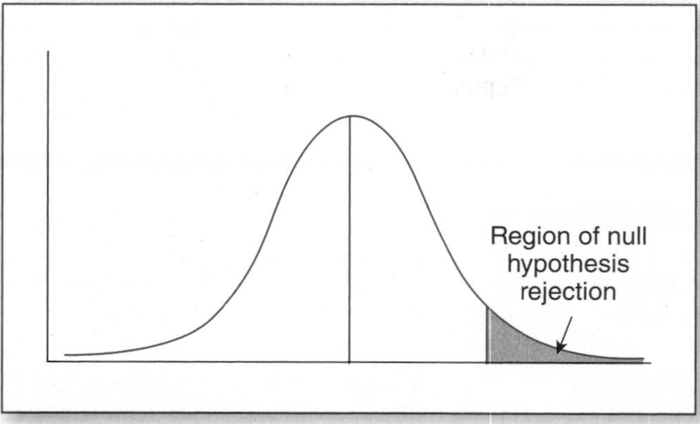

In plain English, the null hypothesis says that we expect no difference between mean SAT scores at your high school and the national mean. The research hypothesis says that we expect mean SAT scores at your high school to be greater (better) than the national mean.

We next need to specify our alpha level. Remember that the alpha level determines the region of null hypothesis rejection and likelihood of committing a Type I error. Let's stick with 5% (.05). As we discussed previously, an alpha level of 5% means we are willing to accept a 5% chance that we reject the null hypothesis when in fact the null hypothesis is true (i.e., we accept a 5% chance of making a Type Ierror). Because this is a directional research hypothesis, we designate 5% of one tail of the distribution of statistical outcomes as the region of null hypothesis rejection, as seen in Figure 6.2.

We now gather our data and calculate a *z* test statistic. Of course, I've provided the data we need. Remember that in this example, we want to know whether average SAT scores at your high school are greater than the U.S. national average. We said that the average SAT score at your high school was 1,560 for a sample of 80 students. The national average SAT score is 1,500 with a standard deviation of 300. Thus, we have two of the three ingredients for the *z* test; all we need to do now is calculate the standard error of the mean, which is the denominator of the *z* test formula. Here again is the formula for the standard error of the mean:

$$\sigma_{\text{x-bar}} = \frac{\sigma}{\sqrt{\text{sample size } (N)}}$$

In our example, $\sigma = 300$ and $N = 80$. Therefore,

$$\begin{aligned} \sigma_{\text{x-bar}} &= \frac{300}{\sqrt{80}} \\ &= \frac{300}{8.944} \\ &= 33.54 \end{aligned}$$

Now, let's conduct our *z* test. Here again is the formula for the *z* test:

$$z = \frac{\overline{x} - \mu}{\sigma_{\text{x-bar}}}$$

Plugging in our ingredients, we get

$$z = \frac{1{,}560 - 1{,}500}{33.54}$$

$$z = \frac{60}{33.54}$$

$$z = +1.79$$

So what does a z of +1.79 mean? First, take a look at Figure 6.3. We need to know whether the mean SAT score of 1,560 is different enough from the population mean of 1,500 to reject the null hypothesis, and therefore conclude that your high school's SAT performance was statistically significantly better than the national average. What we need to do is take this population parameter and sample data and translate them into "z score language" to see whether your high school had higher SAT scores than the national average.

The z of +1.79 is called a **test statistic**. That is, it will be used to test the null hypothesis. We compare our test statistic with what is called a **critical value**. The critical value is used to denote the region of null hypothesis rejection. If the test statistic falls in the region of null hypothesis rejection, we have a statistically significant result (i.e., we reject the null hypothesis). How do we find our critical value? Recall in the previous chapter that when we have a normal distribution of data, as the sampling distribution is, we can determine the proportion of scores falling between two points on the distribution, as well as the relative standing of an individual score on the distribution. We do this by consulting Appendix A. Here you will find the z table that allows us to denote proportions of the normal distribution. Remember that our alpha level for this directional hypothesis test was 5% or .05. So, we need to denote 5% of the normal distribution as the region of null hypothesis rejection. Because we had a directional hypothesis, specifically, that mean SAT scores at your high school are greater than the national average, we need to denote 5% of the right (higher) side of the distribution as the region of null hypothesis rejection. By using Appendix A, and looking at panel C (Area Beyond z in Tail), we find that the z score that denotes the top 5% of the distribution is between 1.64 and 1.65. So, we'll use + 1.645. This is our critical value. Our test statistic is +1.79, which is greater than the critical value of + 1.645. Therefore, we reject the null hypothesis and conclude that mean SAT scores at your high school are greater (better) than the national mean SAT score. If it helps to see what we are talking about, please look at Figure 6.4, which provides this same information we have discussed.

Figure 6.3 Is a Mean Sample SAT Score of 1,560 Significantly Different From a Mean Population SAT Score of 1,500?

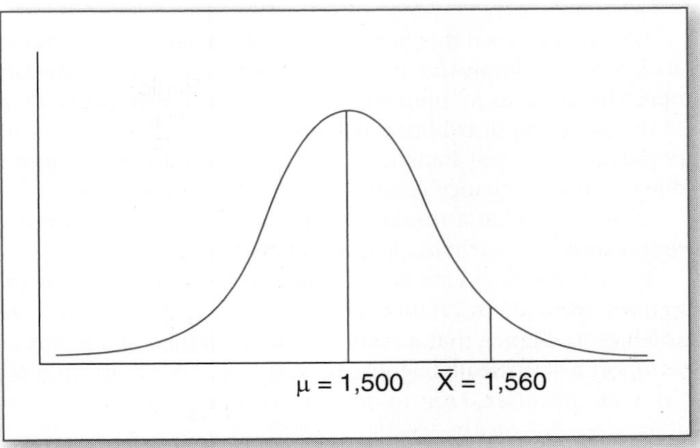

Figure 6.4 Visual Comparison of the Test Statistic (1.79) With the Critical Value (1.645; Because the Test Statistic Falls in the Region of Null Hypothesis Rejection, We Reject the Null Hypothesis)

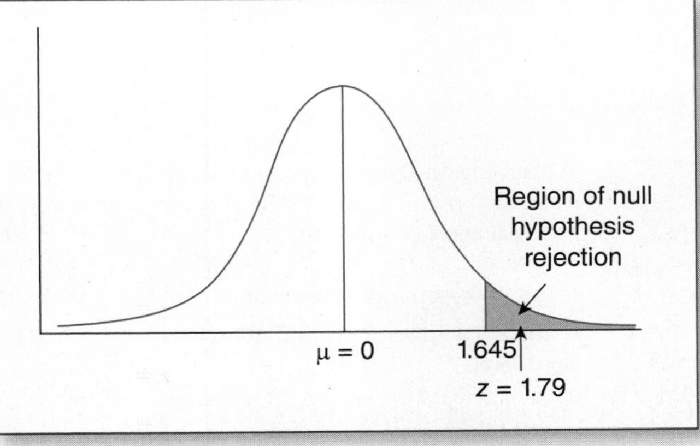

Test statistic: result of using an inferential statistical tool that is compared with a critical value.

Critical value: marks the start of the region of null hypothesis rejection; if a test statistic exceeds the critical value, it falls in the region of null hypothesis rejection.

If we wanted to publish the results of our *z* test, here is how we would do so according to American Psychological Association (APA) style:

$$z\ (N = 80) = 1.79,\ p < .05 \text{ (one-tailed)}$$

Let's break down this presentation. We need to report the sample size. As a consumer of research, one should always want to know the sample size because, in general, the larger the sample size, the better it reflects the population. Therefore, as mentioned in the previous Learning Check, as the sample size increases, the standard deviation of the sampling distribution will be smaller because there will be less discrepancy between the sample and the population. Our test statistic of 1.79 is then reported, followed by the *p* value (probability) that our result occurred due to random, chance factors and is in fact a Type I error.

When you read a research study, you will rarely, if ever, see a critical value reported. Researchers tend to report only the test statistic in published articles.

Remember that a statistically significant result, such as the one we just obtained, is a result that is unlikely to have occurred by chance. Of course, we want our results to be reflective of the population, and we accept a small (5%) chance that a result is due to chance and is not a real phenomenon in the population. If you need to report a statistically significant result in a paper or on a test, be sure to say that the *p* value is less than (i.e., "<") .05. *Too often, I see my students reporting a statistically significant result as "p > .05." Please do not do this.*

LEARNING CHECK

Consider the following research situation:

I want to know whether grades on a recent class exam are better than they have been for the exam on the same information that I've given the past 10 years. The mean for the recent class exam was 90% for a class of 36 students. Historically, the mean for this exam has been 80% with a standard deviation of 15%.

1. State the null and research hypotheses (directional), both symbolically and in plain English.

   A:
   $$H_o\text{: } \mu_{\text{recent class}} = \mu_{\text{historical mean}}$$
   $$H_r\text{: } \mu_{\text{recent class}} > \mu_{\text{historical mean}}$$

   In plain English, the null hypothesis states that there is no difference between my recent class and the historical mean on this exam. The directional research hypothesis states that my recent class performed better than the historical mean on this exam.

2. To test my hypothesis, I use an alpha level of .03. What is my critical value for this test?

   A: There is no precise *z* critical value for an alpha of .03, but +1.89 would be the closest critical value for this alpha level.

3. What is the value of my z test statistic in this example?

A:

$$z = \frac{\bar{X} - \mu}{\sigma_{x\text{-bar}}}$$

and

$$\sigma_{x\text{-bar}} = \frac{\sigma}{\sqrt{N}}$$

So, let's first get the standard error of the mean:

$$\begin{aligned} \sigma_{x\text{-bar}} &= 15/\sqrt{N} \\ &= 15/\sqrt{36} \\ &= \frac{15}{6} \\ &= 2.50 \\ &= \frac{90-80}{2.50} \\ z &= \frac{10}{2.50} \\ z &= +4.00 \end{aligned}$$

4. Do I reject or fail to reject the null hypothesis? What does this mean in plain English?

   A: Because the test statistic of $z = +4.00$ is greater than the critical value of $+1.89$, the test statistic of $+4.00$ falls in the region of null hypothesis rejection, so I reject the null hypothesis. This means it appears my current class did better than the historical mean on this exam.

5. Write this result in proper APA style.

   A: $z\ (N = 36) = 4.00,\ p < .03$ (one-tailed)

Using the z Test for a Nondirectional (Two-Tailed) Hypothesis

Now that we have completed a directional hypothesis test, let's use the z test to conduct a nondirectional hypothesis test. Of course, we first state our hypotheses. For a nondirectional hypothesis test, we have, symbolically,

$$H_o\text{: } \mu_{\text{your high school}} = \mu_{\text{national}}$$

$$H_r\text{: } \mu_{\text{your high school}} \neq \mu_{\text{national}}$$

In plain English, the null hypothesis says that we expect no difference between mean SAT scores at your high school and the national mean. The research hypothesis says that we expect a difference between mean SAT scores at your high school and the national mean. Because this is a nondirectional research hypothesis, we are not specifying whether your high school's mean SAT score will be higher or lower than the national mean, only that it will differ from the national mean.

We will again use our alpha level of 5% (.05) to test the null hypothesis. We have the data we need. Remember that we said that the average SAT score at your high school was 1,560 for a sample of 80 students. The national average SAT score is 1,500 with a standard deviation of 300. So, we are ready to use our data to test the null hypothesis.

Here again is the formula for the z test:

$$z = \frac{\text{sample mean } (\bar{x}) - \text{population mean } (\mu)}{\sigma_{\text{x-bar}}}$$

Plugging in our ingredients, we get

$$z = \frac{1{,}560 - 1{,}500}{33.54}$$

$$z = \frac{60}{33.54}$$

$$z = +1.79$$

As you probably noticed, nothing has changed with the calculations from the directional hypothesis test. We have the same test statistic ($z = +1.79$) as we did previously. Recall that with a nondirectional test, our test statistic must be extreme enough to fall into one of the *two* regions of null hypothesis rejection. Remember also that we are testing for extreme difference, hence, why it is a nondirectional, two-tailed hypothesis test. As we find our critical value with which to compare our test statistic, we will see an important difference between the directional and the nondirectional hypothesis test.

Let's consult Appendix A to find our critical value. Remember that our alpha level for this directional hypothesis test was 5%, but because this is a nondirectional hypothesis test, we need to divide that 5% to include both tails of the distribution. Thus, we need to denote the two regions of null hypothesis rejection with 2.5% of the distribution in each region. Would you expect the critical value to be higher or lower than it was using a directional hypothesis test? Let's look at Appendix A to answer this question. We find that the z score that denotes 2.5% of the distribution is ± 1.96. This is our critical value, and it is indeed larger than it was for our directional hypothesis test. Therefore, rejecting the null hypothesis now requires a larger test statistic. Because we need to denote a region of null hypothesis rejection at both tails of the distribution, this critical value is both positive and negative (i.e., ± 1.96). Figure 6.5 presents a visual depiction of this hypothesis test.

Figure 6.5 Visual Comparison of the Test Statistic (1.79) With the Critical Value (±1.96; Because the Test Statistic Falls Outside the Region of Null Hypothesis Rejection, We Fail to Reject the Null Hypothesis)

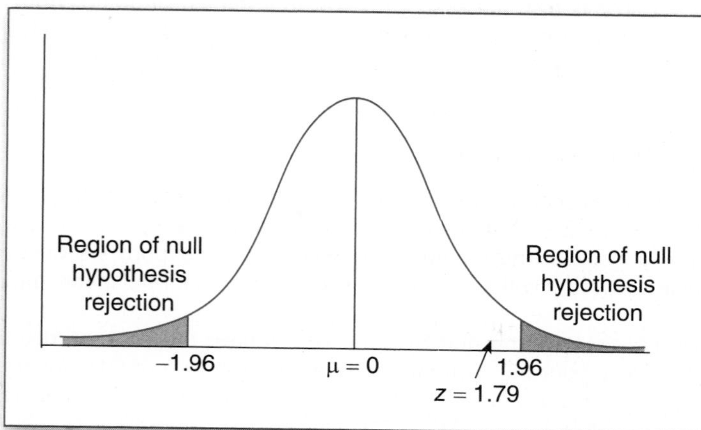

Our test statistic is +1.79, which is less than the critical value of ± 1.96. Therefore, the test statistic falls outside the region of null hypothesis rejection. With the nondirectional hypothesis test, we do not reject the null hypothesis. We conclude that there is no difference between the mean SAT score at your high school and the national mean SAT score. Because we used a nondirectional hypothesis test, only 2.5% of the distribution denotes the "better than the national mean" outcome. In this example, using a nondirectional hypothesis test leads to a different, more conservative, conclusion than when using the directional hypothesis test.

Here is the APA style presentation of our nondirectional (two-tailed) hypothesis test:

$$z\ (N = 80) = 1.79,\ p > .05$$

Notice how these results do not say "two-tailed" after the statistical presentation. When presenting a directional hypothesis test, it is customary to say "one-tailed" after the statistics are reported. Most hypothesis tests are generally assumed to be nondirectional (two-tailed), so researchers only need to indicate when they used a directional (one-tailed) test. Of course, it is not incorrect to say "two-tailed" after presenting the statistics, but it is assumed that a statistical test is two-tailed unless otherwise noted.

LEARNING CHECK

1. Explain why using a nondirectional (two-tailed) hypothesis makes it more difficult to reject the null hypothesis than when using a directional (one-tailed) hypothesis.

   A: A nondirectional test requires that the alpha level accounts for two possible statistical outcomes, whereas a directional test requires the alpha level to account for only one such outcome. Therefore, it is more difficult to detect a statistically significant result when using a nondirectional hypothesis because it is "stretched" in two directions on the distribution of outcomes.

   Let's use the same research situation as that in the previous Learning Check, when I wanted to know whether grades on a recent class exam were better than they have been in the past. As a refresher:

   For my class of 36 students, the mean exam score was 90%.

   Historically, the mean exam score was 80% with a standard deviation of 15%.

2. State the null and research hypotheses (nondirectional), both symbolically and in plain English.

   A:

   $$H_o\!: \mu_{\text{recent class}} = \mu_{\text{historical mean}}$$
   $$H_r\!: \mu_{\text{recent class}} \neq \mu_{\text{historical mean}}$$

   In plain English, the null hypothesis states that there is no difference between my recent class and the historical mean on this exam. The nondirectional research hypothesis states that my recent class performed differently from the historical mean on this exam.

3. To test my hypothesis, I use an alpha level of .03. What is my critical value for this test?

   A: Because this is a nondirectional test, we must denote half of .03 (which is .015) for each tail of the distribution as the region of null hypothesis rejection. The critical value is ±2.17.

4. What is the value of my *z* test statistic in this example?

   A:

   $$z = \frac{\overline{X} - \mu}{\sigma_{\text{x-bar}}}$$

(Continued)

(Continued)

and

$$\sigma_{\text{x-bar}} = \frac{\sigma}{\sqrt{N}}$$

So, first let's get the standard error of the mean:

$$\sigma_{\text{x-bar}} = \frac{15}{\sqrt{36}}$$
$$= \frac{15}{6}$$
$$= 2.50$$
$$z = \frac{90-80}{2.50}$$
$$z = \frac{10}{2.50}$$
$$z = +4.00$$

5. Do I reject or fail to reject the null hypothesis? What does this mean in plain English?

   A: Because the test statistic of $z = 4.00$ is greater than the critical value of ±2.17, the test statistic of 4.00 falls in the region of null hypothesis rejection, and I reject the null hypothesis. That means it appears my current class did score differently (and better) than the historical mean on this exam.

6. Write this result in proper APA style.

   A: $z\ (N = 36) = 4.00,\ p < .03$

ONE-SAMPLE *T* TEST

We have discussed the *z* test, which requires us to know the population parameters to determine whether a sample is different from the population. We will now consider a new inferential statistical tool that is similar to the *z* test, called the one-sample *t* test. In many research contexts, we do not have access to the population standard deviation. When we do not know the population standard deviation, but still want to compare a sample with some benchmark, we use the **one-sample *t* test**. The purpose of the one-sample *t* test is to compare a sample mean to a population mean when the population standard deviation is not known.

One-sample *t* test: parametric statistical tool that allows us to learn whether a sample differs from the population from which it was drawn when the population standard deviation is not known.

The one-sample *t* test was developed by William Gossett, a chemist who worked with the Guinness® Brewing Company (London, U.K.). When working with small samples of beer selected for quality control testing, Gossett found that the sampling distribution of the means was not normally distributed. In general, unless a sample of beer had at least 30 samples to test, the sampling distribution would not be normally distributed. But as the sample size got larger, the sampling distribution became closer and closer to a normal distribution. As we know from Chapter 5, when dealing with data that are normally distributed, we can extract certain information from those data. Thus, in addition to not knowing the population standard deviation, there is another difference between the *z* test and the one-sample *t* test. Specifically, whereas the *z* distribution is normally distributed, the *t* distributions are not normally distributed (although they are bell shaped like a normal distribution). We say "*t* distributions" because they differ for each sample size, and as with the *z* test, we will need to locate specific areas under the *t* distributions.

A Real-World Example of the One-Sample *t* Test

I volunteer at a small local animal rescue organization that removes cats and dogs from shelters at which they might be euthanized and places them in foster homes from which they are adopted. I have been doing this work for more than 10 years, and during this time, this rescue has placed more than 400 dogs into permanent homes. On average, this rescue finds that it takes 22 days from the time a dog is rescued from the shelter to be adopted into a permanent home. Some dogs, of course, are in their foster homes for less than 22 days, and others are in their foster homes for more than 22 days. I am surprised at some of the dogs who need more time to be adopted because they are so well behaved and eager to please people. I began to wonder whether there might be a reason why some dogs take so long to be adopted, and I located an article by Jamie Fratkin and Suzie Baker (2013). These researchers conducted a study in which they had people view photos of either yellow or black Labradors (aka "labs").

The breed is the same, but people felt that the yellow labs had more pleasant personalities than the black labs. Even without interacting with the dog, people drew more negative inferences about black labs. In fact, there is a term *Black Dog Syndrome*, in which it is believed that black dogs get passed over for adoption in favor of non-black dogs. Indeed, Fratkin and Baker's (2013) research suggested that Black Dog Syndrome may exist.

After reading this article, I wondered whether the dogs at the animal rescue who needed a lot of time to get adopted were in fact the black dogs. To find out, I conducted an applied research study of my own with the help of the rescue organization. I tracked how many black dogs came into our rescue and how long it took each one to be adopted during 2014, the year after Fratkin and Baker's (2013) article was published. The time it took for each black dog to be adopted appears in Table 6.2. During the past 10 years, we know that it takes 22 days on average for a dog to be adopted from this rescue.

Photo 6.3 Is this dog at a disadvantage finding a home?

Source: ©iStockphoto.com/Eriklam

Table 6.2 Number of Days Needed for a Black Dog to Be Adopted

x (each datapoint is for one dog/observation)
30 days
35 days
20 days
41 days
58 days
2 days
18 days
28 days
$\sum x = 232$
$\bar{x} = 232 / 8 = 29$ days

Armed with the sample of adoption times for black dogs adopted from the rescue and the mean time until adoption for all dogs at this rescue, we are now in a position to learn about a new statistical tool, the one-sample *t* test.

Ingredients for the One-Sample *t* Test

The formula for the one-sample *t* test is

$$t = \frac{\bar{x} - \mu}{s_{x-bar}}$$

where

$\bar{x}$ is the mean for our sample,

μ is the population mean, and

$s_{x\text{-bar}}$ is the *estimated* standard error of the mean.

This formula might remind you of the *z* test formula. If so, that is good. The numerator is precisely the same. The denominator $s_{x\text{-bar}}$ is the **estimated standard error of the mean**. Recall that for the *z* test, we knew the population standard deviation. Because we do not know that information here, we must have an *estimate* of the standard deviation of the sampling distribution. Here is how we calculate the estimated standard error of the mean:

$$s_{x\text{-bar}} = \frac{\text{estimated standard deviation for a population}}{\sqrt{\text{sample size } (N)}}$$

Of course, before calculating the estimated standard error of the mean, we need the estimated standard deviation (*s*). Here is how we calculate that number:

$$s = \sqrt{\frac{\Sigma(\text{individual score} - \text{mean})^2}{(\text{sample size} - 1)}}$$

Estimated standard error of the mean: estimate of the standard deviation of the sampling distribution.

Let's refer to Table 6.3, which again contains the number of days that each black dog spent in the rescue before being adopted. However, it also contains the calculations we need for the estimated standard deviation of the population. From Table 6.3, we can plug in the numbers to the formula:

$$s = \sqrt{\frac{1954}{(8-1)}}$$

$$s = \sqrt{\frac{1954}{7}}$$

$$s = \sqrt{279.14}$$

$$s = 16.71$$

Now we are in a position to calculate the standard error of the mean. Let's plug in the numbers to the formula:

$$S_{\text{x-bar}} = \frac{\text{estimated standard deviation for a population}}{\sqrt{\text{sample size } (N)}}$$

$$S_{\text{x-bar}} = \frac{16.71}{\sqrt{8}}$$

$$S_{\text{x-bar}} = \frac{16.71}{2.83}$$

$$S_{\text{x-bar}} = 5.90$$

There is one last ingredient that we need to use the one-sample t test. Take a look at Appendix B. Here, we will find our critical values for the t distribution. In the far left column is the abbreviation *df*. This abbreviation stands for "degrees of freedom," which we need to discuss now. **Degrees of freedom** are the numbers of scores in a sample that are allowed to vary. If that definition makes no sense, don't worry; it did not make sense to me either when I was first learning statistics. But an example will help. Look at the data in Table 6.2, which had a mean of 29. Now, if you could change the numbers to any values you wanted, but had to keep the mean of 29, how many numbers are you "free" to change? Let's think about this. We had eight numbers in Table 6.2. If you changed seven of them, then you must change the eighth number to a specific value to keep the mean of 29. Thus, in this example, your degrees of freedom are 7 (or, if you prefer a formula, sample size – 1; in this case, 8 – 1). Again, the notion of degrees of freedom will be vital when locating our critical value with which to compare our test statistic.

Degrees of freedom: number of scores in a sample that can be changed.

Table 6.3 Calculations for the Estimate of the Standard Deviation of the Population

x	$x - \bar{x}$	$(x - \bar{x})^2$
30 days	1	1
35 days	6	36
20 days	−9	81
41 days	12	144
58 days	29	841
2 days	−27	729
18 days	−11	121
28 days	−1	1
$\sum x = 232$		
$\bar{x} = 232 / 8 = 29$ days		$\sum(x - \bar{x})^2 = 1{,}954$

We now have all of our ingredients to conduct a one-sample *t* test and learn whether black dogs spend more time in foster homes than do all dogs in the rescue. But first, let's make sure these ingredients are fresh in our minds.

LEARNING CHECK

1. If the estimated standard deviation for a population is 20, and the sample size is 100, what is the estimated standard error of the mean ($s_{x\text{-bar}}$)?

   A:

$$s_{x\text{-bar}} = \frac{20}{\sqrt{100}} = \frac{20}{10} = 2$$

2. From the previous question, what happens to the value of the estimated standard error of the mean ($s_{x\text{-bar}}$) as the sample size gets larger? That is, with a larger sample size, does $s_{x\text{-bar}}$ increase or decrease in value?

   A: As the sample size gets larger, the estimated standard error of the mean decreases. Exactly as we discussed with the *z* test, the larger the sample size, the better it reflects the population. Therefore, we have less sampling error and a smaller estimated standard error of the mean.

3. Consider the following set of scores on an organic chemistry exam: 50%, 62%, 81%, 78%, 35%, 91%, 69%, 71%, 78%, and 65%. The mean is 68%. What are the degrees of freedom in this example?

   A: With 10 scores, the degrees of freedom are 9 (i.e., 10 − 1). The mean is irrelevant in calculating the degrees of freedom.

4. Explain when researchers should use the *z* test and when they should use the one-sample *t* test. Stated differently, what is the difference between the *z* test and the one-sample *t* test?

   A: The *z* test is used to compare a sample mean with its population mean when the population standard deviation is known. The one-sample *t* test is used to compare a sample mean with its population mean when the population standard deviation is not known.

Using the One-Sample *t* Test for a Directional (One-Tailed) Hypothesis

As always, let's state our hypotheses. Symbolically, we have

$$H_o\!: \mu_{\text{black dogs}} = \mu_{\text{all dogs}}$$
$$H_r\!: \mu_{\text{black dogs}} > \mu_{\text{all dogs}}$$

In plain English, the null hypothesis says that we expect no difference between the time black dogs spend in rescue and the time all dogs spend in rescue before being adopted. The research hypothesis says that black dogs spend more time in rescue before being adopted than do all dogs.

We will use an alpha level of .05, meaning that we are willing to accept a 5% chance that we reject the null hypothesis when in fact the null hypothesis is true. In other words, the likelihood of making a Type I error is 5%. As seen in Figure 6.6, we designate 5% of the distribution of statistical outcomes as the region of null hypothesis rejection.

At last, we can calculate our one-sample *t* test statistic! Here again is that formula:

$$t = \frac{\bar{x} - \mu}{s_{\text{x-bar}}}$$

where

$\bar{x}$ is the mean for our sample (which was 29 days, as seen in Tables 6.2 and 6.3),

μ is the population mean (which was 22 days, as noted at the outset of our discussion of one-sample *t* tests), and

$s_{\text{x-bar}}$ is the estimated standard error of the mean (which we calculated when discussing the ingredients of the one-sample *t* test and is 5.90 in this example).

In our example, we have

$$t = \frac{29 - 22}{5.90}$$

$$t = \frac{7}{5.90}$$

$$t = 1.19$$

Our *t* of 1.19 is the test statistic. As was the case with the *z* test and all other inferential statistical tools to come, we need to compare the test statistic with a critical value that denotes the region of null hypothesis rejection. If our test statistic exceeds the critical value, it falls in the region of null hypothesis rejection, and we reject the null hypothesis.

To locate the critical value, look at Appendix B. Here we will find our critical values for the *t* distributions. In the far left column is the abbreviation *df*, again for "degrees of freedom." Recall that the formula for calculating degrees of freedom for a one-sample *t* test is sample size – 1. In this example, we had a sample of 8 dogs, so we have 7 degrees of freedom (*df*s). This appendix contains the critical values for both directional and nondirectional tests. Here, we need to locate the critical value that corresponds to an alpha level of .05 with 7 degrees of freedom for a directional (one-tailed) test. That critical value is 1.895. As seen in Figure 6.7, our test statistic of 1.19 falls outside of the region of null hypothesis rejection. Therefore,

Figure 6.6 Region of Null Hypothesis Rejection for a Directional One-Sample *t* Test

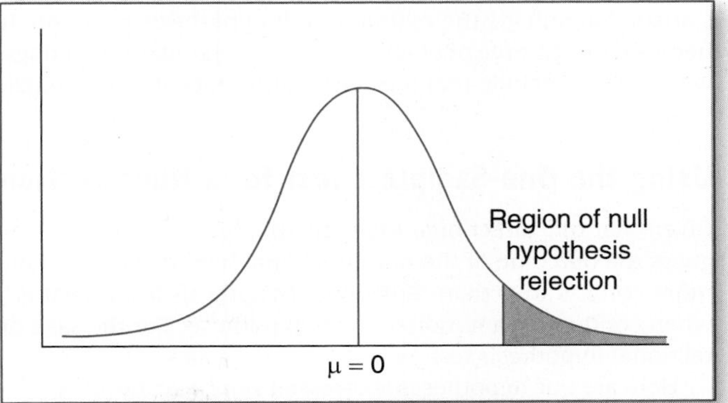

Figure 6.7 Visual Comparison of the Test Statistic (1.19) With the Critical Value (1.895; Because the Test Statistic Falls Outside the Region of Null Hypothesis Rejection, We Fail to Reject the Null Hypothesis)

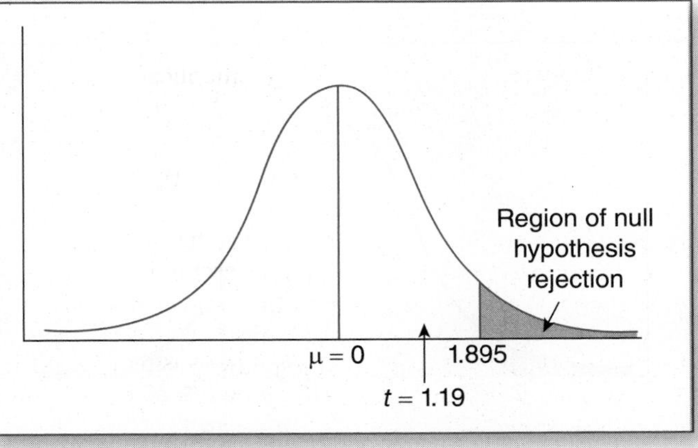

we fail to reject the null hypothesis and conclude that black dogs spend no more time in foster homes than do all dogs in this rescue.

Here is how this statistical test is written according to APA style:

$$t(7) = 1.19, p > .05 \text{ (one-tailed)}$$

Let's break down this presentation and make sure we understand what everything means here. The 7 in parentheses is the degrees of freedom. The larger the sample size, the more degrees of freedom a researcher will have. Of course, the larger the sample size, the less discrepancy there will be between the sample and the population. Therefore, the larger the sample size, the more freedom the researcher will have to make inferences about the population. The test statistic is 1.19. The *p* value of greater than .05 means that the test statistic fell outside the region of null hypothesis rejection. In other words, the difference in adoption times between our sample of black dogs and the population of dogs at this rescue was due to random variation, and we cannot conclude that it is a true difference in the population.

Using the One-Sample *t* Test for a Nondirectional (Two-Tailed) Hypothesis

Given that our directional (one-tailed) hypothesis test was not statistically significant, I bet you can already guess the outcome of the nondirectional hypothesis test. Remember that nondirectional hypothesis tests are more conservative than directional hypothesis tests. That is, it is more difficult to reject the null hypothesis when conducting a nondirectional hypothesis. For the sake of the example, however, let's perform the nondirectional hypothesis test.

Here are our hypotheses, expressed symbolically:

$$H_o: \mu_{\text{black dogs}} = \mu_{\text{all dogs}}$$
$$H_r: \mu_{\text{black dogs}} \neq \mu_{\text{all dogs}}$$

Figure 6.8 Visual Comparison of the Test Statistic (1.19) With the Critical Value (±2.365; Because the Test Statistic Falls Outside the Region of Null Hypothesis Rejection, We Fail to Reject the Null Hypothesis)

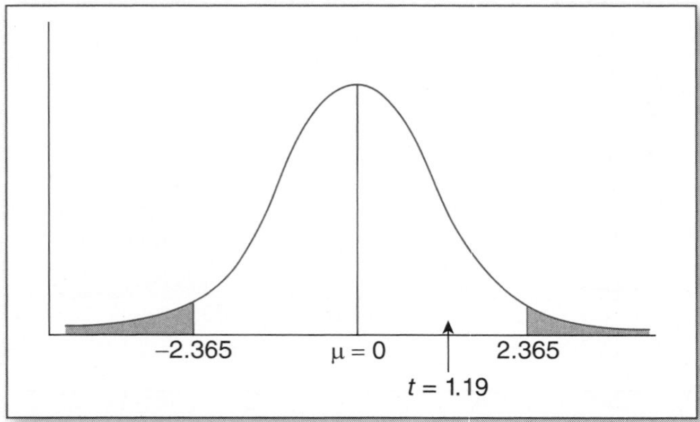

The null hypothesis is the same as it was for our directional hypothesis test. The research hypothesis says that black dogs spend a different amount of time in the rescue before being adopted than do all dogs. We do not specify whether black dogs spend more or less time in rescue before being adopted, only that they spend a different amount of time than all other dogs before being adopted.

As was the case with the *z* test, our *t* test statistic is the same for this nondirectional test as it was for the directional test (i.e., $t = 1.19$). What will change is the critical value with which we compare this test statistic. In using an alpha of .05 and having a nondirectional (two-tailed) hypothesis, we need to find our critical value. Refer again to Appendix B. This time, we need to examine the level of significance for a two-tailed test. Our degrees of freedom are again 7. Thus, our critical value is ± 2.365. With an alpha of .05, that means 2.5% of the statistical outcomes lie beyond this value, denoting the two regions of null hypothesis rejection. This critical value can be positive or negative because we are examining two possible outcomes, that black dogs spend longer in rescue before being adopted and that black dogs spend less time in rescue before being adopted. Because this is a nondirectional test, the critical value is greater than it is for a directional hypothesis test, making it more difficult to reject the null hypothesis. As seen in Figure 6.8, and not surprisingly given the outcome of our directional hypothesis test, the test statistic falls outside the region of null hypothesis rejection. Therefore, we fail to reject the null hypothesis.[2]

LEARNING CHECK

Use the following information to answer question 1:

A researcher has seven datapoints:

10, 7, 9, 3, 10, 6, 4

The population mean is 5.

1. Is her sample data different from the population?

A:
First, state the hypotheses:

$$H_o\text{: } \mu_{sample} = \mu_{population}$$
$$H_r\text{: } \mu_{sample} \neq \mu_{population}$$

Second, we need to select an alpha level. Sticking with convention, let's use .05.
Third, we need to compute our test statistic. Here is what we need to do this:

a) The sample mean is 7.
b) The population mean is 5.
c) We need to find the estimated standard error of the mean:

$$S_{x\text{-bar}} = \frac{\text{estimated standard deviation for a population}}{\sqrt{\text{sample size (N)}}}$$
$$= \frac{2.83}{\sqrt{7}}$$
$$= 1.07$$

d)

$$t = \frac{\bar{x} - \mu}{s_{x\text{-bar}}}$$

$$t = \frac{7-5}{1.07}$$

$$t = 1.87$$

(Continued)

(Continued)

Fourth, we need to find a critical value with which to compare the t test statistic. With a sample size of 7, that gives us 6 degrees of freedom. Look at Appendix B to locate the critical value. We are using a nondirectional (two-tailed) hypothesis test, so our critical value is ±2.447.

Finally, we compare our test statistic (1.87) with the critical value, and we find it falls outside the region of null hypothesis rejection. Therefore, we do not reject the null hypothesis and conclude that the sample was similar to the population from which it was drawn.

2. Would the conclusion we just made (to fail to reject the null hypothesis) have changed had we used a directional (one-tailed) test?

   A: In this case, the critical value would have been +1.943. Although smaller than the critical value for a nondirectional test, in this case, we still would fail to reject the null hypothesis.

ONE-SAMPLE *T* TEST AND SPSS

Let's now see how SPSS handles the one-sample t test. We will use the data from our previous example testing Black Dog Syndrome. These data appear again in Table 6.4. First, we will enter these data into SPSS. Then, we will run the one-sample t test, after which we will interpret the output that SPSS provides.

Table 6.4 Number of Days Needed for Dog to Be Adopted

x (each datapoint is for one black dog/observation)
30 days
35 days
20 days
41 days
58 days
2 days
18 days
28 days

Once you open SPSS, click on *Variable View* in the lower left corner. You will need to name your variable, which is the number of days each of the eight dogs spent in rescue. Perhaps name this variable something such as `Days_in_Rescue`. If you would like to give this variable a label, please do so. Again, I think `Days in Rescue` should be as straightforward as it gets. Make sure your measure is *Scale*. Here is the screenshot of how your *Variable View* setup should look:

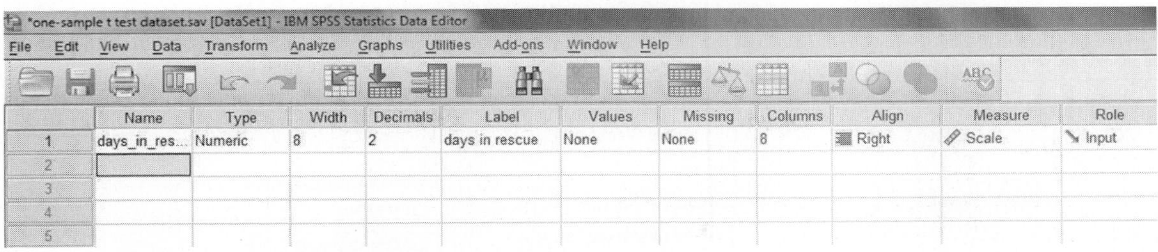

You can now click on *Data View* in the left corner of the screen. We can now enter the data for these eight dogs. Remember that in SPSS, each column is a variable and each row is a datapoint. When you get done entering your data, there should be eight rows of data in one column. Here is what your *Data View* should look like once you've entered your data:

Let's run the one-sample t test. To do so,

1. Click on *Analyze* → *Compare Means* → *One-Sample Test*.

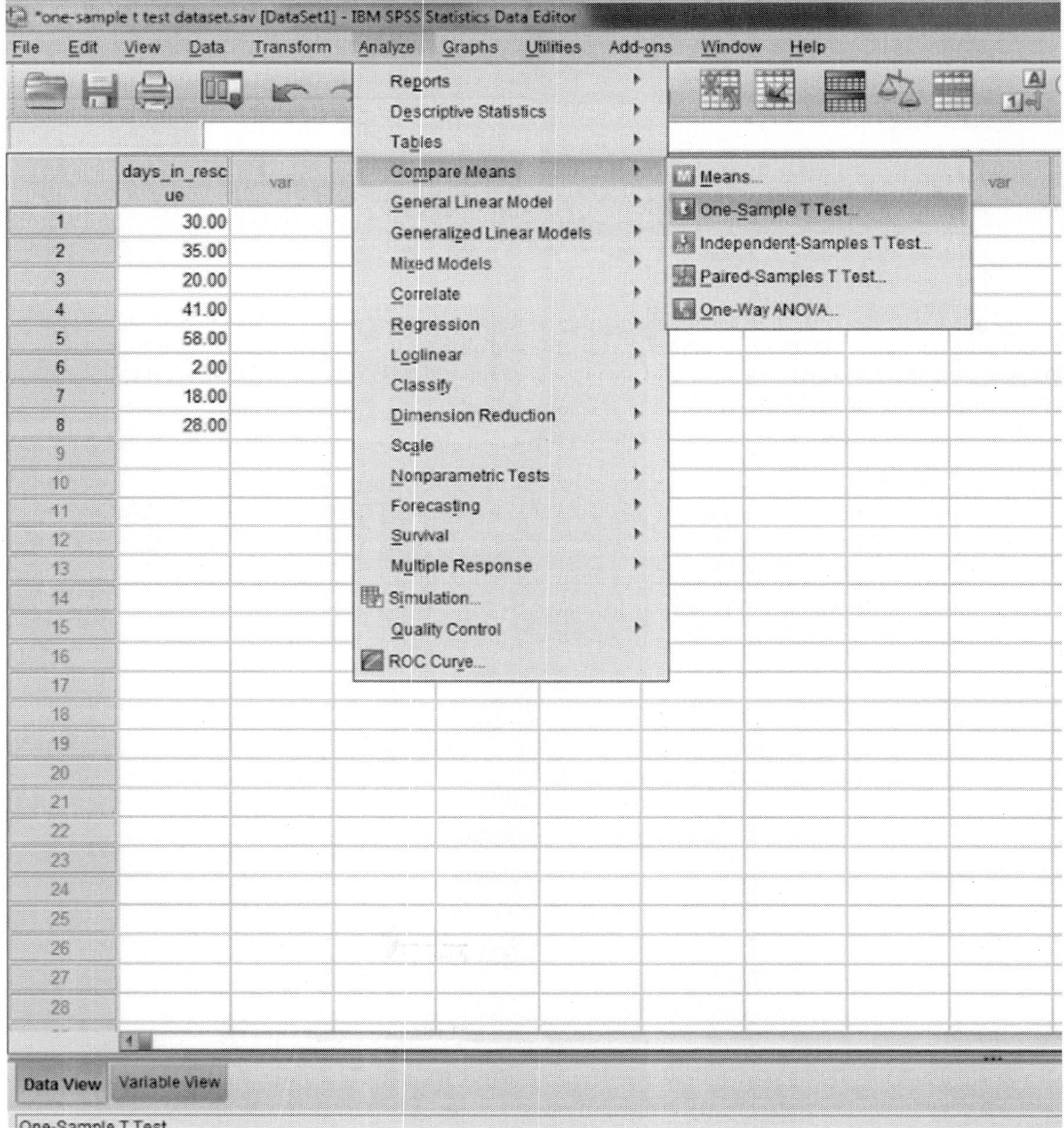

2. Your *Test Variable* is `Days in Rescue` or whatever similar name you gave it.

3. Below the *Test Variables* box, we need to specify a *Test Value*. Here is where we plug in the population mean, which as we discussed earlier is 22.

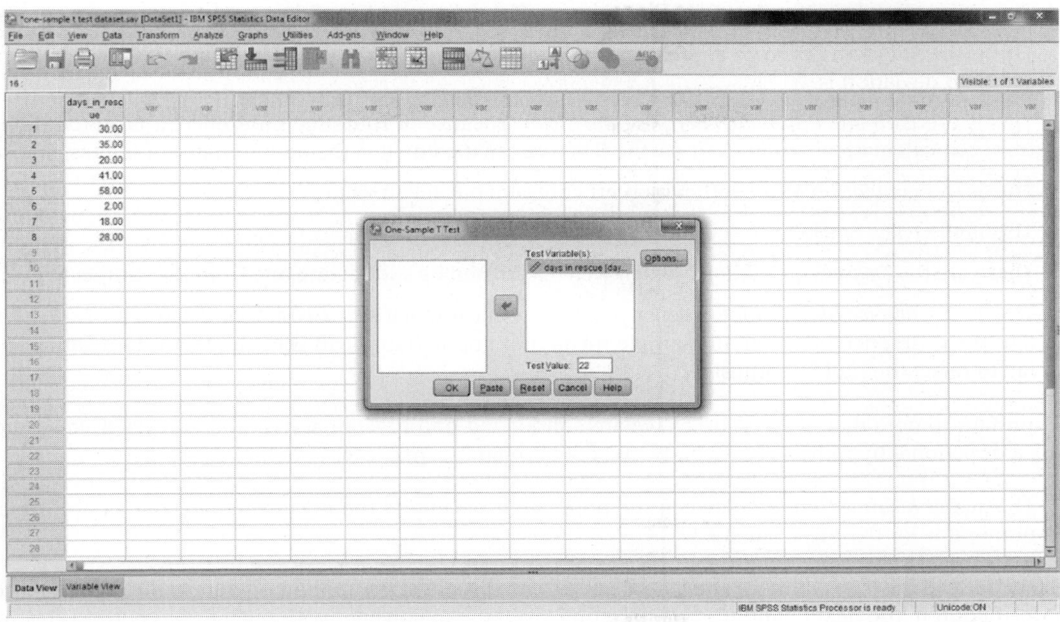

4. Now click *OK*, and your results will soon appear.

Your SPSS output should look like this:

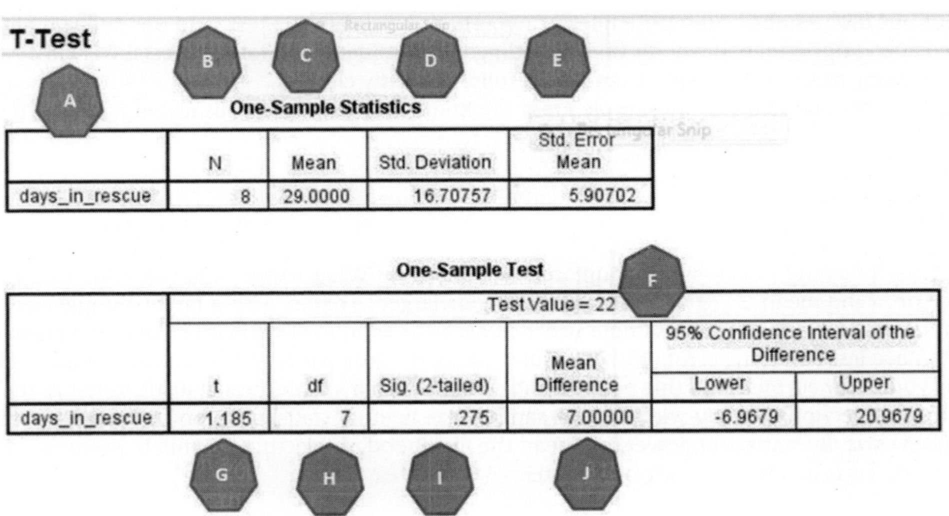

One-Sample Statistics

	N	Mean	Std. Deviation	Std. Error Mean
days_in_rescue	8	29.0000	16.70757	5.90702

One-Sample Test

	Test Value = 22					
					95% Confidence Interval of the Difference	
	t	df	Sig. (2-tailed)	Mean Difference	Lower	Upper
days_in_rescue	1.185	7	.275	7.00000	-6.9679	20.9679

Let's go through this output, taking each label and understanding the information it conveys.

A. This is the *Variable of Interest*, specifically the number of days a dog spent in the rescue.

B. This is the *Sample Size*.

C. This is the *Mean Value* for the variable of interest. The mean number of days a dog spent in rescue was 29.

D. This is the *Standard Deviation* for the variable of interest. Just as we calculated earlier in this chapter, the standard deviation is 16.71.

E. This is the *Estimated Standard Error of the Mean*. Because of rounding difference, it is a little different from our calculation earlier (5.91 vs. the 5.90 we calculated). It is the denominator of the test statistic.

F. This is the *Population Mean* with which we compare our mean value.

G. This is the *t Test Statistic*.

H. These are the *Degrees of Freedom*, which were calculated by subtracting one from the sample size.

I. This is the *Precise Significance Level or p Value* for our test statistic. Given that there is a 27.5% chance that the difference between our sample mean and population mean was due to random variation, we fail to reject the null hypothesis.

It is important to note that SPSS assumes we are conducting nondirectional hypothesis tests. If you are conducting a directional hypothesis test, you would cut this significance level in half.

J. This is the *Mean Difference* between the population mean and the mean value for our sample. It is the numerator for the *t* test statistic.

You likely noticed the `95% Confidence Interval of the Difference` on your output. We will discuss that information in the next chapter, as we have one last issue to consider with regard to hypothesis testing.

STATISTICAL POWER AND HYPOTHESIS TESTING

Throughout our discussions of the principles of hypothesis testing, the *z* test, and the one-sample *t* test, we have hinted at an important concept for understanding and conducting hypothesis tests. We will conclude this chapter by making this concept explicit (and, hopefully, explicitly clear).

Suppose we are conducting a one-sample *t* test. We know the formula for this test is:

$$t = \frac{\overline{x} - \mu}{s_{x-bar}}$$

In an earlier Learning Check, we encountered this question: What happens to the value of the estimated standard error of the mean ($s_{x\text{-}bar}$) as the sample size gets larger? That is, with a larger sample size, does $s_{x\text{-}bar}$ increase or decrease in value? As the sample size increases, the estimated standard error of the mean decreases because we have less sampling error. With a smaller standard error, we get a larger *t* test statistic. A larger test statistic, as you likely surmised by this point, is more likely than a smaller test statistic to fall in the region of null hypothesis rejection. A study with a larger sample size is more statistically powerful than a study with a smaller sample size. By **statistical power,** we mean the likelihood of rejecting the null hypothesis when in fact the null hypothesis is incorrect in the population.

Statistical power: probability of rejecting a null hypothesis that is false in the population.

There are three ways to increase statistical power. First, as we just discussed, use larger sample sizes. Be careful when reading published research, especially if you are reading it from an outlet such as a news source. Make sure you know what sample size a study's conclusions were based on. Statistically significant research results from large samples (e.g., 10,000+ people) may be reported. It is easy to obtain statistically significant results with a large sample size because, again, the larger the sample size, the more it will resemble the population to which we are generalizing our results.

Second, the higher the alpha level that we use, the more power we have. As we have discussed previously, using a lower alpha level (e.g., .01 instead of .05) makes it more difficult to reject the null hypothesis, and therefore, we have less power. The larger the alpha level, the more likely it is we can reject a null hypothesis that should be rejected.

Finally, we discussed at length why it is easier to reject the null hypothesis with a directional (one-tailed) hypothesis test than it is with a nondirectional (two-tailed) hypothesis test. Using one-tailed hypothesis tests also increases power. Suppose we had a t test statistic of 1.80, with the mean difference in the expected direction. Our sample size is 20, so we have 19 degrees of freedom. Looking at Appendix B, we see that for a two-tailed test, our critical value is ± 2.093, and we fail to reject the null hypothesis. However, by using the one-tailed test, we gain power because our critical value is now ± 1.729. So we could reject the null hypothesis in this example using a one-tailed test.

The second and third of these three ways to increase power (using higher alpha levels and using directional hypothesis tests) are things we have said we should not do when conducting research. Please understand, especially with respect to directional and nondirectional tests, statistical work can be subjective. What I am concerned about here and throughout this book is that you are a wise, informed consumer of research. By knowing these considerations about statistical power, it can help you as you encounter claims based on research.

NOTES

1. It is not incorrect to use a directional (one-tailed) hypothesis test. Rather, it is accepted convention to use a nondirectional (two-tailed) hypothesis test. Researchers simply need to be open and explicit when using a nondirectional test.

2. Other research (e.g., Woodward, Milliken, & Humy, 2014) has also called into question the existence of Black Dog Syndrome.

CHAPTER APPLICATION QUESTIONS

1. What is the difference between descriptive statistics and inferential statistics?

2. How is the alpha level (also called the significance level) related to the region of null hypothesis rejection?

3. Why are nondirectional (two-tailed) hypothesis tests considered more conservative than directional (one-tailed) hypothesis tests?

4. Assume you're interested in whether a new medication decreases the severity of symptoms in depressed patients after one month of treatment. Your sample of patients shows a mean depression severity of 12, and the known population mean *without* the medication is $\mu = 15$.

   a) What three additional pieces of information would you need to conduct a hypothesis test to determine whether the new medication lowers the severity of symptoms?

   b) Why is it *not* enough to look at the descriptive statistics to determine whether the new medication decreases symptom severity? (In other words, why is statistical hypothesis testing necessary?)

   c) Would you be more or less likely to reject the null hypothesis if you changed your level of significance from 5% to 10%? Explain your answer by making reference to the concepts of "critical value" and "region of null hypothesis rejection."

   d) What is the link between the alpha level and the Type I error?

5. Lauren is in charge of quality control for the coffee company she works for. Recently she has become worried because of an increase in customer complaints about the acid levels of her company's French Roast coffee. The acid level in her company's French Roast coffee should be normally distributed with a $\mu = 50$ mg/cup and a $\sigma = 20$ mg/cup. She randomly samples 64 bags of French Roast and finds their mean acidity level to be 55 mg/cup. Does Lauren's sample of coffee bags differ significantly from the population? What does this mean for her company?

   a) What are the null and research hypotheses, both symbolically and in plain English?

   b) Is a z test or a one-sample t test appropriate and why?

   c) Is this a directional or a nondirectional test?

   d) What is the value of your test statistic? What is the approximate critical value? What can Lauren conclude from her sample?

6. In a hypothesis test, an extreme z test statistic value, such as $z = 3$ or $z = 4$, ____________.

   a) is probably not in the region of null hypothesis rejection

   b) means you should probably reject the null hypothesis

   c) means you should probably reject the research hypothesis

   d) is very likely to occur

7. A random sample is selected from a population with $\mu = 80$ and $\sigma = 10$. To ensure a standard error of the mean of 2 points or less, the sample size should be at least:

   a) 5.

   b) 10.

   c) 25.

   d) It is impossible to obtain a standard error of 2 points or less with any of the sample sizes in these three choices.

8. Last semester, I decided to start holding weekly review sessions for students in my social psychology class to gather and ask questions. There were 43 students in this class. In the past, I held only monthly review sessions. I wanted to see whether holding weekly review sessions might have helped students do better in the class. I entered the grades from last semester's class into SPSS, and here's what SPSS gave me:

Use the output on this page to answer the following questions:

a) What is the hypothesis that is being tested here? State the null and the research hypotheses, both symbolically and in plain English.

b) What was the mean grade for my recent social psychology class?

c) What was the standard deviation for grades in the class?

d) How was the standard error of the mean calculated?

e) What was the difference in mean grades between my recent class and my classes in the past?

f) What is the test statistic in this analysis?

g) How was this test statistic calculated?

h) How many degrees of freedom are there in this analysis?

i) Although not stated on the SPSS output, locate the approximate critical value.

j) Should I reject or fail to reject the null hypothesis? Explain how you reached this conclusion.

k) Should I continue to hold weekly review sessions or stick with monthly review sessions?

Answers

1. Descriptive statistics provide information about a sample. Inferential statistics allow us to know whether we can make inferences about a population based on sample data.

2. The alpha level determines the region of null hypothesis rejection. The smaller our alpha level, the smaller will be the region of null hypothesis rejection. Therefore, a smaller alpha makes it more difficult to reject the null hypothesis.

3. Nondirectional tests do not specify the nature of the relationship between variables in the population. Therefore, we need to designate a region of null hypothesis rejection in both tails of possible statistical results, forcing us to put half of our alpha level in each tail of that distribution.

4. a) (1) sample size; (2) the estimated standard error of the mean; and (3) the alpha level.

   b) We need to examine the likelihood that the sample data are reflective of the population. Our sample has a lower mean severity than the population, but we need to test whether this difference might be the result of random variation.

   c) With an alpha level of 10% (.10), it is more likely we can reject the null hypothesis than when using an alpha level of 5% (.05) because with a larger alpha level, we will have a smaller critical value. Therefore, a smaller test statistic is more likely to fall in the region of null hypothesis rejection with an alpha of 10% than with an alpha of 5%.

   d) When researchers select the alpha level, they are also stating the Type I error rate. Typically, researchers use an alpha level of .05, meaning they are willing to accept a 5% chance of rejecting the null hypothesis when the null hypothesis is true in the population.

5. a)

$$H_o\text{: } \mu_{\text{Lauren's sample}} = \mu_{\text{all coffee}}$$

$$H_r\text{: } \mu_{\text{Lauren's sample}} > \mu_{\text{all coffee}}$$

In plain English, the null hypothesis states that there will be no difference in acidity levels between Lauren's sample of coffee and the targeted acidity levels at her company. The research hypothesis states that acidity levels will be higher in Lauren's sample than what is targeted at her company.

b) A z test is appropriate because we have access to the population standard deviation.

c) Strictly speaking, Lauren needs to conduct a one-tailed (directional) test because customers have been complaining about too much acidity in their coffee.

d) Recall the formula for the z test:

$$z = \frac{\bar{x} - \mu}{\sigma_{x-bar}}$$

where

$\bar{x}$ is the mean for our sample,

μ is the population mean,

$\sigma_{x\text{-bar}}$ is the standard error of the mean, and

$$\sigma_{x\text{-bar}} = \frac{\sigma}{\sqrt{\text{sample size } (N)}}$$

First let's get the standard error of the mean:

$$= \frac{20}{\sqrt{64}}$$
$$= \frac{20}{8}$$
$$= 2.50$$

Next, let's plug in the ingredient to the z test formula:

$$z = \frac{55 - 50}{2.50}$$
$$z = \frac{5}{2.50}$$
$$z = +2.00$$

Now, let's find the critical value with which to compare this z test statistic. Referring to Appendix A, we see that, for a directional test, our critical value is 1.645.

Because our test statistic exceeds our critical value, the test statistic falls in the region of null hypothesis rejection. Therefore, we reject the null hypothesis.

This conclusion means that the French Roast coffee that Lauren's company is making is indeed more acidic than it is supposed to be and steps should be taken in the production process to reduce these acid levels.

6. b

7. c

8. a)

$$H_o: \mu_{\text{last semester class}} = \mu_{\text{historical}}$$
$$H_r: \mu_{\text{last semester class}} \neq \mu_{\text{historical}}$$

➡ T-Test

One-Sample Statistics

	N	Mean	Std. Deviation	Std. Error Mean
Final course grade	43	83.8140	9.92173	1.51305

One-Sample Test

	Test Value = 80					
					95% Confidence Interval of the Difference	
	t	df	Sig. (2-tailed)	Mean Difference	Lower	Upper
Final course grade	2.521	42	.016	3.81395	.7605	6.8674

In plain English, the null hypothesis states that there is no difference in grades between my social psychology class last semester and the historical mean. The nondirectional research hypothesis states that my social psychology class last semester performed differently than the historical mean on this exam.

NOTE: Yes, I would expect weekly review sessions to facilitate student performance (i.e., they should do better). However, I am using a nondirectional hypothesis test here to be conservative, so that if I can reject the null hypothesis, it would provide stronger evidence than if I had used a directional hypothesis.

b) 83.81%

c) 9.92%

d) $\dfrac{9.92173}{\sqrt{43}}$

e) 83.81% − 80% = 3.81%

f) $t = 2.52$

g) $t = \dfrac{3.81}{1.51305}$

h) 42

i) Using Appendix B, with 42 *dfs*, we see the critical value will be slightly less than ± 2.021, the critical value if we had 40 *dfs*.

j) Reject the null hypothesis because the *t* test statistic of 2.52 exceeds the critical value and, thus, falls in the region of null hypothesis rejection. In addition, the *p* value is given (.016), meaning the test statistic is less than .05 and falls in the region of null hypothesis rejection.

k) Continue with the weekly review sessions; the one-sample *t* test suggested it might have helped student performance.

QUESTIONS FOR CLASS DISCUSSION

1. Provide a null and research hypothesis for each of the following two research studies. Be sure to indicate whether the research hypothesis is directional or nondirectional.
   a) An industrial psychologist wants to know whether people who work first shift perform better than those who work second shift in an automobile factory.
   b) A researcher tests for differences in creativity between left-handed and right-handed people.
2. Suppose you are doing a research study and have decided to use an alpha level of .03. Explain what this means in plain English.
3. Why is it the case that a researcher can never prove a research hypothesis to be correct?
4. What does it mean when we hear that a study had a "statistically significant" finding?
5. The term *error* is used in two different ways in hypothesis testing:
   - Type I error or Type II error
   - standard error of the mean

   a) In words and in symbols, what is the standard error of the mean?
   b) What can a researcher do to influence the size of the standard error of the mean?
   c) Does this action have any effect on the probability of a Type I error? Why or why not?
   d) What can a researcher do to influence the probability of a Type I error?
   e) Does this action in the previous question have any effect on the size of the standard error of the mean? Explain.
6. A psychologist wants to know whether the average length of courtship is different before a second marriage than before a first. Based on previous research, it is known that for courtship before first marriages $\mu = 265$ days. The psychologist collects a sample of 120 people who have just been married for a second time and finds in her sample a mean of 270 days and a standard deviation of 50 days.
   a) What are the null and research hypotheses, both symbolically and in plain English?
   b) Is a *z* test or a one-sample *t* test appropriate, and why?

c) Is this a directional or a nondirectional test?

d) What is the value of your test statistic? What is the approximate critical value? What can the researcher conclude from the sample?

7. Which combination of factors will increase the chances of rejecting the null hypothesis?

a) a large standard error and a large alpha level
b) a large standard error and a small alpha level
c) a small standard error and a large alpha level
d) a small standard error and a small alpha level

8. A very small mean difference can be statistically significant if:

a) The sample size is big, and the sample variability is small.
b) The sample size and sample variability are both big.
c) The sample size is small, and the sample variability is big.
d) The sample size and the sample variability are both small.

CHAPTER 7

Comparing Two Group Means

The Independent Samples t Test

After reading this chapter, you will be able to

- Differentiate between the one-sample *t* test and the independent samples *t* test
- Summarize the relationship among an independent variable, a dependent variable, and random assignment
- Interpret the conceptual ingredients of the independent samples *t* test
- Interpret an APA style presentation of an independent samples *t* test
- Hand-calculate all ingredients for an independent samples *t* test
- Conduct and interpret an independent samples *t* test using SPSS

In the previous chapter, we discussed the basic principles of statistically testing a null hypothesis. We highlighted these principles by introducing two parametric inferential statistical tools, the *z* test and the one-sample *t* test. Recall that we use the *z* test when we want to compare a sample to the population and we know the population parameters, specifically the population mean and standard deviation. We use the one-sample *t* test when we do not have access to the population standard deviation. In this chapter, we will add another inferential statistical tool to our toolbox. Specifically, we will learn how to compare the difference between means from two groups drawn from the same population to learn whether that mean difference might exist in the population.

CONCEPTUAL UNDERSTANDING OF THE STATISTICAL TOOL

The Study

Photo 7.1 A night-light keeps the monsters away.

Source: ©iStockphoto.com/Ryan Kelly

As a little kid, I was afraid of the dark. Of course, this is not an uncommon fear for children to have. I wasn't sure what I was afraid of as the dark contained the same things in my bedroom as the light contained. Of course, we know from developmental psychology research that young children are not yet capable of using this kind of logic. And let's face it: There is something quite functional about fearing the dark, even for adults. My bet is that most of us prefer to be physically alive than the alternative, and the dark is a reminder that we are vulnerable to the world around us. Such is the basic logic of terror management theory (TMT). In a nutshell, this theory contends that as humans, we are cognizant of our eventual deaths. When our ultimate demise is made salient to us, we espouse "worldviews" that allow us to feel our lives have meaning and that we fit into the culture in which we live.

TMT guided an experiment that Tim Kasser and Kennon Sheldon (2000) conducted. In discussing their research, we will walk through what is perhaps the most basic statistical tool needed to analyze data from an experimental study: the independent samples *t* test.

In Kasser and Sheldon's (2000) experiment, a sample of 60 college students was randomly assigned to one of two experimental groups (conditions). Thirty students wrote short essays about their attitudes toward listening to music, whereas the other 30 students wrote short essays about their attitudes toward their deaths. In this experiment, the *essay topic* about which students wrote is called the independent variable.

The independent variable is "variable" because the researchers used random assignment of participants to one of the two essay topics. We introduced the concept of random assignment in Chapter 1 when talking about explanatory research. People can differ from one another in many ways (e.g., gender, religious attitudes, and socioeconomic status). Not that such differences are trivial, but they are not of interest to the researchers in this particular experiment. Therefore, we want to control for their influence on how people in the sample behave, so that we can isolate the effect of the independent variable. Through the process of random assignment, we can minimize the influences of variables other than the independent variable. In doing so, any effects we find (from an independent samples *t* test to be discussed in this chapter) can be linked to the independent variable.

To assess the effects of the essay topic, after writing their essay, students imagined themselves 15 years in the future. In doing so, they made estimates about how much they would expect to spend on clothing, entertainment, and leisure activities (called "pleasure spending"). This estimate should depend on what experimental condition (group) people are randomly assigned to. That is, there should be differences between the two groups on responses about pleasure spending. In this example, pleasure spending is called a dependent variable because it "depends on" the independent variable (i.e., essay topic).According to TMT, people should respond to threats to their existence (i.e., writing essays about their deaths) by enhancing their worldviews. In this experiment, that would mean spending more on clothing, entertainment, and leisure activities. Doing so would suggest they are more successful, at least financially, in their culture.

Here is a visual depiction of this experiment (Figure 7.1):

Figure 7.1 Elements of Kasser and Sheldon's (2000) Experiment

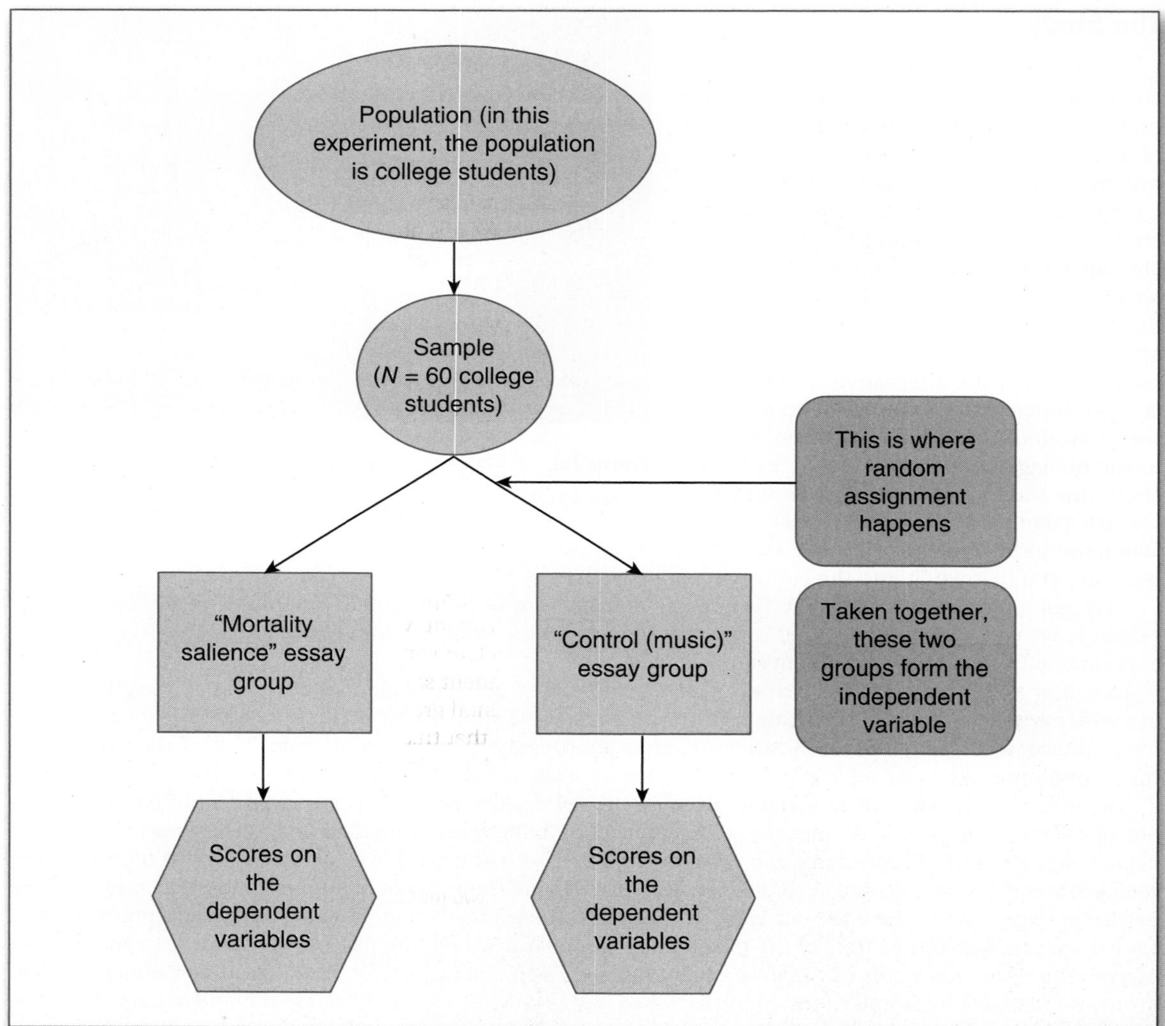

LEARNING CHECK

1. What is the difference between an independent variable and a dependent variable?

   A: The independent variable is manipulated/controlled by the researchers to create two or more groups in an experiment. The independent variable is expected to affect behavior or mental processes. The dependent variable is the behavior or mental process that is influenced by the independent variable. The dependent variable is the outcome of the independent variable.

2. Why is random assignment a critical component of an experiment?

   A: Random assignment allows researchers to isolate the effects of the independent variable on the dependent variable. It does so by arbitrarily placing members of the sample into one of the groups created by the independent variable. Therefore, the differences between people in the sample are minimized, allowing researchers to connect the effects of the independent variable to the dependent variable.

3. Why must an experiment contain at least two groups?

   A: If an experiment contained only one group, there would be no way to compare scores on a dependent variable. To take a simple example, I am 6′ 2″ tall. Am I a tall person? We cannot answer this question without something with which to compare my height. Compared with an average man (who is about 5′ 9″ tall), yes, I am a tall person. Compared with most professional basketball players, no, I am not a tall person.

We will now focus on comparing scores on the dependent variable. Kasser and Sheldon (2000) used "standardized scores" to quantify responses on these dependent variables. "Standardized scores" may sound scary, but you know exactly what that means from reading Chapter 5 and learning about *z* scores. If you are not confident in your *z* score expertise, now is a great chance to go back and review that material in Chapter 5.

The Tool

Remember that the one-sample *t* test is used when we have one sample of data and want to compare its mean with the population mean. In Kasser and Sheldon's (2000) experiment, we have two groups of data (i.e., scores in the dependent variable) created by manipulating the independent variable. In this experiment, we will need to use the **independent samples *t* test**. It is called the "independent samples" *t* test because each member of the sample is randomly assigned to one and only one experimental group. This type of experiment is called a **between-subjects experiment**. Just to avoid confusion, the fact that this statistical tool is called the "independent" samples *t* test has nothing to do with the notion of an independent variable. Rather, *the word "independent" signifies that each member of the sample was randomly assigned to one experimental group.*

Independent samples *t* test: statistical tool used to compare means of two mutually exclusive groups of people.

Between-subjects design: experimental design in which participants are randomly assigned to one and only one experimental group (condition).

Ingredients

What is the logic of the independent samples *t* test? *It is a comparison of whether mean differences in the sample are generalizable to the population from which that sample was drawn.* We will now focus on the conceptual ingredients needed for an independent samples *t* test (which are not difficult to put into practice now that you know the one-sample *t* test).

First, *we must know the mean for each group on a dependent variable*. For instance, did the "death essay" group score higher or lower than the "music essay" group on estimates of future pleasure spending? We would need the mean estimate of pleasure spending for each of these two groups.

Second, not every member of the two groups will have the same score on a dependent variable. There will be variability among individual scores around the mean score for each group. To account for this variability, *we must consider the **standard error of the difference between the means.*** Recall from Chapter 4 the notion of a standard deviation. A *standard deviation* is a measure of how much a group of scores tends to stray from the group's mean. The standard error of the difference between the means serves the same purpose as a standard deviation, within the context of an independent samples *t* test. A standard deviation applies to one group of data; the standard error of the difference *between the means* applies to two groups of data. Like the standard deviation, the standard error of the difference between the means relies in part on the number of people in the groups (i.e., sample size). Thus, *the larger the sample size and the lower the variability of scores around the group means, the lower the standard error of the difference will be.* Therefore, as we said in the previous chapter, larger sample sizes are preferred, statistically speaking, because they reduce the standard error of the difference between the means. They are inherently more representative of the populations from which they were drawn.

Standard error of the difference between the means: standard deviation of a difference between two group means.

In short, to use an independent samples *t* test, we need to know (a) the mean of each group and (b) the standard error of the difference between those means. These two pieces of information give us a "*t* test statistic" that we can use to see whether there is a statistically significant difference between the means of these two groups. Here is the conceptual formula for the independent samples *t* test statistic:

$$t = \frac{\text{Mean difference between the two groups}}{\text{Standard error of the difference between the means}}$$

In thinking through this formula, there are three ways to increase the power of this statistical tool:

1. Larger mean differences (i.e., increase the numerator)
2. Larger sample sizes (i.e., decrease the denominator)
3. Less variability of scores within each group (i.e., decrease the denominator)

Hypothesis from Kasser and Sheldon (2000)

As a refresher from the previous chapter, remember that we are testing the hypothesis that there is no difference in the population between mean scores of the two groups. That is, we are testing the null hypothesis with our statistical tool. To be able to suggest that there are differences in the population based on these two mean scores, we must reject the notion that there is no difference between the mortality salience essay group and the music essay group. In other words, the mean difference between the two groups must be large enough to conclude that there is likely an effect that exists in the population. In plain English, the statistic tested the notion that there will be no difference between the mortality-salience condition and the control condition on scores on the dependent variable. Symbolically,

$$H_o: \mu_{\text{mortality-salience group}} = \mu_{\text{control group}}$$

Published research rarely if ever states a null hypothesis even though, as you know, it is always the null hypothesis that statistical tools are testing. Rather, published research tends to state the research hypothesis. For instance, in Kasser and Sheldon's (2000) article, they predicted that students who wrote essays about death would become more focused on the accumulation of wealth and possessions than would students who wrote about a neutral topic. (p. 348)

Symbolically, we have

$$H_r: \mu_{\text{mortality-salience group}} > \mu_{\text{control group}}$$

LEARNING CHECK

Let's drive home the conceptual logic of the independent samples *t* test with a few examples:

For the first two questions, calculate the *t* test statistic, plugging in the following data from the conceptual formula for the independent samples *t* test:

1. Mean of Group A = 50

   Mean of Group B = 35

   Standard error of the difference between the means = 7.50

   A:
   $$t = \frac{50-35}{7.50}$$
   $$t = \frac{15}{7.5}$$
   $$t = 2.00$$

2. Mean of Group C = 20

   Mean of Group D = 15

   Standard error of the difference between the means = 4

   A:
   $$t = \frac{20-15}{4}$$
   $$t = \frac{5}{4}$$
   $$t = 1.25$$

3. As the sample size increases, all else being equal, will the value of the *t* test statistic increase or decrease? Why?

   A: The *t* test statistic will increase in value because as the sample becomes larger, it will better represent the population from which it was drawn. Therefore, our results have a better chance of being generalized from the sample to the population. Mathematically speaking, a larger sample size decreases the denominator of the *t* test statistic formula (i.e., it decreases the standard error of the difference between the means), making the *t* test statistic bigger.

4. What is the difference between a standard deviation and a standard error of the difference between the means?

   A: The standard deviation is a measure of variability for one group of data. The standard error of the difference between the means is a pooled measure of variability for two groups of data.

Interpreting the Tool

Now that we have laid out all of the ingredients for the independent samples *t* test, let's take a look at Kasser and Sheldon's (2000) results. It might be a good time to take a look back at the visual depiction of this experiment (Figure 7.1). Then, consider the results of their experiment, as they are presented here:

> An independent samples *t* test suggested that participants primed to think about their deaths estimated spending more on pleasure items (M = 0.22, SD = 0.96) than participants primed to think about music (M = −0.27, SD = 0.61), t(52.8) = 2.30, p = .02, d = 0.61, 95% confidence interval (CI) [0.06, 0.92].

What does this text tell us? Let's break it down into its smallest, most digestible bites and indulge in them one at a time. We have the mean (*M*) and standard deviation (*SD*) for each group. Thinking about the ingredients for the *t* test, we of course must have the mean for each group. In addition, we need the standard error of the difference between the means. *To get the standard error of the difference between the means, we need to know the standard deviation for each group, as well as the sample size for each group.* Here, the standard deviation is reported. Although the sample size is not provided in the results, such information should always appear in the Method section of a journal article. In this experiment, the sample size was 60 people.

Recall that the dependent variable in this experiment was called "pleasure spending." It has a *t* test statistic of 2.30. How did that 2.30 magically appear? Let's review the conceptual formula for the *t* test:

$$t = \frac{\text{Mean difference between the two groups}}{\text{Standard error of the difference between the means}}$$

Now, let's fill in this formula with numbers from the results:

$$2.30 = \frac{0.22-(-0.27)}{\text{Standard error of the difference between the means}}$$

The difference between the two group means was 0.49. Remember, we are dealing with *z* scores here, so when we see a difference score of 0.49, it means that there is almost one half of 1 standard deviation difference between the mean scores. It does not matter which mean you subtract from the other.

Typically in reported research, the standard error of the difference between the means is not given. However, with some basic algebra, we can figure it out (if we care to do so; for the purposes of making sense of these results, this step is not necessary, but let's be true to the process). From your algebra days, take 0.49 (the difference between the means of the two groups and the numerator of the *t* statistic) and divide it by 2.30. Voila, 0.213 is your standard error of the difference between the means.

Now that we know where the *t* test statistic comes from, there are some additional pieces of information we need to consider when using this tool. We need to consider *degrees of freedom (df)*, a concept introduced in the previous chapter. Degrees of freedom are the numbers of scores that are free to vary and still have the same mean. *Degrees of freedom are always dependent on the sample size.* The larger the sample, the more degrees of freedom a researcher has. The larger the sample, all else being equal, the more likely it is we can generalize a statistical result from the sample to the population. For an independent samples *t* test, the calculation of degrees of freedom is simple:

$$df = \text{Sample size} - 2$$

Why "minus 2"? Remember, that 2 is *the number of group means being compared* in the independent samples *t* test. Therefore, we are free to vary all but one score in each group (2 scores in total).

If you look at Kasser and Sheldon's (2000) results closely, you will notice something strange about the degrees of freedom that they reported. Remember that the sample size in this experiment was 60; therefore, shouldn't the degrees of freedom be 58 (i.e., 60 – 2)? What is going on here? Now is a good time to examine assumptions that are made when using an independent samples *t* test. Here are those assumptions:

Assumptions of the tool

1. The variability of scores in one group must be equal to the variability of scores in the other group. This assumption is called **homogeneity of variances**. That is, one group should not have a higher standard deviation than the other group (remember from Chapter 4 that the variance of scores in a group is obtained simply by squaring the standard deviation). Take a look back at the results from Kasser and Sheldon's (2000) experiment, and consider the standard deviation for each group. When conducting an independent samples *t* test, these standard deviations should be equal.

Homogeneity of variances: assumption of the independent samples *t* test that the variability of each group is approximately equal.

Indeed, this first assumption of the independent samples *t* test is a problem in this experiment. We will deal with how to tell whether this assumption is violated later in this chapter. For now, we can say that when this assumption is violated, researchers incur a fine when conducting the *t* test, much like a motorist incurs a fine when pulled over for speeding. Specifically, they lose degrees of freedom for this statistical tool. Remember that the higher the number of degrees of freedom a researcher has, the more likely he or she can generalize results from a sample to the population. Therefore, violating this assumption and, thus, losing degrees of freedom makes it less likely that a researcher can generalize results to the population.

In addition to homogeneity of variances, there are three other assumptions of the independent samples *t* test:

2. Perhaps most obvious, each observation (i.e., participant) must be in only one of the two groups.
3. The data were scale (interval or ratio) data; see Chapter 2 for a review of scales of data measurement.
4. The distributions of scores that comprise each group mean are normally distributed (see Chapter 5 for a review of normal data distributions).

Testing the null hypothesis

So, at this point, we have a *t* test statistic and our degrees of freedom. We can use these two pieces of information to tell whether we can generalize our result to the population. To do so, first recall from Chapter 6 that when testing a hypothesis, we need to know how likely some score or outcome was to occur by chance. The assumption that the distributions of scores are normally distributed becomes critical here. As you know, when a distribution of scores is normally distributed, we can specify how likely a specific score is to occur. In this example, we know what our specific score is; ours is the *t* test statistic. The *t* test statistic for pleasure spending was 2.30. As researchers, we want to know, "Can we generalize this outcome from our sample data to the larger population?" Armed with degrees of freedom, we can determine whether this difference between group means generalizes to our population. We must compare our *t* statistic of 2.30 to a critical value to learn whether the *t* statistic is large enough to allow us to draw conclusions about our population from our sample data.

Take a look at Appendix B. It contains the critical values for the distribution of possible t statistics. We need to compare our t test statistic with the correct critical value. It is unusual in a real research study to be able to locate the precise critical value on a table like the one in Appendix B. Of course, for the purposes of understanding the process of the independent samples t test, we can do so here. We have 52.8 degrees of freedom. We must know our alpha level, for which we will continue to use .05.

As we discussed in the previous chapter, statistical tests reported in research are typically two tailed, even with directional hypotheses, as we had; that is, we expected the mortality salience group to indicate higher levels of pleasure spending than the control group. Again, researchers generally prefer two-tailed hypothesis tests because they are more conservative than one-tailed hypothesis tests. To reiterate this point, take a look at the critical values for the t distribution. By using our two-tailed test with an alpha of .05 and 52.8 degrees of freedom, we can look to the degrees of freedom that are provided in this appendix. Here, we can estimate our critical value with the degrees of freedom that are given in the appendix of 40 and 60. By using these two degrees of freedom, we see that our critical value is between ± 2.021 and ± 2.000, which are the critical values for 40 and 60 degrees of freedom, respectively. Had we used a one-tailed test, our critical value would have been between ± 1.684 and ± 1.671. Given a smaller critical value with the one-tailed test, there is a great likelihood of rejecting the null hypothesis.

When conducting actual research, it is indeed unusual for researchers to have the exact number of degrees of freedom that appear on these critical value tables. Fret not, because the good news is that the software program Statistical Package for the Social Sciences (SPSS) has all the critical values memorized for us, and when conducting research, it is software such as SPSS that we will rely on. In the practice of doing research, no one consults critical value tables, but it is good to understand the role they play in the research process.

Let's go back to our t test statistic, which was 2.30. We need to compare this statistic with the critical value for a two-tailed hypothesis test with 52.8 degrees of freedom. Given that critical value is between ± 2.000 and ± 2.021, we see that our t statistic is greater than that critical value. Let's look at Figure 7.2. We are testing the hypothesis that there is no (i.e., 0) difference between the group means in that population. To reject this notion, we need a test statistic that is greater than 0. How much greater is "greater than 0"? If the test statistic meets or exceeds the critical value, the test statistic falls in the region of null hypothesis rejection, and we reject the null hypothesis. As you see in Figure 7.2, our test statistic (2.30) is indeed greater than the critical value (which is between ± 2.000 and ± 2.021). Therefore, in this research, Kasser and Sheldon (2000) were able to reject the null hypothesis and conclude that people in the mortality-salience condition indicated a greater likelihood to spend money on pleasure than did people in the control/music condition.

Figure 7.2 A Visual Comparison of the Test Statistic (2.30) With the Critical Value (±2.01); Because the Test Statistic Falls in the Region of Null Hypothesis Rejection, We Reject the Null Hypothesis

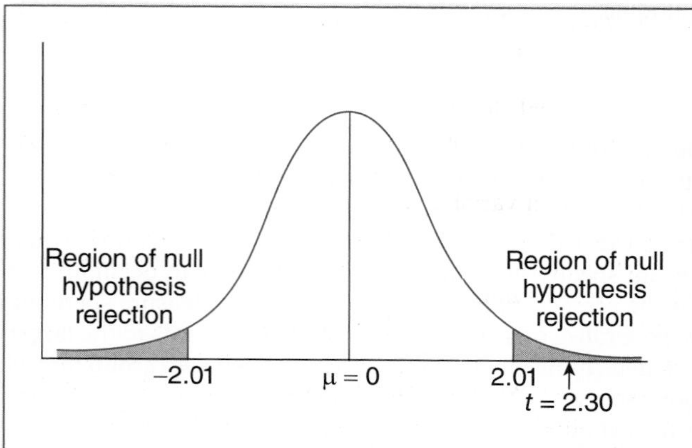

We know that our test statistic exceeds our critical value and we reject the null hypothesis. Referring to Kasser and Sheldon's (2000) results, there are other pieces of information it includes that you should be aware of. Specifically, we should discuss the p value. Remember from the previous chapter that a p value (or "probability" value) tells us how likely a statistical result was obtained because of random variation and is likely to be a Type I error. In other words, was the difference between group means merely a fluke? Researchers generally prefer smaller *p* values because that means there is little chance that the differences between the group means emerged because of chance factors.

We see that the *p* value is $p = .02$. What does that mean in plain English? It means that there is a 2% chance that the difference between the means (i.e., 0.22 and −0.27) was due to random variation. We want this percentage to be as close to 0 as possible. However, there is always a chance that some statistical result was due to random variation. In any *t* test reported, there is almost guaranteed to be some difference between the means. The question is whether that difference is large enough, accounting for variability and sample size, to warrant making conclusions about our larger population. Remember that our "alpha" or "significance level" of 5% means that if there is less than a 5% chance a result in the sample occurred by chance, then we are willing to draw conclusions about our population. We say such results are *statistically significant*. Here, with a *p* value of .02 (i.e., 2%), we can reject the null hypothesis that there will be no difference between the two groups on estimates of pleasure spending in the future. Therefore, we can conclude that participants who wrote essays about their deaths were more likely to think they will spend more money on pleasure in the future than people who did not contemplate their deaths.

Extending our null hypothesis test

In addition to testing the null hypothesis, it is common for researchers to provide two additional pieces of information: (1) an effect size and (2) a confidence interval.

The **effect size** is the amount of variability in a dependent variable that can be traced to the independent variable. In essence, the effect size allows us to learn how big an impact the independent variable has on the dependent variable. In our discussion of critical values, remember that the more degrees of freedom you have, the more likely you will be to reject the null hypothesis. Degrees of freedom are contingent on sample size; thus, so too are the critical values that determine how large the region of null hypothesis rejection will be. If you have a large enough sample size, we can reject almost any null hypotheses, no matter how small a relationship there is in the population. For instance, if my 8 a.m. statistics class exam mean is 75% and my 2 p.m. statistics class exam mean is 74.9%, is that a statistically significant difference? If the sample size was large enough, it could be. However, is a difference of 0.1% a particularly strong effect? Reporting an effect size provides such information.

For the independent samples *t* test, the effect size is normally reported in Cohen's *d* (which is typically reported as simply *d*). As you can see in Kasser and Sheldon's (2000) results, the effect size for the dependent variable of pleasure spending is 0.61. What does this mean? There are benchmarks for determining what constitutes a weak, moderate, and strong effect size. Specifically, Cohen (1992) suggested that an effect size, as measured by Cohen's *d*, of less than 0.20 is trivial; an effect size between 0.20 and 0.50 is weak; an effect size between 0.51 and 0.80 is moderate; and an effect size greater than 0.80 is strong. Thus, in our instance, our effect size of 0.61 is moderate. Therefore, the independent variable has a moderate effect on the dependent variable.

The effect size statistic complements the notion of statistical significance. When we ask whether a result is statistically significant, we are asking whether we can take our result obtained in our sample and draw conclusions about our population from which that sample was drawn. When we speak about effect size, we are asking how powerful an effect (in this case, an independent variable) is in affecting behavior. Remember that a result can be statistically significant because it was found using a large sample. That's because large samples will better reflect the populations than will smaller samples. However, just because a result is statistically significant does not mean it has a powerful effect on behavior.

In addition to knowing effect sizes, it will be helpful to know how **confidence intervals** (CIs) are used in reporting statistical results. A confidence interval is a range of possible differences between group means in which we feel confident that the actual group mean difference will lie in the larger population. Stated differently, if we could test an infinite number of samples and calculate the interval for each sample, 95% of those samples would contain the actual population mean. Let's unpack that explanation.

In Kasser and Sheldon's (2000) results, for the dependent variable of pleasure spending, we have a confidence interval of [0.06, 0.92]. What does that mean? Recall that the mean difference between the two groups on this dependent variable was 0.49. If we could draw an unlimited number of samples, 95% of those samples would contain a mean difference between 0.06 and 0.92. Here is the important part, that *the range of possible mean differences in the population does not include 0*. Why is it so important that this range not include 0? If it did, that would mean it is reasonably possible that the mean difference in the population is 0 (i.e., there is no mean difference in the population).

Confidence intervals complement the notion of statistical significance. Again, when we ask whether a result is statistically significant, we are asking whether we can take our result (here, a difference between two means) obtained in our sample and draw conclusions about our population from which that sample was drawn. *When we add a confidence interval to the test of statistical significance, we learn the range of plausible values that our result could take on in the population.*

Effect size: statistical measurement of how powerful the relationship is between variables (e.g., between an independent variable and a dependent variable).

Confidence interval: interval estimate that contains the population mean a certain percentage of time, based on repeated sampling of that population.

LEARNING CHECK

Now that we've seen the independent samples *t* test in action, let's review our conceptual understanding of this tool. In addition to the dependent variable of pleasure spending that we just discussed in great detail, Kasser and Sheldon (2000) also had a dependent variable called "financial worth." That is, participants provided a dollar estimate of how much they would be worth financially 15 years into the future. Here are the statistical results for this dependent variable:

> An independent samples *t* test suggested that participants primed to think about their deaths estimated they would be worth more money ($M = 0.16$, $SD = 0.94$) than participants primed to think about music ($M = -0.23$, $SD = 0.38$), $t(44.5) = 1.99$, $p = .05$, $d = 0.54$, 95% CI [0.00, 0.77].

Now, answer the following questions. Then check your answers.

1. What is the mean difference between the two groups being examined?
2. What is the *t* test statistic?
3. What is the standard error of the difference between the means? (*HINT:* It is not reported above.)
4. How many degrees of freedom do the researchers have for this analysis?
5. Was the assumption of homogeneity of variance violated or not violated? How do you know?
6. By using Appendix B, approximate the critical value that was used to see whether we reject or do not reject the null hypothesis.
7. What is the probability that the difference between the two groups' means was due to random variation?
8. Did the researchers reject or not reject the null hypothesis?

9. Given your answer to the previous question, what does it mean in plain English?
10. By using Cohen's (1992) guidelines, interpret the effect size.
11. Interpret the 95% confidence interval.

Answers

1. 0.16 – (–0.23) = 0.39
2. 1.99
3. $$1.99 = \frac{0.39}{\text{Standard error of the difference between the means}}$$

   Standard error of the difference between the means = 0.196
4. 44.5
5. Yes, this assumption was violated because normally, for the independent samples *t* test, degrees of freedom are measured "sample size – 2." Had that been the case, there would have been 60 – 2 = 58 degrees of freedom. This assumption was violated because we have only 44.5 degrees of freedom. We lost degrees of freedom because of this violation.
6. We cannot locate the precise degrees of freedom in this appendix, but we can locate critical values for 40 and 60 degrees of freedom. Our 44.5 degrees of freedom falls in between these two parameters, so let's use the critical value for 40 degrees of freedom (which is ±2.021) and 60 degrees of freedom (which is ±2.000). By using these two critical values, we can approximate our critical value to be about ±2.01.
7. $p = .05$ (5% chance the mean difference was due to random variation).
8. The *t* test statistic of 1.99 falls just below the critical value of 2.01; therefore, we fail to reject the null hypothesis. (*NOTE:* The researchers said $p = .05$; therefore, p was *not less than* .05, which it would need to be to reject the null hypothesis.)
9. Writing about one's death or writing about music did not affect college students' estimates of their overall financial worth 15 years into the future.
10. $d = 0.54$ is a moderate effect size.
11. If we could draw an unlimited number of samples from this population, 95% of those samples would contain a mean difference between .00 and .77. Because it contains zero, we cannot be confident that there is a mean difference on this dependent variable in the population.

USING YOUR NEW STATISTICAL TOOL

Now that you have a good understanding of what an independent samples *t* test tells us and how to interpret this tool, let's put it to use!

Hand-Calculating the Independent Samples *t* Test

We will first calculate an independent samples *t* test by hand. Then, you will have the opportunity to practice these calculations in the next Learning Check. Afterward, we will learn how to conduct and interpret the independent samples *t* test with the help of SPSS.

As an extension of Kasser and Sheldon's (2000) experiment, let's add another dependent variable that they could have measured, namely, materialistic values. It seems reasonable, according to Terror Management Theory, that if people just wrote about their deaths, they would likely be more materialistic than if they just wrote about music. One way to fit into Western cultures is to advertise one's status via material possessions. Thus, when reminded that we will in fact die at some point, we might express materialistic values as a means to restore our sense of power over our surroundings.

Step 1: State hypotheses

Remember, we must statistically test the null hypothesis:

$$H_o: \mu_{\text{mortality-salience group}} = \mu_{\text{control group}}$$

In terms of the research hypothesis, we would expect the following:

$$H_r: \mu_{\text{mortality-salience group}} > \mu_{\text{control group}}$$

There are several self-report measures of materialism available. Marsha Richins and Scott Dawson's (1992) 18-item scale has people respond to statements such as "I like to own things that impress people" and "I have all the things I really need to enjoy life" (reverse-coded) using a 1 (*I strongly disagree with the statement*) to 5 (*I strongly agree with the statement*) response range. Thus, scores on this scale can range from 18 to 90. Here are hypothetical data for 12 participants in this experiment:

Experimental Group					
Mortality Salience (Death Essays)			Control (Music Essays)		
72	67	50	51	37	33
44	70	57	78	35	42

Step 2: Calculate the mean for each of the two groups

$$\text{Mortality Salience Group Mean} = \frac{(72 + 67 + 50 + 44 + 70 + 57)}{6} = 60$$

$$\text{Control Mean} = \frac{(51 + 37 + 33 + 78 + 35 + 42)}{6} = 46$$

We now have the numbers needed for the numerator of our *t* statistic:

$$t = \frac{60 - 46}{\text{Standard error of the difference between the means}}$$

Step 3: Calculate the standard error of the difference between the means

These calculations are a little more intricate than calculating the means, but you already know how to do everything because you read Chapter 4, in which we learned about the notions of standard deviation and variance. Recall that the standard deviation for a group of scores is simply the square root of the variance. Or stated another way, the variance is the standard deviation squared.

Here is the formula for the standard error of the difference between the means:

$$s_{x1-x2} = \sqrt{\frac{s_1^2}{n_1} + \frac{s_2^2}{n_2}}$$

where

s_1^2 is the variance for the first group (the mortality salience group),
n_1 is the number of people in the first group,
s_2^2 is the variance for the second group (the control/music group), and
n_2 is the number of people in the second group.

The difficult part is the calculation of the variance for each group (s^2). However, it is not difficult. We did this back in Chapter 4. Here again is what we do:

For each group, take each score and subtract from it the group mean. Doing so will yield a "deviation from the mean" score. So, for the mortality salience group,

Individual Score	Group Mean	(Deviation From Mean)
72	60	12
67	60	7
50	60	−10
44	60	−16
70	60	10
57	60	−3

And for the control (music) group:

Individual Score	Group Mean	(Deviation From Mean)
51	46	5
37	46	−9
33	46	−13
78	46	32
35	46	−11
42	46	−4

As we know from Chapter 4, simply adding together the individual scores' deviations from the mean is pointless as that summation will always be 0. Therefore, we square each deviation from the mean as doing so eliminates the negative numbers.

For the mortality salience group,

Individual Score	Group Mean	(Deviation From Mean)	$(\text{Deviation})^2$
72	60	12	144
67	60	7	49
50	60	−10	100
44	60	−16	256
70	60	10	100
57	60	−3	9

And for the control (music) group,

Individual Score	Group Mean	(Deviation From Mean)	$(\text{Deviation})^2$
51	46	5	25
37	46	−9	81
33	46	−13	169
78	46	32	1,024
35	46	−11	121
42	46	−4	16

Now, we sum the $(\text{deviations})^2$ for each group:

Mortality Salience Group Mean = (144 + 49 + 100 + 256 + 100 + 9) = 658

Control Mean = (25 + 81 + 169 + 1,024 + 121 + 16) = 1,436

We then divide each sum by the number of people in that group, minus 1.

Mortality salience group: $\frac{658}{6-1}$ Control group: $\frac{1{,}436}{6-1}$

Thus, the variance for the mortality salience group is 131.6. The variance for the control group is 287.2. Let's plug these numbers into the formula for the standard error of the difference between the means:

$$\sqrt{\frac{131.6}{n_1}+\frac{287.2}{n_2}}$$

It now gets much easier. The sample size for each group is 6. Let's plug those sample sizes into the formula:

$$\sqrt{\frac{131.6}{6}+\frac{287.2}{6}}$$

Simplifying this equation a little bit gives us

$$\sqrt{21.933+47.867}$$

Simplifying even further gives us

$$\sqrt{69.8}$$

Thus, our standard error of the difference between the means is 8.3546. It's all downhill from here.

Step 4: Calculate the *t* test statistic

Recall from step 2 that our group means were 60 for the mortality salience group and 46 for the control/music group. We have all of our ingredients to perform our independent samples *t* test:

$$t=\frac{\text{Mean difference between the two groups}}{\text{Standard error of the difference between the means}}$$

$$t=\frac{60-46}{8.3546}$$

$$t=1.68$$

What information does this *t* test statistic of 1.68 tell us? Remember, we want to know whether the difference between the means found in our sample is generalizable to the population. Obviously, 60 is greater than 46, but can we conclude that people who contemplated their deaths are more materialistic than those who instead contemplated music?

Step 5: Determine degrees of freedom (*df*s)

We now need to know how much freedom we have to generalize our results to the population. Remember that for an independent samples *t* test, degrees of freedom = sample size – 2. Therefore, given we have data from 12 people, we have 10 degrees of freedom here (i.e., 12 – 2; we are assuming that we have met the four assumptions for the independent samples *t* test). Armed with our degrees of freedom, we must now find our critical value with which to compare our *t* test statistic. If our *t* test statistic exceeds the critical value, we will reject the null hypothesis. If our *t* test statistic is less than the critical value, we do not reject the null hypothesis.

Step 6: Locate the critical value

Consult Appendix B to find our critical value. In returning to our two-tailed test of the null hypothesis with a significance level of .05, our test statistic needs to be greater than ± 2.228 for us to reject the null hypothesis.

Step 7: Make a decision about the null hypothesis

Visually, Figure 7.3 shows how to conceive of using the t test statistic we calculated and the critical value to reject or to fail to reject our null hypothesis. As you can see, our t test statistic of 1.68 falls below our critical value of ± 2.228. Therefore, we cannot reject the null hypothesis. In plain English, we conclude that people express similar levels of materialistic values regardless of whether they had their mortality made salient to them.

Step 8: Calculate an effect size

Remember that we have a fairly small sample size in this example. With a small sample size, it is more difficult to find a statistically significant result than with a larger sample size. However, as we discussed previously, just because we fail to reject the null hypothesis does not mean the effect of the independent variable is nonexistent. Let's calculate the effect size (Cohen's d) for this example. Here is the formula for Cohen's d:

$$d = \frac{\text{Mean difference between the two groups}}{\sqrt{\frac{\text{Variance of group 1}}{2} + \frac{\text{Variance of group 2}}{2}}}$$

We have already calculated all of the information we need to determine Cohen's d:

1. The mean for each group
2. The variance for each group

From step 2 in this section, the mean for the mortality salience group was 60, and the mean for the control (music) group was 46. From step 3, the variance for the mortality salience group was 131.6, and the variance for the control (music) group was 287.2. Let's plug in the numbers for the dependent variable of materialism:

Figure 7.3 A Visual Comparison of the Test Statistic (1.68) With the Critical Value (±2.228); Because the Test Statistic Falls Outside the Region of Null Hypothesis Rejection, We Fail to Reject the Null Hypothesis

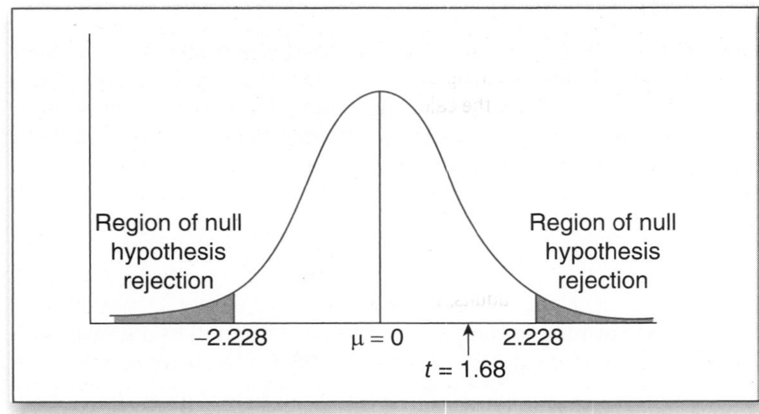

$$d = \frac{60 - 46}{\sqrt{\frac{131.2}{2} + \frac{287.2}{2}}}$$

$$d = \frac{14}{\sqrt{65.6 + 143.6}}$$

$$d = \frac{14}{\sqrt{209.2}}$$

$$d = \frac{14}{14.464}$$

$$d = .97$$

Keep in mind the benchmarks for interpreting Cohen's d. Specifically, Cohen (1992) suggested that an effect size of less than 0.20 is trivial; an effect size between 0.20 and 0.50 is weak; an effect size between 0.51 and 0.80 is moderate; and an effect size greater than 0.80 is strong. Thus, our effect size of 0.97 is strong.

Step 9: Determine the confidence interval

Finally, we must consider the confidence interval around our mean difference. To calculate a 95% CI for an independent samples *t* test, here is our formula:

> 95% CI = (mean of group 1 – mean of group 2) ± critical value for *t* × (standard error of the difference between the means)

We have already calculated all of the ingredients needed to calculate our confidence interval:

Mean of group 1 (mortality salience) = 60

Mean of group 2 (control/music) = 46

Critical value for *t* (which we found while determining the region of null hypothesis rejection) = ±2.228

Standard error of the difference between the means = 8.3546

95% CI = 60 – 46 ± 2.228(8.3546)

95% CI = 14 ± 18.614

95% CI = [–4.614, 32.614]

As you can see, our interval contains 0, which means we cannot be confident that the difference we observed in the sample exists in the population.

Now, we have calculated all sorts of numbers, but they are worthless unless we can communicate them concisely. Here is how we would report the results in the text of an article of the analyses we just conducted, using APA style:

> An independent samples *t* test suggested that participants primed to think about their deaths were no more materialistic (*M* = 60.00, *SD* = 11.47) than were participants primed to think about music (*M* = 46.00, *SD* = 16.95), *t*(10) = 1.68, *p* > .05, *d* = 0.97, 95% CI [–4.61, 32.61].

Remember that the standard deviation (*SD*) is the square root of the variance. We never calculated the *SD* in this section, but we did calculate the variance (in step 3). So here we just took the square root of the variance to get our standard deviation.

LEARNING CHECK

Here are some additional examples to get more practice hand-calculating and interpreting the independent samples *t* tests. The example contains raw data from individual participants, so the calculations are involved. The second example provides summary statistics, so the calculations will be a little less involved than what we've been doing up to this point in this section.

Problem #1

Andrew Christopher and Mark Wojda (2008) conducted a study that examined, among other considerations, sex differences in political attitudes. Specifically, among a sample of 246 working adults, they measured social dominance orientation

(Continued)

(Continued)

(Pratto, Sidanius, Stallworth, & Malle, 1994). Social dominance orientation is a person's preference for social hierarchy and stratification. Participants indicated how negatively or positively they felt about statements such as "Increased economic equality (reverse-coded)" and "Some people are just inferior to others" on a 0 (*very strongly negative*) to 8 (*very strongly positive*) response range. Here are scores from 12 participants on Felicia Pratto and colleagues' (1994) 14-item social dominance measure:

Women	Men
18	51
33	40
42	36
31	60
49	52
25	43

Questions to Answer:

1. What is the hypothesis being tested?
2. What is the mean difference between the two groups being examined?
3. What is the standard error of the difference between the means?
4. What is the *t* test statistic?
5. How many degrees of freedom do the researchers have for this analysis?
6. According to Appendix B, what is the critical value that was used to see whether we reject or fail to reject the null hypothesis?
7. What is the probability that the difference between the two groups' means was due to random variation?
8. Did the research reject or fail to reject the null hypothesis?
9. Given your answer to the previous question, what does that mean in plain English?
10. Calculate the effect size and interpret it according to Cohen's (1992) guidelines.
11. Calculate and interpret the 95% confidence interval.
12. Write these results for the text of an article in proper APA style.

Answers

1. There is no difference between women and men on social dominance orientation scores.
2. Mean for women = 33; mean for men = 47; mean difference = 14

3. 5.85
4. $t = \frac{47 - 33}{5.85}$

   $t = 2.39$
5. 10
6. ±2.228
7. Less than 5% because the t statistic of 2.39 exceeds the critical value of ±2.228.
8. Given the answer to question 7, we reject the null hypothesis.
9. Men scored higher on social dominance orientation than did women.
10. d = 1.38; this is a strong effect size. That is, a person's sex was strongly predictive of his or her social dominance orientation score.
11. The 95% confidence interval is −0.97 to −27.03, meaning that if we could draw an unlimited number of samples from this population, 95% of those samples would contain a mean difference between −0.97 and −27.03. That this interval does not contain 0 means we can be confident there is a difference between women and men on social dominance orientation in the population.
12. Here is the proper APA style write-up:

An independent samples t test suggested that men tended to score higher in social dominance orientation (M = 47.00, SD = 8.90) than did women (M = 33.00, SD = 11.22), $t(10) = 2.39$, $p < .05$, $d = 1.38$, 95% CI [−0.97, −27.03].

This example brings up a methodological point about the independent samples t test. In this example, participants were classified as either female or male. So indeed, participants were in only one of the two groups being compared. However, unlike in Kasser and Sheldon's (2000) research, *participants in Christopher and Wojda's (2008) research were not randomly assigned to groups.* It's not possible to randomly assign someone to be a woman or a man. Although there is no random assignment to groups as there would be in a true experiment, you can still use the independent samples t test whenever you want to compare two mutually exclusive groups.

Problem #2

A forensic psychologist wants to know whether men convicted of robbery receive different sentences if they have an ethnic-sounding first name (e.g., Declan) or a more traditional-sounding first name (e.g., David). After sampling 30 male convicts, 15 with an ethnic-sounding first name and 15 with a more traditional-sounding first name, here is what this researcher found:

a) Mean sentence for men with ethnic-sounding first names = 5.5 years with a standard deviation of 2.5 years
b) Mean sentence for men with more traditional-sounding first names = 4.0 years with a standard deviation of 1.75 years

   1. What is the population being studied?
   2. Why couldn't this researcher use random assignment?

(Continued)

(Continued)

3. What is the hypothesis being tested?
4. What is the mean difference between the two groups being examined?
5. What is the standard error of the difference between the means?
6. What is the *t* test statistic?
7. How many degrees of freedom do the researchers have for this analysis?
8. By using Appendix B, find the critical value that was used to see whether we reject or do not reject the null hypothesis.
9. What is the probability that the difference between the two groups' means was due to random variation?
10. Did the researchers reject or fail to reject the null hypothesis?
11. Given your answer to the previous question, what does that mean in plain English?
12. Calculate the effect size and interpret it according to Cohen's (1992) guidelines.
13. Calculate and interpret the 95% confidence interval.
14. Write these results for the text of an article in proper APA style.

Answers

1. The population is men who have been convicted of robbery.
2. We cannot assign people to be men, nor can we assign them to be robbery convicts. It is simply not practical to use random assignment in this research.
3. There will be no difference between male robbers who have ethnic-sounding first names and male robbers who have more traditional-sounding first names in jail sentences for their crime.
4. Ethnic-sounding first name mean is 5.5 years; more traditional-sounding first name mean is 4.0 years, so the mean difference is 1.5 years.
5. 0.79
6. $t = \frac{1.50}{0.79}$

   $t = 1.90$
7. 28
8. ±2.048
9. Greater than 5% ($p > .05$)
10. Do not reject the null hypothesis because the *t* test statistic is less than the critical value.

11. There was no difference in jail sentences handed down to male burglars who had an ethnic-sounding first name versus those who had a more traditional-sounding first name.

12. d = 0.70. This is a moderate effect size. That is, the relationship between a person's first name and his jail term for robbery was moderately strong.

13. The 95% confidence interval is −0.11 to 3.11, meaning that if we could draw an unlimited number of samples from this population, 95% of those samples would contain a mean difference between −0.11 and 3.11. Because this interval contains 0, we cannot be confident there is a difference between convicted male robbers with ethnic-sounding and more traditional-sounding first names.

14. Here is the proper APA style write-up:

    An independent samples t test suggested that males convicted of robbery were sentenced to similar jail terms, regardless of whether they had an ethnic-sounding first name (M = 5.50 years, SD = 2.50 years) or a more traditional-sounding first name (M = 4.00 years, SD = 1.75 years), $t(28) = 1.90$, $p > .05$, d = 0.69, 95% CI [−0.11, 3.12].

Independent Samples *t* Test and SPSS

Now that you have a handle on the conceptual nature of the independent samples t test and know how to calculate it, let's run our own independent samples t test using SPSS. To do so, let's use some hypothetical data. Suppose that Kasser and Sheldon (2000) had included another dependent variable in their experiment. For instance, it might have been logical to include a measure of anxiety about one's death. Thus, it might make sense that writing about one's death would heighten a person's anxiety about his or her ultimate physical demise compared with writing about music. Jon Hoelter (1979) developed the Multidimensional Fear of Death Anxiety (MFOD) scale, in which people respond on a 1 (*strongly disagree*) to 5 (*strongly agree*) response range to items such as "Discovering a dead body would be a horrifying experience" and "I am afraid I will not have time to experience everything I want to." There are 42 items on this scale, so scores could potentially range from 42 to 210. We could easily use this scale and get an aggregate death anxiety score for each participant. Let's suppose we included this death anxiety scale. Here are the aggregate scores on it for a sample of 30 participants (15 in each experimental group):

Experimental Group					
Mortality Salience (Death Essays)			Control (Music Essays)		
112	75	150	100	75	98
187	100	119	82	90	140
152	112	125	65	115	111
136	162	88	112	133	90
87	147	63	84	68	71

Establishing your spreadsheet

Once you open SPSS, you will need to click on *Variable View* in the lower left corner. You will need to name two variables, namely, the independent variable and the dependent variable. Again, the independent variable is the group to which participants in the sample are randomly assigned, either a mortality salience group (i.e., writing about death) or a control group (i.e., writing about music). Perhaps name this variable something such as `Experimental_Group`. Next, name the dependent variable something such as `Death_Anxiety`. After naming your variables, remember to give them labels. No need to get fancy or creative here. Let's simply label these variables "Experimental Group" and "Death Anxiety."

After naming your variables, you need to let SPSS know whether each participant had been randomly assigned to the mortality salience group or to the control group. To do so, click on *Values for the Experimental Group*. Here, you need to give numerical values to the group participants were randomly assigned to. For the first value, make it a 0 and label it "Mortality Salience" or "Death Essay," or something to that effect. For the next value, make it a 1 and label it "Control" or "Music Essay," or something to that effect. Click *OK* to close the *Values* window. Be sure, as well, that your measure choice is "Scale."

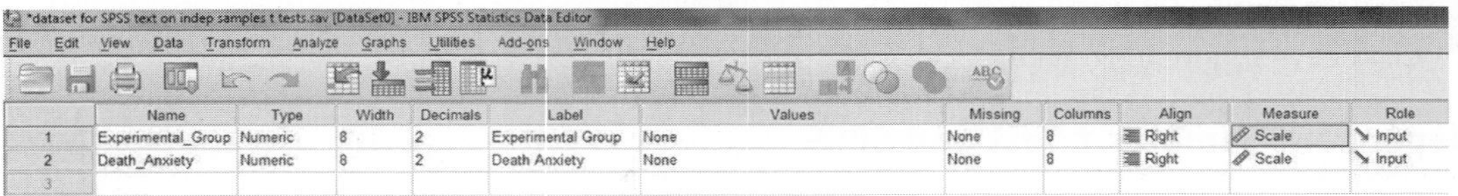

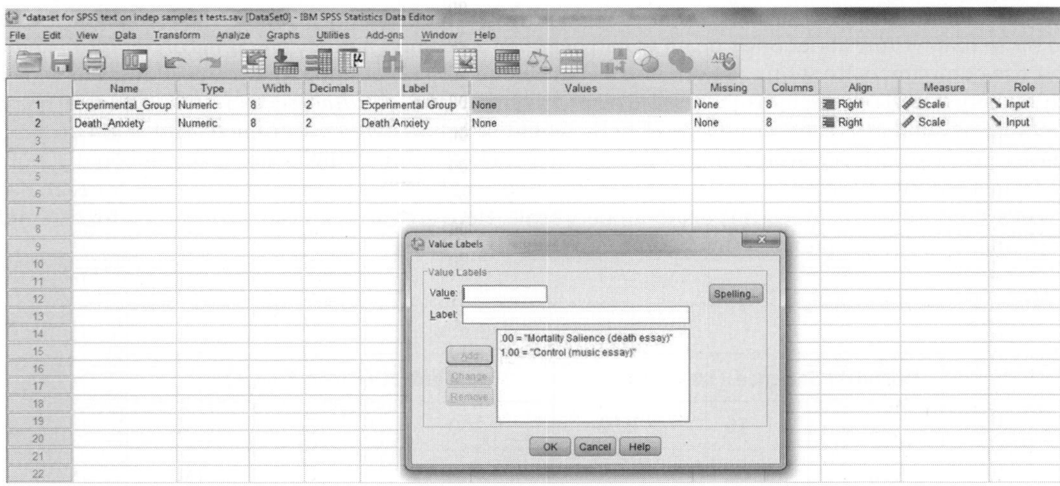

In the left corner of the screen, click on *Data View*. You are now ready to enter the data from these 30 participants. Remember, it makes no difference the order in which you enter data into SPSS. Just be sure to code correctly the experimental group that participants were randomly assigned to (0 or 1); then enter each aggregated score on the dependent variable (i.e., `Death_Anxiety`) for that participant. Here is what your file should look like:

*dataset for SPSS text on indep samples t tests.sav [Da

File Edit View Data Transform Analyze

	Experimental_Group	Death_Anxiety
1	.00	112.00
2	.00	187.00
3	.00	152.00
4	.00	136.00
5	.00	87.00
6	.00	75.00
7	.00	100.00
8	.00	112.00
9	.00	162.00
10	.00	147.00
11	.00	150.00
12	.00	119.00
13	.00	125.00
14	.00	88.00
15	.00	63.00
16	1.00	100.00
17	1.00	82.00
18	1.00	65.00
19	1.00	112.00
20	1.00	84.00
21	1.00	75.00
22	1.00	90.00
23	1.00	115.00
24	1.00	133.00
25	1.00	68.00
26	1.00	98.00
27	1.00	140.00
28	1.00	111.00
29	1.00	90.00
30	1.00	71.00
31		

Running your analyses

Once you have entered all of these data into SPSS, you should have 30 rows of data (one row for each participant) and two columns of data (one for the independent variable and one for scores on the dependent variable). You are now set to run your independent samples *t* test. Here's how you run this analysis:

1. Click on *Analyze → Compare Means → Independent Samples T Test.*

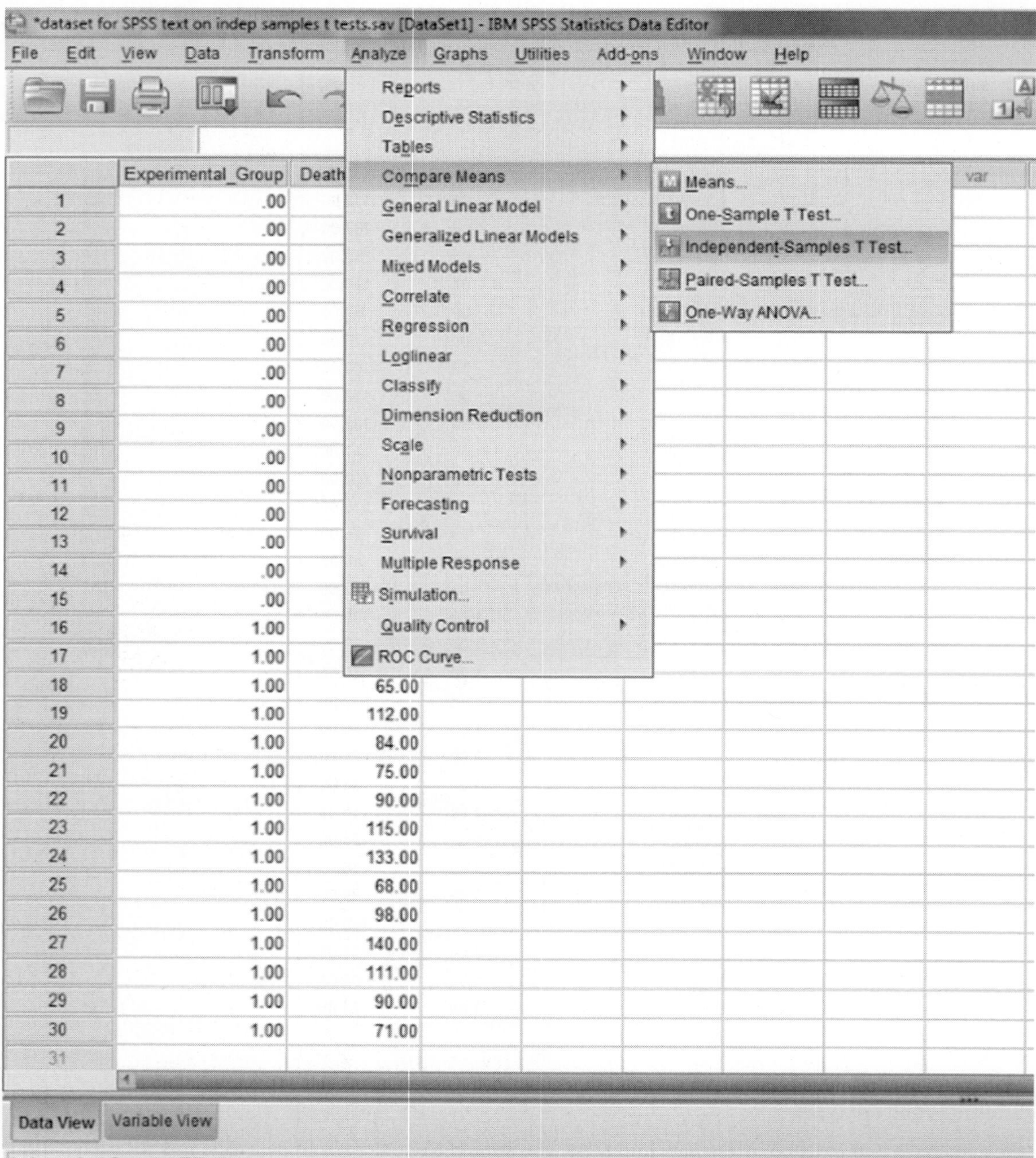

	Experimental_Group	Death
1	.00	
2	.00	
3	.00	
4	.00	
5	.00	
6	.00	
7	.00	
8	.00	
9	.00	
10	.00	
11	.00	
12	.00	
13	.00	
14	.00	
15	.00	
16	1.00	
17	1.00	
18	1.00	65.00
19	1.00	112.00
20	1.00	84.00
21	1.00	75.00
22	1.00	90.00
23	1.00	115.00
24	1.00	133.00
25	1.00	68.00
26	1.00	98.00
27	1.00	140.00
28	1.00	111.00
29	1.00	90.00
30	1.00	71.00
31		

2. Your *Test Variable* is your dependent variable (i.e., `Death_Anxiety`). Your *Grouping Variable* is your independent variable (i.e., `Experimental_Group`).

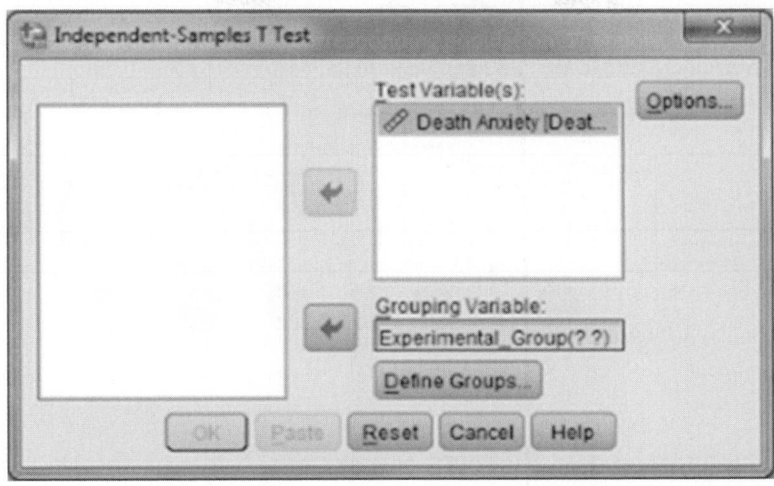

3. Once you click over your *Grouping Variable*, you will need to *Define Groups*, so click on it. It makes no difference what you call group 1 and what you call group 2. However, remember how the independent variable was coded into SPSS (i.e., with `0`s and `1`s). So, for group 1, give it a `0`, and for group 2, give it a `1`. Click *Continue* and then *OK*, and you should soon have your results!

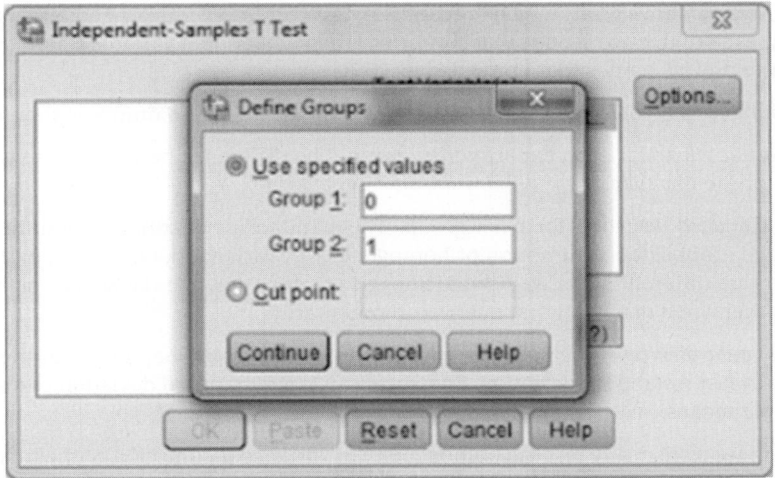

Hopefully, your output looks like this and contains the same numbers as you see here:

T-Test

[DataSet0]

A B C D E F

Group Statistics

	Experimental Group	N	Mean	Std. Deviation	Std. Error Mean
Death Anxiety	Mortality Salience (death essay)	15	121.0000	34.93668	9.02061
	Control (music essay)	15	95.6000	22.97141	5.93119

Independent Samples Test

		Levene's Test for Equality of Variances		t-test for Equality of Means						
		F	Sig.	t	df	Sig. (2-tailed)	Mean Difference	Std. Error Difference	95% Confidence Interval of the Difference	
									Lower	Upper
Death Anxiety	Equal variances assumed	2.674	.113	2.353	28	.026	25.40000	10.79585	3.28569	47.51431
	Equal variances not assumed			2.353	24.199	.027	25.40000	10.79585	3.12814	47.67186

G H I J K L M

What am I looking at? Interpreting your SPSS output

Now, let's make sense of what we see on our output. There are lots of numbers here, of course, so we'll just take one bite at a time.

A. This is the *dependent variable*, `Death_Anxiety` (yes, it would be helpful if it were labeled as such in SPSS, but consider it a daily hassle). Be aware that the name that appears here is the name that I gave the dependent variable. Had I named the dependent variable something other than `Death_Anxiety`, that's what would have appeared here.

B. This is the *independent variable*, which I named `Experimental_Group`. In addition, and perhaps more importantly, each of the two groups that comprised the independent variable is noted here. Again, these names are the precise names that I provided in SPSS.

C. This is the *number of people in each experimental group*. Ideally, these numbers should be equal.

D. This is the *group mean* for each experimental group. The difference between these two numbers is the numerator for the t statistic.

E. This is the *standard deviation* for each group. The standard deviations are assumed to be the same across the two groups (the assumption of homogeneity of variances). Obviously, in this instance, these two numbers are different; what we need to know is whether they are statistically significantly different from each other. We'll deal with that question momentarily.

F. This is the *standard error of the mean* for each group. Recall from Chapter 6 that the standard error of the mean is in fact a standard deviation. Specifically, it is the standard deviation of a sampling distribution of sample means.

G. Here is where we statistically test the homogeneity of variance assumption of the independent samples t test. What would our null hypothesis be? We are testing the null hypothesis that there is no difference in variability between the two experimental groups. If we reject this hypothesis, we would need to conclude that there is a difference between the variability in each group and, therefore, that this assumption would be violated.

In this analysis, the p value is .113. As this p value is greater than .05, we do not reject the null hypothesis and conclude that the variability in the two groups was equivalent (i.e., we did not violate the homogeneity of variances assumption).

Be very careful when examining the Levene's test; it is not the independent samples t test! All the Levene's test does is tell us which line to read when interpreting the independent samples t test. That is, can the assumption of homogeneity of variances be assumed? If so, as was the case in this instance, read the line "Equal variance assumed." If this assumption has been violated, as it was in Kasser and Sheldon's (2000) experiment, then read the "Equal variances not assumed" line.

H. This is your *t test statistic*. Recall how it was calculated:

$$t = \frac{\text{Mean difference between the two groups}}{\text{Standard error of the difference between the means}}$$

In this example, the t statistic is 2.35. How did we get that statistic? Remember the group means under D. We take the difference of those two numbers (i.e., 121.00 and 95.60) and that gives us the numerator of 25.4. The standard error of the difference between the means is, well, hold tight. We'll find that on our output momentarily.

I. Here are our *degrees of freedom*. As we said earlier, the formula for the degrees of freedom is total sample (i.e., 30 in this example) – 2. It's easy enough to figure out when we don't violate the homogeneity of variance assumption. When we do violate this assumption, however, it is like getting a speeding ticket; we have to pay a fine. When we get a speeding ticket, that fine is of course money we must pay. When we violate the homogeneity of variances assumption, that fine is degrees of freedom. We lost some degrees of freedom for violating this assumption. This violation occurred in Kasser and Sheldon's (2000) experiment; hence, that is why the degrees of freedom they reported were not the straightforward "sample size – 2" normally used to calculate degrees of freedom for this statistic.

J. This is the *p value, or significance level,* of the t test statistic. Here, our p value is .026. In other words, there is a 2.6% chance that our observed difference between the two group means was due to random variation. Because this value is less than .05, we can conclude that the difference between the means was not due to random variation. Therefore, we can generalize this result from the sample to the population from which it was drawn.

K. Here is the *difference between the two group means* that are noted under D previously (in case you didn't feel like doing some simple subtraction).

L. This is the *standard error of the difference between the means*. It is the denominator of the t test statistic.

Here is our t test statistic and how it was calculated from this printout:

$$2.35 = \frac{121.00 - 95.60}{10.79585}$$

M. Here is *the 95% confidence interval around the mean difference*. As is the case in published research, the critical values are not specified on the SPSS printout, but they are being used to calculate this confidence interval.

Now, SPSS does not provide one piece of information that is essential when reporting and interpreting an independent samples t test. Specifically, it does not report the effect size. Why SPSS does not do this is an excellent question. I do not have an equally excellent answer. Fortunately, you're a whiz at effect sizes, so let's calculate the Cohen's *d* using information that SPSS does provide:

$$d = \frac{\text{Mean difference between the two groups}}{\sqrt{\frac{\text{Variance of group 1}}{2} + \frac{\text{Variance of group 2}}{2}}}$$

The variance of each group is not given on the SPSS output; however, the standard deviation is provided. Remember that to obtain the variance for a group, you simply square the standard deviation. Now let's calculate the Cohen's *d*:

$$d = \frac{25.4}{\sqrt{\frac{34.94^2}{2} + \frac{22.97^2}{2}}}$$

$$d = \frac{25.4}{\sqrt{\frac{1220.81}{2} + \frac{527.62}{2}}}$$

$$d = \frac{25.4}{\sqrt{610.41 + 263.81}}$$

$$d = \frac{25.4}{\sqrt{874.22}}$$

$$d = \frac{25.4}{29.57}$$

$$d = 0.86$$

In returning to Cohen's (1992) criteria for interpreting an effect size, we see that our *d* of 0.86 is a strong effect size. In plain English, the independent variable had a powerful effect on people's self-reported levels of death anxiety.

There is one other thing that SPSS does not do for us. It does not report the results in APA style. We need to do that ourselves, and so we shall:

> An independent samples *t* test suggested that participants primed to think about their deaths were more anxious about death (M = 121.00, SD = 34.94) than were participants primed to think about music (M = 95.60, SD = 22.97), $t(28)$ = 2.35, p = .026, d = 0.86, 95% CI [3.29, 47.51].

LEARNING CHECK

Now that we've calculated our independent samples *t* test by hand and know how to run one on SPSS, you know what might be fun? Why not enter the data from our hand calculations (in the previous section of this chapter) into SPSS, run the independent samples *t* test, and interpret our output? This would be a great way to test what you learned in the previous two parts of this chapter and will reinforce this information. Here again are those data (which are materialism scores for a sample of 12 people):

Experimental Group					
Mortality Salience (Death Essays)			**Control (Music Essays)**		
72	67	50	51	37	33
44	70	57	78	35	42

Hopefully your SPSS output looks like this:

T-Test

Group Statistics

	Experimental Group	N	Mean	Std. Deviation	Std. Error Mean
Materialism	Mortality salience (death essay)	6	60.0000	11.47170	4.68330
	Control (music essay)	6	46.0000	16.94698	6.91857

Independent Samples Test

		Levene's Test for Equality of Variances		t-test for Equality of Means						
		F	Sig.	t	df	Sig. (2-tailed)	Mean Difference	Std. Error Difference	95% Confidence Interval of the Difference	
									Lower	Upper
Materialism	Equal variances assumed	.344	.571	1.676	10	.125	14.00000	8.35464	-4.61530	32.61530
	Equal variances not assumed			1.676	8.787	.129	14.00000	8.35464	-4.96956	32.96956

Questions to Answer

1. What is the hypothesis being tested?
2. What is the mean difference between the two groups being examined?
3. What is the standard error of the difference between the means?
4. What is the *t* test statistic?
5. Was the assumption of homogeneity of variances violated? How do you know?
6. How many degrees of freedom do the researchers have for this analysis?
7. According to Appendix B, what is the critical value that was used to see whether we reject or fail to reject the null hypothesis?
8. What is the precise probability that the difference between the two groups' means was due to random variation?
9. Did the researchers reject or fail to reject the null hypothesis?
10. Given your answer to the previous question, what does that mean in plain English?
11. What is the effect size?
12. What is the 95% confidence interval?

(Continued)

(Continued)

Answers

1. There will be no difference between the mortality salience condition and the control condition on materialism scores.
2. 60 − 46 = mean difference of 14
3. 8.3546
4. $t = 1.68$
5. The assumption was not violated. We know this because the Levene's Test for Equality of Variances produced a statistically insignificant result, meaning we cannot reject the null hypothesis that the variability between our two groups is equal.
6. 10
7. ±2.228
8. $p = .125$
9. The researchers failed to reject the null hypothesis because the *t* test statistic of 1.68 is less than the critical value of ±2.228.
10. People expressed similar levels of materialistic values in the mortality salience group and the control group.
11. $d = 0.96$
12. [−4.61, 32.61]

CHAPTER APPLICATION QUESTIONS

1. How does a one-sample *t* test differ from an independent samples *t* test?
2. Why would it be impractical to randomly assign people to a socioeconomic status (SES)?
3. Suppose you conducted a two-group study with 11 participants in each group. By using a two-tailed hypothesis test, what would your critical value be?
4. Referring to the previous question, if you used a one-tailed hypothesis test, what would your critical value be?
5. In terms of our ability to reject the null hypothesis, (a) explain how variability can be *a good thing* in an experiment; and (b) explain how variability can be *a bad thing* in an experiment.
6. A statistically significant outcome is defined as an outcome that has a _____ probability of occurring if the _____ hypothesis is true.

   a) small; research c) small; null

   b) large; research d) large; null

7. Which of the following t test statistics will have the strongest effect size?
   a) $t(28) = 2.16$
   b) $t(38) = 2.44$
   c) $t(48) = 2.72$
   d) it is impossible to know without more information

8. Which of the following t test statistics is most likely to be statistically significant?
   a) $t(70) = 2.00$
   b) $t(35) = 2.00$
   c) $t(10) = 2.00$
   d) it is impossible to know without more information

9. All other things being equal, what will happen to the value of the independent samples t test statistic as:
   a) the number of people in each group increases?
   b) the standard error of the difference between the means increases?
   c) the difference between group means increases?

Answers

1. A one-sample t test is used to compare one group of data with some benchmark, normally the population mean. An independent samples t test assesses whether the difference in means between two groups drawn from the same population exists in that population.
2. Socioeconomic status is a participant variable; that is, it is a naturally occurring characteristic that is not possible to assign someone to. A researcher cannot practically take a person who grew up in a middle-class environment and assign him or her to a lower SES status. Such an assignment would likely have no effect on people's behavior or mental processes.
3. ± 2.086
4. $+1.725$
5. With respect to our ability to reject the null hypothesis: (a) Variability is a good thing when there is a large mean difference between the groups in an independent samples t test. (b) Variability can be a bad thing when there is a large variance (and, hence, standard deviation) within each group being statistically analyzed.
6. c
7. d
8. a
9. a) t statistic increases
   b) t statistic decreases
   c) t statistic increases

QUESTIONS FOR CLASS DISCUSSION

1. What is the difference between an independent variable and a dependent variable in an experiment?
2. Why is the independent samples *t* test called an "independent" test?
3. What information does an effect size provide over and above a hypothesis test?
4. What information does a confidence interval provide over and above a hypothesis test?
5. On average, what value is expected for the *t* statistic if the null hypothesis is true?
   a) 0
   b) 1
   c) .05
   d) cannot be determined without sample data
6. You see the following statistical analysis presented from an experiment with two groups to which participants were randomly assigned to one and only one group:

$$t(48) = 3.21, p < .03, d = 0.70, 95\% \text{ CI } [3.00, 10.00]$$

   What can you conclude from this information?

   I. We can generalize this result from our sample to our population.
   II. There is a 70% chance that the independent variable caused an effect on the dependent variable.
   III. There was a statistically significant difference between the two groups' mean scores.
   IV. A total of 48 people's data were included in these analyses.
      a) I and II only
      b) I and III
      c) I, II, and III only
      d) all of the above are correct statements

7. Use this APA style report of an independent samples *t* test to answer the questions that follow it:

   When using a sample of 50 students, an independent samples *t* test suggested that children and adolescents who had a Big Brother-Big Sister mentor had higher grade-point averages ($M = 3.25$, $SD = 0.51$) than did children and adolescents without such a mentor ($M = 2.75$, $SD = 0.60$), $t(48) = 2.99$, $p = .002$, $d = 0.91$, 95% CI [0.19, 0.82].

   a) What was the hypothesis being tested?
   b) What is the mean difference between the two groups being examined?

c) What is the t statistic?

d) What is the standard error of the difference between the means?

e) Was the assumption of homogeneity of variance violated or not violated? How do you know?

f) By using Appendix B, approximate the critical value that was used to see whether we reject or do not reject the null hypothesis. Assume a directional hypothesis.

g) What is the probability that the difference between the two groups' means was due to random variation?

h) Did the researchers reject or not reject the null hypothesis?

i) Given your answer to the previous question, what does that mean in plain English?

j) By applying Cohen's (1992) guidelines, interpret the effect size.

k) Interpret the 95% confidence interval.

CHAPTER 8

Comparing Two Repeated Group Means

The Paired Samples t Test

After reading this chapter, you will be able to

- Differentiate between an independent samples *t* test and a paired samples *t* test
- Interpret the conceptual ingredients of the paired samples *t* test
- Interpret an APA style presentation of a paired samples *t* test
- Hand-calculate all ingredients for a paired samples *t* test
- Conduct and interpret a paired samples *t* test using SPSS

We have discussed one-sample *t* tests (Chapter 6) and independent samples *t* tests with (Chapter 7). Recall that we use the one-sample *t* test when we have only one sample of data and want to compare it with the population mean. We use the independent samples *t* test when want to compare means of two mutually exclusive groups of people. In this chapter, we consider the third and final type of *t* test, *the paired samples* t *test*. Just think about what the phrase "paired samples" should mean intuitively. If you have a pair of shoes on, you have two shoes on (one on each foot, I would think). If you have a pair of samples, you have a person providing a pair of (two) datapoints, just like you have a pair of shoes on. Let's take a quick example. If we conducted a study that compared productivity at different times of day, we could measure people's productivity during the morning, and then again in the mid-afternoon. We could then compare people's performance in the morning with their performance in the mid-afternoon. The same people provided productivity data in the morning and productivity data in the mid-afternoon. Hence, they provided a pair of datapoints, so we'd use the paired samples *t* test.

I am betting you will like the paired samples *t* test even better than the independent samples *t* test. First, you already know the logic of the paired samples *t* test from reading this far into the chapter. Second, it's easier to calculate a paired samples *t* test than an independent samples *t* test. So let's see if my bet is right.

As I said at the start of the previous chapter, I was not a big fan of the dark as a young kid. I was never sure what I was afraid of, but that did not matter. I was afraid of monsters, but for the most part, I outgrew that specific fear at a fairly young age. I say for the most part because there are still some monster-like creatures that I do not particularly care to associate with even now that I am an adult. For example, I know snakes serve a vital purpose in the ecosystem, but candidly, I don't want to be around them. Most snakes where I live (in Michigan) are perfectly harmless, but I still don't like them. I suspect my feelings are shared by many other people. Perhaps it is the way snakes look, move, or feel to the touch (so I've been told), but many people do not like snakes.

Photos 8.1a and 8.2b Which one would be more trouble to "miss"?

Source: ©iStockphoto.com/Wirepec; ©iStockphoto.com/Mark Kostich

CONCEPTUAL UNDERSTANDING OF THE TOOL

The Study

It is against this backdrop of dislike of snakes that we discuss a research study that Brian Stirling, Madeleine Greskovich, and Dan Johnson (2014) conducted. Before we discuss their experiment, however, we need some theoretical background. Signal detection theory is concerned with the ability to detect stimuli in the environment. It relies on people's accuracies and inaccuracies to assess how well they can detect certain stimuli. People are asked whether they detected (e.g., saw, heard) a particular stimulus. For instance, if you were in my office right now and I asked you whether you smelled a coffee aroma, you likely would say "yes" because there is dark-roast coffee brewing. This would be called a "hit" because you detected a stimulus that was present. If you said that you did not smell the coffee, even though it was present, this would be called a "miss" because you did not detect a stimulus that was present. Misses can be bad because there are certainly stimuli you want to be able to detect. If you can't smell the coffee, that's not a huge deal. But if your dorm was on fire, you would definitely want to detect the smell of smoke or hear the fire alarm blaring. In addition to "hits" and "misses," there are what's called "false alarms." Sometimes we think we detect a stimulus when in fact nothing was there. If you said you smelled roses in my office, that would be a "false alarm" because you are detecting a stimulus that does not exist in my office (and there have never been roses in my office, but if you send me some, it would brighten my day).

Now that we have a handle on the basics of signal detection theory, let's return to Stirling et al.'s (2014) research. They used signal detection theory to test the notion that people would display a response bias toward snakes. That is to say, when presented with a stimulus for a brief period of time, people would be likely to respond in ways that indicated they saw a snake rather than some less dangerous stimulus. What would potentially be worse (that is, potentially more dangerous): to think you saw a snake when what you saw was just a cute salamander (a false alarm for snakes), or to not see a snake that was slithering toward you (missing the snake)? I think missing the snake could have more severe consequences than mistaking a salamander for a snake.

In their experiment, Stirling and colleagues (2014) had 15 college students come into a lab and sit at a computer. Pictures of snakes (fear-inducing) and salamanders (harmless) were flashed on the center of the computer screen. In total, 52 images were presented (13 of snakes, 13 of salamanders, and 26 irrelevant images), each for 20 ms. After each stimulus was presented, participants had to indicate whether it was a fear-relevant stimulus (which was a snake) or a fear-irrelevant stimulus (which was a salamander). They did this by pressing the "Z" or "M" key on the computer's keyboard, respectively.

In this experiment, a *false alarm* was recorded if a participant was presented with a salamander (harmless) but indicated that a snake (fear-inducing) was present. This situation is like when I was a kid and thought I saw a monster under my bed, but instead it was just a stuffed animal. A *miss* was recorded if a participant was presented with a snake but indicated that a salamander was present. This situation is like thinking your roommate is playing a joke on you when you find what you think is a plastic spider in your bed, only it turns out to be a real spider. Bad things can happen when we miss a dangerous stimulus; again, it's like failing to see a car coming when crossing the street. Both false alarms and misses are considered mistakes in signal detection theory. Stirling and colleagues (2014) were interested in the types of mistakes that people make.

Figure 8.1 provides a visual depiction of this experiment. Use it and your knowledge gained to this point in the chapter to make sure we understand some basics before moving on.

LEARNING CHECK

1. What is the difference between an independent samples *t* test and a paired samples *t* test?

   A: The independent samples *t* test is used to compare two group means when each person in the sample provides one datapoint (that is, participants are in one and only one group). The paired samples *t* test is used when each person in the sample provides two datapoints.

2. What is the independent variable in Stirling et al.'s (2014) experiment?

   A: The two types of incorrect responses are false alarms and misses.

3. What is the dependent variable in Stirling et al.'s (2014) experiment?

   A: The difference between the proportion of false alarms and the proportion of misses.

The Tool

As noted previously, the name of the statistical tool we need to compare means generated by the same people at different points in time is called the **paired samples *t* test**. It is called "paired samples" because each person in the sample is contributing data to two means. Sometimes you will see the paired samples *t* test referred to as the *dependent samples* t *test*. This too makes sense when contrasting it with the independent samples *t* test, in which each person in the sample is contributing data to only one group mean. Additionally, some researchers like to call it the *correlated samples* t *test*. In this chapter, we will call it the paired samples *t* test, but just be aware of this terminology. Stirling et al.'s (2014) experiment is an example of a **within-subjects design**. A between-subjects design requires that each participant appear in one and only one group. A within-subjects design requires that each participant appear in both groups.

Paired samples *t* test: statistical tool used to compare the difference between two means provided by the same sample of people.

Figure 8.1 Elements of Stirling et al.'s (2014) Experiment

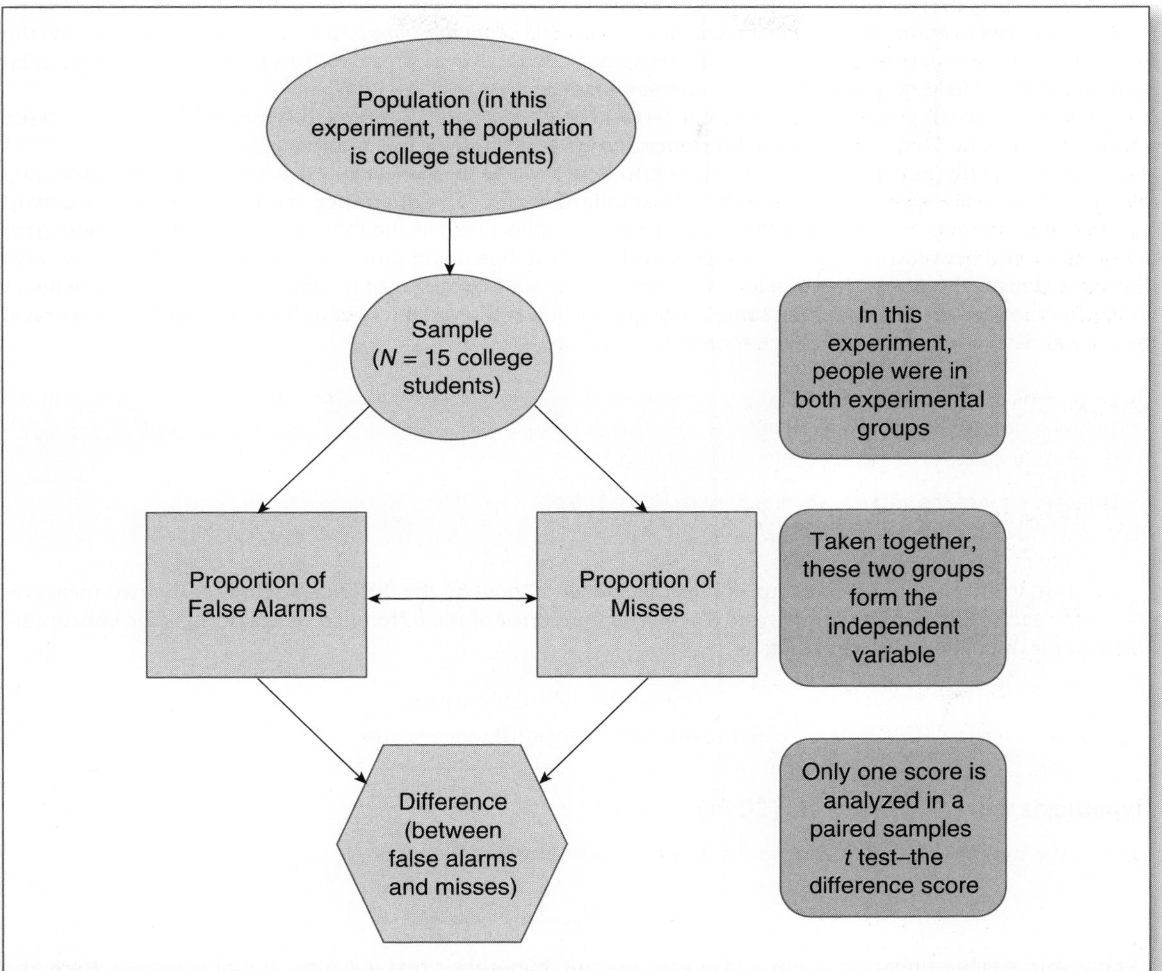

Within-subjects design: research design in which each participant provides at least two responses to be compared. Stated differently, each participant is in every group created by the independent variable.

Ingredients

What is the logic of the paired samples t test? Just like the independent samples t test, *it is a comparison of whether mean differences in the sample are generalizable to the population from which that sample was drawn*. However, with the paired samples t test, each person in the same provides two datapoints. In other words, *the two means being compared are from the same people*; even though it may look like two separate groups in this experiment, please realize that in a within-subjects design, people are "randomly assigned" to all groups in the experiment. Indeed, in a within-subjects design, random assignment is less of a consideration than it is in a between-subjects design. Now let's get to the three conceptual ingredients of the paired samples *t* test.

First, *we need to know each person's score on each variable being measured*. Here, we would need to know the proportion of false alarms (choosing a snake when a salamander was presented) and misses (choosing a salamander when a snake was presented) each person made.

Second, from each person's score on each variable being measured, *we need to derive the difference between those two numbers*. That is, we need a **difference score** between these two numbers.

Third, and finally, as not every person's difference score will be the same, *we need to account for this variability among the difference scores*. Therefore, we need **standard error of the difference scores**. Think of the standard error of the difference scores (used here in the paired samples *t* test) as the fraternal twin of the standard error of the difference between the means (used previously in the independent samples *t* test). Conceptually, they serve the same statistical purpose. Just like its fraternal twin, the standard error of the difference scores is dependent in part on sample size. The larger the sample size and the lower the variability of difference scores, the lower will be the standard error of the difference scores.

Difference score: number that is the difference between a person's performance in one experimental condition and his or her performance in a second experimental condition.

Standard error of the difference scores: standard deviation of a mean difference score within a sample.

In short, to conduct a paired samples *t* test, we need to know (a) the difference score on the two measurements for each person in the sample and (b) the standard error of the difference scores. Here is the conceptual formula for the paired samples *t* test:

$$t = \frac{\text{Mean of the difference scores}}{\text{Standard error of the difference scores}}$$

Hypothesis from Stirling et al. (2014)

What is the hypothesis that Stirling and colleagues (2014) tested? Here it is:

$$H_o: \mu_{\text{flase alarms}} = \mu_{\text{misses}}$$

I know you're sick of hearing it, but it is always the null hypothesis that a statistical tool is testing. Here, the researchers are testing the notion that there will be no difference in the proportion of false alarms (reporting a snake when a salamander was present) and misses (reporting a salamander when a snake was present).

Here is the research hypothesis (H_r) that the authors stated:

> "we hypothesized that individuals would show a response bias toward fear-relevant stimuli (snakes)" (p. 38).
>
> "A response bias toward snakes . . . is present if the proportion of false alarms exceeds the proportion of misses (Macmillan & Creelman, 2005)" (p. 39).

Symbolically, we have

$$H_r: \mu_{\text{flase alarms}} \neq \mu_{\text{misses}}$$

LEARNING CHECK

1. What is the difference between a within-subjects design and a between-subjects design?

   A: In a between-subjects design, each participant is randomly assigned to one and only one group that is being compared. In a within-subjects design, each participant appears in multiple groups that are being compared.

2. Explain why Stirling et al.'s (2014) experiment requires the use of a paired samples *t* test.

   A: Each participant provided two datapoints. That is, each participant had a number of false alarms and a number of misses that the researchers would compare by using a paired samples *t* test.

3. How is the standard error of the difference scores (used in a paired samples *t* test) similar to the standard error of the difference between the means (used in an independent samples *t* test)?

   A: The standard error of the difference scores is similar to the standard error of the difference between the means because they are both the denominator of their respective *t* tests.

4. Ford Motors (Dearborn, MI) has hired you as a world-renowned organizational psychologist and soon-to-be expert on paired samples *t* tests to conduct research to see whether its employees are more productive before lunch or after lunch. You start by sampling the quantity of work of six people using a 1 (*minimal productivity*) to 7 (*a great deal of productivity*) range. Here are the results of your initial research:

Before Lunch	After Lunch	Difference Score (D)
5	4	1
6	7	−1
6	4	2
5	2	3
4	1	3
5	6	−1

   In addition, you find that the standard error of the difference scores is 0.75 (for now, just trust me that it is 0.75). Plug in the numbers to the conceptual formula for the paired samples *t* test (you'll need to figure out the average difference score yourself).

   A:

$$t = \frac{1.167}{0.75}$$

$$t = 1.56$$

Now that we've explained Stirling et al.'s (2014) methodology, the conceptual logic of the paired samples *t* test, and the hypothesis being tested, let's look at their results. Keep in mind that the means being compared are proportions. Sometimes it's easy to get lost in such basic considerations when learning new statistical concepts. Always slow down and read everything carefully so that you don't lose sight of the "big picture" of what statistical analyses tell us in plain English.

Interpreting the Tool

Here is what Stirling et al. (2014, p. 39) found:

> The paired samples t test revealed that the proportion of false alarms ($M = 0.259$, $SD = 0.157$) was significantly greater than the proportion of misses ($M = 0.069$, $SD = 0.060$), $t(14) = 3.76$, $p = .002$, $d = 0.97$, 95% CI [0.08, 0.30].

We'll break down the statistics in a just a moment, but in plain English, people were more likely to report seeing a snake when it was a salamander (commit a false alarm) than they were to report seeing a salamander when it was a snake (commit a miss). How did Stirling et al. (2014) reach this conclusion? Let's break down their statistical presentation, most of which you already know (whether you believe you do or not).

We first have the means and standard deviations for the proportion of false alarms and proportion of misses. On the surface, this reads a little bit like Tim Kasser and Kennon Sheldon's (2000) results we discussed in the previous chapter. It looks like there are two groups, a false alarm group and a misses group. Remember that in this experiment, people in the sample provided both false alarms and misses. No mean difference score is provided, but it would simply be the difference of the two means (0.259 and 0.069, which is 0.19).

Let's look at the t test statistic. How did this test statistic of 3.76 appear? Remember the conceptual formula for the paired samples t test:

$$t = \frac{\text{Mean of the difference scores}}{\text{Standard error of the difference scores}}$$

Let's fill in this formula with the numbers that Stirling et al. (2014) reported:

$$3.76 = \frac{0.259 - 0.069}{\text{Standard error of the difference scores}}$$

Again, similar to the standard error of the difference between the means, the standard error of the difference scores will not be given in published research. We'll calculate this statistic in the next section of this chapter, but for now, use your basic algebra skills to derive it. Take 0.19 (the mean difference score and numerator of the t statistic), and divide it by 3.76. Presto, the standard error of the difference scores is 0.05.

In parentheses after the letter t, you will find the degrees of freedom (*dfs*) for this analysis. Degrees of freedom are dependent on sample size. The more degrees of freedom a researcher has (or, in other words, the larger the researcher's sample size), the more he or she can generalize sample results to the population. The calculation of the degrees of freedom for the paired samples t test is slightly different than for the independent samples t test. Specifically, for the paired samples t test,

$$\text{Degrees of freedom} = \text{Sample size} - 1$$

For the independent samples t test, degrees of freedom were calculated as "sample size – 2." Why is it "– 1" for the paired samples t test? In practice, there is only one group of data being analyzed; specifically, a group of difference scores. Here, the sample size was 15 people, so $15 - 1 = 14$. That's how we got our 14 degrees of freedom.

Testing the null hypothesis

Armed with our t statistic and degrees of freedom, we are ready to see whether we can generalize our result from our sample to the population from which it was drawn. I bet you can answer this question now. This is the p value. Remember that the p value is the likelihood that our mean difference score was due to random variation. Here, that probability was .002 (or .2%). Because this probability is less than .05 (5%), we can indeed reject the null hypothesis and generalize our result from this sample to the population. Easy enough, but let's not forget the "behind-the-scenes" processes that led to this conclusion.

Once again, consult Appendix B, where you will see your old friend, the critical values for the distribution of possible *t* statistics. The *t* statistic that Stirling et al. (2014) obtained (which was 3.76) must be compared with the correct critical value. If the *t* statistic obtained is greater than the critical value, we would reject the null hypothesis and be able to generalize our result from the sample to the population.

By using the conservative two-tailed hypothesis test, we have an alpha level of .05 and 14 degrees of freedom. Coincidentally, in this instance, the precise degrees of freedom are given in the appendix for 14 degrees of freedom. By using an alpha level of .05 and a two-tailed test, we see our critical value is ± 2.145. As displayed in Figure 8.2, our *t* statistic of 3.76 falls in the region of null hypothesis rejection; therefore, we reject the notion that there is no difference between the proportion of false alarms reported and the proportion of misses reported. We conclude that within the population, people are more likely to report seeing a snake (something dangerous) when it was a salamander than they were to report seeing a salamander (something not dangerous) when it was a snake.

Figure 8.2 A Visual Comparison of the Test Statistic (3.76) With the Critical Value (±2.145); Because the Test Statistic Falls in the Region of Null Hypothesis Rejection, We Reject the Null Hypothesis

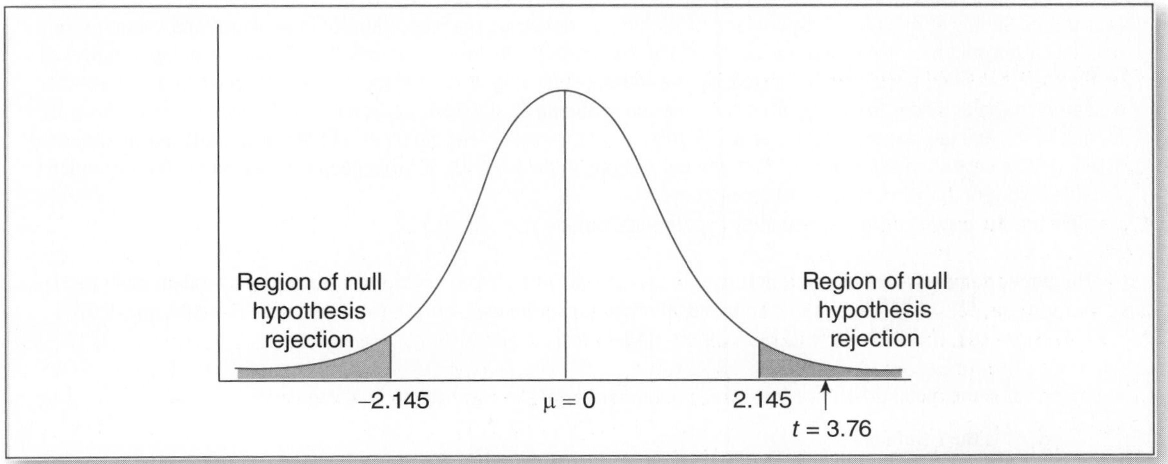

Extending our null hypothesis test

Let's finish this section by examining the last two pieces of Stirling et al.'s (2014) results, the effect size and the confidence interval (CI).

Recall that an effect size is a measure of how powerful the independent variable is in affecting people's behavior. Just as with the independent samples *t* test, the effect size is most frequently reported with a Cohen's *d* (or just *d*). Here, we have a *d* of 0.97. The criteria for interpreting Cohen's *d* (Cohen, 1992) are the same as they are for the independent samples *t* test. That is, a Cohen's *d* of less than 0.20 is trivial; an effect size between 0.20 and 0.50 is weak; an effect size between 0.51 and 0.80 is moderate; and an effect size greater than 0.80 is strong. Thus, in our instance, our effect size of 0.97 is strong. Therefore, the independent variable has a strong effect on the dependent variable.

Finally, we need to consider the 95% confidence interval (CI). Recall that a confidence interval is an estimate that contains the population mean difference a certain percentage of time, assuming we can sample that population repeatedly. Here, the 95% CI is [0.08, 0.30]. If we could draw an unlimited number of samples, 95% of those samples would contain a mean difference between 0.08 and 0.30. Notice that this range does not include 0. In other words, we can be confident that a difference exists in the population. Had the confidence interval included 0, there would be a chance that the difference does not exist in the population.

Assumptions of the tool

As with the independent samples *t* test (and other inferential statistical tools we will learn about in later chapters), there are assumptions that need to be met for us to use the paired samples *t* test. For the paired samples *t* test, these assumptions are the same as they are for the independent samples *t* test with a couple of differences.

First, rather than the distribution of scores within each group being normally distributed, as was the assumption with the independent samples *t* test, for the paired samples *t* test, the difference scores must be normally distributed.

Second, we don't need to worry about the homogeneity of variances because with a paired samples *t* test, each participant contributes data to both group means. Therefore, if the variances of the two groups are different (heterogeneous) in a paired samples *t* test, it cannot be a function of our sample or of random assignment.

LEARNING CHECK

Let's extend Stirling et al.'s (2014) experiment. In addition to measuring the proportions of false alarms and misses as they did, they also could have measured the reaction time that participants took to identify the animal presented. It may well be the case that when asked whether a creature is a snake, people might respond more quickly than when asked whether a creature is a salamander. In this hypothetical extension of Stirling et al.'s work, participants are shown pictures of animals; for half of the animals shown, they are asked, "Is this creature a snake?" For the other half of the animals shown, they are asked, "Is this creature a salamander?" The amount of time, in milliseconds, it takes people to respond is the dependent variable. A lower number indicates a faster response time.

Here are the results of these completely hypothetical data:

The paired samples *t* test revealed that people took longer when asked whether a creature was a salamander ($M = 1{,}500$ ms, $SD = 447$ ms) than when asked whether a creature was a snake ($M = 850$ ms, $SD = 364$ ms), $t(14) = 4.73$, $p < .05$, $d = 1.22$, 95% CI [355.29 ms, 944.71 ms].

1. What is the mean difference score (i.e., the numerator of the *t* statistic to be computed)?
2. What is the *t* statistic?
3. What is the standard error of the difference scores?
4. How were the degrees of freedom computed?
5. According to Appendix B, what is the critical value that was used to see whether we reject or do not reject the null hypothesis?
6. What is the probability that the mean difference was due to random variation?
7. Did the researchers reject or fail to reject the null hypothesis?
8. Given your answer to the previous question, what does that mean in plain English?
9. By using Jacob Cohen's (1992) guidelines, interpret the effect size.
10. Interpret the 95% CI.

Answers

1. 1,500 − 850 = 650 is the mean difference score
2. $t = 4.73$
3. 137.42
4. sample size − 1, so here, we have 15 − 1 = 14 degrees of freedom
5. ±2.145
6. $p < .05$ (less than 5%)
7. Because the t statistic exceeded the critical value, we reject the null hypothesis.
8. We can generalize our result to the population; more specifically, we can conclude that people take longer to identify a creature when asked whether it's a salamander than when asked whether it's is a snake.
9. This is a strong effect size. That is, the creature people were asked to identify had a strong effect on how long it took them to respond.
10. The 95% CI is 355.29 ms to 944.71 ms, meaning that repeated sampling of this population would lead us to find that 95% of those samples would have a mean difference between 355.29 ms and 944.71 ms. Because this interval does not contain 0, it means we can be confident that, in the population, people respond more quickly when asked whether a creature is a snake than when asked whether a creature is a salamander.

USING YOUR NEW STATISTICAL TOOL

Hand-Calculating the Paired Samples *t* Test

As we did with the independent samples *t* test, we will first hand-calculate a paired samples *t* test, after which we will learn how to do and interpret one using the software program Statistical Package for the Social Sciences (SPSS).

Let's take the extension of Stirling et al.'s (2014) experiment that we used in the previous Learning Check. Here are data from six participants:

Experimental Group	
"Did you see a salamander?"	"Did you see a snake?"
500 ms	300 ms
1,000 ms	400 ms
2,000 ms	800 ms
1,500 ms	1,000 ms
1,200 ms	1,200 ms
1,200 ms	700 ms

The independent variable is the type of animal participants were asked about, a salamander or a snake. Because participants were asked about both types of animals, we have a within-subjects design.

Step 1: State hypotheses

Let's use these data to hand-calculate the paired samples *t* test. Always keep in mind the hypothesis that is being statistically tested (yes, the null hypothesis):

$$H_o: \mu_{\text{see a snake?}} = \mu_{\text{see a salamander?}}$$

In terms of a research hypothesis, we would expect to see a difference in reaction time depending on the question being asked. We would likely expect this:

$$H_r: \mu_{\text{see a snake?}} < \mu_{\text{see a salamander?}}$$

Remember that when examining reaction times, a lower number indicates a faster response.

Step 2: Calculate the mean difference score

To get the mean difference score, first obtain the difference score for each participant:

	"Did you see a salamander"	"Did you see a snake"	Difference Score (D)
	500 ms	300 ms	200 ms
	1,000 ms	400 ms	600 ms
	2,000 ms	800 ms	1,200 ms
	1,500 ms	1,000 ms	500 ms
	1,200 ms	1,200 ms	0 ms
	1,200 ms	700 ms	500 ms
Means	1,233.33 ms	733.33 ms	500 ms

$$\text{Mean difference score} = \frac{(200+600+1{,}200+500+0+500)}{6} = \frac{3{,}000}{6} = 500 \text{ ms}$$

That's all we need for the numerator of our *t* statistic:

$$t = \frac{500 \text{ ms}}{\text{Standard error of the difference scores}}$$

Step 3: Calculate the standard error of the difference scores

As was the case with the standard error of the difference between the means when discussing the independent samples *t* test, this is the most involved calculation we need to do in hand-calculating a paired samples *t* test.

Here is the formula for the standard error of the differences scores:

$$S_D = \frac{\text{Standard deviation of the difference scores}}{\text{Square root of the sample size}}$$

To get the standard deviation of the difference scores, we are simply computing a standard deviation, something that is no stranger to us at this point in the class. Let's do it.

Difference Score	Mean Difference Score	Deviation From Mean	Deviation From Mean^2
200 ms	500 ms	−300	90,000
600 ms	500 ms	100	10,000
1,200 ms	500 ms	700	490,000
500 ms	500 ms	0	0
0 ms	500 ms	−500	250,000
500 ms	500 ms	0	0

Now, we need to sum the squared differences scores:

$$(90{,}000 + 10{,}000 + 490{,}000 + 0 + 250{,}000 + 0) = 840{,}000$$

Next, we divide this summation by the sample size − 1. Here, that would be 6 − 1 = 5.

So:

$$\frac{840{,}000}{5} = 168{,}000$$

Of course, we now need to take the square root of the quotient we just calculated:

$$\text{Square root of } 168{,}000 = 409.88$$

Thus, our standard deviation of the difference scores is 409.88. Let's now plug in our numbers to get the standard error of the difference scores:

$$S_D = \frac{409.88}{\text{Square root of the sample size}}$$

Remember that in this example, the sample size was 6. The square root of 6 is 2.45. Thus, our standard error of the difference scores is

$$S_D = \frac{409.88}{2.45}$$

$$S_D = 167.30$$

Step 4: Calculate the *t* test statistic

Recall that the mean difference score was 500, which is the numerator of the paired samples *t* test. We just calculated the denominator of this test, with a standard error of the differences scores of 167.29. Let's plug these numbers into the formula for the paired samples *t* test:

$$t = \frac{500}{167.29}$$
$$t = 2.99$$

Of course, we need to do a little more work to give meaning to our *t* test statistic of 2.99. Specifically, can we generalize our mean difference scores (of 500 ms) from our sample to the population? To answer this question, our next step is to calculate our degrees of freedom, which we will use to locate our critical value with which to compare our *t* test statistic.

Step 5: Determine degrees of freedom (*dfs*)

Remember that for the paired samples *t* test, the degrees of freedom = sample size − 1. So, here, we have a sample size of 6, giving us degrees of freedom = 5. By knowing our degrees of freedom, we can now find our critical value with which to compare our *t* statistic. If our *t* test statistic exceeds the critical value, we would reject the null hypothesis.

Step 6: Locate the critical value

We consult Appendix B to find our critical value. By returning to our two-tailed test of the null hypothesis with a significant level of .05, we see that our critical value is ± 2.571.

Step 7: Make a decision about the null hypothesis

Therefore, our test statistic needs to be greater than ± 2.571 for us to reject the null hypothesis. As Figure 8.3 displays, indeed, our *t* statistic of 2.99 does fall in the region of null hypothesis rejection. We therefore reject the null hypothesis and conclude that people responded more quickly when being asked whether a creature was a snake than when asked whether a creature was a salamander.

Step 8: Calculate an effect size

For the purposes of example, we used a small dataset so that we didn't have to spend all day doing hand calculations. Let's find out just how powerful the effect of the independent variable was on speed of response. Here comes the effect size. For the paired samples *t* test, we calculate Cohen's *d* as follows:

$$d = \frac{\text{Mean difference score}}{\text{Standard deviation of the difference scores}}$$

We've calculated both components of this formula, so let's plug them in:

$$d = \frac{500}{409.88}$$
$$d = 1.22$$

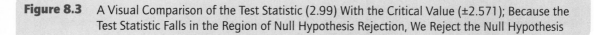

Figure 8.3 A Visual Comparison of the Test Statistic (2.99) With the Critical Value (±2.571); Because the Test Statistic Falls in the Region of Null Hypothesis Rejection, We Reject the Null Hypothesis

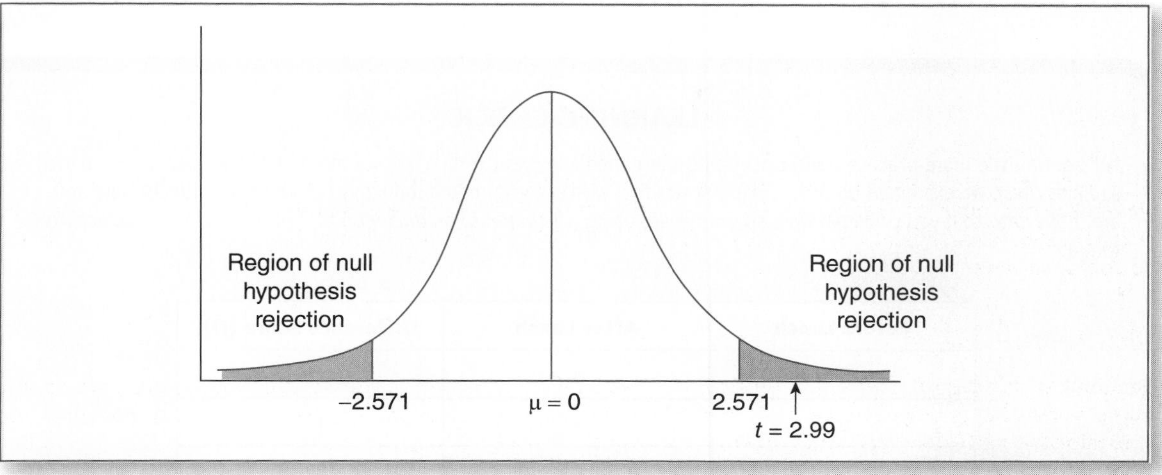

Our effect size (*d*) of 1.22 is strong, according to Cohen's (1992) established criteria discussed previously in this chapter.

Step 9: Determine the confidence interval

Finally, let's take a look at our confidence interval around the mean difference. We want to know with 95% confidence what the range of difference scores will be in the population. Here is the way we calculate the confidence interval for a paired samples *t* test:

$$95\%\ \text{CI} = \text{Mean difference} \pm \text{critical value for } t \times (\text{standard error of the difference scores})$$

As we've calculated all the information we need for this formula, here it all is:

Mean difference = 500 ms

Critical value for $t = \pm 2.571$

Standard error of the mean difference scores = 167.29

$95\%\ \text{CI} = 500 \pm 2.571(167.29)$

$95\%\ \text{CI} = 500 \pm 430.103$

$95\%\ \text{CI} = [69.897, 930.103]$

This range does not contain 0, so we can be confident that the difference we observed in our sample does in fact exist in the population. One note: This looks like a large range, but remember that in this example, we are dealing with milliseconds. Thus, even the high end of the range is less than one full second of time.

Here is how we report this result in APA style:

The paired samples t test revealed that people took longer when asked whether a creature was a salamander (M = 1,233.33 ms, SD = 500.67 ms) than when asked whether a creature was a snake (M = 733.33 ms, SD = 344.48 ms), $t(5) = 2.99$, $p < .05$, d = 1.22, 95% CI [69.90 ms,930.10 ms].

LEARNING CHECK

Let's get a little more practice hand-calculating the paired samples t test. When we discussed "The Tool" of the paired samples t test, we examined data by looking at whether workers were more productive before or after lunch. Here again are those data that you collected from six employees using a 1 (*minimal productivity*) to 7 (*a great deal of productivity*) range.

Before Lunch	After Lunch	Difference Score (D)
5	4	1
6	7	−1
6	4	2
5	2	3
4	1	3
5	6	−1

Questions to Answer:

1. What is the hypothesis being tested?
2. What is the mean difference score?
3. What is the standard error of the difference between the means?
4. What is the t statistic?
5. How many degrees of freedom do the researchers have for this analysis?
6. By using Appendix B, approximate the critical value that was used to see whether we reject or do not reject the null hypothesis.
7. What is the probability that the difference between the two groups' means was due to random variation?
8. Did the researcher reject or fail to reject the null hypothesis?
9. Given your answer to the previous question, what does that mean in plain English?
10. By using Cohen's (1992) guidelines, interpret the effect size.

11. Interpret the 95% CI.
12. Write these results for the text of an article by using proper APA style.

Answers

1. There will be no difference in employee productivity before lunch or after lunch.
2. Mean difference = $\frac{7}{6} = 1.167$
3. 0.75
4. $t = \frac{1.167}{0.75}$

   $t = 1.56$
5. 5
6. ±2.571
7. Greater than 5% because the *t* statistic of 1.56 is less than the critical value of ±2.571.
8. Given the answer to question 7, we do not reject the null hypothesis.
9. Employees were equally as productive before lunch as they were after lunch.
10. $d = \frac{1.167}{1.834}$

    $d = 0.64$. This is a moderate effect size. That is, time of day is moderately predictive of an employee's productivity.
11. The 95% CI is −0.75 to 3.09, meaning that 95% of the samples drawn from the same population would be between −0.75 and 3.09. Because this interval contains 0, we cannot be confident there is a difference in productivity before lunch and after lunch.
12. Here is the proper write-up in APA style:

The paired samples *t* test revealed that people were as productive before lunch ($M = 5.17$, $SD = 0.75$) as they were after lunch ($M = 4.00$, $SD = 2.28$), $t(5) = 1.56$, $p > .05$, $d = 0.64$, 95% CI [−0.75, 3.09].

Paired Samples *t* Test and SPSS

We have gotten a handle on why we use paired samples *t* tests, the logic of this tool, and how to calculate this tool. Next up, we will use SPSS to run and interpret a paired samples *t* test. We have had a lot of data floating around this chapter, so how about we take the dataset we just calculated by hand, enter those data in SPSS, and interpret that output? In addition, the next Learning Check will have another dataset for you to enter into SPSS and test your ability to interpret the output.

Here again are the data we analyzed by hand from six participants. Again, remember what's going on methodologically in this extension of Stirling et al.'s (2014) research. We asked participants whether a creature flashed on the computer screen was a salamander or whether it was a snake. Then we recorded, in milliseconds, how long it took them to respond, hypothesizing that people would respond more quickly when asked whether they had seen a snake.

"Did you see a salamander?"	"Did you see a snake?"
500 ms	300 ms
1,000 ms	400 ms
2,000 ms	800 ms
1,500 ms	1,000 ms
1,200 ms	1,200 ms
1,200 ms	700 ms

Establishing your spreadsheet

Here's how to enter these data into SPSS.

As always, we need to name our variables under *Variable View*, which is in the lower left corner of the screen. We have two variables here: People were asked (1) whether they saw a salamander and (2) whether they saw a snake. So perhaps name the first variable something such as `Salamander` and the second variable something such as `Snake`. After naming each variable, please be sure to give it a label. Again, something such as "Salamander" and "Snake" should work just fine here as well. Be sure your measure is in "Scale" for each variable. Here is what your variable should look like:

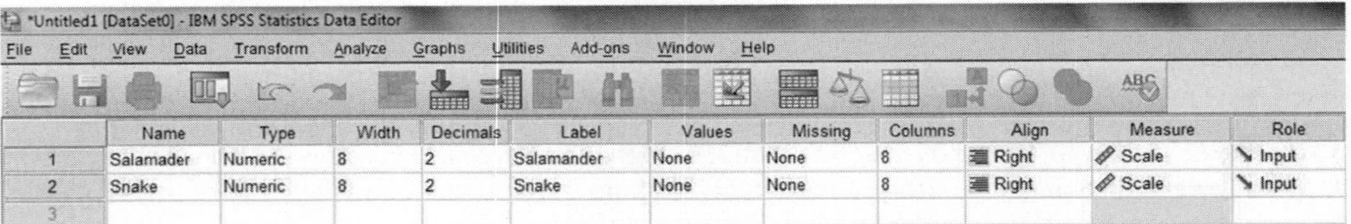

	Name	Type	Width	Decimals	Label	Values	Missing	Columns	Align	Measure	Role
1	Salamader	Numeric	8	2	Salamander	None	None	8	Right	Scale	Input
2	Snake	Numeric	8	2	Snake	None	None	8	Right	Scale	Input
3											

Now, we simply need to enter the data into SPSS. Click on *Data View*, and you can enter these data from these six participants, each of whom provided two datapoints.

Once you have entered these 12 datapoints into SPSS, you should have 6 rows of data, one for each participant, and 2 columns of data, one for each type of question they were asked. Here is what your *Data View* should look like after entering the data from these six participants:

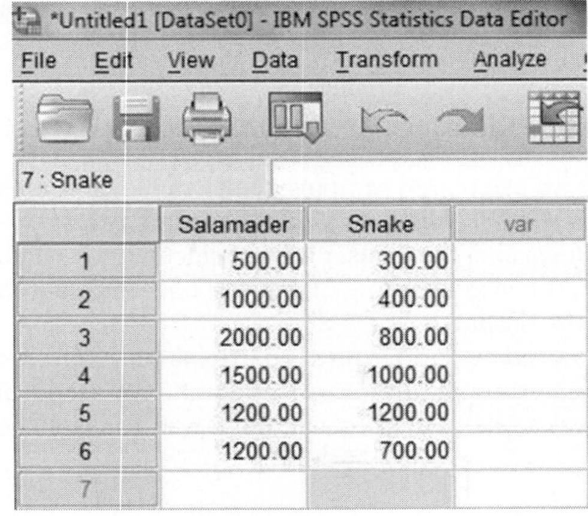

	Salamader	Snake	var
1	500.00	300.00	
2	1000.00	400.00	
3	2000.00	800.00	
4	1500.00	1000.00	
5	1200.00	1200.00	
6	1200.00	700.00	
7			

Running your analyses

You are now set to run your paired samples *t* test. Here's how you do it:

1. Click on *Analyze* → *Compare Means* → *Paired Samples T Test*.

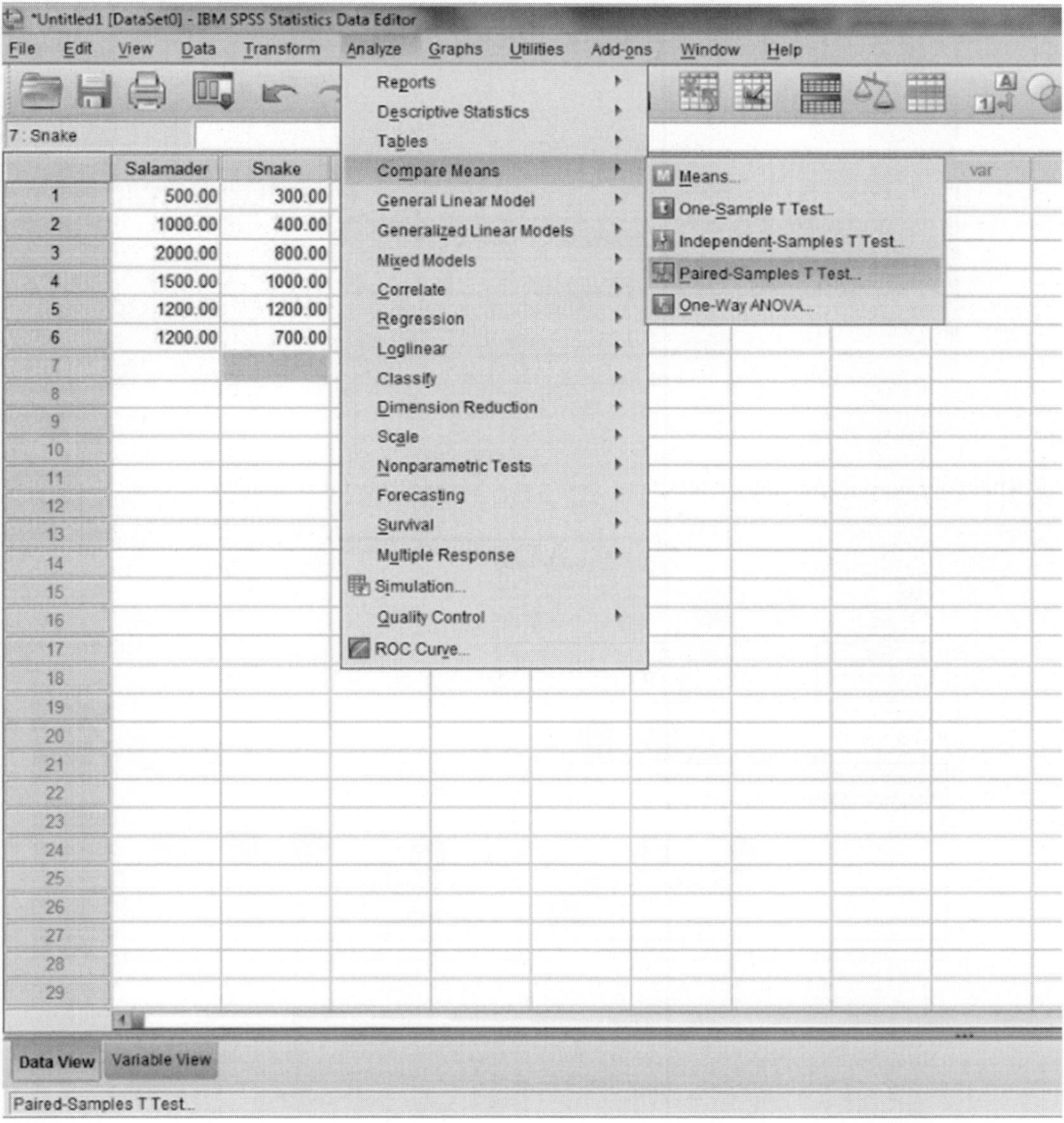

2. Now, you need to identify a "pair" of variables to compare, which is pretty easy in this case. You want to compare the `Salamander` reaction times and the `Snake` reaction times. `Salamander` can be Variable 1, and `Snake` can be Variable 2.

3. Click *OK*, and your paired samples *t* test results should come up!

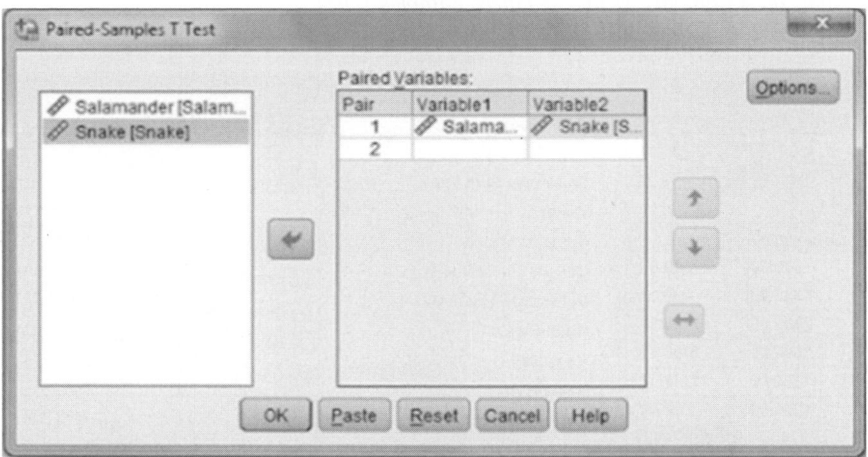

Here is what your output should look like. Let's dissect this analysis one bit at a time.

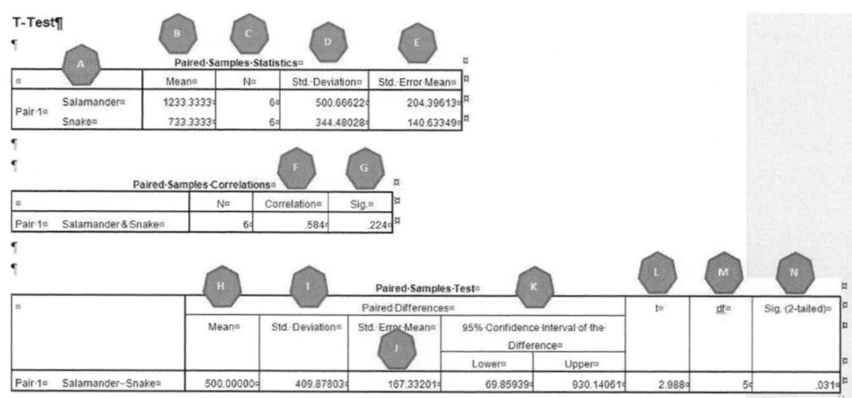

T-Test

Paired Samples Statistics

		Mean	N	Std. Deviation	Std. Error Mean
Pair 1	Salamander	1233.3333	6	500.66622	204.39613
	Snake	733.3333	6	344.48028	140.63349

Paired Samples Correlations

		N	Correlation	Sig.
Pair 1	Salamander & Snake	6	.584	.224

Paired Samples Test

		Paired Differences					t	df	Sig. (2-tailed)
		Mean	Std. Deviation	Std. Error Mean	95% Confidence Interval of the Difference				
					Lower	Upper			
Pair 1	Salamander - Snake	500.00000	409.87803	167.33201	69.85939	930.14061	2.988	5	.031

What am I looking at? Interpreting your SPSS output

A. This is *the independent variable*. More specifically, it is *the two conditions/groups* in which participants were placed in the experiment.

B. These are *the means for each condition/group*.

C. This is *the number of people in each group*. In a paired samples t test, these numbers should almost always be equal because each person is contributing data to each condition/group of the independent variable.

D. This is the *standard deviation* for each condition of the independent variable.

E. This is the *standard error of the mean* for each group. Recall from Chapter 6 that it is the standard deviation of a sampling distribution of means.

The next two pieces of information we'll see on the printout are ones that will make more sense after we cover Chapter 12 on correlations. But let's see if we can make some sense of them now as a preview of coming attractions in Chapter 12.

F. This is the *correlation coefficient between participants' scores* on each condition. Here, people provided reaction times. So, this statistic ($r = .58$) is the correlation between people's reaction times when asked whether a creature was a salamander and when asked whether a creature was a snake. A correlation greater than .50 is considered to be strong, so here, there is a strong relationship between these two variables.

G. This is the *p value, or significance level*, of the correlation coefficient. As you are well versed in the concept of statistical significance, we see that this correlation coefficient is not statistically significant.

At this point, we start getting into the nitty-gritty of the paired samples t test, and you will start to see the numbers that you calculated in the previous section of this chapter. As we continue on, some numbers we see on the printout may not match precisely with our hand calculations. That's all because of rounding, so don't let these differences bother you!

H. This is the *mean difference score*. You could calculate it from B previously, which gave the mean for each condition/group, but SPSS saves you that calculation.

I. This is the *standard deviation of the difference scores*.

J. This is the *standard error of the difference scores*. It was calculated by taking the standard deviation of the difference scores and dividing it by the square root of the sample size.

K. Here is *the 95% CI around the mean difference score*. Again, as is the case in published research, the critical values are not specified on the SPSS printout, but they are being used to calculate this confidence interval. In this case, we see that the confidence interview ranges from 69.86 ms to 930.14 ms. It does not include 0, so we can be confident that in the population, there is a difference in reaction times depending on the type of creature people are asked to identify.

L. This is the *t test statistic*. Recall how it was calculated:

$$t = \frac{\text{Mean of the difference scores}}{\text{Standard error of the difference scores}}$$

Here, the t test statistic was 2.99. Remember the mean of the difference scores was 500, and the standard error of the difference scores was 167.33.

M. These are our *degrees of freedom*. Recall that for a paired samples t test, they are calculated "sample size − 1." Here, that is $6 - 1 = 5$.

N. This is the *p value, or significance level,* of the t test statistic. Our p value here is .031. In other words, there is a 3.1% chance that our t statistic resulted from random variation (i.e., was a fluke outcome). Because it is below .05 (5%), we can reject the null hypothesis and conclude that people respond more quickly when being asked whether a creature was a snake than when asked whether a creature was a salamander.

As was the case with the independent samples *t* test, SPSS does not provide us with effect sizes. We get to calculate that information ourselves.

First, recall that Cohen's *d* is calculated as such:

$$d = \frac{\text{Mean difference scores}}{\text{Standard deviation of the difference scores}}$$

Let's pluck the numbers off the SPSS output and into this equation:

$$d = \frac{500 \text{ ms}}{409.878 \text{ ms}}$$

$$d = 1.22$$

Our *d* is a strong effect size. That is, the type of creature people are asked to identify has a strong effect on how long it takes them to respond to the question.

As a refresher, here is the APA style write-up of these analyses:

> The paired samples *t* test revealed that people took longer when asked whether a creature was a salamander (M = 1,233.33 ms, SD = 500.67 ms) than when asked whether a creature was a snake (M = 733.33 ms, SD = 344.48 ms), $t(5) = 2.99$, $p < .05$, $d = 1.22$, 95% CI [69.90 ms, 930.10 ms].

LEARNING CHECK

A psychological statistics teacher wants to find out how much his students learn from taking his class. To do this, he gives them a test on the first day of class to see what they already know about psychological statistics. Then, on the last day of class, he gives them the same test they took on the first day of class. He expects (and is hoping) that scores are higher when students take the exam on the last day of class than on the first day of class. Test scores are percentages. Here are the data from the 11 students in his class:

Test Score on Day 1	Test Score on Last Day of Class
60	90
50	75
20	85
25	80
45	88
56	65
70	80
20	50
45	65
35	40
80	65

First, enter these data into SPSS and run your analyses. Here is what your output should look like:

T-Test

[DataSet0]

Paired Samples Statistics

		Mean	N	Std. Deviation	Std. Error Mean
Pair 1	Day 1 test score	46.0000	11	19.89975	6.00000
	Last day of class score	71.1818	11	15.91740	4.79928

Paired Samples Correlations

		N	Correlation	Sig.
Pair 1	Day 1 test score & Last day of class score	11	.176	.605

Paired Samples Test

		Paired Differences					t	df	Sig. (2-tailed)
					95% Confidence Interval of the Difference				
		Mean	Std. Deviation	Std. Error Mean	Lower	Upper			
Pair 1	Day 1 test score - Last day of class score	-25.18182	23.19404	6.99327	-40.76379	-9.59985	-3.601	10	.005

Second, use the output to answer the following questions (feel free to use the output to check and make sure you entered the data correctly and ran the proper analysis):

1. What is the hypothesis being tested?
2. What is the mean difference score?
3. What is the standard error of the difference between the means?
4. What is the *t* test statistic?
5. How many degrees of freedom do the researchers have for this analysis?
6. By using Appendix B, locate the critical value that was used to see whether we reject or do not reject the null hypothesis.
7. What is the probability that the difference between the two exam means was due to random variation?
8. Did the researchers reject or fail to reject the null hypothesis?
9. Given your answer to the previous question, what does that mean in plain English?
10. By using Cohen's (1992) guidelines, interpret the effect size.
11. Interpret the 95% CI.
12. Write these results for the text of an article by using proper APA style.

Answers

1. There will be no difference in exam scores at the start of the semester and at the end of the semester.
2. Day 1 mean = 46.00; last day mean = 71.18; mean difference = −25.18
3. 6.99
4. $t = -3.601$

(Continued)

(Continued)

5. $df = 10$
6. ±2.228
7. p value = .005 or 0.5%
8. Because the t test statistic of −3.601 exceeded the critical value of ±2.228, we reject the null hypothesis.
9. Students performed better on the exam after completing their psychological statistics course than before taking this course. Thus, it appears students learned something from taking the class.
10. $d = \frac{-25.18}{23.194}$

    $d = 1.09$. This is a strong effect size. That is, the time at which the exam was taken was strongly predictive of performance on that test.
11. The 95% CI is −40.76 to −9.60, meaning that 95% of the samples drawn from the same population would be between −40.76 and −9.60. This interval does not contain 0, so we can be confident that students perform better on the exam after than before they take a class in psychological statistics.
12. Here is the proper write-up in APA style:

The paired samples t test revealed that students performed better on the exam after taking the class (M = 71.18%, SD = 15.92%) than before taking the class (M = 46.00%, SD = 16.90%), $t(10) = -3.601$, $p = .005$, $d = 1.09$, 95% CI [−40.76, −9.60].

CHAPTER APPLICATION QUESTIONS

1. Why is the paired samples t test called a "paired" test?
2. What would be the degrees of freedom for a paired samples t test with a sample size of 23 people?
   a) 24 c) 23
   b) 22 d) 21
3. Suppose you conducted a paired samples t test with a sample size of 18 people. By using a one-tailed hypothesis test with an alpha level of .05, what would the critical value be?
4. Referring to the previous question, if you used a two-tailed hypothesis test, what would the critical value be?
5. All other things being equal, what will happen to the value of the paired samples t test statistic as:
   a) the sample size decreases?
   b) the standard error of the difference scores decreases?
   c) the mean of the difference scores decreases?

Answers

1. Because the data being analyzed come from people in two (a pair of) groups.
2. b
3. 1.740 or −1.740
4. ±2.110
5. a) *t* statistic decreases
   b) *t* statistic increases
   c) *t* statistic decreases

QUESTIONS FOR CLASS DISCUSSION

1. (a) Methodologically, what is the difference between an independent samples *t* test and a paired samples *t* test? (b) When computing a paired-samples *t* test, how is it different from an independent samples *t* test?
2. Assuming the same number of people is used in both analyses, would the independent samples *t* test or the paired samples *t* test be more likely to yield statistically significant results? Why?
3. A pharmaceutical company is interested in learning whether a new drug reduces postoperative pain. Thirteen patients are asked on a scale of 1 (*no pain*) to 7 (*extreme pain*) how much pain they are experiencing before receiving the drug and two hours after ingesting the drug. Use this APA style report of a paired samples *t* test to answer the questions that follow it:

   The paired samples *t* test revealed that people reported similar levels of pain before taking the drug ($M = 4.77$, $SD = 1.59$) and two hours after taking the drug ($M = 4.00$, $SD = 1.78$), $t(12) = 1.81$, $p = .096$, $d = 0.50$, 95% CI [−0.16, 1.70].

   a) What was the hypothesis being tested?
   b) What is the mean difference score?
   c) What is the *t* test statistic?
   d) What is the standard error of the difference scores?
   e) How many degrees of freedom do the researchers have for this analysis?
   f) By using Appendix B, locate the critical value that was used to see whether we reject or do not reject the null hypothesis.
   g) What is the probability that the difference between the two means was due to random variation?
   h) Did the research reject or fail to reject the null hypothesis?
   i) Given your answer to the previous question, what does that mean in plain English?
   j) By using Cohen's (1992) guidelines, interpret the effect size.
   k) Interpret the 95% CI.

4. Suppose a study was designed to test the hypothesis of equal means on the final examination scores for an experimental teaching method and the traditional lecture method. Participants were randomly assigned to one of the two methods, classes were taught, and final examination scores were recorded. Which type of hypothesis testing tool should be used to assess whether there is a difference in the final exam scores of the two teaching techniques? Explain your choice.

   a) one-sample *t* test
   b) paired samples *t* test
   c) independent samples *t* test

5. Related to the previous question, suppose the researcher had access to only one class. She decided to teach half of the material using the experimental teaching method and the other half of the material using the traditional lecture method. Which type of hypothesis testing tool should be used to assess whether there is a difference in the final exam scores of the two teaching techniques? Explain your choice.

   a) one-sample *t* test
   b) paired samples *t* test
   c) independent samples *t* test

CHAPTER 9

Comparing Three or More Group Means

The One-Way, Between-Subjects Analysis of Variance (ANOVA)

After reading this chapter, you will be able to

- Differentiate between the independent samples *t* test and the one-way, between-subjects ANOVA
- Interpret the conceptual ingredients of the one-way, between-subjects ANOVA
- Interpret an APA style presentation of a one-way, between-subjects ANOVA
- Hand-calculate all ingredients for a one-way, between-subjects ANOVA
- Conduct and interpret a one-way, between-subjects ANOVA using SPSS

Last night, I went to eat at a local pizza place, and when the waitress asked what I wanted to drink, I said "Coke." She asked whether Pepsi® (PepsiCo, Inc., Purchase, NY) was OK, and I said it was. To me, Coke® (Coca-Cola Company, Atlanta, GA) and Pepsi are interchangeable drinks. However, I rarely drink either of these types of soft drinks. I like Dr. Pepper® (Dr. Pepper Snapple Group, Plano, TX) more than Coke or Pepsi. Being a research psychologist, I immediately thought of a research study after the waitress took our drink orders. I bet (i.e., offer a research hypothesis) that if we compared which type of soda people liked best—Coke, Pepsi, or Dr. Pepper—that people would like Dr. Pepper more than Coke or Pepsi.[1] To conduct this study, we could ask people to try a sip of one type of soda, then rate it on a 1 (*do not like it at all*) to 9 (*like it very much*) response range. To analyze the data from this study, which contains three types of soda, we would need to use a tool that we are going to learn about in this and the next two chapters.

In the previous two chapters, we learned about tools to compare means from two groups or samples of data. Indeed, the independent samples and paired samples *t* tests are the foundation for any comparison of group-level data. However, sometimes we need to make more than one group-level comparison. Obviously, we can learn more information from making more comparisons. In our example, we can learn whether people prefer Coke to Pepsi, Coke to Dr. Pepper, and Pepsi to Dr. Pepper. In addition, we can compare multiple treatments to no treatment. For instance, maybe people prefer water to any of these three types of sodas. In this chapter and the next two chapters, we will consider situations in which we have more than two groups of data to analyze.

CONCEPTUAL UNDERSTANDING OF THE TOOL

The Study

Have you ever heard the expression "You are what you eat?" Perhaps there is some truth to this statement, at least that's what I say to get myself to eat vegetables without first dousing them in ranch dressing (and washing them down with Dr. Pepper). In addition to the importance of eating lots of fruits and vegetables, I understand that it is best to eat organic foods. Indeed, there is something that just feels inherently good about eating something that is "organic." I don't know what it is that feels good, but perhaps it is because I am being healthy or because eating organic food is good for the environment. I'm not sure, but when eating organic foods, I just feel like a particularly good person.

I suppose that sounded a bit obnoxious. However, it may well be how people feel in such circumstances. Paul Rozin (1999) contends that our preferences (e.g., for organic foods) may in fact translate into values that affect how we perceive the world around us. For instance, people who don't smoke may "look down upon" people who do smoke as smoking is an unhealthy behavior. Likewise, people who eat organic foods may develop a sense of superiority, just like I felt good about myself when I consume such food. It is this reasoning that was the foundation for an experiment that Kendall Eskine (2012) conducted and that we will discuss now.

In Eskine's (2012) experiment, 62 undergraduate students learned that they were participating in two unrelated studies, a consumer research study and a moral judgment task. Of course, there was just one real experiment. Each participant was randomly assigned to one of three experimental groups. Specifically, participants were randomly assigned to either an "organic food" group, a "comfort food" group, or a control food group. In the *organic food group*, participants received a packet of pictures of four organic foods (i.e., apple, spinach, tomato, and carrot), each labeled as "USDA Organic." The *comfort food group* received a packet of pictures of four comfort foods (ice cream, a cookie, chocolate, and a brownie). Finally, the *control food group* received a packet of pictures of four, for lack of a better term, "nondescript foods" (i.e., oatmeal, rice, mustard, and beans). To make sure people looked at each food item, they had to rate how desirable they felt the food was.

Let me introduce some terminology that you will read in published research that uses the new statistical tool in this chapter. The groups in an experiment are sometimes referred to as **conditions, values**, and **levels** (in addition to just plain "groups"). All of these terms mean the same thing. If we have an experiment with three levels, as we do with Eskine's (2012) experiment, that simply means there are three groups in the experiment.

Conditions: term used to denote the number of groups in an experiment.

Values: term used to denote the number of groups in an experiment.

Levels: term used to denote the number of groups in an experiment.

After completing their desirability ratings of each of the four foods they saw, participants received a packet of six vignettes depicting morally questionable behaviors (e.g., a lawyer walking through a hospital soliciting business from victims or a Congressperson accepting bribes). After reading each vignette, participants rated it on a 1 (*not at all morally wrong*) to 7 (*very morally wrong*) response range. Moral judgment scores were averaged across the six vignettes.

In previous chapters, we encountered the notion of random assignment. Recall that random assignment occurs when an experimenter uses a random process, such as a random number generator, to put members of a sample in one of the experimental groups. We want to focus on the effects of the experimental groups on ratings of the morally questionable behaviors in the vignettes. You might know some people who would likely rate any such behavior as morally wrong. Other people you know will rate such behaviors far less harshly. Likewise, we have an experiment that involves looking at pictures of food. For people who haven't eaten in a while, they might be affected by those pictures in ways that people who just ate may not be affected. The point is that through random assignment, we can help minimize such effects of these preexisting differences among members of the sample and focus on the effects of the experimental groups.

Figure 9.1 provides a visual depiction of this experiment.

Figure 9.1 Examples of Organic, Comfort, and Control Foods in Eskine's (2012) Experiment

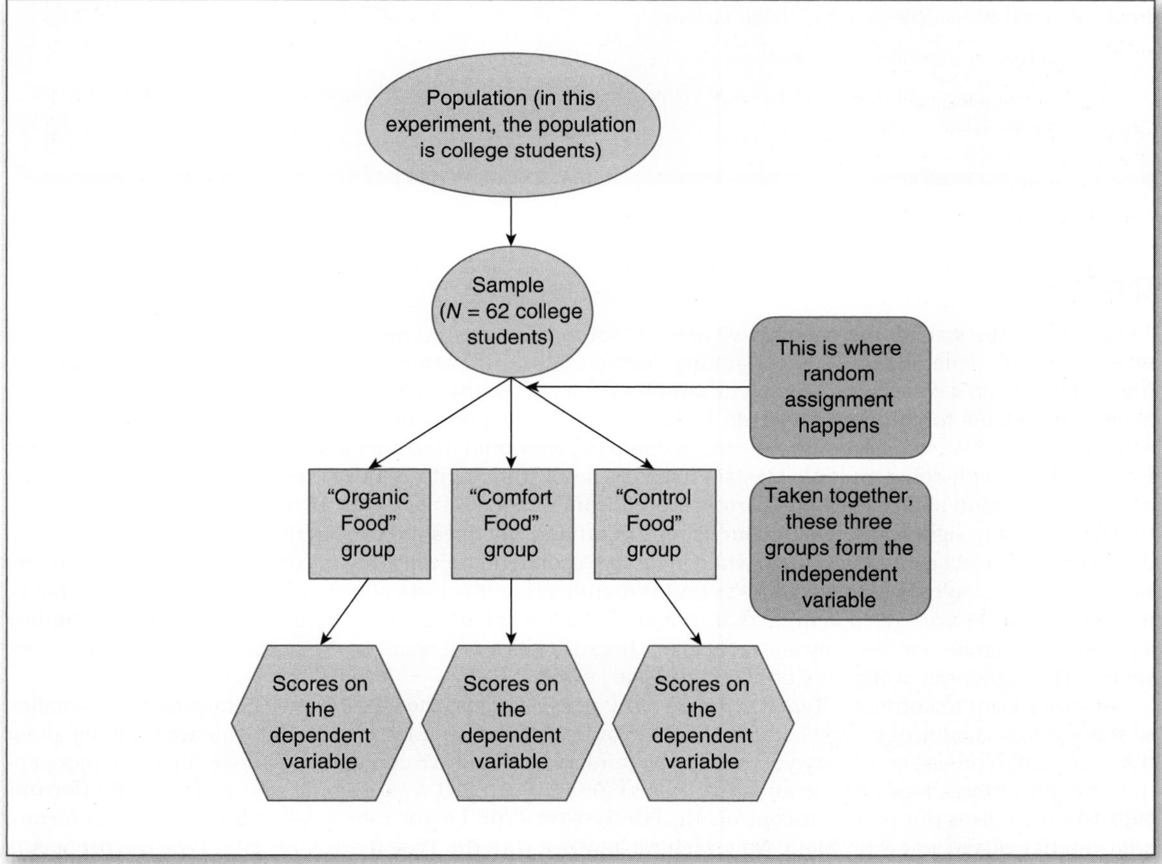

Source: Materials in Eskine's experiment

After viewing one and only one type of food, participants then made their judgments about the morality of questionable behaviors.

LEARNING CHECK

1. Why might a researcher do an experiment with three or more groups instead of only two groups?

   A: We can learn more information about the population by making more comparisons. The more groups that there are in an experiment, the more comparisons that we can make.

2. What is the independent variable in Eskine's (2012) experiment?

   A: Type of food that participants were exposed to

3. What are the groups that were created from the manipulation of this independent variable?

   A: Organic food, comfort food, and control food

4. What is the dependent variable in Eskine's (2012) experiment?

   A: Moral evaluations of actions in the vignettes

5. How was the dependent variable operationalized?

   A: By using a response range of 1 (*not at all morally wrong*) to 7 (*very morally wrong*). Moral judgment scores were averaged across the six vignettes.

The Tool

As we said at the start of the chapter, we need a tool to compare the means of three or more groups to see whether we can generalize differences among these groups from a sample to its population. You might be saying, "Well, just do a series of independent samples t tests to compare each group mean." And we could. If we have three means to compare as we do in Eskine's (2012) experiment, we would need three independent samples t tests. If we had four group means to compare, we would need six independent samples t tests. What is the problem with doing multiple t tests? First, it's a lot of work to do all those t tests. More importantly, think about this situation in terms of Type I errors. Recall from Chapter 6 that a Type I error is the likelihood that we find a statistically significant result in our sample but that result does not exist in the larger population. Stated differently, we reject a null hypothesis when in fact we should not reject it. If you conduct enough independent samples t tests, you're eventually going to find something that is statistically significant by sheer luck (that is, it will be a Type I error). Keep in mind that with an alpha level of .05 (5%), we have a 1-in-20 chance of finding a statistically significant result by sheer luck, not because it is a real result in the population. The more t tests we run, the higher the probability of making a Type I error.

We don't want to commit a Type I error. So, why not just adjust the alpha from .05 to something smaller, so there is less chance of a Type I error? The fact you're asking that question tells me you are thinking about this situation in precisely the way you need to be thinking about it! We could do that; if we run three independent samples t tests, let's just use an alpha level of .05 / 3 = .0167 (1.67%). Doing so is called the **Bonferroni adjustment**. This is not wrong. It controls the **family-wise Type I error** rate at 5%. However, the Bonferroni adjustment leads to a new problem. Now we have an issue with the Type II error. Recall a Type II error occurs when we do not detect a result in our sample that does exist in the population. Stated differently, we fail to reject a null hypothesis when in fact we should reject it. When we reduce the alpha level to .0167, we increase the likelihood of committing a Type II error. So, we need a new tool, a tool that allows us to balance our concern about making Type I and Type II errors. I give you the **analysis of variance** or, as it is typically abbreviated, the **ANOVA**.

Bonferroni adjustment: dividing the alpha level (normally .05) by the number of statistical comparisons being made; this controls the chance of making a Type I error at 5% across all statistical tests being conducted.

Family-wise Type I error: likelihood of detecting at least one statistically significant result when conducting multiple statistical tests. It is called "family-wise" because it is the error rate for a series (family) of statistical tests.

Analysis of variance (ANOVA): statistical tool used to compare means of three or more groups of data.

Recall that in Eskine's (2012) experiment, participants were randomly assigned to see one of three types of foods: organic foods, comfort foods, or control foods. *It is a small but critical point to note that people saw one and only one of these three types of foods.* Therefore, this is a between-subjects design. In addition, the researchers used one independent variable, the type of food that people were exposed to. The precise name for the statistical tool we'll consider in this chapter is the **one-way, between-subjects ANOVA**. It is *one-way* because we are analyzing the effects of one independent variable. It is *between-subjects* because participants were randomly assigned to one and only one experimental group.

One-way, between-subjects ANOVA: analysis in which there is one independent variable and each participant is assigned to one and only one experimental level.

Ingredients

What is the logic of the one-way, between-subjects ANOVA? *It allows us to learn, when comparing three or more group means, whether there are differences between these means within our sample that are generalizable to the population.* As with the previous inferential statistical tools we've discussed, we want to know whether results obtained in our sample are representative of the larger population. Let's focus on the conceptual ingredients for a one-way, between-subjects ANOVA.

Recall that ANOVA is short for "analysis of variance." So perhaps not surprisingly, the ingredients we need to use an ANOVA are sources of variability. In a nutshell, an analysis of variance (ANOVA) will help us conclude whether variability between the experimental groups is due to the independent variable or to some sort of **error variance**. By error variance, we are referring to factors other than the independent variable. For Eskine's (2012) experiment, we mentioned a few such factors (e.g., predisposition to judge others in strict or lenient moral terms). I know what you're thinking, "If people were randomly assigned to experimental groups, doesn't that eliminate error variance?" Well, no, we can never completely eliminate the influence of preexisting differences in our sample, and there could be other sources of error variance in an experiment. For instance, in Eskine's experiment, I wonder whether the time-of-day that experimental sessions were conducted may have influenced people's reactions to the morally questionable behaviors. If it did, then that would be a source of error variance. In sum, *the ANOVA is a competition between (a) variability traceable to the independent variable and (b) variability traceable to factors other than the independent variable.*

Error variance: amount of variability between scores resulting from uncontrolled variables and random variation.

At this point, I think some numbers will be helpful in illustrating these two sources of variability. Keep in mind that the dependent variable in Eskine's (2012) experiment was ratings of the morally questionable behaviors, using a 1 (*not at all morally wrong*) to 7 (*very morally wrong*) response range. Here are hypothetical ratings from 12 participants:

	Type of Food Seen		
	Organic Foods	**Comfort Foods**	**Control Foods**
	6	4	5
	5	4	6
	7	3	4
	4	5	1
Group Mean	5.5	4	4

What should we pay attention to at this point? The two types of variability that we will discuss now.

First, let's look at the organic foods group. Even though each of the four people in this group was exposed to the same set of foods, they each had different scores on the dependent variable. Indeed, the same can be said for participants in the control foods group, and only two people in the comfort foods group had the same score on the dependent variable. Bottom line, *it is important to note that not each participant in each group scored the same on the dependent variable.* Logically, not all people will react the same way to the type of food they were exposed to in the experiment. You might like raw broccoli, but I would definitely have a different reaction to that same food. That is, there is some variability within each group, called **within-groups variability**. If the only factor affecting people's reactions to the morally questionable behaviors in the vignettes was the independent variable, then all the scores within each group would be the same. Obviously, factors other than the independent variable are at work in this example as they are in any experiment.

Within-groups variability: amount of variability between scores *within each experimental group*.

There is a second type of variability we need to pay attention to. The mean of the 12 individual scores is 4.5; this is called the **grand mean** of the experiment. However, not all of the group means are 4.5; in fact, none of the group means equals the grand mean. Therefore, there is some variability between the groups, called **between-groups variability**. Of course, when researchers conduct an experiment, they expect to see differences between their experimental groups. That's the whole idea of an independent variable. Indeed, one reason why we see variability between the groups could be because of the independent variable. As researchers, we assume that between-groups variability is due to manipulation of the independent variable. However, it must be acknowledged that such variability could also be due to other, uncontrolled factors. We mentioned that the time of day that the experimental sessions were conducted could have affected how people behaved in the experiment. Hopefully not all of the experimental sessions in which people were exposed to comfort foods were conducted at 5:30 p.m. when many people might be thinking about dinner. Regardless, the point is that although between-groups variability is generally thought to be a function of the independent variable, it always includes some level of error variability. Therefore, between-groups variability consists of systematic variance (i.e., the independent variable) and error variance.

Grand mean: mean obtained from averaging scores across all groups in an experiment.

Between-groups variability: amount of variability *between scores across groups*; includes an estimate of the effect of the independent variable and error variance.

So, we have variability *within each group* and variability *between the different groups*. We will quantify within-groups variability and between-groups variability a little later in this chapter. For now, here's the conceptual formula for an ANOVA:

$$F = \frac{\text{Between-groups variability}}{\text{Within-groups variability}}$$

Remember, as we discussed, between-groups variability is thought to be a function of the independent variable, but we must acknowledge that differences between groups can emerge from factors other than the independent variable (i.e., some degree of error variability). Therefore, a more complete way of thinking about this ratio is as follows:

$$F = \frac{\text{Systematic variance + error variance}}{\text{Error variance}}$$

By *systematic variance*, we are referring to variance from the independent variable. As with the t tests that we learned about in the previous two chapters, the larger the F ratio is, the more likely it is to be statistically significant, allowing us to generalize our results from our sample to the larger population. Let's think through this conceptual formula a little bit.

The numerator consists of the effects of the independent variable (*systematic variance*) as well as of error variance. Now certainly, we might get a large numerator by having a lot of error variance rather than variability due to the independent variable. However, when we look at the denominator of the F ratio, it is pure error variance. Therefore, if we have a large error variance, which would inflate the numerator, it would also inflate the denominator, offsetting its effect on the numerator. For example, suppose our systematic variance is 3 and our error variance is 9. Here is our F ratio:

$$F = \frac{3+9}{9}$$

$$F = \frac{12}{9}$$

$$F = 1.33$$

If indeed error variance is somehow responsible for the between-groups variability we observed, it will be "wiped out" when it appears in the denominator of the F ratio.

In continuing to look at this conceptual formula, what would happen if the independent variable had no effect on the dependent variable? Plug in a 0 for systematic variability. That leaves us with only error variability. Regardless of how much error variability there is, the F ratio would be 1 because the numerator would consist of only error variability and the denominator would consist of that same amount of error variability. For instance, if systematic variability is 0, and error variance is 15, then our F ratio would look like this:

$$F = \frac{0+15}{15}$$

$$F = \frac{15}{15}$$

$$F = 1$$

When taking this logic a step further, for an F ratio to be statistically significant (that is, to show a statistically significant effect of the independent variable on the dependent variable), it needs to be greater than 1. How much greater than 1, we will see later in this chapter.[2]

I know you're eager to jump into Eskine's (2012) ANOVA details, but before we do, let's pause a moment and consider the assumptions of this statistical tool. Just as we had in the previous two chapters on *t* tests, there are some considerations to make you aware of when using one-way, between-subjects ANOVAs. Given your *t* test prowess, some of these assumptions will seem familiar.

Assumptions of the tool

1. The variability of each group must be approximately equal to the variability of every other group in the analysis. As was the case with *t* tests, we must pay a fine when this assumption is violated, and that fine is a loss of degrees of freedom.

2. The scores on the dependent variable must be normally distributed within each group in the analysis. Fortunately, this assumption is difficult to violate. In Chapter 5, we discussed normal distributions and the properties of such distributions. In Chapter 6, we discussed the central limit theorem, one component of which is that most data distributions will be normally distributed as our samples get larger. We rarely need to worry about violating this assumption.

3. Just as with *t* tests, data must be on an interval or a ratio scale. You might be wondering what to do with data that are not interval or ratio scale. We will learn how to use some tools to use with nominal and ordinal data in Chapter 14, so hang tight on this front.

Hypotheses from Eskine (2012)

Before we examine the results of Eskine's (2012) experiment, let's be sure we're set on the hypothesis that is being tested. As has been drilled into you, ultimately we are testing the hypothesis that there is no difference between the experimental groups, in this case, on the dependent variable of judgments of morally questionable behaviors. Stated differently:

$$H_o: \mu_{\text{organic food group}} = \mu_{\text{comfort food group}} = \mu_{\text{control food group}}$$

To reiterate, to be able to suggest that there are differences in the population based on these three mean scores, we must reject the notion that there is no difference among the organic food group, the comfort food group, and the control food group. That is, the mean differences we find in our sample must be large enough to conclude that there is likely an effect that exists in the population. In plain English, the ANOVA tested the notion that there are no differences among these three groups on the dependent variable of judgments of morally questionable behaviors.

Again, published research will state a research hypothesis and rarely if ever states a null hypothesis. Here is the research hypothesis that Eskine (2012) offered:

> Based on the research from moral licensing, which indicates that people are less likely to act altruistically when their moral identities are salient, ... the present research predicts that those exposed to organic foods would . . . . make harsher moral judgments compared to those exposed to nonorganic foods. (p. 252)

Symbolically, we have:

$$H_r: \mu_{\text{organic food group}} > (\mu_{\text{comfort food group}} = \mu_{\text{control food group}})$$

LEARNING CHECK

1. What is a Type I error? Why is the Type I error an issue when we are comparing three or more group means?

   A: Researchers commit a Type I error when they find a statistically significant result in their sample data that does not exist in the population from which that sample was drawn. The Type I error is problematic when comparing three or more group means because the more statistical comparisons we make, the more likely we are to commit this type of error.

2. Why is Eskine's (2012) experiment considered a "one-way" design? Why is Eskine's (2012) experiment considered a "between-subjects" design?

   A: It was a "one-way" experimental design because it contained one independent variable. It was a "between-subjects" experimental design because participants were randomly assigned to one and only one experimental group created by the manipulation of the independent variable.

3. What are the two components of between-groups variability?

   A: The effects of the independent variable (systematic variance) and error variability

4. Suppose an ANOVA has a systematic variance of 5 and an error of variance of 10. What will the F ratio be?

   A:
$$F = \frac{5+10}{10}$$
$$F = \frac{15}{10}$$
$$F = 1.5$$

5. Suppose an ANOVA has a systematic variance of 20 and an error variance of 20. What will the F ratio be?

   A:
$$F = \frac{20+20}{20}$$
$$F = \frac{40}{20}$$
$$F = 2$$

6. What is the "grand mean" in an ANOVA? Why might the grand mean not simply be the average of all group means?
   A: The grand mean is the mean obtained from averaging scores across all groups in an experiment. The grand mean may not be the average of the group means because there may not be an equal number of participants in each experimental group. A group with 20 participants will have a stronger influence on the grand mean than will a group with, say, 16 participants.

Interpreting the Tool

Now that we have a handle on what an ANOVA (and more specifically, a one-way, between-subjects ANOVA) allows us to do, let's examine in detail the results of Eskine's (2012) experiment. Here are those results, written in APA style:

> [An] ANOVA on averaged moral judgments indicated an overall effect of food type, F (2, 59) = 7.516, p = .001, η_p^2 = .203, and a follow-up Tukey's HSD test showed that those exposed to organic food made

> significantly harsher moral judgments ($M = 5.58$, $SD = .59$) than those exposed to control foods ($M = 5.08$, $SD = .62$), $p < .05$, or comfort foods ($M = 4.89$, $SD = .57$), $p = .001$, with the latter two groups not significantly differing. (p. 253)

In plain English, people who saw organic foods subsequently judged questionable behaviors to be more immoral than people who saw comfort foods or the control food group. More technically, Eskine (2012) rejected the null hypothesis as the organic food group scored higher on the dependent variable than either of the other two groups. Therefore, he could conclude that in the population, people who are exposed to organic foods judge others more harshly than people exposed to comfort foods or control foods. Let's now examine the statistical guts of this plain English conclusion.

Testing the null hypothesis

We have our *F* ratio, which is 7.516. We'll calculate an *F* ratio in the next section, but for now, remember our conceptual formula:

$$F = \frac{\text{Systematic variance} + \text{error variance}}{\text{Error variance}}$$

When reading published research results, we usually won't be told what the systematic variance and the error variance were. All we will be given is the *F* ratio, and for the purposes of drawing conclusions from a research study, that's ultimately what we need (and some other information that we'll discuss now).

In addition to the *F* ratio, we have two numbers in parentheses; specifically, we see "(2, 59)." These are our degrees of freedom. For *t* tests, there was one number for degrees of freedom. But for an ANOVA, there will be two numbers for degrees of freedom reported with an *F* ratio. Given that there are two types of variance, we need a degrees of freedom number for each one. The first one that is reported, here it is 2, is the *between-groups degrees of freedom* (also called the *numerator degrees of freedom*). Here is how it is calculated:

$$df_{\text{between-groups}} = \text{number of groups being compared} - 1$$

So in this instance, we have:

$$df_{\text{between-groups}} = 3 - 1$$

Hence:

$$df_{\text{between-groups}} = 2$$

The second number, 59, is the *within-groups degrees of freedom* (also called the *denominator degrees of freedom*). Here is how it is calculated:

$$df_{\text{within-groups}} = \text{sample size} - \text{number of groups being compared}$$

Recall that the sample size, which is always given in the description of the sample in published research, was 62 in this experiment. So here, we have:

$$df_{\text{within-groups}} = 62 - 3$$
$$df_{\text{within-groups}} = 59$$

Much like we needed the one number for degrees of freedom when finding a critical value for a *t* statistic, we'll need both of these degrees of freedom to find the critical value of our *F* ratio. As was the case with the *t* statistic, we need to compare our *F* ratio to some critical value to see whether it is large enough for us to make inferences about our population from our sample data. Now that we have our *F* ratio and degrees of freedom, let's use this information and find the critical value to compare our *F* ratio to.

Take a look at Appendix C. It contains the critical values for *F* ratios. Across the top of the appendix are columns containing ascending between-groups (numerator) degrees of freedom. Down the left-hand column are rows containing ascending within-groups (denominator) degrees of freedom. In Eskine's (2012) ANOVA, there were 2 between-groups degrees of freedom and 59 within-groups degrees of freedom. As is typically the case, we will use an alpha level of .05. So, let's find the intersection of these two kinds of degrees of freedom with an alpha level of .05. As you will see in Appendix C, we can locate the 2 between-groups degrees of freedom easily enough; however, there is not a row with precisely 59 within-groups degrees of freedom. As you know, critical values are almost never reported in published research. But here, we can see that for 60 within-groups degrees of freedom, we would have a critical value of 3.15. For 44 within-groups degrees of freedom, we would have a critical value of 3.21. So, in Eskine's results, his critical value was somewhere between 3.15 and 3.21. So, let's just take the average of these two critical values and say the critical value is 3.18.[3]

Figure 9.2 The Distribution of *F*-ratio Test Statistics

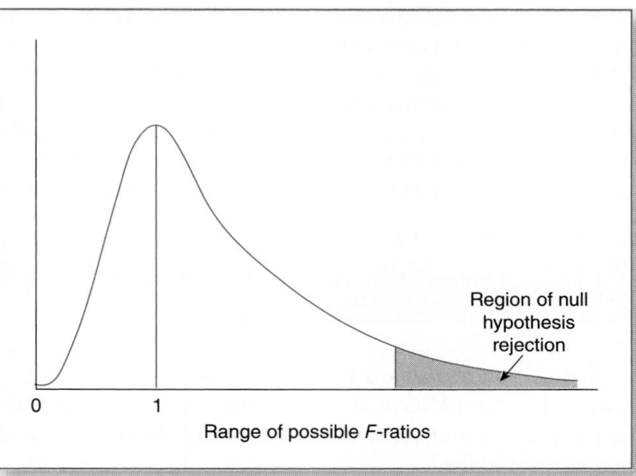

For a visualization of what is going on right now, look at Figure 9.2. Along the *x*-axis we have our possible *F* ratio values. Note here that the lowest value an *F* ratio can take on is 0. Unlike *z* and *t* statistics, which can take positive or negative values, *F* ratios are always positive numbers. As we saw in Chapter 4, and as we'll see in the next section of this chapter, when calculating between-groups variability and within-groups variability, variability can never be a negative number. Therefore, *F* ratios can never be negative numbers. This has an important implication; that is, *all ANOVAs are inherently one-tailed hypothesis tests*. Theoretically, *F* ratios, similar to *t* statistics, can run to infinity. Also, notice that unlike the shape of the distribution of *t* statistics, the distribution of *F* ratios is positively skewed. That is, larger *F* ratios occur with less frequency than do smaller *F* ratios.

Figure 9.3 Comparing Eskine's (2012) *F*-ratio Test Statistic to its Critical Value

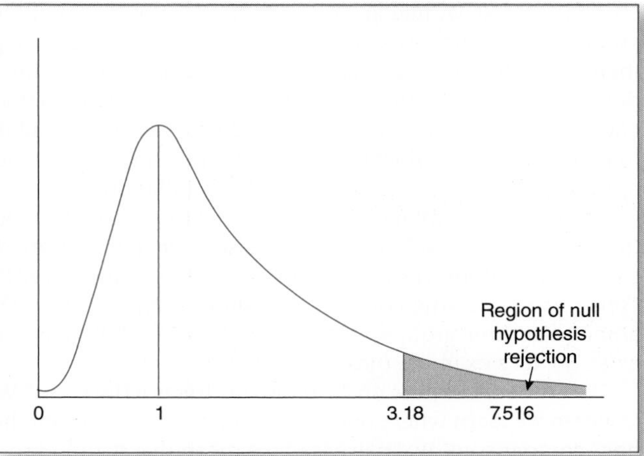

Quick quiz: What percentage of the *F* ratio distribution in Figure 9.2 is shaded? If you said 5%, good for you! Now treat yourself to your favorite comfort food. Indeed, we do not need

to worry about one- or two-tailed statistical tests here. With an ANOVA, all tests are inherently one-tailed. Doing so does not increase the likelihood of making a Type I error as one-tailed tests did with our *z* test and *t* tests.

Now let's apply this logic to Eskine's (2012) results. With a critical value of 3.18 and an *F* ratio of 7.516, we can see in Figure 9.3 that this *F* ratio exceeds the critical value and falls in the region of null hypothesis rejection. As Eskine reported in his results, the *p* value was .001. That is, there was a 0.1% chance the results he obtained were due to random variation. Therefore, we reject the null hypothesis and conclude that there are differences in moral judgments of questionable behaviors based on the type of food people were exposed to.

Extending our null hypothesis test

Finally, we have the "η_p^2" to consider. This is the **partial eta squared**. It is a measure of effect size, just like Cohen's *d* was a measure of effect size for *t* tests. Here, the partial eta squared is .203. This means that 20.3% of the variability in the dependent variable (moral judgments) can be traced to the independent variable (food type). We will discuss how to calculate the partial eta squared in the next section of this chapter.

Quick review: Why do we need to report effect sizes? They give us an estimate of the strength of the effect of the independent variable on the dependent variable. Whereas the concept of statistical significance tells us whether a result in our sample exists in the population, effect sizes tell us how strong the relationship between two variables is. Unlike with Cohen's *d*, the effect size used with *t* tests, there are no established guidelines for establishing weak, moderate, and strong effect sizes measured by partial eta squared.

Partial eta squared: measure of effect size that can be reported in an ANOVA.

Just so you are aware of it, in addition to a partial eta squared, there is another effect size that is often reported with an ANOVA. It is called the eta squared. We will discuss eta squared and compare it with partial eta squared in Chapter 11, where we introduce the tool needed to analyze data when we have two or more independent variables.

Going beyond the *F* ratio: Post hoc tests

Before exploring the rest of Eskine's (2012) results, let's stop and realize what we've just learned. Notice that the ANOVA revealed an "overall effect of food type." This is important. Recall that an ANOVA allows us to compare at least three group means simultaneously, balancing the Type I error rate and the Type II error rate. When we see that an ANOVA had an "overall effect," it means that there is a mean difference somewhere between our groups. The *F* ratio test statistic is an *omnibus test*; that is, it gives us a "big picture" snapshot to tell us whether there are differences among our group means. At this point, though, we do not know which group means were different from each other. Instead, an ANOVA just tells us that there is some statistically significant mean difference between our groups. Frankly, finding a statistically significant ANOVA as Eskine did creates more questions than it answers. We now have to figure out which group means are statistically different from one another to draw any specific inferences about the population.

You might be thinking, like I did when I first learned about ANOVA, something such as, "Wow, that's not really that informative. I want to know precisely what groups are different from each other." OK, we'll get to the specific group differences in just a moment. But, again, an ANOVA allows us to balance the concern of making a Type I error with the concern of making a Type II error. Once we know that a difference exists somewhere among our three groups, we can then do some "follow-up" analyses to learn precisely where those differences exist. So, let's examine these follow-up analyses.

We now concentrate on "a follow-up Tukey's HSD test." What is a **Tukey HSD** test? As you likely guessed, this is where we learn where our precise differences between the group means exist. It is a series of "pairwise **post hoc**" comparisons. By "pairwise," we mean that it compares each group mean to every other group mean, one comparison at a time. By "post hoc," we mean "after the fact." In this context, we are talking about "after an ANOVA." The "HSD" stands for "honestly significantly difference." We call it an "honestly significant difference" at this point when we find two means that are statistically significantly different from one another. This sounds like a test, doesn't it? You are correct, but these post hoc comparisons further allow us to control the Type I error rate. Here, the group means and standard deviations (or another measure of variability, such as the standard error of the mean) are reported. In addition, statistical comparisons are made between the group means. We will need to calculate a *critical mean difference*, which if any mean difference in our sample exceeds, we can conclude that there is a difference between those two groups in our population based on our sample data. In the next section, we will learn how to determine a critical mean difference.

Eskine (2012) found that people who saw organic foods made harsher moral judgments (mean of 5.58) than people who saw the other two types of food (means of 4.89 and 5.08 for the comfort foods group and the control foods group, respectively). Long before you took this class, you knew 5.58 was greater than 4.89 and 5.08, but are these differences generalizable from our sample to the population? Tukey's HSD answered that question by comparing the organic foods group to the other two groups and by revealing a statistically significant difference between the organic foods group and the other two groups, with $p = .001$ in both cases. Of course, given that .001 is less than .05, we can indeed generalize these two mean differences from the sample to the population.

Tukey's HSD post hoc test: procedure used after (hence, "post hoc") an *F* ratio has been calculated. This procedure allows us to learn which group means are significantly different from one another.

LEARNING CHECK

Now that we've run through the conceptual ingredients of a one-way, between-subjects ANOVA, let's take a look at a new research result. Conveniently, Eskine (2012) had a second dependent variable in his experiment. Specifically, after viewing the pictures of one of three types of foods and completing their moral evaluations, participants were told that there was another experiment going on and that those researchers needed volunteers. They were asked to participate in this second experiment with no compensation of any kind provided for as much of 30 minutes as they could spare. Participants indicated how long, up to 30 minutes, they would be willing to volunteer in this subsequent experiment (referred to as "prosocial behavior"). The amount of time people said they would devote to this second experiment was the dependent variable. Here are the results of this one-way, between-subjects ANOVA:

> A between-subjects analysis of variance (ANOVA) revealed an overall effect of food type on prosocial behavior, $F(2, 59) = 8.894$, $p < .001$, $\eta_p^2 = .232$, and a follow-up Tukey's honestly significant difference (HSD) test showed that those exposed to organic food volunteered significantly less time ($M = 13.40$, $SD = 9.38$) than those exposed to control foods ($M = 19.88$, $SD = 10.33$), $p < .05$, or comfort foods ($M = 24.55$, $SD = 5.49$), $p < .001$, with the latter two groups not significantly differing. (Eskine, 2012, p. 252)

1. What were the means being statistically examined?

   A: organic foods = 13.40 minutes; control foods = 19.88 minutes; and comfort foods = 24.55 minutes

2. What is the *F* ratio?

   A: 8.894

(Continued)

(Continued)

3. How many degrees of freedom did the researchers have for this analysis?

   A: 2 between-groups (or numerator) degrees of freedom and 59 within-groups (or denominator) degrees of freedom

4. By using Appendix C, approximate the critical value that was used to see whether we reject or do not reject the null hypothesis.

   A: Slightly larger than 3.15 (the critical value for 2 numerator and 60 denominator degrees of freedom), but smaller than 3.21 (the critical value for 2 numerator and 44 denominator degrees of freedom).

5. What is the probability that the differences among the three groups' means were due to random variation?

   A: Less than .1% ($p < .001$)

6. Did the researchers reject or not reject the null hypothesis?

   A: Because the p value is less than .05, we can conclude there is a small likelihood that the differences among our means were due to random variation. Therefore, we reject the null hypothesis.

7. What is the effect size? Interpret what this number means.

   A: .232. This means that 23.2% of the variability in the dependent variable (time volunteered) is explained by the independent variable (the type of food seen).

8. Given your answer to the previous questions, what does this statistical presentation mean in plain English?

   A: People exposed to organic foods were less willing to indicate they would help someone than were people exposed to comfort foods or control foods.

USING YOUR NEW STATISTICAL TOOL

With our handle on the conceptual nature of the one-way, between-subjects ANOVA, let's now dig into the feast that is using this new tool, first with hand-calculations and then with the software program Statistical Package for the Social Sciences (SPSS).

Hand-Calculating the One-Way, Between-Subjects ANOVA

In full disclosure, my students are not shy about telling me that hand-calculating ANOVAs is a long process. They are correct. However, as we always do when performing our calculations, we will keep our eye on the understanding of why we are calculating what we are calculating. That should make each step in what could feel like a long process a little easier to take. Earlier in this chapter, we saw some hypothetical data from Eskine's (2012) experiment to illustrate within-groups and between-groups variability. Let's use those data to learn how to hand-calculate a one-way, between-subjects ANOVA. Keep in mind that the dependent variable in Eskine's (2012) experiment was moral ratings of the morally questionable

Type of Food Seen		
Organic Foods	**Comfort Foods**	**Control Foods**
6	4	5
5	4	6
7	3	4
4	5	1

behaviors, using a 1 (*not at all morally wrong*) to 7 (*very morally wrong*) response range. Here again are those hypothetical ratings from 12 participants:

Step 1: State hypotheses

It can be easy to forget, once we dive into our data, exactly what it is we are doing. We are ultimately, of course, testing some hypothesis. Here, we are testing the hypothesis that there will be no difference between the experimental groups on the dependent variable of judgments of morally questionable behaviors. If you prefer notation to words, here you go:

$$H_o: \mu_{\text{organic food group}} = \mu_{\text{comfort food group}} = \mu_{\text{control food group}}$$

When offering a research hypothesis, all we need to say is that we expect our group means to not all be equal. We do not have to specify which mean will be greater than another mean; however, in actual research, of course, investigators do have such ideas. So here, in terms of the research hypothesis, we would expect the following:

$$H_r: \mu_{\text{organic food group}} > (\mu_{\text{comfort food group}} = \mu_{\text{control food group}})$$

In plain English, we expect the organic foods group to offer harsher moral judgments than the comfort foods group or the control foods group.

Step 2: Calculate the mean for each group

As you will see a little later in this process, the group mean won't be used in calculating the *F* ratio. However, when this process is complete, these are the numbers we will need to report (and, besides, we'll need them for step 3), so let's calculate them now:

	Type of Food Seen		
	Organic Foods	**Comfort Foods**	**Control Foods**
	6	4	5
	5	4	6
	7	3	4
	4	5	1
Group Means	5.5	4	4

Step 3: Calculate the sums of squares (*SSs*)

Keep in mind, from Chapter 4, that "sums of squares" simply means the sum of the squared deviations from the group mean. Also keep in mind that we are now discussing "analysis of variance." And, finally, recall that we have two types of variance: within-groups variability and between-groups variability. Therefore, we need two sums of squares: within groups and between groups. If you add together the within-groups and between-groups sums of squares, you get a total sums of squares, as shown in Figure 9.4.

I should confess one of my eccentricities at this point. I want to be as sure as I can be that my calculations are correct. As a student, I obsessed over them. When taking a test, I would check and recheck every calculation until my teacher ripped my test from my hands. A homework assignment that took most students an hour to complete, I took easily five hours to do because I would redo my problems to check my original work.

Figure 9.4 Two Types of Variability: Between-Groups and Within-Groups

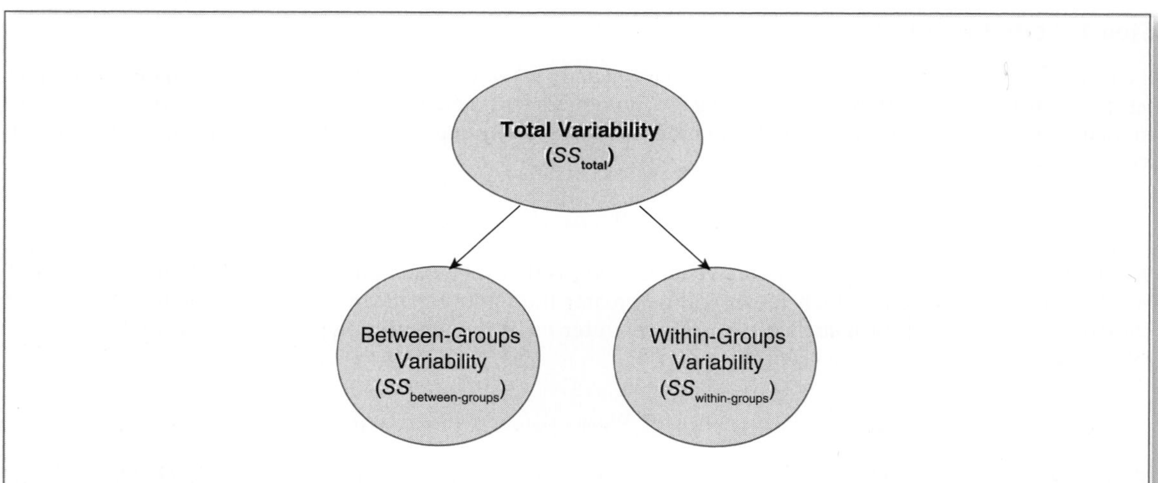

So, indulge me here. Let's calculate our total sums of squares first, then our within-groups and between-groups sums of squares (the latter two should add up to the total sums of squares).

Total Sums of Squares (SS_{total})

When calculating the total sums of squares, we need to look at the grand mean for the set of data. Recall when we first encountered these data, we calculated the grand mean to be 4.5. What we will do now is take each score in the entire set of data, and subtract it from 4.5. Doing so allows us to get an "overall" picture of variability in the experiment, hence, the term "total" sums of squares. Here we go:

Type of Food Seen					
Organic Foods		Comfort Foods		Control Foods	
Score	Deviation	Score	Deviation	Score	Deviation
6	1.5	4	−0.5	5	0.5
5	0.5	4	−0.5	6	1.5
7	2.5	3	−1.5	4	−0.5
4	−0.5	5	0.5	1	−2.5

You know what's next: Square those deviations!

Type of Food Seen								
Organic Foods			Comfort Foods			Control Foods		
Score	Deviation	Deviation^2	Score	Deviation	Deviation^2	Score	Deviation	Deviation^2
6	1.5	2.25	4	−0.5	0.25	5	0.5	0.25
5	0.5	0.25	4	−0.5	0.25	6	1.5	2.25
7	2.5	6.25	3	−1.5	2.25	4	−0.5	0.25
4	−0.5	0.25	5	0.5	0.25	1	−3.5	12.25

Now, sum the squared deviations within each group, leaving us with organic foods = 9; comfort foods = 3; and control foods = 15.

And, finally, summing each group's squared deviation total gives us 9 + 3 + 15 = 27. Our total sums of squares (SS_{total}) is 27. We will next calculate our within-groups sums of squares and then our between-groups sums of squares. Given that there are the two sources of variability in an experiment, in our example, they should add up to 27.

Within-Groups Sums of Squares ($SS_{within\text{-}groups}$)

To calculate the within-groups sums of squares, we need to have each score and the group means that we calculated in step 2. The term *within-groups* means variability in each group and, specifically, variability around the group's mean. So, given that logic, we take each score and subtract it from its respective group mean. Let's recall our group means from step 2:

Organic Foods = 5.5   Comfort Foods = 4   Control Foods = 4

So, let's calculate the deviations of individual scores from their respective group means:

Type of Food Seen					
Organic Foods		Comfort Foods		Control Foods	
Score	Deviation	Score	Deviation	Score	Deviation
6	0.5	4	0	5	1
5	−0.5	4	0	6	2
7	1.5	3	−1	4	0
4	−1.5	5	1	1	−3

You know what's next: Square those deviations.

Type of Food Seen								
Organic Foods			Comfort Foods			Control Foods		
Score	Deviation	Deviation²	Score	Deviation	Deviation²	Score	Deviation	Deviation²
6	0.5	0.25	4	0	0	5	1	1
5	–0.5	0.25	4	0	0	6	2	4
7	1.5	2.25	3	–1	1	4	0	0
4	–1.5	2.25	5	1	1	1	–3	9

Now, sum the squared deviations within each group, leaving us with organic foods = 5; comfort foods = 2; and control foods = 14.

And finally, summing each group's squared deviation total gives us 5 + 2 + 14 = 21. Our within-groups sums of squares ($SS_{\text{within-groups}}$) is 21.

Between-Groups Sums of Squares ($SS_{\text{between-groups}}$)

Now that we calculated our total sums of squares (27) and within-groups sums of squares (21), you can probably guess what our between-groups sums of squares is. However, humor me and let me take you through its calculation.

To get the our between-groups sums of squares, we need the grand mean (which, again, is the mean score on dependent variable across all groups in an experiment; here the grand mean was 4.5) and the mean for each group, which we calculated in step 2. What we do now is take the grand mean and subtract from it each group mean. Of course, we square these deviations. However, after we square the deviations, we need to do one more thing; specifically, *we need to multiply that squared deviation by the number of people in each group* of the ANOVA. In this case, each group had four people, so each group contributed equally to the between-groups sums of squares. However, in many research studies, the number of people in each group many not be equal, so we need to weigh each group's influence on its contribution to the between-groups sums of squares.

We take our squared group deviations from the grand mean, multiplied by the respective number of people in each group, and then sum them to get our between-groups sums of squares. Again, our group means from step 2 were:

Organic Foods = 5.5 Comfort Foods = 4 Control Foods = 4

The grand mean was 4.5:

$$\begin{aligned}
\text{Organic Foods} &= (5.5-4.5)^2 \times 4 \\
&= 1^2 \times 4 \\
&= 1 \times 4 = 4 \\
\text{Comfort Foods} &= (4-4.5)^2 \times 4 \\
&= (-.5)^2 \times 4 \\
&= .25 \times 4 = 1 \\
\text{Control Food} &= (4-4.5)^2 \times 4 \\
&= (-.5)^2 \times 4 \\
&= .25 \times 4 = 1
\end{aligned}$$

Now, sum together these three numbers, and we get 4 + 1 + 1 = 6.

Thus, our between-groups sums of squares ($SS_{between\text{-}groups}$) is 6.

The logic of between-groups variability is to allow us to quantify how much the independent variable and potential confounding variables affect the dependent variable. If there were no differences between the groups (i.e., all group means were equal to each other and, thus, to the grand mean), it would indicate that the independent variable had no effect on the dependent variable.

Step 4: Determine degrees of freedom (*df*s)

As we said in a previous section of this chapter, in an ANOVA, there are two types of degrees of freedom reported: within-groups degrees of freedom and between-groups degrees of freedom. Of course, just like when calculating sums of squares, I also like to calculate a total number of degrees of freedom.

Total Degrees of Freedom (df_{total})

To calculate the total degrees of freedom for the ANOVA, simply take the sample size and subtract 1. So in this example, we have 12 participants, so:

$$df_{total} = \text{sample size} - 1$$

$$df_{total} = 12 - 1 = 11$$

Within-Groups Degrees of Freedom ($df_{within\text{-}groups}$)

To calculate the within-groups degrees of freedom, we take our sample size and subtract from it the number of groups in the ANOVA. In this example, we have a sample size of 12 people and 3 groups being compared. So:

$$df_{within\text{-}groups} = \text{sample size} - \text{number of groups in the ANOVA}$$

$$df_{within\text{-}groups} = 12 - 3 = 9$$

Between-Groups Degrees of Freedom ($df_{between\text{-}groups}$)

To calculate the between-groups degrees of freedom, we take the number of groups in the ANOVA and subtract 1. So in this case with three groups, we have:

$$df_{between\text{-}groups} = \text{number of groups in the ANOVA} - 1$$

$$df_{between\text{-}groups} = 3 - 1 = 2$$

Step 5: Calculate the mean squares (*MS*s)

When we say "mean squares," we are not talking about shapes that are unkind and cold hearted. Rather, we are talking about *average squared deviation scores*. The *MS*s are measurements of variability within the groups and between the groups. There are two *MS*s that we need to calculate, one for within-groups variability and one for between-groups variability. Here is the general *MS* formula:

$$MS = \frac{\text{Sums of squares}(SS)}{df}$$

In steps 3 and 4, we calculated the ingredients to calculate the MSs, so let's put that work to use. To calculate our $MS_{\text{within-groups}}$, our sums of squares was 21 and our degrees of freedom were 9. Thus:

$$MS_{\text{within-groups}} = \frac{21}{9}$$
$$MS_{\text{within-groups}} = 2.33$$

To calculate our $MS_{\text{between-groups}}$, our sums of squares was 6 and our degrees of freedom was 2. Thus:

$$MS_{\text{between-groups}} = \frac{6}{2}$$
$$MS_{\text{between-groups}} = 3$$

We don't need to calculate an MS_{total}. To do so would not give us any meaningful information that we will be using later on.

Step 6: Calculate your *F* ratio test statistic

Remember at this point what information an ANOVA provides us. It is *competition between (a) variability traceable to the independent variable and (b) variability traceable to factors other than the independent variable.* As stated, here is our conceptual formula to calculate the *F* ratio:

$$F = \frac{MS_{\text{between-groups}}}{MS_{\text{within-groups}}}$$

We simply need to plug in our $MS_{\text{between-groups}}$ and our $MS_{\text{within-groups}}$ variability calculated in step 5:

$$F = \frac{3.00}{2.33}$$
$$F = 1.29$$

Like I promised at the outset of this section, there are a lot of numbers to calculate. I hope you haven't been disappointed. What might help us organize all this information is to create what's called a "source table" or an "ANOVA summary table." It's a handy way to present all of the information needed to compute an *F* ratio. Here it is for our data:

Source of variability	*SS*	*df*	*MS*	*F*
Between-groups	6	2	3	1.29
Within-groups	21	9	2.33	
Total	27	11		

Make sure you understand where the numbers in this ANOVA summary table came from in our calculations. In the next Learning Check, you will see an ANOVA summary table and need to be able to answer questions about it.

Step 7: Locate the critical value

I know that it feels like we should catch our breath after all these calculations. However, we're now at the fun part, making sense of this F ratio of 1.29. Remember, as with any inferential statistical test, we want to know whether we can generalize our result from our sample to the larger population. Clearly, the organic food group scored higher than did the other two groups on moral judgments in our example data, but is that difference generalizable to our population? We need to compare the F ratio we obtained to some critical value to see whether we can reject our null hypothesis and make an inference about our population based on our sample data.

When locating a critical value, we need to know our alpha level and our degrees of freedom. My guess is that, by now, an alpha level of .05 is indented into your cerebral cortex. When calculating an ANOVA, we had to determine our degrees of freedom in step 4 for both within-groups and between-groups variability. Here are those degrees of freedom:

$$df_{\text{within-groups}} = 12 - 3 = 9$$
$$df_{\text{between-groups}} = 3 - 1 = 2$$

Armed with our alpha level of .05, our $df_{\text{between-groups}}$ of 2, and our $df_{\text{within-groups}}$ of 9, let's consult Appendix C. As we discussed earlier in this chapter, with ANOVAs, we are always conducting one-tailed hypothesis tests. In Appendix C, we have $df_{\text{between-groups}}$ in columns across the page and $df_{\text{within-groups}}$ in rows down the page. We need to look for the intersection of 2 between-groups degrees of freedom and 9 within-groups degrees of freedom with an alpha level of .05. Doing so gives us a critical value of 4.26. Remember that we need to compare our calculated F ratio to this critical value. If our calculated F ratio exceeds the critical value, we reject the null hypothesis. If our calculated F ratio test statistic is less than the critical value, we fail to reject the null hypothesis.

Step 8: Make a decision about the null hypothesis

Visually, Figure 9.5 displays how to think about using our F ratio we calculated to reject or to fail to reject our null hypothesis offered in step 1. As you can see in this figure, our F ratio of 1.29 falls below our critical value

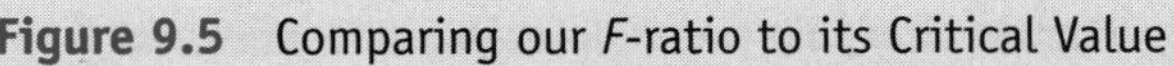

Figure 9.5 Comparing our *F*-ratio to its Critical Value

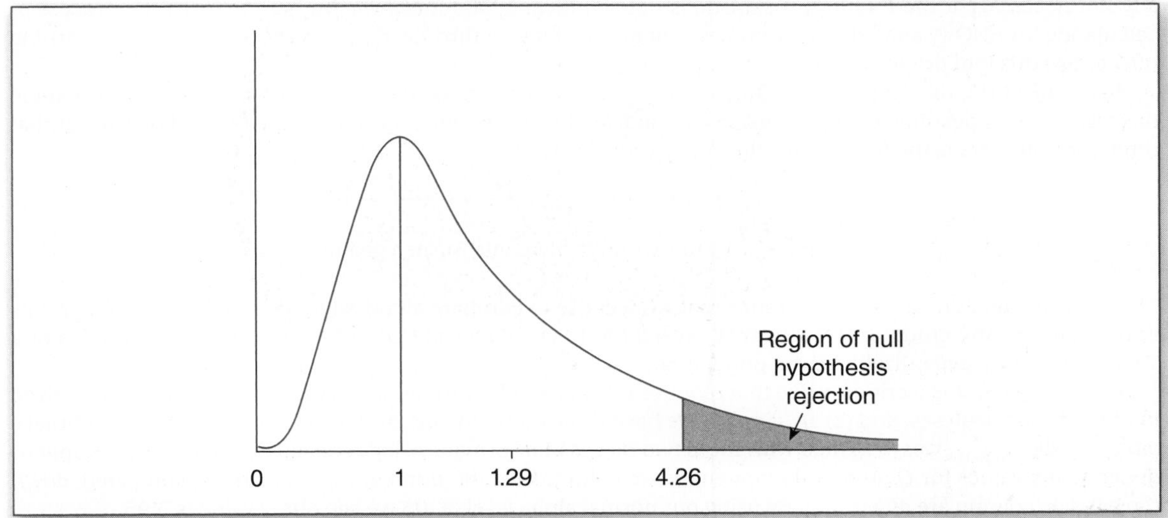

of 4.26. Therefore, we cannot reject the null hypothesis. In plain English, we conclude that the organic food group, the comfort food group, and the control food group expressed similar levels of moral judgments of ethically questionable behaviors.

Step 9: Calculate an effect size

Although our result was not generalizable from our sample to the population in these hypothetical data, keep in mind that this lack of statistical significance could well be a function of our small sample size. To keep the hand-calculations from getting too cumbersome, we had data from only 12 participants. As we've said before, any effect in a sample can be statistically significant if the sample is large because a larger sample will better represent the population than will a smaller sample. However, a lack of statistical significance does not mean the independent variable was unrelated to the dependent variable. So, let's calculate an effect size to see how strongly related the independent variable is to the dependent variable.

For the partial eta squared (η_p^2), here is the formula:

$$\eta_p^2 = \frac{SS_{\text{between-groups}}}{SS_{\text{between-groups}} + SS_{\text{within-groups}}}$$

From step 3 of these calculations, we see that $SS_{\text{between-groups}}$ was 6 and $SS_{\text{within-groups}}$ was 21. So for the partial eta squared (η_p^2), we have:

$$\eta_p^2 = \frac{6}{6+21}$$

$$\eta_p^2 = \frac{6}{27}$$

$$\eta_p^2 = .22$$

Step 10: Perform post hoc tests

Remember what the F ratio tells us. That is, it tells us whether there are mean differences between our groups. Now we need to learn which group means are significantly different from one another. Post hoc tests are generally not necessary if the F ratio test statistic is not significant. Of course, we are here to learn the process of calculating an ANOVA and what that process entails. So, let's go through this process for the sake of learning how to use this tool properly.

As Eskine (2012) did, let's examine Tukey's HSD post hoc tests. As we'll see in the next section of this chapter, there are several post hoc tests available to us, and we'll discuss some of the most used post hoc tests at that time. For now, here is the formula for the Tukey post hoc test:

$$\text{HSD} = Q \times \sqrt{\frac{MS_{\text{within-groups}}}{\text{number of participants in each group}}}$$

The "HSD" is the critical mean difference that we will use to compare all possible differences between groups in our sample. Any group differences that exceed the HSD are considered to be honestly different (i.e., not a Type I error) and generalizable to the population.

Think of Q as being a critical value that requires two pieces of information: (1) the number of means involved in the post hoc analyses; and (2) $df_{\text{within-groups}}$. We have three group means, and recall from our ANOVA summary table that $\text{df}_{\text{within-groups}}$ was 9. Armed with these two pieces of information, let's consult Appendix D. This appendix contains values for Q. Across the appendix are columns for the number of means being compared; down the left-side column are $df_{\text{within-groups}}$. By using our normal alpha level of .05,we see our Q value is 3.95.

Our $MS_{within\text{-}groups}$ was 2.333, and we had 4 people in each group. Thus:

$$\sqrt{\frac{2.333}{4}}$$

We now have the square root of 0.58325, which is 0.764.

When taking all of the ingredients, we need:

HSD = 3.95 × 0.764

HSD = 3.0178

What does this HSD = 3.0178 mean in plain English? It means that for a two-group mean in our sample to be generalizable to the population, those two means must differ by at least 3.0178. Here again are our group means:

Organic Foods = 5.5 Comfort Foods = 4 Control Foods = 4

As none of them differ by at least 3.0178, there are no statistically significant differences among these three groups.

As we know, all these results are meaningless unless they are communicated. Here is the APA style write-up of these analyses:

> A one-way, between-subjects ANOVA on moral judgments indicated no effect of food type, $F(2, 9) = 1.29$, $p > .05$, $\eta_p^2 = .22$, and a follow-up Tukey's HSD test showed that those exposed to organic food made moral judgments ($M = 5.50$) similar to those exposed to control foods ($M = 4.00$), $p > .05$, and comfort foods ($M = 4.00$), $p > .05$, with the latter two groups also not significantly differing.

LEARNING CHECK

Problem #1

Use this ANOVA summary table to answer the questions that follow it:

Source of variability	*SS*	*df*	*MS*	*F*
Between-groups	14	4	3.50	0.91
Within-groups	184	48	3.83	
Total	198	52		

1. What is the sample size for this analysis? Explain how you know.

   A: 53 because the df_{total} is 52, and it was calculated by taking the sample size − 1. Therefore, for df_{total} to be 52, the sample size had to be 53.

(Continued)

(Continued)

2. How many groups were analyzed in this ANOVA? Explain how you know.

   A: There were 5 groups in the experiment. The $df_{between\text{-}groups}$ was 4, and it was calculated by taking the total number of groups − 1. Therefore, for $df_{between\text{-}groups}$ to be 4, the total number of groups had to be 5.

3. How was the $MS_{between\text{-}groups}$ calculated?

   A:
$$\frac{SS_{between\text{-}groups}}{df_{between\text{-}groups}}$$
$$\frac{14}{4} = 3.50$$

4. How was the $MS_{within\text{-}groups}$ calculated?

   A:
$$\frac{SS_{within\text{-}groups}}{df_{within\text{-}groups}}$$
$$\frac{184}{48} = 3.83$$

5. How was the F ratio test statistic calculated?

   A:
$$\frac{MS_{between\text{-}groups}}{MS_{within\text{-}groups}}$$
$$\frac{3.50}{3.83} = 0.91$$

Here are two additional examples to get practice calculating and interpreting a one-way, between-subjects ANOVA. The first example contains raw data from individual participants, and the second example provides summary statistics to work with.

Problem #2

A medical researcher is interested in testing the effectiveness of a new drug in reducing depressive symptomology. To do so, she randomly assigns clinically depressed people to one of three groups: one group that receives the experimental drug, one group that receives a placebo, and one group that receives nothing at all. The researcher gathers data from 15 people. Depressive symptoms are rated on a 1 (*low*) to 9 (*high*) response range. Here are the data from these 15 participants:

Type of Drug		
Experimental Drug	**Placebo**	**Nothing**
9	6	6
6	6	8
5	5	6
6	3	6
9	8	9

Questions to Answer:

1. What is the hypothesis being tested?
2. What alpha level will you use?
3. Interpret what this alpha level means.
4. What are the means being compared in this analysis?
5. (a) What is the total sums of squares? (b) What is the within-groups sums of squares? (c) What is the between-groups sums of squares?
6. (a) What are the total degrees of freedom? (b) What are the within-groups degrees of freedom? (c) What are the between-groups degrees of freedom?
7. (a) What is the within-groups mean square (*MS*)? (b) What is the between-groups mean square (*MS*)?
8. What is your *F* ratio?
9. Put the data you have calculated into an ANOVA summary table.
10. What is the critical value for this analysis?
11. Do you reject or fail to reject the null hypothesis?
12. What is the effect size (partial eta squared) for this analysis?
13. Find the HSD. What does this number mean in plain English?
14. Based on your answer to question 13, were any of the three types of drugs significantly different from each other?
15. In plain English, what do these analyses tell us?
16. Write this result in APA style.

Answers

1. There is no difference in depressive symptomology based on the drug that people ingested.
2. We'll use the usual .05.
3. An alpha of .05 means that we are accepting a 5% chance of rejecting the null hypothesis when in fact the null hypothesis is true in the population (i.e., we accept a 5% chance of making a Type I error).
4. Mean for Experimental Drug = 7.0; mean for Placebo = 5.60; mean for Nothing = 7.0
5. (a) 41.73; (b) 35.20; (c) 6.53
6. (a) 14; (b) 12; (c) 2
7. (a) 2.93; (b) 3.27
8. $F = \frac{3.27}{2.93} = 1.12$
9.

Source of variability	*SS*	*df*	*MS*	*F*
Between-groups	6.53	2	3.27	1.12
Within-groups	35.20	12	2.93	
Total	41.74	14		

(Continued)

(Continued)

10. For an alpha level of .05, the critical value is 3.89.
11. We fail to reject the null hypothesis because the F ratio is less than the critical value
12. $\eta_p^2 = \frac{6.53}{6.53 + 35.20}$

    $\eta_p^2 = .157$

13. $\text{HSD} = Q \times \sqrt{\frac{MS_{\text{within-groups}}}{\text{number of participants in each group}}}$

    $= 3.78 \times \sqrt{\frac{2.93}{5}}$

    $= 3.78 \times 0.7655$

    $= 2.89$

This number of 2.89 means that for a mean difference between any two groups to be statistically significant, that mean difference must be at least 2.89.

14. No, none of the mean differences were statistically different from each other.
15. There are no differences in depressive symptomology based on which one of the three drugs that people ingested.
16. A one-way, between-subjects ANOVA on depressive symptomology indicated no effect of type of drug, $F(2, 12) = 1.12$, $p > .05$, $\eta_p^2 = .157$. A follow-up Tukey's HSD test showed that those who ingested the experimental drug ($M = 7.0$) had similar levels of depressive symptomology as people who ingested the placebo ($M = 5.60$) and who ingested nothing ($M = 7.0$), both having $p > .05$. There was also no difference in depressive symptomology for the placebo and no drug groups, $p > .05$.

Problem #3

A researcher wants to compare the means of four groups. After collecting data from 48 people in a between-subjects design, here are summary statistics needed to test this hypothesis that there is no difference among those four group means, using an alpha of .05:

Group A mean = 30; Group B mean = 25; Group C mean = 20; Group D mean = 15

Within-groups sums of squares ($SS_{\text{within-groups}}$) = 50; Between-groups sums of squares ($SS_{\text{between-groups}}$) = 25

Questions to Answer:

1. Put these data into an ANOVA summary table.

A:

Source of variability	*SS*	*df*	*MS*	*F*
Between-groups	25	3	8.33	7.31
Within-groups	50	44	1.14	
Total	75	47		

(Continued)

2. What is the critical value in this analysis?

   A: Given our between-groups degrees of freedom (3) and within-groups degrees of freedom (44), and an alpha level of .05, we consult Appendix C and see that our critical value is 2.82.

3. Do you reject or fail to reject the null hypothesis in this example?

   A: Given that our *F* ratio test statistic is greater than the critical value, we reject the null hypothesis.

4. Calculate the effect size

   A:

$$\eta_p^2 = \frac{SS_{\text{between-groups}}}{SS_{\text{between-groups}} + SS_{\text{within-groups}}}$$

$$= \frac{25}{75}$$

$$= .33$$

5. Regarding post hoc tests, calculate the HSD for this example. Assume each group had 12 people in it. Explain in plain English what this HSD number means in relation to our example.

   A:

$$\text{HSD} = Q \times \sqrt{\frac{MS_{\text{within-groups}}}{\text{number of participants in each group}}}$$

$$= 4.20 \times \sqrt{\frac{1.14}{12}}$$

$$= 4.20 \times .308$$

$$= 1.29$$

This number of 1.29 indicates that for a mean difference between any two groups to be statistically significant, that mean difference must be at least 1.29. In this example, all mean differences are greater than 1.29; therefore, we conclude that each group was statistically significantly different from every other group.

One-Way, Between-Subjects ANOVA and SPSS

Now that you have a handle on the conceptual nature of the one-way, between-subjects ANOVA and know how to calculate it by hand, let's run our ANOVA using SPSS. As we've done previously, we will use some hypothetical data. Suppose that Eskine (2012) had included a third dependent variable in his experiment. For instance, when examining the effects of exposure to different types of food, he could have included a measure of self-esteem. By self-esteem, we mean a person's global evaluation of themselves. It might make sense that exposure to organic foods would result in higher levels of self-esteem than would exposure to control foods. Morris Rosenberg (1965) developed a widely used measure of self-esteem, in which people can respond on a 1 (*strongly disagree*) to 5 (*strongly agree*) response range to items such as "I am able to do things as well as most other people" and "I wish I could have more respect for myself (reverse-coded)." There are 10 items on this scale, so scores could potentially range from 10 to 50. We could easily use this scale and get an aggregate self-esteem score for each participant. Let's suppose we included this self-esteem scale as a dependent variable in Eskine's (2012) research. Here are the aggregate scores on it for a sample of 45 participants (15 in each experimental group):

Type of Food Seen					
Organic Foods		**Comfort Foods**		**Control Foods**	
48	37	25	26	15	45
25	41	41	18	35	28
42	36	35	40	25	24
50	45	46	24	40	31
30	31	22	48	25	29
47	29	35	35	34	38
41	44	42	28	42	32
38		26		22	

Establishing your spreadsheet

Once you open SPSS, you will need to click on *Variable View* in the lower left corner. You will need to name two variables, namely, the independent variable and the dependent variable. Again, the independent variable is the type of food to which people were exposed, either organic foods, comfort foods, or a control group of foods. Perhaps name this variable something such as `Type_of_Food_Seen`. Be sure to give it a label, too. I would just use the Label "Type of Food Seen." Next, name the dependent variable something such as `Self_Esteem`, and give it the same label. Remember that by giving labels to variables, it will make the SPSS output much easier to understand.

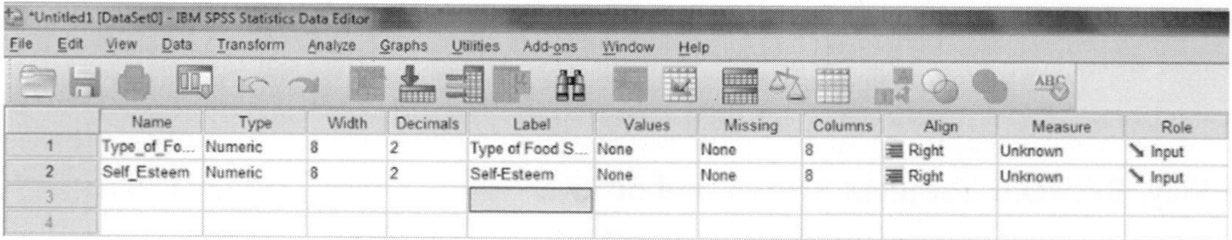

After naming your variables, we need to tell SPSS which experimental condition each participant was randomly assigned to. To do so, click on *Values for the Type of Food Seen*. Here, we must give numerical values to the group each participant was in during the experiment. These values are arbitrary, but for the sake of illustration here, let's all do the same thing: For the Organic Foods group, give it a `0`, and then give it a value label of "organic foods." For the Comfort Foods group, give it a `1`, and then give it a value label of "comfort foods." Finally, for the Control Foods group, give it a `2`, and then give it a value label of "control foods." Finally, make sure your measures are labeled appropriately, with the independent variable being nominal data and the dependent variable being scale.

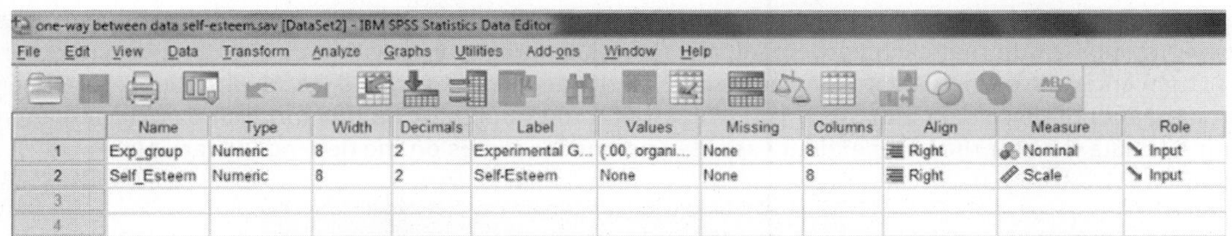

In the left corner of the screen, click on *Data View*. You are now ready to enter the data from these 45 participants.

As usual, it does not matter the order in which you enter these data. But of course, you must code correctly the experimental group that each participant was randomly assigned to (with a `0`, `1`, or `2` as described previously); then enter the participant's aggregated score on the dependent variable (i.e., `Self_Esteem`). Once you have entered all of these data into SPSS, you will have 45 rows of data (one row for each participant) and two columns of data (one for the independent variable and one for scores on the dependent variable).

*Untitled1 [DataSet0] - IBM SPSS Statistics Data Editor

File Edit View Data Transform Analyze Graphs Utiliti

10 :

	Type_of_Food_Seen	Self_Esteem	var	var
10	.00	31.00		
11	.00	47.00		
12	.00	29.00		
13	.00	41.00		
14	.00	44.00		
15	.00	38.00		
16	1.00	25.00		
17	1.00	26.00		
18	1.00	41.00		
19	1.00	18.00		
20	1.00	35.00		
21	1.00	40.00		
22	1.00	46.00		
23	1.00	24.00		
24	1.00	22.00		
25	1.00	48.00		
26	1.00	35.00		
27	1.00	35.00		
28	1.00	42.00		
29	1.00	28.00		
30	1.00	26.00		
31	2.00	15.00		
32	2.00	45.00		
33	2.00	35.00		
34	2.00	28.00		
35	2.00	25.00		
36	2.00	24.00		
37	2.00	40.00		

Data View Variable View

Note: Not all participants' data could be displayed on the screenshot

Running your analysis

We are now ready to run our one-way between-subjects ANOVA. To run the analyses:

1. Click on *Analyze → General Linear Model → Univariate.*

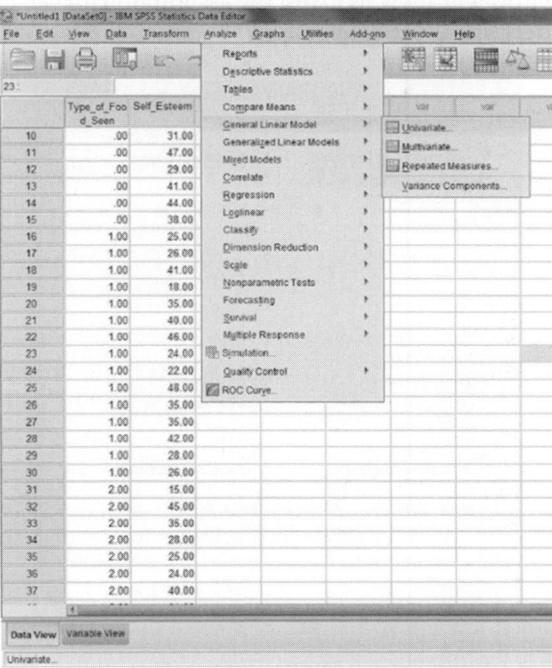

Be sure you keep in mind what the independent variable is and what the dependent variable is.

2. Click the independent variable (i.e., `Type_of_Food_Seen`) into the *Fixed Factor(s)* box.
3. Then, click over the dependent variable (i.e., `Self_Esteem`) into the *Dependent Variable* box.

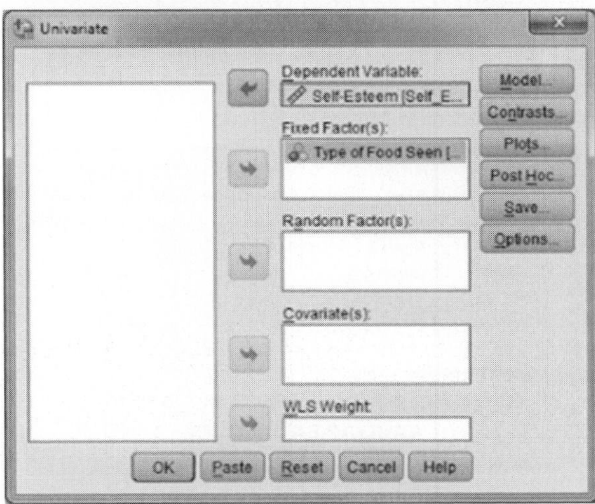

4. Click on *Options*. In the *Display* area on the lower half of this box, click on:
   a) *Descriptive statistics* (this will give us means and standard deviations),
   b) *Estimates of effect size*, and
   c) *Homogeneity tests* (this will allow us to test the assumption that all groups have equal variability on scores on the dependent variable).

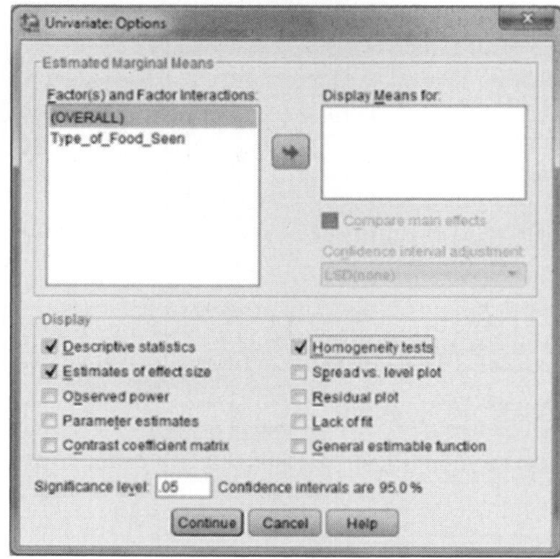

Then, Click *Continue*.

5. Now click on *Post Hoc*. Ask for post hoc tests for the independent variable (`Type_of_Food_Seen`). We are going to assume that the variances of the three groups are equal. We have lots of choices available to us for post hoc tests. Choose *Tukey* (in the second column of choices). Then click *Continue*.

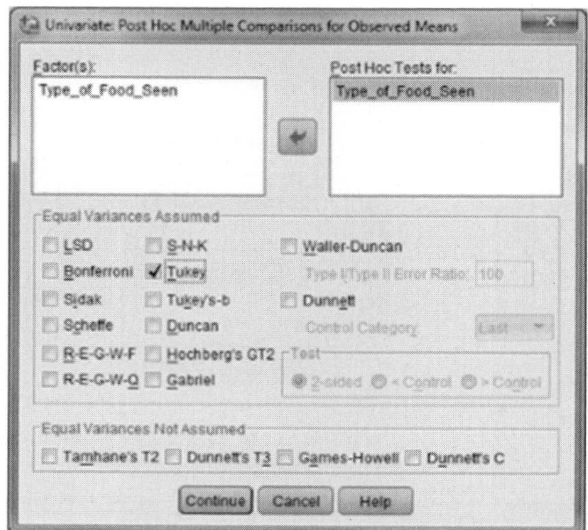

6. Then click *OK*, and your analyses will run.

Your output should look exactly like this (except without the notations that I will guide you through right now):

Univariate Analysis of Variance

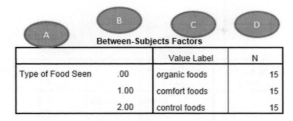

Between-Subjects Factors

		Value Label	N
Type of Food Seen	.00	organic foods	15
	1.00	comfort foods	15
	2.00	control foods	15

Descriptive Statistics

Dependent Variable: Self-Esteem

Type of Food Seen	Mean	Std. Deviation	N
Organic foods	38.9333	7.55425	15
comfort foods	32.7333	9.30796	15
control foods	31.0000	8.21149	15
Total	34.2222	8.89047	45

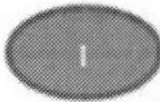

Levene's Test of Equality of Error Variances[a]

Dependent Variable: Self-Esteem

F	df1	df2	Sig.
.760	2	42	.474

Tests the null hypothesis that the error variance of the dependent variable is equal across groups.

a. Design: Intercept + Type_of_Food_Seen

Tests of Between-Subjects Effects

Dependent Variable: Self-Esteem

Source	Type III Sum of Squares	df	Mean Square	F	Sig.	Partial Eta Squared
~~Corrected Model~~	~~521.911[a]~~	~~2~~	~~260.956~~	~~3.708~~	~~.033~~	~~.150~~
~~Intercept~~	~~52702.222~~	~~1~~	~~52702.222~~	~~748.847~~	~~.000~~	~~.947~~
Type_of_Food_Seen	521.911	2	260.956	3.708	.033	.150
Error	2955.867	42	70.378			
~~Total~~	~~56180.000~~	~~45~~				
Corrected Total	3477.778	44				

a. R Squared = .150 (Adjusted R Squared = .110)

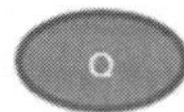

Post Hoc Tests

Type of Food Seen

Multiple Comparisons

Dependent Variable: Self-Esteem
Tukey HSD

(I) Type of Food Seen	(J) Type of Food Seen	Mean Difference (I-J)	Std. Error	Sig.	95% Confidence Interval Lower Bound	95% Confidence Interval Upper Bound
organic foods	comfort foods	6.2000	3.06328	.119	-1.2422	13.6422
	control foods	7.9333*	3.06328	.034	.4911	15.3756
comfort foods	organic foods	-6.2000	3.06328	.119	-13.6422	1.2422
	control foods	1.7333	3.06328	.839	-5.7089	9.1756
control foods	organic foods	-7.9333*	3.06328	.034	-15.3756	-.4911
	comfort foods	-1.7333	3.06328	.839	-9.1756	5.7089

Based on observed means.
The error term is Mean Square(Error) = 70.378.
*. The mean difference is significant at the .05 level.

What am I looking at? Interpreting your SPSS output

Let's make sense of what we see on this output, one step at a time.

A. This is the *independent variable,* which was the type of food to which participants were exposed. Keep in mind that the name that appears here, "Type of Food Seen," is what I labeled the independent variable in SPSS.

B. This is the arbitrary *numerical value I assigned to each experimental group* when I entered the data into SPSS.

C. This is *the name that I gave each group*, according to the numerical value that I assigned to it, in SPSS.

D. This is the *number of people in each experimental group*.

E. As SPSS was kind enough to state explicitly, this is the *dependent variable*.

F. First, the independent variable `Type_of_Food_Seen` is provided. More importantly at this point, these are the *levels of the independent variable*. In other words, there are the *groups created by manipulating the independent variable*.

G. This is the *mean for each experimental group*. In addition, there is a ***"Total" mean***, which is the ***grand mean*** for the experiment.

H. This is the *standard deviation for each experimental group*.

Although these data are very basic to you at this point in the class, remember that we ultimately need the group means and the group standard deviations when reporting our ANOVA results.

I. Here is where we test the assumption of ANOVA that there is homogeneity of variability between the groups in the analysis. Just as with t tests, this assumption is tested with a Levene's Test of Equality.

For this statistical test, *we are testing the hypothesis that there is no difference in variability across the three groups in our analysis*. If we reject this hypothesis, we would need to conclude that there is a difference between the variability among the three groups, and therefore, this assumption would be violated.

Here, the *p* value ("Sig" on the SPSS printout) is .474. Because this *p* value is above .05, we do not reject the null hypothesis and conclude that the variability across the three groups was the same (in other words, we did not violate this assumption).

J. This column contains the *sources of variability* in the experiment. As discussed previously, there are two sources of variability in any experiment: (1) between-groups variability and (2) within-groups variability. Summed together, they give us the total variability in the experiment. Why then are there six sources of variability in this column? For our purposes of interpreting this output, we can ignore the first two rows, *Corrected Model*, *Intercept*, and the second-to-last row, *Total*. However, pay close attention to the other three rows. In this example:
   a. `Type_of_Food_Seen` is the between-groups variability. Regardless of what you named it in the *Variable View* tab, the between-groups variability will appear as the third row in the *Test of Between-Subjects Effects*.
   b. *Error* is the within-groups variability.
   c. *Corrected Total* is the sum of the between-groups variability and the within-groups variability (that is, it is the total variability in the experiment).

K. This column quantifies *the between-groups sums of squares* ($SS_{between\text{-}groups}$), *the within-groups sums of squares* ($SS_{within\text{-}groups}$), *and the total sums of squares* (SS_{total}) in the experiment. When we hand-calculated an ANOVA in the previous section of this chapter, this is step 3 of that process. In this case:
   a. Between-groups sums of squares is 521.911.
   b. Within-groups sums of squares is 2955.867.
   c. Total sums of squares is the sum of between-groups and within-groups variability, so here, total variability is 3477.778.

L. This column contains the *degrees of freedom (df) for each source of variability* in the experiment. This is step 4 from our hand-calculations in the previous section of this chapter. Again, we only care about the same three rows of information. Let's refresh how these numbers get calculated:
   a. $df_{between\text{-}groups}$ is calculated by taking the number of groups in the ANOVA, less 1. So here, $df_{between\text{-}groups} = 2$ because there were 3 groups in the analysis, and $3 - 1 = 2$.
   b. $df_{within\text{-}groups}$ is calculated by taking our sample size and subtracting from it the number of groups in the ANOVA. So here, $df_{within\text{-}groups} = 42$ because the sample was 45 people and there were 3 groups: $45 - 3 = 42$.
   c. Finally, df_{total} is calculated by taking our sample size, less 1. Here, $df_{total} = 44$ because the sample size was 45, and $45 - 1 = 44$.

M. Here are our *mean squares* (*MS*s). This is step 5 of the hand-calculations. Just so you know where, in general, these numbers came from, keep in mind the general formula for *MS*s:

$$\frac{\text{Sums of squares } (SS)}{df}$$

So in our example:

$$MS_{\text{between-groups}}: \frac{521.911}{2}$$
$$= 260.956$$

$$MS_{\text{within-groups}}: \frac{2955.867}{42}$$
$$= 70.378$$

There is no need to calculate a total *MS*, so SPSS does not do so.

N. This is our *F ratio*. There are three listed here, but the only one that's relevant to us is the one in the between-groups row (the third one down in this column), $F = 3.708$. Here again is the general formula for the *F* ratio, which we presented in step 6 of our hand-calculations:

$$F = \frac{MS_{\text{between-groups}}}{MS_{\text{within-groups}}}$$

Here is how our *F* ratio of 3.708 appeared on the output:

$$3.708 = \frac{260.956}{70.378}$$

O. This is the *p value, or significance level,* of our *F* ratio. Here, our *p* value was .033. This is a combination of steps 7 and 8 from our hand-calculations. SPSS does not provide us with a critical value to compare our *F* ratio to; however, it is using one, I promise. Here, there is a 3.3% chance that our obtained *F* ratio was due to random variation and not to the independent variable. Because this value is less than .05, we can conclude that there is a significant difference between at least two group means in the ANOVA (i.e., we can generalize our results from the sample to the population). Of course, as we know from the previous section of this chapter, we need to dig a little deeper to see which means are significantly different from each other. We'll do that digging in just a bit.

P. But first we need to examine our *effect size*. Our partial eta squared (η_p^2) is .15. Here is how that statistic was derived:

$$\eta_p^2 = \frac{SS_{\text{between-groups}}}{SS_{\text{between-groups}} + SS_{\text{within-groups}}}$$

$$= \frac{521.911}{521.911 + 2955.867}$$
$$= \frac{521.911}{3477.778}$$
$$= .15$$

Q. Here is where we learn which group means are significantly different from each other. These are our *post hoc tests*; again, they are "post hoc" because we do them after we obtain our *F* ratio.

R. and S. In a sense, these two columns are interchangeable. Each one lists, side by side, the groups being compared in the ANOVA. SPSS does this because we need to examine the difference between each pair of group means.

T. This is the difference between the two means listed in R and S in that row. SPSS takes the group mean under R and subtracts from it the group mean under S. Now, it would nice if SPSS put the means being compared in this table, but it does not. We need to refer back to the means listed at the start of the output to see what two means constitute the difference listed here. For instance, the mean self-esteem level for the organic foods group was 38.93. The mean self-esteem level for the comfort foods groups was 32.73. The difference between these means is 6.20.

One word of minor caution: There is redundant information here. All meaningful information is presented twice. Here, it simply depends on which mean is subtracted from which other mean. For instance, the first row in this table takes organic foods and subtracts from it comfort foods. However, look down to the third row, and you'll see that it takes comfort foods and subtracts from it organic foods. The absolute value of the mean difference is the same, but the direction will be different (positive or negative). The important thing is to examine the absolute value of the mean difference.

U. This is the *p* value, or significance level, of the mean difference in T. This is where we learn which pair(s) of group means are and are not significantly different. Here we see that the difference between the organic food group and the comfort food group (a mean difference of 6.20) was not statistically significant, with a *p* value of .119. The difference between the organic food group and the control food group (a mean difference of 7.93) was statistically significant, with a *p* value of .034. Finally, the difference between the comfort food group and the control food group (a mean difference of 1.73) was not statistically significant with a *p* value of .839. Therefore, the only means that were different from each other with statistical significance were the organic foods group mean of 38.93 and the control foods group mean of 31.00.

V. Finally, SPSS provides us with 95% confidence intervals around the difference between each pair of group means. Interestingly, however, these confidence intervals are not always, or as best I can tell, even usually reported in research studies that use ANOVAs. This is interesting, given that they tend to be reported in the world of *t* tests. But given that SPSS provides this output with post hoc tests, now you're aware of it.

Please do not forget that SPSS output means nothing if we do not communicate what the output is trying to tell us. Here are the results of this analysis in APA style:

A one-way, between-subjects analysis of variance (ANOVA) revealed an overall effect of food type on self-esteem, $F(2, 42) = 3.71$, $p = .033$, $\eta_p^2 = .150$. A follow-up Tukey's honestly significant difference (HSD) test showed that those exposed to organic food had higher self-esteem ($M = 38.93$, $SD = 7.50$) than those exposed to control foods ($M = 31.00$, $SD = 8.21$), $p = .034$. No other comparisons were statistically significant.

LEARNING CHECK

Now that you have a good idea of how to digest the SPSS output for a one-way, between-subjects ANOVA, let's drive home that understanding. Let's use our dataset from the hand-calculations in the previous section to generate SPSS output and to make sure it's sinking in. Here again are those data; enter them into SPSS, and run your one-way, between-subjects ANOVA.

Experimental Group		
Organic Foods	**Comfort Foods**	**Control Foods**
6	4	5
5	4	6
7	3	4
4	5	1

Here is what your output should look like:

Univariate Analysis of Variance

Between-Subjects Factors

		Value Label	N
Type of Food Seen	.00	organic foods	4
	1.00	comfort foods	4
	2.00	control group	4

Descriptive Statistics

Dependent Variable: Moral Evaluations

Type of Food Seen	Mean	Std. Deviation	N
organic foods	5.5000	1.29099	4
comfort foods	4.0000	.81650	4
control group	4.0000	2.16025	4
Total	4.5000	1.56670	12

Levene's Test of Equality of Error Variances[a]

Dependent Variable: Moral Evaluations

F	df1	df2	Sig.
1.286	2	9	.323

Tests the null hypothesis that the error variance of the dependent variable is equal across groups.

a. Design: Intercept + Type_of_Food_Seen

Tests of Between-Subjects Effects

Dependent Variable: Moral Evaluations

Source	Type III Sum of Squares	df	Mean Square	F	Sig.	Partial Eta Squared
Corrected Model	6.000[a]	2	3.000	1.286	.323	.222
Intercept	243.000	1	243.000	104.143	.000	.920
Type_of_Food_Seen	6.000	2	3.000	1.286	.323	.222
Error	21.000	9	2.333			
Total	270.000	12				
Corrected Total	27.000	11				

a. R Squared = .222 (Adjusted R Squared = .049)

Post Hoc Tests

Type of Food Seen

Multiple Comparisons

Dependent Variable: Moral Evaluations

Tukey HSD

(I) Type of Food Seen	(J) Type of Food Seen	Mean Difference (I-J)	Std. Error	Sig.	95% Confidence Interval	
					Lower Bound	Upper Bound
organic foods	comfort foods	1.5000	1.08012	.386	-1.5157	4.5157
	control group	1.5000	1.08012	.386	-1.5157	4.5157
comfort foods	organic foods	-1.5000	1.08012	.386	-4.5157	1.5157
	control group	.0000	1.08012	1.000	-3.0157	3.0157
control group	organic foods	-1.5000	1.08012	.386	-4.5157	1.5157
	comfort foods	.0000	1.08012	1.000	-3.0157	3.0157

Based on observed means.

The error term is Mean Square(Error) = 2.333.

(Continued)

(Continued)

1. What is the hypothesis being tested?
2. What is the mean for each of the three groups?
3. What is the standard deviation for each group?
4. Was the assumption of homogeneity of variances violated?
5. What are the two sources of variability in these data?
6. Plug in the numbers needed to obtain the *F* ratio test statistic of 1.286.
7. According to Appendix C, and assuming an alpha level of .05, what is the critical value that was used to see whether we reject or do not reject the null hypothesis?
8. What is the precise probability that the differences among our group means were due to random variation?
9. Did the researchers reject or not reject the null hypothesis?
10. Given your answer to question 9, what does that mean in plain English?
11. What is the effect size?
12. Which means, if any, are statistically different from one another?

Answers

1. That there is no difference in moral evaluations based on the type of food to which people were exposed.
2. Organic foods = 5.50; Comfort foods = 4.00; Control Foods = 4.00
3. Organic foods = 1.29; Comfort foods = 0.82; Control Foods = 2.16
4. Looking at the Levene's Test of Equality of Error Variances, we see that the *p* value, which is denoted as "Sig.", is greater than .05. Therefore, we fail to reject the notion that variances are similar across our three groups. In plain English, this assumption was not violated.
5. We have (a) between-groups variability and (b) within-groups variability, which SPSS labels *Error*.
6. $F = \frac{3}{2.33}$
7. With 2 between-groups degrees of freedom, 9 within-groups degrees of freedom, and using an alpha level of .05, our critical value is 4.26.
8. The "Sig" level (*p* value) of .323 means that there is a 32.3% chance that the differences between our means are due to random variation.
9. The researchers failed to reject the null hypothesis because, as noted in the previous answer, the *p* value exceeded .05.
10. There is no difference in people's moral evaluation of behavior based on whether they were exposed to organic foods, comfort foods, or a control group of foods.
11. The effect size is the partial eta squared, which is 0.222.
12. Because the *F* ratio test statistic was not statistically significant, we know that none of the means are different from each other. To confirm this is the case, examination of the post hoc tests confirms that all mean differences fall outside the region of null hypothesis rejection (in others words, all *p* values are greater than .05).

NOTES

1. I have no reason to think that Dr. Pepper will be preferred to Coke or Pepsi other than the fact that Dr. Pepper has its headquarters in my hometown of Plano, Texas, and that it is my favorite type of soda. Clearly, we should not base a research hypothesis on such personal anecdotes.
2. If you're wondering why the ANOVA is an "*F*" ratio, the tool was developed by Sir Ronald Fisher. If you want to learn more about this person, you should read Joan Box's (1978) biography of him.
3. The critical value would be closer to 3.15 given that 59 within-groups degrees of freedom is obviously closer to 60 than it is to 44. However, to be conservative and make it difficult to reject our null hypothesis, I want us to stack the deck against rejecting the null hypothesis. Therefore, the critical value of 3.18 is slightly biased against rejecting the null hypothesis.

CHAPTER APPLICATION QUESTIONS

1. When would a researcher use a one-way, between-subjects ANOVA instead of an independent samples *t* test?
2. Related to the previous question, why is an ANOVA preferable to conducting multiple *t* tests?
3. Why is the one-way, between-subjects ANOVA called "one-way?" Why is it called "between-subjects?"
4. Why can the *F* ratio test statistic never be less than zero?
5. Suppose you conducted a study with 5 groups and a sample size of 25 people. What is your critical value for this ANOVA (a) using an alpha level of .05 and (b) using an alpha level of .01? Why is the critical value larger for an alpha level of .01 than it is for an alpha level of .05?
6. If you have a statistically significant *F* ratio test statistic, what must you do after calculating the effect size? Why do you have to do this?
7. You see the following statistical analysis presented from an experiment to which participants were randomly assigned to one and only one group:

$$F(3, 120) = 3.78, p < .05, \eta_p^2 = .21$$

   What can you conclude from this information?

   I. The sample size was 123.
   II. The result can be generalized from the sample to the population.
   III. We need to conduct post hoc tests now.

   a) I only
   b) II and III
   c) I and III
   d) none of the above can be concluded.
8. On average, what value is expected for the *F* ratio test statistic if the null hypothesis is true?

9. Below is the distribution of *F* ratio test statistics:

Figure 9.6

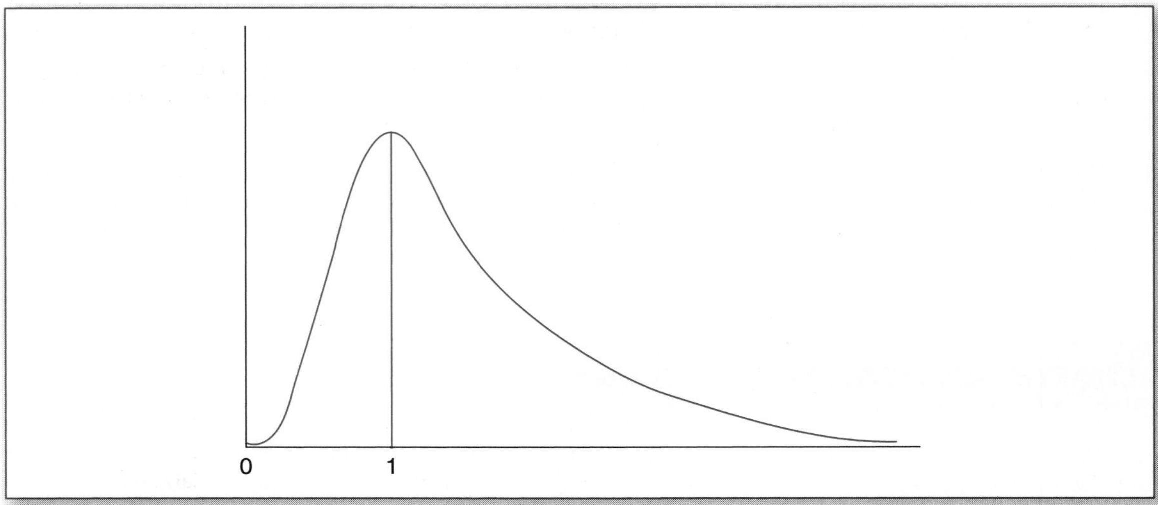

It is _____ skewed because _____.

a) positively; it is normal to have a large test statistic
b) negatively; it is normal to have a small test statistic
c) positively; it is rare to have a large test statistic
d) negatively; it is rare to have a small test statistic

10. What is the purpose of a post hoc test?
    a) to determine whether a Type I error was made in the ANOVA
    b) to determine whether a Type II error was made in the ANOVA
    c) to determine which groups are significantly different from each other
    d) to determine the effect size of the analysis

Answers

1. When there are three or more group means to compare, the ANOVA is the better analytic tool to use.
2. The ANOVA is the better analytic tool because it balances the risk of making a Type I error and a Type II error while performing multiple comparisons.
3. It is "one-way" because it analyzes the effects of one independent variable. It is "between-subjects" because each participant provides data to one and only one experimental group.
4. The *F* ratio is as follows:

$$F = \frac{\text{Systematic variance} + \text{error variance}}{\text{Error variance}}$$

Because variance can never be negative, an *F* ratio can never be less than zero.

5. A: Remember that $df_{\text{between-groups}}$ is calculated as the number of groups being compared, minus 1. So here, we have 5 – 1 = 4. In addition, $df_{\text{within-groups}}$ is calculated as the sample size minus the number of groups being compared. So here, we have 25 – 5 = 20. Now consult Appendix C. (a) For an alpha level of .05, our critical value is 2.87. (b) For an alpha level of .01, our critical value is 4.43. (c) The critical value is larger for an alpha level of .01 because the larger the alpha level, the less willing we are to accept making a Type I error. The larger the critical value, the less chance we have of making a Type I error.
6. Conduct post hoc tests. The *F* ratio provides an omnibus test; that is, it tells us there is some significant difference between group means somewhere in the data, but it does not tell us precisely what means are different. Post hoc tests allow us to learn which means are different from each other.
7. b
8. 1
9. c
10. c

QUESTIONS FOR CLASS DISCUSSION

1. Differentiate between the concepts of between-groups variability and within-groups variability.
2. Below is a partially completed ANOVA summary table.

Source of variability	*SS*	*df*	*MS*	*F*
Between-groups	20	4	????	?????
Within-groups	225	????	????	
Total	????	94		

   a. Fill in the missing pieces of information.
   b. What was our sample size in this analysis?
   c. How many groups were in this analysis?
   d. By applying a .05 significance level, what is the approximate critical value in this analysis?
   e. Do you reject or fail to reject the null hypothesis in this example?
   f. What is the effect size?

3. All other things being equal, what will happen to the value of the *F* ratio test statistic as:
   a. the sample size increases?
   b. the between-groups variability decreases?
   c. the within-groups variability increases?
   d. you use an alpha level of .01 instead of .05?
4. Here is a description of a research study, followed by an APA style report of its results. Use the write-up to answer the questions that follow it.

Paul Cherulnik and Scott Wilderman (1986) examined the impressions that people form of a person living in either a lower middle-class, a middle-class, or an upper middle-class home. Higher numbers indicate a more positive impression of the homeowner. Hypothetical results from their research are as follows:

> A one-way, between-subjects analysis of variance (ANOVA) revealed an overall effect of socioeconomic level of housing on impressions formed of occupants $F(2, 66) = 4.56$, $p < .03$, $\eta_p^2 = .17$. Tukey's honestly significant difference (HSD) test showed that participants formed more positive impressions of a person when that person lived in a middle-class house ($M = 20.00$, $SD = 5.00$) than when living in a lower middle-class house ($M = 15.13$, $SD = 4.25$), $p < .05$, or an upper middle-class house ($M = 10.33$, $SD = 3.62$), $p < .001$. In addition, people formed more positive impressions of a person living in a lower middle-class house than in an upper middle-class house, $p < .05$.

Questions to Answer

a. What was the hypothesis being tested in this research?

b. What were the means being statistically examined?

c. What is the *F* ratio?

d. How many degrees of freedom do the researchers have for this analysis?

e. According to Appendix C, and using an alpha level of .05, approximate the critical value that was used to see whether we reject or do not reject the null hypothesis.

f. What is the probability that the differences among the three groups' means were due to random variation?

g. Did the researchers reject or not reject the null hypothesis?

h. What is the effect size? Interpret what this number means.

i. Given your answer to the previous questions, what does this statistical presentation mean in plain English?

Answers

a. The hypothesis being tested is that there is no difference in impressions of people who live in lower middle-class, middle-class, or upper middle-class houses.

b. Lower middle-class = 20; middle-class = 15.13; upper middle-class = 10.33

c. $F = 4.56$

d. $df_{\text{between-groups}} = 2$; $df_{\text{within-groups}} = 66$

e. The critical value would be slightly less than 3.15, which is the critical value for $df_{\text{within-groups}}$ of 60 and $dfs_{\text{between-groups}}$ of 2.

f. $p < .03$ means that there is less than a 3% chance that the difference among the group means was due to random variation.

g. Because the *F* ratio test statistic of 4.56 exceeded the critical value, the null hypothesis was rejected.

h. .17, which means that 17% of the variability in impressions formed was due to the type of house the occupant lived in.

i. People formed the most positive impression of a person when that person lived in a middle-class house. In addition, people formed more positive impressions of a person living in a lower middle-class house than in an upper middle-class house.

CHAPTER 10

Comparing Three or More Repeated Group Means

The One-Way, Repeated-Measures Analysis of Variance (ANOVA)

After reading this chapter, you will be able to

- Differentiate between the one-way, between-subjects ANOVA and the one-way, repeated-measures ANOVA
- Interpret the conceptual ingredients of the one-way, repeated-measures ANOVA
- Contrast the unique conceptual ingredients of the one-way, repeated-measures ANOVA with the one-way, between-subjects ANOVA
- Interpret an APA style presentation of a one-way, repeated-measures ANOVA
- Hand-calculate all ingredients for a one-way, repeated-measures ANOVA
- Conduct and interpret a one-way, repeated-measures ANOVA using SPSS

Recall from Chapters 7 and 8 that we have two types of *t* tests. One of these *t* tests is used when participants are assigned to one and only one group. This is the independent samples *t* test. The one-way, between-subjects ANOVA that we examined in the previous chapter is an extension of the independent samples *t* test. We use the one-way, between-subjects ANOVA when we have one independent variable with three or more levels and each participant is assigned to one, and only one, of those levels.

The second type of *t* test is the paired samples *t* test. It is used when participants provide two datapoints in a study. As you may have guessed, some studies have participants provide three or more datapoints in a study. In these situations, we need what's called a **one-way, repeated-measures ANOVA**. Let's take a simple example of this statistical tool. As a teacher, I of course keep track of my students' grades on exams and other assignments throughout the semester. Each fall, I give three exams in my "Introductory Psychology" class. With each course, I look (and hope) to see that students' grades improve after the first exam, which is often a hard one for new college students. Therefore, to see whether there was a statistically significant difference among the exam scores for my class, I would use a one-way, repeated-measures ANOVA with each student in the class providing three datapoints, that is, their scores on the three exams.. The one independent variable is the exam number (first, second, and third), and the dependent variable is exam scores.

One-way, repeated-measures ANOVA: analysis in which there is one independent variable and each participant contributes data to all levels of the experiment.

In the first major section, as in the previous three chapters, we will start by discussing a published research study that used our new statistical tool. Then, we will learn about the conceptual nature of the tool. Finally, we will discover how to interpret published results that used this tool. In the next major section, we will do our hand-calculations and learn how to use this tool with the software program Statistical Package for the Social Sciences (SPSS).

CONCEPTUAL UNDERSTANDING OF THE TOOL

The Study

When psychologists studied the topic of racial prejudice during the 1950s and 1960s, they used measures such as the Multifactor Racial Attitudes Inventory (Woodmansee & Cook, 1967). Items from this scale include "The problem of racial prejudice has been greatly exaggerated by a few black agitators" and "I would rather not have blacks live in the same apartment building I live in." Even if someone agreed with such statements, at some level, most people know they shouldn't feel this way. And even if someone did feel this way, probably know that they shouldn't express such feelings overtly. Most people want to appear nonprejudiced, both to themselves and to other people (Crandall & Eshleman, 2003). This is called the justification-suppression model of the expression of prejudice. Unlike 60 or 70 years ago, racism and discrimination manifest themselves today in subtle ways that may be difficult to discern. So, psychologists have had to devise more creative ways to study the topic of prejudice.

It is against this societal and empirical backdrop that we consider a study that Donte Bernard, Jessica McManus, and Donald Saucier (2014) conducted. At the time of their research, people were still (and still are) feeling the effects of the 2008-2009 stock market collapse and resulting Great Recession. As a result of that, most of us became worried about our finances and started watching our money more carefully. As I don't need to tell you, going to college is not an inexpensive endeavor. In addition to tuition, books, lab/studio fees, other supplies, and perhaps room and board, another expense most students need to cover is what are called, among other things, "privilege fees," "student life fees," or "campus access fees." These fees are ones that support campus services such as the student union, the recreation and workout center, the health center, and various student organizations on campus. Each student pays this fee, and that sum then gets divided up by campus administrators and, hopefully, student government representatives to support these various campus functions.

Bernard and his colleagues (2014) conducted an experiment in which 204 White students at Kansas State University were asked to allocate the University's $300 student life fee and allocate it among 15 different student organizations: Agricultural Student Council, Architecture Planning and Design, Black Student Union, College of Business Ambassadors, Dairy Science Club, Engineering Student Council, Arts & Sciences Student Council, History Club, International Buddies, Kinesiology Student Association, Economics Club, Math Club, International Honor Society of Psychology, Social Work Organization, and Union Program Council. Thus, each participant allocated some amount of money to each of thesestudent groups. Participants could allocate $0 to some of these groups if they so desired. That was the experiment. It had one independent variable, student organization. This independent variable had 15 groups, each student organization to which participants allocated money.

Figure 10.1 Materials Used in Bernard et al.'s Research

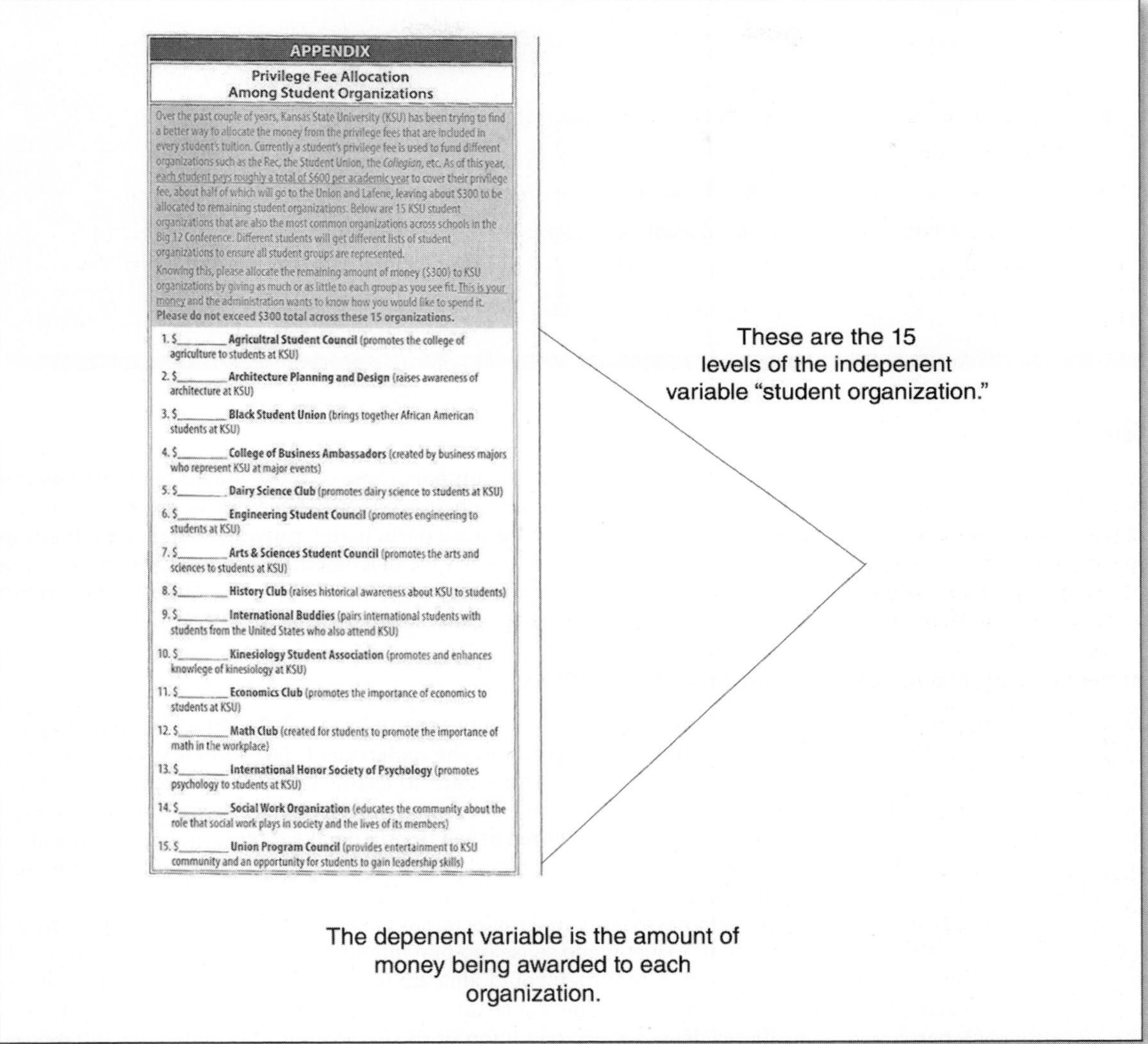

APPENDIX

Privilege Fee Allocation Among Student Organizations

Over the past couple of years, Kansas State University (KSU) has been trying to find a better way to allocate the money from the privilege fees that are included in every student's tuition. Currently a student's privilege fee is used to fund different organizations such as the Rec, the Student Union, the *Collegian*, etc. As of this year, each student pays roughly a total of $600 per academic year to cover their privilege fee, about half of which will go to the Union and Lafene, leaving about $300 to be allocated to remaining student organizations. Below are 15 KSU student organizations that are also the most common organizations across schools in the Big 12 Conference. Different students will get different lists of student organizations to ensure all student groups are represented.

Knowing this, please allocate the remaining amount of money ($300) to KSU organizations by giving as much or as little to each group as you see fit. This is your money and the administration wants to know how you would like to spend it. **Please do not exceed $300 total across these 15 organizations.**

1. $________ **Agricultral Student Council** (promotes the college of agriculture to students at KSU)
2. $________ **Architecture Planning and Design** (raises awareness of architecture at KSU)
3. $________ **Black Student Union** (brings together African American students at KSU)
4. $________ **College of Business Ambassadors** (created by business majors who represent KSU at major events)
5. $________ **Dairy Science Club** (promotes dairy science to students at KSU)
6. $________ **Engineering Student Council** (promotes engineering to students at KSU)
7. $________ **Arts & Sciences Student Council** (promotes the arts and sciences to students at KSU)
8. $________ **History Club** (raises historical awareness about KSU to students)
9. $________ **International Buddies** (pairs international students with students from the United States who also attend KSU)
10. $________ **Kinesiology Student Association** (promotes and enhances knowlege of kinesiology at KSU)
11. $________ **Economics Club** (promotes the importance of economics to students at KSU)
12. $________ **Math Club** (created for students to promote the importance of math in the workplace)
13. $________ **International Honor Society of Psychology** (promotes psychology to students at KSU)
14. $________ **Social Work Organization** (educates the community about the role that social work plays in society and the lives of its members)
15. $________ **Union Program Council** (provides entertainment to KSU community and an opportunity for students to gain leadership skills)

These are the 15 levels of the indepenent variable "student organization."
The depenent variable is the amount of money being awarded to each organization.

Source: Stimulus materials from Bernard et al.'s (2014) research: Bernard, D. L., McManus, J. L., & Saucier, D. A. (2014). Blacks in the red: Racial discrimination in funding allocations. *Psi Chi Journal of Psychological Research, 19,* 28–36.

Why was this experiment considered to be "repeated measures?" Each of the 204 participants had to make an allocation to each 1 of the 15 student organizations listed. Thus, each participant provided 15 datapoints to the experiment. A between-subjects experiment would have asked each participant to provide a dollar amount to just one student organization, and as you might be thinking, that would not have been a terribly realistic situation as funding allocations are typically made among multiple groups. Figure 10.1 contains a visual depiction of this experiment.

LEARNING CHECK

1. What is the independent variable in Bernard et al.'s (2014) experiment?
   A: Student organization
2. How many conditions were created from the manipulation of this independent variable?
   A: 15
3. What is the dependent variable in Bernard et al.'s (2014) experiment?
   A: Amount of money allocated to each student organization
4. How was the dependent variable operationalized?
   A: Allocation of $300 among the 15 student organizations

The Tool

As noted previously, the name of the statistical tool we need to compare three or more means generated by the people is called the *one-way, repeated-measures ANOVA*. To refresh, it is *one-way* because we are analyzing the effects of one independent variable. It is *repeated-measures* because participants provided data for each group in the experiment. As with the one-way, between-subjects ANOVA we discussed in the previous chapter, the one-way, repeated-measures ANOVA allows us to learn, when comparing three or more group means, if there are differences among these means within our sample that are generalizable to the population.

Between-subjects versus repeated-measures ANOVAs

The repeated-measures ANOVA has a key advantage over the between-subjects ANOVA. In a between-subjects ANOVA, a participant is assigned to one and only one group in the experiment. For some experiments, it is necessary, from a methodological standpoint, to do this. Think back to Eskine's (2012) research, in which he had people view one of three types of foods (organic, comfort, or control) before making moral evaluations. Had he exposed his participants to all three types of food and then asked them to make their moral judgments after seeing each type of food, that would have probably seemed weird to participants. I bet they could have guessed what was going on in that experiment. That would have been a huge confounding variable.

Bernard et al. (2014) had each participant necessarily make allocations to each of the 15 student organizations (i.e., all 15 groups in the experiment). Doing so just made sense (no pun intended) from a methodological standpoint. If participants had just one organization that they could allocate the $300 to, we would not be able to compare their relative feelings toward all the clubs. The statistical beauty of the repeated-measures ANOVA is that because each participant contributes data to every condition of the experiment, *the individual differences that can be problematic in a between-subjects research design are less problematic in a repeated-measures research design*. Certainly, participants still differ in many ways, but those differences exist across all experimental conditions, so they have far less effect than they do in a between-subjects ANOVA.

Recall that an ANOVA is a competition between (a) variability traceable to the independent variable and (b) variability traceable to factors other than the independent variable. In the big picture, nothing has changed moving from between-subjects to repeated-measures ANOVA. On a more detailed level, however, there is now, in a repeated-measures ANOVA, less variability traceable to factors other than the independent variable because participant individual differences exist across all conditions of the experiment. For example, I tend to have a high level of agreeableness (Costa & McCrae, 2008). That is, I don't like to upset people and want everyone to get along with each other. Thus, had I been a participant in Bernard et al.'s (2014) experiment, I likely would have divided up the $300 equally between the groups, not because I was equally interested in them, but because I didn't want to upset anyone associated with them. My agreeable tendencies would have existed across all 15 experimental conditions, and it would not have influenced my allocation to any one student organization alone. The bottom line to remember is that *there is less within-groups variability in a repeated-measures ANOVA than in a between-subjects ANOVA.*

Assumptions of the tool

Of course, as with our previous inferential statistical tools, we have some assumptions that we need to be aware of when conducting a repeated-measures ANOVA. The first three assumptions are the same as they are for the between-subjects ANOVA, so we'll list them quickly here:

1. The variability of each group must be approximately equal to the variability of every other group in the analysis.
2. Scores on the dependent variable must be normally distributed.
3. The data for the dependent variable must be measured on an interval or a ratio scale.
4. There is a fourth assumption of the repeated-measures ANOVA. Specifically, this assumption is that each participant does not undergo some sort of drastic change throughout the course of the research study. For instance, suppose a participant in Bernard et al.'s (2014) research got a phone call in the middle of allocating funds to each student organization. This phone call was from the participant's mom, who said their family was moving 2,000 miles away because of a new job opportunity. Might such a development affect the participant's behavior in this experiment? Perhaps, or maybe not. Regardless, because each participant is providing multiple datapoints, things can happen during the time it takes to provide multiple datapoints, and those developments can affect peoples' behaviors and cognitions.

In returning to Bernard et al.'s (2014) research, as you may have noticed when you examined Figure 10.1, one of these student organizations in this experiment is one that explicitly supports a racial minority group (that is, the Black Student Union). This is the group that was of particular interest in Bernard et al.'s research. As we noted at the start of our discussion of the one-way, repeated-measures ANOVA, researchers have needed to develop subtle ways to examine prejudice. In this experiment, there was $300 to be allocated among 15 student organizations. On average, that would mean $20 would be allocated to each student organization. Of course, some participants might give more money to organizations in which they had a particular interest, but on average, we should see $20 allocated to each organization. If an organization, such as the Black Student Union, was allocated significantly less than other organizations, it could be a sign of prejudice against that group. Indeed, this was precisely what Bernard and his colleagues were studying in this experiment.

Hypothesis from Bernard et al. (2014)

Of course, statistically, we always test the null hypothesis. In this research, the null hypothesis is that there is no difference in money allocated to the 15 student organizations. Think about how this null hypothesis would look symbolically; you will have a chance to write it out in the next Learning Check.

Here is the research hypothesis that Bernard et al. (2014) offered:

> We hypothesized that a student organization that supported a racial minority group would be allocated significantly less money than student organizations that did not support a racial minority group. (p. 31)

Think about how to express this research hypothesis symbolically, and move on to the Learning Check.

LEARNING CHECK

1. How are the one-way, between subjects ANOVA and one-way, repeated-measures ANOVA similar? How are these two analytic tools different?

   A: They are similar in that they both compare differences among three or more group means. They are different because in a between-subjects ANOVA, each person contributes data to one and only one group being analyzed. In a repeated-measures ANOVA, each person will have contributed data to each group being analyzed. In Bernard et al.'s (2104) research, each participant provided 15 datapoints, one for each student organization to which he or she allocated money (even if he or she did not allocate any money to a student organization, it was still a datapoint of $0).

2. What is the primary advantage of using a one-way, repeated-measures ANOVA instead of the one-way, between-subjects ANOVA?

   A: The repeated-measures ANOVA contains less within-group variability than does the between-subjects ANOVA. Because each person contribute data to all groups being analyzed, participant individual differences are less influential in a repeated-measures ANOVA than they are in a between-subjects ANOVA.

3. Given this advantage of the one-way, repeated-measures tool, why would a researcher ever use the one-way, between-subjects ANOVA?

   A: It may not be practical to use a repeated-measures design. For instance, if you wanted to study how exposure to physically attractive models influences how much people are willing to pay for a product that the model is advertising, it would probably not be a good idea to have the same participants respond to the same product being advertised by an attractive model and again by a less attractive model. Doing so will make it easy to guess the purpose of the research, something researchers don't want to have happen.

4. By using symbols, state the null (H_o) and research (H_r) hypotheses in Bernard et al.'s (2014) research.

   A:

   $$H_o\text{: } \mu_{\text{agricultural}} = \mu_{\text{architecture}} = \mu_{\text{Black Student Union}} = \mu_{\text{College of Business}} = \mu_{\text{Dairy Science}} = \mu_{\text{Engineering}} = \mu_{\text{Arts \& Sciences}} = \mu_{\text{History}} = \mu_{\textit{Int'lBuddies}} = \mu_{\text{Kinesiology}} = \mu_{\text{Economics}} = \mu_{\text{Math}} = \mu_{\text{Intlhonorpsychology}} = \mu_{\text{Socialwork}} = \mu_{\text{Unionprogram}}$$

   $$H_r\text{: } \mu_{\text{Black Student Union}} < (\mu_{\text{agricultural}} = \mu_{\text{architecture}} = \mu_{\text{College of Business}} = \mu_{\text{Dairy Science}} = \mu_{\text{Engineering}} = \mu_{\text{Arts \& Sciences}} = \mu_{\text{History}} = \mu_{\textit{Int'lBuddies}} = \mu_{\text{Kinesiology}} = \mu_{\text{Economics}} = \mu_{\text{Math}} = \mu_{\text{Intlhonorpsychology}} = \mu_{\text{Socialwork}} = \mu_{\text{Unionprogram}})$$

5. Referring back to the previous question, just as a refresher, what does μ stand for?

   A: This is the symbol for the population mean. We use sample data to draw conclusions about the population because it is ultimately the population that we want to learn about and, hence, make hypotheses about.

Interpreting the Tool

Let's look at Bernard et al.'s (2014) statistical presentation. Then we will break down their presentation into its conceptual parts:

> The ANOVA revealed differences in average amount of money allocated across the 15 student organizations, $F(14, 2842) = 9.93$, $p < .001$,$(\eta_p^2) = .047$. This significant main effect was probed using Bonferroni multiple comparison procedures. Through these analyses, it was found that the BSU (Black Student Union) was allocated less money ($M = 11.70$, $SD = 12.47$) . . . than nine of the 14 other student organizations ($M = 17.41$ to 34.97, $SD = 19.65$ to 47.49), $ps < .022$. (p. 32)

In plain English, people allocated less money to the Black Student Union than to 9 of the other 14 student organizations that requested funding. More technically, Bernard et al. (2014) rejected the null hypothesis and concluded that in the population of college students, people are less likely to allocate money to an organization that supports racial minority interests. Let's now examine the statistical inner workings of these results.

Testing the null hypothesis

We have an *F* ratio of 9.93. I don't mean to insult your *F* ratio test statistic expertise, but keep the conceptual formula in mind:

$$F = \frac{\text{Systematic variance + error variance}}{\text{Error variance}}$$

When we hand-calculate a repeated-measures ANOVA and learn how to use this statistical tool with SPSS, we will examine systematic and error variance in more detail. For now, remember that a portion of the error variance is participant individual differences. As we discussed earlier in this chapter, participant individual differences have less of an impact in a repeated-measures design than in a between-subjects design. Therefore, all else being equal, there is less error variance in a repeated-measures design, thus, reducing the denominator of the *F* ratio test statistic.

Next up and in parentheses are our degrees of freedom, specifically, "(14, 2842)." Just as in the between-subjects ANOVA, we have two types of degrees of freedom. They have slightly different names in a repeated-measures ANOVA, but they are otherwise conceptually similar. Specifically, the "14" is our *between degrees of freedom* and the "2842" is our *error degrees of freedom*. Let's see how these numbers were calculated.

For between degrees of freedom, we calculate it just as we calculated the $df_{\text{between-groups}}$ in a between-subjects ANOVA. Specifically, we have the number of experimental conditions minus 1. So here, we have:

$$df_{\text{between}} = 15 - 1$$

Hence:

$$df_{\text{between}} = 14$$

The error degrees of freedom are a little more involved. Recall that in the between-subjects ANOVA, $df_{\text{within-groups}}$ was calculated as the sample size minus the number of groups being compared. For a repeated-measures ANOVA, we still need to calculate $df_{\text{within-groups}}$, but to do so, we take the total number of responses and subtract the number of groups being compared. Recall that in a repeated-measures analysis, each participant makes multiple responses. Therefore, we need to multiply the sample size by the number of groups being compared. Recall that our sample size is 204 people and that there are 15 groups being compared. That gives us $204 \times 15 = 3{,}060$. In other words, there were 3,060 responses made in Bernard's et al.'s (2014) research. With 15 groups, we have $df_{\text{within-groups}}$ of $3{,}060 - 15 = 3{,}045$.

Of course, 3,045 is not what's reported. How did we get to 2,842? Remember that a key advantage to a repeated-measures design is that we reduce the role of participant individual differences in the experiment. We must therefore remove "participant individual differences" from this number. To do so, we take our sample size and subtract 1. With a sample size of 204, that gives us $204 - 1 = 203$. Now, we can calculate df_{error} as $df_{\text{within-groups}} - df_{\text{participant}}$ or, in this example, as $3{,}045 - 203 = 2{,}842$.

With degrees of freedom, we now need to find our critical value to compare our *F* ratio test statistic to. We use Appendix C, just as we did for the between-subjects ANOVAs. Across the top of the appendix are columns containing ascending between (numerator) degrees of freedom. Down the left-hand column are rows containing ascending error (denominator) degrees of freedom. This appendix does not contain the precise critical value for $df_{\text{between}} = 14$ and $df_{\text{error}} = 2842$. So, we'll have to estimate it, and we will do so using the usual alpha level of .05. If we use $df_{\text{between}} = 10$ and df_{error} of 120, we have a critical value of 1.91. As visualized in Figure 10.2, our test

Figure 10.2 Comparing Bernard et al's (2014) *F*-ratio Test Statistic to Its Critical Value

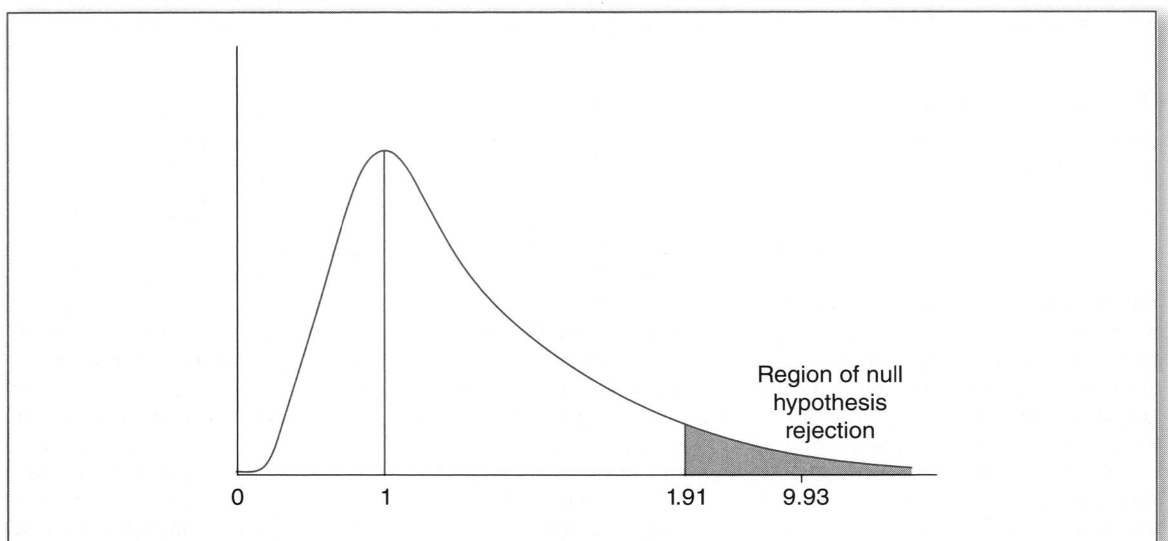

statistic of 9.93 is clearly greater than this critical value. Therefore, we reject the null hypothesis that there is no difference in funds allocated across the 15 different student organizations.

As you look at Figure 10.2, let's review three key ideas about ANOVAs. First, remember that this is a positively skewed distribution. In other words, large *F* ratios are rare. To reject a null hypothesis, an *F* ratio must be large enough to fall in the region of null hypothesis rejection, which contains the upper 5% of the distribution. Second, ANOVAs are always one-tailed tests. Third and related to the second idea, *F* ratios can never be less than 0. This is because variability can never be negative.

Extending our null hypothesis test

In returning to Bernard et al.'s (2014) results, we have our partial eta squared (η_p^2) of .047. This is the effect size. Recall that an effect size provides information beyond what the hypothesis test provides. Whereas the hypothesis test tells us whether a result found in a sample can be generalized to the population, an effect size tells us how strong the relationship is between two variables, in this case, between the student organization and funding allocations. Here, 4.7% of the variability in funding allocations can be traced to the independent variable, which was the student organization.

Going beyond the *F* ratio: Post hoc tests

Remember from the previous chapter that the *F* ratio is an omnibus inferential statistical tool. That is, it tells us whether there is some difference, somewhere, among our group means that is generalizable to the population. To determine precisely where the statistically significant differences among our means exist, we now need to do post hoc tests. Recall from the previous chapter that for the between-subjects ANOVA, we used what was called Tukey's HSD tests for our post hoc tests. For repeated-measures ANOVA, we can still use Tukey (and will do so when we hand-calculate a one-way, repeated-measures ANOVA later in this chapter). However, when using SPSS (as Bernard et al. [2014] surely did), it is customary to use a different type of post hoc test. Bernard et al. (2014) used what is called the "Bonferroni-corrected" method of post hoc tests. As mentioned briefly in the previous chapter, the Bonferroni-corrected method considers the total number of comparisons being made. This is important because the more comparisons we run using an alpha level of .05, the more likely we are to find statistically significant differences by sheer luck and not because they are real differences in the population (i.e., we increase the likelihood of making a Type I error). Thus, the Bonferroni-corrected method of a post hoc test controls this family-wise Type I error rate by taking into account the number of comparisons being made.

Bernard et al. (2014) compared the mean amount of money allocated to the Black Student Union ($11.70) to the mean amount of money allocated to the other 14 student organizations. They found that the mean amount of money allocated to the BSU was less than it was for 9 of the other organizations and that such differences were statistically significant. Because Bernard et al. controlled the Type I error rate by using the Bonferroni-corrected procedure, we can be more confident in this conclusion than if they had not done so.

As we conclude this section on interpreting the one-way, repeated-measures ANOVA, I want to make you aware of what some researchers consider to be a controversy when using any type of ANOVA. Recall that after we obtain our *F* ratio test statistic and compare it to the appropriate critical value, we either reject or fail to reject the null hypothesis. If we reject the null hypothesis, we know that there are significant differences somewhere among our group means. However, we do not know precisely what means are significantly different from each other because the *F* ratio and comparison to the critical value is an omnibus test; that is, it just gives us the "big picture" of what is going on in our data. Some researchers contend that if the *F* ratio is statistically significant, then when examining the post hoc tests, we do not need to be particularly concerned about the Type I error rate. Of course, other researchers argue we still need to account for Type I errors. I bring up this controversy because, as noted previously in this section, there are many types of post hoc tests available and each one deals with Type I errors in a slightly different way. The important thing to know, from the perspective of understanding statistical presentations of ANOVA research findings, is why we need post hoc tests.

LEARNING CHECK

Let's take another example of a presentation of a one-way, repeated-measures ANOVA. To do so, let's consider a research study that Mary Hassandra and her colleagues (2009) conducted. Specifically, Hassandra et al. assessed the effectiveness of a program called "I do not smoke, I exercise." This program was aimed at middle-school (7th grade) students to help them see exercise as a preferable behavior to smoking. Among the data that Hassandra and colleagues collected was a measure of knowledge about the health consequences of smoking. This knowledge measure contained 22 items, answering true or false to statements such as "Smoking has been demonstrated to cause breathing difficulties while playing sports." Participants got a point for each item answered correctly, so scores could range from 0 to 22.

How is this research an example of a one-way, repeated-measures ANOVA? Hassandra et al. (2009) measured the 7th graders' knowledge of smoking at three different points in time: the first time (T1) was prior to the start of the program, the second time (T2) was immediately after the program ended, and the third time (T3) was 12 months after the program ended. Therefore, each student provided data to each "point in time," which serves as the independent variable in this research. Scores on the knowledge of smoking tests serves as the dependent variable.

Here are the results of Hassandra et al.'s (2009) one-way, repeated-measures ANOVA on 7th graders' knowledge of smoking when they are put into an APA style write-up:

> The repeated-measures ANOVA revealed a significant time effect, $F(2, 186) = 129.825$, $p < .001$, $\eta_p^2 = .414$. Examination of the within-subjects contrasts revealed that knowledge increased from T1 ($M = 14.33$) to T2 ($M = 18.65$), $p < .001$, and although there was a significant decrease from T2 to T3 ($M = 17.56$), $p < .001$, the differences between T1 and T3 remained significant, $p < .001$.

(Continued)

(Continued)

Use this presentation to answer the following questions:

1. What were the means being statistically examined?

   A: For T1, 14.33; for T2, 18.65, for T3, 17.56
2. What was the *F* ratio test statistic?

   A: 129.825
3. How many degrees of freedom did the researchers have for this analysis?

   A: 2 between (or numerator) *df*s and 186 error (or denominator) *df*s
4. By using Appendix C, approximate the critical value that was used to see whether we reject or do not reject the null hypothesis.

   A: We do not have a critical value of df_{error} of 186, so let's use df_{error} of 120, the next available critical value, which will be more conservative than df_{error} of 186. With $df_{between}$ of 2, and assuming our usual alpha level of .05, that gives us a critical value of 3.07.
5. What is the probability that the differences among the three group means were due to random variation?

   Less than .1% ($p < .001$)
6. Did the researchers reject or fail to reject the null hypothesis?

   A: Because the *p* value was less than .05, we reject the null hypothesis because there is only an acceptably small chance that the differences among our means were due to random variation.
7. What is the effect size? Interpret what it means.

   A: 0.414. This means that 41.4% of the variability in the dependent variable of knowledge about smoking was explained by the independent variable of point in time.
8. Explain these results in plain English to someone who knows nothing about ANOVAs or post hoc tests.

   A: 7th graders had more knowledge about smoking after completing the program than before being part of the program. However, a year after the program was over, they had less knowledge about smoking than immediately after the program ended. Fortunately, these students still knew more about smoking a year after the program ended than they did before being part of the program. Thus, it does appear this program had a long-term impact on 7th graders knowledge about smoking.

USING YOUR NEW STATISTICAL TOOL

With our grip on the conceptual nature of the one-way, repeated-measures ANOVA, let's now do our hand-calculations; after which, we'll learn how to use this tool with SPSS.

Hand-Calculating the One-Way, Repeated-Measures ANOVA

I have some excellent news for you. Because you know how to calculate a one-way, between-subjects ANOVA from Chapter 9, you know almost all you need to know to calculate the one-way, repeated-measures ANOVA. So let's get started.

You might have noticed several examples in this book that are related to food. I love to cook and eat. One of my favorite foods is pizza. In the small town I live in, we have three local (not a chain) pizza places: Gena's, Cascarelli's, and Charlie's. I sampled seven of my students and asked them to rate how much they liked the pizza at each of these restaurants, using a 1 (*do not like it at all*) to 9 (*like it a lot*) response range. Here are those data:

	Pizza Place		
Student #	**Gena's**	**Cascarelli's**	**Charlie's**
1	7	8	8
2	8	6	9
3	4	4	4
4	9	9	9
5	7	7	9
6	9	7	8
7	9	9	8

When conducting a repeated-measures ANOVA by hand, I tend to put each participant (or in this case, student) number in the left hand-column. Doing so helps me remember that each participant contributed data to each level of the independent variable.

Step 1: State the hypothesis

We are testing the hypothesis that there will be no differences in how much students like the pizza at the three pizza restaurants. Notationally, we have:

$$H_o: \mu_{\text{Gena's}} = \mu_{\text{Cascarelli's}} = \mu_{\text{Charlie's}}$$

Frankly, I am not sure there is a viable theoretically grounded research hypothesis in this example. We all have our favorite restaurants, but of course, we should not base our research hypotheses on personal experience (see Chapter 1 for reminders of why this is the case). So, this example is an instance of purely exploratory research.

Step 2: Calculate the mean for each group

As was the case with the one-way, between-subjects ANOVA, the mean for each group is not used to calculate the test statistic. But we do need group means when we report our results.

	Pizza Place		
Student #	**Gena's**	**Cascarelli's**	**Charlie's**
1	7	8	8
2	8	6	9
3	4	4	4
4	9	9	9
5	7	7	9
6	9	7	8
7	9	9	8
Group Means	7.57	7.14	7.86

Step 3: Calculate the sums of squares (*SS*s)

At the outset of this section, I said that you already know, from reading the previous chapter, almost all of the calculations needed to do a one-way, repeated-measures ANOVA. When calculating the various sums of squares, here is where we meet one difference in calculations between the two tools. If you want to see the logic of the calculations in the section (which are the most involved of any step in this process), take a look at Figure 10.3. Let's first calculate our total sums of squares and then our between sums of squares. After doing so, we'll deal with the within-groups sums of squares, which is where we will see a difference from the previous chapter.

Total Sums of Squares (SS_{total})

The process of calculating the total sums of squares for a one-way, repeated-measures ANOVA is the same as it was for the one-way, between-subjects ANOVA. Recall that the grand mean is the mean for all scores on a dependent variable in a research study. In this example, the grand mean is 7.52. We need to take each of the 21 individual scores in the dataset and subtract from it the grand mean. Let's do this now.

Figure 10.3 "Partitioning" Forms of Variability in a Repeated-Measure ANOVA

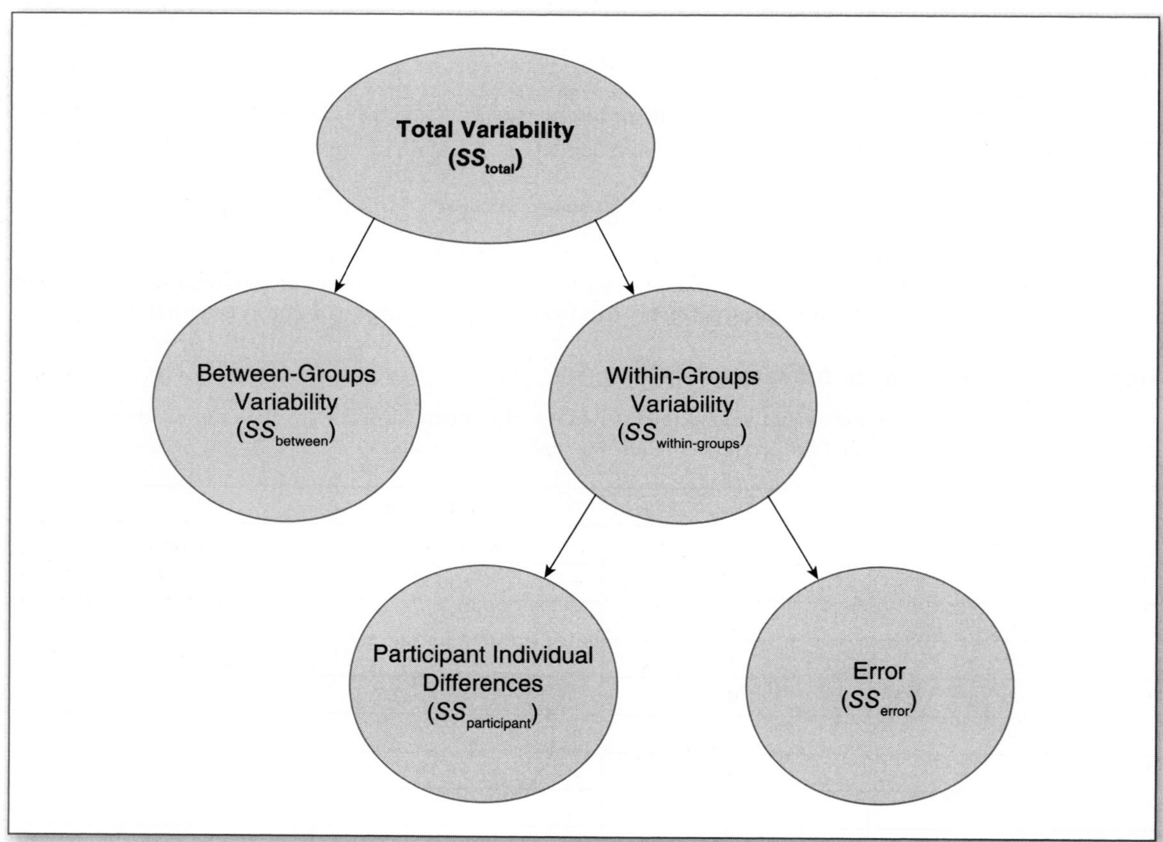

Pizza Place					
Gena's		Cascarelli's		Charlie's	
Score	Deviation	Score	Deviation	Score	Deviation
7	−.52	8	.48	8	.48
8	.48	6	−1.52	9	1.48
4	−3.52	4	−3.52	4	−3.52
9	1.48	9	1.48	9	1.48
7	−.52	7	−.52	9	1.48
9	1.48	7	−.52	8	.48
9	1.48	9	1.48	8	.48

I am willing to bet you know what to do next, but allow me to say it anyway: Square the deviation scores.

Pizza Place								
Gena's			Cascarelli's			Charlie's		
Score	Deviation	Deviation^2	Score	Deviation	Deviation^2	Score	Deviation	Deviation^2
7	−.52	.27	8	.48	.23	8	.48	.23
8	.48	.23	6	−1.52	2.31	9	1.48	2.19
4	−3.52	12.39	4	−3.52	12.39	4	−3.52	12.39
9	1.48	2.19	9	1.48	2.19	9	1.48	2.19
7	−.52	.27	7	−.52	.27	9	1.48	2.19
9	1.48	2.19	7	−.52	.27	8	.48	.23
9	1.48	2.19	9	1.48	2.19	8	.48	.23

Now, we sum the squared deviations within each group, leaving us with Gena's = 19.73; Cascarelli's = 19.85; and Charlie's = 19.65.

To get our total sums of squares, we add the summed squared deviations for each group, giving us 19.73 + 19.85 + 19.65 = 59.23. Thus, our total sums of squares (SS_{total}) is 59.23.

Between Sums of Squares ($SS_{between}$)

In the one-way, between-subjects ANOVA, each participant provided data to one and only one group mean. In the one-way, repeated-measures ANOVA, each participant provides data to each group mean, so there is really only one group of participants. Therefore, what was called between-groups sums of squares in the previous chapter, we will call simply *between sums of squares* as this measure of variability is "between" the different pizza places being compared.

To calculate our $SS_{between}$, we need our grand mean (7.52 in this example) and the mean for each group, which we calculated in step 2. Here's what we do now:

a) We take the grand mean and subtract it from each group mean.

b) We then square that deviation.

c) Multiply that squared deviation by the number of people that contributed to the group mean (which, yes, in this example, will be the same number of people for each group, in this case, 7).

Our group means from step 2 were:

Gena's = 7.57 Cascarelli's = 7.14 Charlie's = 7.86

The grand mean was 7.52.

$$\text{Gena's} = (7.57 - 7.52)^2 \times 7$$
$$= .05^2 \times 7$$
$$= 0.0175$$
$$\text{Cascarelli's} = (7.14 - 7.52)^2 \times 7$$
$$= -.38^2 \times 7$$
$$= 1.0108$$
$$\text{Charlie's} = (7.86 - 7.52)^2 \times 7$$
$$= .34^2 \times 7$$
$$= 0.8092$$

Now we sum these three numbers (0.0175 + 1.0108 + 0.8092), giving us 1.8375. Thus, our between sums of squares ($SS_{between}$) is 1.8375.

Error Sums of Squares (SS_{error})

You may have noticed from this section heading that we have a "new" type of sums of squaresto calculate. We are about to get to it, but before we do, let's do something we already know how to do: Calculate the within-group sums of squares. We will need it to determine our error sums of squares.

Recall that the within-group sums of squares is a measure of variability around a group mean. We need each score and the group means. We take each score and subtract it from its respective group mean. Our group means from step 2:

Gena's = 7.57 Cascarelli's = 7.14 Charlie's = 7.86

Now we need to calculate the deviations of individual scores for their respective group means:

Pizza Place					
Gena's		Cascarelli's		Charlie's	
Score	Deviation	Score	Deviation	Score	Deviation
7	−.57	8	.86	8	.14
8	.43	6	−1.14	9	1.14
4	-3.57	4	-3.14	4	-3.86

9	1.43	9	1.86	9	1.14
7	−.57	7	−.14	9	1.14
9	1.43	7	−.14	8	.14
9	1.43	9	1.86	8	.14

To rid ourselves of the negative deviation scores, we square all deviation scores:

Pizza Place								
Gena's			Cascarelli's			Charlie's		
Score	Deviation	Deviation^2	Score	Deviation	Deviation^2	Score	Deviation	Deviation^2
7	−.57	.32	8	.86	.74	8	.14	.02
8	.43	.18	6	−1.14	1.30	9	1.14	1.30
4	−3.57	12.75	4	−3.14	9.86	4	−3.86	14.90
9	1.43	2.04	9	1.86	3.46	9	1.14	1.30
7	−.57	.32	7	−.14	.02	9	1.14	1.30
9	1.43	2.04	7	−.14	.02	8	.14	.02
9	1.43	2.04	9	1.86	3.46	8	.14	.02

We now sum the squared deviations within each group, leaving us with Gena's = 19.69; Cascarelli's = 18.86; and Charlie's = 18.86.

Summing each group's squared deviation total gives us 19.69 + 18.86 + 18.86 = 57.41. Our within-group sums of squares ($SS_{\text{within-group}}$) is 57.41.

Remove "participant individual differences" from within-group sums of squares

And now here comes that difference from between-subjects ANOVAs. Recall from the previous chapter that within-group variability is partly a function of participant individual differences. In a between-subjects analysis, those individual differences can influence how people react to the factor (independent variable) we are studying. In a within-subjects analysis, those individual differences still exist, but they exist across all experimental conditions (here, the pizza place being evaluated). Therefore, individual differences are not as big of a concern in a repeated-measures analysis as they are in a between-subjects analysis. We now need to account for this consideration in calculating the within-group sums of squares.

As the right side of Figure 10.3 displays, we will remove variability traceable to participant individual differences from the within-group sums of squares, thereby decreasing this number (which was 57.41 in our current example). To do so, we need to get (a) a mean rating for each participant and (b) the grand mean. Let's get our mean rating for each participant:

Pizza Place				
Student #	Gena's	Cascarelli's	Charlie's	Mean Rating
1	7	8	8	7.67
2	8	6	9	7.67
3	4	4	4	4.00

(Continued)

(Continued)

Pizza Place				
Student #	Gena's	Cascarelli's	Charlie's	Mean Rating
4	9	9	9	9.00
5	7	7	9	7.67
6	9	7	8	8.00
7	9	9	8	8.67

Recall that the grand mean for this study was 7.52. We need to take the grand mean and subtract each participant's mean rating. Participants with a high mean rating have a tendency to like pizza places, whereas participants with a low mean rating have a tendency to dislike pizza places. We are currently removing such tendencies from the within-group sums of squares.

And of course, we square the difference between the participant's mean rating and the grand mean:

Pizza Place					
Student #	Gena's	Cascarelli's	Charlie's	Mean Rating	(Mean Rating – Grand Mean)^2
1	7	8	8	7.67	$.15^2 = .02$
2	8	6	9	7.67	$.15^2 = .02$
3	4	4	4	4.00	$-3.52^2 = 12.39$
4	9	9	9	9.00	$1.48^2 = 2.19$
5	7	7	9	7.67	$.15^2 = .02$
6	9	7	8	8.00	$.48^2 = .23$
7	9	9	8	8.67	$1.15^2 = 1.32$

There is one last calculation we need to perform here. Specifically, we need to multiply our squared deviation score by the number of conditions (in this case, the number of pizza places) in the analysis. We do this because this number is a function of the number of conditions to which the participant provided data. So let's do that now:

Pizza Place					
Student #	Gena's	Cascarelli's	Charlie's	Mean Rating	(Mean Rating – Grand Mean)^2 × # of Groups
1	7	8	8	7.67	$.02 \times 3 = .06$
2	8	6	9	7.67	$.02 \times 3 = .06$
3	4	4	4	4.00	$12.39 \times 3 = 37.17$
4	9	9	9	9.00	$2.19 \times 3 = 6.57$
5	7	7	9	7.67	$.02 \times 3 = .06$
6	9	7	8	8.00	$.23 \times 3 = .69$
7	9	9	8	8.67	$1.32 \times 3 = 3.96$

We now sum these numbers to get a subject individual differences sums of squares. Here, we have $.06 + .06 + 37.17 + 6.57 + .06 + .69 + 3.96 = 48.57$. Our participant individual difference sums of squares ($SS_{participant}$) is 48.57.

We now must remove the participant individual difference sums of squares from the within-group sums of squares, *which will leave us with only error variability*. Recall that our $SS_{\text{within-group}}$ was 57.41 and our $SS_{\text{participant}}$ was 48.57. Thus, our error sums of squares (SS_{error}) is 57.41 − 48.57 = 8.84.

I will highlight this fact again later in this section, but for now, trust me that by removing subject individual difference variability, it increases the power of our tool, making it more likely that we can reject the null hypothesis than we could with a between-subjects design assuming the sample size remains constant for both types of analyses.

Step 4: Determine degrees of freedom (*df*s)

We now calculate total degrees of freedom, between degrees of freedom, and error degrees of freedom.

Total Degrees of Freedom (df_{total})

We take the total number of responses and subtract 1. In this example, we had seven participants, each of whom rated three pizza places. Therefore, we have 21 responses:

$$df_{\text{total}} = \text{total number of responses} - 1$$
$$df_{\text{total}} = 21 - 1$$
$$df_{\text{total}} = 20$$

Between Degrees of Freedom ($df_{between}$)

To calculate the between degrees of freedom, we take the number of conditions to which participants responded and subtract 1. So in this case, with three pizza places being rated, we have:

$$df_{\text{between}} = \text{number of conditions} - 1$$
$$df_{\text{between}} = 3 - 1$$
$$= 2$$

Error Degrees of Freedom (df_{error})

Of course, with the new calculations of the within-group sums of squares (now called *error variance*), there are some new calculations needed in the error degrees of freedom. First, let's get our within-groups degrees of freedom, which is calculated similarly to how it was for the between-subjects ANOVA:

$$df_{\text{within-groups}} = \text{total number of responses} - \text{number of conditions to which participants responded}$$

$$df_{\text{within-groups}} = 21 - 3$$
$$= 18$$

Now we need to remove the participant individual differences degrees of freedom ($df_{\text{participant}}$), just like we needed to remove the subject individual differences variability. To calculate the participant individual difference degrees of freedom, we take the sample size and subtract 1. Therefore, we have:

$$df_{\text{participant}} = \text{sample size} - 1$$
$$df_{\text{participant}} = 7 - 1$$
$$= 6$$

Figure 10.4 "Partitioning" Degrees of Freedom in a Repeated-Measure ANOVA

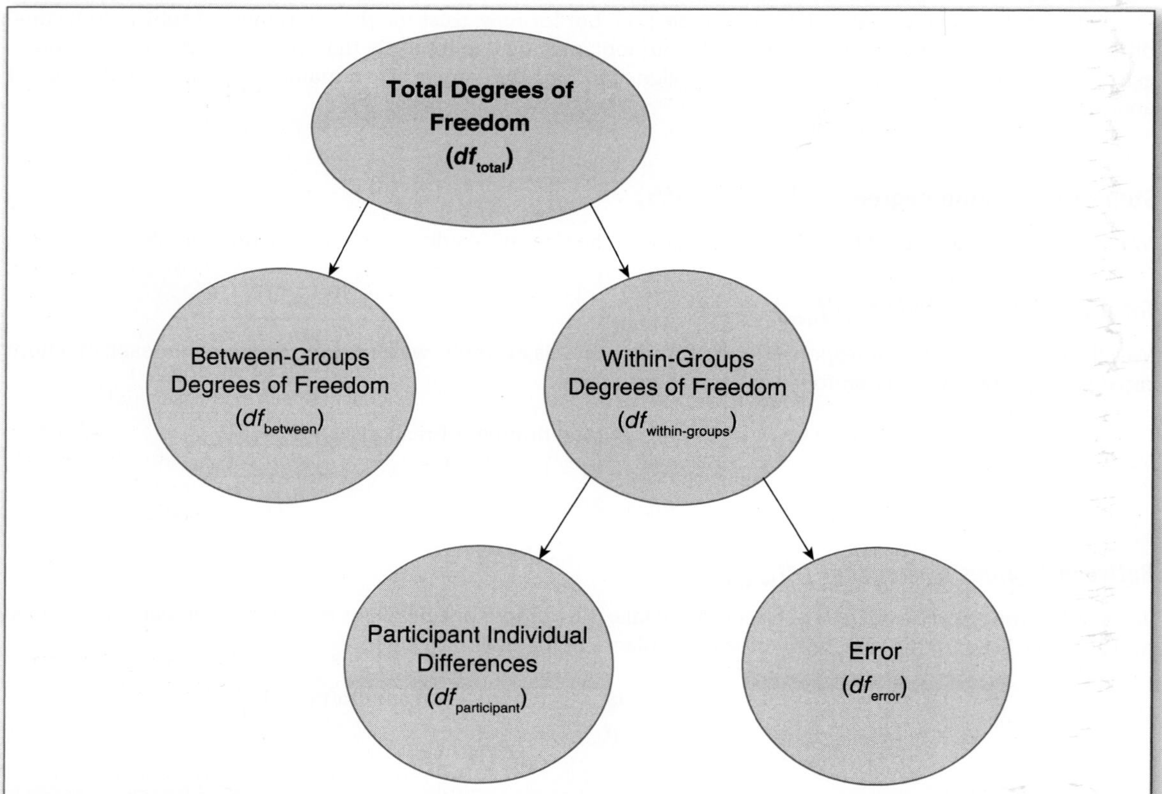

To get our error degrees of freedom (df_{error}), we take our $df_{within\text{-}group}$ and subtract from it the $df_{participant}$. Therefore:

$$df_{error} = df_{within\text{-}group} - df_{participant}$$

$$df_{error} = 18 - 6$$
$$= 12$$

To visualize the process we just experienced, take a look at Figure 10.4. Similar to Figure 10.3 that displayed how to divvy up variability in a repeated-measures design, Figure 10.4 displays how degrees of freedom are organized in a repeated-measures design.

Step 5: Calculate the mean squares (*MS*s)

As we did for between-subjects ANOVAs, we will calculate two *MS*s here, $MS_{between}$ and MS_{error}. *MS*s are average deviation scores, and the general *MS* formula is:

$$MS = \frac{\text{Sums of squares}}{df}$$

To calculate our $MS_{between}$, our sums of squares was 1.84 and our degrees of freedom were 2. Thus:

$$MS_{between} = \frac{1.84}{2}$$
$$MS_{between} = 0.92$$

To calculate our MS_{error}, our sums of squares was 8.84 and our degrees of freedom were 12. Thus:

$$MS_{error} = \frac{8.84}{12}$$
$$MS_{error} = 0.74$$

Keep in mind that MS_{error} will be the denominator in the F ratio calculation that we are about to do. Because we removed participant individual differences from its calculation, it is smaller than it otherwise would have been. A smaller MS_{error} means that the F ratio will be larger than it otherwise would be. Of course, larger F ratios are more likely to be statistically significant than are smaller F ratios.

Step 6: Calculate your *F* ratio test statistic

Now is a good time to reiterate what purpose an ANOVA serves. Remember that it is a competition between (a) variability traceable to the independent variable and (b) variability traceable to factors other than the independent variable.

We plug in our $MS_{between}$ and MS_{error} calculated in step 5, and that gives us our F ratio test statistic:

$$F = \frac{0.92}{0.74}$$
$$F = 1.24$$

As we did at this point in the calculation of our between-subjects ANOVA, let's summarize our calculations in an ANOVA summary table. I like these sorts of tables because they present a lot of information (as you know from calculating it all) quickly.

Source of Variability	*SS*	*df*	*MS*	*F*
Participant Individual Differences	48.57	6	—	
Between	1.84	2	0.92	1.24
Error	8.84	12	0.74	
Total	59.23	20		

There are two observations about this summary table. First, please note that the *SS*s in this example do not add to the SS_{total} because of rounding. Second, there is no $MS_{participant}$ number because it is not needed to calculate the F ratio test statistic.

Step 7: Locate the critical value

Now that we have our test statistic of $F = 1.24$, we need to see whether we can generalize from our sample to the population. When we look back at our means in step 2, we see differences in how the three pizza places were rated, but are these differences extreme enough to conclude such differences likely exist in the population? Let's find our critical value and compare our test statistic to it.

We consult Appendix C. It is the same set of critical values that we used in between-subjects ANOVAs. With an alpha level of .05, $df_{between}$ of 2, and df_{error} of 12, we can locate our critical value of 3.89.

Step 8: Make a decision about the null hypothesis

Visually, Figure 10.5 displays the comparison between our *F* ratio test statistic and our critical value. As you can see in the figure, our test statistic of 1.24 is smaller than the critical value of 3.89. Therefore, we fail to reject the null hypothesis. In plain English, we conclude that students rated the pizza at the three local restaurants to be of similar quality.

Step 9: Calculate an effect size

Although not statistically significant, we should always calculate an effect size with any inferential statistical test. Remember that an effect size provides an indication of how strong the relationship is between two variables. As we did for the one-way, between-subjects ANOVA, we will again calculate the partial eta squared for our effect size. Here is the formula for partial eta squared:

$$\eta_p^2 = \frac{SS_{\text{between}}}{SS_{\text{between}} + SS_{\text{error}}}$$

From step 3, SS_{between} was 1.84 and SS_{error} was 8.84. So, to calculate our partial eta squared, we have:

$$\eta_p^2 = \frac{1.84}{1.84 + 8.84}$$

$$\eta_p^2 = .17$$

Figure 10.5 Comparing Our *F*-ratio to Its Critical Value

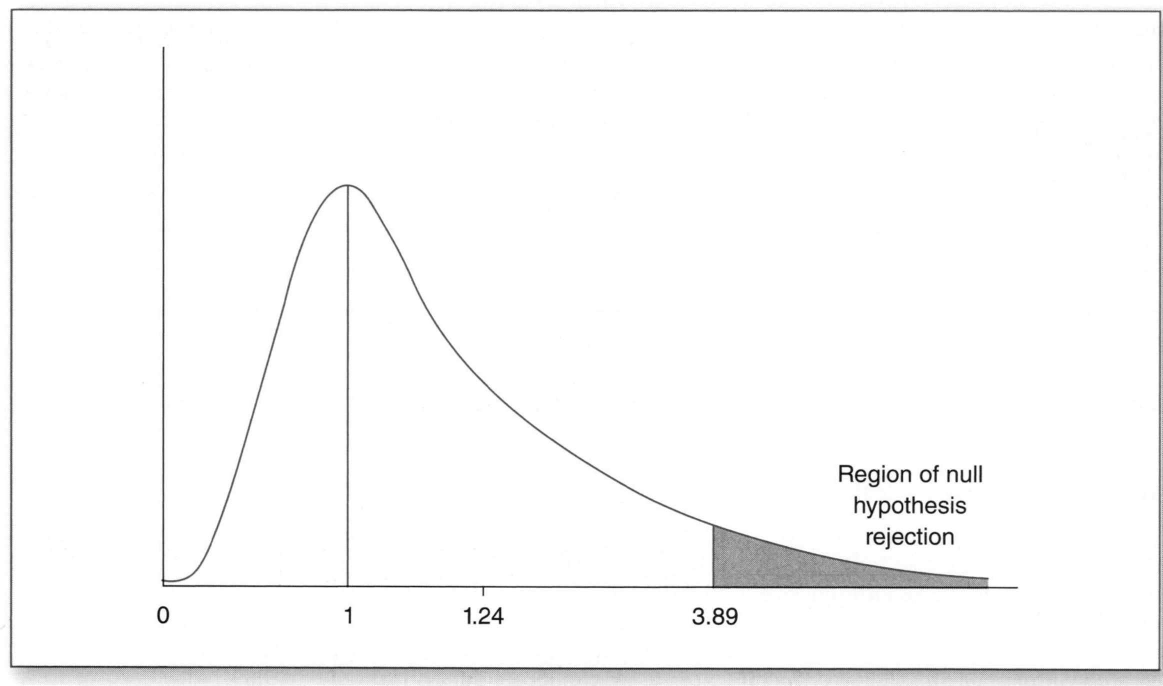

This means that 17% of the variability in the dependent variable (pizza quality ratings) can be explained by the independent variable (restaurant). You might think that seems like a large percentage of variability explained, and indeed, it is. Remember that effect sizes provide *different* information than does our hypothesis test (which in this case was not statistically significant). Because of a fairly small sample size, we did not reject the null hypothesis. Although not relevant to our example, it is possible to have a situation in which we reject the null hypothesis but the effect size is trivial. Think about why that might be; we will pick up this situation again in the next Learning Check.

As mentioned only briefly in the previous chapter, for ANOVAs, there are two effect sizes you see reported, the partial eta squared (η_p^2) that we have been discussing and the eta squared (η^2). When conducting a one-way, between-subjects or a one-way, repeated-measures ANOVA, they will provide the same information, specifically, the percentage of variability in the dependent variable that is accounted for by the independent variable. Thus, for any one-way ANOVA, it technically does not matter whether you report a partial eta squared or an eta squared. In the next chapter, we will deal with the eta squared in more detail.

Step 10: Perform post hoc tests

In Bernard et al.'s (2014) research, they used a procedure called "Bonferroni-corrected." Many different types of post hoc tests are available to researchers (as you might have noticed in the previous chapter when we were learning about ANOVAs using SPSS). Here, we will stick with Tukey's honestly significant difference (HSD) post hoc tests, which is conceptually the same procedure we used for one-way, between-subjects ANOVAs.

Remember that for post hoc tests, we need to find a critical mean difference, which if any mean difference in our sample exceeds, we can conclude that there is a difference between those two groups in our population based on our sample data. To calculate our critical mean difference, we use this formula:

$$= Q \times \sqrt{\frac{MS_{\text{error}}}{\text{number of participants in each group}}}$$

Recall that Q requires two pieces of information: (1) the number of means involved in the post hoc analyses and (2) df_{error}. We have three group means, and recall from our ANOVA summary table that df_{error} was 12. Armed with these two pieces of information, let's consult Appendix D. This appendix contains values for Q. Across the appendix are columns for the number of means being compared; down the left-side column are df_{error}. By using our normal alpha level of .05, we see our Q value is 3.77.

Our MS_{error} was 0.74, and we had seven people in each group. Thus:

$$\sqrt{\frac{0.74}{7}}$$

$$\sqrt{1.1057}$$

$$= 0.325$$

Taking all of the ingredients we need to calculate our critical mean difference, we have:

$$= 3.77 \times 0.325$$

$$= 1.225$$

If a difference between any two of our group means exceeds 1.225, we conclude it was an honestly significant difference, and thus, we can generalize that difference from the sample to the population.

Here again are our group means:

Gena's = 7.57 Cascarelli's = 7.14 Charlie's = 7.86

As none of them differ by at least 1.225, there are no statistically significant differences among these three groups. This is not surprising because our omnibus F ratio test statistic was not statistically significant.

You might be thinking, would we ever report the results of a pizza preference survey in APA style? Our example is a nice one that would interest consumer psychologists, so in a word, "yes." Here is the APA style presentation of our one-way, repeated-measures ANOVA:

> A one-way, repeated-measures ANOVA on quality of the pizza revealed no effect of restaurant, $F(2, 12) = 1.24$, $p > .05$, $\eta_p^2 = .17$. Tukey's post hoc tests revealed that the quality of pizza at Gena's ($M = 7.57$), Cascarelli's ($M = 7.14$), and Charlie's ($M = 7.86$) were all equivalent, for all three comparisons, $p > .05$.

LEARNING CHECK

1. All else being equal, why is the repeated-measures ANOVA more powerful than the between-subjects ANOVA? Stated differently, why is it more likely we will reject the null hypothesis using a repeated-measures ANOVA than when using a between-subjects ANOVA?

   A: The repeated-measures ANOVA removes participant individual differences from the MS_{error}, which is the denominator of the F ratio. Thus, reducing the denominator of a fraction makes the quotient of that fraction larger. With a larger F ratio, we are more likely to reject the null hypothesis than we are with a smaller F ratio.

2. As initially discussed in step 9 in this section, why is it possible we could reject the null hypothesis but have an extremely small effect size? In your response, explain what is meant when we say we "reject the null hypothesis" and "effect size."

   A: If the sample size is large enough, any group mean difference could be significant even if it is not a huge difference. However, in such cases, the effect size will be fairly small, indicating that although we have a statistically significant effect that exists in the population, it is not a powerful effect in the population.

Problem #1

Use this ANOVA summary table to answer the questions that follow it:

Source of Variability	*SS*	*df*	*MS*	*F*
Participant Individual Differences	18	6	–	
Between	24	4	6	5.13
Error	75	64	1.17	
Total	117	74		

1. How many conditions were there in this analysis? Explain how you know.

   A: We know that $df_{between}$ (4) is the number of conditions to which people responded, minus 1. Therefore, there were 5 conditions in this analysis.

2. What is the sample size for this analysis? Explain how you know.

   A: Sample size was 15. Remember that df_{total} (74) is the number of responses in the research study, minus 1. Therefore, there were 75 total responses. From the previous question, we also know that $df_{between}$ (4) is the number of conditions to which people responded, minus 1. Therefore, there were 5 conditions in this analysis. If we have 75 total responses and 5 conditions, we now divide 75 by 5, giving us our sample size of 15.

3. How was the $MS_{between}$ calculated?

A:

$$\frac{SS_{between}}{df_{between}}$$

$$\frac{24}{4}=6$$

4. How was the MS_{error} calculated?

A:

$$\frac{SS_{error}}{df_{error}}$$

$$\frac{75}{64}=1.17$$

6. How was the F ratio test statistic calculated?

A:

$$\frac{MS_{between}}{MS_{error}}$$

$$\frac{6}{1.17}= 5.13$$

7. Suppose this had been a one-way between-subjects ANOVA. What would the error variability (SS_{error}) have been had this summary table presented a between-subjects ANOVA? Explain what this means for the F ratio; would the F ratio have been greater than, the same as, less than what is now in the source table?

A: For a between-subjects ANOVA, SS_{error} would have been 75+ participants individual difference, which here was $SS_{participant}$ = 18. Thus, in a between-subjects ANOVA, SS_{error} would have been 75 + 18 = 93. This is the numerator for the calculation of MS_{error}, which would have been 93/64 = 1.45. Of course, 1.45 is greater than the current MS_{error} of 1.17. MS_{error} is the denominator of the F ratio test statistics, and whenever we increase the value of a denominator, we decrease the resulting ratio, so our F ratio test statistic would have been 6/1.45 = 4.14. This illustrates the statistical beauty of repeated-measures designs; they are more powerful (i.e., more likely to lead us to reject the null hypothesis) than are between-subjects designs.

Problem #2

A researcher wants to compare the means of four conditions. After collecting data from 25 people in a repeated-measures design, here are summary statistics needed to test her hypothesis, using an alpha level of .05, that there is no difference among the means of these four conditions:

Group A mean = 10; Group B mean = 8; Group C mean = 6; Group D mean = 4

$SS_{between}$ = 36; SS_{error} = 216

Questions to Answer:

1. Put these data in an ANOVA summary table. (*NOTE*: $SS_{participant}$ cannot be determined from the information provided; it's already figured in the calculation of SS_{error}.)

(Continued)

(Continued)

A:

Source of Variability	*SS*	*df*	*MS*	*F*
Participant Individual Differences	–	24	–	
Between	36	3	12	4.00
Error	216	72	3	
Total	252	99		

2. What is the approximate critical value in this analysis?

   A: Given our $df_{between}$ of 3, df_{error} of 72, and alpha level of .05, we consult Appendix C and see that our critical value is going to be between 2.68 (the critical value of df_{error} of 120) and 2.76 (the critical value of df_{error} of 60). To be conservative, we can use 2.76 as the critical value. Doing so makes it as difficult as possible to reject the null hypotheses given our degrees of freedom.

3. Do you reject or fail to reject the null hypothesis?

   A: Given that our *F* ratio test statistic is greater than the critical value, we reject the null hypothesis.

4. Calculate the effect size.

   A:

$$\eta_p^2 = \frac{SS_{between}}{SS_{between + SS_{error}}} = \frac{36}{36+216} = .14$$

Regarding post hoc tests, calculate the HSD for this example. Explain in plain English what this HSD number means.

A:

$$\text{HSD} = Q \times \sqrt{\frac{MS_{error}}{\text{number of participants in each group}}}$$

In Appendix D, there is not a value available given our df_{error}. Let's use df_{error} of 60, which will make *Q* larger than it otherwise would be with df_{error} of 72. A larger *Q* will make the HSD larger, and a larger HSD requires more extreme mean differences for us to detect statistical significance:

$$= 3.75 \times \sqrt{\frac{3}{25}}$$
$$= 3.75 \times 0.346$$
$$= 1.30$$

This number of 1.30 indicates that for a mean difference between any two conditions to be statistically significant, that mean difference must be at least 1.30. In this example, all mean differences are greater than 1.30; therefore, we conclude that each group had a statistically significant difference from every other group.

One-Way, Repeated-Measures ANOVA and SPSS

At the outset of this chapter, I gave the example of using my students' test scores as a situation in which a one-way, repeated-measures ANOVA would be an appropriate statistical tool to use. Let's use this example as we learn to use SPSS to conduct this type of analysis.

Here is each of the three test scores, in percentages, for 20 students in my "Introductory Psychology" class this past fall semester (completely hypothetical, of course):

	Test Number		
Student	**First Test**	**Second Test**	**Third Test**
1	84	85	91
2	69	77	80
3	99	97	92
4	80	88	96
5	82	73	95
6	60	77	76
7	74	86	87
8	90	93	98
9	87	92	100
10	75	75	77
11	48	60	65
12	88	98	95
13	70	71	85
14	85	74	82
15	55	81	80
16	74	92	98
17	58	64	69
18	79	80	83
19	90	98	95
20	74	68	83

Establishing your spreadsheet

Once you open SPSS, you will need to click on *Variable View* in the lower left corner. Entering data into SPSS is a different process in repeated-measures ANOVA than it was in between-subjects ANOVAs, so please take your time setting up your SPSS spreadsheet.

You will need to name three variables, namely, the groups created by the independent variable. You do not need a variable for a student number. In this example, the independent variable is `Test_number`. You can name the first test `Test_1`, the second test `Test_2`, and the third test `Test_3`, or something to that effect. Be sure to give each test number a label, too. I would just use the labels "First test score", "Second test score", and "Third test score" as those labels seem straightforward to me. Make sure your measures are labeled as "Scale" variables.

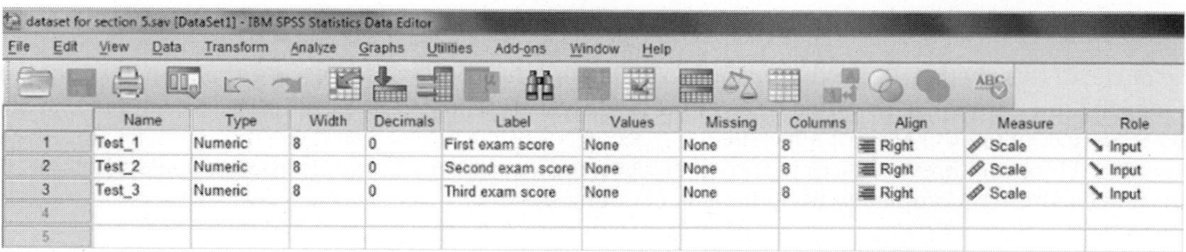

	Name	Type	Width	Decimals	Label	Values	Missing	Columns	Align	Measure	Role
1	Test_1	Numeric	8	0	First exam score	None	None	8	Right	Scale	Input
2	Test_2	Numeric	8	0	Second exam score	None	None	8	Right	Scale	Input
3	Test_3	Numeric	8	0	Third exam score	None	None	8	Right	Scale	Input
4											
5											

In the left corner of the screen, click on *Data View*. You are now ready to enter the three test scores for each of these 20 students.

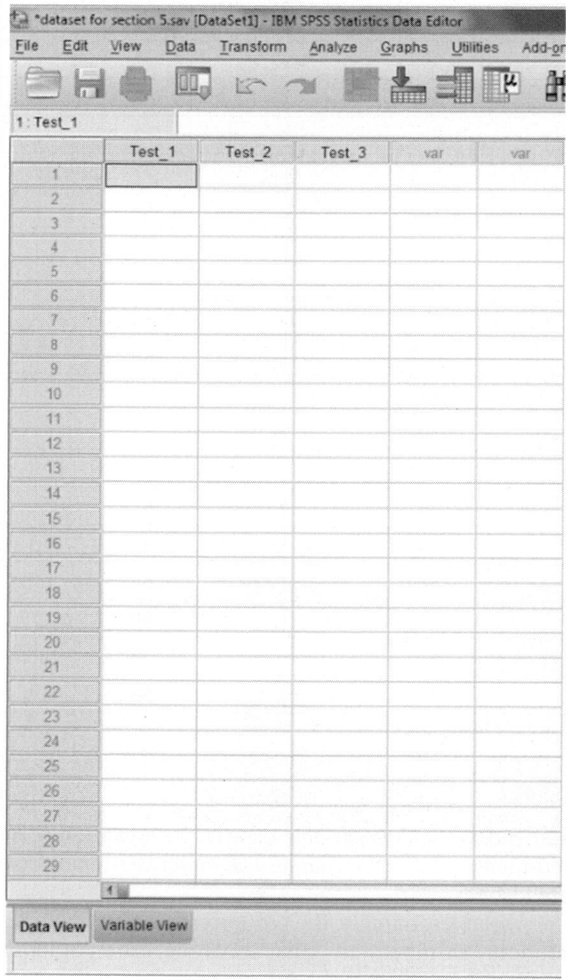

For each student, enter their first, second, and third test scores. Once you have entered all of these data into SPSS, you will have 20 rows of data (one row for each student) and three columns of data (one column for each test score).

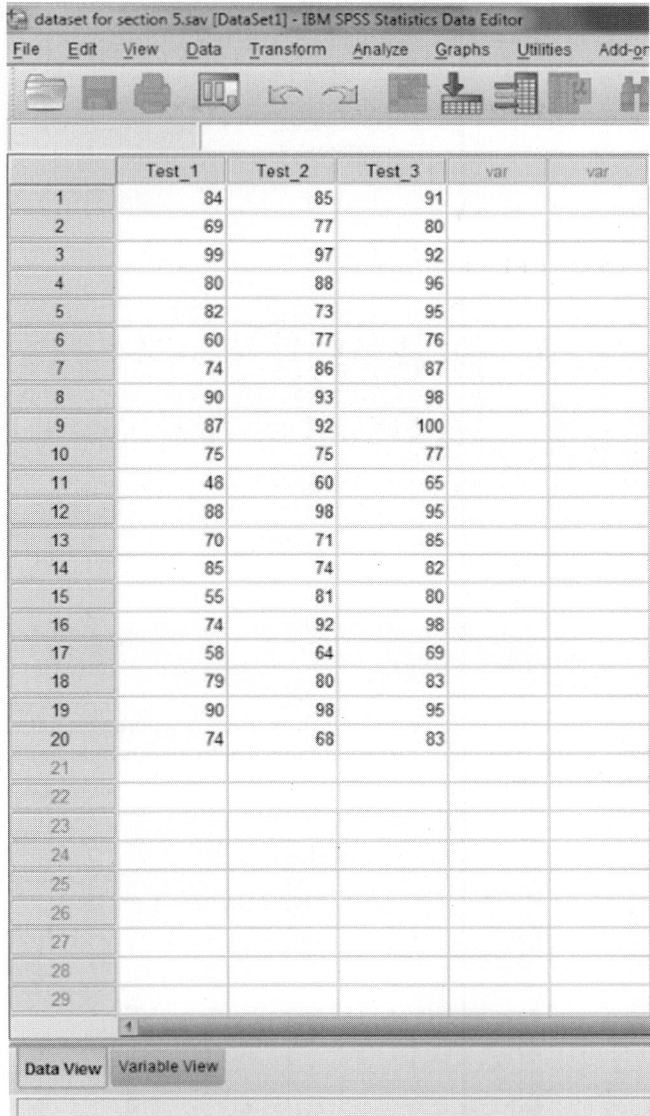

	Test_1	Test_2	Test_3	var	var
1	84	85	91		
2	69	77	80		
3	99	97	92		
4	80	88	96		
5	82	73	95		
6	60	77	76		
7	74	86	87		
8	90	93	98		
9	87	92	100		
10	75	75	77		
11	48	60	65		
12	88	98	95		
13	70	71	85		
14	85	74	82		
15	55	81	80		
16	74	92	98		
17	58	64	69		
18	79	80	83		
19	90	98	95		
20	74	68	83		

The process of entering data for a one-way, repeated-measures ANOVA may seem simpler than the process for a one-way, between-subjects ANOVA. However, now that we want to run our analysis, things are a bit different than they were in the previous chapter. Slow down, read carefully, and we'll get our analysis completed with no problem.

Running your analysis

To run our one-way, repeated-measures ANOVA:

1. Click on *Analyze* → *General Linear Model* → *Repeated Measures*.

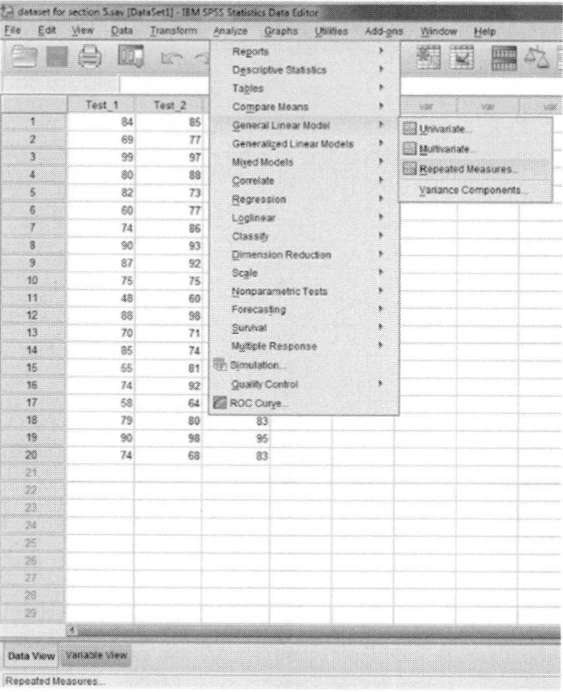

2. You will see a *Within-Subject Factor Name* dialogue box. Here is where you name your independent variable and tell SPSS how many levels (groups) it contains. Let's call our independent variable `Test_number`, and of course, it has three levels.

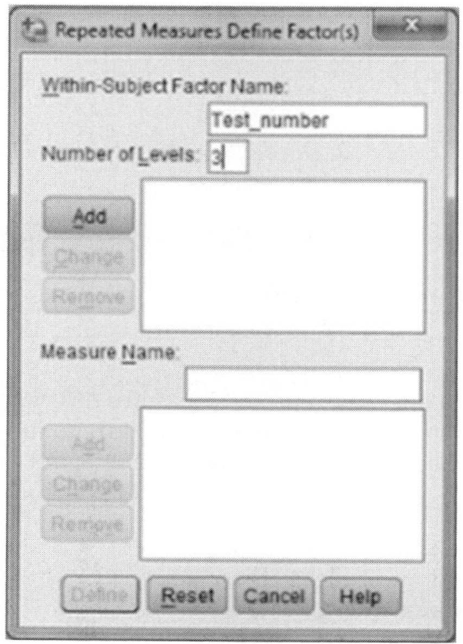

3. Once you have named the independent variable and specified the number of groups it contains, click on *Add*. Then click on *Define*. You will be taken to a *Repeated Measures* dialogue box. Here, you need to tell which groups of the independent variable you want to compare.

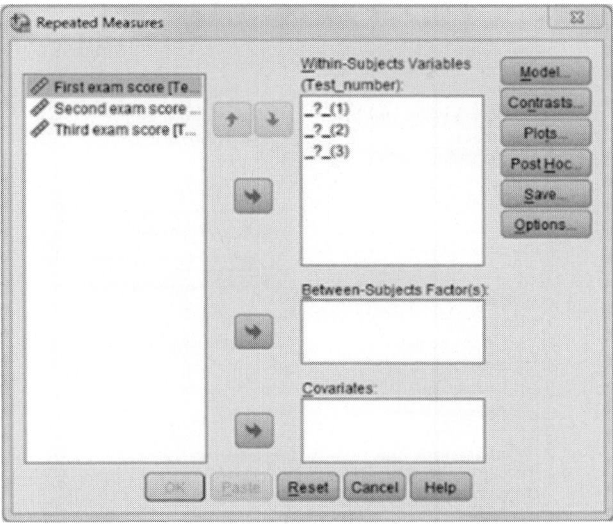

4. Of course, we want to compare all three test score means, so click each variable in the *Within-Subjects Variable* box. It would be best if you clicked them over in order, or else things will get confusing reading the printout.

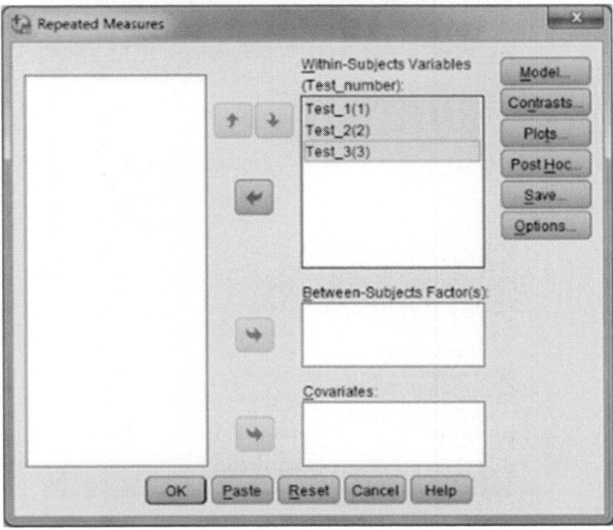

5. Now click on *Options*. The *Repeated Measures Options* dialogue box has a top section called *Estimated Marginal Means*. There are two things to do here. First, click the factor (`Test_number`) into the *Display Means For* box. Second, click on *Compare main effects*, and then choose the *Confidence interval adjustment → Bonferroni*. What you have done is obtain the mean for each group and have asked SPSS to compare them statistically.

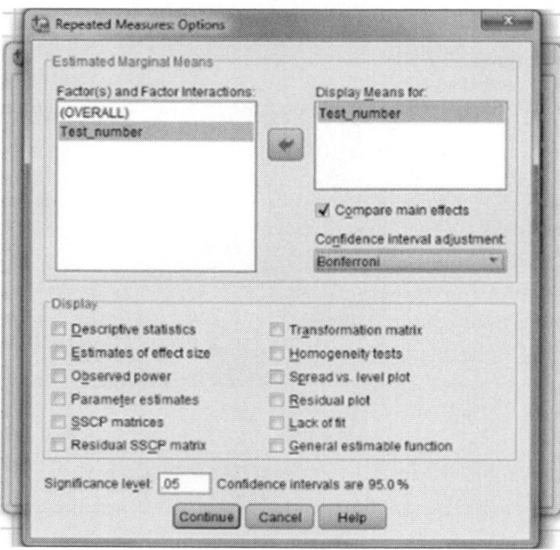

6. The bottom section of the *Repeated Measures Options* box is called *Display*. Ask SPSS to display (a) *Descriptive statistics* and (b) *Estimates of effect size*. Here is what your completed *Repeated Measures Options* dialogue box should look like:

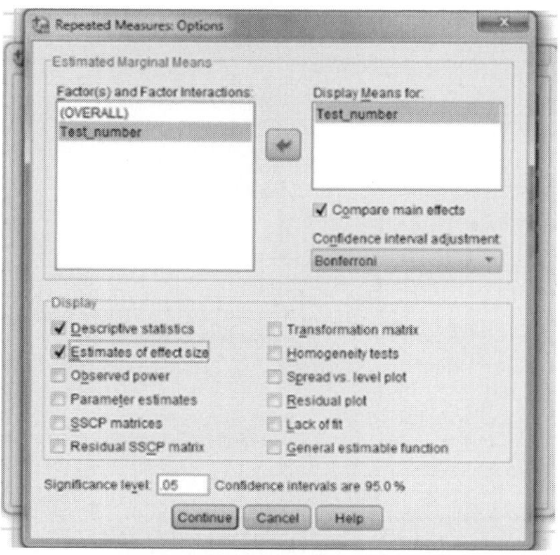

7. Click *Continue* and then *OK*. Your output should soon appear:

General Linear Model

Within-Subjects Factors

Measure: MEASURE_1

Exam_number	Dependent Variable
1	Test_#1
2	Test_#2
3	Tesst_#3

Descriptive Statistics

	Mean	Std. Deviation	N
First exam score	76.05	13.169	20
Second exam score	81.45	11.441	20
Third exam score	86.35	10.012	20

Multivariate Tests[a]

Effect		Value	F	Hypothesis df	Error df	Sig.	Partial Eta Squared
Exam_number	Pillai's Trace	.667	18.022[b]	2.000	18.000	.000	.667
	Wilks' Lambda	.333	18.022[b]	2.000	18.000	.000	.667
	Hotelling's Trace	2.002	18.022[b]	2.000	18.000	.000	.667
	Roy's Largest Root	2.002	18.022[b]	2.000	18.000	.000	.667

a. Design: Intercept
Within Subjects Design: Exam_number

b. Exact statistic

Mauchly's Test of Sphericity[a]

Measure: MEASURE_1

Within Subjects Effect	Mauchly's W	Approx. Chi-Square	df	Sig.	Epsilon[b]		
					Greenhouse-Geisser	Huynh-Feldt	Lower-bound
Exam_number	.865	2.600	2	.273	.881	.965	.500

Tests the null hypothesis that the error covariance matrix of the orthonormalized transformed dependent variables is proportional to an identity matrix.

a. Design: Intercept
Within Subjects Design: Exam_number

b. May be used to adjust the degrees of freedom for the averaged tests of significance. Corrected tests are displayed in the Tests of Within-Subjects Effects table.

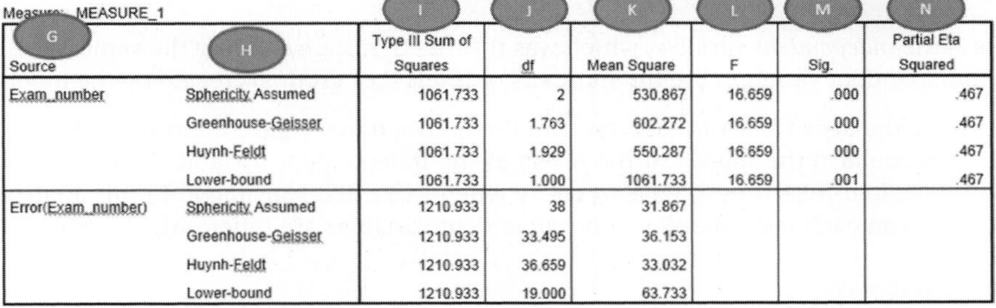

Tests of Within-Subjects Effects

Measure: MEASURE_1

Source		Type III Sum of Squares	df	Mean Square	F	Sig.	Partial Eta Squared
Exam_number	Sphericity Assumed	1061.733	2	530.867	16.659	.000	.467
	Greenhouse-Geisser	1061.733	1.763	602.272	16.659	.000	.467
	Huynh-Feldt	1061.733	1.929	550.287	16.659	.000	.467
	Lower-bound	1061.733	1.000	1061.733	16.659	.001	.467
Error(Exam_number)	Sphericity Assumed	1210.933	38	31.867			
	Greenhouse-Geisser	1210.933	33.495	36.153			
	Huynh-Feldt	1210.933	36.659	33.032			
	Lower-bound	1210.933	19.000	63.733			

Tests of Within-Subjects Contrasts

Measure: MEASURE_1

Source	Exam_number	Type III Sum of Squares	df	Mean Square	F	Sig.	Partial Eta Squared
Exam_number	Linear	1060.900	1	1060.900	33.590	.000	.639
	Quadratic	.833	1	.833	.026	.874	.001
Error(Exam_number)	Linear	600.100	19	31.584			
	Quadratic	610.833	19	32.149			

Tests of Between-Subjects Effects

Measure: MEASURE_1

Transformed Variable: Average

Source	Type III Sum of Squares	df	Mean Square	F	Sig.	Partial Eta Squared
Intercept	396418.817	1	396418.817	1163.144	.000	.984
Error	6475.517	19	340.817			

Estimated Marginal Means

Exam_number

Estimates O

Measure: MEASURE_1

Exam_number	Mean	Std. Error	95% Confidence Interval	
			Lower Bound	Upper Bound
1	76.050	2.945	69.887	82.213
2	81.450	2.558	76.096	86.804
3	86.350	2.239	81.664	91.036

Pairwise Comparisons P

Measure: MEASURE_1

(I) Exam_number	(J) Exam_number	Mean Difference (I-J)	Std. Error	Sig.[b]	95% Confidence Interval for Difference[b]	
					Lower Bound	Upper Bound
1	2	-5.400*	2.052	.049	-10.788	-.012
	3	-10.300*	1.777	.000	-14.965	-5.635
2	1	5.400*	2.052	.049	.012	10.788
	3	-4.900*	1.480	.011	-8.784	-1.016
3	1	10.300*	1.777	.000	5.635	14.965
	2	4.900*	1.480	.011	1.016	8.784

Based on estimated marginal means

*. The mean difference is significant at the .05 level.

b. Adjustment for multiple comparisons: Bonferroni.

What am I looking at? Interpreting your SPSS output

There is of course a lot of output here. Being generous, SPSS provides us with more output than we need, and we will focus on only the parts that we need to test our hypothesis.

A. This is the *independent variable*, which was the `Test_number` during the semester. Below the names of the independent variables are the numbers of levels (i.e., groups) created by the independent variables.

B. These are the *dependent variables* and are the names that we gave them in SPSS. You might be thinking that they are also the names of the levels of the independent variable. That is correct, and it is why I found repeated-measures to be a bit tricky when I was first learning it. In this analysis, we are comparing scores on each test; therefore, our dependent variables are inherently the levels of our independent variable.

C. These are the *labels of the dependent variable* that we provided.

D. These are the *means for each dependent variable*.

E. These are the *standard deviations for each dependent variable*.

F. This is the *number of respondents* who completed each dependent variable. Remember that this is a repeated-measures design; therefore, it is the same people completing each dependent variables.

G. This column contains the *sources of variability* in this analysis. To refresh, we have two sources of variability: between and error. Between is variability traceable to our independent variable, and error is variability traceable to factors other than our independent variable.

H. As we discussed earlier in this chapter, there are certain assumptions that must be met to use a repeated-measures ANOVA. For our purposes here, we will assume these assumptions are met and *use the "Sphericity Assumed" line* for both sources of variability.

I. The column quantifies *the between sums of squares* ($SS_{between}$) *and the error sums of squares* (SS_{error}). When we hand-calculated the one-way, repeated-measures ANOVA in the previous section of this chapter, this was step 3 of that process. In this example:

   a) $SS_{between} = 1061.733$

   b) $SS_{error} = 1210.933$

   Unlike the one-way, between-subjects ANOVA, SPSS does not provide us with SS_{total}.

J. This column contains the *degrees of freedom* (df) *for each source of variability*. This is step 4 from our hand-calculations. Let's refresh how these *df*s were calculated:

   a. $df_{between}$ is calculated by taking the number of conditions to which people responded (which here was three because there were three test grades being analyzed) and subtracting 1. Hence, $df_{between}$ is 2.

   b. To get df_{error}, we first need to find $df_{within-groups}$, which is the total number of responses, less the number of conditions to which people responded. With 3 tests and 20 students, that gives us 60 responses: 60 − 3 = 57.

   c. But wait, there's more. We need to remove subject individual difference degrees of freedom. These are calculated by taking the sample size (of 20 in this case) and subtracting 1. Our participant individual difference degrees of freedom are 20 − 1 = 19.

      Now to get df_{error}, take $df_{within\text{-}groups}$ and subtract $df_{individual\ difference}$. That gives us 57 − 19, which is 38. Hence, $df_{error} = 38$.

K. Here are our *mean squares* (MSs). This is step 5 of the hand-calculations. Just so you know where, in general, these numbers came from, recall the general formula of *MS*s:

$$\frac{\text{Sums of squares}(SS)}{df}$$

   On our SPSS output:

   a. $MS_{between}$:

$$\frac{1061.733}{2} = 530.867$$

   MS_{error}:

$$\frac{1210.933}{38} = 31.867$$

L. This is our *F* ratio test statistic. It was step 6 in our hand-calculations. Here is the general formula for this ratio:

$$F = \frac{MS_{\text{between}}}{MS_{\text{error}}}$$

Here is how our *F* ratio test statistic of 16.659 appeared on the output:

$$16.659 = \frac{530.867}{31.867}$$

M. This is the *p value, or significance level,* of our *F* ratio test statistic. This was a combination of steps 6 and 7 in our hand-calculation. Here, our *p* value reads as .000. Because it is less than .05, we can conclude that there are differences between the dependent variables. Because the *F* ratio test statistic is an omnibus test, it only tells us that a difference exists; it does not tell us which test score(s) was better than another test score.

Be careful when you see SPSS report a *p* value of .000. There is **never** an inferential statistical test performed in which there is a 0% chance our results were a function of random variability. Because of rounding, SPSS spits out .000, but in reality, there is a number down there somewhere. We'll see how to report *p* values in APA style when SPSS gives us .000.

N. This is our effect size. Here is how this value of .467 appeared on the output:

$$\eta_p^{\;2} = \frac{SS_{\text{between}}}{SS_{\text{between}} + SS_{\text{error}}}$$

$$= \frac{1061.733}{1061.733 + 1210.933}$$

$$= .467$$

O. Here again are our *means for each dependent variable*. We asked for them here in part for convenience as we will next explore which dependent variables are significantly different from each other. Here, we also have the standard error of the mean for each dependent variable mean, as well as the 95% confidence interval.

P. And, finally, here are our *post hoc tests (called pairwise comparisons)*. There are many different post hoc tests available, but for repeated-measures ANOVA, Bonferroni is commonly used (as Bernard et al. [2014] did). Reading these post hoc tests requires the same process as for the between-subjects ANOVA post hoc tests. Specifically, on the left side of the comparisons are listed each dependent variable. Looking at `Exam_number 1`, it is compared to `Exam_number 2` and then to `Exam_number 3`. Then `Test_number 2` is compared to the other two tests, and the same goes for `Test_number 3`.

The *Mean Difference* column is the difference between each pair of means listed in O previously.

We next have a standard error of the mean difference, followed by the *p* value (Sig.) of each mean comparison being made. This is where we learn which mean differences are statistically significant from each other. As you see here, all mean differences are statistically significant.

For everything SPSS can do, there is one thing it cannot do. It does not communicate our results in APA style. Let's do that ourselves right now:

The one-way, repeated-measures ANOVA revealed that there were significant differences among the scores on the three exams, $F(2, 38) = 16.66$, $p < .001$, $\eta_p^2 = .467$. Bonferroni-corrected multiple comparisons revealed that students scored better on the third exam ($M = 86.35$, $SD = 10.01$) than on the second exam ($M = 81.45$, $SD = 11.44$), $p = .011$. In addition, they scored better on the second exam than on the first exam ($M = 76.05$, $SD = 13.14$), $p = .049$. The first and third exams were also significantly different, $p < .001$.

LEARNING CHECK

Let's check our understanding of one-way, repeated-measures ANOVAs using SPSS. Below I have inserted an SPSS printout from Bernard et al.'s (2014) research. Rather than include all 15 student organizations that they studied, I included data from just 4 organizations (my apologies if you feel cheated, but the point here is to learn how to read and interpret SPSS output, not to flood you with SPSS output). Here is that output:

General Linear Model

Within-Subjects Factors

Measure: MEASURE_1

Student_Group	Dependent Variable
1	Black_Student_Union
2	Kinesiology_Student_Association
3	Math_Club
4	Social_Work_Organization

Descriptive Statistics

	Mean	Std. Deviation	N
Black Student Union	11.6961	12.47009	204
Kinesiology Student Association	17.4118	19.65007	204
Math Club	13.3922	16.10994	204
Social Work Organization	19.1471	22.21875	204

Tests of Within-Subjects Effects

Measure: MEASURE_1

Source		Type III Sum of Squares	df	Mean Square	F	Sig.	Partial Eta Squared
Student_Group	Sphericity Assumed	7310.863	3	2436.954	7.960	.000	.038
	Greenhouse-Geisser	7310.863	2.664	2744.143	7.960	.000	.038
	Huynh-Feldt	7310.863	2.703	2704.807	7.960	.000	.038
	Lower-bound	7310.863	1.000	7310.863	7.960	.005	.038
Error(Student_Group)	Sphericity Assumed	186437.637	609	306.137			
	Greenhouse-Geisser	186437.637	540.826	344.727			
	Huynh-Feldt	186437.637	548.692	339.786			
	Lower-bound	186437.637	203.000	918.412			

(Continued)

(Continued)

Student_Group

Estimates

Measure: MEASURE_1

Student_Group	Mean	Std. Error	95% Confidence Interval Lower Bound	95% Confidence Interval Upper Bound
1	11.696	.873	9.975	13.418
2	17.412	1.376	14.699	20.124
3	13.392	1.128	11.168	15.616
4	19.147	1.556	16.080	22.214

Pairwise Comparisons

Measure: MEASURE_1

(I) Student_Group	(J) Student_Group	Mean Difference (I-J)	Std. Error	Sig.[b]	95% Confidence Interval for Difference[b] Lower Bound	95% Confidence Interval for Difference[b] Upper Bound
1	2	-5.716*	1.516	.001	-9.755	-1.676
	3	-1.696	1.344	1.000	-5.277	1.885
	4	-7.451*	1.779	.000	-12.191	-2.711
2	1	5.716*	1.516	.001	1.676	9.755
	3	4.020	1.806	.163	-.793	8.832
	4	-1.735	1.901	1.000	-6.800	3.329
3	1	1.696	1.344	1.000	-1.885	5.277
	2	-4.020	1.806	.163	-8.832	.793
	4	-5.755*	1.965	.023	-10.991	-.519
4	1	7.451*	1.779	.000	2.711	12.191
	2	1.735	1.901	1.000	-3.329	6.800
	3	5.755*	1.965	.023	.519	10.991

Based on estimated marginal means

*. The mean difference is significant at the .05 level.

b. Adjustment for multiple comparisons: Bonferroni.

Questions:

1. What is the hypothesis being tested?
2. What is the mean for each of the four groups?
3. What is the standard deviation for each group?
4. What are the two sources of variability in these data?
5. What is the *F* ratio test statistic?
6. Plug in the numbers needed to obtain the *F* ratio test statistic.
7. What is the effect size? Interpret what this number means.
8. According to Appendix C, what is the approximate critical value that was used to see whether we reject or do not reject the null hypothesis?
9. What is the precise probability that the differences among our group means were due to random variation?
10. Did the researchers reject or not reject the null hypothesis?
11. Which means, if any, are statistically different from one another?
12. Given your answer to questions 10 and 11, what does that mean in plain English?
13. Write the result in APA style.

Answers

1. The hypothesis being tested is that there is no difference in funding allocations among the Black Student Union, the Kinesiology Student Association, the Math Club, and the Social Work Organization.
2. Black Student Union = \$11.70; Kinesiology Student Association = \$17.41; Math Club = \$13.39; Social Work = \$19.15.
3. Black Student Union = \$12.47; Kinesiology Student Association = \$19.65; Math Club = \$16.11; Social Work = \$22.22.
4. The Student Group is the between variability, and of course, we have error variability.
5. $F = 7.96$
6. $\frac{2436.95}{306.14} = 7.96$
7. $\eta_p^2 = .038$. This means that 3.8% of the variability in funding allocations is accounted for by the student organization.
8. With $df_{between} = 3$, $df_{error} = 609$, and an alpha level of .05, our critical value is between 2.60 and 2.65.
9. With the output saying $p = .000$, we report $p < .001$. In other words, there is less than a 0.1% chance that the differences among the means emerged due to random variation.
10. Because our F ratio exceeds the critical value, the null hypothesis was rejected.
11. After examining the pairwise comparisons, we determined that the Black Student Union was awarded less money than both the Kinesiology Student Association and Social Work Organization. Also, the Math Club was awarded less money than the Social Work Organization.
12. The Black Student Union was awarded less money than the Kinesiology Student Association and the Social Work Organization, respectively. Furthermore, the Math Club was awarded less money than the Social Work Organization.
13. The one-way, repeated-measures ANOVA revealed that there was a significant difference in funds allocated to the four student organizations, $F(3, 609) = 7.96$, $p < .01$, $\eta_p^2 = .038$. Bonferroni-corrected multiple comparisons revealed that the Black Student Union ($M = 11.70$, $SD = 12.47$) was awarded less money than the Kinesiology Student Association ($M = 17.41$, $SD = 19.65$), $p = .001$, and the Social Work Organization ($M = 19.15$, $SD = 22.22$), $p < .001$, respectively. In addition, the Math Club ($M = 13.39$, $SD = 16.10$) was awarded less money than the Social Work Organization, $p = .023$. No other comparisons were significant.

CHAPTER APPLICATION QUESTIONS

1. If an ANOVA is a "one-way" ANOVA, what information does that provide us?
2. Read the description of the research study below, and then use the APA style report of its results to answer the questions that follow it.

   One of my senior thesis students, Jason Jones, examined the impact of first names on a variety of interpersonal perceptions that we make about people. One such impression is how socially outgoing (extraverted) people are. Jones (2001) examined estimations of people's level of extraversion based on their first names. He used 30 different names that varied in terms of generational popularity. Ten names were the most popular given first names during the 1940s; 10 names were the most popular given first names during the 1960s; and 10 names were the most popular given first names during the 1980s. For each first name, participants estimated how socially outgoing a person with that name would be, using a 1 (*not at all extraverted*) to 7 (*very extraverted*) response range. Here are Jones's results, reported in APA style:

> The one-way, repeated-measures ANOVA revealed that there was a significant difference in perceptions of extraversion based on the generation of the first name, $F(2, 344) = 4.99$, $p < .01$, $\eta_p^2 = .125$. Bonferroni-corrected multiple comparisons revealed that names popular in the 1940s ($M = 3.33$, $SD = 2.89$) were rated as less extraverted than were names popular in the 1960s ($M = 5.14$, $SD = 1.77$) or the 1980s ($M = 5.21$, $SD = 1.91$), for both comparisons, $p < .01$. There were no differences in perceived level of extraversion for people with names from the 1960s and the 1980s, $p = .893$.

Answers

1. It means that there is one independent variable in the research study.

Questions to Answer

a. What was the hypothesis being tested in this research?

b. What were the means being statistically examined?

c. What is the F ratio?

d. How many degrees of freedom do the researchers have for this analysis?

e. By using Appendix C, approximate the critical value that was used to see whether we reject or do not reject the null hypothesis. Use an alpha level of .05.

f. What is the probability that the differences among the three groups' means were due to random variation?

g. Did the researchers reject or not reject the null hypothesis?

h. What is the effect size? Interpret what this number means.

i. Given your answer to the previous questions, what do these results mean in plain English?

Answers

a. There will be no effect of name generational popularity on perceptions of extraversion.

b. 1940s names = 3.33; 1960s names = 5.14; 1980s names = 5.21

c. F = 4.99

d. $df_{between} = 2$; $df_{error} = 344$

e. The critical value is between 3.00 and 3.07.

f. p value of < .01 means that there is less than a 1% chance the mean differences were due to random variation.

g. The researchers rejected the null hypothesis.

h. An effect size of .125 means that 12.5% of the variability in the dependent variable (perceptions of extraversion) is accounted for by the independent variable (name generational popularity).

i. People with first names that were popular in the 1940s are perceived to be less extraverted than are people with first names that were popular in the 1960s and the 1980s. There was no difference in perceived extraversion for people with first names popular in the 1960s and those with first names popular in the 1980s.

QUESTIONS FOR CLASS DISCUSSION

1. Why is a repeated-measures ANOVA more powerful than a between-subjects ANOVA?

2. Consider the following research situation, and then answer the questions that follow it:

   You have been hired by one of the local pizza places in my town to determine which of its three sauces customers like the most: regular tomato sauce, spicy tomato sauce, and white sauce. You asked 12 customers to taste and rate each type of sauce, using a 1 (*hated it*) to 7 (*loved it*) response range. Here are the means for each type of sauce:

Sauce	Mean
Regular tomato	5.57
Spicy tomato	4.67
White	2.21

Here is the corresponding ANOVA summary table:

Source of Variability	*SS*	*df*	*MS*	*F*
Participant Individual Differences	4	???	—	???
Between	200	???	???	
Error	53	???	???	
Total	257	???	—	

a) Complete the ANOVA summary table.

b) What is the critical value using an alpha level of .05? What is the critical value using an alpha level of .01? Why is the critical value larger when using an alpha of .01?

c) Do you reject or fail to reject the null hypothesis?
d) Calculate and interpret the effect size.
e) Perform any necessary post hoc tests.
f) Write your result in APA style.

CHAPTER 11

Analyzing Two or More Influences on Behavior

Factorial Designs for Two Between-Subjects Factors

After reading this chapter, you will be able to

- Differentiate between a one-way and a two-way ANOVA
- Interpret the conceptual ingredients of the two-way, between-subjects ANOVA
- Distinguish unique ingredients of a two-way, as opposed to a one-way, between-subjects ANOVA
- Interpret an APA style presentation of a two-way, between-subjects ANOVA
- Hand-calculate all ingredients for a two-way, between-subjects ANOVA
- Conduct and interpret a two-way, between-subjects ANOVA using SPSS

In the previous four chapters, we discussed how to analyze data when we have one factor (i.e., one independent variable) influencing behavior or cognitions. Of course, behaviors and cognitions often have more than one factor influencing them. As I think about what to have for dinner tonight, I consider what food I have available at home, what I ate earlier today, and how much I have (or have not) exercised today. These are but three factors on what might be for dinner tonight. In a research study, when we have two or more factors influencing behavior, we have what is called a **factorial design**. In this chapter, we will consider the two-way, between-subjects ANOVA. That is, we will consider how to analyze data when researchers examine two factors on behavior and cognitions.

Factorial design: research design that examines two or more influences on behavior.

CONCEPTUAL UNDERSTANDING OF THE TOOL

When I was about 6 years old, my parents decided it was time for me to start helping with certain "grown up" tasks around the house. I always enjoyed helping in the kitchen, in large part, because I liked to eat, but also because I was fascinated with how food was made. So, when I was about 6 years old, my parents decided I could make the family dinner one night each week. Of course, at that age, making dinner meant taking a frozen pizza, adding some preshredded cheese on top, and throwing it in the oven. But as I got older and more capable (and less dangerous) in the kitchen, I honed my pizza making skills, so that by the time I was about 10, I could make a "real" homemade pizza. From that time until I graduated from high school, I made homemade pizza for dinner once each week.

Pizza is a versatile food. So many people like it because there are so many different items and combinations of items that you can put on a pizza. For instance, my favorite pizza combination is pepperoni, red onions, black olives, jalapenos, all on tomato sauce, with mozzarella and provolone cheeses, and topped with chili lime sauce. However, the amount of each of these toppings can alter the taste of the pizza. For instance, using two jalapeno peppers on a 12-inch pizza makes it almost too spicy for me to eat; however, one jalapeno pepper is perfect (to me) on that pizza. Indeed, it is not only the specific toppings and combination of toppings on the pizza that affects its taste but also the amount of each topping that affects its taste. That may seem like an obvious point, but keep it in mind as we encounter our next statistical tool, the two-way, between-subjects ANOVA, in this chapter.

The Study

Since I started learning how to prepare dinner at 6 years old, pizza has been my favorite food. I think because it was my "go to" meal when I began cooking for my family, making and eating pizza now brings me a certain level of "comfort" or feeling of happiness. Indeed, most of us probably have some sort of "comfort food" that reminds of us of special people in our lives. My grandmother always made leg-of-lamb when her grandkids visited her at her house, so leg-of-lamb is another comfort food for me. Perhaps the smell of cookies baking is a comfort food to you. Or maybe there was a special meal that you got to enjoy with your family as a kid and eating it now brings back those same positive emotions. Many people have particular "comfort foods" that bring them a certain emotional delight when they eat those foods.

One reason why certain foods bring us a certain comfort is that, via associations in the sensory system in the brain, they are associated with particular experiences in our lives (Barsalou, 1999). One primary motivation we as human beings have is to form relationships to avoid feelings of loneliness. Indeed, a great deal of research shows that feelings of connectedness with other people help us avoid a variety of negative outcomes, such as depression (Ayduk, Downey, & Kim, 2001) and physical problems (MacDonald & Leary, 2005). Even when we cannot be with people we love, we do things to compensate for their physical absence. For instance, you may have a picture of your family in your dorm room or pictures on your phone of your friends and family that remind you of their presence in your life. And, of course, you might eat certain foods that remind you of those special people.

Even though I do not make dinner for my parents now as I did when I was a kid, making pizza today activates those pleasant childhood memories for me and, in doing so, helps stave off the negative outcomes mentioned previously. It is against this backdrop of comfort foods that we consider an experiment that Jordan Troisi and Shira Gabriel (2011) conducted.

At the start of the semester in which they conducted this experiment, Troisi and Gabriel (2011) asked all students in "Introductory Psychology" classes at their university whether they considered chicken noodle soup to be a comfort food, using a 1 (*not much at all*) to 5 (*very much so*) response range. They did this so they could classify people in the experiment into one of two groups: those who considered chicken noodle soup to be a comfort food and those who did not consider it to be a comfort food. Specifically, respondents who gave chicken noodle soup a 4 or 5 comfort food rating were classified as the "comfort food" group. Respondents who gave chicken noodle soup a 1 rating were classified as the "noncomfort food" group.

About 4 to 6 weeks after students provided these ratings, Troisi and Gabriel (2011) conducted their experiment. They had a sample of 111 undergraduate students from the "Introductory Psychology" classes; 58 of these people indicated that chicken noodle soup was a comfort food, and 53 indicated that it was not a comfort food. Upon arriving at the experimental session, participants were randomly assigned to perform a task while either eating a bowl of chicken soup alone or completing the experiment alone with no chicken soup provided.

Let's make sure we understand the two factors being studied or not in this research. One factor is whether people considered chicken noodle soup to be a comfort food or not. The second factor is the group people were randomly assigned to in the experimental session—consuming chicken noodle soup or not consuming chicken noodle soup.

Troisi and Gabriel (2011) told participants who were given the soup that they were participating in a pilot taste test before they completed the "real" experiment. After receiving or not receiving a bowl of chicken noodle soup, participants performed a word completion task. They saw a list of word fragments, six of which can be seen in Figure 11.1. Let's look at the top three word fragments. These are the ones of interest to this research. Each fragment could be completed as a relationship-related word or nonrelationship-related word. Look at the first relationship-related fragment. It could be completed as a relationship-oriented word (Include) or as a nonrelationship-related word (Incline). These three "relationship-oriented" word fragments served as the dependent variable in this experiment. Thus, scores on this dependent variable could range from 0 to 3.

Figure 11.1 Word Fragments That Troisi and Gabriel (2011) Used in Their Research

3 relationship-oriented fragments:
Participants saw:
I N C L _ _ _
L I _ _
W E L _ _ _ _

Each fragment could be completed with a relationship-related word, which appears first:
INCLUDE (or INCLINE)
LIKE (or LIFE, LIST, LINE, etc.)
WELCOME (or WELFARE, WELDING, etc.)

3 control word-fragments (i.e., could not be completed as relationship-focused words):
Participants saw:
T H E _ _
Q U _ _ _
C A _ _

Possible words from each fragment:
(e.g., THEME, THERE, THEIR, THESE)
(e.g., QUEST, QUEEN, QUICK, QUOTE)
(e.g., CALL, CARD, CATS, CANE)

Now let's consider the bottom word fragments. These fragments could not be completed as relationship-oriented words. Why would the researchers include fragments that could not be completed as relationship-related words? Doing so made it more difficult for participants to determine the purpose of the research.

Figure 11.2 presents a visual depiction of this experiment. As you can see, for a two-way research study, we can visualize it by "crossing" the conditions of the two independent variables. Thus, there are a total of four groups in this experiment. Each participant was randomly assigned either to eat chicken noodle soup or not to eat it. In addition, each participant considered chicken noodle soup to be a comfort food or not a comfort food. The mean score on the dependent variable will be within each of the four cells of this design.

Figure 11.2 Elements of Troisi and Gabriel's (2011) Experiment

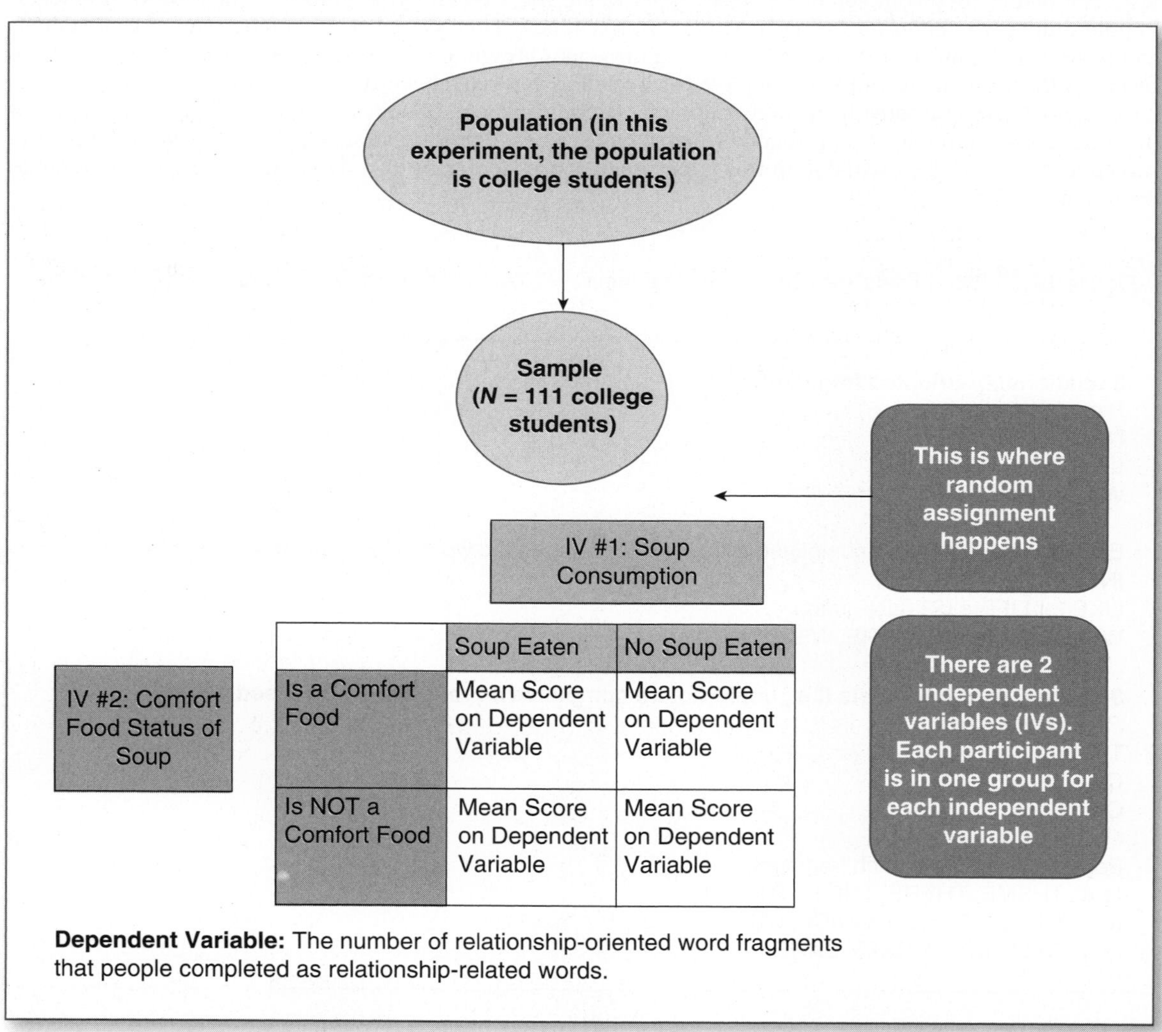

LEARNING CHECK

1. Explain why a two-way ANOVA is called "two-way."

   A: Because it is analyzing the effects of two independent variables (factors).

2. What are the independent variables in Troisi and Gabriel's (2011) experiment?

   A: Soup consumption and comfort food status of soup

3. What are the conditions that were created from the manipulation of these independent variables?

   A: There are four conditions created by manipulating these two independent variables. As displayed in Figure 11.2, one group ate soup and considered soup to be a comfort food; another group ate soup but did not consider soup to be a comfort food; a third group did not eat soup but did consider soup to be a comfort food; finally, one group did not eat soup nor did they consider soup to be a comfort food.

4. Why might the independent variable of "comfort food status of soup" not be considered a true independent variable (*HINT*: Think about random assignment)?

   A: Participants were not randomly assigned to the levels of this independent variable. Much like people cannot be randomly assigned to be male or female, people cannot be randomly assigned to find a food to be a type of comfort food or not. Returning to our original example to open this chapter, you might not find pizza to be a comfort food, but I do. You cannot be, practically speaking, randomly assigned to find pizza to be a comfort food, and I cannot be randomly assigned to not find pizza to be a comfort food.

   "Comfort food status of soup" is a quasi-independent variable. We discussed quasi-independent variables in Chapter 1. This does not in any way affect how we use our statistical tools.

5. What is the dependent variable in Troisi and Gabriel's (2011) experiment?

   A: Relationship-related word fragments that people completed as relationship words.

6. How was the dependent variable operationalized?

   A: There were three word fragments that could have been completed as relationship words. The number of such word fragments that participants completed (minimum of 0, maximum of 3) was how the dependent variable was operationalized.

The Tool

I have some good news for you. You already know almost everything there is to know about factorial designs from reading the previous two chapters. I know that I said something similar in the previous chapter, and we still did a lot of work. But truly, we are just building on your foundation of inferential statistical tools. In this section, we will introduce some terminology and concepts that are unique to factorial ANOVAs. In doing so, and in the next section, we will apply these concepts to Troisi and Gabriel's (2011) research.

Recall that a *factorial design* is an analysis that examines two or more influences (independent variables) on behavior and cognitions (the dependent variable/s). When we examine the effects of two or more independent variables, we tend to call the independent variables **factors**. That is, we have two or more factors influencing behavior and cognitions.

Factor: variable that is expected to influence behavior or cognitions; factor is another name for *independent variable.*

Factorial notation

Recall also that for a factor to be a variable, it must have at least two levels (or groups). Without at least two levels, nothing varies, and a researcher cannot make any comparisons. Given that a factor must have at least two levels, and that a factorial design by definition has at least two factors, the simplest factorial design possible is one in which there are two levels of two factors. Indeed, if you look at Figure 11.2 again, you will see that this is the type of factorial design that Troisi and Gabriel (2011) used. They had two factors: Consumption of Soup and Comfort Food Status of the Soup. Each of these factors had two levels. For the factor of Consumption of Soup, participants were randomly assigned to eat it or not eat it before completing the word fragment completion task. For the factor of Comfort Food Status of Soup, participants had rated it either as a comfort food or as not a comfort food.

Troisi and Gabriel's (2011) experiment is an example of a "2×2" factorial design. This should be pronounced "2 by 2" and not "2 times 2" as is tempting to do from our math classes. Let's break down this "2 by 2" notation into its smallest parts.

1. Each number represents the presence of a factor in the research design. Here we have two numbers, so there are two factors.
2. Each factor is separated by an "×".
3. Each number tells us the number of levels (groups) created by a factor. Thus, the first "2" means that this factor has two levels. The second "2" means that this factor has two levels.

You will see this type of **factorial notation** in any two-way ANOVA presentation. So, I want to make sure you don't make some of the common mistakes people make when they are first learning about factorial notation. Let's discuss four common mistakes to avoid:

1. I often see people think that the first number in two-way factorial notation is the number of independent variables and the second number is the number of levels of that independent variable. This is wrong; please do not do this. Instead, to determine the number of independent variables (factors) in the notation, simply count how many numbers there are. For example, say you see a 2 × 2 × 2 notation. How many factors are there? How many levels does each factor contain? There are three factors, and each factor has two levels. As another example, you see a 5 × 7 notation. Here, there are two factors, the first has five levels and the second has seven levels.
2. To determine the number of factors, do not multiply the numbers together. It is tempting to do so, but remember, the number of factors is noted by whole numbers, each separated with an " × ," which in the world of factorial designs is pronounced "by."
3. As an extension of the previous caution, how many groups were there in Troisi and Gabriel's (2001) experiment? A careful look at Figure 11.1 reveals four total groups: (1) those who ate soup and thought it was a comfort food; (2) those who did not eat soup but thought it was a comfort food; (3) those who ate soup but did not think it was a comfort food; and (4) those who did not eat soup and did not think it was a comfort food. When you see factorial notation, you can figure out the number of groups by multiplying together the numbers in that notation. For example, in a 3×3 design, how many groups are there? If you said 9, nice! How about in a 2×2×2 design, how many groups are there? If you said 8, you've got a great handle on this information.
4. We have discussed factorial notation with respect to independent variables (factors) and the number of groups formed from these factors. However, we have yet to discuss dependent variables. There is a good reason we have not discussed dependent variables here. That good reason is because we cannot tell from a stated factorial notation how many dependent variables there are in an experiment. Certainly, there has to be at least one, but a 2×2 design could have, in theory, an infinite number of dependent variables. We simply do not obtain this information from factorial notation.

Factorial notation: shorthand that tells us how many independent variables (factors) and how many levels of each independent variable (factor) a research study has.

Main effects and interactions

Let's introduce two concepts that you need to know to make sense of factorial designs later in this chapter. Remember that right now we are studying the effects of two factors on behavior and cognitions. It is possible that one factor has an effect; it is possible that the other factor has an effect. When examining the effect of one independent variable on a dependent variable, we say that there was a **main effect** of that factor. For example, in Troisi and Gabriel's (2011) research, there were two main effects: the effect of soup consumption and the effect of comfort food status of soup. There are always as many main effects as there are independent variables (factors) in the study. Please understand that we are not saying any of these main effects will be statistically significant, only that we will analyze them.

Main effect: effect of one factor on a dependent variable.

In addition to main effects, we need to understand that *factors can interact* to produce effects on behavior and cognitions. The concept of an **interaction** is one you likely understand but perhaps not in terms of statistics. Let's take some common examples of an interaction before returning to Troisi and Gabriel's (2011) research. Specifically, whenever you take a medication, it is a good idea to see whether there are foods you should avoid eating or be sure to eat enough of because, depending on the medication, certain foods can enhance or detract from the benefit of the drug. For instance, many people take an iron supplement each day. Certainly there is a main effect of taking iron. That is, iron increases oxygen levels in our bodies. However, if one takes an iron supplement with a drink full of Vitamin C, such as orange juice, the effects of the iron are enhanced because the Vitamin C increases the body's absorption of the iron. Similarly, people who take MAO inhibiting antidepressant drugs need to stay away from foods that contain tyramine (e.g., beer, some processed meats, and avocados) because tyramine slows down the body's ability to metabolize the MAO inhibitors and can result in dangerously high blood pressure. There is nothing wrong with foods containing tyramine in terms of blood pressure (main effect of tyramine) unless you factor in the use of MAO inhibitors. In my own case, I have occasional allergies, and I find that Benadryl® (Johnson & Johnson, New Brunswick, NJ), without fail, eliminates my allergic reactions. Of course, it also makes me extremely groggy (a main effect). If I ingest alcohol along with my Benadryl, the alcohol will greatly intensify the grogginess that the Benadryl brings on. There is nothing wrong (I don't think) with a glass or two of wine, but when Benadryl is involved, that can be a dangerous combination, even if I am not driving.

Interaction: occurs when the effect of one factor depends on the levels of a second factor.

When we get to statistical interactions, it will be important to see, literally, what we are talking about. Graphs are essential in helping me understand interactions, so let's take a look at what some of these examples of interactions look like. Figure 11.3 contains the interaction between taking an iron supplement and Vitamin C consumption on oxygen levels. Let's examine this figure closely. We are assuming that we have done an experiment that examined the effects of iron consumption and Vitamin C consumption on oxygen levels in the body. On the *y*-axis is the dependent variable or outcome of the factors. Here, it is oxygen level.

Figure 11.3 Illustration of an Interaction Between Two Factors

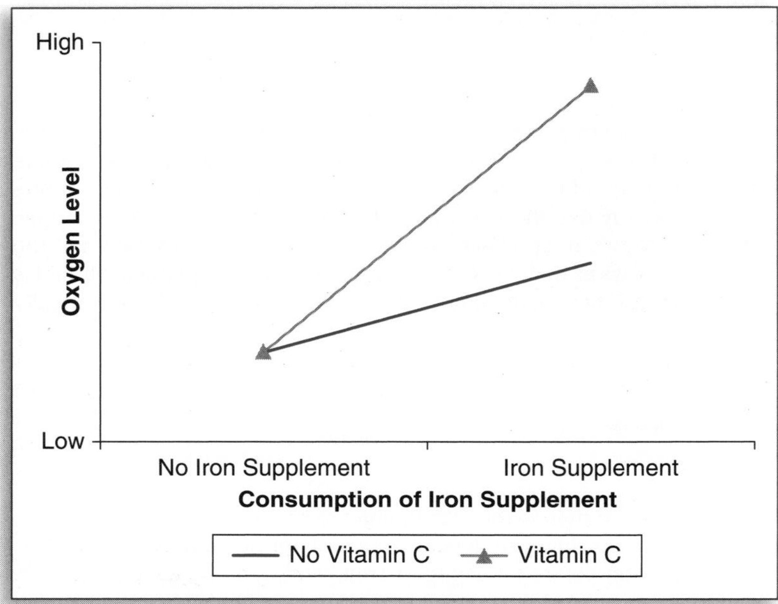

Our factors are iron consumption and Vitamin C consumption. The levels of one factor are placed on the *x*-axis. Here, people either did not or did consume an iron supplement. The other factor we need to represent with lines, one line for each level of that factor. So, we will have two lines, one for people who consumed Vitamin C and one for people who did not consume Vitamin C.

To interpret this graph, let's look at each level of the factor on the *x*-axis. First, we have people who did not take an iron supplement. These people who did not take an iron supplement also either consumed Vitamin C or did not consume Vitamin C. There is very little difference in oxygen levels among people who did not take an iron supplement based on whether they did or did not consume Vitamin C.

When we move to the other level of the factor on the *x*-axis, we see that we have people who did take an iron supplement. These people who took an iron supplement also either consumed Vitamin C or did not consume Vitamin C. There is a large difference in oxygen levels among people who took an iron supplement based on whether they did or did not consume Vitamin C.

What do we take away from this graph? The effects of the iron supplement *depend on* whether people are also ingesting Vitamin C. If people are taking Vitamin C, the effects of the iron supplement on oxygen levels are more powerful than they are when people are not taking Vitamin C. The key words here are that the effects of one factor *depend on* the levels of a second factor. Here, the effects of iron *depend on* whether people are taking Vitamin C.

Think about this "depends on" phrase in a more mundane situation. I ask you whether you would like a piece of cheesecake. If you like and can eat cheesecake, you would probably say "yes." However, what if you had just had a big meal and a rich dessert? What if you were about to go for a 10-mile run? Under these circumstances, you probably would not feel like eating cheesecake. Therefore, whether you eat the cheesecake *depends on* other factors (i.e., how full you already feel and whether you're about to exercise). Let's see whether we can graph this interaction. The dependent variable always goes on the *y*-axis. The dependent variable is the likelihood you eat the cheesecake. One factor is whether you like and can eat cheesecake. We can put this factor on the *x*-axis with the levels "no" and "yes." The other factor is, to take only one, whether you're about to exercise. We draw one line for "not going to exercise" and one line for "about to go exercise." Figure 11.4 contains what this interaction looks like.

When we have a 2 × 2 factorial design, there are a total of eight possible outcomes from our analyses. Remember that a 2 × 2 design has two independent variables (main effects) that may or may not be statistically significant. In addition, there is an interaction that may or may not be statistically significant. Figure 11.5 contains the eight possible outcomes from a 2 × 2 design using Troisi and Gabriel's (2011) factors.

In a given study, only one of these outcomes will occur. Take a look at each of the eight panels (possible outcomes) and see whether you can tell which ones present an interaction between two factors. (Seriously, take some time to do this, and then read on from here.)

Panels e, f, g, and h all display interactions. That is, the effects of soup consumption on the number of relationship words completed depend on whether people think soup is a comfort food. Let's look specifically at panel f. On the x-axis are the two levels of the factor soup consumption. Look first at the level of "soup eaten." Here, people who considered soup to be a comfort food completed more relationship words than did people who did not consider soup to be a comfort food. Now look at the level of "no soup eaten." Here, people who considered soup to be a comfort food completed fewer relationship words than did people who did not consider soup to be a comfort food. In other words, the effect of eating the soup on the number of relationship words completed *depends on* whether people considered soup a comfort food.

Figure 11.4 Illustration of an Interaction Between Cheesecake Preference and Exercising on Likelihood of Eating Cheesecake

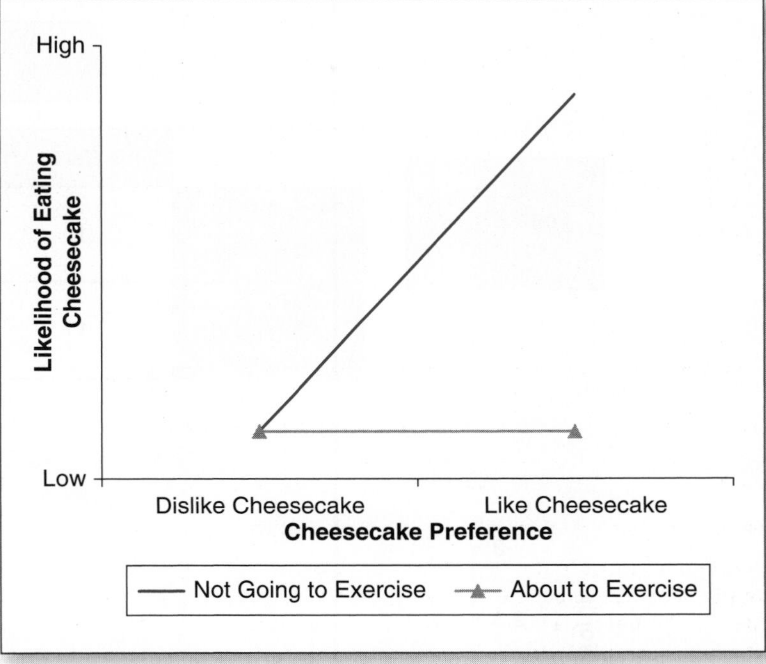

Please look at panels e, g, and h again. In the next Learning Check, you will have a chance to interpret one of these interactions.

Hypotheses for Troisi and Gabriel (2011)

In the next section, we will examine Troisi and Gabriel's (2011) results. Here, let's look at their hypotheses. Recall from Figure 11.2 that there were two factors: soup consumption and comfort food status of soup. In addition, there is an interaction between these two factors. So in all, three hypotheses are being tested, one for each main effect and one for the interaction. Here are the null hypotheses being tested:

For the main effect of soup consumption on the number of relationship-related words completed:

$$H_o: \mu_{\text{not-consumed}} = \mu_{\text{consumed}}$$

For the main effect of comfort food status of soup on the number of relationship-related words completed:

$$H_o: \mu_{\text{not comfort food}} = \mu_{\text{comfort food}}$$

Figure 11.5a Eight Possible Outcomes for 2×2 Factorial Design With the Independent Variables of Soup Consumption and Comfort Food Status of Soup

IV #1: Soup Consumption

IV #2: Comfort Food Status of Soup

	Soup Eaten	No Soup Eaten
Is a Comfort Food	1	1
Is NOT a Comfort Food	1	1

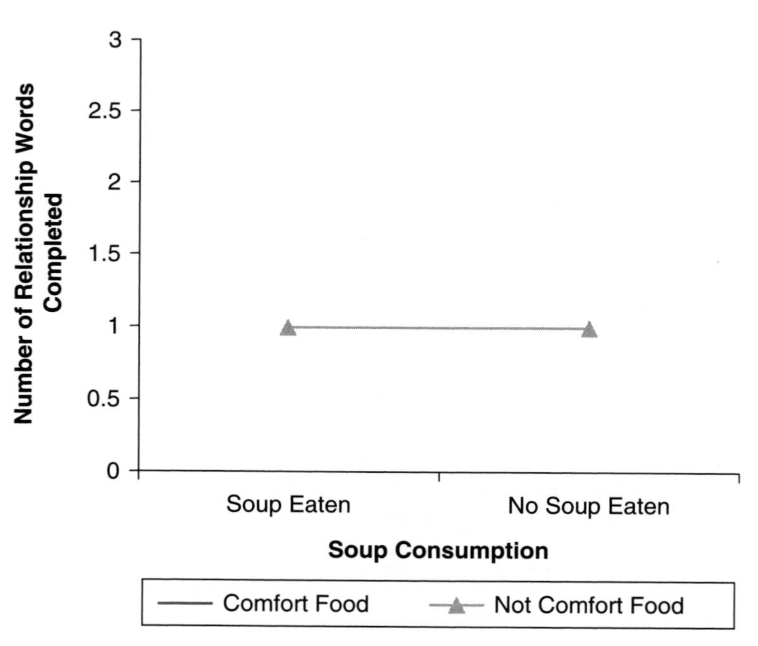

Note: The Comfort Food and Not Comfort Food likes overlap.

Figure 11.5b

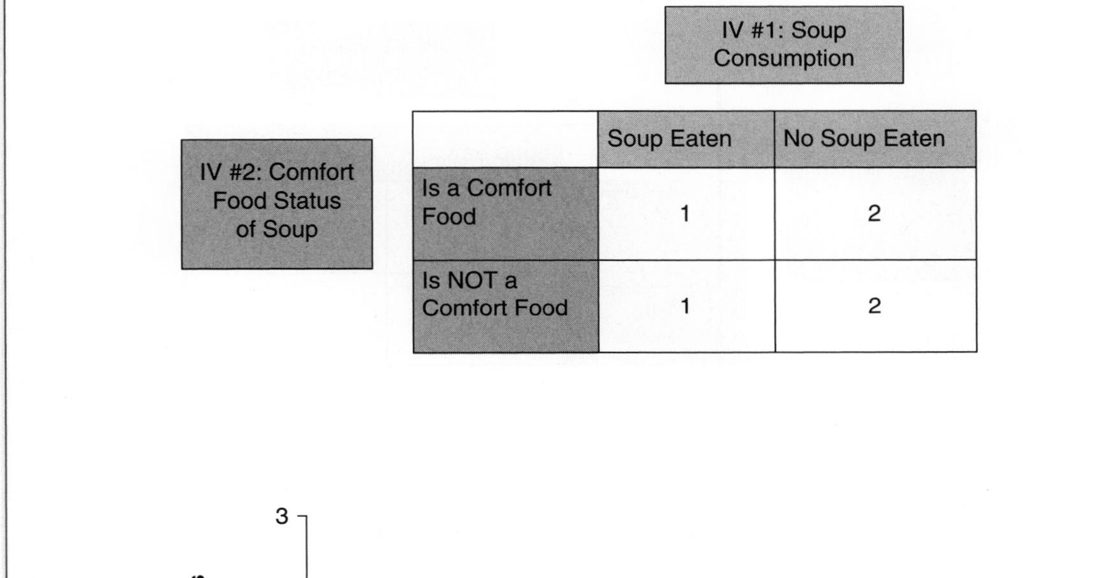

	Soup Eaten	No Soup Eaten
Is a Comfort Food	1	2
Is NOT a Comfort Food	1	2

Note: The Comfort Food and Not Comfort Food likes overlap.

Figure 11.5c

IV #1: Soup Consumption

IV #2: Comfort Food Status of Soup

	Soup Eaten	No Soup Eaten
Is a Comfort Food	1	1
Is NOT a Comfort Food	3	3

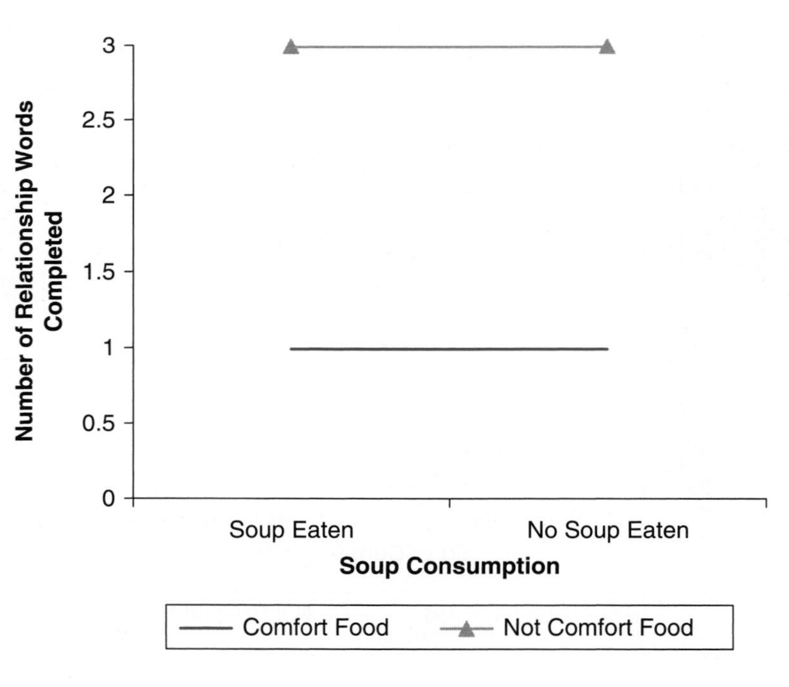

Figure 11.5d

IV #2: Comfort Food Status of Soup		IV #1: Soup Consumption	
		Soup Eaten	No Soup Eaten
	Is a Comfort Food	2	3
	Is NOT a Comfort Food	1	2

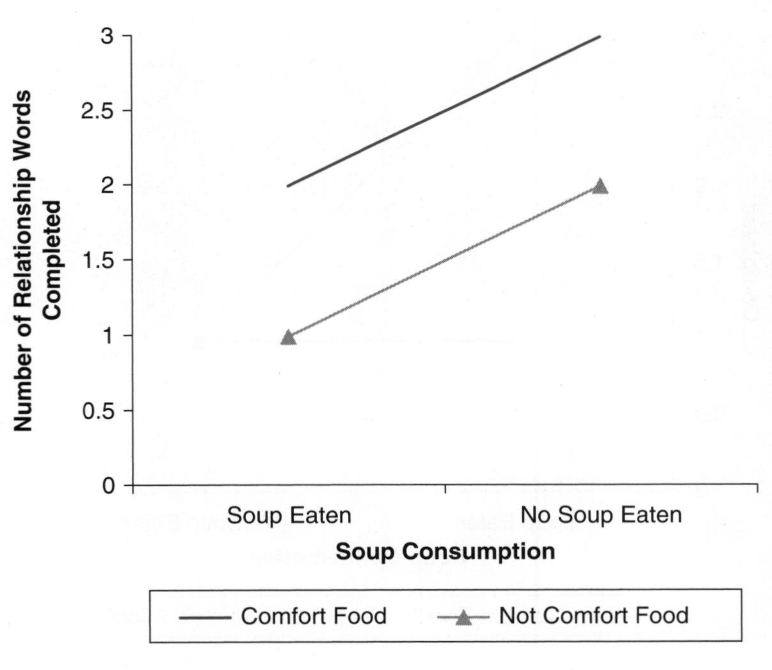

Figure 11.5e

IV #1: Soup Consumption

IV #2: Comfort Food Status of Soup

	Soup Eaten	No Soup Eaten
Is a Comfort Food	1	1
Is NOT a Comfort Food	3	1

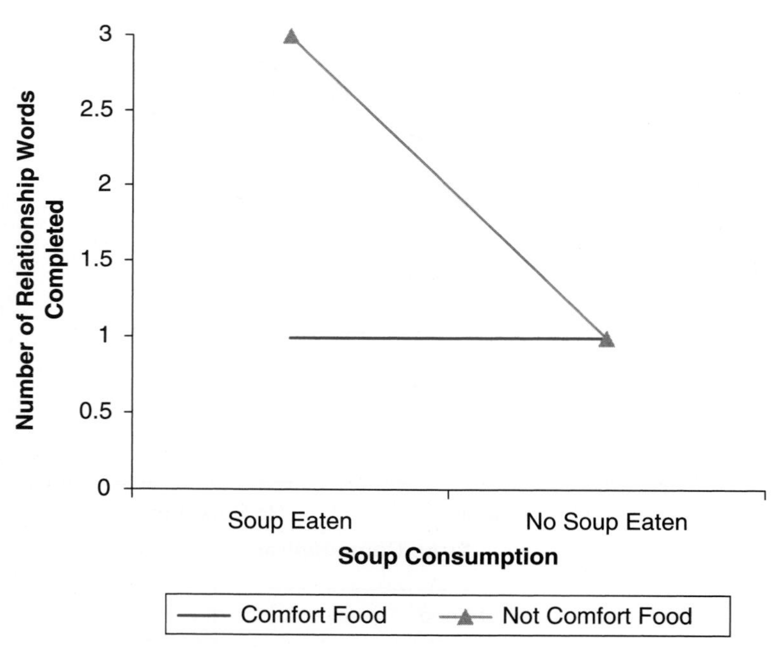

Figure 11.5f

IV #2: Comfort Food Status of Soup	IV #1: Soup Consumption	
	Soup Eaten	No Soup Eaten
Is a Comfort Food	3	1
Is NOT a Comfort Food	2	2

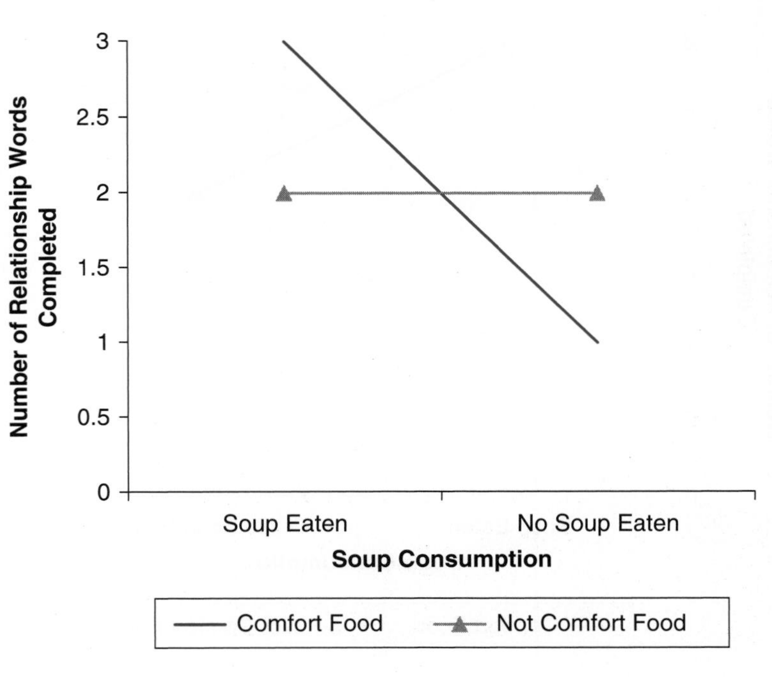

Figure 11.5g

IV #2: Comfort Food Status of Soup	IV #1: Soup Consumption	
	Soup Eaten	No Soup Eaten
Is a Comfort Food	3	2
Is NOT a Comfort Food	1	2

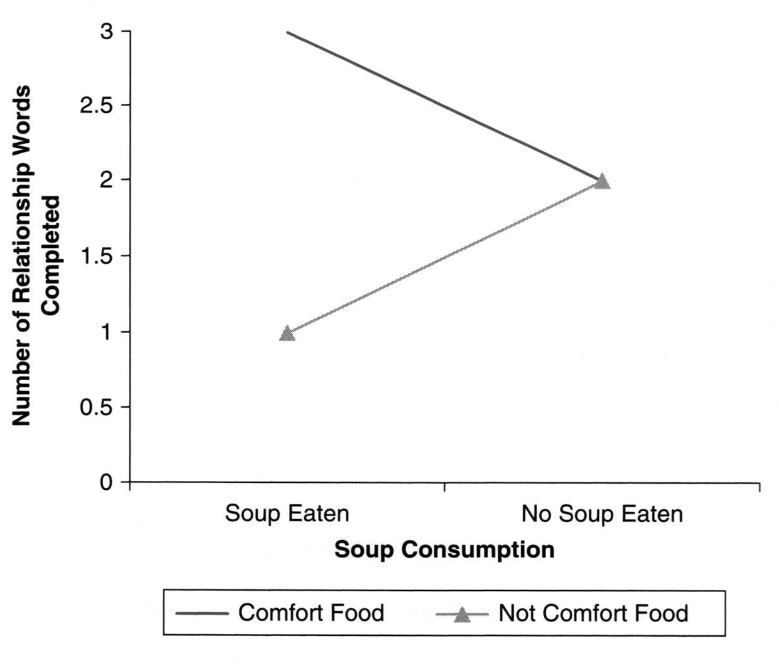

Figure 11.5h

	IV #1: Soup Consumption	
IV #2: Comfort Food Status of Soup	Soup Eaten	No Soup Eaten
Is a Comfort Food	3	1
Is NOT a Comfort Food	1	3

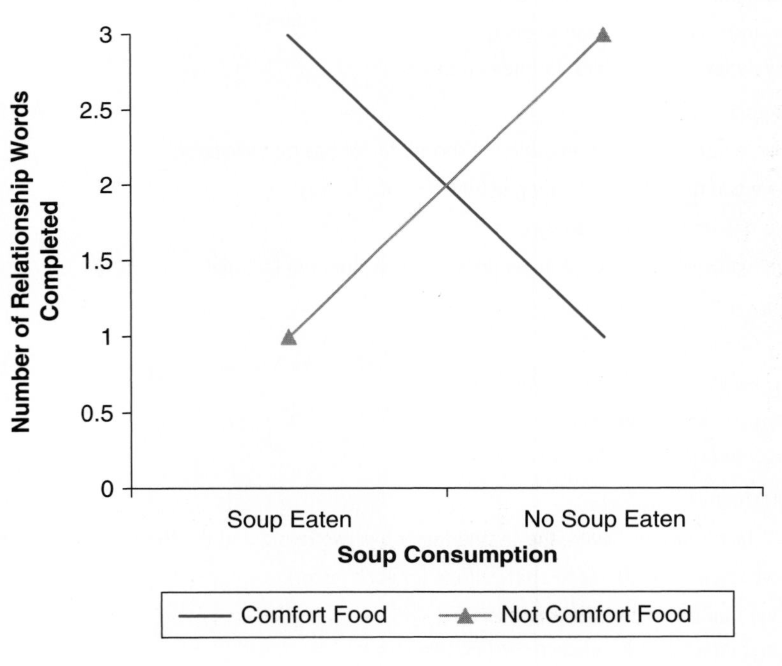

For the interaction:

H_o: There is no interaction between soup consumption and comfort food status of soup on the number of relationship-related words completed.

Troisi and Gabriel (2011) offered the research hypothesis "that comfort foods are associated with relationships" (p. 748). Therefore, if people find a certain food (i.e., chicken noodle soup) to be a comfort food, then when eating that food, relationship-related words will be more accessible and they will tend to complete word fragments in terms of relationship-oriented words. In other words, the effect of eating soup *depends on* whether people think of soup as a comfort food.

LEARNING CHECK

1. What is the difference between a main effect and an interaction?

   A: A main effect is the effect of one and only one factor on a dependent variable. An interaction occurs when the effect of one factor depends on the levels of a second factor. That is, the first factor does not "tell the whole" story about its precise relationship to the dependent variable. We need to examine the levels of the second factor to understand how that first factor affects the dependent variable.

2. Suppose we have a "3×4" factorial design.
   a) How many factors do we have?
   b) How many levels of each factor do we have?
   c) How many main effects are there to analyze?
   d) How many interactions are there to analyze?
   e) How many dependent variables are there in this analysis?

   A: a) Two factors
   b) The first factor has three levels, and the second factor has four levels.
   c) There are two main effects to analyze (one for each factor).
   d) There is one interaction to analyze.
   e) We don't know the number of dependent variables from the factorial notation.

3. Suppose we have a "2×2×2" factorial design.
   a) How many factors do we have?
   b) How many levels of each factor do we have?
   c) How many main effects are there to analyze?
   d) How many interactions are there to analyze?

   A: a) Three factors
   b) The first factor has two levels; the second factor has two levels; and the third factor has two levels.
   c) There are three main effects to analyze (one for each factor).
   d) There are four interactions to analyze:
   The first interaction is between the first two factors.
   The second interaction is between the first and third factors.
   The third interaction is between the second and third factors.
   The fourth interaction is among all three factors.

4. Look at Figure 11.5, panel g. Interpret what this interaction means in plain English.

   A: People who ate soup and who considered soup to be a comfort food completed more relationship words than people who ate soup but did not consider soup to be a comfort food. Among people who did not eat soup, there was no difference in the number of relationship words completed between people who considered soup to be a comfort food and people who did not consider soup to be a comfort food.

5. Look at Figure 11.5, panels a, b, c, and d. Why are these examples of main effects but not interactions?

   A: In all four panels, the effects of one factor do not depend on the levels of the second factor. For instance, in panel a, among people who ate soup, there is no difference in the number of relationship words completed between people who did and did not consider soup to be a comfort food. Among people who did not eat soup, again, there is no difference in the number of relationship words completed between people who did and did not consider soup to be a comfort food. In other words, the effects of Soup Consumption on the number of relationship words completed have nothing to do with whether people considered soup to be a comfort food.

   Notice that in all four panels that the lines for the levels of the factor Comfort Food Status of Soup are parallel to each other. When we see the lines for a factor being parallel, it indicates that there is not interaction. In a line graph, interaction is displayed with nonparallel lines. Of course, the only way we can ever know whether an interaction is statistically significant is to use the appropriate tool, which we will learn later in this chapter.

6. Look at Figure 11.5, panel c. Interpret what this main effect means in plain English.

   A: Among people who ate soup, those who did not consider soup to be a comfort food completed more relationship words than those who considered soup to be a comfort food. Among people who did not eat soup, those who did not consider soup to be a comfort food completed more relationship words than those who considered soup to be a comfort food.

   Notice the language to describe the two levels of the factor Comfort Food Status of Soup. They are the same. That's because the levels of this factor do not interact with the factor of Soup Consumption. In this example, the effects are the same for Soup Consumption no matter how people felt about soup as a comfort food.

Interpreting the Tool

In the previous section, we discussed concepts specific to factorial designs, specifically, main effects and interactions. We will now examine the results of Troisi and Gabriel's (2011) factorial design. Before we do so, it might be good to refresh yourself on the factors and the dependent variable in this experiment by consulting Figure 11.2.

For any two-way ANOVA, we will have three effects tested statistically: the two main effects and the one interaction that results from those two factors. Keep this in mind as we see the results of this research:

> A two-way ANOVA on this variable (the number of relationship-related word fragments that participants completed as relationship words) revealed no significant main effect of soup consumption, $F(1, 107) = 0.24$, $p = .627$, $\eta^2 = .002$, and no significant main effect of comfort food status of soup, $F(1, 107) = 3.74$, $p = .056$, $\eta^2 = .032$. However, there was an interaction between soup consumption and comfort food status, $F(1, 107) = 4.48$, $p = .037$, $\eta^2 = .042$. (Troisi & Gabriel, 2011, p. 748)

There are more results to examine. But let's stop here and interpret these results. Then we will deal with the remaining results and accompanying statistics. In plain English, neither main effect (i.e., factor) had a statistically significant effect on the dependent variable. However, the two factors did have a statistically significant interactive effect on the dependent variable.

I know that we want to get to the take-home message from these results. However, recall from Chapter 9 that the F ratio test statistic, which is what we have here so far, simply tells us whether there are significant differences somewhere in our data (hence, why it is often called an omnibus F test). What we know at this point is that neither factor by itself produced a significant effect on how many relationship words people completed). We also know that the interaction between the two factors was statistically significant, but we need do some more work to understand what this interaction means in plain English. We will first see how the numbers in the results presented thus far were calculated. Then, we will do that wok on our interaction.

Testing the null hypothesis

To reiterate, for any two-way ANOVA, we will have three effects tested statistically: the two main effects (because we have two factors in the ANOVA) and the one interaction that results from those two factors. Troisi and Gabriel (2011) presented results on the two main effects, followed by the interaction. Let's look at the main effect of soup consumption:

$$F(1,\ 107) = 0.24,\ p = .627,\ \eta^2 = .002$$

Our F ratio test statistic is 0.24. Recall the conceptual formula for an F ratio test statistic:

$$F = \frac{\text{Systematic variance} + \text{error variance}}{\text{Error variance}}$$

To refresh from the previous two chapters, systematic variance is variance in scores on the dependent variable that is traceable to the independent variable, whereas error variance is the variance attributable to uncontrolled variables and random variation. We will of course calculate F ratios in the next section.

We have "(1, 107)" in parentheses. These are our degrees of freedom. The first number is our between-groups (or numerator) degrees of freedom, and the second number is our within-groups (or denominator) degrees of freedom. From Chapter 9, you might recall how to calculate them, but as we are dealing with factorial designs now, a little guidance might help.

First, the within-groups ANOVA is calculated precisely as it was for the one-way, between-subjects ANOVA. Specifically:

$$df_{\text{within-groups}} = \text{sample size} - \text{number of groups being compared}$$

Keep in mind that we have a total of four groups in this analysis (Figure 11.2). Therefore, with 111 participants, we have:

$$df_{\text{within-groups}} = 111 - 4$$
$$df_{\text{within-groups}} = 107$$

Second, the $df_{\text{between-groups}}$ is just a bit more involved than it was for a one-way, between-subjects ANOVA. We need to calculate an overall $df_{\text{between-groups}}$, but then we must divvy up that overall $df_{\text{between-groups}}$ into a $df_{\text{between-groups}}$ for each main effect and interaction in our ANOVA.

The overall $df_{\text{between-groups}}$ is calculated exactly as it was for the one-way, between-subjects ANOVA. Specifically:

$$df_{\text{between-groups}} = \text{number of groups in the analysis} - 1$$

We have 4 total groups in this experiment, so:

$$df_{\text{between-groups}} = 4 - 1$$
$$df_{\text{between-groups}} = 3$$

Now it's time to divvy up the overall $df_{\text{between-groups}}$. For each main effect, we calculate a $df_{\text{between-groups}}$ by taking the number of level of each factor and subtracting 1. For the main effect of soup consumption, we have two levels (ate the soup or did not eat the soup). And, of course, 2 − 1 = 1. Therefore, $df_{\text{soup consumption}} = 1$. For the main effect of comfort food status of soup, we also have two levels (was a comfort food or was not a comfort food). Therefore, $df_{\text{comfort food status}} = 2 - 1 = 1$.

To summarize, we have an overall $df_{\text{between-groups}}$ of 3 and a $df_{\text{between-groups}}$ for each main effect 1. That leaves us just 1 $df_{\text{between-groups}}$ for the interaction of the two factors. Of course, we should understand how to calculate a *df* for the interaction. We multiply together the *df*s for the two main effects:

$$df_{\text{interaction}} = df_{\text{soup consumption}} \times df_{\text{comfort food status}}$$
$$df_{\text{interaction}} = 1 \times 1$$
$$df_{\text{interaction}} = 1$$

Now that we have our degrees of freedom, we can locate a critical value to compare to our *F* ratio. We will examine both main effects and then the interaction between the two factors. In published research, you normally will not see a critical value reported, but as you know, it is the comparison of the *F* ratio test statistic to the critical value that determines whether our statistical result is significant and generalizable from the sample to the population.

To find our critical value, we need to consult Appendix C. We've seen this appendix in the previous two chapters when discussing one-way ANOVAs. Nothing has changed here, except now we need to find three critical values: one for the main effect of soup consumption, one for the main effect of comfort food status, and one for the interaction of these two factors. We know that the $df_{\text{between-groups}}$ is 1 for each main effect and the interaction. In addition, the $df_{\text{within-groups}}$ is 107 for the entire analysis. In looking at Appendix C, we can locate the 1 $df_{\text{between-groups}}$ column. However, there is not a precise row for $df_{\text{within-groups}}$ of 107. We will estimate it to be between the critical values for $df_{\text{within-groups}}$ of 60 and 120. With our normal alpha level of .05, we can use a critical value of 3.96 (which is somewhat conservative because that is the average of the critical values associated with 60 and 120 $df_{\text{within-groups}}$ even though we have more $df_{\text{within-groups}}$ than that average).

We now compare our critical value of 3.96 to each of the three *F* ratio test statistics. These comparisons are displayed in Figure 11.6. The top two sections of Figure 11.6 show the comparisons of the *F* ratio test statistics for the two main effects to the critical value. As you can see (and perhaps remember from reading Troisi and Gabriel's [2011] results), the *F* ratios for both main effects are less than the critical value. Because they fall outside the region of null hypothesis rejection, Troisi and Gabriel failed to reject the two null hypotheses for the main effects. When we examine the *F* ratio for the interaction in the bottom of Figure 11.6, we see that the *F* ratio exceeds the critical value. It falls in the region of null hypothesis rejection, so Troisi and Gabriel rejected the null hypothesis for the interaction.

After our *F* ratio test statistic and degrees of freedom appears our precise *p* value. Recall this number is the probability that a statistical result occurred by random variation. We want this number to be low, and as you may be sick of hearing by now, when it is less than .05, we can generalize a statistical result in our sample to the larger population. For the main effect of soup consumption, with a *p* value of .627, that means there is a 62.7% chance that the result occurred by random variation, and so we cannot generalize it from the sample to the population. For the main effect of comfort food status, with a *p* value of .056, that means there is a 5.6% chance that the result occurred by random variation, and again, it cannot be generalized. I know you might be thinking .056 is close to .05, as evidenced in the middle of Figure 11.6. Close only counts in playing darts and horseshoes, not in testing hypotheses. However, for the interaction (as you already know from Figure 11.6), there is a 3.7% chance this effect was produced from random variation, which lead Troisi and Gabriel (2011) to reject the null hypothesis.

Extending the null hypothesis tests

And last but not least is our effect size. In the previous two chapters, I issued a warning for this chapter about effect sizes. When dealing with one-way ANOVAs, we used an effect size called partial eta squared (η_p^2). This effect size is acceptable for a one-way ANOVA. However, when we have a factorial design, we must use an effect size called eta squared (η^2). Given your familiarity with the concept of sums of squares, let's see how both η_p^2 and η^2 are calculated; then we will discuss when each one can or must be used.

Figure 11.6 Panels (a) and (b) Provide Comparisons for the Two Main Effects. Panel (c) Provides the Comparison for the Interaction

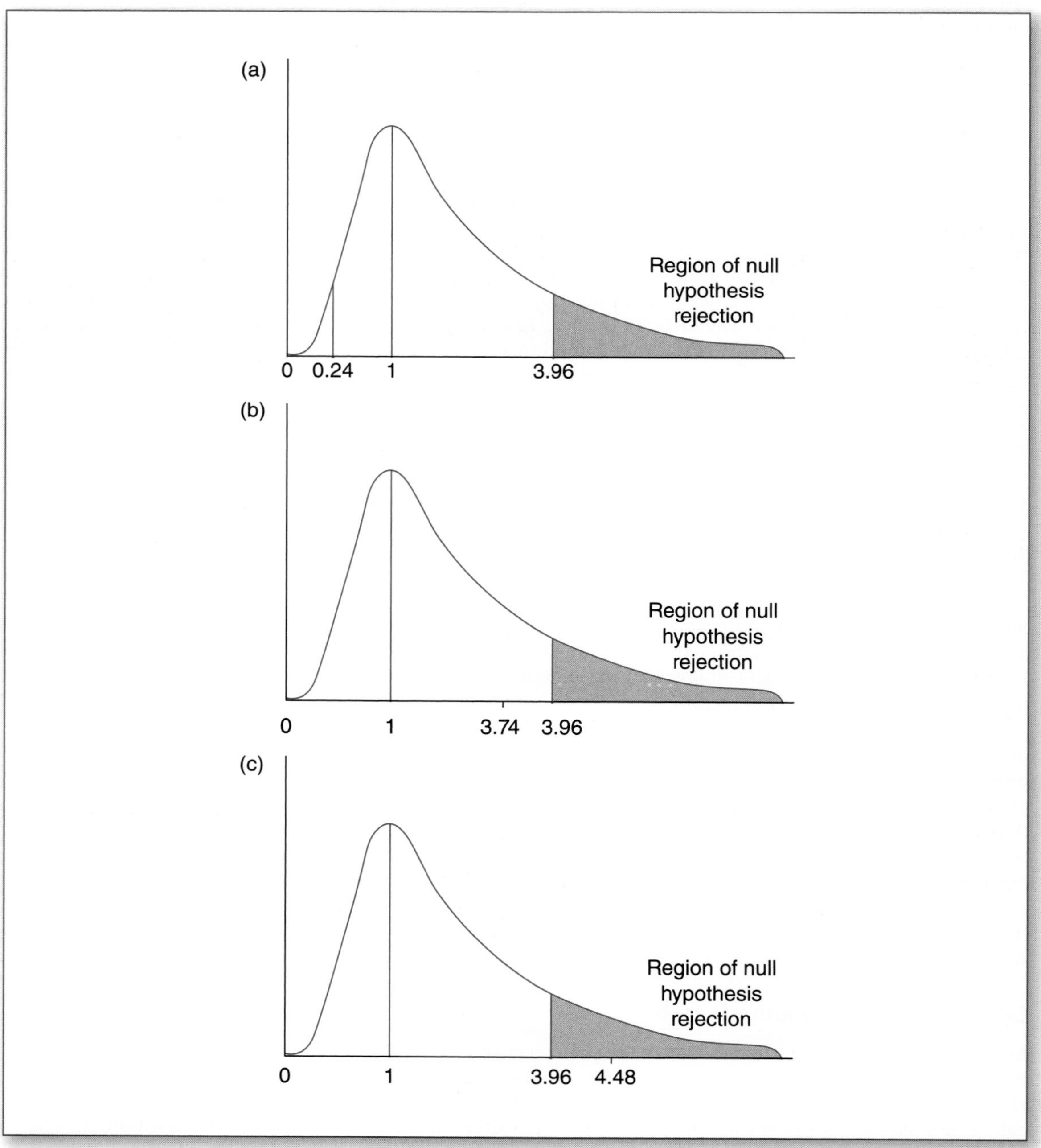

From the previous two chapters, here is the formula for η_p^2:

$$\eta_p^2 = \frac{SS_{between-groups}}{SS_{between-groups} + SS_{within-groups}}$$

Now, here is the formula for η^2:

$$\eta^2 = \frac{SS_{between-groups}}{SS_{total}}$$

If you look at the denominators of these two formulas, you might wonder, doesn't $SS_{between\text{-}groups} + SS_{within\text{-}groups} = SS_{total}$, which is the denominator of the η^2? Well, sort of. Let me explain what I mean by "sort of."

With a one-way ANOVA, we have one factor we are analyzing. Without a second factor, there can be no interaction. Therefore, the only between-groups variability must be due to the one factor. So in a one-way ANOVA, $SS_{between\text{-}groups}$ will be the same for η_p^2 as it is for η^2.

With a two-way ANOVA, we have two factors we are analyzing. With two factors, there is going to be an interaction to analyze as well. Therefore, between-groups variability can be due to three sources: the main effect of the first factor, the main effect of the second factor, and the interaction between the two factors. If we use η_p^2 for two-way ANOVAs, then $SS_{between\text{-}groups} + SS_{within\text{-}groups}$ does not equal SS_{total} because the $SS_{between\text{-}groups}$ is specific to a main effect or to the interaction. Let's take a hypothetical example to demonstrate why we must use η^2 with factorial ANOVAs.

Suppose we have the following *SS*s for a one-way ANOVA:

$$SS_{between\text{-}groups} = 30$$
$$SS_{within\text{-}groups} = 25$$

Of course, in this instance, SS_{total} would be 55. If we calculate η_p^2, we have:

$$\frac{30}{30 + 25}$$
$$\eta_p^2 = .545$$

If we calculate η^2, we have:

$$\frac{30}{55}$$
$$\eta^2 = .545$$

So, for a one-way ANOVA, it does not matter which effect size is reported. Let's turn our attention to a two-way ANOVA; here are the *SS*s for this two-way ANOVA:

$$SS_{between\text{-}groups} \text{ for factor 1} = 10$$
$$SS_{between\text{-}groups} \text{ for factor 2} = 10$$
$$SS_{between\text{-}groups} \text{ for the interaction} = 10$$
$$SS_{within\text{-}groups} = 25$$

Let's just focus on the first factor. If we calculate η_p^2 for this first factor, we have:

$$\frac{10}{10 + 25}$$
$$\eta_p^2 = .286$$

Here is the problem with reporting η_p^2 in a factorial design: ***It excludes the variability traceable to the other factor and the interaction between the two factors.*** We need to include all variability in the calculation of our effect size, and η^2 does this with its denominator of SS_{total}. In this example, our correct effect size is:

$$\frac{10}{10+10+10+25}$$

$$\eta^2 = .182$$

If you're wondering why we even bothered discussing η_p^2, there are two reasons. First, it is often reported in research (whether it should be or not). Second, as you have seen, this is the effect size that the software program Statistical Package for the Social Sciences (SPSS) reports. When we learn to do factorial analyses using SPSS, we will have to calculate η^2 ourselves.

Please do not forget what the η^2 is telling us; that is, it is the percentage of variability in the dependent variable that is accounted for by the independent variable or interaction of independent variables. Recall that when discussing one-way ANOVAs in the previous two chapters, we would now discuss post hoc tests to determine where the significant differences exist between our group means. In Troisi and Gabriel's (2011) research, we do not need to do post hoc tests for two reasons. First, the two omnibus *F* tests for the two main effects were not statistically significant. Strictly speaking, we only need post hoc tests when we have a significant omnibus *F* test. Second, in this research, there were only two levels of each factor. Had one of the two main effects been statistically significant, we then could have just looked at the two means for that factor to figure out which one was larger and generalized that difference to the population.

Dissecting a statistically significant interaction

Although we do not need to do post hoc tests, we are not done with these results. Recall that the interaction between the two factors (soup consumption and comfort food status of soup) was statistically significant. Troisi and Gabriel (2011) rejected the null hypothesis that there was no interaction between these factors, saying:

> there was an interaction between soup consumption and comfort food status, $F(1, 107) = 4.48$, $p = .037$, $\eta^2 = .042$. (p. 748)

This is great, but what does that tell us? *When we have a statistically significant interaction, we need to dissect that interaction to understand what it is telling us.* Let's look at how Troisi and Gabriel (2011) reported the interaction in the text of their article:

> Among participants for whom chicken noodle soup was a comfort food, those who had consumed it completed more relationship-related words ($M = 1.60$, $SD = 0.56$) than did those who had not consumed it ($M = 1.29$, $SD = 0.53$), $t(56) = -2.18$, $p < .05$, $d = 0.57$. However, among participants for whom chicken noodle soup was not a comfort food, there were no differences in the number of relationship words completed between those who had consumed the soup ($M = 1.11$, $SD = 0.75$) and those who had not ($M = 1.31$, $SD = 0.68$), $t(51) = 1.00$, $p = .32$, $d = 0.28$. Thus, participants given a chance to consume their comfort food showed increased cognitive activation of relationship-related words. (p. 749)

This text may seem a little overwhelming at first reading; however, we have discussed all the statistical tools needed to understand it. As I said in the previous section, I find that for interactions, we need to see a graph. And, indeed, these researchers agreed as they provided one, which you can see in Figure 11.7.

Let's walk through their text, making specific reference to this figure as we do so.

Along the x-axis, we have the factor of comfort food status with its two levels. For the other factor, soup consumption, we have shaded bars for its two levels. On the y-axis, we have the dependent variable of number of relationship words completed.

Let's go through Troisi and Gabriel's (2011) presentation of the interaction in the order in which they presented it. Starting with the Comfort Food group, we see that people who consumed the soup had higher scores on the dependent variable than people who did not consume the soup. You know that if you want to compare two means to see whether one is significantly different from the other, you conduct a t test. That is what these researchers did in the first four lines of these results:

> Among participants for whom chicken noodle soup was a comfort food, those who had consumed it completed more relationship-related words (M = 1.60, SD = 0.56) than did those who had not consumed it (M = 1.29, SD = 0.53), $t(56) = -2.18$, $p < .05$, $d = 0.57$. (p. 749)

Figure 11.7 Interaction on Number of Relationship Words Completed in Troisi and Gabriel (2011)

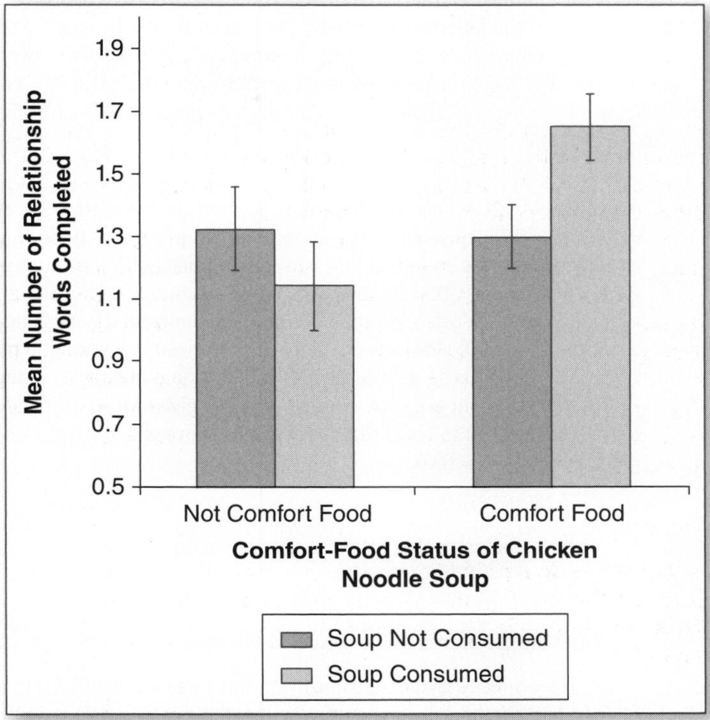

Source: Troisi, J. D., & Gabriel, S. (2011). Chicken soup really is good for the soul: "Comfort food" fulfills the need to belong. *Psychological Science, 22,* 747–753.

As you can see, the difference in number of relationship words completed between people who did and did not eat soup was statistically significant among participants who considered soup to be a comfort food.

But what about people who did not consider soup to be a comfort food? Was there a statistically significant difference in the number of relationship words that these participants completed? To find out, we need to do another t test, this one to compare people who did and did not consume soup among those who did not consider soup to be a comfort food. Here is what Troisi and Gabriel (2011) reported:

> However, among participants for whom chicken noodle soup was not a comfort food, there were no differences in the number of relationship words completed between those who had consumed the soup (M = 1.11, SD = 0.75) and those who had not (M = 1.31, SD = 0.68), $t(51) = 1.00$, $p = .32$, $d = 0.28$. (p. 749)

Among participants who did not consider soup to be a comfort food, there was no significant difference in the number of relationship words completed based on whether they ate soup.

In sum, when people considered soup to be a comfort food, they completed more relationship-related words after eating soup than after not eating soup. When people did not consider soup to be a comfort food, it made no difference whether they ate soup. Therefore, the hypothesized interaction between the two factors was supported.

LEARNING CHECK

A social psychologist is interested in studying how offensive people find certain types of profanity to be based on the ethnicity of the person who uttered the profanity. She conducts an experiment in which participants interacted with either a White male, Black male, or Asian male who utters either an ethnically derogatory slur or a nonethnic curse word. Participants were asked how offensive they found the profanity (ethnically derogatory or nonethnic curse word), using a 1 (*not at all offensive*) to 4 (*extremely offensive*) response range. Here are the results of this experiment:

> A two-way ANOVA on offensiveness suggested no main effect of ethnicity of the person cursing, $F(2, 149) = 1.30$, $p = .276$, $\eta^2 = .016$, and no main effect of type of curse word, $F(1, 149) = 0.19$, $p = .662$, $\eta^2 = .001$. However, there was an interaction between ethnicity of the person cursing and type of curse word, $F(2, 149) = 4.33$, $p = .015$, $\eta^2 = .054$. Participants found a White male making an ethnically derogatory slur ($M = 2.77$, $SD = 0.31$) to be more offensive than a White male making a nonethnic slur ($M = 2.48$, $SD = 0.32$), $t(45) = 3.06$, $p = .004$, $d = 0.90$. However, participants perceived a Black male making an ethnically derogatory slur ($M = 2.65$, $SD = 0.40$) to be as offensive as a Black male making a nonethnic slur ($M = 2.44$, $SD = 0.36$), $t(47) = -1.86$, $d = -0.54$. In addition, participants perceived an Asian male making an ethnically derogatory slur ($M = 2.50$, $SD = 0.47$) to be as offensive as an Asian male making a nonethnic slur ($M = 2.49$, $SD = 0.49$), $t(46) = .05$, $p = .971$, $d = 0.01$.

1. What is the factorial notation for this experiment?

   A: 3×2

2. What are the names of the factors in this experiment? How many levels does each factor have?

   A: The ethnicity of the person cursing has three levels (White, Black, or Asian), and the type of curse word has two levels (ethnically derogatory or nonethnic curse word)

3. What is the dependent variable?

   A: How offensive the type of curse word was perceived to be, operationally defined using a 1 (*not at all offensive*) to 4 (*extremely offensive*) response range

4. How were the degrees of freedom for the interaction calculated?

   A: The $df_{between\text{-}groups}$ was 2 for ethnicity of the person cursing, and the $df_{between\text{-}groups}$ was 1 for the type of curse word. To get the $df_{interaction}$, we multiply together the *df*s for the factors. That gives us $2 \times 1 = 2$.

5. How much variability in the dependent variable is accounted for by the interaction?

   A: Examining the eta squared (η^2) for the interaction, we see it is .054. So, 5.4% of the variability in offensiveness of the curse word was accounted for by the interaction between our two factors.

6. Use the means provided and make a line graph of the interaction. Plot the levels of the ethnicity of the person cursing on the *x*-axis.

A:

Figure 11.8 One Independent Variable (Ethnicity of Person Cursing) Appears on the x-Axis; We Made Separate Lines for the Levels of the Second Independent Variable (Type of Obscenity); and the Dependent Variable (Level of Offensiveness) Appears on the y-Axis

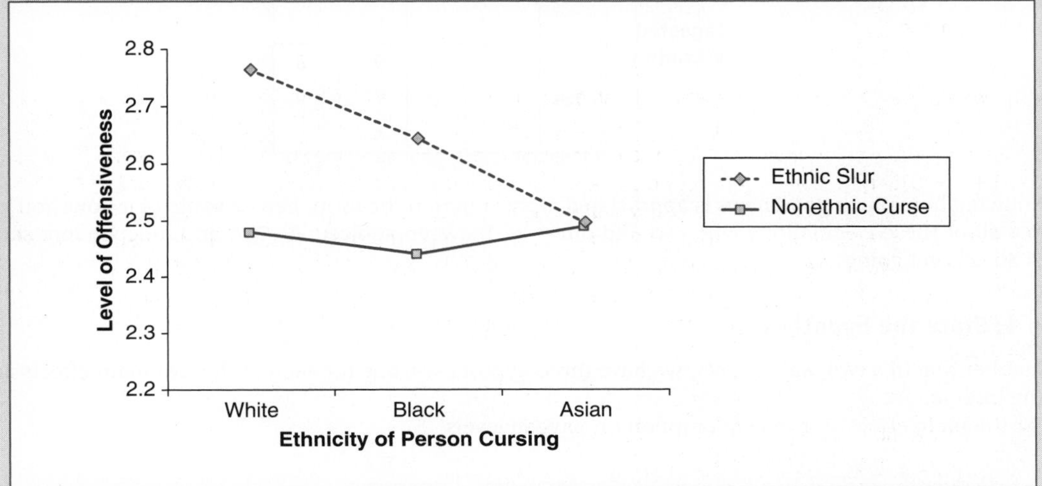

7. With the graph you just drew, interpret this interaction in plain English.

   A: People were more offended when a White man uttered an ethnic slur than a nonethnically charged curse word. There were no differences in how offended people were when hearing a racial slur or nonethnically charged curse word from a Black or an Asian man.

USING YOUR NEW STATISTICAL TOOL

Hand-Calculating the Two-Way, Between-Subjects ANOVA

We mentioned earlier in this chapter that iron supplements are popular in part because they raise oxygen levels in our bodies, and increased oxygen levels help us feel more energetic. We also said that consuming an iron supplement with a drink high in Vitamin C enhances the effects of the iron supplement. Let's take some data pertaining to iron supplements and Vitamin C ingestion and their effects on oxygen levels to learn how to hand-calculate a two-way, between-subjects ANOVA. A researcher has a sample of 20 people whom she randomly assigned to two factors: iron supplement and Vitamin C consumption. Specifically, people were randomly assigned either to take an iron supplement or not to take an iron supplement. In addition, people were also randomly assigned either to consume a glass of orange juice (which is high in Vitamin C) or not to consume a glass of orange juice. The researcher uses a pulse oximetry to measure oxygen levels as the dependent variable (to keep the calculations simple, we are using intentionally hypothetical numbers for oxygen levels). Here are the scores on oxygen levels for each of the 20 people in this research study:

Took Iron Supplement

Ingested Vitamin C		No		Yes	
	No	3	2	4	6
		2	2	5	6
		4		5	
	Yes	1	3	9	8
		3	2	7	9
		3		8	

Knowing how much good news is appreciated at this point in the term, here is some of it now: You've done almost all of these calculations when we did one-way, between-subjects ANOVA and independent samples *t* tests! So let's get going.

Step 1: State the hypotheses

Remember that in a two-way ANOVA, we have three hypotheses, one for each of the two main effects and one for the interaction.

For the main effect of iron consumption on oxygen levels:

$$H_o: \mu_{\text{iron not consumed}} = \mu_{\text{iron consumed}}$$

For the main effect of Vitamin C consumption on oxygen levels:

$$H_o: \mu_{\text{Vitamin C not consumed}} = \mu_{\text{Vitamin C consumed}}$$

For the interaction:

H_o: There is no interaction between iron consumption and Vitamin C consumption on oxygen levels.

Step 2: Calculate the mean for each group and the marginal means

Here, we have the means presented in tabular fashion as the individual scores were presented at the outset of this section:

Took Iron Supplement

Ingested Vitamin C		No	Yes
	No	2.60	5.20
	Yes	2.40	8.20

In addition to calculating the mean for each of the four groups, we should calculate what is called the *marginal means.* The marginal means provides us with the means for each level of a factor. The marginal means for the factor of taking the iron supplement are highlighted in blue. The marginal means for the factor of ingesting Vitamin C are highlighted in gray.

Took Iron Supplement

Ingested Vitamin C		No	Yes	
	No	2.60	5.20	3.90
	Yes	2.40	8.20	5.30
		2.50	6.70	

To figure out whether there is a statistically significant main effect of taking an iron supplement on oxygen levels, we will compare the marginal means in blue. To figure out whether we have a statistically significant main effect of ingesting Vitamin C on oxygen levels, we will compare the marginal means in gray.

Step 3: Calculate the Sums of Squares (*SS*s)

As you know, there are two sources of variability: between-groups and within-groups (which sum to total variability). We now need to calculate $SS_{between\text{-}groups}$ for each main effect and the interaction, in addition to an $SS_{within\text{-}groups}$. We will start with SS_{total}, then derive each of our $SS_{between\text{-}groups}$, and finish with our one $SS_{within\text{-}groups}$.

Total Sums of Squares (SS_{total})

The process of calculating SS_{total} is the same for a two-way as for a one-way ANOVA. We need the grand mean, and then take each score in the entire set of data and subtract it from the grand mean. The grand mean is 4.6. Now, here is each score in the dataset:

3, 2, 4, 2, 2, 1, 3, 3, 3, 2, 4, 5, 5, 6, 6, 9, 7, 8, 8, 9

We will find the deviation of each score from the grand mean, then square that deviation score, and finally sum those squared deviations to get SS_{total}. Let's do it:

Score	Deviation from Grand Mean	Deviation^2
3	−1.6	2.56
2	−2.6	6.76
4	−0.6	0.36
2	−2.6	6.76
2	−2.6	6.76
1	−3.6	12.96
3	−1.6	2.56
3	−1.6	2.56
3	−1.6	2.56
2	−2.6	6.76
4	−0.6	0.36
5	0.4	0.16
5	0.4	0.16
6	1.4	1.96

Score	Deviation from Grand Mean	Deviation²
6	1.4	1.96
9	4.4	19.36
7	2.4	5.76
8	3.4	11.56
8	3.4	11.56
9	4.4	19.36

Summing the squared deviation scores gives us 122.80. Thus, our total sums of squares (SS_{total}) is 122.80. Just remember that as we calculate our three $SS_{between\text{-}groups}$ and one $SS_{within\text{-}groups}$, these numbers must total 122.80.

Within-Groups Sums of Squares ($SS_{within\text{-}groups}$)

As there is only one $SS_{within\text{-}groups}$ to calculate, let's tackle it now.

We need each score and the group means from step 2. Remember that within-groups variability means variability within each group. So, we take each score and subtract it from its respective group mean. Then, of course, we square those deviations, and finally sum the squared deviations across all participants.

To start calculating $SS_{within\text{-}groups}$, here are the group means from step 2:

		Took Iron Supplement	
		No	Yes
Ingested Vitamin C	No	2.60	5.20
	Yes	2.40	8.20

We have four groups in all. We first take the no iron supplement, no Vitamin C group with its mean of 2.60.

Score	Deviation from Group Mean	Deviation²
3	0.4	0.16
2	−0.6	0.36
4	1.4	1.96
2	−0.6	0.36
2	−0.6	0.36

Let's go ahead and sum our squared deviations for each group, which here would give us 3.20.

Now for the no iron supplement, ingested Vitamin C group with its mean of 2.40.

Score	Deviation from Group Mean	Deviation²
1	−1.4	1.96
3	0.6	0.36
3	0.6	0.36
3	0.6	0.36
2	−0.4	0.16

Summing the squared deviations for this group gives us 3.20.

Next up is the took an iron supplement, but no Vitamin C group with its mean of 5.20

Score	Deviation from Group Mean	Deviation^2
4	−1.2	1.44
5	−0.2	0.04
5	−0.2	0.04
6	0.8	0.64
6	0.8	0.64

Summing the squared deviations for this group gives us 2.80.

Finally, we took an iron supplement and ingested Vitamin C group with its mean of 8.20

Score	Deviation from Group Mean	Deviation^2
9	0.8	0.64
7	−1.2	1.44
8	−0.2	0.04
8	−0.2	0.04
9	0.8	0.64

Summing the squared deviations for this last group gives us 2.80.

Now, to get our $SS_{\text{within-groups}}$, we sum each of the four numbers we calculated as the squared deviation quantity for each group. That gives us 3.20 + 3.20 + 2.80 + 2.80 = 12. Therefore, our $SS_{\text{within-groups}}$ is 12.

Between-Groups Sums of Squares ($SS_{between\text{-}groups}$)

Remember that we have two main effects and an interaction to analyze. Each main effect and the interaction could be related to the dependent variable of oxygen level. Therefore, there are three sources of between-groups variability we need to calculate here. We will calculate an overall $SS_{\text{between-groups}}$, and then divvy it up between the two main effects and the interaction.

Calculate overall $SS_{between\text{-}groups}$

We need the grand mean, which was 4.60, and the mean for each group. We take the grand mean and subtract it from each group mean. Then we of course square that deviation. As was the case for one-way ANOVA, we again need to multiply that squared deviation by the number of people in each group, which in this example was 5. We multiply the squared deviations by the number of people in each group because in many research studies, the number of people in each group is not the same, so we need to weigh each group's influence on its contribution to $SS_{\text{between-groups}}$.

To start calculating $SS_{\text{between-groups}}$, here are the group means from step 3:

		Took Iron Supplement	
		No	**Yes**
Ingested Vitamin C	**No**	2.60	5.20
	Yes	2.40	8.20

Let's do our calculations!

$$\begin{aligned}\text{No iron, no Vitamin C} &= (2.60 - 4.60)^2 \times 5\\ &= 2^2 \times 5\\ &= 4 \times 5\\ &= 20\end{aligned}$$

$$\begin{aligned}\text{No iron, yes Vitamin C} &= (2.40 - 4.60)^2 \times 5\\ &= 2.2^2 \times 5\\ &= 4.84 \times 5\\ &= 24.20\end{aligned}$$

$$\begin{aligned}\text{Yes iron, no Vitamin C} &= (5.20 - 4.60)^2 \times 5\\ &= 0.60^2 \times 5\\ &= 0.36 \times 5\\ &= 1.80\end{aligned}$$

$$\begin{aligned}\text{Yes iron, yes Vitamin C} &= (8.20 - 4.60)^2 \times 5\\ &= 3.60^2 \times 5\\ &= 12.96 \times 5\\ &= 64.80\end{aligned}$$

Now, to get our $SS_{\text{between-groups}}$, we sum each of the four numbers we calculated as the squared deviation, multiplied by the number of people in each group, for each group. That gives us 20 + 24.20 + 1.80 + 64.80 = 110.8. Therefore, our $SS_{\text{between-groups}}$ is 110.8

Recall that SS_{total} was 122.80. This number is the sums of $SS_{\text{within-groups}}$ and $SS_{\text{between-groups}}$. And sure enough our $SS_{\text{within-groups}}$ was 12, and $SS_{\text{between-groups}}$ was 110.8, which indeed sum to 122.80 (whew).

Now we need to take our $SS_{\text{between-groups}}$ and divvy it up between the two main effects and the interaction. First, recall that our marginal means allow us to test the main effect of a factor. So here, to learn whether there is a main effect of iron supplements on oxygen levels, we would compare those who did not take an iron supplement (marginal mean of 2.50) with those who did take an iron supplement (marginal mean of 6.70).

	Took Iron Supplement		
	No	**Yes**	
Ingested Vitamin C	2.60	5.20	3.90
	2.40	8.20	5.30
	2.50	6.70	

For each main effect, we take the marginal means for a factor and subtract from each marginal mean the grand mean. We square this deviation, and multiply this deviation by the number of people in each group. Because a factor must have two or more marginal means, we then sum these two scores. Yes, I am betting it will make more sense once we do it.

Calculate SS_{iron}

Here you go:

$$[(2.50 - 4.60)^2 \times 10] + [(6.70 - 4.60)^2 \times 10]$$

Some explanation here might be helpful. The 2.50 is the marginal mean for the no iron supplement group; the 6.70 is the marginal mean for the group that took an iron supplement. To see whether there is a main effect of taking iron on oxygen levels, we compare these two means. Recall that 4.60 is the grand mean. Now, where are we getting 10 people in each group? When calculating $SS_{\text{between-groups}}$ for one factor, we ignore the other factor, like it does not exist. There were 10 people who did not take an iron supplement and 10 people who did take an iron supplement. That's how we arrived at 10 people in each group.

Continuing our calculations, we have:

$$\begin{aligned}\text{No Iron} &= [2.1^2 \times 10] + [2.1^2 \times 10]\\ &= [4.41 \times 10] + [4.41 \times 10]\\ &= 44.1 + 44.1\\ &= 88.2\end{aligned}$$

Therefore, $SS_{\text{iron}} = 88.20$

Calculate $SS_{VitaminC}$

$$\begin{aligned}&[(3.90 - 4.60)^2 \times 10] + [(5.30 - 4.60)^2 \times 10]\\ &= [0.7^2 \times 10] + [0.7^2 \times 10]\\ &= [0.49 \times 10) + [0.49 \times 10]\\ &= 4.90 + 4.90\\ &= 9.80\end{aligned}$$

Therefore, $SS_{\text{VitaminC}} = 9.80$

Calculate $SS_{interaction}$

Now recall that $SS_{\text{between-groups}}$ was 110.8. We now know that SS_{iron} was 88.2 and SS_{VitaminC} was 9.80. So, I am betting you know (or can easily determine) what $SS_{\text{interaction}}$ is. Here is a hint:

$$SS_{\text{between-groups}} = SS_{\text{iron}} + SS_{\text{VitaminC}} + SS_{\text{interaction}}$$

We know three of the four parts of this equation, so we fill in that missing part, which of course is $SS_{\text{interaction}}$:

$$\begin{aligned}110.8 &= 88.20 + 9.80 + SS_{\text{interaction}}\\ 110.8 - 88.20 - 9.80 &= SS_{\text{interaction}}\\ 12.80 &= SS_{\text{interaction}}\end{aligned}$$

Congratulations, you have just completed the most detailed calculations for this chapter!

Step 4: Determine degrees of freedom (*df*s)

Total Degrees of Freedom (df_{total})

As was the case with one-way, between-subjects ANOVAs, we take the sample size and subtract 1. With 20 participants in this analysis, we have:

$$\begin{aligned}df_{\text{total}} &= \text{sample size} - 1\\ &= 20 - 1\\ &= 19\end{aligned}$$

Within-Groups Degrees of Freedom ($df_{within\text{-}groups}$)

As was also the case with one-way, between-subjects ANOVAs, we take the sample size and subtract from it the number of groups in the analysis. So here we have:

$$\begin{aligned} df_{\text{within-groups}} &= \text{sample size} - \text{number of groups in the ANOVA} \\ &= 20 - 4 \\ &= 16 \end{aligned}$$

Between-Groups Degrees of Freedom ($df_{between\text{-}groups}$)

With df_{total} of 19 and $df_{\text{within-groups}}$ of 16, you know that the $df_{\text{between-groups}}$ is 3. To calculate it, remember that we have

number of groups in the analysis – 1

We have 4 total groups in this experiment, so:

$$\begin{aligned} df_{\text{between-groups}} &= 4 - 1 \\ df_{\text{between-groups}} &= 3 \end{aligned}$$

But of course, we have to divvy up the overall $df_{\text{between-groups}}$ between the two main effects and the interaction. For each main effect, we calculate a $df_{\text{between-groups}}$ by taking the number of levels of each factor and subtracting 1. Each factor has two levels, so for main effect, we have 1 *df*. That leaves us just 1 $df_{\text{between-groups}}$ for the interaction of the two factors. Recall that to calculate the $df_{\text{interaction}}$, we multiply together the *df*s for the two main effects:

$$\begin{aligned} df_{\text{interaction}} &= df_{\text{iron}} \times df_{\text{VitaminC}} \\ df_{\text{interaction}} &= 1 \times 1 \\ df_{\text{interaction}} &= 1 \end{aligned}$$

Step 5: Calculate the mean squares (*MS*s)

Now we need to compute average squared deviation scores. We will have one *MS* for within-groups variability, one *MS* for each main effect, and one *MS* for the interaction. Recall the general formula for these calculations:

$$MS = \frac{SS}{df}$$

$$\begin{aligned} MS_{\text{within-groups}} &= \frac{12}{16} \\ &= 0.75 \end{aligned}$$

$$\begin{aligned} MS_{\text{iron}} &= \frac{88.2}{1} \\ &= 88.2 \end{aligned}$$

$$\begin{aligned} MS_{\text{Vitamin C}} &= \frac{9.8}{1} \\ &= 9.80 \end{aligned}$$

$$\begin{aligned} MS_{\text{intersection}} &= \frac{12.8}{1} \\ &= 12.80 \end{aligned}$$

Step 6: Calculate your *F* ratio test statistics

Remember at this point what information an ANOVA provides us. It is a *competition between (a) variability traceable to the independent variable and (b) variability traceable to factors other than the independent variable.* Here once again is our general formula to calculate the *F* ratio:

$$F = \frac{MS_{\text{between-groups}}}{MS_{\text{within-groups}}}$$

We simply need to plug in our appropriate *MS*s calculated in step 5. We will have three *F* ratios to calculate, one for each main effect and one for the interaction:

$$F_{\text{iron}} = \frac{88.2}{0.75}$$
$$F_{\text{iron}} = 117.6$$

$$F_{\text{Vitamin C}} = \frac{9.8}{0.75}$$
$$F_{\text{Vitamin C}} = 13.07$$

$$F_{\text{intersection}} = \frac{12.8}{0.75}$$
$$F_{\text{intersection}} = 17.07$$

We have performed a lot of calculations in this. Let's summarize our calculations in an ANOVA summary table. Be aware that it looks a little different from the ones we saw in the previous two chapters because now we have three sources of between-groups variability (taking iron supplement, ingesting Vitamin C, and the interaction between these two factors).

Source of Variability	*SS*	*df*	*MS*	*F*
Iron supplement	88.20	1	88.20	117.60
Vitamin C	9.80	1	9.80	13.07
$\text{Interaction}_{\text{IronXVitaminC}}$	12.80	1	12.80	17.07
Within-groups	12.00	16	0.75	
Total	122.80	19		

Step 7: Locate the critical values

Of course, we now need to determine whether the *F* ratio test statistics we worked so hard to calculate are statistically significant. To make this decision, we first need to find the critical values to compare our *F* ratio test statistics to. As with an inferential statistical tool, if a test statistic exceeds its critical value, we have a statistically significant result and can generalize our result from the sample to the larger population.

Remember that when locating a critical value, we need to know our alpha level and degrees of freedom. Our alpha level is .05. From step 4, here were our *df*s:

$$df_{\text{within-groups}} = 16$$
$$df_{\text{iron}} = 1$$
$$df_{\text{VitaminC}} = 1$$
$$df_{\text{interaction}} = 1$$

Be aware that we need a critical value for each *F* ratio test statistic. Consult Appendix C to find the critical values for each main effect and interaction (there will be three critical values in all). In this example, all $dfs_{\text{between-groups}}$ are the same, so our critical values will be the same number in each case. We need to look for the intersection of 1 df_{between} and 16 df_{within}. With an alpha of .05, we see that our critical value is 4.49. We will compare each *F* ratio test statistic to this critical value.

Step 8: Make a decision about each null hypothesis

As you can see in Figure 11.9, all of our *F* ratios exceed 4.49. Therefore, we reject all three null hypotheses stated in step 1. In plain English, we can conclude the following:

Figure 11.9 Testing Three Null Hypotheses for a Two-Way ANOVA: (a) Main Effect of an Iron Supplement; (b) Main Effect of Taking Vitamin C; and (c) Interaction Between These Two Factors

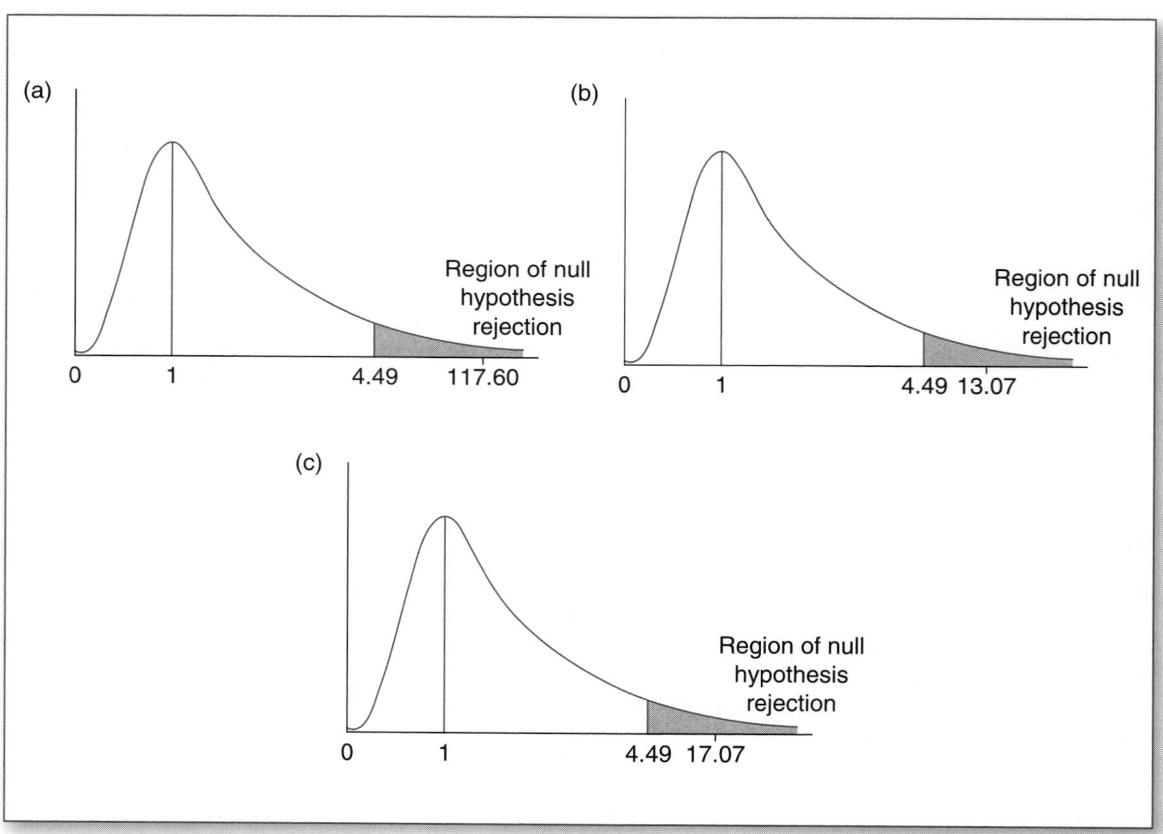

1. There was a difference in oxygen levels between people who took an iron supplement and those who did not take an iron supplement.

   If we examine the marginal means, we can tell, without further analyses because there are only two groups to compare, that people who took an iron supplement had higher oxygen levels than people who did not take an iron supplement.

2. There was a difference in oxygen levels between people who ingested Vitamin C and those who did not ingest Vitamin C.

   Again, with only two levels of this factor, we do not need post hoc tests to see that people who ingested Vitamin C had higher oxygen levels than people who did not ingest Vitamin C.

3. There was a significant interaction between taking an iron supplement and ingesting Vitamin C on oxygen levels. I am not sure this qualifies as "plain English" as we will need to do a little more work here to make sense of this interaction. We'll first calculate our effect sizes and then do this follow-up work.

Step 9: Calculate the effect sizes

Recall that for a factorial design such as the one we have here, we must use an effect size called eta-squared. Here is that formula:

$$\eta^2 = \frac{SS_{\text{between-groups}}}{SS_{\text{total}}}$$

We calculated *SS*s in step 4; here are the results of those calculations:

$$SS_{\text{total}} = 122.80$$
$$SS_{\text{iron}} = 88.20$$
$$SS_{\text{VitaminC}} = 9.80$$
$$SS_{\text{interaction}} = 12.80$$

Now let's calculate three effect sizes, one for each main effect and one for the interaction:

For the main effect of iron, we have:

$$\eta^2 = \frac{88.20}{122.80}$$
$$= .718$$

For the main effect of Vitamin C, we have:

$$\eta^2 = \frac{9.80}{122.80}$$
$$= .080$$

For the interaction, we have:

$$\eta^2 = \frac{12.80}{122.80}$$
$$= .104$$

Remember what effect sizes tell us here. That is, they tell us the percentage of variability in the dependent variable that is accounted for by each factor and interaction of the factors. So, here, 71.8% of the variability in oxygen levels was accounted for by whether people took an iron supplement. Another 8% was accounted for by whether people ingested Vitamin C, and 10.4% was accounted for by the interaction between these two factors.

Speaking of that interaction, we have a little more work to do to be able to explain it in plain English.

Step 10: Perform follow-up tests

When we discussed one-way ANOVAs in the previous two chapters, we did post hoc tests after determining whether our *F* ratio test statistic was statistically significant. If any one of our factors had three or more levels, then we would move into post hoc tests here. However, with only two levels of each factor, there is no need to do post hoc tests. If the *F* ratio for a factor is statistically significant, we simply look at the marginal means for that factor and see which one is larger. Simple enough.

But what about our statistically significant interaction? Recall that when we discussed Troisi and Gabriel's (2011) results, and more specifically, how they made sense of their statistically significant interaction, we saw they performed independent samples *t* tests, something we encountered in Chapter 7. Given all the calculations we've done up to this point, we will not do those *t* tests here. Instead, I will provide you with a graph of our results, and then we will walk through how to interpret this interaction.

Figure 11.10 contains the visual display of our statistically significant interaction. To create this figure, I simply took the means for each of our four groups and plotted them. Just as we did when interpreting Troisi and Gabriel's (2011) results, let's start our interpretation of Figure 11.10 off by moving along the levels of

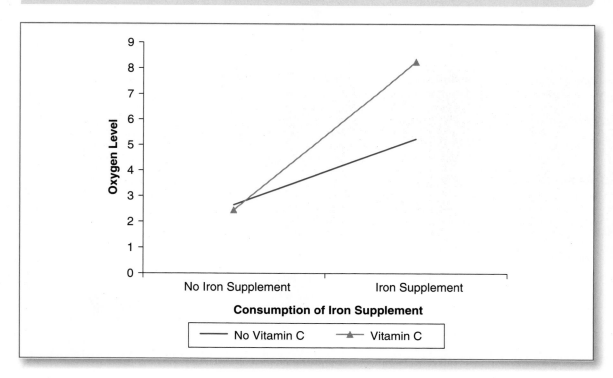

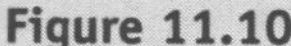
Figure 11.10

the x-axis. Among people who did not take an iron supplement, we see that oxygen levels were similar based on whether they ingested Vitamin C or did not ingest Vitamin C (we would run a t test to compare these two means, expecting them to not be significantly different). Among people who did take an iron supplement, we see that oxygen levels were higher for those who also ingested Vitamin C than for those who did not ingest Vitamin C (we would run a t test to compare these two means, expecting them to be significantly different). Therefore, the effect of taking an iron supplement *depends on* whether people also ingest Vitamin C.

As with any statistical tool we use, we must tell others what the work means by using APA style:

> A two-way, between-subjects ANOVA on oxygen levels revealed a significant main effect of taking an iron supplement $F(1, 16) = 117.60$, $p < .05$, $\eta^2 = .718$, such that people who took an iron supplement ($M = 6.70$) had higher oxygen levels than people who did not take an iron supplement ($M = 2.50$). There was also a significant main effect of ingesting Vitamin C, $F(1, 16) = 13.07$, $p < .05$ $\eta^2 = .08$, such that people who ingested Vitamin C ($M = 5.30$) had higher oxygen levels than people who did not ingest Vitamin C ($M = 3.90$). Finally, there was a significant interaction between these two factors, $F(1, 16) = 17.07$, $p < .05$, $\eta^2 = .104$. Among participants who did not take an iron supplement, there was no difference in oxygen levels based on whether they did ($M = 2.40$, $SD = 0.89$) or did not ($M = 2.60$, $SD = 0.89$) ingest Vitamin C, $t(8) = 0.35$, $p > .05$, $d = 0.22$. Among participants who did take an iron supplement, those who also ingested Vitamin C had higher oxygen levels ($M = 8.20$, $SD = 0.84$) than those who did not ingest Vitamin C ($M = 5.20$, $SD = 0.84$), $t(8) = -5.67$, $p < .001$, $d = 3.57$. Thus, the effects of iron on oxygen levels appear to be stronger when also ingesting Vitamin C.

If you're wondering where the t tests results came from to understand the interaction, I ran them on SPSS. But don't worry; you will have a chance to do so after a Learning Check.

LEARNING CHECK

Problem #1

Use this ANOVA summary table to answer the questions that follow it:

Source of Variability	*SS*	*df*	*MS*	*F*
Factor A	50	1	50	5.00
Factor B	2	1	2	0.20
$\text{Interaction}_{\text{AxB}}$	15	1	15	1.50
Within-groups	440	44	10	
Total	507	47		

1. What is the sample size for this analysis?

   A: 48; we know this because $df_{\text{total}} = 47$. This number was calculated by taking the sample size – 1. Therefore, to get $df_{\text{total}} = 47$, the sample size has to be 48.

(Continued)

(Continued)

2. How many groups were analyzed in this ANOVA?

   A: 4; we know this because for both main effects, the *df*s are 1. To get this number, we must take the number of levels for the factor and subtract 1. There are thus two levels of each factor. As we know from Figure 11.2 and from the example we just used, this is called a 2×2 factorial design, which has four groups.

3. How was $SS_{\text{InteractionAxB}}$ calculated?

   A: $SS_{\text{total}} = SS_{\text{within-groups}} + \text{all } SS_{\text{between-groups}}$. So here we have $SS_{\text{total}} = 507$, $SS_{\text{within-groups}} = 440$, $SS_{\text{FactorA}} = 50$, and $SS_{\text{FactorB}} = 2$. By plugging in the numbers, we get:

$$507 = 440 + 50 + 2 + SS_{\text{interactionAxB}}$$
$$15 = SS_{\text{interactionAxB}}$$

4. How was $df_{\text{InteractionAxB}}$ calculated?

   A: We take the *df*s for each factor and multiply them together. That gives us 1 × 1 = 1.

5. How was $MS_{\text{InteractionAxB}}$ calculated?

   A: $$\frac{SS_{\text{Interaction AxB}}}{df_{\text{Interaction AxB}}} = \frac{15}{1} = 15$$

6. How was $F_{\text{InteractionAxB}}$ calculated?

   A: $$\frac{MS_{\text{Interaction AxB}}}{MS_{\text{within-groups}}} = \frac{15}{10} = 1.50$$

Problem #2

Fill in the missing pieces of information from this ANOVA summary table:

Source of Variability	*SS*	*df*	*MS*	*F*
Factor A	10	2	????	????
Factor B	50	2	????	????
$\text{Interaction}_{\text{AxB}}$	40	????	????	????
Within-groups	800	????	????	
Total	900	408		

A:

Source of Variability	*SS*	*df*	*MS*	*F*
Factor A	10	2	5	2.50
Factor B	50	2	25	12.50
$\text{Interaction}_{\text{AxB}}$	40	4	10	5.00
Within-groups	800	400	2	
Total	900	408		

Two-Way, Between-Subjects ANOVA and SPSS

As with previous inferential statistical tools, we conclude our discussion with how to use it with the help of SPSS. Given how involved the hand-calculations were in this chapter, I think running the same analysis on SPSS would be helpful in reinforcing the basic principles of the two-way ANOVA. So, here again are our data from each of the 20 participants:

		Took Iron Supplement			
		No		**Yes**	
Ingested Vitamin C	**No**	3	2	4	6
		2	2	5	6
		4		5	
	Yes	1	3	9	8
		3	2	7	9
		3		8	

Establishing your spreadsheet

We will open SPSS, and then as always, first click on *Variable View*. You will need to name a total of three variables: the two independent variables (factors) and the dependent variable. Name one of the factors something such as `Iron_supplement`, and name the other factor `Vitamin_C`. Of course, both factors need Labels. I used "IronSupplement?" and "Vitamic C?" as my labels. Then of course we have to name and label our dependent variable. I used the Name `oxygen_level` and label "oxygen level" (I know I am not a creative person). Be sure that all three variables are numeric under the *Type* column.

We now need to tell SPSS which levels of each factor people were randomly assigned to. To do so, click on *Value* for the first factor, which I Labeled "IronSupplement?" I gave a `0` to people assigned to the "no supplement" condition and a `1` to people assigned to the "supplement" condition. Now click on *Value* for the second factor, which I Labeled "Vitamin C?" I gave a `0` to people who ingested "no Vitamin C" and a `1` to people who ingested "8 oz fruit juice". Finally, please make sure that all of your measures are labeled as "Scale" variables.

*Section 5 dataset.sav [DataSet1] - IBM SPSS Statistics Data Editor

File Edit View Data Transform Analyze Graphs Utilities Add-ons Window Help

	Name	Type	Width	Decimals	Label	Values	Missing	Columns	Align	Measure	Role
1	Iron_supplement	Numeric	8	0	Iron Supplement?	{0, no supplement}...	None	8	Right	Scale	Input
2	Vitamin_C	Numeric	8	0	Vitamin C?	{0, no Vitamin C}...	None	8	Right	Scale	Input
3	oxygen_level	Numeric	8	0	oxygen level	None	None	8	Right	Scale	Input
4											
5											

We are now ready to enter our data. Click on *Data View*, and let's get to it.

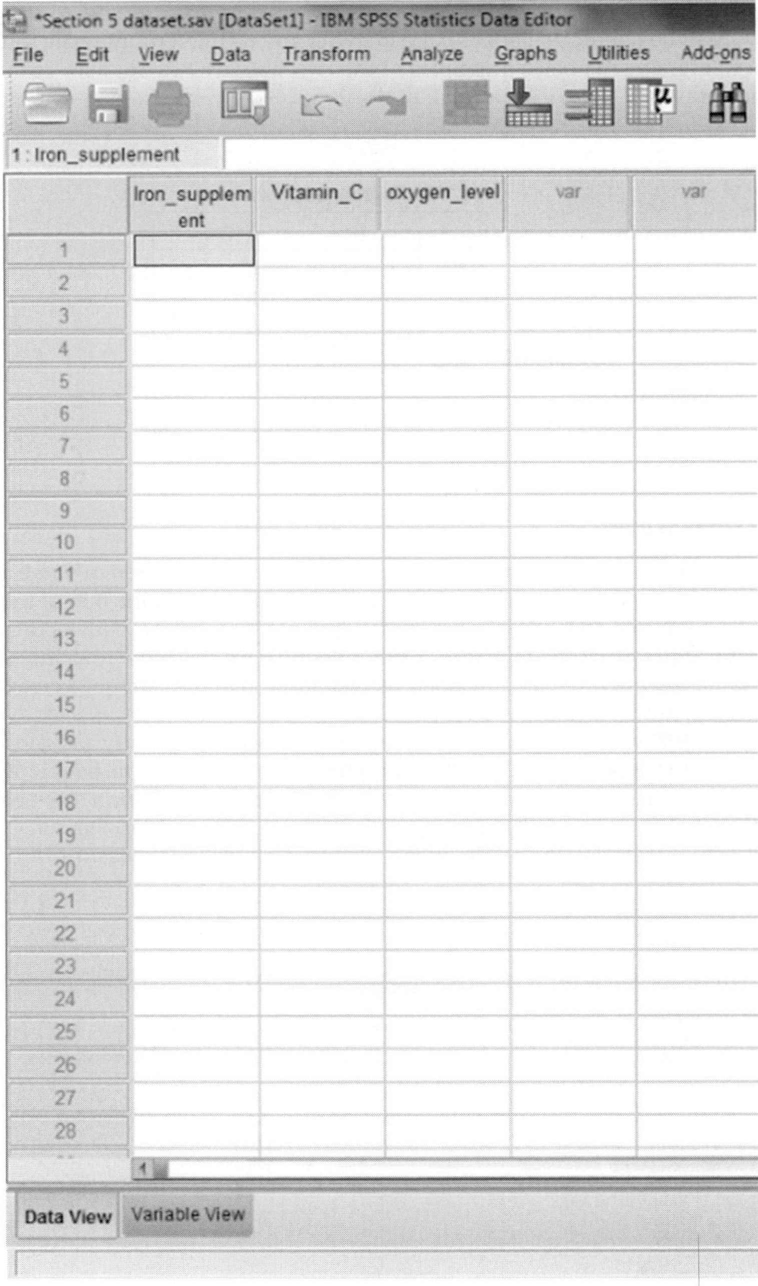

With a factorial design as we have here, I would advise you to enter each "cell" of data at once. I started by entering the scores for the "no supplement, no Vitamin C" cell. Each level of these two factors was given a value of 0 in the *Variable View*. So now, I just entered a 0 for both of these columns here. After entering these five pieces of data, here is what my file looks like (and I am hoping yours does too):

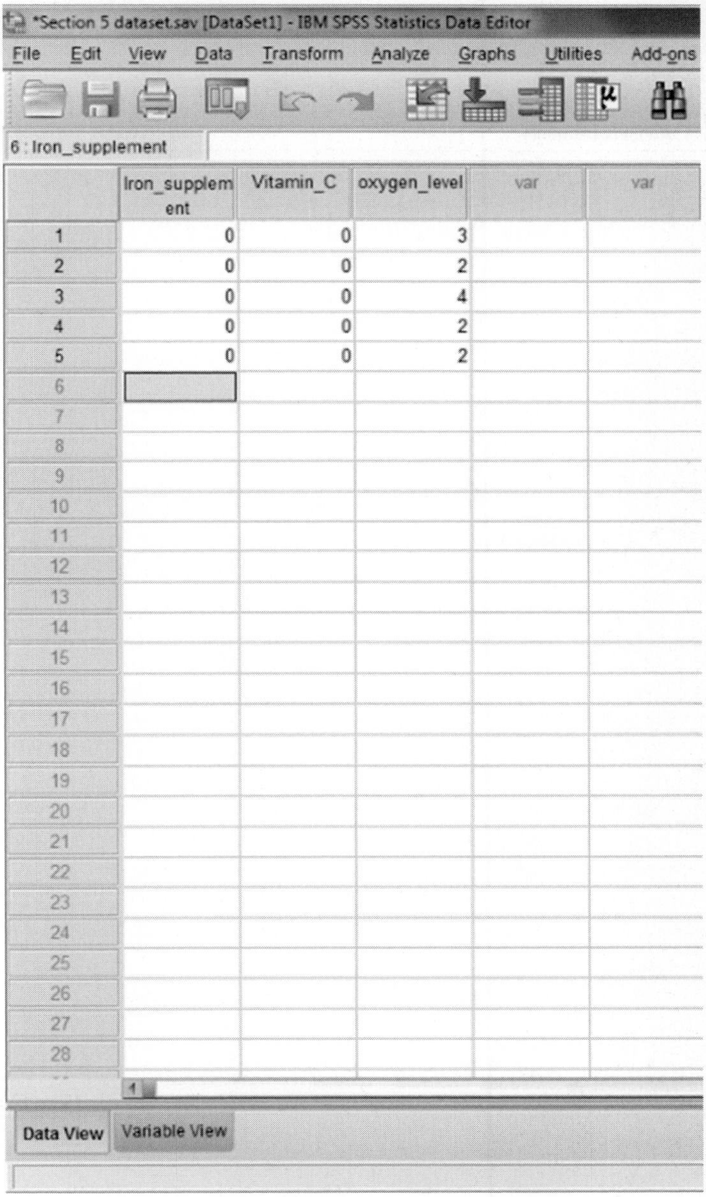

*Section 5 dataset.sav [DataSet1] - IBM SPSS Statistics Data Editor

File Edit View Data Transform Analyze Graphs Utilities Add-ons

6 : Iron_supplement

	Iron_supplement	Vitamin_C	oxygen_level	var	var
1	0	0	3		
2	0	0	2		
3	0	0	4		
4	0	0	2		
5	0	0	2		

Data View Variable View

Next I entered the data for people in the "no supplement, 8 oz fruit juice" cell. Again, the "no supplement" level of this factor was coded as 0. The "8 oz fruit juice" level of the Vitamin C factor was coded as 1. After entering these five pieces of data, here is what my file looks like:

*Section 5 dataset.sav [DataSet1] - IBM SPSS Statistics Data Editor

File Edit View Data Transform Analyze Graphs Utilities Add-ons

11 : Iron_supplement

	Iron_supplement	Vitamin_C	oxygen_level	var	var
1	0	0	3		
2	0	0	2		
3	0	0	4		
4	0	0	2		
5	0	0	2		
6	0	1	1		
7	0	1	3		
8	0	1	3		
9	0	1	3		
10	0	1	2		
11					
12					
13					
14					
15					
16					
17					
18					
19					
20					
21					
22					
23					
24					
25					
26					
27					
28					

Data View Variable View

Then I moved to the "supplement, no Vitamin C" cell and entered those data; after which, I entered the data for the last cell, "supplement, 8 oz fruit juice." Here is what my spreadsheet looks like (and hopefully yours does too):

Section 5 dataset.sav [DataSet1] - IBM SPSS Statistics Data Editor

File Edit View Data Transform Analyze Graphs Utilities Add-ons

16 :

	Iron_supplement	Vitamin_C	oxygen_level	var	var
1	0	0	3		
2	0	0	2		
3	0	0	4		
4	0	0	2		
5	0	0	2		
6	0	1	1		
7	0	1	3		
8	0	1	3		
9	0	1	3		
10	0	1	2		
11	1	0	4		
12	1	0	5		
13	1	0	5		
14	1	0	6		
15	1	0	6		
16	1	1	9		
17	1	1	7		
18	1	1	8		
19	1	1	8		
20	1	1	9		
21					
22					
23					
24					
25					
26					
27					
28					

Data View Variable View

Running your analysis

Now it's time to run our two-way, between-subjects ANOVA.

1. Click on *Analyze* → *General Linear Model* → *Univariate.*

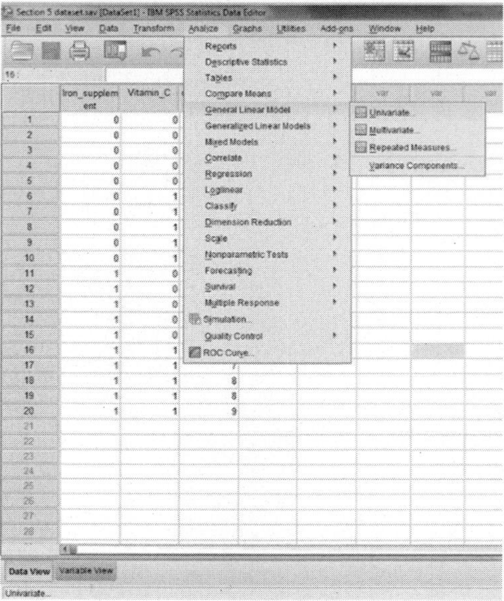

2. Click the two independent variables into the *Fixed Factor(s)* box.
3. Then click the dependent variable into the *Dependent Variable* box.

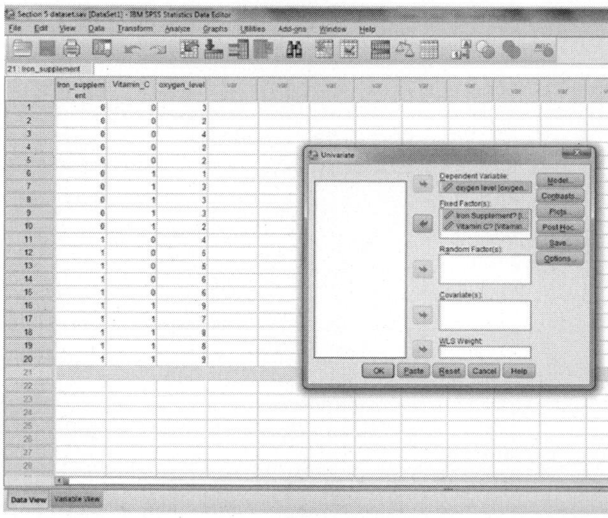

4. Click on *Options*. In the *Estimated Marginal Means* area in the top portion of this dialogue box, please select both factors and their interactions and click into the *Display Means* box (no need to select *OVERALL*).

5. In the *Display* area in the lower half of this box, click on:
   a. *Descriptive statistics*,
   b. *Estimates of effect size*, and
   c. *Homogeneity tests* (this will allow us to test the assumption that all groups have equal variability on scores on the dependent variable.

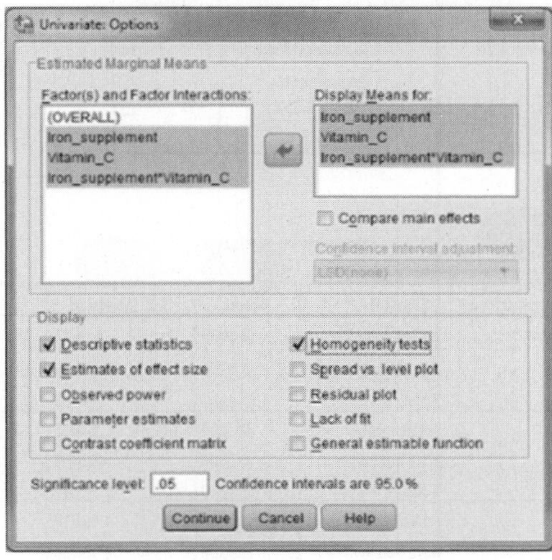

Click *Continue*.

I would like you to ask SPSS to provide one more piece of output. On the right side of the *Univariate* dialogue box, click on *Plots*. Here, we can make a graphical display of our results (and, in particular, the interaction). On the horizontal axis (*x*-axis), put `Iron_supplement`. Click *Vitamin_C into Separate Lines*. Then click on *Add* and *Continue*.

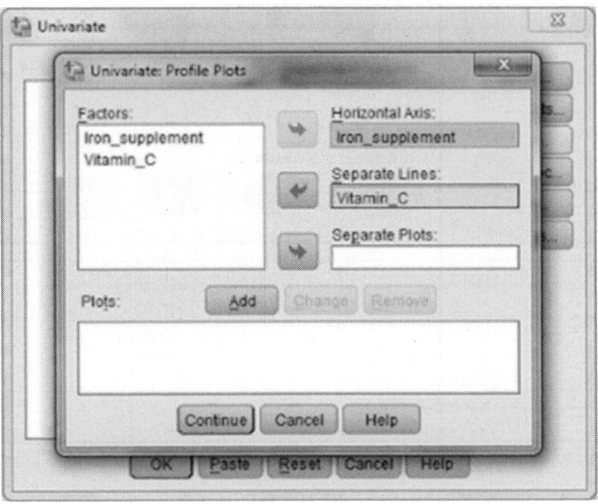

Now click *OK*, and our analysis will run and output will soon appear.
Here is what your SPSS output should look like:

Univariate Analysis of Variance

A B C D

Between-Subjects Factors

		Value Label	N
Iron Supplement?	0	no supplement	10
	1	supplement	10
Vitamin C?	0	no Vitamin C	10
	1	8 oz fruit juice	10

E H I F G

Descriptive Statistics

Dependent Variable: oxygen level

Iron Supplement?	Vitamin C?	Mean	Std. Deviation	N
no supplement	no Vitamin C	2.6000	.89443	5
	8 oz fruit juice	2.4000	.89443	5
	Total	2.5000	.84984	10
supplement	no Vitamin C	5.2000	.83666	5
	8 oz fruit juice	8.2000	.83666	5
	Total	6.7000	1.76698	10
Total	no Vitamin C	3.9000	1.59513	10
	8 oz fruit juice	5.3000	3.16403	10
	Total	4.6000	2.54227	20

J

Levene's Test of Equality of Error Variances[a]

Dependent Variable: oxygen level

F	df1	df2	Sig.
.063	3	16	.979

Tests the null hypothesis that the error variance of the dependent variable is equal across groups.
a. Design: Intercept + Iron_supplement + Vitamin_C + Iron_supplement * Vitamin_C

Tests of Between-Subjects Effects

Dependent Variable: oxygen level

K L M N O P Q

Source	Type III Sum of Squares	df	Mean Square	F	Sig.	Partial Eta Squared
~~Corrected Model~~	~~110.800[a]~~	~~3~~	~~36.933~~	~~49.244~~	~~.000~~	~~.902~~
~~Intercept~~	~~423.200~~	~~1~~	~~423.200~~	~~564.267~~	~~.000~~	~~.972~~
Iron_supplement	88.200	1	88.200	117.600	.000	.880
Vitamin_C	9.800	1	9.800	13.067	.002	.450
Iron_supplement * Vitamin_C	12.800	1	12.800	17.067	.001	.516
Error	12.000	16	.750			
~~Total~~	~~546.000~~	~~20~~				
Corrected Total	122.800	19				

a. R Squared = .902 (Adjusted R Squared = .884)

What am I looking at? Interpreting your SPSS output

Now let's interpret this information.

A. These are *the factors* (independent variables).

B. These are the arbitrary *numerical values we assigned to each level of each factor* when we coded what group each participant was in.

C. This is the *name I gave each level of the factors*.

D. This is the *number of people in each experimental group for each level of each independent variable*.

E. This is the *dependent variable* (in case you didn't know from SPSS calling it "Dependent Variable").

F. and G. Here we have *each factor, with the levels of each factor under it*. You can see the four groups (i.e., no iron supplement/no Vitamin C; no iron supplement/8 oz orange juice; iron supplement/no Vitamin C; and iron supplement/8 oz orange juice).

H. This is the *mean for each experimental group*. In addition, there is a "Total" mean at the very bottom of this column, and that is the grand mean.

I. This is the *standard deviation for each group*.

J. Here is where we test the assumption of ANOVAs that there is homogeneity of variability between the groups being analyzed. For this test, *we are testing the hypothesis that there is no difference in variability across the four groups*. Here, the p value is .979. Obviously this p value is greater than .05, so we fail to reject the null hypothesis; in other words, we conclude there is no difference in the variability across groups and this assumption is not violated.

K. Here are the *sources of variability* in the analysis. As was the case with one-way, between-subjects and repeated-measures ANOVA, SPSS gives us more sources of variability than we care about. The five sources of variability we need to pay attention to are:

a) `Iron_supplement`

b) `Vitamin_C`

c) `Iron_supplement * Vitamin C`

d) `Error`

e) `Corrected Total`

Just so you know and perhaps already figured out, `Iron_supplement * Vitamin C` is the interaction between the two factors.

L. This column *quantifies the* SSs we calculated in step 3 of our hand-calculations. Here are the *SS*s for each source of variability:

`Iron_supplement` = 88.200

`Vitamin_C` = 9.800

`Iron_supplement * Vitamin C` = 12.800

`Error` = 12.000

`Corrected Total` = 122.80

M. Here are our *degrees of freedom* for each source of variability. These we calculated in step 4 of the previous section. Here are the *df*s for each source of variability:

Iron_supplement = 1

Vitamin_C = 1

Iron_supplement * Vitamin C = 1

Error = 16

Corrected Total = 19

N. Here are our *mean squares* (MSs). This was step 5 of our hand-calculations. Remember the general formula for calculating an *MS*:

$$MS = \frac{SS}{df}$$ Here are the *MS*s for each meaningful source of variability:

Iron_supplement = 88.200

Vitamin_C = 9.800

Iron_supplement * Vitamin C = 12.800

Error = .750

O. Here are our *F ratio test statistics*, which we calculated in step 6 of the previous section. Keep in mind the general formula for the *F* ratio:

$$F = \frac{MS_{\text{between-groups}}}{MS_{\text{within-groups}}}$$

Here are the *F* ratio test statistics for each meaningful source of variability:

Iron_supplement = 117.60

Vitamin_C = 13.07

Iron_supplement * Vitamin C = 17.07

P. These are the *p values for each F ratio test statistic*. This is a combination of steps 7 and 8 in our hand-calculations. SPSS has all the critical values memorized for us. So, here, it can tell us the probability that a mean difference was due to random variation. Here are the significance levels for each source of between-groups variability:

Iron_supplement: $p < .001$

Vitamin_C: $p = .002$

Iron_supplement * Vitamin C: $p = .001$

Q. Here are the partial eta squareds (i.e., effect sizes). But as you know from the second section of this chapter, we have a problem; that is, we must use eta squared (η^2). SPSS does not provide this effect size for us, so we need to get it ourselves. Luckily, it's not hard to do. Here is the formula for eta squared:

$$\eta^2 = \frac{SS_{\text{between-groups}}}{SS_{\text{total}}}$$

We already know the *SS*s:

$$SS_{\text{iron}} = 88.20$$
$$SS_{\text{Vitamin C}} = 9.80$$
$$SS_{\text{interaction}} = 12.80$$
$$SS_{\text{total}} = 122.80$$

So we can calculate our eta squareds:

For the main effect of iron, we have:

$$\eta^2 = \frac{88.20}{122.80} = .718$$

For the main effect of Vitamin C, we have:

$$\eta^2 = \frac{9.80}{122.80} = 0.080$$

For the interaction, we have:

$$\eta^2 = \frac{12.80}{122.80} = .104$$

I am thinking that perhaps some or even all of this printout seems familiar given your expertise with one-way, between-subjects ANOVAs. There are of course some differences (two factors instead of one factor, the interaction, the issue with SPSS not reporting η^2), but there have been many more similarities than radical differences, until now.

With a statistically significant omnibus *F* ratio for the interaction, we need to do some more work to make sense of what this interaction means. As mentioned in the previous section, we now need to "dissect" the interaction. We do this dissection with our old friend, the independent samples *t* test. I know you understand *t* tests and how to do them in SPSS from Chapter 7, so I want to guide you through the process of dissecting an interaction, with specific emphasis on using *t* tests to do so.

Dissecting interactions in SPSS

To dissect the interaction, it might help to have a graph of it. We made that graph when doing our analyses, so let's look at it again now, seeing how SPSS made it for us:

When we interpreted the interaction in Troisi and Gabriel's (2011) research, we examined a graph and, specifically, made comparisons at each level of the factor on the *x*-axis. That's exactly what we do here, except we're being more formal and conducting independent samples *t* tests. So we conduct one *t* test to compare people who did and did not ingest Vitamin C with no iron supplement (the first level of the factor on the *x*-axis). We conduct a second *t* test to compare people who did and did not ingest Vitamin C with an iron supplement.

Profile Plots

Estimated Marginal Means of oxygen level

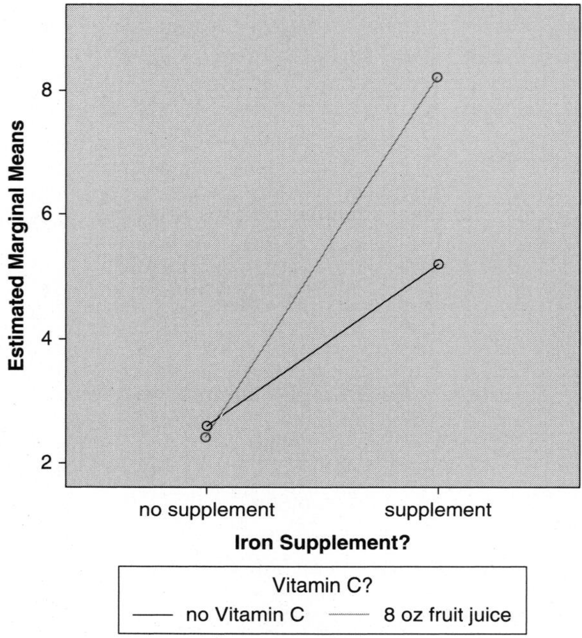

Here are the results of these two independent samples *t* tests.

T-Test for no iron supplement condition

Group Statistics

	Vitamin C?	N	Mean	Std. Deviation	Std. Error Mean
oxygen level	no Vitamin C	5	2.6000	.89443	.40000
	8 oz fruit juice	5	2.4000	.89443	.40000

Independent Samples Test

		Levene's Test for Equality of Variances		t-test for Equality of Means						
									95% Confidence Interval of the Difference	
		F	Sig.	t	df	Sig. (2-tailed)	Mean Difference	Std. Error Difference	Lower	Upper
oxygen level	Equal variances assumed	.000	1.000	.354	8	.733	.20000	.56569	-1.10447	1.50447
	Equal variances not assumed			.354	8.000	.733	.20000	.56569	-1.10447	1.50447

T-Test for iron supplement condition

Group Statistics

	Vitamin C?	N	Mean	Std. Deviation	Std. Error Mean
oxygen level	no Vitamin C	5	5.2000	.83666	.37417
	8 oz fruit juice	5	8.2000	.83666	.37417

Independent Samples Test

		Levene's Test for Equality of Variances		t-test for Equality of Means						
									95% Confidence Interval of the Difference	
		F	Sig.	t	df	Sig. (2-tailed)	Mean Difference	Std. Error Difference	Lower	Upper
oxygen level	Equal variances assumed	.000	1.000	-5.669	8	.000	-3.00000	.52915	-4.22022	-1.77978
	Equal variances not assumed			-5.669	8.000	.000	-3.00000	.52915	-4.22022	-1.77978

The first t test (titled *T-Test for no iron supplement condition*) compares people who did and did not ingest Vitamin C, none of whom took an iron supplement. As you can see, we have our means for these two groups stated explicitly in the *Group Statistics* box. The t test appears in the *Independent Samples Test* box. With a t test statistic of .354, we see the p value is .733. Therefore, there is not a significant difference between people ingesting and not ingesting Vitamin C, all of whom did not take an iron supplement.

Our second t test (titled *T-Test for iron supplement condition*) compares people who did and did not ingest Vitamin C, all of whom took an iron supplement. The means for these two groups are stated explicitly, followed by the actual t test. With a t statistic of –5.669 and a p value of $< .01$, there is a significant difference between people ingesting and not ingesting Vitamin C, all of whom took an iron supplement.

Taken together, these t tests tell us that iron's effect on oxygen levels *depends on* the presence of Vitamin C. Taking an iron supplement with Vitamin C increases oxygen levels more than taking an iron supplement without Vitamin C.

LEARNING CHECK

Below is the SPSS output from Troisi and Gabriel's (2011) experiment discussed at the outset of this chapter. Use this printout, and answer the questions that follow it.

Between-Subjects Factors

		Value Label	N
IV: Consume chicken soup or not?	.00	no food	54
	1.00	food	57
IV: Yes or No: Chicken Soup is a comfort food.	.00	soup not cf	53
	1.00	soup is cf	58

Descriptive Statistics

Dependent Variable: DV: Belongingness word stems completed

IV: Consume chicken soup or not?	IV: Yes or No: Chicken Soup is a comfort food.	Mean	Std. Deviation	N
no food	soup not cf	1.3077	.67937	26
	soup is cf	1.2857	.53452	28
	Total	1.2963	.60281	54
food	soup not cf	1.1111	.75107	27
	soup is cf	1.6000	.56324	30
	Total	1.3684	.69774	57
Total	soup not cf	1.2075	.71679	53
	soup is cf	1.4483	.56731	58
	Total	1.3333	.65134	111

Tests of Between-Subjects Effects

Dependent Variable: DV: Belongingness word stems completed

Source	Type III Sum of Squares	df	Mean Square	F	Sig.	Partial Eta Squared
Corrected Model	3.547[a]	3	1.182	2.934	.037	.076
Intercept	194.664	1	194.664	483.054	.000	.819
Cond	.096	1	.096	.238	.627	.002
cf	1.508	1	1.508	3.743	.056	.034
Cond * cf	1.806	1	1.806	4.480	.037	.040
Error	43.119	107	.403			
Total	244.000	111				
Corrected Total	46.667	110				

a. R Squared = .076 (Adjusted R Squared = .050)

(Continued)

(Continued)

T-Test

Group Statistics

IV: Yes or No: Chicken Soup is a comfort food.		IV: Consume chicken soup or not?	N	Mean	Std. Deviation	Std. Error Mean
soup not cf	DV: Belongingness word stems completed	no food	26	1.3077	.67937	.13323
		food	27	1.1111	.75107	.14454
soup is cf	DV: Belongingness word stems completed	no food	28	1.2857	.53452	.10102
		food	30	1.6000	.56324	.10283

Independent Samples Test

			Levene's Test for Equality of Variances		t-test for Equality of Means						
										95% Confidence Interval of the Differen	
IV: Yes or No: Chicken Soup is a comfort food.			F	Sig.	t	df	Sig. (2-tailed)	Mean Difference	Std. Error Difference	Lower	Upper
soup not cf	DV: Belongingness word stems completed	Equal variances assumed	.103	.750	.998	51	.323	.19658	.19696	-.19883	.591
		Equal variances not assumed			1.000	50.807	.322	.19658	.19658	-.19811	.591
soup is cf	DV: Belongingness word stems completed	Equal variances assumed	1.035	.313	-2.176	56	.034	-.31429	.14441	-.60358	-.024
		Equal variances not assumed			-2.180	55.982	.033	-.31429	.14415	-.60305	-.025

Questions to Answer

1. What are the hypotheses being tested?
2. Fill in the means for each of the four groups in this experiment:

<table>
<tr><td></td><td></td><td colspan="2">Soup Consumption</td></tr>
<tr><td></td><td></td><td>Yes</td><td>No</td></tr>
<tr><td rowspan="2">Comfort Food Status of Soup</td><td>Comfort Food</td><td></td><td></td></tr>
<tr><td>Not Comfort Food</td><td></td><td></td></tr>
</table>

3. What are the marginal means?
4. What are the four sources of variability in these data?
5. The p value for the main effect of comfort food status of soup (cf) is .056. Explain what this number means.
6. Plug in the numbers needed to obtain the F ratio test statistic of 4.48 for the interaction between the two factors.
7. According to Appendix C, what is the approximate critical value that was used to see whether we reject or do not reject the null hypothesis for each main effect and for the interaction? Assume an alpha level of .05.
8. What is the probability that the interaction was due to random variation?
9. Did the researchers reject or not reject the null hypotheses? Answer for each hypothesis being tested.
10. What are the effect sizes for both main effects and the interaction?

Answers

1. Remember that there are three hypotheses for a 2×2 factorial design. One hypothesis for the first main effect, one hypothesis for the second main effect, and one hypothesis for the interaction.

For the main effect of soup consumption on the number of relationship-related words completed:

$$H_o: \mu_{\text{not-consumed}} = \mu_{\text{consumed}}$$

For the main effect of comfort food status of soup on the number of relationship-related words completed:

$$H_o: \mu_{\text{not comfort food}} = \mu_{\text{comfort food}}$$

For the interaction:

H_o: There is no interaction between soup consumption and comfort food status of soup on the number of relationship-related words completed.

2.

		Soup Consumption	
		Yes	**No**
Comfort Food Status of Soup	**Comfort Food**	1.60	1.29
	Not Comfort Food	1.11	1.31

3.

		Soup Consumption		
		Yes	**No**	
Comfort Food Status of Soup	**Comfort Food**	1.60	1.29	1.45
	Not Comfort Food	1.11	1.31	1.21
		1.37	1.30	

4. The four sources of variability are (1) the main effect of soup consumption; (2) the main effect of comfort food status of soup; (3) the interaction between these two factors; and (4) within-groups variability.

5. A p value of .056 means that there is a 5.6% chance that the difference between the two means (1.45 and 1.21) for the factor of comfort food status is due to random variation.

6. $F = \frac{1.806}{.403} = 4.48$

7. Both main effects and the interaction have $df_{\text{between-groups}} = 1$ and $df_{\text{within-groups}} = 107$. By consulting Appendix C, we find that the approximate critical value to compare all F ratio test statistics to is between 3.92 and 4.00.

8. .037 or 3.7%

9. The researchers failed to reject the null hypotheses for the two main effects; however, they rejected the null hypothesis for the interaction.

10. Be very careful here; remember that we cannot use the partial eta squared that SPSS provides. Instead, we must use the eta squared, which we must calculate for ourselves. Here again is the eta squared (η^2) formula:

$$\eta^2 = \frac{SS_{\text{between-groups}}}{SS_{\text{total}}}$$

(Continued)

(Continued)

For each main effect and the interaction, we plug in our numbers from the SPSS printout:
Main effect of Soup Consumption:

$$\eta^2 = \frac{.096}{46.667}$$
$$= .002$$

Main effect of Comfort Food Status of Soup:

$$\eta^2 = \frac{1.508}{46.667}$$
$$= .032$$

Interaction between the two factors:

$$\eta^2 = \frac{1.806}{46.667}$$
$$= .039$$

CHAPTER APPLICATION QUESTIONS

1. Figure 11.11 comes from research that Ross O'Hara and colleagues (O'Hara, Walter, & Christopher, 2009) conducted in which they examined individual differences as predictors of political interest.

   Use Figure 11.11 to answer the following questions:

   a) What is the dependent (outcome) variable in this research?
   b) What are the factors in this research?
   c) What are the levels of each factor?
   d) Interpret this interaction.

2. In a 2 × 2 × 3 factorial ANOVA, there are ____ main effects to test and ___ interactions to test:

   a) 12; 3
   b) 3; 4
   c) 3; 3
   d) 3; 12

3. Suppose you want to run a 2 × 4 experiment using a between-subjects design, and you want 25 participants in each group created by manipulation of the independent variables. How many participants will you need to run this experiment?

   a) 25
   b) 50
   c) 100
   d) 200

Figure 11.11 Interaction of Need for Cognition and Conscientiousness on Political Interest

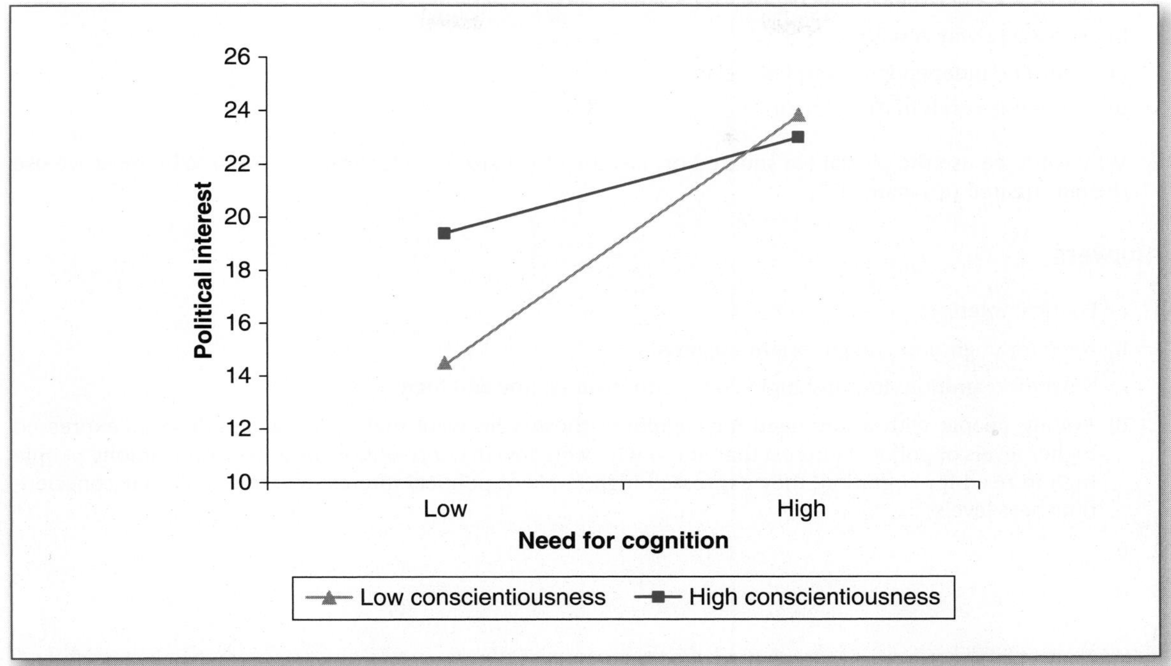

Source: Reprinted with permission from O'Hara et al., 2009; O'Hara, R. E., Walter, M. I., & Christopher, A. N. (2009). Need for cognition and conscientiousness as predictors of political interest and voting. *Journal of Applied Social Psychology, 39,* 1397–1416.

4. What are the $df_{\text{within-groups}}$ in a 4 × 2 between-subjects ANOVA with 10 people in each group?

   a) 8 c) 72

   b) 10 d) 80

5. By using the same information as in the previous question, what are the degrees of freedom for the first factor listed in the experimental design notation?

   a) 4 c) 2

   b) 3 d) 1

6. A significant interaction between factors A and B indicates:

   a) either the main effect for factor A or the main effect for factor B is also significant, but not both

   b) both the main effect for factor A and factor B must also be significant

   c) neither of the two main effects is significant

   d) the significance of the interaction has no implications for the main effects.

7. Kim has found a significant interaction in her 2 × 3 between-subjects factorial experimental design. What should Kim do next?

   a) run a 2 × 2 between-subjects factorial ANOVA
   b) run a one-way ANOVA
   c) compute independent samples t tests
   d) write this result in APA format

8. Why can't we use the partial eta squared (η_p^2) as the effect size with factorial ANOVAs? Why must we use the eta squared (η^2) instead?

Answers

1. a) Political interest
   b) Need for cognition and conscientiousness
   c) Need for cognition: low and high; conscientiousness: low and high
   d) Among people with a low need for cognition, those who were high in conscientiousness expressed higher levels of political interest than those who were low in conscientiousness. However, among people high in need for cognition, they expressed high levels of political interest regardless of their conscientiousness levels.
2. b
3. d
4. c
5. b
6. d
7. c
8. Here are the formulas for η_p^2 and η^2:

$$\eta_p^2 = \frac{SS_{\text{between-groups}}}{SS_{\text{between-groups}} + SS_{\text{within-groups}}}$$

$$\eta^2 = \frac{SS_{\text{between-groups}}}{SS_{\text{total}}}$$

   η_p^2 excludes the variability traceable to other factors and interactions between the two factors in the factorial design. We need to include all variability in the calculation of our effect size, and η^2 does this with its denominator of SS_{total}.

QUESTIONS FOR CLASS DISCUSSION

1. Suppose an experiment has a 2 × 3 × 4 design. Given this information, answer the following six questions:

   a) How many factors (independent variables) are there in this experiment?

b) How many levels are there for ***each*** factor (independent variables)?

c) How many dependent variables are there in this experiment?

d) How many total groups were created through the manipulation of the independent variable(s)?

e) How many main effects are there in this experiment?

f) How many interactions are there in this experiment?

2. Figure 11.12 comes from research that Peter Glick and colleagues (Glick, Larsen, Johnson, & Branstiter, 2005) conducted in which they measured people's perceptions of women based on their appearance and occupation.

Figure 11.12

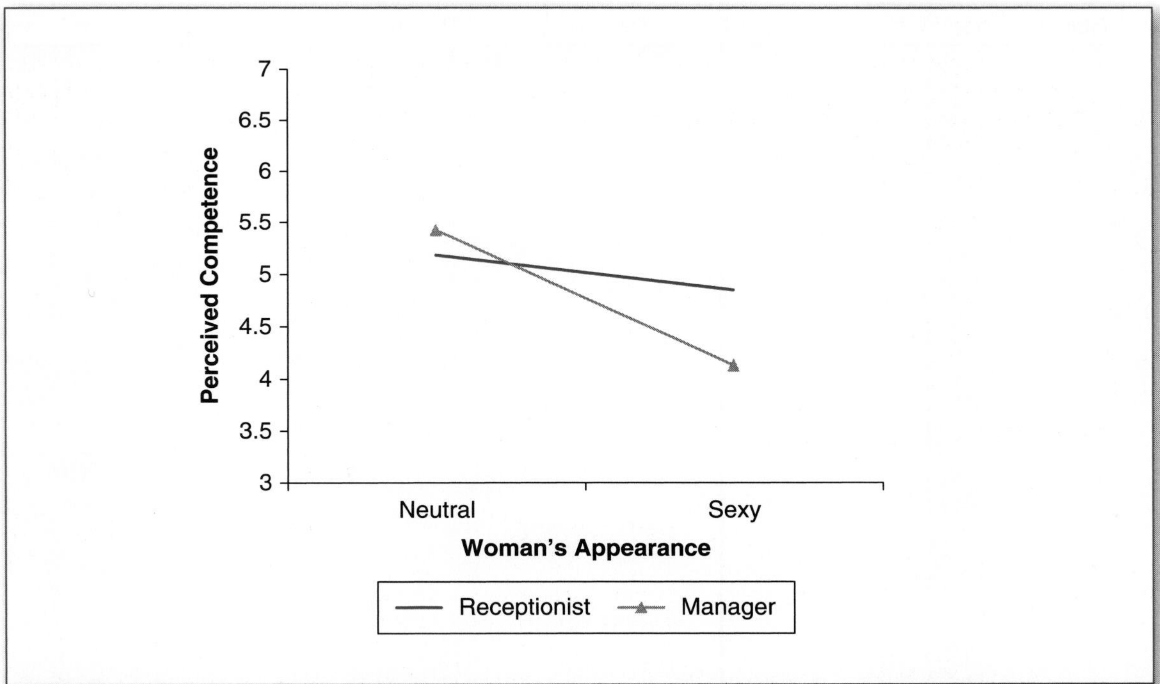

Use Figure 11.12 to answer the following questions:

a) What is the dependent (outcome) variable in this research?

b) What are the factors in this research?

c) What are the levels of each factor?

d) Interpret this interaction.

3. In the third Learning Check in this chapter, we used the following research result:

   A two-way ANOVA on offensiveness suggested no main effect of ethnicity of the person cursing, $F(2, 149) = 1.30$, $p = .276$, $\eta^2 = .016$, and no main effect of type of curse word, $F(1, 149) = 0.19$, $p = .662$, $\eta^2 = .001$. However, there was an interaction between ethnicity of the person cursing and type of curse word, $F(2, 149) = 4.33$, $p = .015$, $\eta^2 = .054$.

   Use this information to complete the following ANOVA summary table:

Source of Variability	***SS***	***df***	***MS***	***F***
Ethnicity of Person Cursing	0.430	???	???	???
Type of Curse Word	0.032	???	???	???
$\text{Interaction}_{\text{PersonxCurseword}}$	1.429	???	??	???
Within-groups	24.635	???	???	
Total	???	???		

CHAPTER 12

Determining Patterns in Data

Correlations

After reading this chapter, you will be able to

- Differentiate among predictor, independent, outcome, and dependent variables
- Explain the four different types of correlations
- Contrast the type of correlation with the strength of a correlation
- Identify three common uses of correlations
- Discuss limitations in interpreting correlations
- Hand-calculate a Pearson moment correlation coefficient
- Use SPSS to conduct and interpret SPSS output for a Pearson moment correlation coefficient

In the previous five chapters, we learned to interpret and use statistical tools when we want to compare nominal groups, sometimes created by the researchers and other times naturally occurring, on a scale outcome. In this chapter and the next chapter, we will learn about tools to use when we want to examine the relationships between scale variables. In this chapter, we will learn to use a statistical tool called the *Pearson moment correlation coefficient* (which is abbreviated as an italicized r: *r*). The Pearson correlation coefficient is typically used to measure the relationship between naturally occurring (not experimentally manipulated) variables, such as length of study time and grade-point average (GPA), education and socioeconomic status, or vegetable consumption and health outcomes.

CONCEPTUAL UNDERSTANDING OF THE TOOL

The Study

As I get older, I marvel more and more at how my students can learn and use new social media and technology so effortlessly, at least compared to how much effort I need to put into learning such technological advances.

Perhaps I am showing signs of getting older by saying this, but when I "talk" to people, that means picking up the phone and calling them or sitting down together and having a conversation. Apparently, though, some people have a broader, more-inclusive definition of "talking" to someone than I do. For instance, as you likely know, people can chat with each other on instant messaging services, exchange numerous texts in a short period of time, and tweet their activities to many people at once. To me, these do not qualify as talking to or socializing with someone, but perhaps for other people, these methods of communication serve the purpose of fulfilling social needs, a truly basic need (Lambert et al., 2013).

One particularly popular social media tool is Facebook (Facebook, Inc., Menlo Park, CA). Even if you do not use Facebook, I bet you are familiar with its basic premise, to allow people to communicate with each other through pictures, videos, and written text. There are numerous ways to interact with people, either privately or publicly, using Facebook. Since Facebook began in 2004, many studies have been conducted on its use. One study, by Russell Clayton, Randall Osborne, Brian Miller, and Crystal Oberle (2013), examined personal characteristics and behaviors that predicted Facebook usage. Specifically, these researchers examined feelings of loneliness, anxiety, alcohol use, and marijuana use as predictors of "Facebook intensity," a term we will elaborate on in just a little while.

In Clayton et al.'s (2013) study, 229 undergraduate students completed measures of loneliness, anxiousness, alcohol use, and marijuana use. To operationalize loneliness, respondents completed the 20-item Russell (1996) UCLA Loneliness Scale. This scale contains items, such as "How often do you feel that no one really knows you well?" People answer using a 1 (*never*) to 5 (*almost daily*) response range. To operationalize anxiousness, respondents completed Allan Fenigstein, Michael Scheier, and Arnold Buss's (1975) 23-item measure by responding to items, such as "It takes me time to overcome my shyness in new situations" using a 1 (*extremely uncharacteristic of me*) to 5 (*extremely characteristic of me*) response range. To operationalize alcohol use, participants completed 14 items, such as "How often do you drink alcohol when you are nervous?" Finally, to operationalize marijuana use, participants completed a 6-item measure (Hoffman, Hunt, Rhodes, & Riley, 2003) that includes questions, such as "How often have you used marijuana to relieve emotional discomfort such as sadness, anger, or hostility?" The response ranges used for both the alcohol and the marijuana use were 0 (*never*) to 5 (*daily or almost daily*).

In addition to measuring these personal characteristics, Clayton et al. (2013) used the Facebook Intensity Scale (Ellison, Steinfield, & Lampe, 2007). This scale is "designed to tap the extent to which the participant was emotionally connected to Facebook and the extent to which Facebook was integrated into her daily activities" (Ellison et al., p. 1150). When completing this scale, participants use a 1 (*strongly disagree*) to 5 (*strongly agree*) response range to respond to items, such as "Facebook has become part of my daily routine." In addition, this scale asks respondents to indicate the number of friends they have on Facebook and the number of minutes each day that they spend on Facebook.

If we look carefully in the previous two paragraphs at how Clayton et al. (2013) measured all of the variables in their research, we notice that they are all scale variables. I bring up this point because, as we will see, to use the tool we will learn about in this chapter, our variables should be measured on a scale measurement.

In research that uses correlational tools, such as Clayton et al.'s (2013) work, it is important to make a couple of subtle distinctions from experimental research. Recall from Chapter 1 that in experimental research, we have independent and dependent variables. An independent variable is a variable that a researcher creates by manipulating some aspect of the experimental setting. The researcher then randomly assigns participants to the conditions created by that manipulation. A dependent variable is measured as the outcome of the manipulation of the independent variable.

In nonexperimental research, such as the work of Clayton et al. (2013), there are no manipulated independent variables. The variables of loneliness, anxiety, alcohol use, and marijuana use are not ones that we can easily manipulate and randomly assign people to. They are called **predictor variables** because researchers can still measure them, but they cannot manipulate them, so they are not true independent variables. Predictor variables tend to be naturally occurring variables, such as a college student's year in school (i.e., first-year, sophomore, junior, or senior). In addition to using the term "predictor variable" instead of the term "independent variable," nonexperimental research tends to use the term **outcome variable** or *criterion* rather than "dependent variable."

Predictor variable: nonmanipulated variable that is used to forecast an outcome variable.

Outcome variable: variable that is measured as a function of the predictor variable; also called a *criterion* variable.

These are minor semantic issues but ones that a wise consumer of research needs to know about. That said, when you read nonexperimental research, it is possible that you will still see the terms "independent variable" and "dependent variable" used; however, I just want you to know that in such studies, there is no manipulated independent variable.

LEARNING CHECK

1. What is the difference between an independent variable and a predictor variable?

   A: An independent variable is manipulated by the researcher, whereas a predictor variable tends to be naturally occurring and cannot be easily manipulated by the researchers.

2. What is the difference between a dependent variable and an outcome variable (also called a criterion)?

   A: This is a matter of wording, but the term "dependent variable" tends to be used in experimental research, whereas the term "outcome variable" or "criterion" tends to be used in nonexperimental research. With that said, you will often still see nonexperimental research using terms such as "independent variable" and "dependent variable." Just be aware of the methodology and whether a variable was manipulated by the researchers.

3. What is (are) the predictor variable(s) in Clayton et al.'s (2013) research?

   A: feelings of loneliness, anxiety, alcohol use, and marijuana use

4. What is (are) the outcome variables in Clayton et al.'s (2013) research?

   A: Facebook intensity

5. Why would it have been impossible (or least extremely difficult for both practical and ethical reasons) for Clayton and his colleagues (2013) to do an experiment, given the focus of their research?

   A: It was not practical (or possible to do ethically) to manipulate the variables of feelings of loneliness, anxiety, alcohol use, and marijuana use. Imagine the problems (legally, practically, and ethically) of randomly assigning a participant to be in the "alcohol consumption" group! Given the nature of this study, an experiment was not possible to do.

The Tool

To analyze their data, Clayton and colleagues (2013) needed to use a statistical tool called the **Pearson moment correlation coefficient.** This statistical tool provides a measurement of the *type* (also called direction) and *strength* of relationship between two variables. We will refer to this tool as simply a "correlation" or "correlation coefficient" throughout this chapter.

In this section, we will examine four types of correlations, how to interpret the strength of a correlation, the assumptions required to use the Pearson correlation, and common research uses for correlations. To frame our discussion in the next section, we will finish this section by examining the hypotheses that Clayton et al. (2013) tested in their research.

Pearson moment correlation coefficient: statistic that quantifies the linear relationship between two scale variables; often referred to simply as a correlation coefficient.

Types (directions) of correlations

We will discuss four types of correlations. Each one is displayed in the four panels of Figure 12.1. When visually displaying a correlation, we do so using a scatterplot, in which the values of one variable appear on the x-axis (horizontal), and the values of the other variable appear on the y-axis (vertical). Technically, it does not matter which variable is placed on which axis. However, in psychological research using correlations, it is typical to place the predictor variable on the x-axis and to place the outcome variable on the y-axis. For instance, suppose we want to examine the correlation between high-school grade-point-average and college grade-point average. Typically, college admissions committees use high-school GPA to predict college GPA, so college GPA would be placed on the y-axis and high-school GPA would be placed on the x-axis.

In Figure 12.1, panel a displays a **positive correlation** between two variables. As you can see, as the values of the variable on the x-axis increase, the values of the variable on the y-axis tend to increase as well. Stated differently, as the values of the variable on the x-axis decrease, the values of the variable on the y-axis tend to decrease as well. In short, with a positive correlation, the two variables tend to move in the same direction. For instance, we know that as outdoor temperatures increase, acts of aggression and violence tend to increase as well (Bushman, Wang, & Anderson, 2005; Reifman, Larrick, & Fein, 1991). That is, there is a positive correlation between the variable of temperature and the variable of aggression.

Positive correlation: results when two variables tend to vary together in the same direction.

Before moving on to panel b in Figure 12.1, I want to draw your attention to two critical words in the definition of a positive correlation (or any other type of correlation we are going to discuss). Specifically, the words *tend to* are vital to understand. In general, we see more acts of aggression when the temperatures are hotter, but there are exceptions to this trend. Take another example of a positive correlation. There is, as you could probably guess, a positive correlation between the number of hours that students study and their GPAs. However, do you know someone who parties a lot and seems to study a lot less than most people, yet still has a high GPA? I certainly knew a few such people when I was in college (and was jealous of these rare people), but they are the exceptions to the trend. Of course, they are easy to recall, but that's because they are, by definition, rare.

Now, when we return to Figure 12.1, we see that panel b displays a **negative correlation**. A negative correlation exists when the values of the two variables tend to move in opposite directions. That is, as values of the variable on the x-axis tend to increase, the values of the variable on the y-axis tend to decrease (and vice versa). For instance, people who feel lonely tend to report being less happy than people who feel less lonely (Yan, Su, Zhu, & He, 2013). That is, as feelings of loneliness increase, happiness levels tend to decrease.

Negative correlation: increases in one variable tend to be accompanied by decreases in a second variable. In other words, the two variables tend to relate in the opposite direction.

To clarify, when we say "positive" correlation or "negative" correlation, we do not mean "good" correlation or "bad" correlation. *The words "positive" and "negative" refer to slope of the relationship between the two variables.*

Figure 12.1a Positive Correlation

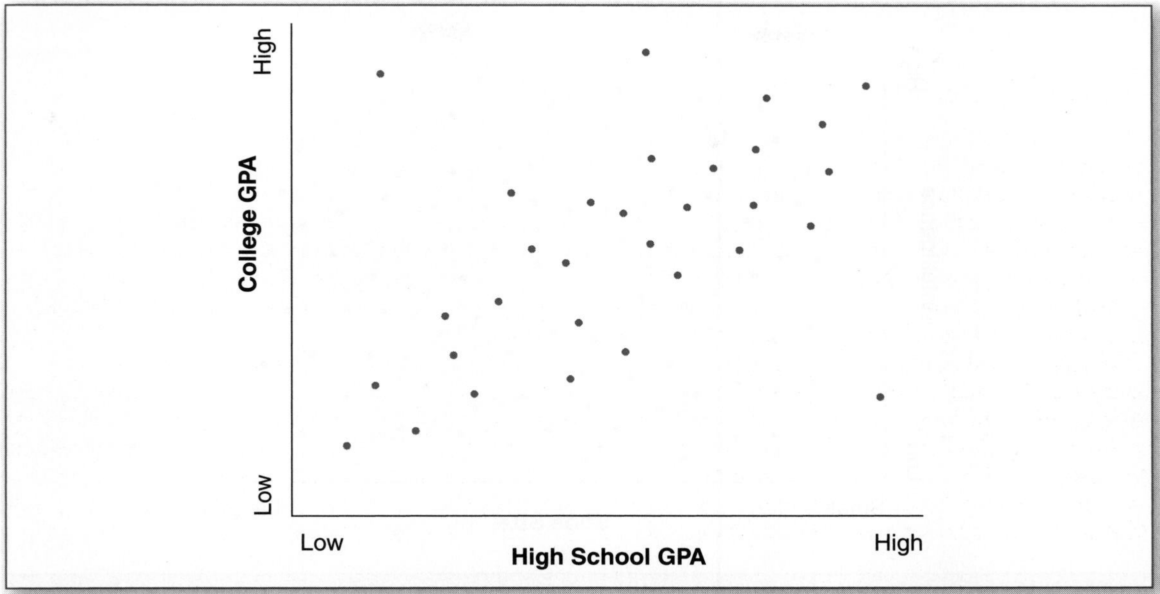

Figure 12.1b A Negative Correlation

Figure 12.1c Zero (no) Correlation

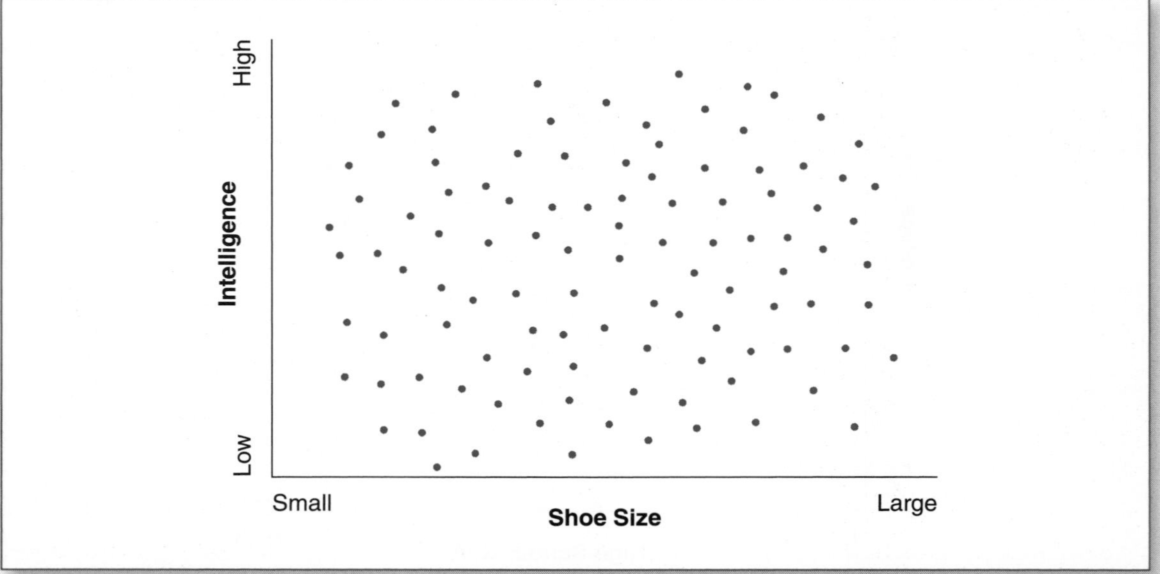

Figure 12.1d Curvilinear Relationship

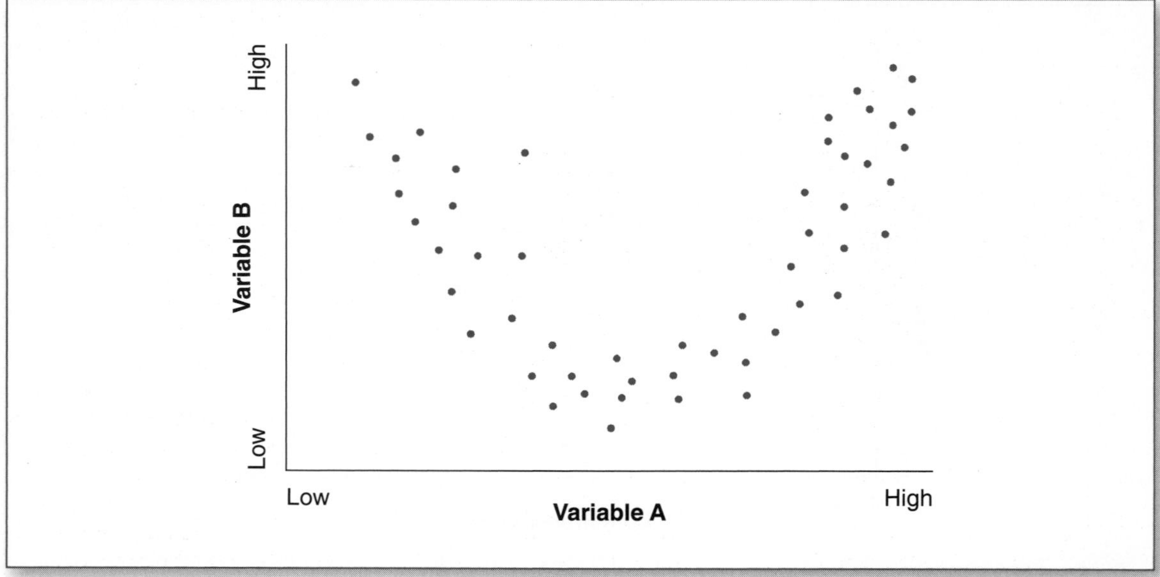

Panel c presents a situation in which there is a **zero correlation** between the two variables. As you can see, the datapoints are scattered in a random fashion. As you know from Chapter 1, our minds tend to impose relationships even when they don't exist (called illusory correlations), so I have a hard time thinking of examples in which there is not a relationship between two variables. However, I doubt there is a relationship between shoe size and intelligence.

Finally, panel d presents what's called a **curvilinear relationship** between two variables. A curvilinear relationship exists when the values of the two variables tend to be positively correlated up to a certain value, but then the variables are negatively correlated after that certain value. Let's take a couple of examples that might make the notion of curvilinear relationship clearer. Perhaps in your "Introductory Psychology" class you were introduced to the notion of Yerkes-Dodson's Law (1908). This law states that performance on a task (e.g., taking a test or an athletic performance) is at its best when we are "optimally" aroused, that is, motivated but not overly motivated to do well. The visual display of Yerkes-Dodson's Law can be seen in Figure 12.2. At lower levels of arousal (or motivation), performance increases up to a certain point. This makes sense. If you really don't care about doing well on a test, or how your team does in a game, your performance won't be very good. However, once we reach a certain level of arousal, additional arousal (or motivation) starts to hurt performance. This also makes sense. If you're so stressed (aroused) about a test that you cannot concentrate on the information you need to understand, your performance is likely to suffer.

Figure 12.2 Graph of the Yerkes-Dodson Law: A Curvilinear Relationship

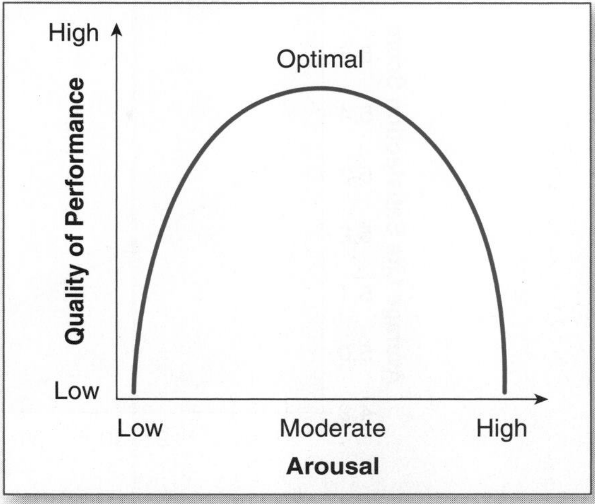

Curvilinear relationship: results when the relationship between two variables is not a linear relationship.

Yerkes-Dodson's Law is an "inverted U" relationship. Curvilinear relationships can also take on a "U relationship." For example, as seen in Figure 12.3, there is a curvilinear relationship between age and happiness, such that we are happiest at younger and older ages. David Blachflower and Andrew Oswald (2008) found that this relationship between age and happiness existed across 72 countries. Although there were some country-specific differences (e.g., happiness bottoms out at age 46 in the United States, whereas it bottoms out at age 62 in the Ukraine), the general pattern of the relationship was the same across nations.

Strength of correlations

In addition to the type of the relationship between the two variables, a correlation coefficient provides us with information about the strength of the relationship between the two variables. Take a look at Figure 12.4, which displays the correlation between marijuana use and alcohol use in Clayton et al.'s (2013) research. You know that this is a positive correlation because as the values of marijuana use increase, the values of alcohol use tend to increase. But how strong of a positive correlation do we have here? For the correlation in Figure 12.4, we want a number that tells us how strong this relationship is.

The strength of the relationship between two variables can range from 0, meaning there is no relationship, which we saw in panel c of Figure 12.1, to 1, meaning there is a "perfect" relationship between the two variables.

Figure 12.3 The Relationship Between Age and Life Satisfaction

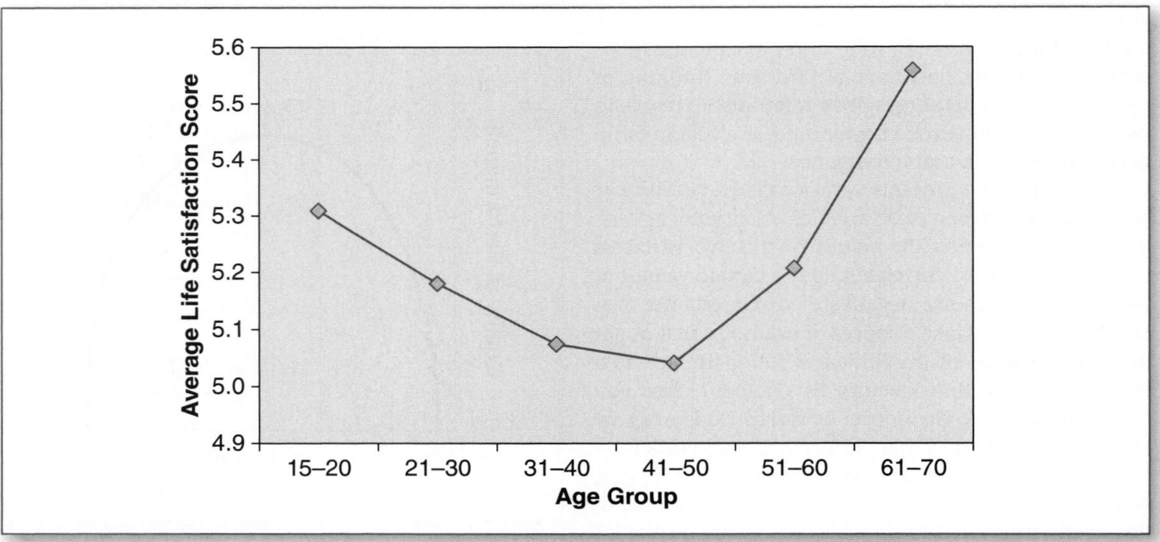

Figure 12.4 Relationship Between Marijuana Use and Alcohol Use in Clayton et al.'s (2013) Research

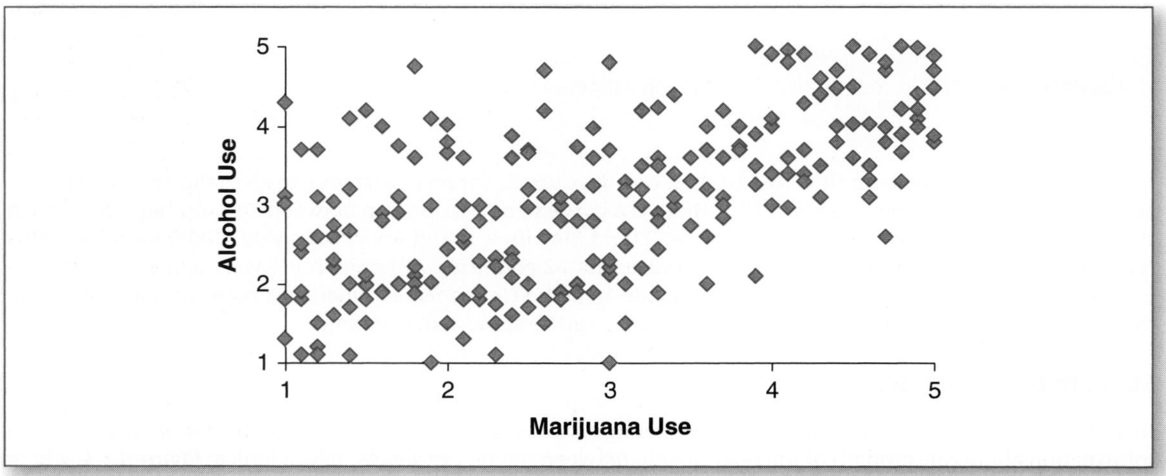

The closer the correlation coefficient is to the absolute value of 1, the stronger the relationship is between the two variables. We will learn how to calculate and generate correlation coefficients using the software program Statistical Package for the Social Sciences (SPSS) in the latter part of this chapter. For now, trust me that the correlation between marijuana use and alcohol use is +.61.

Table 12.1 Guidelines for Classifying Correlation Coefficients (Cohen, 1988)

Correlation Coefficient	Strength of the Relationship
0 to ±.29	None (.00) or Weak
±.30 to ±.49	Moderate
±.50 to ±1.00	Strong

What does an $r = +.61$ tell us? Just as there were guidelines for interpreting effect sizes for *t* tests and ANOVAs, we have guidelines for interpreting the strength of correlation coefficients. Table 12.1 contains these guidelines. A correlation of +.61 is a strong correlation. Realize that by its very definition, a correlation coefficient is an effect size. Indeed, this subsection's heading, "Strength of Correlations," indicates we are dealing with effect sizes in this chapter.

Assumptions of the Pearson correlation

As with any inferential statistical tool, there are certain conditions that need to exist before the Pearson correlation coefficient can be used. We consider three assumptions now:

1. Both variables are quantified by using a scale measurement. We cannot use this tool with nominal or ordinal data (Chapter 14 will provide us with tools for nominal and ordinal data).

   You will sometimes see correlations reported in research that are not quantified by using a scale measurement. This is not a mistake on the part of researchers. What's going on in such cases is that there are different types of correlations available to researchers. In this Chapter, we focus on the most common correlation, the Pearson correlation coefficient. In Chapter 14, we will visit the Spearman rank-order correlation. Here, we will briefly visit two other types of correlations, just so you are aware of them.

   The *point-biserial correlation coefficient* is used when one variable in the analysis is measured on a nominal scale. For instance, suppose we want to learn whether college first-years or seniors are experiencing more stress in their lives. Class standing (i.e., first-year or senior) is a nominal variable, and stress is a scale variable. Thus, we could use the point-biserial correlation.

   The *phi coefficient* is used when both variables are nominal. By extending the previous example, we could simply ask first-years and seniors whether they are feeling stressed. Such a response ("yes" or "no") is a nominal measurement. Therefore, with two nominal measurements, the researcher would need the phi coefficient.

   Now back to the assumptions of our focus in this chapter, the Pearson correlation:

2. There is a linear relationship between the two variables. As we saw when discussing curvilinear relationships earlier in this section, Pearson correlations are not useful for understanding nonlinear relationships, such as Yerkes-Dodson's Law.
3. Scores on both variables are normally distributed. As we have noted in previous chapters, this assumption is normally satisfied when sample sizes are at least 25–30 participants.

Uses for correlations

We now discuss three common uses for correlations in research.

Use 1: Study naturally occurring relationships

We've discussed this use previously in this chapter, but it is essential to reiterate it. Think about the nature of Clayton and colleagues' (2013) research; that is, they wanted to study personal characteristics such as loneliness and anxiety and how they are related to Facebook use. As discussed, it is not realistic to manipulate these variables experimentally, for instance, randomly assigning some participants to be lonely and others to be not lonely. It might be possible, but I think it would be at best ethically questionable to do so. However, these variables and their relationships to certain behaviors are obviously important. For research that involves variables that are impossible or unethical to manipulate experimentally, research can use correlations and Clayton and his colleagues did.

Another area of research in which correlations are used is in examining the relationship between standardized tests, such as the Scholastic Aptitude Test (SAT®; College Board, New York, NY) and the American College Testing (ACT®; ACT, Inc., Iowa City, IA) exam, with academic performance in college-level classes. We cannot, practically speaking, randomly assign high-school students to an SAT score and then measure how well they do in their college classes. Instead, we must use their "naturally occurring" scores on these standardized tests and correlate them with college grades.[1]

Use 2: Basis for predictions

We will be discussing the results of Clayton et al.'s (2013) research in the next section. For now, take a look at Figure 12.5. As you see in this Figure, we placed the variable of anxiousness on the x-axis and the variable of Facebook intensity on the y-axis. We said previously that when presenting the scatterplot of the relationship between two variables, it technically does not matter which variable we place on each axis. However, in practice, we place the predictor variable on the x-axis and the outcome variable on the y-axis. In Clayton et al.'s research, anxiousness was used to predict Facebook intensity; therefore, we placed the two variables on the axes of the scatterplot that we did.

Regarding the relationship between performance on standardized tests and academic performance in college, researchers use SAT or ACT scores to predict academic performance in college. You could use academic

Figure 12.5 Anxiousness as a Predictor of Facebook Intensity

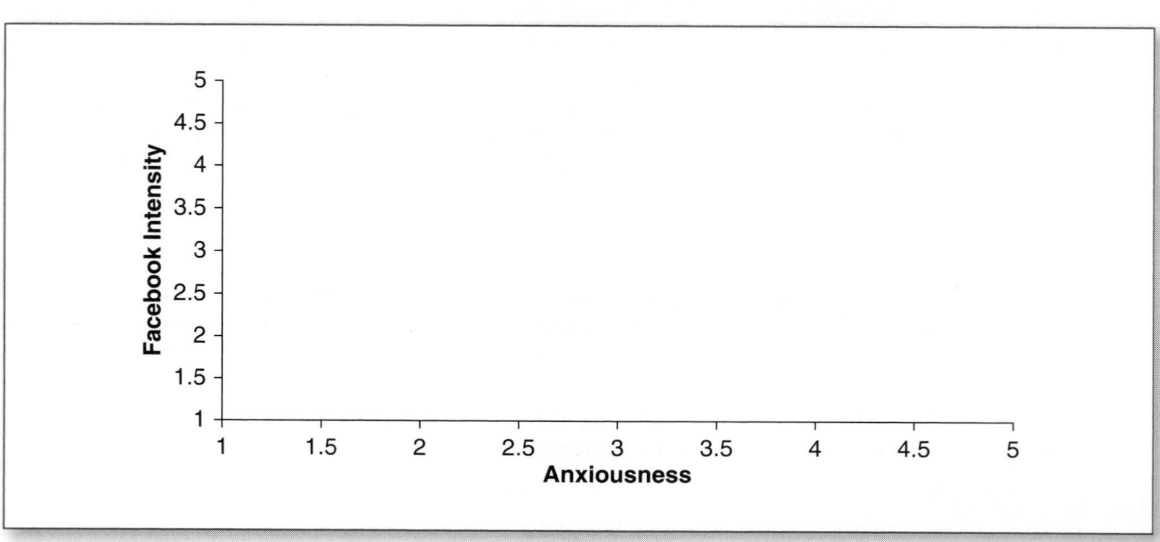

performance to predict SAT or ACT scores, but I don't think that would be meaningful to do (what good does it do to predict a past event, such as SAT score?). Therefore, SAT scores goes on the x-axis and academic performance in college goes on the y-axis.

We will expand on using correlations to make predictions in the next chapter. For now, just understand that the predictor variable goes on the x-axis and the outcome variable goes on the y-axis.

Use #3: Establishing measurement reliability and validity

In Chapter 2, we discussed the importance of measurements possessing reliability and validity. If you want a complete review of these concepts, please reread the section titled "Scales of Measurement: How We Measure Variables" in Chapter 2. If not, just remember that reliability refers to the extent to which a measurement tool produces consistent results, and validity refers to the extent to which a measurement is appropriate to use in a given research situation. Notice that both definitions have the phrase "extent to which" in them. Here is where correlations come into play. Correlation coefficients provide a measurement of the extent to which a measure is reliable and valid.

Let's suppose we want to learn whether the SAT is a reliable measurement tool and is a valid predictor of academic performance in college. To understand these processes, we will consider two figures. First, look at Figure 12.6. On the x-axis, we have SAT scores the first time students take the test. Of course, many students take this test a second time. For these students, we have a second SAT score, which appears on the y-axis. If the SAT is reliable, there should be a fairly strong positive correlation between students' scores on the first test and students' scores on the second test. Generally, a correlation of $r = +.70$ or stronger indicates an acceptable level of reliability for a measurement tool.

Regarding the validity of the SAT, take a look at Figure 12.7. On the x-axis, we again have SAT scores. On the y-axis, we have college grades. We examine the correlation between these two variables. Assuming it is at least a moderately strong correlation, we can conclude that the SAT has validity in predicting academic achievement in college. Generally, a correlation of $r = +.40$ or stronger indicates an acceptable level of validity for a measurement tool.

Hypotheses from Clayton et al. (2013)

Let's finish this section by examining the hypotheses from Clayton et al.'s (2013) research. Recall that they studied four predictors of Facebook intensity, specifically, loneliness, anxiousness, alcohol use, and marijuana use. Thus, these researchers offered four hypotheses, one for each predictor variable and its relationship to Facebook intensity.

Just as with the previous inferential statistical tools we've discussed, we are testing a null hypothesis when we use a Pearson correlation. In this case, the null hypothesis would be that a predictor variable is not correlated with Facebook intensity. For instance, one specific null hypothesis is that loneliness and Facebook intensity will be uncorrelated. Notationally, we have:

$$H_o: r = 0$$

But, of course, published research will state a research hypothesis instead of a null hypothesis. Here are the four research hypotheses, one for each predictor variable's relationship to Facebook intensity, that Clayton et al. (2013) offered:

H_r: Loneliness and Facebook intensity will be positively correlated.

H_r: Anxiousness and Facebook intensity will be positively correlated.

H_r: Alcohol use and Facebook intensity will be positively correlated.

H_r: Marijuana use and Facebook intensity will be negatively correlated.

Figure 12.6 Establishing Reliability of the SAT

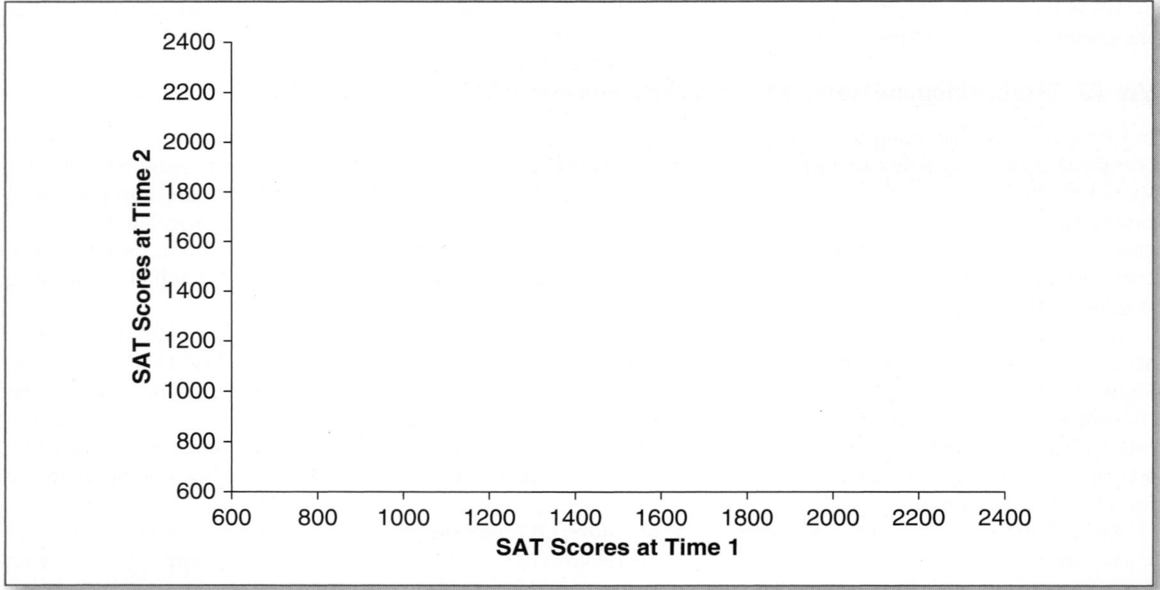

Figure 12.7 Establishing Validity of the SAT

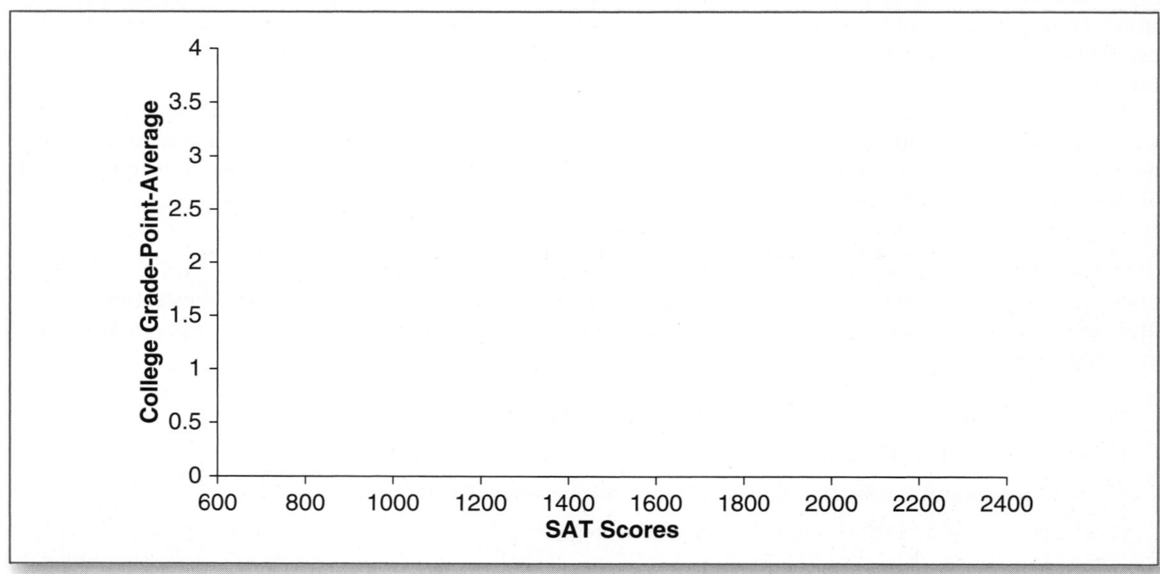

LEARNING CHECK

1. Define "positive" and "negative" in the context of correlation coefficients.

   A: These terms deal with the slope of the association between the two variables. A positive correlation means that there is a positive slope (i.e., the values of both variables tend to move in the same direction), and a negative correlation means that there is a negative slope (i.e., the values of both variables tend to move in the opposite direction).

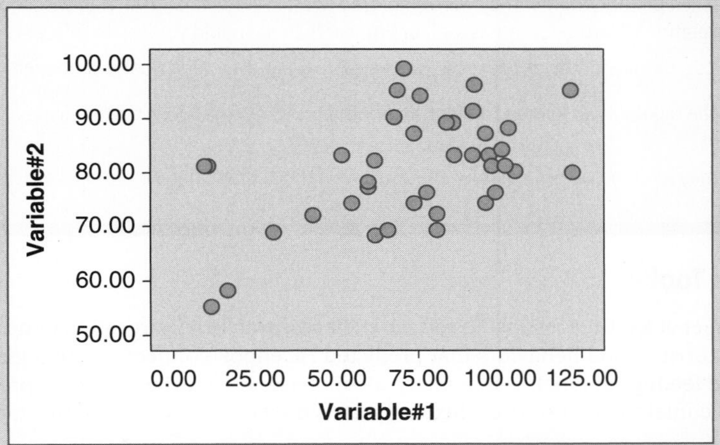

2. Consider the above scatterplot. Which of the following correlation coefficients is the BEST estimate of the coefficient that would represent the data in the above scatterplot?

   a) −1.25　　c) +1.25
   b) −.50　　d) +.50

   A: d

3. Which of the following is the **strongest** correlation coefficient?

   a) +.25　　c) −.07
   b) −.86　　d) +1.35

   A: b; remember that correlations cannot be stronger than the absolute value of 1.0, so if you chose d, understand why it is wrong.

4. You would probably find a **POSITIVE** correlation between:

   a) the number of hours studying for a test and scores on that test.
   b) distance from the equator and average daily high temperature.
   c) frequency of brushing your teeth and amount of plaque buildup on your teeth.
   d) levels of depression and levels of physical activity.

   A: a

(Continued)

(Continued)

5. According to Jacob Cohen's (1988) classification scheme of correlation sizes, a correlation of $r = -.45$ would be considered:

   a) weak. c) strong.

   b) moderate. d) none of the above.

   A: b

6. A recent survey asked people whether they were employed and to rate their satisfaction with life on a scale measurement. Which correlation (Pearson, point-biserial, or Phi) coefficient should you use to analyze this data?

   A: Point-biserial correlation coefficient because one variable (employment status) is a nominal variable.

7. If you're testing the reliability of a measurement and find an $r = .00$, what does that indicate about the reliability of this measurement?

   A: It means the measurement is not reliable, and thus, we cannot draw any meaningful conclusions from its use.

Interpreting the Tool

Let's dive into Clayton et al.'s (2013) results. To refresh their research briefly, recall that these researchers examined personal characteristics and behaviors that predicted Facebook connection strategies. Specifically, these researchers examined feelings of loneliness, anxiety, alcohol use, and marijuana use as predictors of "Facebook intensity." Table 12.2 contains the results of this study. Let's dissect what we see in this table.

Table 12.2 Results of Clayton et al.'s (2013) Research

	M	*SD*	1	2	3	4	5
1. Loneliness	3.33	0.47	(.70)				
2. Anxiousness	3.23	0.57	.47***	(.86)			
3. Alcohol Use	1.60	0.55	.04	−.06	(.95)		
4. Marijuana Use	1.52	0.86	.11	.01	.61***	(.92)	
5. Facebook Intensity	3.46	0.90	.11	.18**	.16*	−.05	(.86)

Abbreviations. M = mean; *SD* = standard deviation.

* $p < .05$. ** $p < .01$. *** $p < .001$.

Source: Clayton, R. B., Osborne, R. E., Miller, B. K., & Oberle, C. D. (2013). Loneliness, anxiousness, and substance abuse as predictors of Facebook use. *Computers in Human Behavior, 29*, 687–693.

Testing the null hypothesis

Researchers often present a set of correlations in what's called a **correlation matrix**, as we have here. The first column of the correlations matrix contains the name of each variable that was included in the analyses. The second and third columns, as is the case here, often present the mean (*M*) and standard deviation (*SD*) for each variable. Although it has been a while since we discussed measures of central tendency and measures of variability (Chapter 4), realize that such simple information helps readers understand the nature of the sample used and, hence, the population being studied.

Correlation matrix: visual display of correlation coefficients.

Appearing after the means and standard deviations, we have five more columns. The numerical headings for the columns correspond to the number and associated variable in each row. Thus, the column with a "1" is the variable of loneliness. As we move down that column, we see the correlation coefficients between loneliness and each of the other variables in the matrix. For example, the correlation between loneliness and Facebook intensity was .11. Notice that in the matrix, there are no "+" signs. When reporting correlations, researchers typically do not include a "+" to indicate a positive correlation as we have here. They do, though, use a "–" sign to indicate a negative correlation, as you can see in the relationship between marijuana use and Facebook intensity.

Notice that for the variable of loneliness, there is a "(.70)" that appears at the intersection of the first row and the first numbered column. We discussed in Chapter 2 the notion of *internal reliability*, which is how consistent scores are on a single measurement instrument that is administered one time. In its simplest terms, we can correlate scores on each half of the individual items on a measurement tool. Of course, there are often many ways to divide the items on a measurement in half (e.g., odds and evens and first half and last half). Therefore, we can find a mean correlation from the correlations between all possible halves of the test. Doing so provides a common indicator of internal reliability called **Cronbach's alpha**. For variables of anxiousness, the internal reliability is .86. Internal reliabilities are often reported in a matrix this way, and I want to be sure you understand what you are seeing when you come across them. As we said earlier in this chapter, a reliability of +.70 or stronger is considered to be acceptable. Internal reliabilities are of no importance to the conceptual nature of the research, but of course, researchers want to be sure their measures are reliable. With the help of SPSS, internal reliabilities for our measures are simple to generate. This chapter contains an addendum that shows you how to generate and interpret a Cronbach's alpha using SPSS.

Cronbach's alpha: measure of internal reliability; it is the mean correlation of all correlations between different possible halves of a measurement tool.

Finally, you will see some correlation coefficients with one or more asterisks (*) after them. Take a look at the bottom of the table. These asterisks are used to indicate which correlations are statistically significant. If there is no asterisk next to a correlation coefficient, it means that correlation was not statistically significant. So in the case of the relationship between loneliness and Facebook intensity, the correlation of .11, although in the direction hypothesized (a positive correlation), was not statistically significant. Thus, Clayton et al. (2013) failed to reject the null hypothesis for this relationship.

In addition to presenting many correlations using a correlation matrix, sometimes you will see correlations reported in the text of a research article. Here is how to report correlations in the text by using the result Clayton et al. (2013) found between alcohol use and Facebook intensity:

> There was a positive correlation between alcohol use and Facebook intensity, $r(227) = .16, p < .05$.

The number in parentheses, 227, is the degrees of freedom for this analysis. It was calculated by taking the sample size, which was 229, and subtracting 2.

Cautions in interpreting correlations

Correlations are a frequently used tool in a wide variety of fields, not just psychology. Therefore, as we learn about correlations, there are five cautions I want to make you aware of. I issue these cautions so that you understand not only the strengths but also the limitations of this widely used research tool. I sometimes see incredibly bright people make some of these mistakes when interpreting or using correlational data, and I don't want you to be among them (meaning I don't want you to make these mistakes; I definitely want you to be incredibly bright).

Caution 1: Don't confuse type (direction) and strength of a correlation

The directional sign (positive or negative) of the correlation says nothing about the strength of the relationship between the two variables. For instance, suppose we have a correlation coefficient of −.78 (there is no need to put a 0 before the decimal point because correlations can never be greater than 1.0). The "-" sign indicates it is a negative correlation. The ".78," according to Cohen's (1988) guidelines, means that there is a strong relationship between the two variables. Now suppose we have a different correlation coefficient of .27. As we said previously, researchers typically do not include a "+" to indicate a positive correlation as we have here. The ".27" is a weak relationship according to our guidelines.

On the number line, it is true that ".27" is greater than "−.78." In the world of correlations, forget the number line. *It is the absolute value of the number that determines the strength of the correlation*. The closer to 1.0 that absolute value is, the stronger the relationship is between the two variables. The direction does not matter whatsoever.

Caution 2: Range restriction

Suppose we want to examine the correlation between a professional basketball player's height and his or her performance playing basketball. We will operationalize "performance playing basketball" as the number of rebounds that a player grabs, on average each game (adjusted for number of minutes played). Do you see a potential problem in determining the correlation between these two variables? How many people who are of typical height (e.g., 5 feet, 9 inches tall for men) play professional basketball?

Here is an example of range restriction. *Range restriction occurs when we do not or cannot measure the entire range of values that a variable (such as height) can take on.* There are few people of average height, much less people who are short, playing professional basketball. Let's see what range restriction can do to a correlation coefficient. If we measure professional basketball players' heights and number of rebounds per minute played each game, we would get a scatterplot that looks like the one in Figure 12.8. On the x-axis is height, in inches. On the y-axis is the variable we want to predict, rebounds. If the average height of a man is 5 feet, 9 inches (which is 69 inches), where are all the players of average height? There weren't any as the shortest player in this sample was 5 feet, 11 inches (71 inches) tall.

In Figure 12.8, we have a correlation between height and number of rebounds of .48. Thus, it is a positive correlation, as we would expect, and of moderate strength according to Cohen's (1988) guidelines in Table 12.1. However, in this situation, we have a restricted range of values for the variable of height. *When we have range restriction as we do here, the correlation between the two variables is smaller than it likely would be if we could measure all of the values of both variables.* If more professional male basketball players were of average (5 feet, 9 inches) or below-average height, we would see a stronger relationship between height and rebounding because those short players would tend not to get many rebounds.

Let's illustrate range restriction by extending this example. Let's suppose we study only particularly tall male professional basketball players, that is, those who stand at least 6 feet, 10 inches tall (82 inches tall). Figure 12.9 displays the scatterplot of these data. Now our correlation between height and rebounds fall to .32. Without players between 5 feet, 11 inches and 6 feet, 9 inches tall, there just isn't much dispersion in either of our variables. As we know from previous chapters, variability is essential to detecting relationships

Figure 12.8 Scatterplot Displaying the Relationship Between Basketball Players' Height and Number of Rebounds per Game

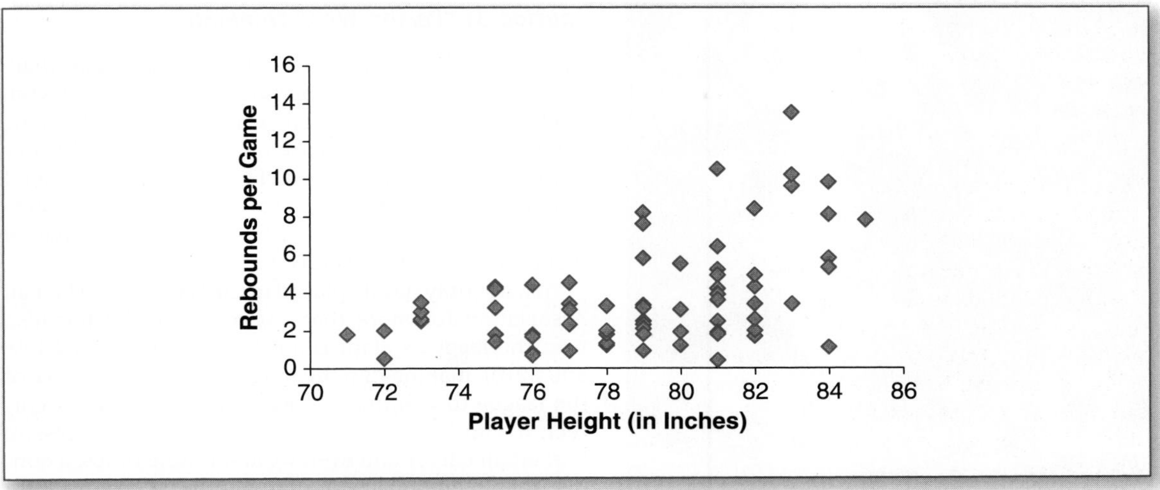

Source: Data retrieved from 2014 -2015 Yahoo Sports player profiles for the National Basketball Association's Memphis Grizzlies, Chicago Bulls, Golden State Warriors, Charlotte Hornets, and Detroit Pistons.

Figure 12.9 Range Restriction: Without Variability in the Heights of Basketball Players, We Have More Difficulty Detecting a Relationship Between Height and Number of Rebounds per Game

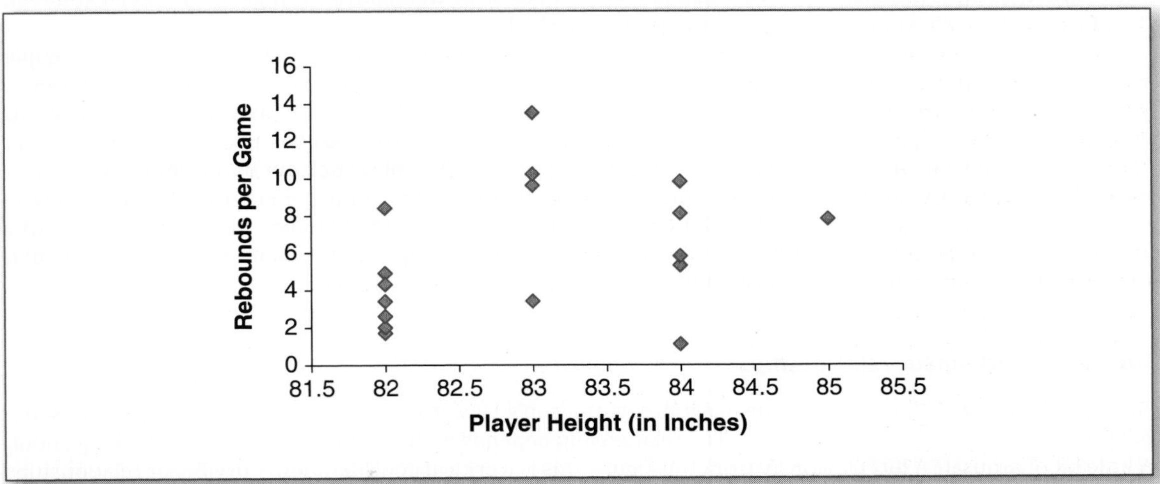

Source: Data retrieved from 2014 -2015 Yahoo Sports player profiles for the National Basketball Association's Memphis Grizzlies, Chicago Bulls, Golden State Warriors, Charlotte Hornets, and Detroit Pistons.

"Little" Nate Robinson with teammates

Source: Bruce Bennett/Getty Images Sport/Getty Images

between variables, and this is the problem that range restriction presents, a lack of variability in our variables being correlated.

Caution 3: "Person-Who" thinking

Even if you don't follow professional men's basketball, I bet you've heard of people such as Shaquille O'Neal, Michael Jordan, and LeBron James. They are, or were, some of the best men's basketball players in the history of the sport. Have you heard of Nate Robinson? If not, I am surprised, especially if you follow men's professional basketball. You see, Robinson is in fact 5 feet, 9 inches tall, a man of average height.

Yet, not only has he played in the National Basketball Association for more than 10 years, but he has also won the league's Slam Dunk Contest (in 2006, 2009, and 2010), making him the only player in the history of the league to win this contest three times. That's correct, a man of average height has had a successful basketball career and even won, multiple times, a contest that seems to favor particularly tall people in a sport filled with tall people to start with.

I am 6 feet, 2 inches tall, so given Robinson's success playing basketball, perhaps I should consider a career change from college professor to professional basketball player. Why might this be a bad idea for me to consider (much less do)? Think about this in terms of the law of small numbers, which we discussed at length in Chapter 1. Can one man of average height be a professional basketball star? Of course, such things do happen, but in this case, Robinson is the exception to the rule that most professional basketball players tend to be of well above-average height. Even at 6 feet, 2 inches tall, I am short in the world of professional basketball.

To take another example of "person-who" thinking, one we discussed previously in this chapter, people who spend more time studying tend to earn higher grades than people who spend less time studying. However, you likely know a student who spends more time partying or playing video games than studying and yet earns great grades in his or her classes. Such a student is an outlier;[2] that is, he or she goes against the trend of what is the case for most people or situations. Of course, exceptions to the rules stick out in our minds, so we can recall these "person-who" instances better than instances that conform to the general rule. You know many more students who get grades that reflect how much time they invest in their studies, but such people simply aren't memorable because, by definition, they are similar to most people. In the same way, given his height, Nate Robinson is an outlier in the world of professional basketball.

Caution 4: Curvilinear relationships

Take a look back at Figure 12.2 that displays Yerkes-Dodson's Law. It is a curvilinear relationship. That is, the relationship is not linear (straight-lined). The relationship depends on how much arousal we are talking about. A little bit of arousal? A lot? Obviously from this figure, this is a critical consideration. Curvilinear relationships present a problem when interpreting and using correlations. That is because when dealing with correlations, researchers assume that there is a linear (straight-lined) relationship between the two variables being investigated. If they had used correlations as we've discussed them to this point, Yerkes and Dodson would have missed the nature of the relationship between arousal and performance. That is, they would have concluded that there is no correlation between arousal and performance. However, if we look more deeply at the relationship, then indeed, we detect an important relationship between these two variables.[3]

Caution 5: Spurious correlations

You may have heard at some point that "correlation does not equal causation." Let's examine what that means. Take an example: Did you know that there is a relationship between the number of kitchen appliances in the home and use of birth control? That is, the more kitchen appliances people have, the more likely they are to use birth control. So if we want to curb teenage pregnancy, it appears we need to go to the local middle and high schools and give those students blenders (what Keith Stanovich cleverly called "Birth control by the toaster method" [2004, p. iv]).

This is an example of a **spurious correlation**. By spurious, we mean "deceptive" (Haig, 2003). Birth control use and number of kitchen appliances are indeed related. However, there are outside factors, which are not stated, that are responsible for the real relationship that we observe. Why do you think that people who have lots of kitchen appliances are more likely to use birth control? Or stated the other way, why are people who have few appliances less likely to use birth control? What does one need to get appliances? To get access to birth control? In both cases, people need money. Wealthier people, relative to poorer people, tend to have more kitchen appliances (because they can afford them), and they tend to use birth control more often (because they can afford to do so). Therefore, the relationship between using birth control and the number of kitchen appliances in the home exists because of a connection to socioeconomic status (SES). Of course, SES is related to a variety of other behaviors and outcomes, such as education. There could be (and likely are) numerous "third factors" that are responsible for an observed relationship between two other factors.

> **Spurious correlation**: real relationship between two variables or events that exists because both variables are correlated to a third, unmeasured variable.

Consider the following news headline, "Birth season affects traits." This story summarized findings of several research studies. For example, people with birthdays in the spring or summer tend to be more optimistic than people with birthdays in autumn or winter. However, people with spring or summer birthdays are also more likely to experience more frequent and rapid mood swings than people born in the winter. These findings are real relationships between when during the year people were born and their temperaments. However, it is a spurious correlation. What do you think might be a third, unmeasured factor in these relationships? Environmentally, outdoor temperature, light exposure, a mother's level of physical activity, and types of pathogens (to name but a handful) differ by season. Thus, it could be some of these factors (or others) that are contributing to the relationship between birth season and personality.

The bottom line here is that just because two events are related does not mean one caused the other. Season of birth does not cause personality differences. As just discussed, there could be, and typically are, other factors that need to be considered. When you see language in news headlines or elsewhere such as "There is a link between," "Research supports a connection between," or "There is a relationship between," it is normally indicative of a correlation between two factors. That does not mean that one event caused the other event to occur. Spurious correlations are real relationships between two variables or events, but again, we need to think more deeply about why such connections exist. There is a relationship between ice cream cone sales and number of drownings in the United States. However, a third, unstated factor is at work here (think about what that third factor might be, and we will discuss it in the next Learning Check). Correlations are in fact powerful statistical tools and are staples in social science research. However, their interpretation requires some caution.

LEARNING CHECK

1. Here are the null hypotheses that Clayton et al. (2013) tested:

   #1. H_0: Loneliness and Facebook intensity will be uncorrelated.

   #2. H_0: Anxiousness and Facebook intensity will be uncorrelated.

   #3. H_0: Alcohol use and Facebook intensity will be uncorrelated.

   #4. H_0: Marijuana use and Facebook intensity will be uncorrelated.

Take a look at the correlation matrix of their results (Table 12.2). For each hypothesis, (a) state the correlation between the two variables in the hypothesis; (b) state whether the hypothesis was rejected or not rejected; and (c) state the *p* value associated with each correlation used to test that hypothesis.

A: #1: $r = .11$; not rejected because the *p* value was greater than .05

#2: $r = .18$; rejected because the *p* value was less than .01

#3: $r = .16$; rejected because the *p* value was less than .05

#4: $r = -.05$; not rejected because the *p* value was greater than .05

2. Explain why a restricted range makes a correlation coefficient smaller than it would have been had the range of values for one or both variables not been restricted.

   A: To detect patterns in data, there must be a range of the values (or scores) of the variables we are studying. It becomes progressively more difficult to detect relationships as the amount of variability declines. Imagine we want to study how the number of hours that students sleep correlates with performance on a quiz in class the next morning. If every student scored the same on the quiz, it would be impossible to detect any relationship between these two variables.

3. Why is it the case that no matter how strong the correlation is between two variables, we can NEVER, EVER conclude that a change in one variable CAUSED a change in the other variable?

   A: There is always the possibility that both variables being correlated are each related to some third, unmeasured variable. It is this third, unmeasured variable that ultimately is responsible for the correlation we found.

4. Why is it a fact that the more ice cream cones that are sold correlates to more people who drown in backyard pools?

   A: Think about the time of year during which people tend to eat ice cream cones and the time of year people swim in an outdoor pool. Both events tend to occur during the summer months; hence, it is the time of year that is the factor responsible for the relationship between ice cream cone sales and the number of drownings in backyard pools.

5. Which of the following is the **weakest** correlation coefficient?

   a) .49 c) .07

   b) −.86 d) −1.00

   A: c

6. Explain why choice c was the best answer to question 5.

   A: The strength of a correlation is determined by how close the coefficient is to 1.0, regardless of whether it is +1.0 (a perfect positive correlation) or −1.0 (a perfect negative correlation). Therefore, choice c provides the coefficient furthest from 1.0, and hence, why it is the weakest correlation coefficient.

USING YOUR NEW STATISTICAL TOOL

With a conceptual understanding of correlations, let's now learn how to calculate them by hand; after which, we will learn how to use this tool with the help of SPSS.

Hand-Calculating the Pearson Correlation Coefficient (*r*)

We will walk through some hypothetical data to illustrate the calculation of a correlation coefficient. Specifically, we will use data from 10 participants who completed a measure of anxiousness and self-reported the number of times they checked Facebook each day. Here are these hypothetical data for these 10 people:

Anxiousness Score	Number of Facebook Check-Ins per Day (Facebook Intensity)
35	3
75	5
50	4
40	4
55	1
35	3
80	7
60	6
50	2
70	5

In practice, we are interested in predicting Facebook usage from anxiety scores. Therefore, when making a scatterplot of these data, we will put scores on the variable of anxiousness on the x-axis and scores on the variable of Facebook check-ins each day on the y-axis. Figure 12.10 contains a scatterplot of these data. We will then calculate the statistic that summarizes this scatterplot.

Step 1: State hypotheses

H_o: There will be no relationship between anxiousness and the number of times people check Facebook each day.

H_r: There will be a relationship between anxiousness and the number of times people check Facebook each day.

Notationally, we have:

$$H_o: r = 0$$
$$H_r: r \neq 0$$

Notice that the research hypothesis is a two-tailed hypothesis. Of course, based on what we already know from Clayton et al.'s (2013) research, we expect anxious people to check Facebook more than less anxious people;

Figure 12.10 Scatterplot of the Relationship Between Anxiousness and Daily Facebook Check-Ins

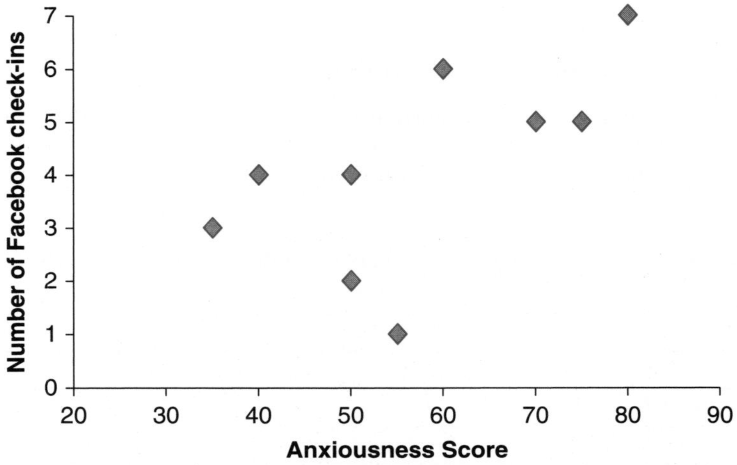

that is, we expect a positive correlation between anxiousness and the number of times people check Facebook each day. But as has been drilled into you in this class, a two-tailed hypothesis is more conservative than a one-tailed hypothesis.

Step 2: For both variables, find each participant's deviation score and then multiply them together

One way to think about a positive correlation is that, for each participant, scores on both variables tend to be above or below the means of both variables; that is, scores on both variables tend to deviate from their group means in the same way. Conversely, a negative correlation emerges when scores above the mean on one variable tend to be associated with scores below the mean on the other variable. That is, scores on the two variables tend to deviate from their group means in opposite ways.

So now, we need to find the mean for each variable, and then each participant's deviation score from the mean.

Anxiety Score *Mean = 55.0*	Anxiety Deviation Score	Facebook Intensity *Mean = 4.0*	Facebook Deviation Score
35	−20	3	−1
75	20	5	1
50	−5	4	0
40	−15	4	0
55	0	1	−3
35	−20	3	−1

Anxiety Score *Mean = 55.0*	**Anxiety Deviation Score**	**Facebook Intensity** *Mean = 4.0*	**Facebook Deviation Score**
80	25	7	3
60	5	6	2
50	−5	2	−2
70	15	5	1

We now need to multiply the two deviation scores that we just calculated:

Anxiety Score *Mean = 55.0*	**Anxiety Deviation Score**	**Facebook Intensity** *Mean = 4.0*	**Facebook Deviation Score**	**Product of Deviation Scores**
35	−20	3	−1	−20 × −1 = 20
75	20	5	1	20 × 1 = 20
50	−5	4	0	−5 × 0 = 0
40	−15	4	0	−15 × 0 = 0
55	0	1	−3	0 × −3 = 0
35	−20	3	−1	−20 × −1 = 20
80	25	7	3	25 × 3 = 75
60	5	6	2	5 × 2 = 10
50	−5	2	−2	−5 × −2 = 10
70	15	5	1	15 × 1 = 15

Step 3: Sum the products in step 2

We now simply sum the 10 products in the far right column of step 2:

$$= 20 + 20 + 0 + 0 + 0 + 20 + 75 + 10 + 10 + 15$$
$$= 170$$

What have we just calculated? Recall when we discussed analysis of variance (ANOVA) in the previous three chapters that we had a ratio of "between-groups" variability divided by "error" variability. What we have just done in steps 2 and 3 is find the correlational equivalent of between-groups variability. It will be the numerator of the ratio that provides us with the correlation coefficient, which we will calculate in step 6. Look closely at the products of deviation scores. Notice how they are all positive numbers (or zero)? As scores on one variable tend to be above that group mean, scores on the other variable also tend to be above that group mean (and vice versa). That should be a clue as to whether we will obtain a positive or negative correlation after our calculations are finished.

Now, we must calculate the correlational equivalent of error variability.

Step 4: Calculate the sums of squares for both variables

To get our sums of squares, we take each score's deviation from its group mean, and then square it.

Anxiety Score *Mean* = *55*	Anxiety Deviation Score	(Anxiety Deviation Score)^2	Facebook Intensity *Mean* = *4.0*	Facebook Deviation Score	(Facebook Deviation Score)^2
35	−20	400	3	−1	1
75	20	400	5	1	1
50	−5	25	4	0	0
40	−15	225	4	0	0
55	0	0	1	−3	9
35	−20	400	3	−1	1
80	25	625	7	3	9
60	5	25	6	2	4
50	−5	25	2	−2	4
70	15	225	5	1	1

Now we sum each column of squared deviation scores. For the anxiety deviation scores, we have:

$$= 400 + 400 + 25 + 225 + 0 + 400 + 625 + 25 + 25 + 225$$
$$= 2{,}350$$

And for the Facebook deviation scores, we have:

$$= 1 + 1 + 0 + 0 + 9 + 1 + 9 + 4 + 4 + 1$$
$$= 30$$

Step 5: Multiply the two sums of squares and then take the square root

(a) First, we multiply 2,350 by 30, which gives us 70,500

(b) Second, because we squared the deviations from the mean, we need to "unsquare" them; that is, take the square root of the quotient we just calculated. The square root of 70,500 is 265.52.

What we have just calculated in steps 4 and 5 (i.e., 265.52) is the denominator of the formula for the correlation coefficient. I realize I have not yet provided you with that formula. Please go to step 6 now.

Step 6: Calculate the correlation coefficient (r) test statistic

Here is the formula for the correlation coefficient:

$$r = \frac{\text{sum the product of the deviation scores in step 3}}{\sqrt{(\text{sums of squares for one variable} \times \text{sums of squares for the other variable})} \text{ in step 5b}}$$

To get our r for our data, let's plug our numbers into this formula:

$$r = \frac{170}{265.52}$$
$$r = .64$$

Step 7: Locate the critical value

As with our previous inferential statistical tools, we need to compare our test statistic to its critical value. Go to Appendix E, which contains the critical values for Pearson correlation coefficients. With a sample size of 10, our degrees of freedom are 8 (sample size – 2, just as it was for the independent samples t test). We see in Appendix E that for a two-tailed hypothesis with 8 degrees of freedom and an alpha of .05, our critical value is .632.

Step 8: Make a decision about the null hypothesis

Just as in previous chapters about inferential statistical tools, we reject the null hypothesis when the test statistic exceeds the critical value. We fail to reject the null hypothesis when the statistic is less than the critical value. Here, our test statistic of .64 exceeds the critical value of .632. Therefore, the test statistic falls in the region of null hypothesis rejection and we reject the null hypothesis. In plain English, as people tend to be more anxious, they are more likely to use Facebook. Furthermore, given Cohen's (1988) guidelines, this is a strong correlation between anxiousness and daily Facebook check-ins.

In the previous section, we interpreted correlations when they were presented in a correlation matrix. Sometimes researchers report correlations in textual format. Here is how to do so:

> There was a positive correlation between anxiousness and Facebook intensity, $r(8) = .64$, $p < .05$.

Notice that, just as with t tests, the degrees of freedom appear in parentheses immediately after the statistical symbol.

Before we enter the next Learning Check, I want to make you aware that in the next chapter, we will be extending our discussion of correlations to learn more precisely how we use correlational data to make predictions. We will encounter this same dataset again not only in the next section of this chapter, but in the next chapter as well.

LEARNING CHECK

1. In our example data, suppose each participant checked Facebook four times each day. If that was the case, what would the correlation have been between loneliness and the number of Facebook check-ins each day?

   A: It would be impossible to calculate a correlation because there is now only one variable. If every participant checked Facebook four times each day, then it is no longer a variable; rather, it is a constant and cannot be analyzed. This is an example (and an extreme example at that) of range restriction that we discussed earlier.

2. Suppose Clayton et al. (2013) had included a measure of extraversion as a predictor of Facebook intensity. Extraversion is one's tendency to seek out social stimulation in the form of other people and social events, such as parties. Extraversion can be measured with an instrument like the one that Paul Costa and Robert McCrae (2008) developed. Their extraversion measure contains items such as "I like to be where the action is," to which people respond using a 1 (*not at all descriptive of me*) to 7 (*very much descriptive of me*) response range. Below are hypothetical data for 10 participants. Use these data to calculate the correlation between extraversion and the number of times people check Facebook each day.

(Continued)

(Continued)

Extraversion Score	Facebook Intensity
6	4
3	2
3	5
2	3
4	1
4	6
5	2
5	7
1	3
7	2

Answer the following questions:

a) What is the hypothesis that is being tested?

A: H_0: There will be no relationship between extraversion and the number of times people check Facebook each day.

b) What is the mean of each variable?

A:

$$M_{\text{extraversion}} = 4.0$$
$$M_{\text{Facebook}} = 3.5$$

c) What is the *r* test statistic?

A: $r = .03$

d) How many degrees of freedom are there in this analysis?

A: $df = 8$

e) Use Appendix E to determine the critical value to compare the test statistic to.

A: When we use a two-tailed hypothesis test with an alpha of .05, we have a critical value of .6319.

f) Do we reject or fail to reject the null hypothesis?

A: Because the test statistic is less than the critical value, the test statistic falls outside the region of null hypothesis rejection. We fail to reject the null hypothesis.

g) Classify the strength of this relationship by using Cohen's (1988) guidelines.

A: $r = .03$ is a weak relationship.

h) What does this result mean in plain English?

A: There is no relationship between extraversion levels and frequency of checking Facebook each day.

i) Write this result in proper APA style.

A: There was no correlation between extraversion and frequency of checking Facebook each day, $r(8) = .03$, $p > .05$.

Just as a note of caution, the test statistic you calculated ($r = .03$) is obviously less than .05. However, please be careful to not confuse a weak correlation (of $r < .05$) with a p value of < .05; r and p refer to two different statistics."

The Pearson Correlation (*r*) and SPSS

Now that you are familiar with how to interpret and calculate correlations, let's see how to use this tool in SPSS. We will use the same dataset as we did in our hand calculations.

Anxiousness Score	Facebook Intensity
35	3
75	5
50	4
40	4
55	1
35	3
80	7
60	6
50	2
70	5

Establishing your spreadsheet

After opening SPSS, go to *Variable View* to set up your spreadsheet. We have two variables for which to enter data into SPSS. First, we have anxiety scores, and second, we have Facebook Intensity scores. Go ahead and provide a name and a label to each one. We do not need to provide values for either variable because both variables contain numeric data on a scale measurement. Here is about what your *Variable View* should look like:

*dataset for hand calcs.sav [DataSet1] - IBM SPSS Statistics Data Editor

File Edit View Data Transform Analyze Graphs Utilities Add-ons Window Help

	Name	Type	Width	Decimals	Label	Values	Missing	Columns	Align	Measure	Role
1	Anxiousness	Numeric	8	2	Anxiety Score	None	None	8	Right	Scale	Input
2	Facebook	Numeric	8	2	Facebook Intensity	None	None	8	Right	Scale	Input
3											
4											

Let's enter our data. Click on *Data View*, and then enter the data. As always, be extremely careful in this process; SPSS can only be helpful if we give it the correct data in the first place. After you enter the data from these 10 people, here is what your *Data View* should look like:

dataset for hand calcs.sav [DataSet1] - IBM SPSS Statistics Data Editor

File Edit View Data Transform Analyze Graphs Uti

11 : Anxiousness

	Anxiousness	Facebook	var	var
1	35.00	3.00		
2	75.00	5.00		
3	50.00	4.00		
4	40.00	4.00		
5	55.00	1.00		
6	35.00	3.00		
7	80.00	7.00		
8	60.00	6.00		
9	50.00	2.00		
10	70.00	5.00		
11				
12				
13				
14				
15				
16				
17				
18				
19				
20				
21				
22				
23				
24				
25				
26				
27				
28				
29				

Data View Variable View

Running your analysis

Now we are ready to generate our Pearson correlation coefficient. Here is how we do so:

1. Click on *Analyze → Correlate → Bivariate.*

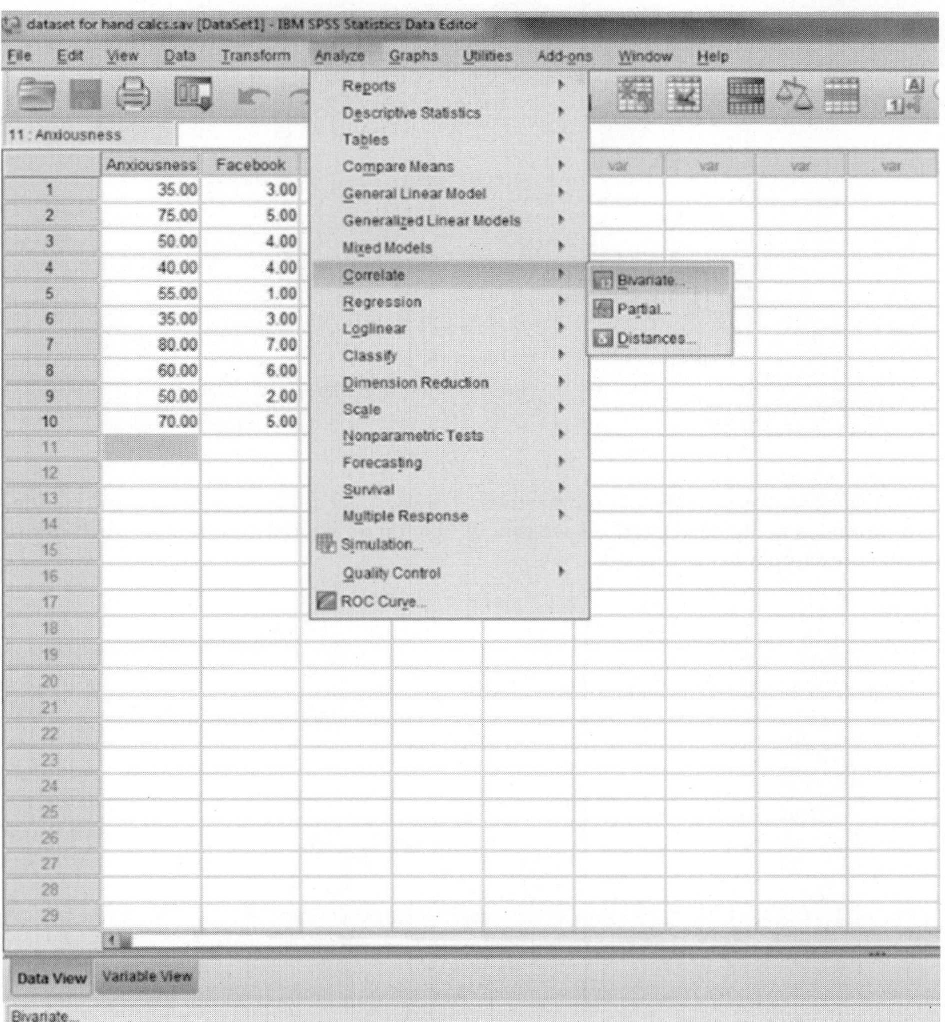

2. Click on *Anxiety Score* and *Facebook Intensity* in the *Variables* box.
3. There are several types of correlations, one more of which we will learn about in Chapter 14. Realize that SPSS's default is to the one we need here, the Pearson correlation. Notice that SPSS also automatically "flags" correlations that are significant at an alpha level of .05 or less.

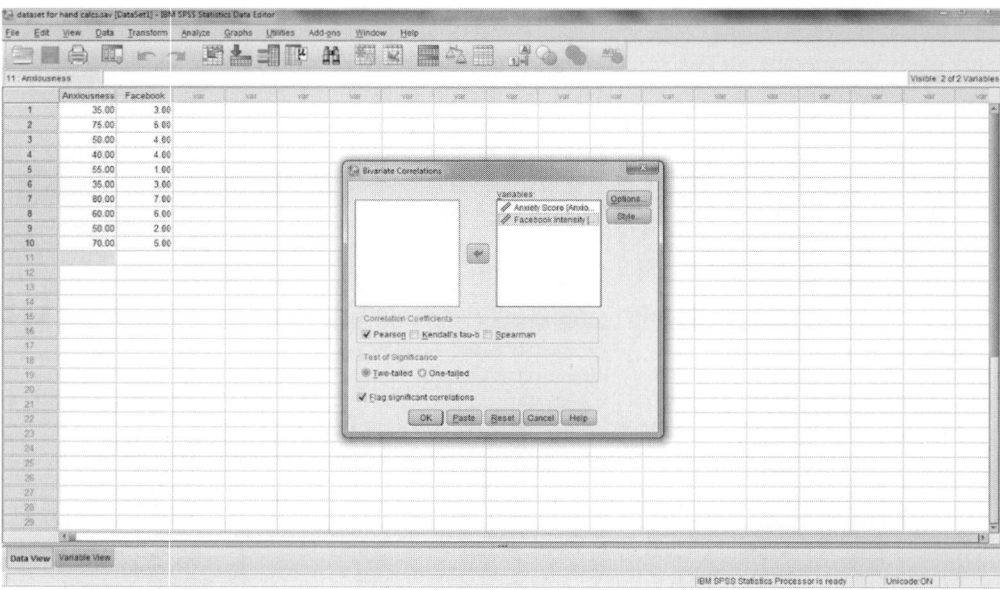

4. Click on *Options*. For the sake of completeness, I always like to have the means and standard deviations of the variables being correlated. As we saw in Clayton et al.'s (2013) research, such information helps describe the sample being studied.

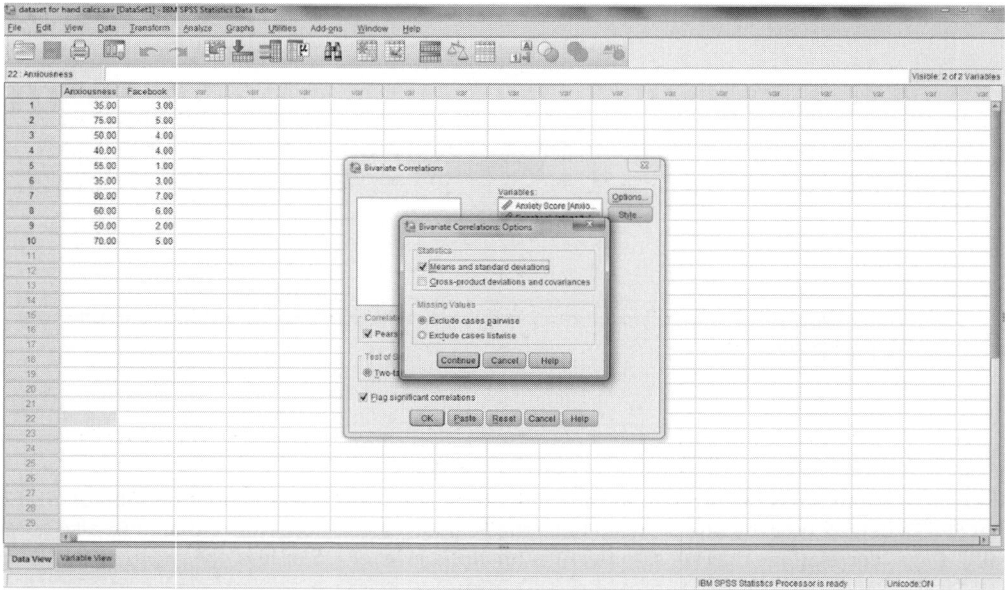

After clicking *Continue*, and then clicking *OK*, your output should appear and look like this:

Correlations

A

Descriptive Statistics

	Mean	Std. Deviation	N
Anxiety Score	55.0000	16.15893	10
Facebook Intensity	4.0000	1.82574	10

B

2

Correlations

		Anxiety Score	Facebook Intensity
Anxiety Score	Pearson Correlation	1	.640*
	Sig. (2-tailed)		.046
1	N	10	10
Facebook Intensity	Pearson Correlation	.640* ← a	1
	Sig. (2-tailed)	.046 ← b	
	N	10 ← c	10

*. Correlation is significant at the 0.05 level (2-tailed).

What am I looking at? Interpreting your SPSS output

Here is the information that SPSS has provided for us:

A. We have our descriptive statistics for the variables being correlated.

B. Here is our correlation matrix.

   1. Each row is one variable.

   2. Likewise, each column is also one variable.

What we need to do to determine the correlation between two variables is look for the intersection between the row of one variable and the column of the other variable. In this example, that is pretty simple to do. If we go to the first column (Facebook Intensity) and second row (Anxiety Score), we have three pieces of information presented to us:

a) *Pearson Correlation* is exactly that, the correlation between the two measures.

b) *Sig. (2-tailed)* is the significance level of the correlation coefficient. It is the p value you see reported in research. Here, that value is $p = .046$.

c) *N* is the number of people who completed both measures being correlated.

There is one caution I want to issue as you examine this SPSS output. As mentioned at the end of the previous Learning Check, please do not confuse the correlation coefficient with the p value. I see my students do so all too often, and it is easy to make this mistake. After all, both pieces of information are always no greater than 1.0. Just read the output carefully, and you should be fine.[4]

Before you close this SPSS spreadsheet, please save it so that you can use it again. We will need it in the next chapter.

LEARNING CHECK

Kevin Zabel and his colleagues (Zabel, Christopher, Marek, Wieth, & Carlson, 2009) conducted a study in which they asked people to invest hypothetical money among mutual fund choices that varied in how risky they were. That is, some mutual funds offered potential for large payoffs but carried a lot of risk, whereas other mutual funds were fairly safe investments but offered less chance for large payoffs. Zabel et al. wanted to see whether people's age and sensation-seeking tendencies were correlated with the riskiness of the investments selected. Sensation was measured with the Hoyle, Stephenson, Palmgreen, Lorch, and Donohew (2002) 8-item Brief Sensation Seeking Scale on which participants responded to items such as "I would love to have new and exciting experiences, even if they are illegal" on a 1 (*not at all characteristic of me*) to 7 (*extremely characteristic of me*) response range. Here is the SPSS output from their analyses:

Correlations

Descriptive Statistics

	Mean	Std. Deviation	N
Age	35.8717	18.95206	265
Sensation Seeking	3.4034	1.28190	298
Risk-taking	9.2620	3.45799	294

Correlations

		Age	Sensation Seeking	Risk-taking
Age	Pearson Correlation	1	-.589**	-.225**
	Sig. (2-tailed)		.000	.000
	N	265	265	260
Sensation Seeking	Pearson Correlation	-.589**	1	.239**
	Sig. (2-tailed)	.000		.000
	N	265	298	293
Risk-taking	Pearson Correlation	-.225**	.239**	1
	Sig. (2-tailed)	.000	.000	
	N	260	293	294

**. Correlation is significant at the 0.01 level (2-tailed).

Answer the following questions:

1. Why is the correlation between the first row (variable `Age`) and the first column (variable `Age`) precisely 1?

   A: That's because it is reporting a correlation between `Age` (in the first row) and `Age` (in the first column). This is simply a function of how SPSS generates a correlation matrix. If you look carefully at this matrix, you will see that it contains the correlations between all of the variables in two separate places in the matrix. For example, the correlation between `Age` and `Sensation Seeking` is $r = -.589$. This correlation is displayed twice in the matrix, just so you know what's going on.

2. What is the mean age of participants in this sample?

   A: 35.87 years old

3. What is the correlation between age and risk taking?

   A: $r = -.225$ (rounded to $r = -.23$)

4. Is this correlation statistically significant? How do you know?

   A: yes, it is statistically significant because the p value is less than .05

5. SPSS says the p value is .000. Why should the p value be reported as "$p < .001$" in an APA style write-up?

   A: Because the p value indicates the probability that a result we obtained in the sample was due to random variation and is not a true effect in the population. There can never be a 0% chance of random variation explaining a statistical outcome, so we must report some probability, no matter how small, of this being the case.

6. Interpret the correlation between `Age` and `Risk-taking` in plain English.

   A: As people get older, they tend to take fewer risks with their investments.

7. How many people completed the measures of `Sensation Seeking` and `Risk-taking`?

   A: 293

NOTES

1. Be aware that we can use our other statistical tools, such as *t* tests and ANOVAs, to analyze data from naturally occurring groups. For instance, suppose you wanted to study life satisfaction among college first-years, sophomores, juniors, and seniors. You would have life satisfaction as an outcome variable and year in college as the predictor variable. Most researchers would analyze these data by using a one-way between-subjects ANOVA with four groups. These are naturally occurring groups because students cannot be randomly assigned to a year in college. The point here is that any statistical tool can be used to analyze naturally occurring relationships between variables; it is the research question and design under consideration that determine what statistical tool is needed.

2. To classify an instance as an "outlier," researchers typically see how many standard deviations an instance is from its mean. For example, an outlier could be operationalized as being 2 standard deviations above or below the group mean.

3. There are advanced statistical tools beyond the scope of our discussion that are available to see whether we may have a curvilinear relationship between two variables. If you are interested in such tools, a good place to start learning about them is Brett Pelham's (2013) book, *Intermediate Statistics*, and in particular, pages 96–99 of that book.

4. We mentioned earlier in this chapter the notion of a Cronbach's alpha, which is a commonly reported statistic of a measurement's internal reliability. You can generate this statistic using SPSS. However, to do so, you must enter scores from each item on the measurement tool. For our illustrative purposes, we entered only the composite anxiety score. If you are interested in learning to calculate a Cronbach's alpha using SPSS, see the Addendum to this chapter.

CHAPTER APPLICATION QUESTIONS

1. What is the difference between a predictor variable and an outcome (criterion) variable?
2. How does a point-biserial correlation differ from a Pearson correlation?
3. Why are correlations useful in a study of naturally occurring phenomena, such as SES?
4. Why do outliers make it difficult to interpret relationships between variables?
5. A researcher observed that drinking coffee improved performance on complex math problems up to a point. The researcher also noted, however, that excessive coffee drinking interferes with problem solving. What type of relationship was observed?

   a) positive linear
   b) negative linear
   c) curvilinear linear
   d) counterintuitive

6. You would probably find a **NEGATIVE** correlation between:

   a) the number of hours studying for a test and scores on that test.
   b) distance from the equator and average daily high temperature.
   c) caffeine consumption and blood pressure.
   d) height and weight

7. If two variables are related so that as values of one variable increases, the values of the other also tend to increase, then the relationship is said to be:

   a) positive
   b) negative
   c) curvilinear
   d) spurious

8. The type (direction) of a linear relationship between two variables is given by _____ of *r*.

   a) the numerical value
   b) the plus or minus sign
   c) both the sign and the numerical value
   d) neither the sign nor the numerical value

9. A perfect linear relationship of variables *X* and *Y* would result in a value of *r* equal to:

   a) zero
   b) a large value but not +1.00 or −1.00
   c) a small value but not zero
   d) either +1.00 or −1.00

10. For the test for significance of a correlation, the null hypothesis states:

    a) the population correlation is zero
    b) the population correlation is not zero
    c) the sample correlation is zero
    d) the sample correlation is not zero

11. A psychologist has found a correlation of .54 between measures of need for achievement and college grade-point average. Given this knowledge, you would expect that:

a) if you knew a student's need for achievement score, you could predict the student's grade point average perfectly.

b) as need for achievement scores decrease, there is a tendency for college grade point to decrease.

c) as need for achievement scores increase, there is a tendency for college grade point to decrease.

d) there is no relationship between need for achievement and college grade point average.

12. There is a reliable correlation between being outgoing and being satisfied with life. This may be explained if the variable "having more friends" leads people to be both more outgoing and more satisfied with life. In this example, "having more friends" is called a(n) _____ variable, and the resulting correlation may be a(n) _____ correlation.

    a) independent; illusory
    b) independent; spurious
    c) third; illusory
    d) third; spurious

13. What are the degrees of freedom for a Pearson correlation calculated with a sample size of 55 people?

    a) 57
    b) 55
    c) 54
    d) 53

Answers

1. The predictor variable is the one for which we have information we are using to make a prediction. The outcome (criterion) variable is what we want to predict with the information that we have.
2. The point-biserial correlation is a correlation between two variables when one variable is measured on a nominal (categorical) scale, and the other variable is a scale variable.
3. It is not practical to manipulate certain variables, such as SES. It would be meaningless to use random assignment to assign people to different levels of SES. It would be meaningful, however, to study SES as a naturally occurring variable.
4. Outliers tend to stand out in our minds, so even when we see data that suggest a relationship between variables in the population, we question it because outliers are easier to understand than are data. For instance, I knew someone who smoked all his life and lived to be 98 years old. So, smoking can't be all that bad, right? Well, of course, this person was an outlier, but as I knew him personally, that relationship makes more of an impression on my judgment (potentially) than hearing about research establishing a relationship between smoking and premature death.
5. c
6. b
7. a
8. b
9. d
10. a
11. b
12. d
13. d

QUESTIONS FOR CLASS DISCUSSION

1. How is a positive correlation different from a negative correlation?
2. How does a Phi coefficient differ from a Pearson correlation?
3. Here are four correlation coefficients: –.05, .26, –.97, .84. Put them in order, showing the strongest to weakest relationship.
4. Why does the notion of a spurious correlation make interpreting a correlation between two variables difficult?

ADDENDUM TO CHAPTER 12

Obtaining a Cronbach's Alpha Using SPSS

Please open the SPSS dataset titled "Cronbach's Alpha and SPSS." We will use it to calculate a Cronbach's alpha using SPSS.

These data are from Zabel et al.'s (2009) research. They are the scores for each of the eight items of the sensation-seeking measure that they used, for all participants in their research. When calculating Cronbach's alpha using SPSS, you must have the scores from every item on a measurement tool. In this book, we have focused primarily on using total scores on measurement tools for the sake of illustrating various statistical tools using SPSS. But for calculating a Cronbach's alpha using SPSS, again, you must have each participant's score on each item on the measurement tool.

Here is how to generate a Cronbach's alpha using SPSS.

1. Click on *Analysis* → *Scale* → *Reliability Analysis*.

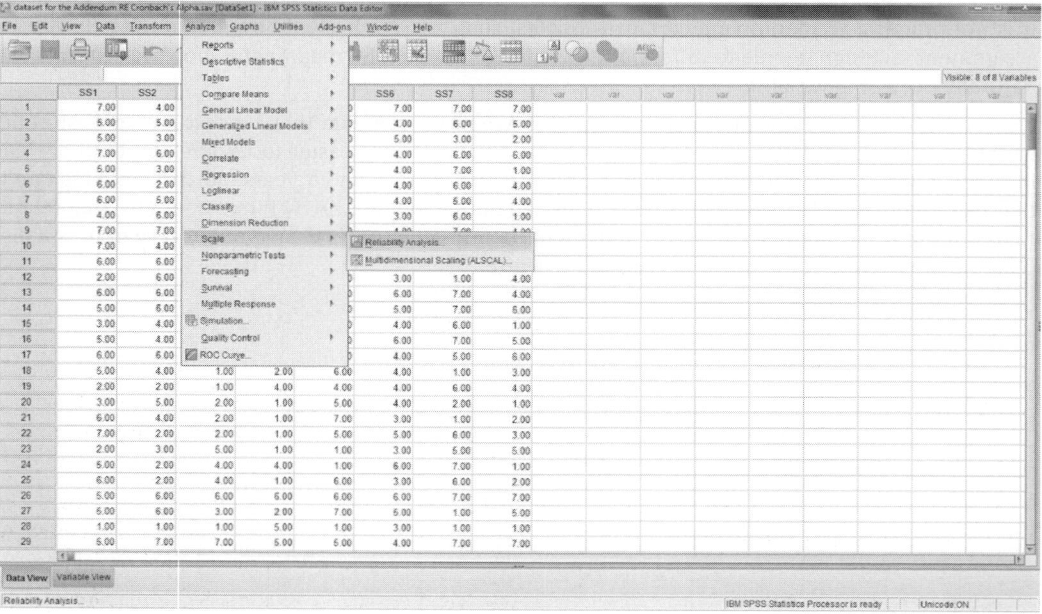

2. Enter each item for the scale into the *Items:* dialogue box.

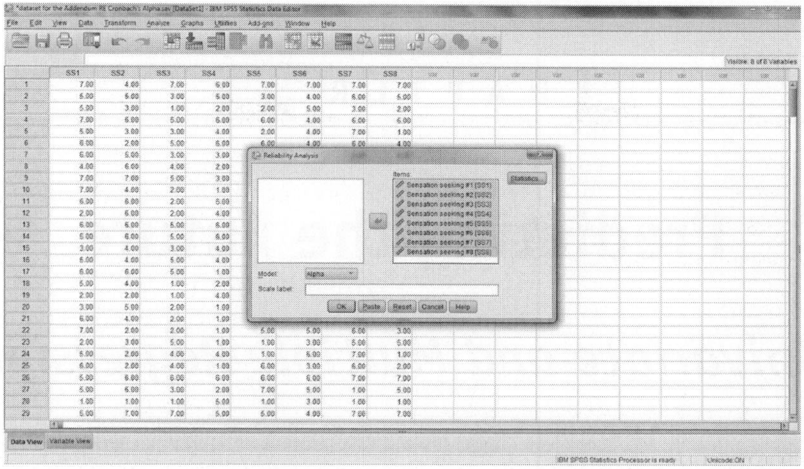

3. Click *OK*, and here should be your output:

Reliability

Scale: ALL VARIABLES

Case Processing Summary

		N	%
Cases	Valid	289	96.7
	Excluded[a]	10	3.3
	Total	299	100.0

a. Listwise deletion based on all variables in the procedure.

A

Reliability Statistics

Cronbach's Alpha	N of Items
.811	8

B C

Let's make sense of what SPSS had provided us.

A. Here we have sample summary statistics. Specifically, the total sample was 299, but 10 people were excluded. This happened because each of these 10 people did not complete all eight items on the measurement scale. Thus, the analysis is based on 289 datapoints.

B. Here is the Cronbach's alpha. In addition to seeing it presented in correlation matrices, as we discussed earlier in this chapter, sometimes you will see it reported in the text of a research article as α. So here, we have $\alpha = .81$.

C. This is simply the number of items in the analysis. We knew it was eight going into the analysis, but it's always good to check this number to make sure we did not leave out or include any extra items that aren't supposed to be involved in the analysis.

CHAPTER 13

Predicting the Future

Univariate and Multiple Regression

After reading this chapter, you will be able to

- Understand the components of a univariate regression equation
- Conduct a univariate regression analysis using SPSS
- Conduct and interpret SPSS output for a univariate regression equation
- Understand the components of a multiple regression equation
- Conduct a multiple regression equation using SPSS
- Conduct and interpret SPSS output for a multiple regression equation

In the previous chapter, we learned about the Pearson correlation coefficient (*r*). We discussed several uses for this statistical tool, one of which was that it is the basis for making predictions about one variable (called the outcome variable or criterion) based on information from a second variable (called the predictor variable). In that chapter, I promised you that we would expand on using correlations to make predictions in this chapter. Without further ado, let's get started on learning how to make predictions using a new statistical tool called regression.

We will learn two types of regression by continuing our discussion of Russell Clayton and colleagues' (Clayton, Osborne, Miller, & Oberle, 2013) research on predictors of Facebook intensity. We will first extend our knowledge of correlations to what is called univariate regression, which allows us to make predictions based on one predictor variable. Then, we will learn a second tool called multiple regression, which allows us to make predictions based on two or more predictor variables.

In the previous chapter, we discussed a tool that allowed us to learn the strength and type (direction) of a relationship between two variables. Correlations are the basis for making predictions, and in this chapter, we will focus on this use of correlations. Knowing that, for instance, high-school grade-point average (GPA) is positively correlated with academic performance in college is wonderful, but through using regression techniques, we can derive an equation that will allow us to predict a student's academic performance in college using his or her high-school GPA.

UNIVARIATE REGRESSION

In a situation in which we have one predictor variable, such as high-school GPA, we use **univariate regression** to predict the outcome variable, in this case, academic performance in college.

Univariate regression: statistical tool in which we use one predictor variable to forecast scores on an outcome variable.

Ingredients

In a nutshell, with univariate regression, we use data from a predictor variable (which if you recall is placed on the *x*-axis of a scatterplot) and an outcome variable (placed on the *y*-axis of a scatterplot) to calculate an equation for a linear relationship. Then, we can take any score from the predictor variable and find a predicted score on the outcome variable. Sounds pretty simple, doesn't it?

Before we jump into calculating a regression equation, let's illustrate what we will be doing. We used these data to hand-calculate a correlation coefficient in the previous chapter:

Anxiousness Score	Number of Facebook Check-ins per Day (Facebook Intensity)
35	3
75	5
50	4
40	4
55	1
35	3
80	7
60	6
50	2
70	5

Take a look at Figure 13.1, which displays the scatterplot of these data that we first saw in Figure 12.10. In the previous chapter, we found a statistically significant correlation coefficient of .64. Furthermore, the linear relationship between anxiety and number of Facebook check-ins each day means that we can draw a straight line through these data to represent their relationship. This is a **regression line**; as you see in Figure 13.1, it best represents the relationship between our two variables. The regression line summarizes the relationship between the two variables by passing through the center of the scatterplot. Of course, as you see in Figure 13.1, not all datapoints fall on the regression line. The total distance of those points below the line equals the total distance of those points above the line. Think of the regression line as a summary of all the datapoints.

Regression line: straight line that best fits (summarizes) the datapoints in a scatterplot. Also call the line of best fit.

Figure 13.1 Regression Line (Also Called "Line of Best Fit") on a Scatterplot

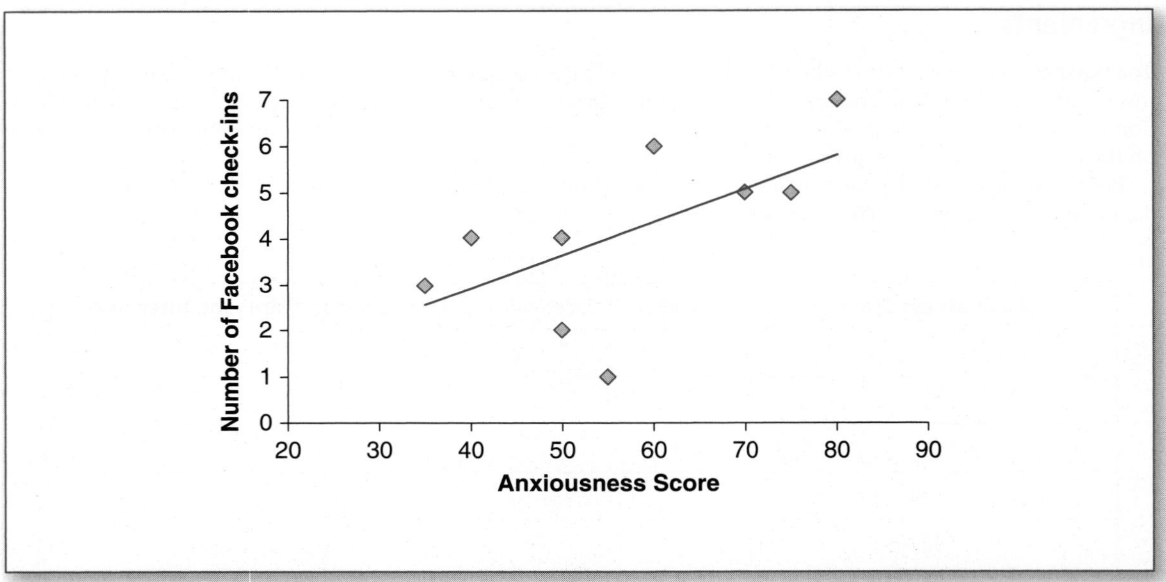

Whether by hand or using the software program Statistical Package for the Social Sciences (SPSS), we will be determining the regression line for our data. The equation for the regression line might look familiar from geometry or algebra classes. For regression, only the symbols differ:

$$\hat{Y} = b(x) + a$$

where

$\hat{Y}$ is the predicted value on the outcome variable

b is the slope of the line

x is an individual score on the predictor variable

a is the y-intercept

Hand-Calculating a Univariate Regression

We will use the same data from the previous chapter to hand-calculate a univariate regression equation so that we take anxiety scores (the predictor variable) and predict the daily number of Facebook check-ins (the outcome variable).

Anxiousness Score	Facebook Intensity
35	3
75	5
50	4
40	4
55	1
35	3
80	7
60	6
50	2
70	5

Step 1: Calculate the slope of the line (*b*)

We must calculate the slope of the line first as it is a necessary component for calculating the y-intercept. Here is the formula for calculating the slope:

$$b = r \times \frac{\text{standard deviation of the outcome variable}}{\text{standard deviation of the predictor variable}}$$

We calculated the correlation coefficient in the previous chapter. It was $r = .64$. Now, we did not calculate the standard deviation of the predictor and outcome variables, but we came close. If you look back at step 4 for hand-calculating the correlation coefficient, you will see that for the anxiety deviation scores, we had a sum of squares of 2,350, and for the Facebook check-ins deviation scores, we had a sum of squares of 30.

Recall our standard deviation formula using sum of squares from Chapter 4, and we have:

For anxiety: $\sqrt{\frac{2{,}350}{10-1}}$

standard deviation = 16.15893

For Facebook check-ins: $\sqrt{\frac{30}{10-1}}$

standard deviation = 1.82574

We now have all three ingredients needed to calculate the slope of our regression line:

$$\begin{aligned} b &= .64 \times \frac{1.82574}{16.15893} \\ &= .64 \times 0.112986442 \\ &= 0.072311323 \end{aligned}$$

If she loves you more each and every day,
by linear regression she hated you before you met.

Source: http://stdioe.blogspot.com/2013/08/linear-regression-revisited.html; http://www.smbc-comics.com/?id=2328

Step 2: Calculate the *y*-intercept (*a*)

Here is the formula for the *y*-intercept:

$$a = \text{Mean of the outcome variable} - (\text{slope} \times \text{mean of the predictor variable})$$

We just calculated the slope, and we calculated the means for each variable in the previous chapter. So, we now have our ingredients to calculate the *y*-intercept:

Mean of the outcome (Facebook) variable = 4.0

Slope (b) = 0.072311323

Mean of the predictor (anxiousness) variable = 55.0

$$a = 4 - (0.072311323 \times 55)$$

$$a = 4 - (3.977122765)$$

$$a = 0.023$$

Thus, our regression equation is:

$$\hat{Y}\text{(daily Facebook check-ins)} = 0.072 \times \text{score on anxiety measure} + 0.023$$

Step 3: Make predictions

Now that we have our equation, we use it to predict how many times a person will check Facebook each day, based on his or her anxiety score. Suppose a person had an anxiety score of 50. By using the equation we just derived, we would have:

$$
\begin{aligned}
\text{Predicted Daily Facebook check-ins} &= 0.072\,(50) + 0.023 \\
&= 3.60 + 0.023 \\
&= 3.623
\end{aligned}
$$

Thus, if a person has an anxiety score of 50, we would predict his or her daily number of Facebook check-ins to be 3.623.

For a person with an anxiety score of 30, what would we predict that person's daily number of Facebook check-ins to be? If you got 2.183, excellent work!

Univariate Regression and SPSS

Let's now use SPSS to perform univariate regression by using our same dataset with anxiousness and daily number of Facebook check-ins. You will be pleased to know that you have already set up your *Variable View* and your *Data View*. We can use the SPSS spreadsheet that you created in the SPSS section of the previous chapter. If you did not save that spreadsheet or cannot locate it, you will need to set it up again. If you need assistance doing so, please review the section titled "The Pearson Correlation (r) and SPSS" in Chapter 12.

Running your analysis

Once you have opened your spreadsheet from the previous chapter or have reestablished it, we are in position to conduct our univariate regression. To do so:

1. Click on *Analysis* → *Regression* → *Linear*.

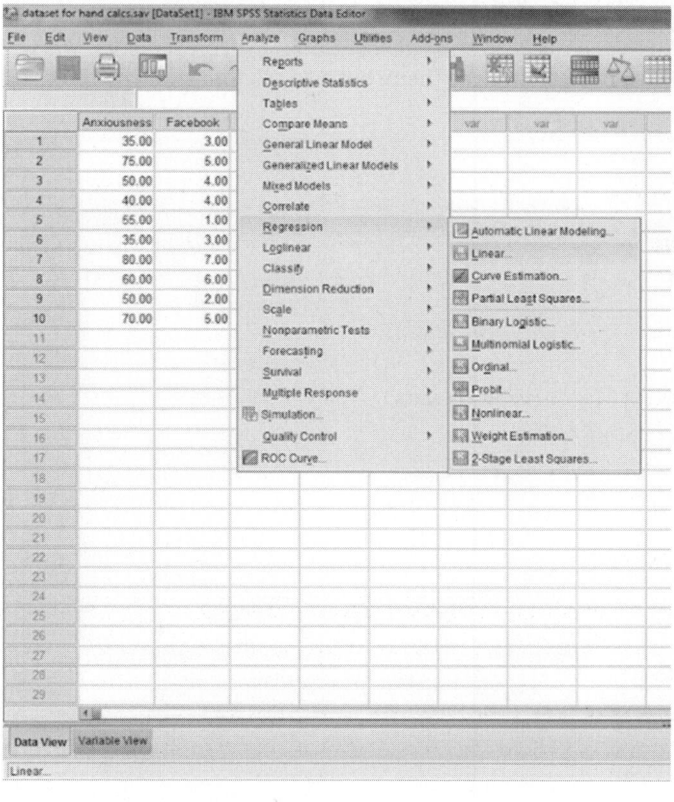

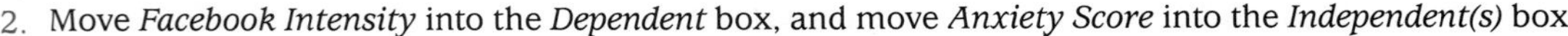

2. Move *Facebook Intensity* into the *Dependent* box, and move *Anxiety Score* into the *Independent(s)* box.

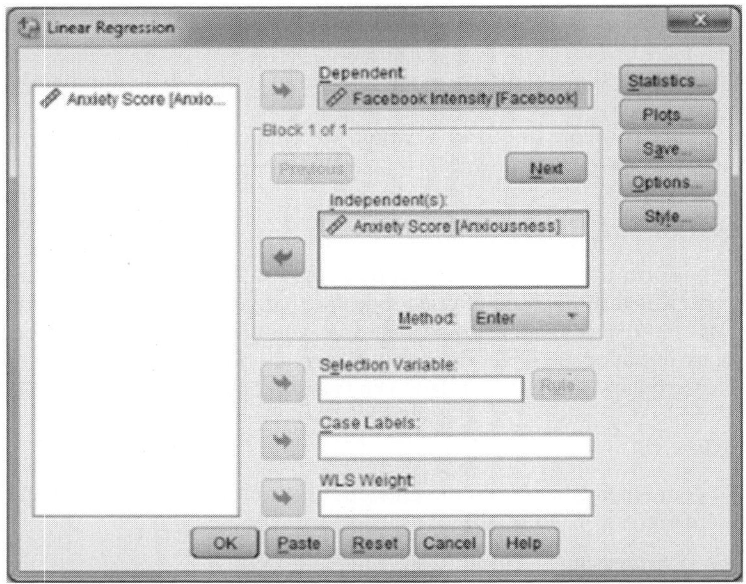

3. On the right side of the *Linear Regression* dialogue box, click on *Statistics.* You will see that *Estimates* and *Model Fit* are selected by default. Keep them, but also ask for *Confidence Intervals*, with a *95% Level*.

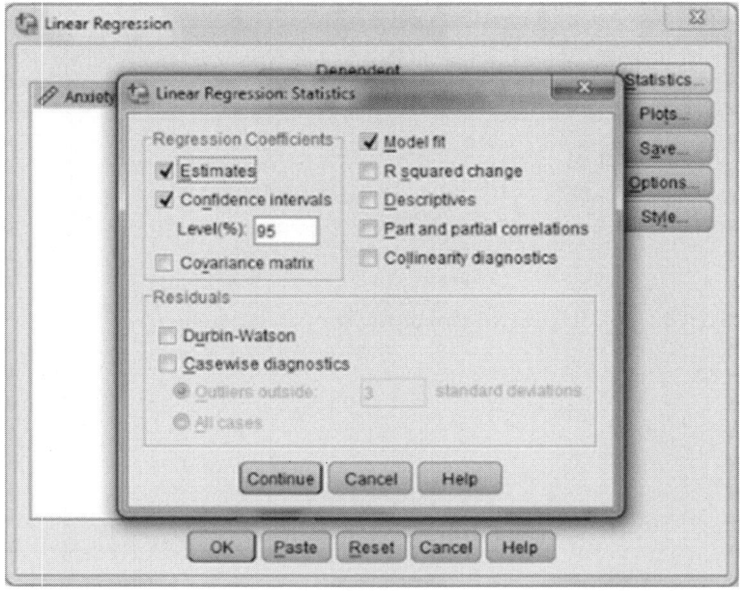

4. Click *Continue*, and then *OK*. Your output will look like this:

Regression

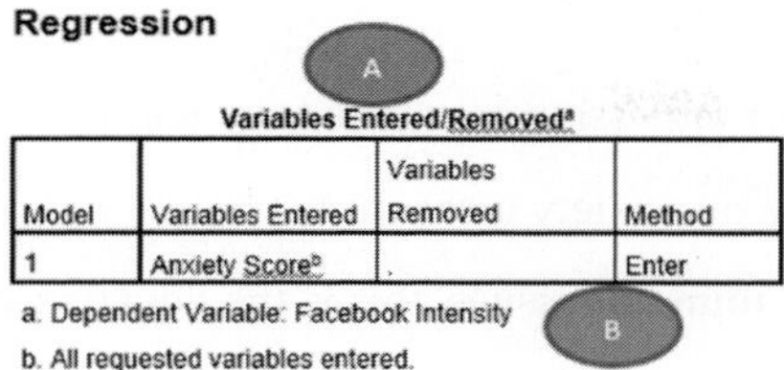

Variables Entered/Removed[a]

Model	Variables Entered	Variables Removed	Method
1	Anxiety Score[b]	.	Enter

a. Dependent Variable: Facebook Intensity

b. All requested variables entered.

Model Summary

Model	R	R Square	Adjusted R Square	Std. Error of the Estimate
1	.640[a]	.410	.336	1.48754

a. Predictors: (Constant), Anxiety Score

ANOVA[a]

Model		Sum of Squares	df	Mean Square	F	Sig.
1	Regression	12.298	1	12.298	5.558	.046[b]
	Residual	17.702	8	2.213		
	Total	30.000	9			

a. Dependent Variable: Facebook Intensity

b. Predictors: (Constant), Anxiety Score

Coefficients[a]

Model		Unstandardized Coefficients		Standardized Coefficients	t	Sig.	95.0% Confidence Interval for B	
		B	Std. Error	Beta			Lower Bound	Upper Bound
1	(Constant)	.021	1.752		.012	.991	-4.019	4.061
	Anxiety Score	.072	.031	.640	2.357	.046	.002	.143

a. Dependent Variable: Facebook Intensity

What am I looking at? Interpreting your SPSS output

Here is the information that SPSS has provided us:

A. This is the *predictor variable* that has been entered into the equation. With univariate regression, there is only one predictor. When we learn about multiple regression in the next section of this chapter, there will be more than one predictor variable in this area of the output.

B. This is the *outcome variable*, the variable that we are trying to predict.

C. This is the *R*-squared (R^2). I bet that was obvious. R^2 *is the percentage of variability in the outcome variable that is accounted for by the predictor variable(s).* In univariate regression, it is calculated by taking the correlation coefficient and squaring it (hence, the name R^2). Our correlation was .64, and $.64^2 = .4096$, so with rounding, SPSS tells us that 41% of the variability in Facebook intensity scores were accounted for by anxiety scores.

D. SPSS calls the predictor variable(s) entered into the regression equation a `Model`. In our case, our model consists of one predictor variable, `Anxiety Scores`. In addition, you see a `(Constant)` in the model. That is going to be important in just a moment as it is relevant to our *y*-intercept.

E. Here we have two important pieces of information. First, for the `(Constant)` row, the value of .021 is our y-intercept.[1] Second, for the `Anxiety Scores` row, the value of .072 is the slope of our regression line.

At this point, we have the information that we need to write our regression equation. Here it is:

$$\hat{Y}\text{ (daily Facebook check-ins)} = 0.072 \times \text{score on anxiety measure} + 0.021$$

Aside from the y-intercept being slightly different because of rounding issues, this is the equation we calculated in the previous section.

F. This is the *standard error of the slope* of the line. Think of the slope as a mean value around which our data are dispersed. The standard error of the slope serves the same purpose as a standard deviation serves with its mean. It is a measure of variability around the value of the slope.

G. The *standardized regression coefficient* is the predicted change in the outcome variable in terms of standard deviations for a 1 standard deviation increase in the predictor variable. It is reported in research with the symbol β and is often called a "beta" or a "beta weight." It is "standardized" because, just like z scores (see Chapter 5), it is measured in standard deviation units. Therefore, no matter how a predictor variable was measured, the standardized regression coefficient allows us to see the strength of the relationship between a predictor and an outcome in a "common measurement language" of standard deviation units. Let's discuss its calculation now.

To calculate a beta weight, we use this formula:

$$\beta = \text{slope} \times \frac{\text{square root of sum of squares of the predictor variable}}{\text{square root of the sum of squares of the outcome variable}}$$

We calculated the slope in the previous section (and yes, it appeared previously on this output as well). We calculated the sums of squares for anxiety scores and for Facebook intensity in the previous chapter. For anxiety scores, sum of squares was 2,350, and for Facebook intensity, it was 30. Let's plug these ingredients into our formula for the beta weight:

$$\begin{aligned}\beta &= 0.072 \times \sqrt{\frac{2{,}350}{30}} \\ &= 0.072 \times \frac{48.4768}{5.4772} \\ &= 0.072 \times 8.85065 \\ &= 0.64\end{aligned}$$

Recall that the correlation between anxiety scores and Facebook intensity was .64. In univariate regression, the correlation coefficient and the standardized beta weight will be the same. This will not be the case in the next section when we discuss multiple regression.

H. In regression, researchers typically do not report a t test statistic as they do with t tests (Chapters 7 and 8). However, just be aware SPSS gives you one for the constant and each predictor variable in the equation. This t test statistic is calculated as follows:

$$t = \frac{\text{Unstandardized beta weight}}{\text{Standard error of the unstandardized beta weight}}$$

So for our predictor variable of anxiety scores, the t of 2.357 was calculated as such:[2]

$$2.357 = \frac{0.072}{0.031}$$

I. This is the *p value of the standardized regression coefficient* (β). It tells us whether the predictor variable is a statistically significant predictor of the outcome variable. This p value of .046 is the same as it was when we ran the correlation between these two variables in SPSS in the previous chapter. This will not be the case in the next section when we discuss multiple regression.

J. Here is the *95% confidence interval for the slope* of the equation.

Before working on the Learning Check, please be sure you save this SPSS spreadsheet. We will use it yet again later in this chapter.

LEARNING CHECK

1. Explain the concept of a regression line.

   A: It is the line that illustrates the nature of the relationship between two variables. It is the line above which there is the same amount of distance as there is below that line; from this perspective, the regression line is similar to a mean.

2. Use the following regression equation to predict the yearly salary (in thousands) from the number of years of higher education:

$$\hat{Y} = 3X + 22$$

   a) Jeremy has had 0 years of higher education. Estimate his annual salary.

      A: 22 ($22,000)

   b) Andrea has had 11 years of higher education. Estimate her annual salary.

      A: 55 ($55,000)

   c) What is the slope of this regression equation?

      A: 3 ($3,000)

   d) What is the *y*-intercept of this regression equation?

      A: 22 ($22,000)

3. In the previous chapter, we used data from Kevin Zabel et al. (Zabel, Christopher, Marek, Wieth, & Carlson, 2009) in the Learning Check to check our understanding of correlations using SPSS. We will again use their research here to check our understanding of univariate regression using SPSS. As a refresher on this research, recall that these researchers conducted a study in which they asked people to invest hypothetical money among mutual fund choices that varied in how risky they were. That is, some mutual funds offered potential for large payoffs but carried a lot of risk, whereas other mutual funds were fairly safe investments but offered less chance for large payoffs. For our purposes discussing univariate regression, Zabel et al. wanted to see whether people's age predicted the riskiness of the investments selected. Here is the SPSS output from their analyses:

(Continued)

(Continued)

Regression

Variables Entered/Removed[a]

Model	Variables Entered	Variables Removed	Method
1	Age[b]	.	Enter

a. Dependent Variable: Risk-taking

b. All requested variables entered.

Model Summary

Model	R	R Square	Adjusted R Square	Std. Error of the Estimate
1	.225[a]	.051	.047	3.26911

a. Predictors: (Constant), Age

ANOVA[a]

Model		Sum of Squares	df	Mean Square	F	Sig.
1	Regression	146.993	1	146.993	13.754	.000[b]
	Residual	2757.271	258	10.687		
	Total	2904.264	259			

a. Dependent Variable: Risk-taking

b. Predictors: (Constant), Age

Coefficients[a]

Model		Unstandardized Coefficients		Standardized Coefficients	t	Sig.
		B	Std. Error	Beta		
1	(Constant)	10.702	.440		24.343	.000
	Age	-.041	.011	-.225	-3.709	.000

a. Dependent Variable: Risk-taking

a) What is the predictor variable in this analysis?

A: age

b) What is the outcome variable in this analysis?

A: risk-taking

c) What percentage of variability in the outcome variable was accounted for by the predictor variable?

A: 5.1%; you can see this number (.051) in the *R Square of the Model Summary* box.

d) Write the regression equation for this analysis.

A: Risk-taking = −0.041 × age + 10.702

e) Interpret the standardized beta coefficient in plain English.

A: The $\beta = -.225$ means that for a 1 standard deviation increase in age, we can expect risk-taking scores to decline by .225 standard deviations. We can expect risk-taking to decline because the sign of the β is negative.

f) Is age a statistically significant predictor of risk-taking? How do you know?

A: Yes, age is a statistically significant predictor of risk-taking because the *p* value associated with the standardized beta coefficient is less than .05.

g) How was the *t* test statistic calculated? Plug in the appropriate numbers to the appropriate formula.

A:
$$t = \frac{B}{SE_B}$$

$$t = \frac{-0.041}{0.011}$$

MULTIPLE REGRESSION

In many research situations, there will be more than one predictor variable of interest. In such situations, we need to understand the logic behind **multiple regression**. Whereas univariate regression uses one predictor variable, multiple regression uses two or more predictor variables to forecast an outcome variable. In a sense, univariate regression is similar to one-way analyses of variance (ANOVAs; see Chapters 9 and 10) in that both analyses have one predictor or independent variable. Multiple regression is similar to factorial ANOVAs (see Chapter 11) in that both analyses have two or more predictor or independent variables.

Multiple regression: statistical tool in which we use two or more predictor variables to forecast scores on an outcome variable.

Understanding Multiple Regression in Research

When using multiple regression, we are still generating an equation to predict some outcome. But now that outcome is a linear *combination of predictor variables*. As we discussed when learning about factorial ANOVAs, there are usually many influences on (predictors of) behavior and cognition, and multiple regression allows us to assess multiple predictors at the same time.

Clayton and colleagues (2013) used multiple regression to test their four predictors (i.e., loneliness, anxiousness, alcohol use, and marijuana use) of Facebook intensity. The results of this analysis appear in Table 13.1. At first glance, there is a lot of information here! However, you already know most of it from the previous section. Let's first walk through each of the five columns and what information each one contains. Then, we will discuss the three rows that appear at the bottom of this table.

A. The first column contains the *y*-intercept (i.e., the `Constant`) and the four predictor variables entered into the equation.

B. The second column contains the numerical values for the *y*-intercept (i.e., the `Constant`) and the slope for each of the four predictor variables. Notice that three of the slopes are positive (for loneliness, anxiety, and alcohol use), meaning they are positively related to the outcome variable. One slope is negative (for marijuana use), meaning it is negatively related to the outcome variable.

Table 13.1 Multiple Regression on Facebook Intensity

A	B	C	D	E
Variable	**B**	**SE_B**	**β**	**95% confidence interval (CI)**
Constant	1.77	.48		.84, 2.71
Loneliness	.14	.14	.07	−.10, .41
Anxiety	.25	.12	.16*	.02, .48
Alcohol Use	.52	.13	.32***	.26, .78
Marijuana Use	−.27	.08	−.26**	−.43, −.10
F-score$_{(df1,\ df2)}$	$6.16_{(4,\ 224)}$***	F		
R^2	.10 G			
Adjusted R^2	.08 H			

* $p < .05$. ** $p < .01$. *** $p < .001$.

Source: Clayton, R. B., Osborne, R. E., Miller, B. K., & Oberle, C. D. (2013). Loneliness, anxiousness, and substance abuse as predictors of Facebook use. *Computers in Human Behavior, 29,* 687–693.

C. Here is the standard error of the y-intercept and for the slopes of each of the four predictor variables.

D. This is the standardized beta weight. Recall from the previous section that a standardized beta weight is the predicted change in the outcome variable in terms of standard deviations for a 1 standard deviation increase in the predictor variable. After some of the βs, you will notice one or more asterisks. As you can see in the notes of the table, these asterisks signify whether a predictor was a statistically significant predictor of the outcome variable.

E. This is the 95% confidence interval around our slope of each predictor variable.

So far, all we have done is add predictor variables to our regression equation. We now have the regression equation (although they are often not explicitly presented in research articles). Here is that equation:

$$\begin{aligned}\hat{Y}\,(\text{Facebook intensity}) = {} & (0.14 \times \text{score on loneliness measure}) + \\ & (0.25 \times \text{score on anxiety measure}) + \\ & (0.52 \times \text{score on alcohol use measure}) + \\ & (-0.27 \times \text{score on marijuana use measure}) + 1.77\end{aligned}$$

Toward the bottom of the table are three additional rows of data that we will consider now.

F. This F ratio test statistic tells us whether the set of predictors, taken together, is statistically significant. The F ratio of 6.16 was calculated conceptually as we did in chapters on ANOVA, with the mean square between variance divided by an error (residual) variance.

With this F ratio, we have two degrees of freedom, the first being the numerator degrees of freedom (which was 4) and the second being the denominators degrees of freedom (which was 224). Here is how both numbers were calculated:

$$df_{\text{numerator}} = \text{number of predictor variables in the regression equation}$$
$$= 4$$
$$df_{\text{denominator}} = \text{sample size} - \text{number of predictor variables} - 1$$
$$= 229 - 4 - 1$$
$$= 224$$

G. The R^2 is the percentage of variability that the predictor variables account for in the outcome variables. In this case, the four predictor variables accounted for a total of 10% of the variability in Facebook intensity. We know from the F ratio of 6.16 that this model of predictors was statistically significant.

H. Often, researchers report what is called "an adjusted R^2". The calculation of this statistic is well beyond what we need to do here; however, I do want you to understand the purpose of an adjusted R^2. Let's suppose that in addition to the four predictors of Facebook intensity, Clayton and colleagues (2013) had included as predictors a person's height and how much he or she liked the movie *Ted*. Is there any reason to think that height and the liking of a particular movie would be related to Facebook usage? Probably not. However, when we add predictor variables to a regression equation, the R^2 value will only increase; it can never decrease as predictor variables are added. So why not throw in basketball-playing ability and the number of letters in a person's last name as predictor variables? Yes, this is getting ridiculous, and that's where the adjusted R^2 comes into play.

The adjusted R^2 takes into account the number and quality of predictor variables entered into the regression. If we add a lot of "junk" predictor variables, such as the number of letters in a person's last name, the adjusted R^2 will reflect this. That is, the adjusted R^2 will be lower if there are a lot of predictor variables and if these predictor variables do a poor job forecasting the outcome variable. Think of adjusted R^2 as a "quality assurance check" on the set of predictor variables. Adjusted R^2 will always be lower than R^2 because it is, practically speaking, impossible to have a perfect set of predictor variables.[3]

Multiple Regression and SPSS

With an understanding of multiple regression and the statistical information it provides us, let's do a multiple regression analysis with SPSS and interpret the resulting output. When discussing correlations in the previous chapter and univariate regression earlier in this chapter, we used anxiousness as the predictor variable and Facebook check-ins as the outcome variable. Now, we will extend those data by adding a second predictor variable into the regression equation: loneliness scores.

Anxiousness Score	Loneliness Score	Facebook Intensity
35	30	3
75	27	5
50	58	4
40	35	4
55	42	1
35	40	3
80	85	7
60	48	6
50	55	2
70	61	5

The anxiousness scores and Facebook intensity scores are the same as in the previous SPSS exercises. Let's use that spreadsheet once again.

Establishing your spreadsheet

First, go to the *Variable View* because we need to insert a new variable (loneliness scores). To do so, highlight the *Facebook Intensity* variable row. Then click on *Edit, Insert Variable*. This will insert a new variable immediately before the *Facebook Intensity* variable.

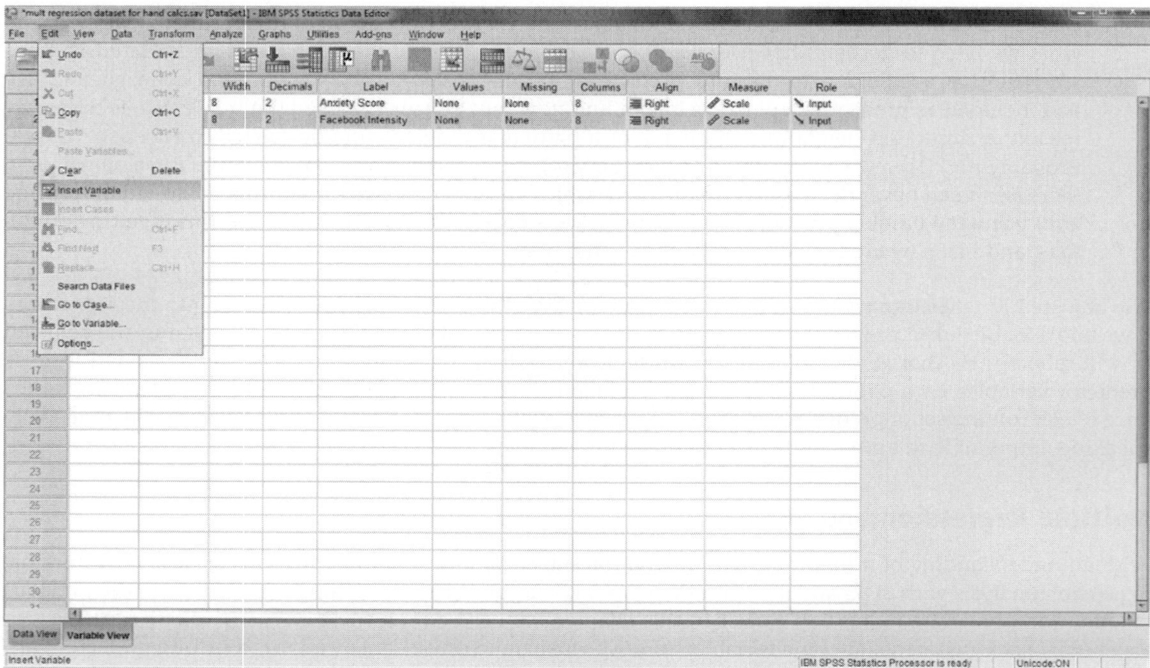

Here is what your *Variable View* will look like:

*mult regression dataset for hand calcs.sav [DataSet1] - IBM SPSS Statistics Data Editor

File Edit View Data Transform Analyze Graphs Utilities Add-ons Window Help

	Name	Type	Width	Decimals	Label	Values	Missing	Columns	Align	Measure	Role
1	Anxiousness	Numeric	8	2	Anxiety Score	None	None	8	Right	Scale	Input
2	VAR00001	Numeric	8	2		None	None	8	Right	Unknown	Input
3	Facebook	Numeric	8	2	Facebook Intensity	None	None	8	Right	Scale	Input
4											
5											

Now you need to provide SPSS with the information about our new variable of loneliness scores. Go ahead and format the *Name*, *Label*, and *Measure* aspects of this variable. After doing so, your *Variable View* should look something like this:

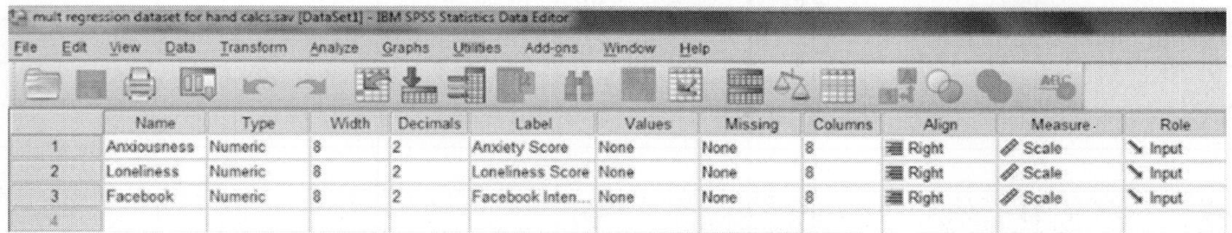

	Name	Type	Width	Decimals	Label	Values	Missing	Columns	Align	Measure	Role
1	Anxiousness	Numeric	8	2	Anxiety Score	None	None	8	Right	Scale	Input
2	Loneliness	Numeric	8	2	Loneliness Score	None	None	8	Right	Scale	Input
3	Facebook	Numeric	8	2	Facebook Inten...	None	None	8	Right	Scale	Input
4											

When you click on *Data View*, you will see that you need to enter scores on the loneliness variable.

	Anxiousness	Loneliness	Facebook	var
1	35.00	.	3.00	
2	75.00	.	5.00	
3	50.00	.	4.00	
4	40.00	.	4.00	
5	55.00	.	1.00	
6	35.00	.	3.00	
7	80.00	.	7.00	
8	60.00	.	6.00	
9	50.00	.	2.00	
10	70.00	.	5.00	

Enter the loneliness score for each of the 10 participants, which you can view again here:

Anxiousness Score	Loneliness Score	Facebook Intensity
35	30	3
75	27	5
50	58	4
40	35	4
55	42	1
35	40	3
80	85	7
60	48	6
50	55	2
70	61	5

Running your analysis

When you have updated your *Data View*, we can run our multiple regression. The procedure for doing so is identical to running a univariate regression, with one exception. That is, we have two predictor variables (or in some analyses more than two, but just two predictor variables in this case) instead of only one predictor variable. After you call up the regression dialogue box (see the previous section if you need a refresher), enter the predictor variables and the outcome variable as such:

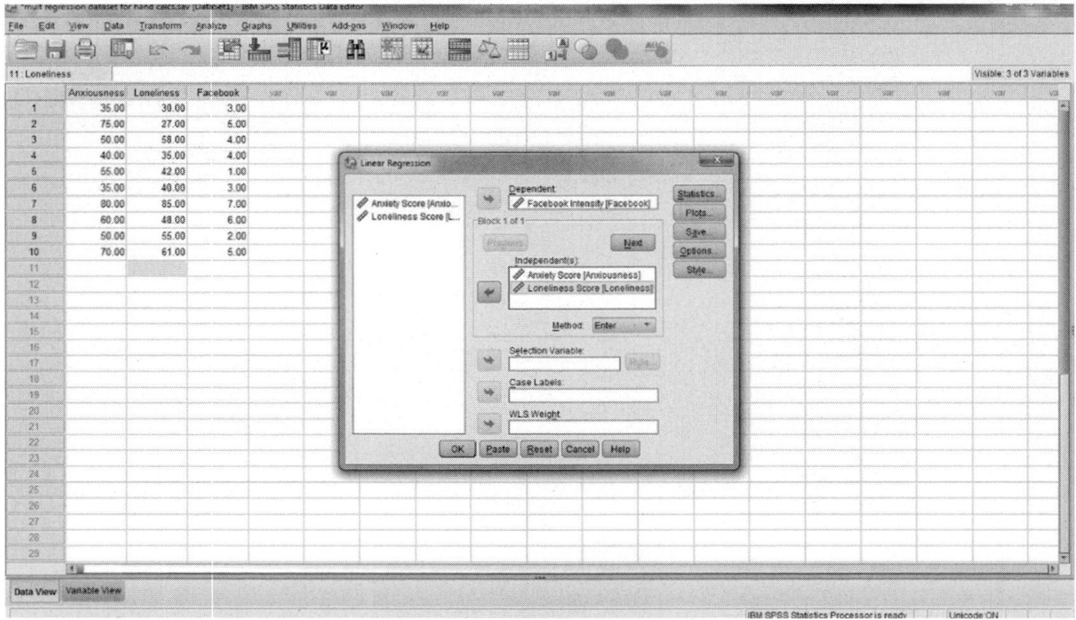

Under the *Statistics* tab, be sure to ask for the 95% confidence interval as we did in our univariate analysis.

Once you click *Continue*, and then *OK*, your output will soon appear.

Variables Entered/Removed[a]

Model	Variables Entered	Variables Removed	Method
1	Loneliness Score, Anxiety Score[b]	.	Enter

a. Dependent Variable: Facebook Intensity

b. All requested variables entered.

Model Summary

Model	R	R Square (A)	Adjusted R Square (B)	Std. Error of the Estimate
1	.658[a]	.433	.271	1.55905

a. Predictors: (Constant), Loneliness Score, Anxiety Score

ANOVA[a]

Model		Sum of Squares	df	Mean Square	F	Sig.
1	Regression	12.985	2	6.493	2.671	.137[b] (C)
	Residual	17.015	7	2.431		
	Total	30.000	9			

a. Dependent Variable: Facebook Intensity

b. Predictors: (Constant), Loneliness Score, Anxiety Score

Coefficients[a]

Model		Unstandardized Coefficients (D)		Standardized Coefficients	t	(E)	95.0% Confidence Interval for B	
		B	Std. Error	Beta		Sig.	Lower Bound	Upper Bound
1	(Constant)	-.296	1.931		-.153	.882	-4.861	4.269
	Anxiety Score	.062	.038	.547	1.633	.146	-.028	.151
	Loneliness Score	.019	.035	.178	.532	.611	-.064	.102

a. Dependent Variable: Facebook Intensity

What am I looking at? Interpreting your SPSS output

This output will hopefully look somewhat familiar. I have highlighted certain aspects of this output that we need to consider in the context of multiple regression. After discussing these points on the printout, the Learning Check will give you more opportunities to make sure you understand multiple regression output.

A. Here is the R^2. In this analysis, the predictor variables accounted for 43.3% of the variability in Facebook intensity scores. This is slightly more than was accounted for when only anxiety was a predictor variable. Remember, that as we add predictor variables into the regression equation, R^2 can only increase.

B. Recall that the "Adjusted R^2" takes into account the number and quality of predictor variables entered into the regression. If we enter predictor variables that do a poor job predicting the outcome variable, the adjusted R^2 will fall in value. Indeed, here our adjusted R^2 was 27.1%. If you look back at the adjusted R^2 when only anxiety was entered in the equation, the adjusted R^2 was 33.6%. By adding loneliness as a predictor, our R^2 increased but our adjusted R^2 decreased. This is a sign that adding loneliness as a predictor did not buy us much predictive ability over and above anxiousness.

C. Here is an ANOVA table. Indeed, it looks similar to the ones we saw in the ANOVA chapters. Clayton and colleagues (2013) reported degrees of freedom, the F ratio test statistic, and its significance level in their results. ANOVA table tells us whether our overall model of predictor variables was statistically significant. In this case, the F ratio of 2.671 has a corresponding p value of .137, so it is not statistically significant. In other words, our model of predictor variables does not statistically significantly predict Facebook intensity.

If you look back at our SPSS output for the univariate regression, you will notice that the F ratio was in fact statistically significant. Why is the model of predictor variables now not statistically significant? It's because we now have two predictors that, *taken together*, do not do a good job predicting the outcome relative to only one predictor. That is, anxiety alone is a more parsimonious (i.e., better) predictor of the outcome than is both anxiety and loneliness. For a model of predictor variables to be statistically significant, the quality of each predictor is important.

D. We have our slope and standard error of the slope for each predictor variable. Remember that multiple regression uses a linear combination of predictor variables to forecast some outcome variable. Thus, the slope and standard error of the slope of a given predictor variable will change when more predictor variables are added to the equation. This is why the slope and its standard error for anxiety scores differ here from the univariate regression analyses we conducted in the first half of this chapter.

At this point, we can write our regression equation:

$$\hat{Y}\text{(Facebook intensity)} = (0.062 \times \text{score on anxiety measure}) + (0.019 \times \text{score on loneliness measure}) - 0.296$$

E. Here we have the p value for each predictor variable's standardized regression coefficient. As you can see, neither predictor is a statistically significant predictor of the outcome variable. You might recall that in the univariate regression, anxiety was a statistically significant predictor of this same outcome variable. What happened? Anxiety is correlated with the other predictor variable (loneliness; see Table 12.2). Therefore, anxiety is less predictive of Facebook intensity because some of its correlation with Facebook intensity is "removed" by its correlation to loneliness.

Let's look at Figure 13.2 to make visual sense of these results. In the top portion of Figure 13.2 is a diagram of the correlation between anxiousness and Facebook intensity. Where the two variables overlap is the correlation between them.

Now look at the bottom portion of Figure 13.2. Here, we introduce loneliness and its relationships with both anxiousness and Facebook intensity. As you can see, loneliness "eats up" some of the overlap between anxiousness and Facebook intensity. By doing so, loneliness reduces the strength of the relationship between anxiousness and Facebook intensity to the point where it is no longer statistically significant.

At first glance, it may seem like it was a bad idea to introduce loneliness into the regression equation. After all, now we have no significant predictors of Facebook intensity, and the model is not statistically significant. But wait, not so fast. We learned something. To start, remember that as a predictor variable by itself, anxiousness did predict Facebook intensity. But when loneliness was introduced as a predictor into the regression equation, anxiousness was no longer a significant predictor of Facebook intensity. In this example, loneliness acts as a

Figure 13.2

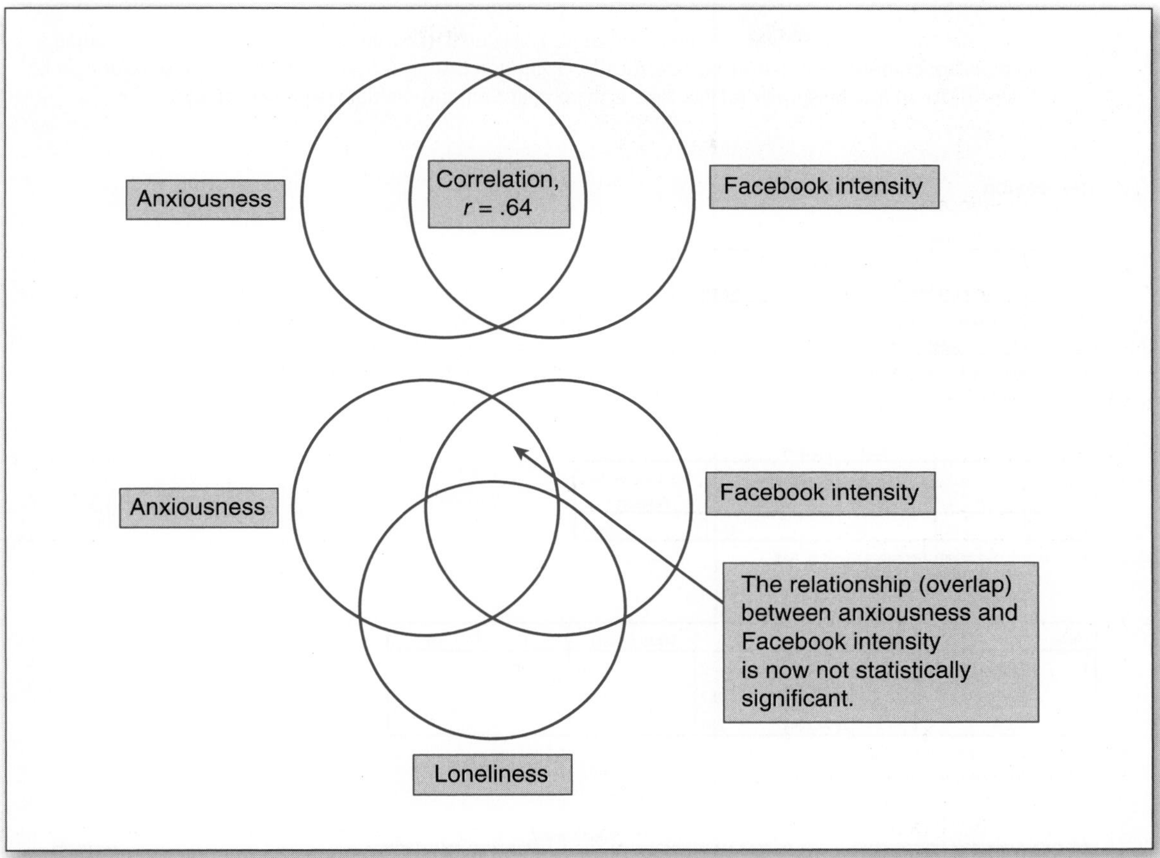

mediating variable between anxiousness and Facebook intensity. That is, once we introduce a third variable (in this case, loneliness) into the equation, the original predictor variable (in this case, anxiousness) is no longer significantly related to the outcome variable.

Mediating variable: variable that helps explain the relationship between two other variables.

In Chapter 12, we discussed the notion of spurious correlations. That is, we can never conclude from a correlation that one variable caused a change in the other variable. That is still the case and always will be; however, when we can measure a "third variable" such as loneliness, we can introduce it into a multiple regression equation to see whether it reduces the strength of the relationship between the predictor variable and the outcome variable. If it does, we have statistical evidence that the original correlation was indeed a spurious one.

LEARNING CHECK

1. We will extend the univariate regression analysis that we considered in our previous Learning Check by adding a second predictor of investment risk-taking. Specifically, in addition to age, Zabel et al. (2009) used sensation seeking as a predictor of investment risk-taking. Here is the output from this multiple regression analysis:

Regression

Variables Entered/Removed[a]

Model	Variables Entered	Variables Removed	Method
1	Sensation Seeking, Age[b]	.	Enter

a. Dependent Variable: Risk-taking

b. All requested variables entered.

Model Summary

Model	R	R Square	Adjusted R Square	Std. Error of the Estimate
1	.270[a]	.073	.066	3.23665

a. Predictors: (Constant), Sensation Seeking, Age

ANOVA[a]

Model		Sum of Squares	df	Mean Square	F	Sig.
1	Regression	211.961	2	105.981	10.117	.000[b]
	Residual	2692.302	257	10.476		
	Total	2904.264	259			

a. Dependent Variable: Risk-taking

b. Predictors: (Constant), Sensation Seeking, Age

Coefficients[a]

Model		Unstandardized Coefficients		Standardized Coefficients	t	Sig.	95.0% Confidence Interval for B	
		B	Std. Error	Beta			Lower Bound	Upper Bound
1	(Constant)	8.378	1.030		8.138	.000	6.351	10.406
	Age	-.022	.013	-.120	-1.640	.102	-.048	.004
	Sensation Seeking	.483	.194	.183	2.490	.013	.101	.864

a. Dependent Variable: Risk-taking

a) How much variability in risk-taking was accounted for by the predictor variables?

A: 7.3%

b) Was this amount of variability statistically significant? How do you know?

A: Yes, because the *F* ratio of 10.12 is statistically significant, $p < .001$.

c) Refer back to Table 13.1 and use Clayton et al.'s (2013) format to make a table of the results from Zabel et al. (2009), using the SPSS output.

A:

Variable	B	SE_B	β	95% Confidence Interval (CI)
Constant	8.378	1.03		6.351, 10.406
Age	−.022	.013	−.12	−.048, .004
Sensation Seeking	.483	.194	.183*	.101, .864
F score$_{(df1,\ df2)}$	$10.12_{(2,\ 257)}$**			
R^2	.073			
Adjusted R^2	.066			

* $p < .05$. ** $p < .001$.

d) Which predictor(s), if any, were statistically significant predictors of risk-taking?

A: Sensation seeking

2. Explain the difference, conceptually, between an R^2 statistic and an adjusted R^2 statistic.

A: The adjusted R^2 takes into account the number of predictor variables, as well as how well those predictor variables forecast the outcome variable. R^2 can only increase in value as predictor variables are added to the regression equation, but the adjusted R^2 can decrease as we add predictor variables, especially ones that do a poor job forecasting the outcome variable.

NOTES

1. This number is slightly different than the one in our hand-calculations because of rounding.
2. Because SPSS rounds to three decimal places, the slope divided by the standard error of the slope as shown on this output does not quite give us the t test statistic that you see. The t test statistic you see is correct.
3. You may have noticed that Clayton et al. (2013) did not present t statistics for the predictor variables. Often, researchers using multiple regression present only the slope (B) and the standard error of the slope (SE_B). From these two numbers, you can derive a t statistic if you want it. The slope and standard error of the slope are sufficient for well-informed readers like you to make sense of the analysis.

CHAPTER APPLICATION QUESTIONS

1. Use the following scatterplots, and answer the questions that follow them:

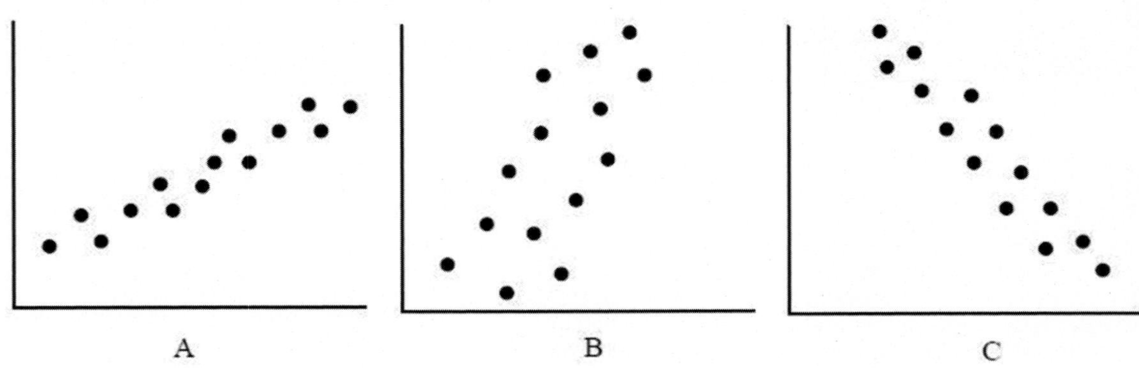

   a) If you were to compute a correlation between the variables for each of the three sets of data, which set of data would yield a correlation closest to zero?

   b) If you were to construct a regression equation using the *X* variable to predict the *Y* variable for each of the three sets of data, for which set of data would the regression equation have the strongest positive slope?

   c) If you were to construct a regression equation using the *X* variable to predict the *Y* variable for each of the three sets of data, for which set of data would the regression equation have the strongest negative slope?

2. Suppose the correlation between hot chocolate sales and weather temperature is –0.80. What proportion (or percentage) of the variability is predicted by the relationship with weather?

   a) 80%
   b) 40%
   c) 20%
   d) 64%

3. In a regression analysis, when $\hat{Y}$ increases by two units for each equal single-unit increase in x, then

   a) the slope equals +2.00
   b) the slope equals +0.50
   c) the y-intercept equals +0.50
   d) the y-intercept equals +2.00

4. How well do Scholastic Aptitude Test (SAT®; College Board, New York, NY) scores predict college GPA? Your college's admissions office wants an answer to this question. It provides you with data from 25 students who have just completed their first year at your school (see below for these data). Enter these data into SPSS, run both bivariate correlational and univariate regression analyses, and then answer the questions that follow these data:

SAT Score (composite)	First-year GPA
1700	3.36
1640	2.10
1520	2.25
1580	2.75
1890	3.20
2110	3.56
2090	2.25
1590	2.40
1680	2.45
1650	3.40
1530	2.85
1880	3.00
1810	2.50
1770	2.86
1410	3.85
1900	3.52
1660	3.35
1450	3.10
1500	2.35
1710	2.95
1380	1.80
1750	3.12
1650	3.00
2220	3.80
1990	4.00

a) What is the correlation between SAT scores and first-year college GPA?

b) Is this correlation statistically significant? Give the precise p value for this analysis.

c) What percentage of the variability in first-year college GPA is accounted for by SAT scores?

d) Write the regression equation for these data.

e) Now, provide your admissions office with an answer to its question: Does SAT score predict first-year college GPA?

5. Your admissions office is interested not only in SAT scores but also in how well leadership activity in high school (as measured by admissions counselor ratings of personal statements that applicants provide) predicts college GPA. In addition to the SAT scores, the admissions office provides you with a "leadership score" for each of the 25 students. Leadership was rated on a 1 (*hardly any leadership experiences*) to 9 (*a great deal of leadership experiences*) response range. Here are all of those data (with SAT scores and GPA repeated here for the sake of completeness and organization):

SAT Score (Composite)	Leadership Experience	First-year GPA
1700	4	3.36
1640	2	2.10
1520	5	2.25
1580	3	2.75
1890	8	3.20
2110	5	3.56
2090	4	2.25
1590	2	2.40
1680	9	2.45
1650	8	3.40
1530	5	2.85
1880	6	3.00
1810	1	2.50
1770	8	2.86
1410	5	3.85
1900	4	3.52
1660	6	3.35
1450	3	3.10
1500	5	2.35
1710	7	2.95
1380	9	1.80
1750	7	3.12
1650	8	3.00
2220	2	3.80
1990	5	4.00

Update your SPSS spreadsheet from the previous example, run a multiple regression, and then answer the following questions:

a) What percentage of the variability in first-year college GPA is accounted for by SAT scores and leadership rating?

b) Looking back at your univariate regression analysis, how much additional variability was accounted for by adding leadership rating to the regression equation?

c) Explain why the adjusted R^2 decreased from 13.5% in the univariate regression to 9.9% in the multiple regression.

d) Write the regression equation for these data.

e) Give your admissions office a "bottom line" message from these data. That is, should they use both or only GPA to forecast first-year college GPA?

Answers

1. a) b
   b) a
   c) c
2. d
3. a
4. a) $r = .413$ ($r = .41$ rounded)
   b) yes; $p = .04$
   c) 17.1%
   d) first-year college GPA = .001 × (SAT score) + 1.074
   e) Yes, SAT score does predict this outcome. It is statistically significant, indicating that SAT scores should be used as a predictor of first-year college GPA.
5. a) A: 17.4%
   b) 0.3% (17.4% – 17.1%)
   c) We have twice as many predictor variables now, and the new predictor variable (leadership ratings) did not account for much additional variability in predicting the outcome.
   d) first-year college GPA = .001 × (SAT score) + .014 × (leadership rating) + 0.961
   e) GPA should be used, but leadership rating should not be used, to predict first-year college GPA.

QUESTIONS FOR CLASS DISCUSSION

1. How does univariate regression extend Pearson correlation coefficients that we discussed in the previous chapter?
2. How does multiple regression extend univariate regression?
3. Why is the "beta weight" (β) a *standardized* regression coefficient?
4. Explain how two predictor variables could have the same slope but only one of them is statistically significant.

CHAPTER 14

When We Have Exceptions to the Rules

Nonparametric Tests

After reading this chapter, you will be able to

- Explain when nonparametric tools are needed
- Compare the chi-square goodness-of-fit test with the chi-square test of independence
- Hand-calculate all ingredients for nonparametric tools
- Interpret nonparametric tools using SPSS
- Explain what nonparametric tool to use for a given research design

Starting in Chapter 6 with the basics of hypothesis testing, we learned how to interpret and use several parametric inferential statistical tools. By "parametric," we mean that parametric tools make assumptions about the population from which the sample is drawn. For example, they all require the dependent (or outcome) variable to be measured using a scale measurement (that is, be ratio or interval data; see Chapter 2 for a refresher on scales of measurement). What happens when these assumptions are violated? First, we cannot use the tools we have learned about up to this point. Second, we can use the tools we are about to discuss in this chapter.

In this chapter, we will discuss four common nonparametric tools. That may sound like a lot to add to our kit. However, these nonparametric tools are less cumbersome to hand-calculate and use on the software program Statistical Package for the Social Sciences (SPSS) than their parametric counterparts.

Before we begin discussing specific nonparametric tools, let's make sure we understand when we need these tools as opposed to the parametric tools we have already discussed. There are three circumstances under which nonparametric tests should be used. First, as mentioned, when a dependent (outcome) variable is measured on a nominal scale, we need a nonparametric test. You may have noticed in Chapters 7–13 that all of our dependent variables were measured on a scale measurement. That is, people did not fall into a category on a dependent variable. For instance, in Chapter 9, we described a study by Kendall Eskine (2012) in which participants made judgments of morally questionable behaviors that used a response range of 1 to 7. In this chapter, we will deal with data in which the outcome is categorical (nominal).

The second situation in which we need nonparametric tools is if either the independent (or predictor) variable or the dependent (or outcome) variable is measured on an ordinal scale. Remember that by "ordinal" we mean "ranked" data. For instance, in some graduate-level programs, they do not assign numerical grades, but rather, they assign class rankings. To be able to draw conclusions from such data, we cannot use any of our parametric tools.

Finally, we use nonparametric tools with particularly small sample sizes and when the population being studied is from a non-normal distribution (i.e., is from a skewed distribution; see Chapter 5 for a quick refresher on skewed distributions and examples of data distributions that tend to be skewed). For example, a medical researcher or clinical psychologist studying a rare disease may need to use a nonparametric tool because almost by definition, a "rare" disease implies a small sample size.

Just as there are many types of parametric tools, there are many types of nonparametric tools. As with parametric tests, each nonparametric tool has a specific purpose, depending on the type of data we have to work with. Four nonparametric tools are summarized in Table 14.1. We will discuss each one in this chapter. For each statistical tool we discuss, we will understand when to use it, how to calculate and interpret it, and then how to generate it with the help of SPSS.

Table 14.1 Summary of Nonparametric Tools

	χ^2 Goodness-of-Fit	χ^2 test of independence	Spearman correlation	Mann Whitney *U* Test
When to Use	One nominal variable	Two nominal variables	Ordinal variables	Ordinal outcome variable
What It Does	Tests how well observed frequencies in a sample match/fit expected patterns of frequencies in the population	Tests differences in frequencies on two between-group variables	Correlates rank-ordered data	Tests two-group differences on an ordinal dependent (outcome) variable

CHI-SQUARE (χ^2) TESTS

As you saw in Table 14.1, there are two types of what are called chi-square (pronounced "k-eye square") tests: the goodness-of-fit test and the test of independence. We will discuss each one starting momentarily. But first, just as there are assumptions with all parametric tests, there are assumptions of the chi-square tests. First, scores must be independent; that is, one score cannot influence or determine another score. Second, we generally want at least five people in each group of the analysis. Finally, data are collected on a nominal scale; that is, data are categorical.

Chi-Square (χ^2) Goodness-of-Fit Test

We use the chi-square test for goodness of fit when we have ***one nominal outcome variable***. By "goodness of fit," we are testing to learn whether nominal data from a sample fit the population distribution. If there is a "good fit," then we will fail to reject the null hypothesis. To reject the null hypothesis, we need a "bad fit" between our sample data and the population.

Recall that we began Chapter 9 with a situation in which we wanted to compare how much people liked Coke®, Pepsi®, and Dr. Pepper®. If you look back at the beginning of that chapter, you will see that in that example, we proposed to measure how much people liked each type of soda using a scale measurement. However, there is another way to measure the outcome of this research. Why not just ask people which one of three sodas they like most? If we do this, we now have a nominal outcome because each person's preference will fall into one category (i.e., one type of soda). With a χ^2 test for goodness of fit, we want to know whether the soda preferences expressed in our sample reflect those in the population. We will see how well our sample's soda preferences fit the population proportions specified by the null hypothesis.

Hand-calculating the χ^2 goodness-of-fit test

Let's use some hypothetical data to see whether people prefer Coke, Pepsi, or Dr. Pepper. As consumer psychologists who are soon-to-be experts at the χ^2, we sample 210 people, asking them to try each one of three beverages (of course, clearing their palates with water in between each tasting). Then we ask them which one of the three beverages they liked the most. We find that 70 people prefer Coke, 75 people prefer Pepsi, and 65 people prefer Dr. Pepper. As with all statistical tools, we will walk through a series of steps to learn whether there is a soda preference in our sample that may be generalizable to the population.

Step 1: State hypotheses

Before stating our null hypothesis, let's think about how many sodas we are comparing. Given that we are comparing three sodas, it might seem reasonable to expect that roughly one third of the population would prefer Coke, one third would prefer Pepsi, and one third would prefer Dr. Pepper. If that was the case, then there would be no preference for one type of soda in our population. "No preference" should be a hint as to our null hypothesis:

H_o: There will be no preference expressed among the three types of soda

H_r: There will be a preference expressed among the three types of soda

Because we are comparing frequencies, it is a bit clumsy to state our hypotheses for χ^2 tests notationally, so we will not do so at all.

Step 2: Determine degrees of freedom (dfs)

Up to this point in the class, degrees of freedom have been based on sample size. With a χ^2 test, that is not the case. Here, degrees of freedom are calculated as:

$$\text{Number of categories} - 1$$

With three categories (type of soda), we have:

$$df = 3 - 1$$
$$df = 2$$

Step 3: Calculate the χ^2 test statistic

Of course, calculating the χ^2 statistic is the most involved step in the process of using our new tool. Table 14.2 contains the calculations we need to perform to get our χ^2 test statistic. Let's refer to this table and walk through these calculations. Here is the formula for the χ^2 test for goodness of fit:

$$\chi^2 = \Sigma: \frac{(\text{observed frequencies} - \text{expected frequencies})^2}{\text{expected frequencies}}$$

We stated at the outset of the hand-calculations that we know how many people preferred each type of soda. These preferences are listed in the "Observed Preference" column. Next is the "Expected Preference" column. How did we get 70 for each observed frequency? With a sample size of 210, and three sodas to choose from, we would expect, on average, 70 people to prefer each soda (i.e., 210 divided by 3). Please note that it could be that a researcher might believe that the expected frequencies could vary among each category. If that is the case, then the expected frequencies would not be the same for all categories. As long as there is good reason to believe the expected frequencies should be different, they do not all have to be the same number.

We next take the difference between the observed frequency and the expected frequency. Then, much like we square deviation scores when computing sums of squares, we square the difference between observed and expected frequencies (otherwise, the sum of the differences would of course be 0).

As seen in the last column of Table 14.2, we take the squared difference score for each category and divide it by the expected frequency for that category. The sum of these quotients will be our χ^2 test statistic. Thus, we have 0 + 0.36 + 0.36, which gives us a χ^2 test statistic of 0.72.

Step 4: Find the critical value and make a decision about the null hypothesis

As was the case with parametric tools, we need our alpha level and degrees of freedom to obtain the critical value to compare our test statistic to. Appendix F contains the critical values for the χ^2 goodness-of-fit test. By using our alpha level of .05 and 2 *df*s, we see our critical value is 5.99. To reject the null hypothesis, our χ^2 test statistic must be larger than 5.99. Of course, our χ^2 test statistic was 0.72, which is less than the critical value. Therefore, we do not reject the null hypothesis. That is, the observed data are a good fit to the expected data. In plain English, people have no preference among Coke, Pepsi, and Dr. Pepper.

Note that like our *F* ratio tests when conducting an analysis of variance (ANOVA), χ^2 test statistics and critical values can never be negative. This is because we cannot arrive at negative numbers in the calculation of the test statistics. When we squared the differences between observed and expected frequencies, we eliminated the negative numbers.

As always, we must communicate our results in APA style:

> A chi-squared goodness-of-fit test revealed no significant preference for any of the sodas, χ^2 (2, N = 210) = 0.72, p > .05. People tended to report liking each type of soda with equal frequency.

Table 14.2 χ^2 Goodness-of-Fit Hand-Calculations

Soda Preference	Observed Preference	Expected Preference	Observed – Expected	(Observed – Expected)^2	$\frac{(\text{Observed} - \text{Expected})^2}{\text{Expected Preference}}$
Coke	70	70	0	0	$\frac{0}{70} = 0$
Pepsi	75	70	5	25	$\frac{25}{70} = 0.36$
Dr. Pepper	65	70	-5	25	$\frac{25}{70} = 0.36$
					$\chi^2 = 0.72$

χ^2 goodness-of-fit test and SPSS

Now that we know how to hand-calculate the χ^2 test for goodness of fit, we will learn how to conduct and interpret this test using SPSS. We will use data collected by a health psychologist who surveyed students at her college about their dietary habits. In her survey, she asked 100 students to name their favorite vegetable. Here are those data, with the number after the vegetable name indicating how many students listed that vegetable as their favorite.

Carrots: 26

Broccoli: 18

Red peppers: 16

Asparagus: 13

Spinach: 11

Turnip greens: 10

Peas: 6

Establishing your spreadsheet

Let's open SPSS, set up our spreadsheet, enter our data, run our analysis, and interpret the output.

Once you open SPSS, go into *Variable View* to set up the spreadsheet. There is only one variable here, which I gave the name `Vegetable_Preferred`. Make sure under *Type*, that it is a *Numeric* variable. For each category (vegetable), let's give it a value. I started at the top of the list, giving a `1` for carrots, a `2` for broccoli, and so on down the list of vegetables. The only other vital consideration is that the measure must be *Nominal*. Your *Variable View* should look like this:

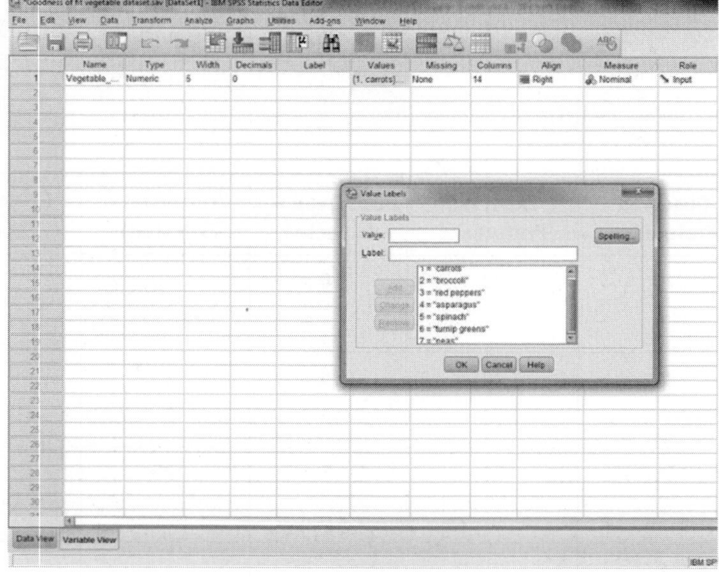

Let's go into *Data View*, and here's what you will see:

For each category (vegetable), we enter a number for each participant who fell into that category (preferred that vegetable). For each of the 26 people who preferred carrots, I entered a 1. For each of the 18 people who preferred broccoli, I entered a 2, and so on, with each of the six people preferring peas being entered as a 7.

In all, you will have 100 rows of data because there were 100 respondents. Go ahead and carefully enter each respondent's preference. Here is a partial screenshot of what your *Data View* should look like once you have entered all 100 respondents' preferences.

*Goodness of fit vegetable dataset.sav [DataSet1] - IBM SPSS St

File Edit View Data Transform Analyze Graphs

	Vegetable_Preferred	var	var
72	4		
73	4		
74	5		
75	5		
76	5		
77	5		
78	5		
79	5		
80	5		
81	5		
82	5		
83	5		
84	5		
85	6		
86	6		
87	6		
88	6		
89	6		
90	6		
91	6		
92	6		
93	6		
94	6		
95	7		
96	7		
97	7		
98	7		
99	7		
100	7		

Data View Variable View

Note: Not all cases can be seen in one screengrab.

Running your analysis

To conduct our χ^2 test for goodness of fit, here is what we need to do:

1. Click on *Analyze → Nonparametric Tests → Legacy Dialogues → Chi_Square.*

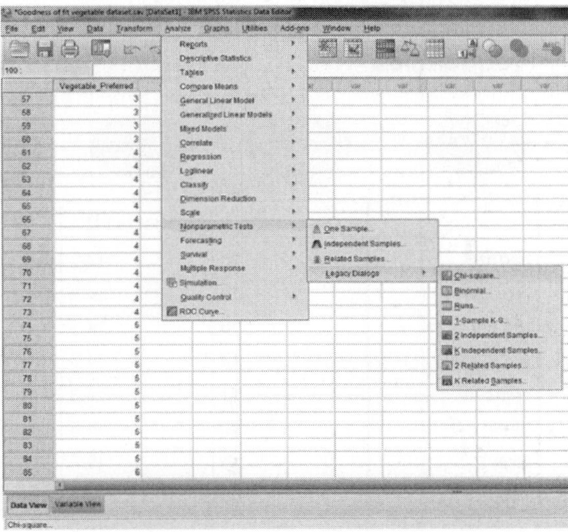

2. Click on our variable in the *Test Variable List* box.
3. Directly under the *Test Variable List* box is where we enter our expected values, one for each category in the analysis. We will use *All Categories Equal*, which is the default for this analysis. Had we expected different values among our vegetables, this is where we would provide our expected values for each category.

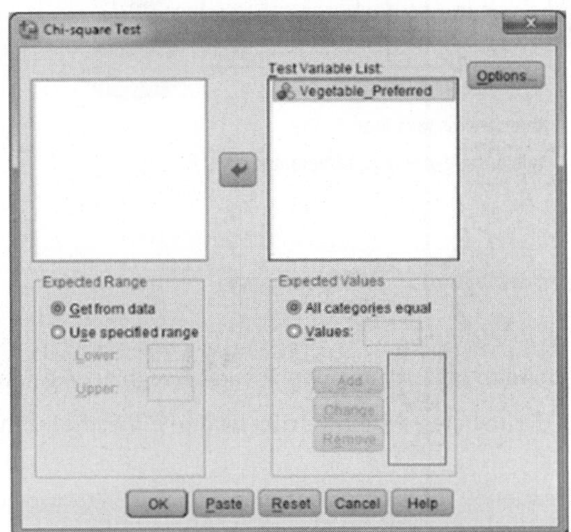

Click *OK*, and the output will soon appear, looking like this:

NPar Tests

Chi-Square Test

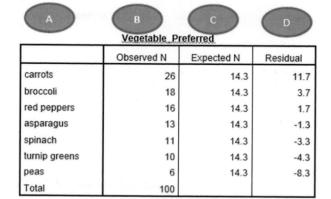

Frequencies

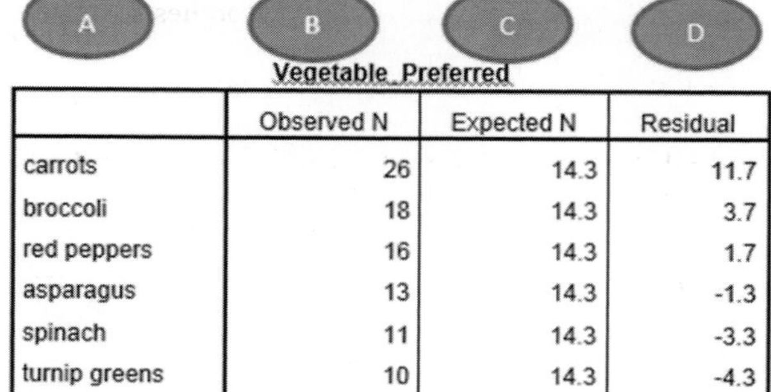

Vegetable_Preferred

	Observed N	Expected N	Residual
carrots	26	14.3	11.7
broccoli	18	14.3	3.7
red peppers	16	14.3	1.7
asparagus	13	14.3	-1.3
spinach	11	14.3	-3.3
turnip greens	10	14.3	-4.3
peas	6	14.3	-8.3
Total	100		

Test Statistics

	Vegetable_Preferred
Chi-Square	17.740[a]
df	6
Asymp. Sig.	.007

a. 0 cells (0.0%) have expected frequencies less than 5. The minimum expected cell frequency is 14.3.

E

F

G

What am I looking at? Interpreting your SPSS output

The output tells us the following information:

A. These categories correspond to the order in which each category (vegetable) was entered into SPSS.

B. These are the observed frequencies, which in this example are the number of people who preferred each type of vegetable.

C. We have the expected frequency for each category. We told SPSS to use equal values for each category, so that is why they are all the same in this example.

D. This is the difference between the observed and expected frequencies, which is calculated as:

observed frequency – expected frequency

E. Here is the χ^2 test statistic, in this case, of 17.74.

F. Here are the degrees of freedom, which were calculated from the number of categories, minus 1. With seven categories, we have 7 – 1, giving us our 6 *df*s.

G. The significance level of our test statistic. As with the previous statistical tools we have discussed, SPSS is comparing the test statistic it calculated (in this case, $\chi^2 = 17.74$) against a critical value. Because the significance level is less than .05, we reject the null hypothesis.

We must take it upon ourselves to write our result in APA style:

A chi-squared goodness-of-fit test revealed significant differences in students' vegetable preferences, χ^2 $(6, N = 100) = 17.74, p = .007$.

LEARNING CHECK

1. Explain what is meant by a test for "goodness of fit?" In other words, what is being "fitted" and to what is it being "fitted?"

   A: We are "fitting" sample data to the population. If the data are a good fit, it suggests that the null hypothesis is correct and cannot be rejected. If the data are a bad fit, it suggests that the null hypothesis is incorrect and should be rejected.

2. How is the χ^2 test for goodness of fit different from both the independent and paired samples *t* tests?

   A: It differs from the independent samples *t* test because the χ^2 test for goodness of fit compares frequencies of nominal data, whereas the independent samples *t* test compares two distinct groups on a scale outcome measure. In addition, the paired samples *t* test compares scores in a repeated-measures design in which each respondent provides two datapoints as opposed to the one datapoint each respondent provides in the χ^2 test for goodness of fit.

3. The Humane Society is interested in learning whether more small dogs (less than 25 pounds) or large dogs (more than 25 pounds) end up in shelters. After conducting a national survey of animal shelters across the United States, the Society learned that of a total of 1,000 dogs that ended up in their shelters, 450 were small dogs and 550 were large dogs.

   Conduct a χ^2 test of goodness of fit to see whether there is a difference between the frequency of small and the frequency of large dogs in the shelters. Assume that the expected frequencies are equal, and use an alpha of .05.

Questions to Answer:

a) What is the hypothesis that is being tested?

   A: There will be no difference between the number of small dogs and the number of large dogs in shelters.

(Continued)

(Continued)

b) What are the degrees of freedom?

A: df = Number of categories − 1

= 2 − 1

= 1

c) What are the observed frequencies for each category?

A: 450 for small dogs; 550 for large dogs

d) What are the expected frequencies for each category?

A: 500 for both sizes of dogs

e) What is the test statistic?

A: $\chi^2 = 10$

f) What is the critical value?

A: 3.84

g) Is the test statistic statistically significant?

A: Because our test statistic of 10 exceeds the critical value of 3.841 our result is statistically significant. In plain English, it appears that more large dogs than small dogs end up at the shelter.

h) Write this result in APA style.

A: A χ^2 goodness-of-fit test revealed that more large dogs than small dogs tended to end up in a shelter, χ^2 (1, N = 1000) = 10.00, $p < .05$.

Chi-Square (χ^2) Test of Independence

With the chi-squared goodness-of-fit test, we learned that people do not express a difference in preference among Coke, Pepsi, and Dr. Pepper. However, might there be geographical differences in soda preference? That is, maybe people in a certain part of the United States prefer one type of soda, whereas people in another part of the country prefer a different type of soda. We could explore our data in more detail, breaking down soda preference by the geographic region in which respondents lived. If we did this, we would have *two nominal variables*: the soda preferred and the geographic region of the respondent. When we have two nominal variables, we use the chi-squared test of independence. By "independence," we are looking to see whether the two variables (in this case, type of soda preferred and geographic location) are independent from and not dependent on each other. It does not matter which variable we consider to be the independent or predictor variable when using this tool. We simply are looking to see whether they are "independent" from each other.

Hand-calculating the χ^2 test of independence

To learn whether there are geographic differences in soda preferences, we will divide our data based on the geographic region in which a respondent lived. For the sake of example, we will assume respondents were

Table 14.3 Observed Frequencies for Soda Preference by Geographic Region

	Region		
Soda	**Southeastern U.S.**	**Southwestern U.S.**	
Coke	52	18	70
Pepsi	38	37	75
Dr. Pepper	15	50	65
	105	105	

either from the southeastern (SE) United States or the southwestern (SW) United States. Table 14.3 contains preferences for our three types of soda, divided into these two geographic regions. These are our observed preference frequencies.

Let's now hand-calculate a χ^2 test of independence to learn whether soda preference is independent or not independent from geographic region. The formula is the same as it was for the goodness-of-fit-test:

$$\chi^2 = \Sigma : \frac{(\text{observed frequencies} - \text{expected frequencies})^2}{\text{expected frequencies}}$$

Step 1: State hypotheses

This is a test of "independence" between two nominal variables. Therefore, our null hypothesis will be that these two variables (soda preference and geographic region) are independent of (not dependent on) each other.

H_o: Soda preference does not depend on geographic region.

H_r: Soda preference depends on geographic region.

In other words, these research hypotheses say that the two variables are not independent.

Step 2: Determine degrees of freedom (dfs)

In our χ^2 test for goodness of fit, we calculated degrees of freedom by taking the number of categories and subtracting 1. In the χ^2 test for independence, we need to do that for both variables. In Table 14.3, we have three rows of data. So our degrees of freedom for the rows is:

$$3 - 1 = 2$$

We have two columns of data, so our degrees of freedom for the columns is:

$$2 - 1 = 1$$

To get total *df*s, we simply multiply our df_{rows} by the df_{columns}, giving us:

$$2 \times 1 = 2$$

Therefore, our $df_{\text{total}} = 2$.

Step 3: Calculate expected frequencies

Our observed frequencies are straightforward to obtain. The data in Table 14.3 simply display people's preferences broken down by geographic region. Obtaining the expected frequencies is a little more involved. We first need to determine the *percentage of total responses* within each column (region). Here, that is pretty simple, as it is 50% for each region (105 responses in a region divided by 210 total responses). When working with non-example data, it is likely these numbers will not each be 50%.

We now need to take that percentage for each region and multiply it by the observed frequencies, which appear in the far right side of Table 14.3. So for the SE region, we have:

$$\text{Coke: } 70 \times 50\% = 35$$
$$\text{Pepsi} = 75 \times 50\% = 37.50$$
$$\text{Dr. Pepper} = 65 \times 50\% = 32.50$$

We repeat this process for the SW region:

$$\text{Coke: } 70 \times 50\% = 35$$
$$\text{Pepsi} = 75 \times 50\% = 37.50$$
$$\text{Dr. Pepper} = 65 \times 50\% = 32.50$$

We now need to organize each calculation by type of soda and geographic region. Doing so gives us the expected frequencies that appear in Table 14.4.

Table 14.4 Expected Frequencies for Soda Preference by Geographic Region

	Region		
Soda	**Southeastern U.S.**	**Southwestern U.S.**	
Coke	35	35	70
Pepsi	37.5	37.5	75
Dr. Pepper	32.5	32.5	65
	105	105	

Step 4: Calculate the χ^2 test statistic

From here on out, we follow the same process that we followed in the χ^2 goodness-of-fit test. Table 14.5 presents the six categories we now have (type of soda for each region), along with our observed and just-calculated expected frequencies. Let's use this table as we calculate our test statistic.

As we did in the previous section, we find the difference between these two frequencies, and then we square those differences for each category. We take each squared difference score and divide it by its respective expected frequency. These quotients are displayed in the last column of Table 14.5.

We sum these quotients, which give us a χ^2 test statistic of 35.38.

Table 14.5 Calculating the χ^2 Test for Independence

Category	Observed Preference	Expected Preference	Observed – Expected	(Observed – Expected)^2	$\frac{(\text{Observed} - \text{Expected})^2}{\text{Expected Preference}}$
Coke, SE	52	35	17	289	$\frac{289}{35} = 8.26$
Coke, SW	18	35	−17	289	$\frac{289}{35} = 8.26$
Pepsi, SE	38	37.5	0.5	0.25	$\frac{0.25}{37.5} = 0.01$
Pepsi, SW	37	37.5	−0.5	0.25	$\frac{0.25}{37.5} = 0.01$
Dr. Pepper, SE	15	32.5	−17.5	306.25	$\frac{306.25}{32.5} = 9.42$
Dr. Pepper, SW	50	32.5	17.5	306.26	$\frac{306.25}{32.5} = 9.42$
					$\chi^2 = 35.38$

Step 5: Find the critical value and make a decision about the null hypothesis

With an alpha level of .05 and a df_{total} of 2, we see in Appendix F that our critical value is 5.99. Our χ^2 test statistic of 35.38 exceeds this critical value. Therefore, we reject the null hypothesis and conclude that these two nominal variables are not independent of each other. In plain English, soda preference depends on (i.e., it varies by) geographic region. People in the southeastern United States tend to prefer Coke; people in the southwestern United States tend to prefer Dr. Pepper. Preference for Pepsi varies less by geographic region than does preference for Coke and Dr. Pepper.

Step 6: Calculate an effect size

For the χ^2 test of independence, two effect sizes are typically used: the Phi coefficient (ϕ) and the Cramer's *V*. We use the Phi coefficient when both variables contain two categories. In our example, that is not the case, as one category (type of soda) has three categories. So, we will compute Cramer's *V*:

The formula for Cramer's *V* is:[1]

$$\text{Cramer's } V = \sqrt{\frac{\chi^2 \text{ test statistic}}{\text{sample size} \times df}}$$

We have all the ingredients we need to calculate this effect size.

$$= \sqrt{\frac{35.38}{210 \times 2}}$$

$$= \sqrt{\frac{35.38}{420}}$$

$$= \sqrt{0.842}$$

$$= 0.29$$

Table 14.6 Cohen's (1992) Guidelines for Interpreting Strength of Effect Size for Cramer's V

Effect size	smaller $df = 1$	smaller $df = 2$	smaller $df = 3$
Weak	0.10	0.07	0.06
Moderate	0.30	0.21	0.17
Strong	0.50	0.35	0.29

Note: The "smaller *df*" means whether the df_{rows} or the $df_{columns}$ is smaller

Table 14.6 contains guidelines for interpreting effect sizes for the test of independence. As we see, we need to know whether our *df*s were smaller for the rows or for the columns. Our df_{rows} was 2 and our $df_{columns}$ was 1, so our "smaller *df*" is 1. Therefore, a Cramer's *V* of 0.29 is a small, almost moderate, effect size.

Here is our APA style write-up:

> A chi-squared test for independence revealed significant geographic differences in soda preferences, χ^2 (2, $N = 210$) = 35.38, $p < .05$, Cramer's $V = 0.29$.

χ^2 test for independence and SPSS

To learn how to use this tool with SPSS, let's consider a situation in which a college wants to know whether there are differences between class of student (first-years, sophomores, juniors, and seniors) and whether they play a varsity sport. That is, the college wants to know whether playing a sport is independent from a student's class standing. To do so, the college's Registrar surveys 80 students on campus, 20 from each class. Table 14.7 contains the responses from these 80 students.

Let's go into SPSS, set up our spreadsheet, enter our data, run our analysis, and interpret the output.

Table 14.7 Observed Frequencies for Sport Participation by Class of Student

	Play a Varsity Sport?		
Class	**Yes**	**No**	
First-year	15	5	20
Sophomore	12	8	20
Junior	7	13	20
Senior	3	17	20
	37	43	

Establishing your spreadsheet

As always, we will start in *Variable View*. We have two variables for each respondent: class standing and whether or not he or she plays a sport. I provided a name to each variable called `Class` and `Sport`. Both types of variables are numeric. I provided a label for each variable, labeling `Class` "Class Standing" and labeling `Sport` "Does Student Play a Sport?"

We need to have values for each category of each variable. There are four categories for the `Class` variable. For first-year respondents, I gave a value of `1`. For sophomore respondents, I gave a value of `2`, junior respondents a `3`, and senior respondents a `4`. There are two categories for the `Sport` variable. If he or she did play a sport, the response was a `1`. If the student did not play a sport, the response was a `0`. Finally, be sure that under *Measure*, both variables are *Nominal*.

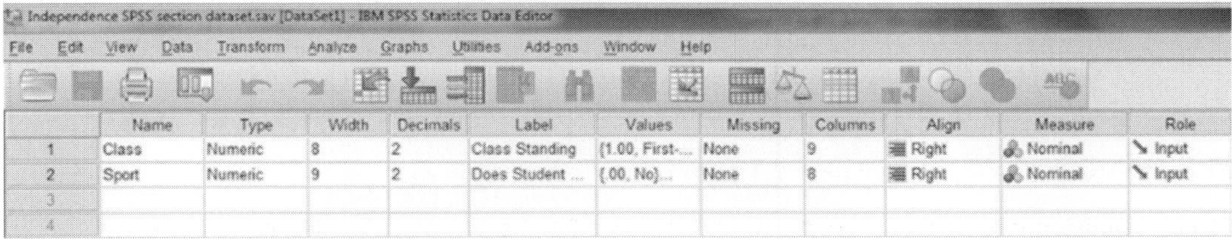

	Name	Type	Width	Decimals	Label	Values	Missing	Columns	Align	Measure	Role
1	Class	Numeric	8	2	Class Standing	{1.00, First-...	None	9	Right	Nominal	Input
2	Sport	Numeric	9	2	Does Student ...	{.00, No}...	None	8	Right	Nominal	Input
3											
4											

Let's go into *Data View*, which will look like this:

We must enter a value for each of the two categories for all 80 respondents. We have 15 first-year respondents who play a sport. For these respondents, we enter a 1 for Class and a 1 for Sport. For the five first-years who do not play a sport, they also receive a 1 for Class, but a 0 for Sport. Let's next enter responses from the 20 sophomore respondents. Here, 12 sophomores played a sport, for whom we enter a 2 for Class and a 1 for Sport. The remaining eight sophomores received a 2 for Class and a 0 for Sport. Go ahead and enter the data for the junior and senior respondents. Here is a partial screenshot of what your *Data View* should look like:

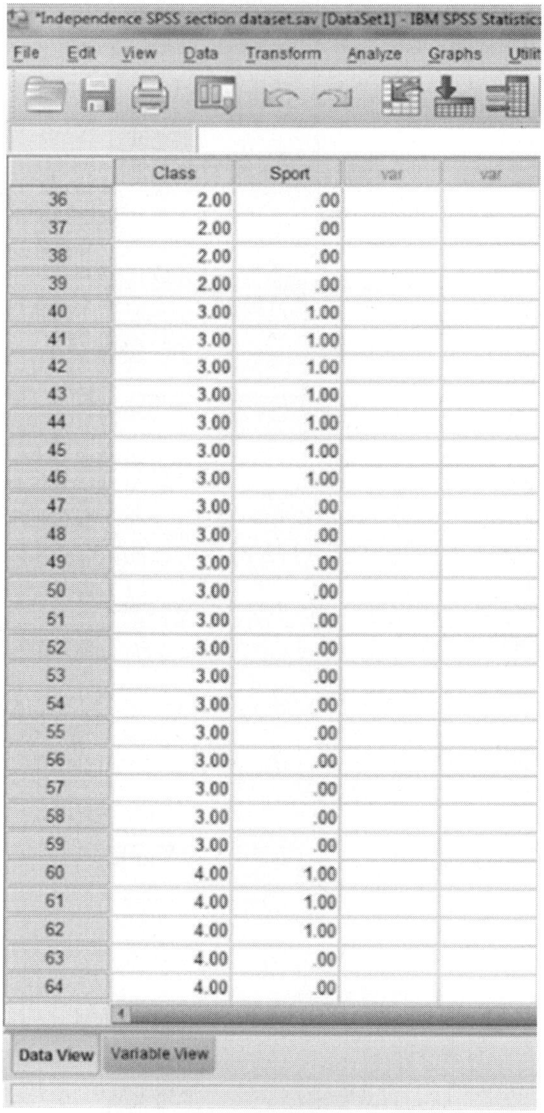

*Independence SPSS section dataset.sav [DataSet1] - IBM SPSS Statistics

File Edit View Data Transform Analyze Graphs Utilit

	Class	Sport	var	var
36	2.00	.00		
37	2.00	.00		
38	2.00	.00		
39	2.00	.00		
40	3.00	1.00		
41	3.00	1.00		
42	3.00	1.00		
43	3.00	1.00		
44	3.00	1.00		
45	3.00	1.00		
46	3.00	1.00		
47	3.00	.00		
48	3.00	.00		
49	3.00	.00		
50	3.00	.00		
51	3.00	.00		
52	3.00	.00		
53	3.00	.00		
54	3.00	.00		
55	3.00	.00		
56	3.00	.00		
57	3.00	.00		
58	3.00	.00		
59	3.00	.00		
60	4.00	1.00		
61	4.00	1.00		
62	4.00	1.00		
63	4.00	.00		
64	4.00	.00		

Data View Variable View

Note: Not all data appear in this screenshot.

Running your analysis

To conduct our χ^2 test for independence, here is what we need to do:

1. Click on *Analysis → Descriptive Statistics → Crosstabs.*

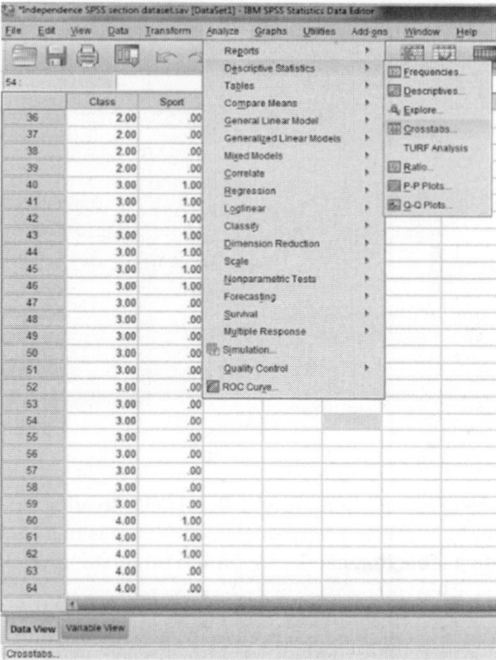

2. We now need to enter one variable as a *Row* and the other variable as a *Column*. It does not matter which variable you click into each, but for the sake of consistency with Table 14.7, let's put `Class` into *Row* and `Sport` into *Column*.

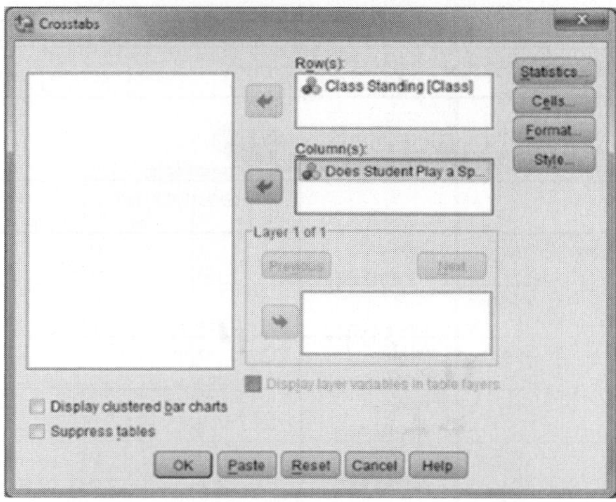

3. Click on *Statistics* in the upper right portion of the *Crosstabs* box. Ask for *Chi-Square*. Immediately below the *Chi-Square* is a *Nominal* box with four choices. This is where we ask for an effect size. Choose *Phi* and *Cramer's* V.

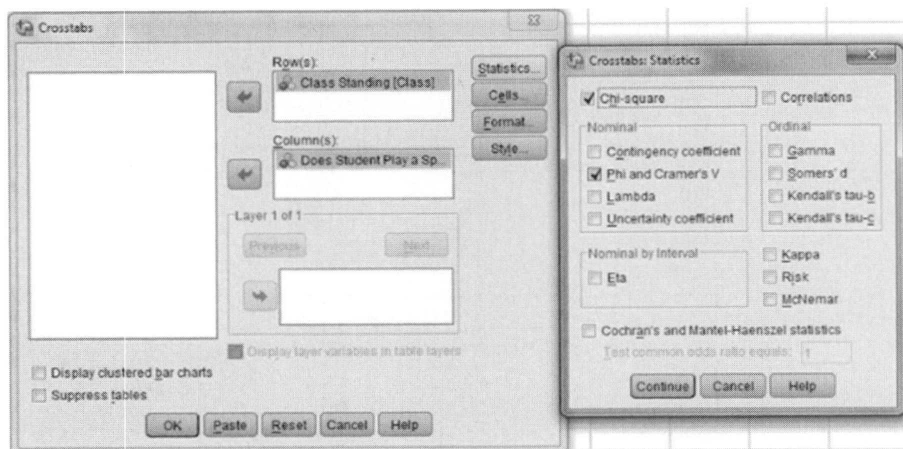

4. Click *Continue* to return to the *Crosstabs* box. Now click on *Cells*. In addition to the observed frequencies that are displayed by default, ask for expected frequencies. This step is not necessary to conduct this statistical test, but it allows us to create a table that can be helpful in understanding our output.

5. Click *Continue* to get back to the *Crosstabs* box, and then click *OK*. Your output should look like this:

Crosstabs

Case Processing Summary

	Cases					
	Valid		Missing		Total	
	N	Percent	N	Percent	N	Percent
Class Standing * Does Student Play a Sport?	80	100.0%	0	0.0%	80	100.0%

A

Class Standing * Does Student Play a Sport? Crosstabulation

			Does Student Play a Sport?		
			.00	Yes	Total
Class Standing	First-Year	Count	5	15	20
		Expected Count	10.8	9.3	20.0
	Sophomore	Count	8	12	20
		Expected Count	10.8	9.3	20.0
	Junior	Count	13	7	20
		Expected Count	10.8	9.3	20.0
	Senior	Count	17	3	20
		Expected Count	10.8	9.3	20.0
Total		Count	43	37	80
		Expected Count	43.0	37.0	80.0

Chi-Square Tests

	Value	df	Asymp. Sig. (2-sided)
Pearson Chi-Square	17.046[a]	3	.001
Likelihood Ratio	18.233	3	.000
Linear-by-Linear Association	16.694	1	.000
N of Valid Cases	80		

a. 0 cells (.0%) have expected count less than 5. The minimum expected count is 9.25.

Symmetric Measures

		Value	Approx. Sig.
Nominal by Nominal	Phi	.462	.001
	Cramer's V	.462	.001
N of Valid Cases		80	

What am I looking at? Interpreting your SPSS output

What does this output tell us?

A. Here is our table of observed and expected frequencies. It looks a little bit like Table 14.7, except here we have our expected values for each of the eight cells in the analysis.

B. This box contains our χ^2 test of independence.

C. The Pearson chi-square is the row of information we need to examine. There are three pieces of information here that are important to understand:

1. The value of the χ^2 test statistic is 17.05.
2. There are three degrees of freedom. Remember how this number was calculated. We need our df_{rows} and $df_{columns}$, both of which are calculated as the number of categories minus 1. With four rows, we have $df_{rows} = 3$; with two columns, we have $df_{columns} = 1$.

We need to multiply the df_{rows} and the $df_{columns}$, which gives us $3 \times 1 = 3$. The df_{total}, which is displayed here, is 3.

3. The significance level is .001, meaning we reject the null hypothesis that year in college and playing a sport are independent of each other (that is, they do appear to depend on each other).

D. Here we see our effect size. Because one of our variables has more than two categories, we need to report the Cramer's V, which is 0.462.

And of course, we must not forget that SPSS does nothing more than give us numbers to interpret and present in an organized (APA) format:

> A chi-squared test for independence revealed significant college class differences in sports participation, χ^2 (3, N = 80) = 17.05, p = .001, Cramer's V = 0.462.

LEARNING CHECK

1. How is the χ^2 goodness-of-fit test similar to the χ^2 test for independence? How are these two tests different?

   A: Both tools are used to analyze nominal data. The goodness-of-fit test uses one nominal variable to see how well those data fit the population. The test for independence uses two nominal variables to see whether scores on each of those two variables are independent of each other, or whether the scores on each of the two variables depend on each other.

2. How is the χ^2 test for independence different from a two-way analysis of variance (ANOVA)?

   A: To use the χ^2 test for independence requires frequency data from two nominal variables. The two-way ANOVA uses two nominal variables (either manipulated independent variables or nonmanipulated predictor variables) to see whether they have an effect on or are related to some outcome (dependent) variable that is a scale variable.

3. At the end of the previous section, we explored whether there were differences in vegetable preference among a sample of 100 university students. Let's now explore differences between men and women for favorite vegetables. Here are those data, this time broken down by respondent sex (male or female):

	Men	**Women**	**Totals**
Carrots	21	5	26
Broccoli	9	9	18
Red peppers	3	13	16
Asparagus	11	2	13
Spinach	6	5	11
Turnip greens	5	5	10
Peas	2	4	6
	57	43	100

   Enter these data in SPSS. Run the analyses to generate this output. Then, answer the questions that appear after the output, which should look like this:

   a) What is the hypothesis that is being tested?

      A: There will be no differences between men and women in their vegetable preferences.

   b) How many men were in the sample? How many women were in the sample?

      A: 57 men and 43 women

   c) What are the expected frequencies for each category?

      A: Men carrots = 14.8; Women carrots = 11.2

Crosstabs

Case Processing Summary

	Cases					
	Valid		Missing		Total	
	N	Percent	N	Percent	N	Percent
Vegetable * Person's Sex	100	100.0%	0	0.0%	100	100.0%

Vegetable * Person's Sex Crosstabulation

			Person's Sex		Total
			men	women	
Vegetable	carrots	Count	21	5	26
		Expected Count	14.8	11.2	26.0
	broccoli	Count	9	9	18
		Expected Count	10.3	7.7	18.0
	red peppers	Count	3	13	16
		Expected Count	9.1	6.9	16.0
	asparagus	Count	11	2	13
		Expected Count	7.4	5.6	13.0
	spinach	Count	6	5	11
		Expected Count	6.3	4.7	11.0
	turnip greens	Count	5	5	10
		Expected Count	5.7	4.3	10.0
	peas	Count	2	4	6
		Expected Count	3.4	2.6	6.0
Total		Count	57	43	100
		Expected Count	57.0	43.0	100.0

Chi-Square Tests

	Value	df	Asymp. Sig. (2-sided)
Pearson Chi-Square	21.547[a]	6	.001
Likelihood Ratio	22.989	6	.001
Linear-by-Linear Association	2.801	1	.094
N of Valid Cases	100		

a. 4 cells (28.6%) have expected count less than 5. The minimum expected count is 2.58.

Symmetric Measures

		Value	Approx. Sig.
Nominal by Nominal	Phi	.464	.001
	Cramer's V	.464	.001
N of Valid Cases		100	

(Continued)

(Continued)

Men broccoli = 10.3; Women broccoli = 7.7

Men red peppers = 9.1; Women red peppers = 6.9

Men asparagus = 7.4; Women asparagus = 5.6

Men spinach = 6.3; Women spinach = 4.7

Men turnip greens = 5.7; Women turnip greens = 4.3

Men peas = 3.4; Women peas = 2.6

d) What are the degrees of freedom?

A: 6

e) What is the test statistic?

A: $\chi^2 = 21.55$

f) What is the critical value that SPSS used to compare the test statistic to?

A: With $df = 6$ and assuming an alpha of .05, we consult Appendix F and find a critical value of 12.59.

g) Is the χ^2 test statistic statistically significant?

A: Yes, our test statistic exceeds our critical value, so it is statistically significant, meaning that men and women appear to differ in their preference for particular vegetables.

h) Write this result in APA style.

A: A chi-squared test for independence revealed significant sex differences in vegetable preferences, χ^2 $(6, N = 100) = 21.55$, $p = .001$, Cramer's $V = 0.464$.

SPEARMAN RANK-ORDER CORRELATION COEFFICIENT

In Chapter 12, we encountered the Pearson moment correlation coefficient. It is used to determine the nature and strength of the relationship between two variables. Two critical assumptions for the Pearson correlation is that the data are normally distributed for both variables and that both variables are scale measures. What happens when one or both of the variables are not normally distributed or are ranked-ordered, that is, when they are ordinal? In such situations, we need a new tool. *For ordinal data, we use the Spearman rank-order correlation coefficient.*

To understand the Spearman rank-order correlation, let's consider a study that Angel Wong and her colleagues (2014) conducted. These researchers investigated the relationship between drug prescription rates for Autism Spectrum Disorder and gross domestic product (GDP, which is the total value of goods and services produced in a country) in 25 countries and geographic regions around the world. These 25 countries appear in far left column of Table 14.8.

Hand-Calculating the Spearman Rank-Order Correlation

Wong et al. (2014) collected data about the prescription rates for Autism Spectrum Disorder per 100,000 people in each country. These prescription rates appear in the second column of Table 14.8. For the purpose of understanding our new statistical tool, I have ranked them in order from highest to lowest. We are going to correlate

Table 14.8 Prescription Data and GDP Ranks from Wong et al. (2014)

Country	Prescriptions per 100,000 Residents	Prescription Rate Rank	Per Capita GDP Rank
The Netherlands	36.36	1	3
Belgium	31.75	2	6
Switzerland	15.35	3	1
South Korea	14.36	4	11
Portugal	10.01	5	10
Thailand	9.98	6	21
New Zealand	8.13	7	8
Colombia	6.41	8	20
Ireland	5.94	9	4
Slovakia	5.59	10	14
Finland	4.01	11	7
Poland	3.97	12	17
Czech Republic	3.91	13	12
Austria	3.89	14	5
Australia	2.74	15	2
Hungary	1.69	16	15
Greece	1.34	17	9
South Africa	1.32	18	19
Central America	1.17	19	24
Venezuela	0.83	20	16
Turkey	0.82	21	18
Egypt	0.74	22	23
Saudi Arabia	0.51	23	13
Indonesia	0.40	24	22
Pakistan	0.04	25	25

these rankings of prescription rates with the GDP per capita for each one of these 25 countries. In the far right column of Table 14.8 are the rank orderings of per capita GDP for each country. We will now correlate these two ordinal variables.

Step 1: State the hypothesis

First, Wong et al.'s (2014) null hypothesis is straightforward. That is, there will be no relationship between prescription rates for Autism Spectrum Disorder and per capita GDP. Notationally, we have:

$$H_o: r_s = 0$$

Notice that for a Spearman correlation, it is written as *r* subscript s.

As with Pearson correlations, we have to consider one- and two-tailed research hypotheses. My personal preference, as you know by now, is to always have two-tailed research hypotheses because they are more conservative than one-tailed research hypotheses. In words, our two-tailed research hypothesis is that there will be a relationship between prescription rates for Autism Spectrum Disorder and per capita GDP. Notationally, we have:

$$H_r: r_s \neq 0$$

I realize that it seems reasonable to predict a positive relationship between these two variables; after all, countries with higher GDPs should have more resources available to treat psychological conditions. However, for the sake of being conservative, we are sticking with a two-tailed research hypothesis.

Step 2: Calculate the difference (*D*) score between each pair of rankings

Let's calculate the difference score between the two rankings of prescription rate and per capita GDP (see Table 14.9). Of course, we know from our days learning about difference scores that summing them would be meaningless because they will of course sum to zero. So, guess what the next step will be.

Table 14.9 Differences in Rankings for Each Country from Wong et al. (2014)

Country	Prescriptions per 100,000 Residents	Prescription Rate Rank	Per Capita GDP Rank	Difference Between the Ranks (D)	Difference^2
The Netherlands	36.36	1	3	−2	4
Belgium	31.75	2	6	−4	16
Switzerland	15.35	3	1	2	4
South Korea	14.36	4	11	−7	49
Portugal	10.01	5	10	−5	25
Thailand	9.98	6	21	−15	225
New Zealand	8.13	7	8	−1	1
Colombia	6.41	8	20	−12	144

Country	Prescriptions per 100,000 Residents	Prescription Rate Rank	Per Capita GDP Rank	Difference Between the Ranks (D)	Difference^2
Ireland	5.94	9	4	5	25
Slovakia	5.59	10	14	−4	16
Finland	4.01	11	7	4	16
Poland	3.97	12	17	−5	25
Czech Republic	3.91	13	12	1	1
Austria	3.89	14	5	9	81
Australia	2.74	15	2	13	169
Hungary	1.69	16	15	1	1
Greece	1.34	17	9	8	64
South Africa	1.32	18	19	−1	1
Central America	1.17	19	24	−5	25
Venezuela	0.83	20	16	4	16
Turkey	0.82	21	18	3	9
Egypt	0.74	22	23	−1	1
Saudi Arabia	0.51	23	13	10	100
Indonesia	0.40	24	22	2	4
Pakistan	0.04	25	25	0	0
					Sum of D^2s = 1023

Step 3: Square and sum the difference scores in step 2

Of course, you know to square those difference scores, which we have done in the far right column of Table 14.9. Once we square the difference scores, we sum them. As seen at the bottom of the far right column in Table 14.9, that sum is 1,023.

Step 4: Calculate the Spearman correlation coefficient (r_s) test statistic

To calculate the Spearman r, here is our formula:

$$r_s = \frac{1 - 6(\text{sum of } D^2\text{s})}{\text{sample size (sample size}^2 - 1)}$$

The only ingredients we need to calculate r_s are (a) the squared sum of the difference scores and (b) the sample size. Everything else, including the number 6 in the numerator, is a given in this formula.

By using this formula and the information in Table 14.9, we have:

$$r_s = 1 - \frac{6(1023)}{25(25^2 - 1)}$$

$$r_s = 1 - \frac{6138}{25(624)}$$

$$r_s = 1 - \frac{6138}{15,600}$$

$$r_s = 1 - .393$$

$$r_s = .607$$

Step 5: Locate critical value and make a decision about the null hypothesis

Of course, we need to decide whether our test statistic in the previous step is statistically significant. To do so, we need our sample size, alpha level, and access to Appendix G. With a sample size of 25, an alpha level of .05, and a two-tailed research hypothesis, Appendix G tells us that our critical value is $r_s = .398$. Given that our test statistic, $r_s = .607$, exceeds that critical value, we reject the null hypothesis and conclude that there is a positive correlation between per capita GDP and rates of prescriptions for Autism Spectrum Disorder.

Please keep in mind that just as with Pearson correlations, a statistically significant Spearman correlation does not mean that one variable caused a change in the other. In this example, it is tempting to conclude that a larger GDP causes more prescriptions to be made for Autism Spectrum Disorder. However, it could be that a third variable, such as expenditures on autism research, is a mediating variable that is responsible for the observed correlation between GDP and prescription rates. If so, this would mean the relationship between GDP and prescription rates is an example of a spurious correlation, which is a concept that has been covered in the previous two chapters.

And of course, none of this work means anything until we communicate it:

> There was a positive correlation between per capita GDP and rates of prescriptions for Autism Spectrum Disorder, r_s (25) = .61, $p < .05$.

This may look a lot like the APA write-up for the Pearson correlation; however, there are two differences. First, perhaps obviously, we report r_s, not r. Second and perhaps less obvious, we report the sample size in parenthesis, not the degrees of freedom as we did with the Pearson correlation.

Spearman's Rank-Order Correlation and SPSS

Let's finish this section by using SPSS to generate r_s. We learned how to do Pearson's correlations on SPSS in Chapter 12; prepare to be amazed by how much you already know about using SPSS for r_s.

Establishing your spreadsheet

Let's use our data from Table 14.8 and enter them into SPSS. After opening SPSS, go to *Variable View* to set up our spreadsheet. Of course, we will need our two ranked-ordered variables (if you enter the actual prescription rates from the table, SPSS will convert them into rankings). However, I would also like to have the country name in the spreadsheet, just to allow me to check and make sure I entered my data correctly. You do not need to have this variable to conduct your analysis, but just be aware I am including it.

I called the country name variable `Country`. It is a string (nominal variable), and I widen it to fit the full name of each country when I enter the data. Then I created a `Prescription_Rank` variable followed by a `GDP_Rank` variable. These last two variables are numeric data, with an ordinal measure. Here is what your *Variable View* should look like:

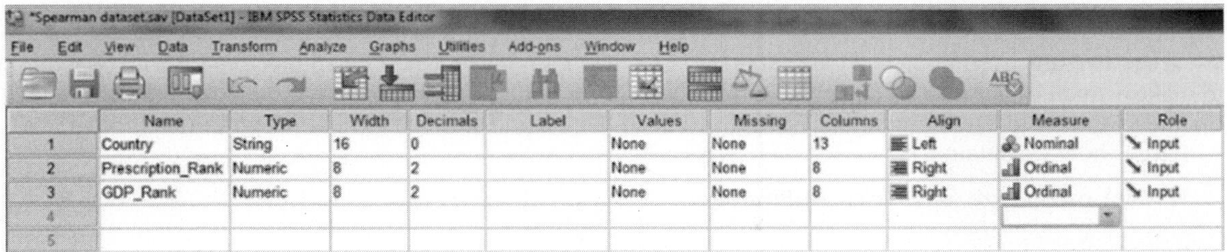

	Name	Type	Width	Decimals	Label	Values	Missing	Columns	Align	Measure	Role
1	Country	String	16	0		None	None	13	Left	Nominal	Input
2	Prescription_Rank	Numeric	8	2		None	None	8	Right	Ordinal	Input
3	GDP_Rank	Numeric	8	2		None	None	8	Right	Ordinal	Input

Now we can enter our data from Table 14.8. Click on our *Data View*, and then enter the data, being careful while you do so. I find it is easy for me to misread so many rankings. Be sure to check your work in SPSS against the data in the table. Here is what your *Data View* will look like after entering the data:

*Spearman dataset.sav [DataSet1] - IBM SPSS Statistics Data Editor

	Country	Prescription_Rank	GDP_Rank	var
1	The Netherlands	1.00	3.00	
2	Belgium	2.00	6.00	
3	Switzerland	3.00	1.00	
4	South Korea	4.00	11.00	
5	Portugal	5.00	10.00	
6	Thailand	6.00	21.00	
7	New Zealand	7.00	8.00	
8	Colombia	8.00	20.00	
9	Ireland	9.00	4.00	
10	Slovakia	10.00	14.00	
11	Finland	11.00	7.00	
12	Poland	12.00	17.00	
13	Czech Republic	13.00	12.00	
14	Austria	14.00	5.00	
15	Australia	15.00	2.00	
16	Hungary	16.00	15.00	
17	Greece	17.00	9.00	
18	South Africa	18.00	19.00	
19	Central America	19.00	24.00	
20	Venezuela	20.00	16.00	
21	Turkey	21.00	18.00	
22	Egypt	22.00	23.00	
23	Saudi Arabia	23.00	13.00	
24	Indonesia	24.00	22.00	
25	Pakistan	25.00	25.00	
26				
27				
28				

Data View | Variable View

Running your analysis

We are now ready to run our analyses and generate our r_s. I am not much of a gambler, but I would be willing to make a small wager that you can take it from here, given your experiences with correlations in Chapter 12. Go ahead and try to run our analyses now; if you need help, it will start in the next paragraph.

Here is how we obtain a r_s:

1. Click on *Analyze* → *Correlate* → *Bivariate*.

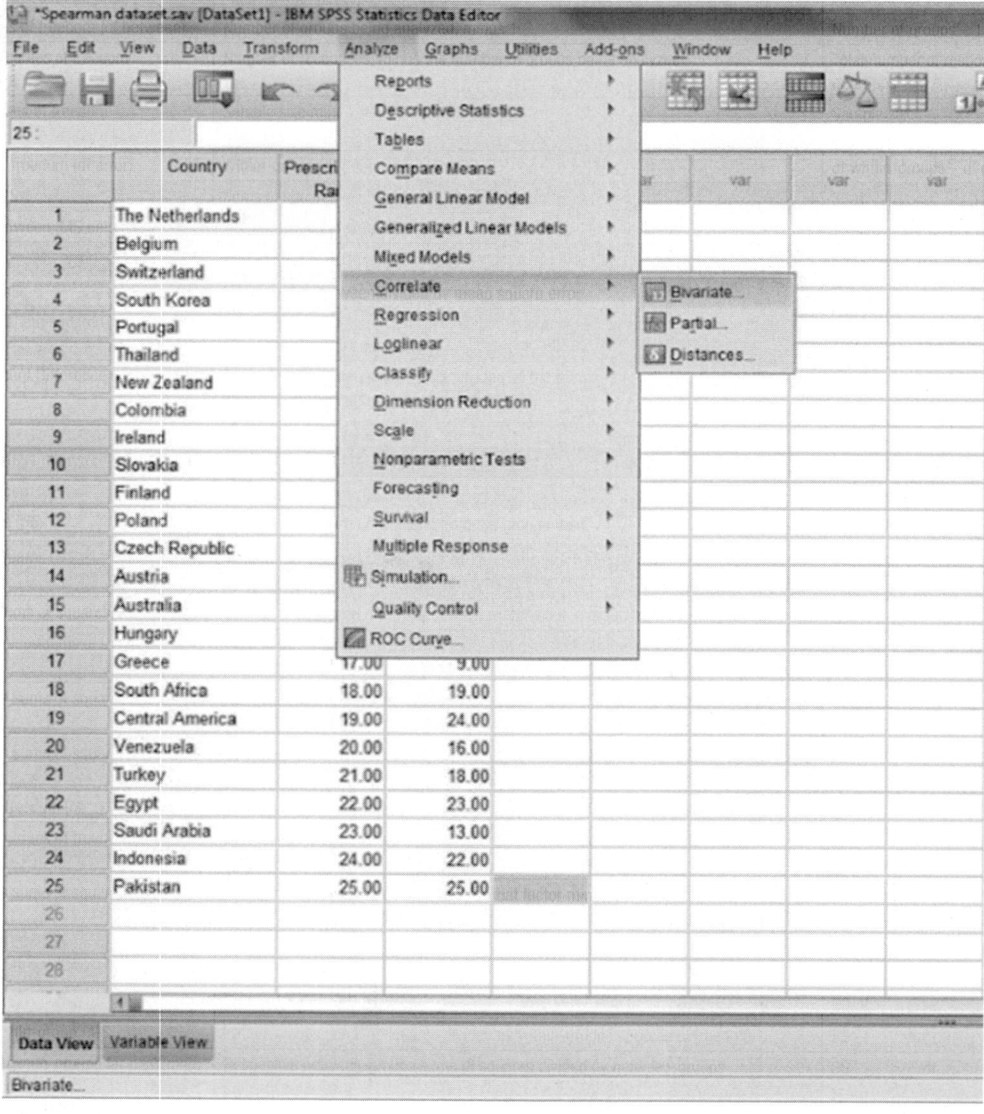

2. We have only our two ranked variables to use, so click on them in the *Variables* box.
3. SPSS's default is to provide us with the Pearson correlation; therefore, we must take control and tell it to give us the Spearman correlation. In addition, please click off the Pearson correlation, just to help avoid confusion when we get our output.

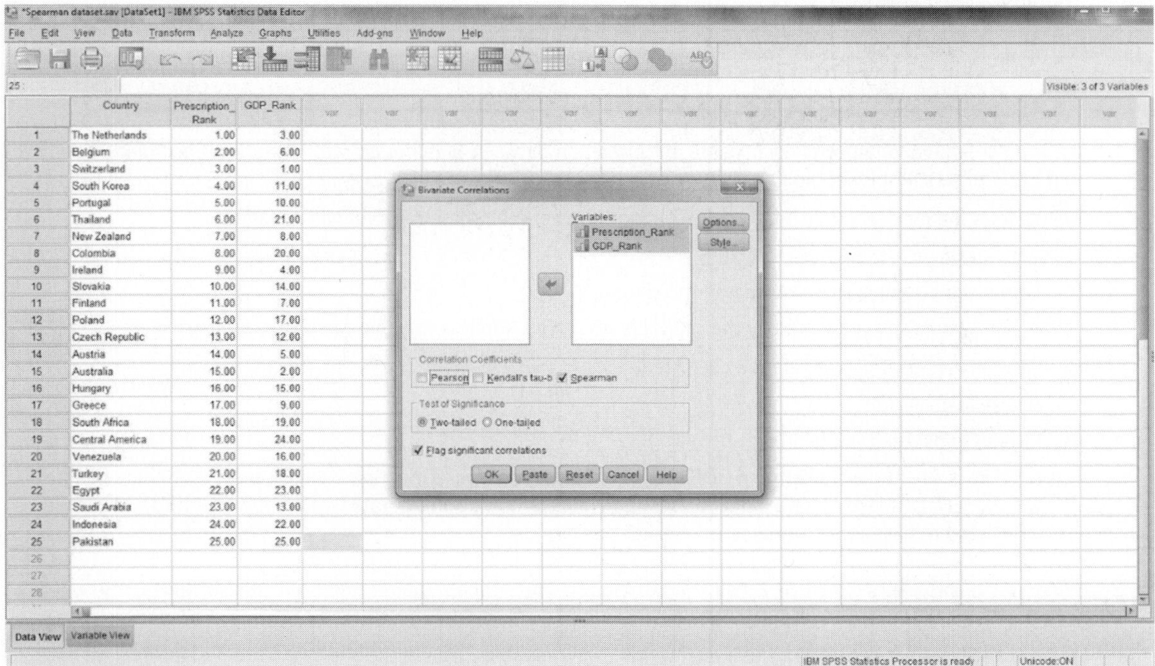

After clicking *OK*, your output should appear. It will look like this:

Nonparametric Correlations

Correlations

			Prescription_Rank	GDP_Rank
Spearman's rho	Prescription_Rank	Correlation Coefficient	1.000	.607**
		Sig. (2-tailed)	.	.001
		N	25	25
	GDP_Rank	Correlation Coefficient	.607**	1.000
		Sig. (2-tailed)	.001	.
		N	25	25

**. Correlation is significant at the 0.01 level (2-tailed).

What am I looking at? Interpreting your SPSS output

This output will appear almost identical to that from the Pearson correlation output we examined in Chapter 12. Rather than explaining what you already read there, let's use this output and check your understanding in the upcoming Learning Check. Please keep in mind when interpreting output that you understand this correlation resulted from two ordinal variables, whereas our old friend the Pearson correlation is used when we have two scale variables.

LEARNING CHECK

1. By using your SPSS printout for the Spearman correlation between prescription rate for Autism Spectrum Disorder and per capita GDP, answer the following questions:
   a) What is the precise significance level of relationship between these two ordinal variables?
      A: $p = .001$
   b) Where is the sample size provided on this printout?
      A: The sample size is denoted by the capital letter *N*. The *N* in this example was 25.
   c) What is the Spearman correlation coefficient (r_s)?
      A: $r_s = .607$
   d) Interpret this result in plain English.
      A: There is a relationship between GDP and prescription rates for Autism Spectrum Disorder, such that countries with larger GDPs tend to have higher prescription rates for this disorder. Stated differently, countries with smaller GDPs tend to have lower prescription rates for this disorder.
2. What is the difference between a Pearson correlation and a Spearman correlation? Stated differently, when would a researcher use a Pearson correlation and when would a researcher use a Spearman correlation?
   A: We use the Pearson correlation when we have two scale variables. We use the Spearman correlation when we have two ordinal (ranked) variables. It is possible you will see a Spearman correlation reported in published research when the variables being correlated are scale variables. This will happen when one or more of the assumptions of the Pearson correlation have been violated.
3. What is the difference between a Spearman correlation and a chi-squared (χ^2) test for independence? Stated differently, when would a researcher use each one of these two tools?
   A: Whereas the Spearman correlation requires two ordinal variables, the χ^2 test for independence requires two nominal variables.
4. If I select an alpha level of .035, what does that mean in plain English?
   A: It means that we are accepting a 3.5% chance that our statistical result is a Type I error; that is, we accepted a 3.5% chance that we find a relationship between variables in our sample that does not exist in the population from which that sample was drawn.

MANN-WHITNEY *U* TEST

In Chapter 7, we discussed the independent samples *t* test. It is used to determine whether the mean difference between two groups is generalizable from a sample to the population. Two critical assumptions of the independent samples *t* test are that (1) the dependent (or outcome) variable is on a scale measurement and (2) that scores on the dependent variable are normally distributed. However, sometimes we have an outcome variable that is on an ordinal scale of measurement or is not normally distributed. In such cases, we use the Mann-Whitney *U* Test. *To use this tool, our outcome variable must be ordinal data.* In published research, you will see results from this tool reported with an italicized letter *U*.

Hand-Calculating the Mann-Whitney *U* Test

In our discussion of the Spearman rank-order correlation, we used data from 25 countries. What we will do now is use some of those data again, but this time, we will focus on the 13 countries in Europe and their prescription rates for Autism Spectrum Disorder. Table 14.10 has the prescription rate data displayed for these 13 countries by "Region," in which a country is either a member of the Eurozone economy or not in the Eurozone economy. We will be comparing prescription rates based on membership in the Eurozone economy.

Step 1: State hypotheses

With the Mann-Whitney *U* test, we are comparing distributions rather than means, as we did with an independent samples *t* test. Therefore, hypotheses are tricky to state notationally, so we will just state them with words.

H_0: There will be no difference in Autism Spectrum Disorder prescription rates between European countries in the Eurozone and European countries not in the Eurozone.

H_r: There will be a difference in Autism Spectrum Disorder prescription rates between European countries in the Eurozone and European countries not in the Eurozone.

Notice that the language of the research hypotheses means it is a two-tailed hypothesis.

Table 14.10 Prescription Rates for European Nations in Wong et al.'s (2014) Research

Country	Prescriptions per 100,000 Residents	Prescription Rate Rank	Region
The Netherlands	36.36	1	Eurozone
Belgium	31.75	2	Eurozone
Switzerland	15.35	3	Not Eurozone
Portugal	10.01	4	Eurozone
Ireland	5.94	5	Eurozone
Slovakia	5.59	6	Eurozone
Finland	4.01	7	Eurozone
Poland	3.97	8	Not Eurozone
Czech Republic	3.91	9	Not Eurozone
Austria	3.89	10	Eurozone
Hungary	1.69	11	Not Eurozone
Greece	1.34	12	Eurozone
Turkey	0.82	13	Not Eurozone

Step 2: Calculate the ranks for categories being compared

Look at the far right two columns in Table 14.11. What we've done is put each country's prescription rank in its respective category (group) of "Eurozone" or "Not Eurozone." There were no tied scores, but if there were tied scores, we would have taken the average of the two rankings they would have had and applied it to the appropriate category. We have separated the ranks in the far two right columns to make the next step a little easier.

Step 3: Sum the ranks for each category

For the Eurozone ranks, we have:

$$1 + 2 + 4 + 5 + 6 + 7 + 10 + 12 = 47$$

For the Not Eurozone ranks, we have:

$$3 + 8 + 9 + 11 + 13 = 44$$

Table 14.11 Prescription Data and Category Ranks from Wong et al. (2014)

Country	Prescriptions per 100,000 Residents	Prescription Rate Rank	Region	"Eurozone" Ranks	"Not Eurozone" Ranks
The Netherlands	36.36	1	Eurozone	1	
Belgium	31.75	2	Eurozone	2	
Switzerland	15.35	3	Not Eurozone		3
Portugal	10.01	4	Eurozone	4	
Ireland	5.94	5	Eurozone	5	
Slovakia	5.59	6	Eurozone	6	
Finland	4.01	7	Eurozone	7	
Poland	3.97	8	Not Eurozone		8
Czech Republic	3.91	9	Not Eurozone		9
Austria	3.89	10	Eurozone	10	
Hungary	1.69	11	Not Eurozone		11
Greece	1.34	12	Eurozone	12	
Turkey	0.82	13	Not Eurozone		13

Step 4: Find the *U* for each group

Remember that the Mann-Whitney *U* test is communicated with a *U*. Each group will have a *U*, and here is the general formula for it. The *n* stands for the sample size of a particular group.

$$U_{\text{group 1}} = (n \text{ group 1}) \times (n \text{ group 2}) + \frac{(n \text{ group 1}) \times (n \text{ group 1} + 1)}{2} - \text{sum of group 1 rankings}$$

Remember that each group has its own *U*. By "group 1" we are referring to the group for which we are calculating a *U*. Group 2 is the group for which we are not calculating a *U*.

Let's calculate the *U* for the Eurozone countries now:

$$U = (8) \times (5) + \frac{(8) \times (8+1)}{2} - 47$$

$$U = 40 + \frac{72}{2} - 47$$

$$U = 40 + 36 - 47$$

$$U \text{ for Eurozone countries} = 29$$

Now we will calculate the *U* for the Not Eurozone countries:

$$U_{\text{group 2}} = (5) \times (8) + \frac{(5) \times (5+1)}{2} - 44$$

$$U = 40 + \frac{30}{2} - 44$$

$$U = 40 + 15 - 44$$

$$U \text{ for Not Eurozone countries} = 11$$

Step 5: Locate the critical value and make a decision about the null hypothesis

Appendix H contains the critical values for the Mann-Whitney *U* test. There are two tables, one for an alpha level of .05 and one for an alpha level of .01. Of course, we will use the table for an alpha of .05. Across the top row, we need the sample size for our first group, and down the left side, we need the sample size for our second group. It does not matter at this point which group is the "first" group and which group is the "second" group. Looking for the intersection of 8 (the number of Eurozone countries) and 5 (the number of Not Eurozone countries) gives us a critical value of 6 for our two-tailed hypothesis test.

We have two *U* values. What we need to do is *compare the smaller U test statistic* to our critical value. In addition, to reject the null hypothesis, *the test statistic must be smaller than the critical value*. This is, of course, the reverse of the other statistical tools we have learned about.

With a test statistic of $U = 11$ and a critical value of 6, the test statistic is larger than the critical value. Therefore, we do not reject the null hypothesis. In other words, there is no difference in prescription rates for Autism Spectrum Disorder between European countries in the Eurozone and European countries not in the Eurozone.

Here is our APA style write-up:

> A Mann-Whitney *U* test indicated that there were no differences in prescription rates between Eurozone and non-Eurozone countries, $U = 11$, $p > .05$.

Mann-Whitney *U* Test and SPSS

We conclude this chapter by using SPSS to conduct this analysis and understand the output generated. Let's go into SPSS and have some fun. We will use the data from Table 14.11 that we just used in our hand calculations.

Establishing your spreadsheet

As always, start in *Variable View*. We have two variables: the region a country falls in (with two levels, in Eurozone or not in Eurozone) and the prescription rates for Autism Spectrum Disorder. We can name the first variable `Region` and the second variable `Prescription_Rates`. Both variables are numeric types of variables. We should provide a label to each variable, which I have creatively done as "Region" and "Prescription Rates". We need to provide values for the `Region` variable. I coded Eurozone countries with a `1` and non-Eurozone countries with a `2`. Under *Measures*, be sure the `Region` variable is nominal, and that the `Prescription Rates` variable is ordinal. Here is what your *Variable View* should look like:

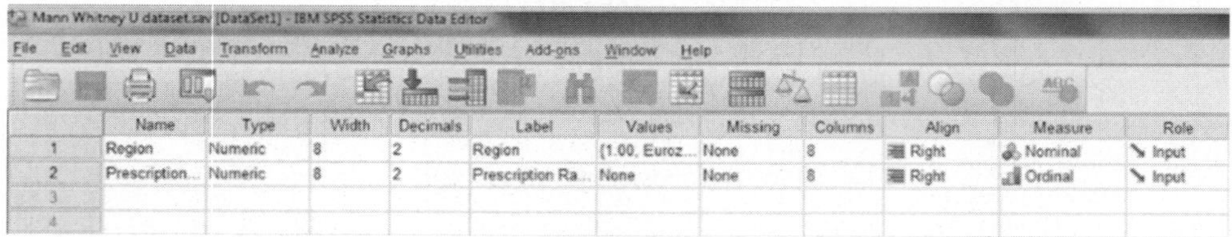

	Name	Type	Width	Decimals	Label	Values	Missing	Columns	Align	Measure	Role
1	Region	Numeric	8	2	Region	{1.00, Euroz...	None	8	Right	Nominal	Input
2	Prescription...	Numeric	8	2	Prescription Ra...	None	None	8	Right	Ordinal	Input
3											
4											

Running your analysis

Let's switch into *Data View*. For the nominal variable of `Region`, we enter a `1` if the country is in the Eurozone and a `2` if the country is not in the Eurozone. In addition, for each country, we must enter its prescription rate ranking.

In all, you will have 13 rows and 2 columns of data that should look like this:

	Region	Prescription_Rates
1	1.00	1.00
2	1.00	2.00
3	2.00	3.00
4	1.00	4.00
5	1.00	5.00
6	1.00	6.00
7	1.00	7.00
8	2.00	8.00
9	2.00	9.00
10	1.00	10.00
11	2.00	11.00
12	1.00	12.00
13	2.00	13.00

We can now put our statistical tool to use. Here's how:

1. Click on *Analyze* → *Nonparametric Tests* → *Legacy Dialogues* → *2 Independent Samples*.

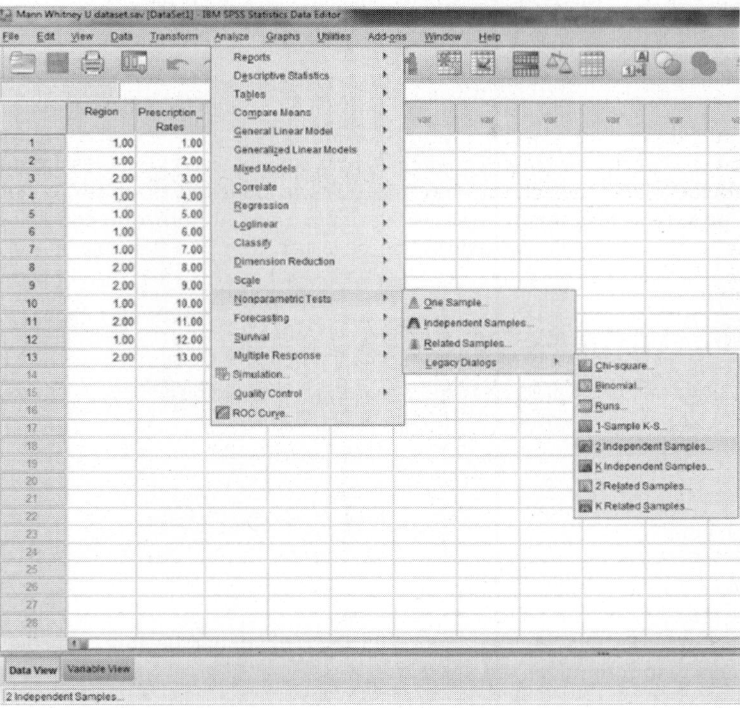

2. In the *Test Variable List*, we want our outcome variable of `Prescription Rates`. In the *Grouping Variable*, we want our predictor variable of `Region`.

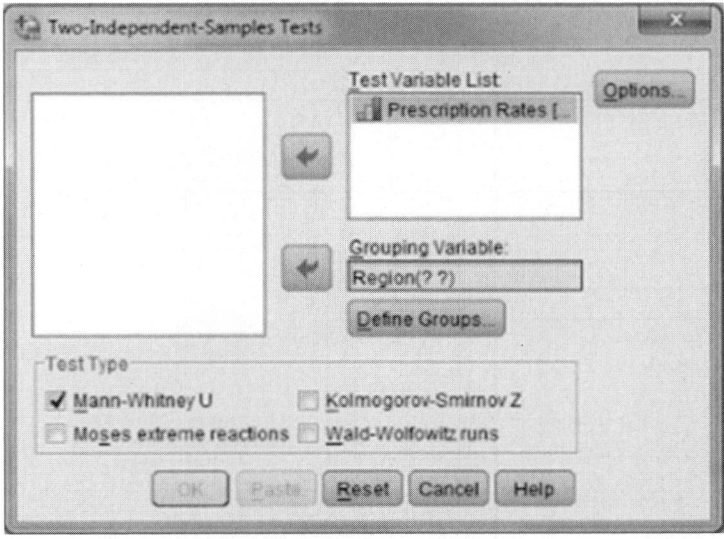

3. We next need to click on *Define Groups*. We must tell SPSS how we coded the nominal predictor variable. It does not matter which group you give a 1 and a 2 to.

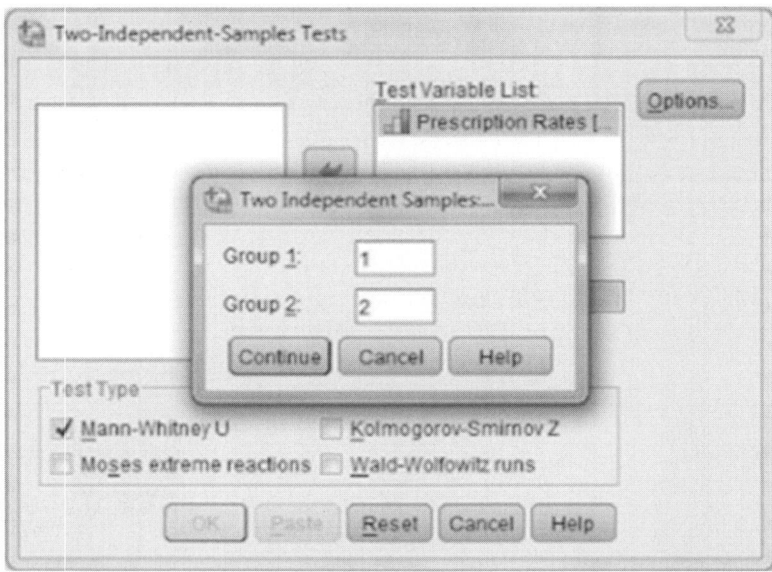

4. By default, SPSS provides us with the Mann-Whitney *U* (test). Just be sure it is checked before pressing *OK* and producing your output, as seen here:

NPar Tests

Mann-Whitney Test

Ranks

	Region	N	Mean Rank	Sum of Ranks
Prescription Rates	Eurozone	8	5.88	47.00
	Not Eurozone	5	8.80	44.00
	Total	13		

Test Statistics[a]

	Prescription Rates
Mann-Whitney U	11.000
Wilcoxon W	47.000
Z	-1.317
Asymp. Sig. (2-tailed)	.188
Exact Sig. [2*(1-tailed Sig.)]	.222[b]

a. Grouping Variable: Region

b. Not corrected for ties.

What am I looking at? Interpreting your SPSS output

Let's make sure we understand what SPSS has just done for us:,

A. This is the outcome variable.

B. This is the predictor variable and its levels.

C. This is the sample size for each level of the predictor variable, as well as the total sample size.

D. This is the sum of the rankings, which we did in step 3 of the hand-calculations.

E. This is the smaller of the two *U* values that we calculated in step 4 of the hand-calculations. It is our test statistic.

F. This is our *p* value. Given that it is greater than .05, we fail to reject the null hypothesis and conclude that there is no difference between countries in and not in the Eurozone economy with respect to prescription rates for Autism Spectrum Disorder.

LEARNING CHECK

1. How is the Mann-Whitney *U* test similar to the independent samples *t* test? How are these two tools different?

   A: These tools are similar in that they both compare two groups on some outcome. They differ based on the measurement of the outcome being analyzed. The independent samples *t* test is used when the outcome is a scale variable. The Mann-Whitney *U* test is used when the outcome is an ordinal variable.

2. How is the Mann-Whitney *U* test similar to the Spearman rank-order correlation? How are these two tools different?

   A: These tools are similar in that they both use ordinal data. They differ in that the Spearman rank-order correlation examines two ordinal variables and tests for a relationship between them. The Mann-Whitney *U* test uses a nominal variable and tests for differences between the two categories on ordinal outcome data.

NOTE

1. Here is the formula to calculate the Phi coefficient:

$$\phi = \sqrt{\frac{\chi^2 \text{ test statistic}}{\text{sample size}}}$$

CHAPTER APPLICATION QUESTIONS

1. Explain the difference among nominal, ordinal, and scale data.
2. What type of data are needed to conduct a χ^2 test?
3. How does a χ^2 goodness-of-fit test differ from a χ^2 test of independence?

4. What is the difference between expected frequencies and observed frequencies?

5. Explain when a researcher should use each of the following statistical tools:
   a) the Spearman rank-order correlation
   b) the χ^2 test for independence
   c) the Mann-Whitney U Test
   d) the χ^2 goodness-of-fit test

6. At the start of every season in every major college sport, "experts" predict which teams will do well and which teams will do poorly. Here are the 2014-2015 predicted and final rankings for each Big Ten men's basketball team:

2014-2015 Predicted Finish	2014-2015 Actual Finish
1. Wisconsin	1. Wisconsin
2. Michigan State	2. Maryland
3. Ohio State	3. Michigan State
4. Michigan	3. Iowa
5. Minnesota	5. Purdue
6. Nebraska	6. Ohio State
7. Iowa	7. Indiana
8. Illinois	8. Illinois
9. Indiana	9. Michigan
10. Maryland	10. Minnesota
11. Purdue	11. Northwestern
12. Penn State	12. Nebraska
13. Northwestern	13. Penn State
14. Rutgers	14. Rutgers

   a) What statistical tool would you use to learn whether the expert predictions are valid predictors of actual ranking at the end of the season?

Answer the following questions:

   b) What is the hypothesis being tested in this analysis?
   c) What is the strength of the relationship between the expert predictions and actual ranking at the end of the season?
   d) What is the precise significance level of relationship between these two ordinal variables?
   e) Interpret what the r_s and significance level mean in plain English.

Answers

1. Nominal data are measured categorically; for instance, a person was born in one country, and another person was born in another country. We can code such data numerically, but the numbers are only category markers and mean nothing statistically.

   Ordinal data are ranked-ordered data. We can rank our top five all-time favorite movies, giving our favorite a 1 and our fifth favorite a 5. However, these numbers are "place holders" and do not tell us how much more we like one movie than another.

   Scale data are meaningful numeric data. If we rate each of our five favorite movies on a 1-to-7 response range, then the numbers tell us how much we prefer one movie to another.

2. Nominal data make use of both types of χ^2 tests.

3. The goodness-of-fit test assesses whether sample data fit the population distribution. The test of independence assesses whether two variables are independent from and not dependent on each other.

4. Expected frequencies are patterns we expect to find in the population; observed frequencies are the actual sample data we have obtained (observed).

5. a) When one or both variables are not normally distributed or are ranked-ordered, that is, when they are ordinal

   b) A: When we have two nominal variables

   c) When we have an outcome variable that is on an ordinal scale of measurement or that is not normally distributed

   d) When we have one nominal variable

6. a) Spearman's rank-order correlation coefficient because both variables (predicted finish and actual finish) are measured on an ordinal scale

   Enter these data into SPSS and conduct the appropriate analysis. Be aware that two teams (Michigan State and Iowa) tied for third place in the actual conference rankings at season's end. Therefore, when you enter data into SPSS, you need to give each one of them a 3.5, which is the mean of third and fourth place.

   b) There is no relationship between predicted rankings at the start of the season and the actual rankings at the end of the season.

   c) $r_s = .52$

   d) $p = .057$

   e) This is a strong correlation that is not statistically significant. We cannot reject the null hypothesis. That is, there is no statistically significant relationship between predicted rankings at the start of the season and the actual rankings at the end of the season.

This example also brings up a recurring theme in statistics. Recall from Chapter 12 that correlations greater than .50 are considered to indicate strong relationships between variables. Why then was it not statistically significant? Remember that the relationship between any two variables will be statistically significant if our sample size is large enough. As a measure of effect size, a correlation of .52 as we found here is strong. Of course, we should not draw conclusions based on the small amount of data we had here (think about the law of small numbers from Chapter 1).

QUESTIONS FOR CLASS DISCUSSION

1. Each year, *U.S. News & World Reports* provides rankings of colleges and universities along various dimensions. One such dataset includes rankings of primary care medical school programs. Here is a listing of the top 18 programs in the western and midwestern United States (data are from 2015):

   1. University of Washington (West)
   2. University of California at San Francisco (West)
   3. University of Nebraska Medical Center (Midwest)
   4. Oregon Health and Science University (West)
   5. University of California at Los Angeles (West)
   6. University of Wisconsin at Madison (Midwest)
   7. University of Minnesota—Twin Cities (Midwest)
   8. Baylor College of Medicine (Midwest)
   9. Michigan State University College of Osteopathic Medicine (Midwest)
   10. University of Iowa (Midwest)
   11. University of Texas Southwestern Medical Center (Midwest)
   13.5. University of California at Davis (West)
   13.5. University of California at San Diego (West)
   13.5. University of Chicago (Midwest)
   13.5. University of Hawaii at Manoa (West)
   16. Washington University in St. Louis (Midwest)
   17.5. Stanford University (West)
   17.5. University of Kansas Medical Center (Midwest)

   Here is the research question to answer: *Are there differences in the ranking of primary care medical schools in the western and midwestern United States?*

   a) What statistical tool would you use to learn whether the rankings of primary care medical schools are different for those in the West versus those in the Midwest?
   b) What is the hypothesis being tested?
   c) What is the predictor variable in this analysis? What are the levels of this predictor variable? What is the sample size for each level of the predictor variable?
   d) What is the test statistic in this analysis?
   e) By using Appendix H, find the critical value that SPSS implicitly used in this analysis.
   f) What is the precise significance level of the relationship between these two variables? What does this statistic tell us?
   g) Interpret what these results mean in plain English.

2. A potential sponsor would like to know whether local viewers prefer some evening news programs over others. The sponsor conducts a viewer preference survey based on a simple random sample of 1,000 households. The results are given below. Perform the appropriate test on these data, using an alpha of .05, and provide the sponsor with nonstatistical advice based on your analysis.

KFOX	KMSN	KMTV	KCNN
200	275	300	225

CHAPTER 15

Bringing It All Together

Using Your Statistical Toolkit

After reading this chapter, you will be able to

Apply statistical tools to real research studies to analyze data from those studies

Congratulations! You have now made it through the nuts and bolts of using some very powerful tools. In this chapter, we will use your expertise to figure out the appropriate use of many of the tools you've learned about in this class. This chapter presents research hypotheses and accompanying methodologies of six published studies. After each presentation, we will dissect the data the researcher collected and figure out what statistical tools are appropriate to use in that research. Throughout this chapter, we will highlight specific statistical tools, their accompanying chapters, and where appropriate, specific page numbers in the book that can refer to if you want to review and refresh yourself on specific information.

After reading about these six research studies, there will be descriptions of three more research studies that will provide you with an opportunity to act as a "statistical consultant" to help determine which statistical tool(s) are needed to test the research hypotheses offered. After each one of these three research studies will be a series of questions for you to answer to help you decide on the appropriate statistical tool for each study.

DECIDING ON THE APPROPRIATE TOOL: SIX EXAMPLES

We will present six research studies with an emphasis on the research hypothesis it offered and the methodology it used to test its hypothesis(ses). In doing so, we will reason through what statistical tools should be used to test the hypothesis(ses). We will not use any statistical tools in this section as we did in the previous 14 chapters. Rather, we will get to use your statistical toolkit and play the role of statistical consultant to each of these researchers in helping them decide how to analyze their data.

To help in our role as statistical consultant, please examine Figure 15.1 carefully. It provides information about how to determine what statistical tools to use, given the hypothesis being tested and scale of measurement (i.e., nominal, ordinal, scale) for the variables in the research study. For each study we are about to read, we will walk through Figure 15.1. Doing so will lead us to the appropriate way to analyze the data for each study. In an actual consulting role, you could refer to the appropriate material discussed in this class and conduct and

Figure 15.1 Flowchart for Choosing the Correct Statistical Tool

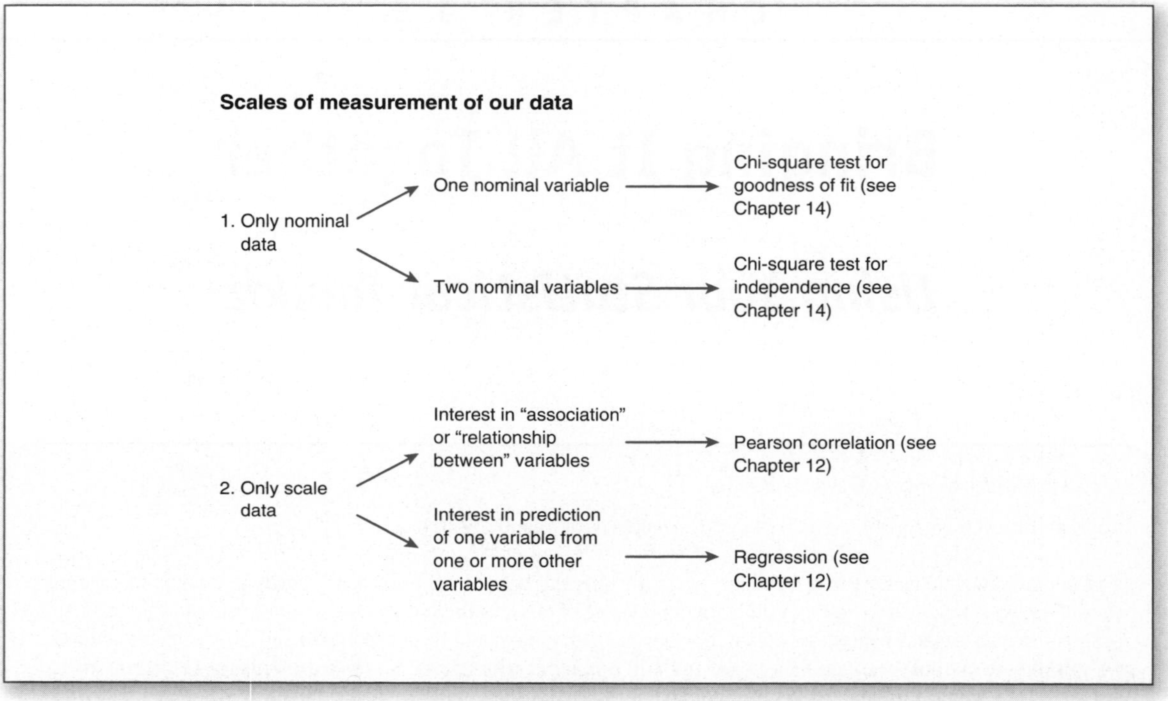

Scales of measurement of our data
1. Only nominal data
One nominal variable
Chi-square test for goodness of fit (see Chapter 14)
Two nominal variables
Chi-square test for independence (see Chapter 14)
2. Only scale data
Interest in "association" or "relationship between" variables
Pearson correlation (see Chapter 12)
Interest in prediction of one variable from one or more other variables
Regression (see Chapter 12)

15.1(a)

3. Presence of one or more ordinal variables
Nominal independent/ predictor variable with ordinal outcome variable
Mann Whitney U test (see Chapter 14)
Two ordinal variables
Spearman rank-order correlation (see Chapter 14)

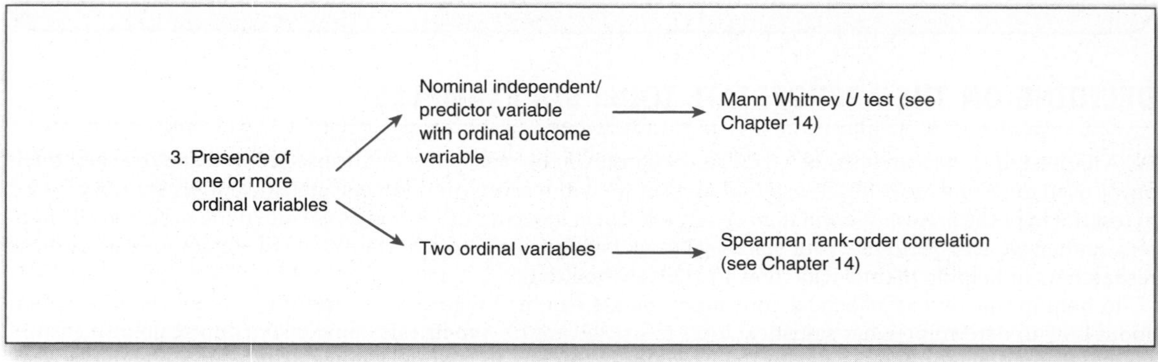

15.1(b)

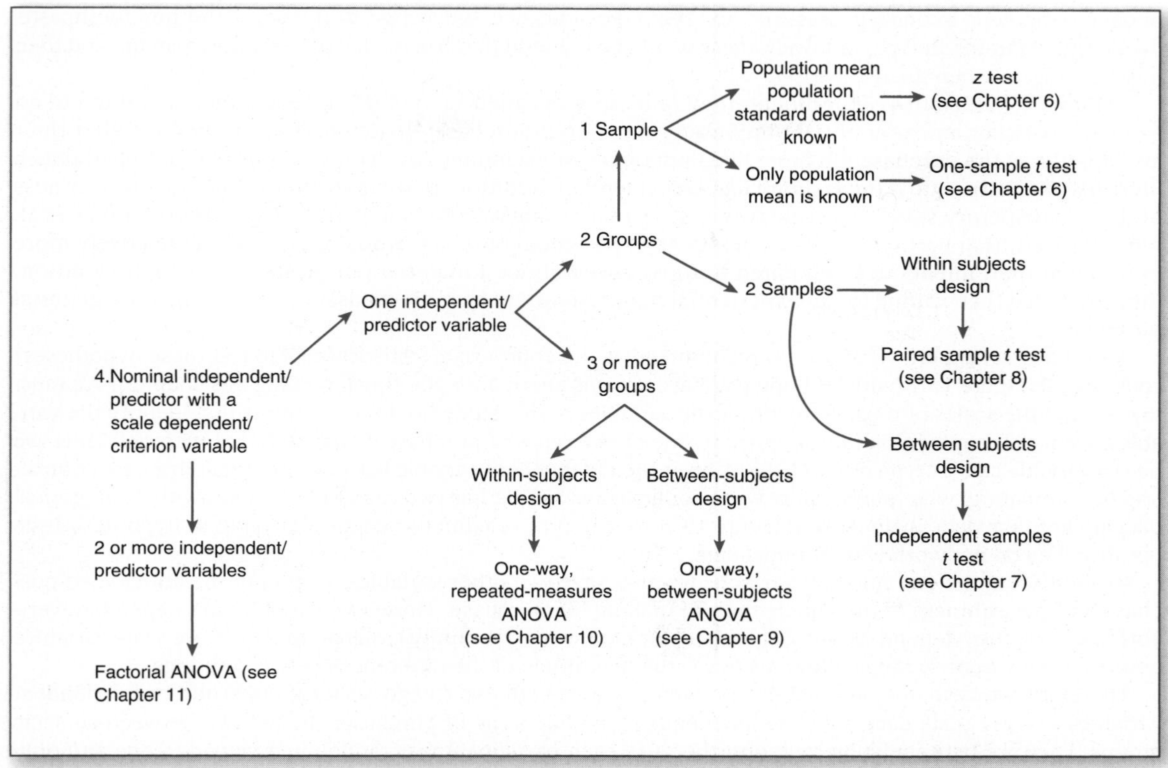

15.1(c)

interpret the statistical analyses for the researcher. Indeed, the skills and abilities you have gained in this class are in demand by both employers and graduate programs; now is a chance to put them to use.

Study 1: "Waiting for Merlot: Anticipatory Consumption of Experiential and Material Purchases"

Most of us probably do not like waiting. For example, when I go shopping, I generally like to check out as quickly as possible and get on with my day. However, might there be some instances in which waiting can be a pleasant experience? This is the notion that Amit Kumar and colleagues (Kumar, Killingsworth, & Gilovich, 2014) tested in their research.

Kumar and colleagues (2014) differentiated between experiential purchases and material purchases. An *experiential purchase* is one that is "made with the primary intention of acquiring a life experience: an event or series of events that one personally encounters or lives through" (p. 1925). For instance, if I book a trip to Boston (my favorite American city), that would be an experiential purchase. I get to explore the city and its historic treasures, go to a Red Sox baseball game, and eat at its many wonderful neighborhood restaurants. A *material purchase* is one that is "made with the primary intention of acquiring a material good: a tangible object that is obtained and kept in one's possession" (p. 1925). For instance, when I go to the store and buy toothpaste, deodorant, vitamins, and paper towels, these would be material purchases. I keep them, use them up, and then buy them again when the need arises.

In Kumar et al.'s (2014) experiment, they randomly assigned each of 97 college students to think of an example of either an experiential purchase or a material purchase. Participants then rated whether their anticipation of the purchase felt more like impatience or excitement by using a response range of –4 (*much more like impatience*) to 4 (*much more like excitement*). In addition, participants indicated the pleasantness of their anticipatory state on a scale from –4 (*extremely unpleasant*) to 4 (*extremely pleasant*). Kumar et al. hypothesized "that participants asked about an experiential purchase would report feeling relatively more excitement than impatience compared to those asked about a material purchase" (p. 1925). In addition, they predicted that waiting for an experiential purchase would be more pleasant than waiting for a material purchase.

As a statistical expert, what do you recommend as the appropriate statistical tool to test these hypotheses? Let's consult Figure 15.1 (which I hope you have dreams about after you finish reading this chapter). We must understand the scales of measurement for the variables in this study. To do so, we must first identify the variables. We have people randomly assigned to one of two types of purchases: *experiential* or *material*. Thus, we have a variable called "type of purchase." This is the independent variable because the researchers are controlling (manipulating) what participants write about. This variable has two categories; we know that categorical data are nominal data. By looking at Figure 15.1, we can now rule out two of the four types of hypothesis tests because they do not work with nominal data.

In addition to the one nominal variable, we also have two other variables: feeling of the anticipated purchase and pleasantness of the anticipation of making the purchase. These two variables are dependent variables because they depend on which group a participant was randomly assigned to. These are scale variables because their response range allows us to see the magnitude of the differences between ratings.

Therefore, we have one nominal independent variable with two categories (or groups) and two dependent variables that are scale data. The one independent variable (type of purchase) created two between-subjects groups. They are between-subjects groups because each participant was randomly assigned to one and only one of the two groups. Thus, as we can see in Figure 15.1, we should use independent samples *t* tests to test these two hypotheses (see Chapter 7 for the details of an independent samples *t* test).

There is one other thing to consider in this experiment. There are two dependent variables, so we need to conduct two independent samples *t* tests. Recall from Chapter 6 what happens when we conduct many statistical tests. The Type I error rate can increase when we run a lot of hypothesis tests. That is, the more statistical tests we run, the more likely we are to find a statistically significant result by sheer chance alone. In other words, we found something in our sample data that does not reflect the population from which that sample was drawn. As you know, we typically use an alpha level of .05 (5%) to denote the region of null hypothesis rejection. In this case, perhaps we should lower that alpha level to .025 (2.5%) for each independent samples *t* test being conducted.

Study 2: "Evaluations of Sexy Women in Low- and High-Status Jobs"

In this study, Peter Glick and colleagues (Glick, Larsen, Johnson, & Branstiter, 2005) examined whether people make inferences about a woman's competence and intelligence based on the type of job she holds and what she wears to that job. These researchers asked 66 participants to view a video of a woman who, participants were told, would talk about herself for a research study in interpersonal perception. The purpose of the video was to convey information about the person's career and appearance. Specifically, the person's career in half the videos was *low status* (a receptionist), and in the other half of the videos, *high status* (a manager). Participants learned that the woman in the video was either "a receptionist for an advertising firm in Chicago whose duties include typing letters, contacting clients, answering phones, and setting up business appointments" or "a senior manager for an advertising firm in Chicago whose duties include heading client meetings, supervising a department of thirty people, overseeing projects, and evaluating employee performance" (p. 391).

In addition to manipulating the status of the woman's career, Glick et al. (2005) manipulated the appearance of the woman in the video to appear as either *neutral* or *sexy*. "For the neutral condition, the woman wore little makeup, black slacks, a turtleneck, a business jacket, and flat shoes. In the sexy condition, the same woman wore makeup and her hair was tousled. She wore a tight, knee-length skirt, a low-cut shirt with a cardigan over it, and high-heeled shoes" (p. 391).

Participants were randomly assigned to watch one and only one of these videos (of a high-status, sexily dressed woman; a high-status, neutrally dressed woman; a low-status, sexily dressed woman; or a low-status, neutrally dressed woman). After watching a video, participants completed a measure of their perceptions of the woman's *competence*. Specifically, they used a 1 (*not at all*) to 7 (*extremely*) response range to rate the woman on the traits of capable, efficient, intelligent, skillful, responsible, inept, and irresponsible. In addition to perceptions of competence, participants gave their impression of the woman's *intelligence*. To do so, they estimated her college grade-point average and estimated the selectivity of the college she attended using a 1 (*not at all selective*) to 5 (*extremely selective*) response range.

The researchers hypothesized that the female manager who dressed in a sexy fashion would be perceived as less competent and less intelligent than a female manager who dressed in a neutral fashion. In addition, the female manager dressed in a sexy fashion would be perceived as less competent and less intelligent than a female receptionist, regardless of how that female receptionist was dressed.

With the hypotheses and methodology in front of us, what statistical tool should Glick et al. (2005) have used to test their hypothesis? Again, let's use Figure 15.1 as a guide to making this decision. We start by determining the scales of measurement for the variables in the study. Let's make sure we know what the variables are in this experiment. People are randomly assigned to read about the professional status of a woman, either low- or high-status. Thus, one variable is professional status. This is an independent variable because the researchers manipulated it. We have a second independent variable. That is, the appearance of the woman in the video, either sexy or neutral.

Both of our independent variables are nominal variables because each participant was randomly assigned to one and only one group (the video that was seen). What about our dependent variable(s)? After watching a video, participants completed measures of perceived competence and intelligence of the woman in the video. These are our two dependent variables, both of which are scale variables.

We have two nominal independent variables and scale-dependent variables. By consulting Figure 15.1, we see that we need to use a factorial analysis of variance (ANOVA) to test the hypothesis. We have a 2 (status of woman) × 2 (appearance of woman) factorial design. Chapter 11 contains the details on how to conduct and interpret such analyses on each dependent variable. As we discussed in the prior research study, with two dependent variables, we need to conduct two factorial ANOVAs, which does increase our Type I error rate.

Study 3: "Evil Genius? How Dishonesty Can Lead to Greater Creativity"

During the financial crisis of 2008 and 2009, a friend of mine who works in the financial services field told me that there was too much "creative financing" going on in the United States. Of course, people such as Bernie Madoff, who stole hundreds of millions of dollars from trusting investors, probably aren't perceived as "creative" but rather as "dishonest." Yet, as Francesca Gino and Scott Wiltermuth (2014) said, "dishonest and creative behavior have something in common: They both involve breaking rules" (p. 973). These researchers conducted a series of experiments to examine the hypothesis that acting dishonestly leads to greater creativity in subsequent behavior. Let's discuss one of their experiments now.

In their experiment, Gino and Wiltermuth (2014) asked 129 people to complete anagram tasks. That is, people needed to form words from a seemingly random set of letters (e.g., *lixobam* can make *mailbox*). The researchers informed participants that performance on this task predicts verbal intelligence, which is positively related to career potential. Thus, participants had reason to complete as many of the anagrams as possible in the 3 minutes they were given to do them. Each anagram in this experiment had multiple correct solutions. However, the researchers told participants that the computer program could not validate more than one answer to each anagram. Therefore, participants needed to self-report to the researchers how many total anagram solutions they generated during the 3-minute period.

After participants finished solving anagrams for 3 minutes, Gino and Wiltermuth (2014) randomly assigned people to one of two conditions. These conditions provided different reference points for participants to self-report their anagram performance. These researchers had tested their anagrams with a different sample of participants and found that most people solved between 5 and 8 anagrams in the 3-minute period. In the "likely-cheating" condition, participants were given reason to lie about their performance. They were told that scores of 0–8 were "lower verbal learners," scores of 9–14 were "average for students in good colleges," scores of 15–20 were "typical for students in Ivy League colleges," and scores of 21 and better were "common for English professors and novelists" (p. 976). Remember that in reality, people rarely got more than 8 anagrams correct in a previous study. Therefore, in this "likely-cheating" condition, most people were tempted to self-report a number that was higher than it really was because the standards that they were provided would make them look bad otherwise.

In addition to the "likely-cheating" condition, there was a control condition that presented participants with different reference points prior to self-reporting their anagram performance. In the control condition, participants learned that scores of 0–5 were "average for students in good colleges," scores of 6–10 were "typical for students in Ivy League colleges," and scores of 11 and better were "common for English professors and novelists" (p. 976). No one's anagram performance would be bad given these standards; thus, they had no reason to lie in self-reporting their anagram performance.

After completing the anagram task and self-reporting their performance, participants were given a creativity task. Specifically, participants completed the Remote Association Task (RAT; Mednick, 1962). The RAT requires people to identify associations between words. Each of the 17 RAT items consists of a set of three words (e.g., sore, shoulder, and sweat) and people must find the word that is linked to them. What word is linked to "sore," "shoulder," and "sweat?" If you said "cold," nice work!

Gino and Wiltermuth (2014) hypothesized that people in the "likely-cheating" condition would be more creative than people in the control condition. Before we examine what statistical tool to use in testing this hypothesis, I have a question: How do we know that people in the "likely-cheating" condition did inflate their self-report anagram performance more than people in the control condition? This is an extremely important assumption[1] to test; if people in the "likely-cheating" condition did not inflate their self-report anagram performance more than people in the control condition, the experiment is not valid.[2]

Let's again turn to Figure 15.1. First, we want to know whether the experiment is valid; that is, did more people in the "likely-cheating" condition cheat more than people in the control condition? How do we answer this question? We have a nominal variable, the condition to which participants were randomly assigned. Based on which group (category) participants were randomly assigned to, we expect to see differences in self-reported anagram performance. Thus, we need to test the actual (observed) self-report performance against what we would expect to see given two groups of participants. This requires use of the chi-square goodness-of-fit test, which we discussed in the previous chapter.

In addition to testing whether people in the "likely-cheating" condition inflated their performance more than people in the control condition, we need to figure out how to test the hypothesis that people in the "likely-cheating" condition were more creative, as operationalized by performance on the RAT, than people in the control condition. Let's again consult Figure 15.1. We have one independent variable that is nominal (condition to which people were randomly assigned) and a scale-dependent variable (creativity, as operationalized by RAT scores). Thus, let's look at the bottom of Figure 15.1 in detail.

Two groups are created by this one independent variable. Furthermore, these two groups are two samples that the researchers want to compare. As participants were randomly assigned to one and only one of the two samples, we have a between-subjects design. Given this research design, we need to use the independent samples *t* test to test the hypothesis.

Figure 15.1 Flowchart for Choosing the Correct Statistical Tool

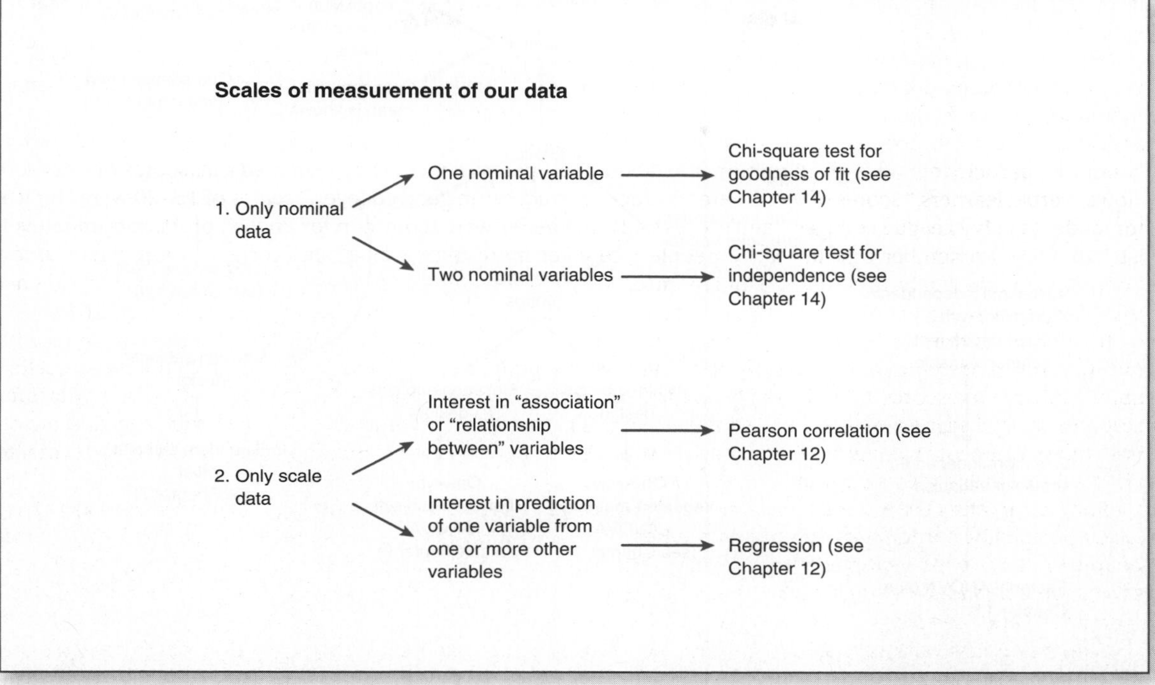

15.1(a)

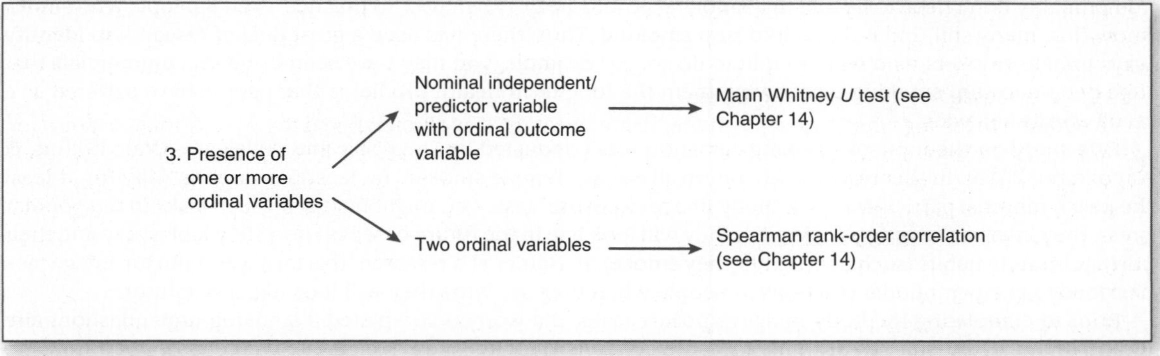

15.1(b)

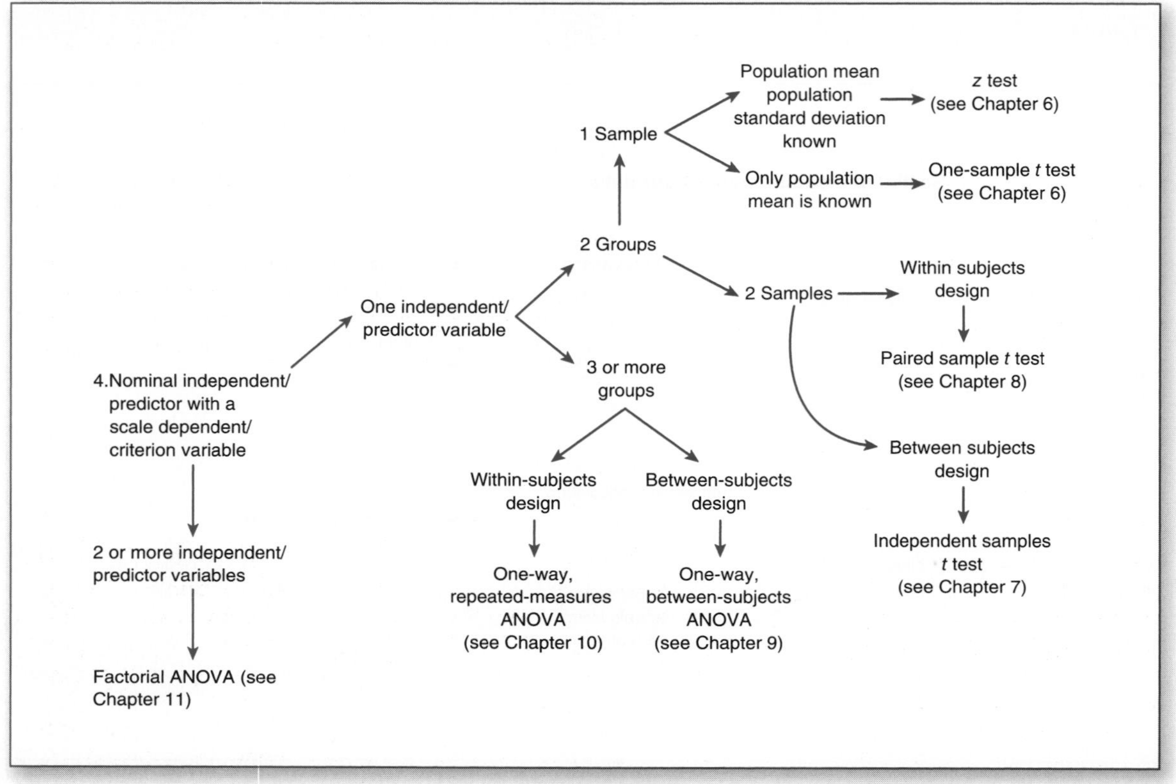

15.1(c)

Study 4: "Differential Effects of a Body Image Exposure Session on Smoking Urge Between Physically Active and Sedentary Female Smokers"

You probably don't need to be told that smoking is not a healthy behavior to practice. Even if people who smoke know this, many still find it difficult to stop smoking. Thus, there has been a great deal of research to identify ways to help smokers who want to quit to do so. For example, you may have seen or heard commercials that urge people to stop smoking by showing them the long-term health problems that people have suffered as a result of this behavior.

One study on the topic of smoking cessation was conducted by Uma Nair and colleagues (Nair, Collins, & Napolitano, 2013). In this research, 21 physically active female smokers (at least 5 cigarettes daily for at least the past 6 months) participated in a "body image exposure" task. You might have seen such tasks in the popular press; they involve showing people what they will look like in the future based on how they look today and their current lifestyle habits (such as whether they smoke). In Nair et al.'s research, this task was a mirror-image task designed to elicit emotional reactions in people when they see what they will look like in the future.

Prior to completing the body image exposure tasks, the women completed a smoking urge questionnaire (Cox, Tiffany, & Christen, 2001). This measure contains such items as "A cigarette would taste good now," to which respondents used a 1 (*strongly disagree*) to 7 (*strongly agree*) response range. Nair and colleagues (2013) wanted to see whether the body image exposure task would reduce women's urge to smoke. So after completing the body image exposure task, participants again completed the measure of smoking urge. The hypothesis was that women would have a lower urge to smoke after the body image exposure task than before completing that task.

To figure out what statistical tool to use, we turn to Figure 15.1. We have a variable, that being of time. That is, participants completed the measure before the body image intervention and again after the body image intervention. It is a nominal variable. It is also our predictor variable; that is, time of completing the measure of interest (smoking urge) is hypothesized to predict scores on that measure. Indeed, we have a second variable, that of smoking urge scores, which serves as the criterion variable. This variable is measured on a scale measurement. Thus, we need to examine the fourth category of data in Figure 15.1.

We have one predictor variable with two groups, pre-intervention and post-intervention. We have two samples, pre-intervention smoking urge scores and post-intervention smoking urge scores. Because the participants in this study completed the criterion variable (smoking urge scores) twice, before the intervention and again after the intervention, we have a within-subjects design. Therefore, to test this hypothesis, we use the paired samples t test, the details of which appear in Chapter 8.

Study 5: "Texting While Stressed: Implications for Students' Burnout, Sleep, and Well-Being"

Texting has become such an omnipresent behavior in recent years that it has become difficult for me to remember a time when there was no such thing as sending a text to someone. Indeed, sending and receiving text messages is a great way to stay socially connected when you cannot be in physical proximity to someone or do not have time to talk with them on the phone. However, given the sheer volume of texts that many people receive and send each day, research has started to examine the association between texting habits and well-being. Karla Klein Murdock (2013) conducted one such study, which we will discuss now.

In her research, she asked 83 first-year undergraduate students to complete three measures. Specifically, participants completed the Bergen Social Relationships Scale (Mittelmark, Aarø, Henricksen, Siqveland, & Torsheim, 2004). It contains six items, such as "There is someone I care about that expects more of me than I can manage," designed to measure stress in close interpersonal relationships. A 1 (*describes me very well*) to 4 (*does not describe me at all*) response range was used. In addition, participants indicated the number of text messages they send and receive in a typical day. Finally, participants completed a version of the Pittsburgh Sleep Quality Index (Buysse, Reynolds, Monk, Berman, & Kupfer, 1989). There are 21 items on this scale that operationalize different aspects of sleep quality (i.e., subjective sleep quality, amount of time needed before falling asleep, duration of uninterrupted sleep, sleep efficiency, sleep disturbances, use of sleep medications, and daytime dysfunction from fatigue). An overall score for sleep quality was obtained by summing all 21 items.

Let's examine two of Murdock's (2013) hypotheses. First, "higher levels of interpersonal stress were expected to be associated with poorer functioning" (p. 210) in the form of lower sleep quality. Second, "above and beyond the variance accounted for by interpersonal stress, higher levels of text messaging were expected to be associated with poorer functioning" (p. 210) in the form of lower sleep quality.

What statistical tool should Murdock (2013) use to test each of her two hypotheses? Let's begin by examining the scales of measurement for the data that she collected on each of the three variables described. The Social Relationship Scale is measured with scale data. There is an ordering of participants' scores on this measure, but because we know the difference in units of measurement between the numbers, it is scale data. The same is true of the variable of number of text messages sent and received on a typical day. If a person sent and received 80 text messages in a typical day, we know how many more texts a person sent and received than someone who sent and received 60 text messages. And finally, sleep quality is also a scale variable as we can determine interpretable differences between scores on this measure. Thus, examination of Figure 15.1 leads us to use the path that begins will all scale variables.

Let's examine each hypothesis and determine the statistical tool to use to test it. The first hypothesis contains a key word that provides a critical clue as to the tool we need. That word is "association." Because Murdock (2013) was interested in the association between interpersonal stress and sleep quality, she should use the Pearson correlation, which we discussed in Chapter 12. For the second hypothesis, the information "above and beyond variance accounted for by interpersonal stress" contains the clue as to what tool she should use to test this hypothesis. In the latter part of Chapter 13, we learned about multiple regression. That is, we learned about using multiple variables (here, interpersonal stress and number of text messages) to predict some outcome (here, sleep quality). Murdock is predicting sleep quality from the number of text messages *after* controlling for the relationship between interpersonal stress and sleep quality. That is why she needs to use multiple regression to test her second hypothesis.

Study 6: "How Handedness Direction and Consistency Relate to Declarative Memory Task Performance"

One of the unique features of the human brain is its contralateral functioning (Gazzaniga & LeDoux, 1978). That is, the right hemisphere of our brain controls the left half of our body, and the left hemisphere of our brain controls the right half of our body. If you write with your right hand, is it the left portion of your brain that makes it possible to move your right arm (and vice versa for people who write with their left hands)?

Of the many mysteries of the human brain, one heavily researched area is that of how memories are processed physiologically. One major type of memory is called explicit memories, that is, memories that require conscious effort to recall. Within this category of explicit memories are two subtypes of memories called episodic memories and semantic memories. *Episodic memories* are composed of specific experiences that are of a certain time and place in a person's life. For instance, if I asked you to recall the night of your high-school prom, you would need to recall this information consciously, and such memories would be different among different people. *Semantic memories* are composed of general knowledge about the world. For instance, if I asked you what the capital of the state of Florida is, you would need to recall this information consciously, and the correct answer for everyone would be the same (i.e., Tallahassee).

In the human brain, it appears that for recall of episodic memories, both the right and left prefrontal cortexes need to work together. For recall of semantic memories, we require only the left prefrontal cortex to be activated. Because this is the side of the brain that controls the right side of the body, it might be expected that right-handed people would be superior to left-handed people at recalling semantic information.[3]

In their research, Alessandra McDowell, Janet Trammell, and Elizabeth Krumrei-Mancuso (2015) explored how handedness is related to recall of episodic memories and semantic memories. To do so, they presented each of their 106 participants with two tasks, one to test episodic memory and one to test semantic memory. To test episodic memory, the researchers presented participants with an associative recognition task (Lyle, Hanaver-Torrez, Hackländer, & Edlin, 2012). This task involves being able to recognize whether you've seen a word pairing previously or not. McDowell and colleagues used a 100 word-pair list. After studying the list of 100 word pairings, participants took a recognition test that contained "30 intact pairs (the same pairs that appeared on the study list) and 30 rearranged pairs (different pairings of words as compared to those on the study list" (p. 231). Participants had to indicate whether each word pair on the test list was intact or rearranged relative to the test list they had studied. Possible scores on this memory task could range from 0 to 60.

To test semantic memory, participants listed as many countries as they could think of in 5 minutes. As there were 196 countries at the time of their study, scores on this variable could range from 0 to 196.

As you might have guessed from our discussions of contralateral functioning and the physiology of recalling semantic memories, McDowell et al. (2015) hypothesized that "right-handed participants would perform better than left-handed participants on a semantic memory task" (p. 230).

What statistical tool should these researchers use to test their hypothesis? Let's begin, as we always do, by examining how the data were measured. McDowell et al. (2015) compared left-handed and right-handed people. In this case, we have a nominal variable because people tend to use one hand predominantly over the other in everyday tasks such as writing.[4] In addition, the memory measures are both scale variables. The difference in units of measurement between the numbers makes both the episodic and semantic memory measures scale variables. For instance, a person who listed 40 countries has a semantic memory that is twice as good as someone who listed 20 countries. In examining Figure 15.1, we have a nominal predictor variable and scale criterion variables.

Figure 15.1 Flowchart for Choosing the Correct Statistical Tool

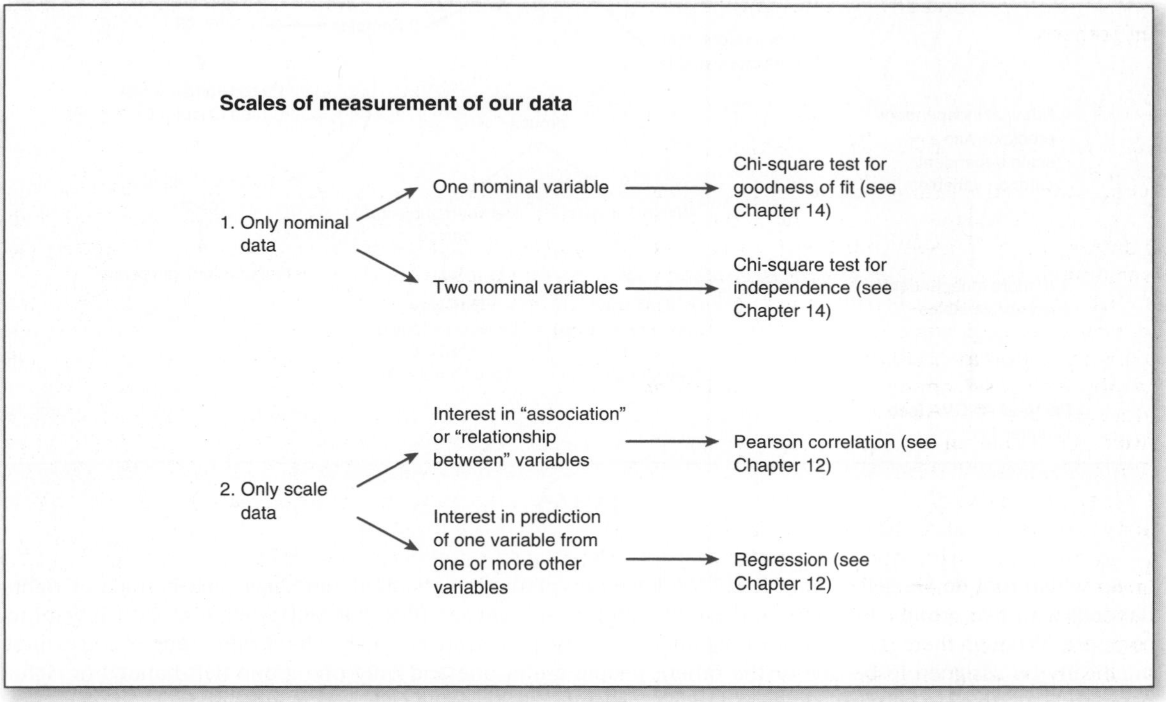

Scales of measurement of our data
1. Only nominal data
One nominal variable
Chi-square test for goodness of fit (see Chapter 14)
Two nominal variables
Chi-square test for independence (see Chapter 14)
2. Only scale data
Interest in "association" or "relationship between" variables
Pearson correlation (see Chapter 12)
Interest in prediction of one variable from one or more other variables
Regression (see Chapter 12)

15.1(a)

3. Presence of one or more ordinal variables
Nominal independent/ predictor variable with ordinal outcome variable
Mann Whitney U test (see Chapter 14)
Two ordinal variables
Spearman rank-order correlation (see Chapter 14)

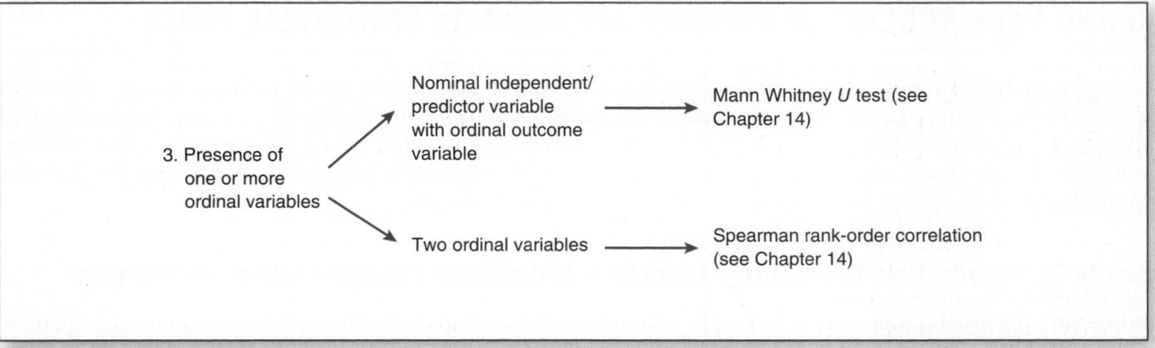

15.1(b)

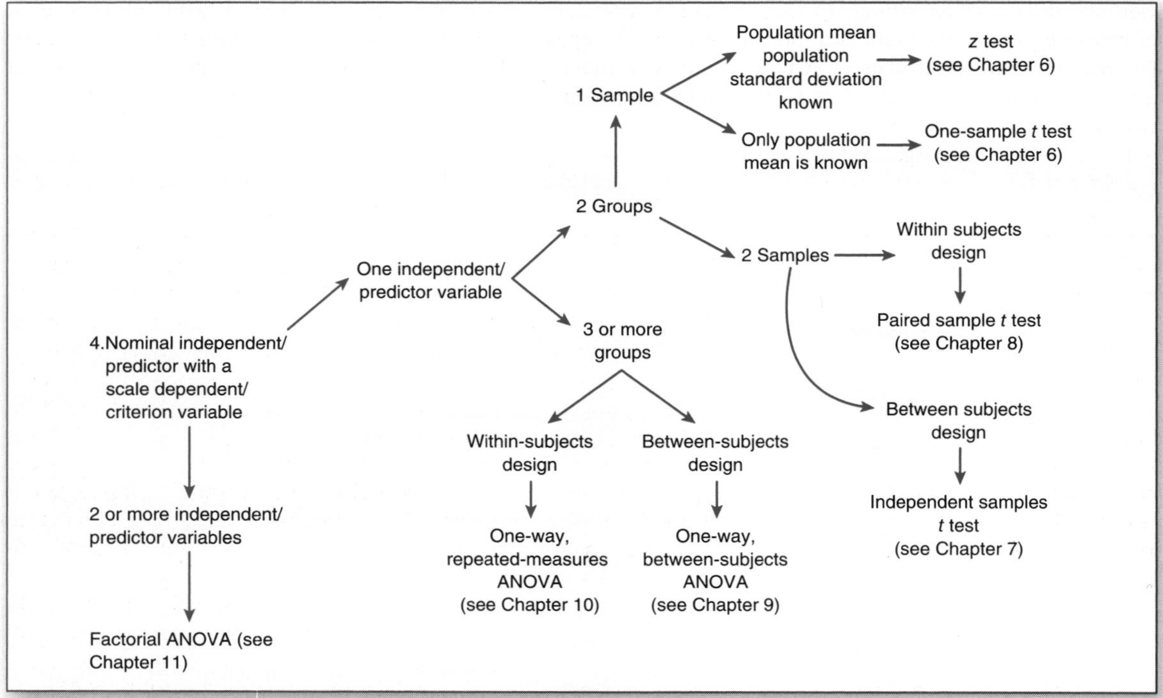

15.1(c)

So which tool do we select from here? We have one predictor variable (handedness: left-handed or right-handed) with two groups. In addition, these two groups are two samples that McDowell et al. (2015) want to compare. Although there is no random assignment (because people are naturally left- or right-handed and cannot practically be assigned to be one or the other), people are in one and only one group (left-handed or right-handed). Thus, this is a between-subjects design. Therefore, this research calls for the independent samples *t* test.

USING YOUR TOOLKIT TO IDENTIFY APPROPRIATE STATISTICAL TOOLS

Now that we have worked together through six research studies, it's time for you to consider additional studies and to determine for yourself what the appropriate statistical tool(s) would be for each study. This section will include descriptions of three research studies. After each one, you will be asked questions to help you determine which statistical tool(s) to use and why the tool you selected is appropriate in each instance. The answers to these questions appear in the third and final sections of this chapter.

Study 7: "Borderline Personality Disorder: Attitudinal Change Following Training"

Borderline personality disorder is a disease characterized by unpredictability in interpersonal relationships, wildly impulsive behavior, and instability in mood and self-image. According to Ronald Comer (2015), many people who arrive at mental health emergency facilities suffer from borderline personality disorder and have tried to injure themselves. Furthermore, people with this disorder tend to form intense but conflict-ridden relationships, in which they vacillate between idealizing and loathing the person they are in that relationship with. People with borderline personalities also "try on" many different identities, often changing their aspirations, friends, and interests. It is considered a particularly serious and difficult-to-treat personality disorder (Goodman, Edwards, & Chung, 2014).

Perhaps not surprisingly, borderline personality disorder is a serious disease for both the person suffering from it and those around him or her. From just our brief description of it here, there is a lot that a clinician must deal with in helping people with this personality disorder. To help clinicians learn more about how to treat people with this disease, Roy Krawitz (2004) helped design and assess the effectiveness of a two-day workshop. Specifically, this workshop was designed to help clinicians learn commonly accepted techniques demonstrated to be effective in alleviating the problems associated with this disorder. The workshop also sought to help clinicians learn how to implement these techniques within existing systemic and medicolegal frameworks. Finally, the workshop attempted, through these educational opportunities, to achieve a positive change in clinicians' attitudes toward clients with borderline personality disorder.

A total of 910 clinicians attended this workshop over an 18-month period. At the start of the workshop, the clinicians rated their willingness, optimism, enthusiasm, confidence, theoretical knowledge, and clinical skills in working with clients with borderline personality disorder. These ratings were made on a 1 (*poor*) to 5 (*excellent*) scale. The attendees made these same ratings again at the conclusion of the workshop and then again 6 months after the workshop. Krawitz (2004) wanted to see whether clinicians' attitudes and perceptions changed from the time they started the workshop to the time it concluded, as well as whether these changes remained 6 months after the workshop.

To determine the statistical tool that Krawitz (2004) should use, be sure to consult Figure 15.1 as you think about and answer these questions:

1. Let's examine the type of data we have. Do we have any nominal variable(s)? Ordinal variable(s)? Scale variable(s)? Be sure to state explicitly the type of data we have for each variable in this research.
2. How many independent/predictor variable(s) do we have in this study? What is (are) the independent/predictor variable(s)?
3. How many groups are being compared in this analysis?
4. Is this a between-subjects or a within-subjects research design?
5. What is (are) the dependent variable(s)/criterion variable(s)?
6. Based on your answers to the first five questions, what statistical tool(s) do you suggest Krawitz (2004) use to make sense of these data?

Study 8: "Effects of Gender and Type of Praise on Task Performance Among Undergraduates"

Most of us probably like to receive feedback that reflects well on us. For instance, if you have been spending a lot of time and energy on a class presentation, it feels good to have your teacher acknowledge your hard work or tell you how great your presentation was. After all, such feedback can make us feel good and could potentially be informative as it tells us that we are making progress on whatever task it is we are working on.

However, not all feedback, no matter how positive it may sound, is helpful. For instance, after your presentation, suppose your teacher told you, "You're a great presenter!" That's nice to hear I suppose, but such feedback does little to help you as it assumes people are either great presenters or not great presenters. There isn't any direction on how to continue to make great presentations (or improve even further). Now, if your teacher tells you, "You sure put a lot of time and thought into your presentation," that provides some information to help you continue to make excellent presentations. That is, you need to invest time and mental effort into them.

Indeed, comments such as "You're a great presenter" are what Leah Lessard and her colleagues (Lessard, Grossman, & Syme, 2015) called *person praise*. That is, such feedback focuses on the person. If you do poorly on a test "because you are dumb," that doesn't indicate how you can do better on the next test. However, comments such as "You sure put a lot of time and thought into your presentation" is an example of *process praise*. That is, such feedback focuses on the actions a person has taken or could take. If you do poorly on a test "because you didn't study for it," now you have some idea how to do better on the next test. Indeed, person praise tends to be associated with a fixed mindset, whereas process feedback tends to be associated with a growth mindset.

It is against this theoretical background that Leah Lessard and her colleagues (2015) conducted an experiment. They wanted to test "how gender and type of praise (person vs. process) affects young adults' performance on a hidden-item puzzle task" (p. 13). To do so, these researchers asked 48 undergraduate students (24 women and 24 men) to complete a series of Nina puzzles. These puzzles are a compilation of 10 cartoon-like drawings by Al Hirschfeld. The word *Nina* is hidden between 2 and 40 times within each drawing. For each drawing, participants were asked to locate the word *Nina* every time it appeared. "Task performance" was operationalized as the number of times a participant found the word *Nina* in the drawings, with higher scores indicating better performance than lower scores.

The experiment began with an experimenter (who was of the same sex as the participant) introducing the Nina puzzle task and helping the participant with two practice puzzles. The participant then did two more practice puzzles on their own. For these second two practice puzzles, the participant had 1 minute to work on them. After that minute was over, the experimenter examined the participant's work and provided either person praise or process praise. Person praise was provided with the feedback "Great! You are really good at these!" Process praise was provided with the feedback "Great! You are really working hard!" After receiving one of these two types of feedback, the participant received six more Nina puzzles to solve in 3 minutes.

Lessard et al. (2015) hypothesized "an interaction between type of praise and gender, such that process praise would be significantly more effective for women than men" (p. 13).

1. Let's examine the type of data we have. Do we have any nominal variable(s)? Ordinal variable(s)? Scale variable(s)? Be sure to state explicitly the type of data we have for each variable in this research.
2. How many independent/predictor variable(s) do we have in this study? What is (are) the independent/predictor variable(s)?
3. How many groups are being compared in this analysis?
4. Is this a between-subjects or a within-subjects research design?
5. What is (are) the dependent variable(s)/criterion variable(s)?
6. Based on your answers to the first five questions, what statistical tool(s) do you suggest Lessard et al. (2015) use to make sense of these data?

Study 9: "Please Respond ASAP: Workplace Telepressure and Employee Recovery"

As you might have surmised at various points in this book, I am not up on the latest technological developments. For instance, I did not own a cell phone until two years ago, and even now as I type this in my office, I realize I left it at home today. Among emails, texts, and Facebook notes, there is a lot of telecommunication I feel that I need to keep up with (and I bet you use more telecommunication mechanisms than I do). Someone texts me, and I feel the need to respond right away. Such a feeling is what Larissa Barber and Alecia Santuzzi (2015) termed *workplace telepressure*, that is, a "preoccupation and urge to immediately respond to work-related (information and communication technology; ICT) messages" (p. 172). Indeed, you may experience workplace telepressure as well, particularly if you tend to use a lot of telecommunication mediums. As Barber and Santuzzi reported, almost half of all Americans check email regularly while on vacation. Indeed, the technology that in some ways makes our lives easier also ties us more tightly to our responsibilities.

With this background in mind, Barber and Santuzzi (2015) conducted research in which they wanted to learn how personal factors and work environment factors are related to and predictive of workplace telepressure. To do so, they developed a 6-item measure of workplace telepressure that included items such as "I have a strong need to respond to others immediately" and "I concentrate better on other tasks once I've responded to my messages." Their sample of 303 adults responded to these items using a 1 (*strongly disagree*) to 5 (*strongly agree*) response range.

In addition to the measure of workplace telepressure, Barber and Santuzzi (2015) measured three other variables. Specifically, they measured *conscientiousness, affective organizational commitment,* and *job involvement*. As you might know if you took a course in personality psychology, conscientiousness is a trait that encompasses how organized, diligent, hard-working, and responsible a person tends to be. In Barber and Santuzzi's research, conscientiousness was measured with 10 items from the International Personality Item Pool (Goldberg et al., 2006). An example item is "make plans and stick to them," to which participants responded using a 1 (*strongly disagree*) to 5 (*strongly agree*) range.

Affective organizational commitment and job involvement are constructs you would have encountered in a course on industrial/organizational psychology. Affective organizational commitment occurs when an employee has a strong emotional attachment to the organization he or she works for. People with high levels of affective organizational commitment tend to work harder and longer than people with lower levels of affective organizational commitment. To operationalize this construct, Barber and Santuzzi (2015) used a 6-item scale that Natalie Allen and John Meyer (1997) developed. An example item is "I feel as if my organization's problems are my own," to which participants responded using a 1 (*strongly disagree*) to 5 (*strongly agree*) range.

A person with a high degree of job involvement tends to be inherently motivated to work for the sake of the work itself. The work itself is the end state of one's job, not money, awards, or other external incentives. To operationalize this construct, Barber and Santuzzi (2015) used a 10-item scale that Rabindra Kanungo (1982) developed. An example item is "I consider my job to be very central to my existence," to which participants responded using a 1 (*strong disagree*) to 5 (*strongly agree*) range.

Barber and Santuzzi (2015) hypothesized that conscientiousness, affective organizational commitment, and job involvement would each be positively correlated with workplace telepressure.

1. Let's examine the type of data we have. Do we have any nominal variable(s)? Ordinal variable(s)? Scale variable(s)? Be sure to state explicitly the type of data we have for each variable in this research.
2. How many independent/predictor variable(s) do we have in this study? What is (are) the independent/predictor variable(s)?
3. How many groups are being compared in this analysis?
4. What is (are) the dependent variable(s)/criterion variable(s)?
5. Based on your answers to the first five questions, what statistical tool(s) do you suggest Barber and Santuzzi (2015) use to make sense of these data?

ANSWERS TO STUDIES 7, 8, AND 9

In this third and final section of the chapter, we will walk through each research study you read about in the previous section. By the time we finish doing so, we will have a good understanding of what statistical tool(s) need to be used with each study. Of course, Figure 15.1 would be excellent to consult throughout this process.

Study 7: "Borderline Personality Disorder: Attitudinal Change Following Training"

1. Let's examine the type of data we have. Do we have any nominal variable(s)? Ordinal variable(s)? Scale variable(s)? Be sure to state explicitly the type of data we have for each variable in this research.

   Answer: In this case, we do have a nominal variable; that is time. Measurements were made before (pre-) the workshop, again immediately after (post-) the workshop, and then 6 months later. In addition, we have a scale variable; that is, the participants rated their willingness, optimism, enthusiasm, confidence, theoretical knowledge, and clinical skills in working with clients with borderline personality disorder using a 1-to-5 response range.

2. How many independent/predictor variable(s) do we have in this study? What is (are) the independent/predictor variable(s)?

   Answer: There is one predictor variable. The predictor variable is time (pre-, post-, and 6 months later). Krawtiz (2004) wanted to examine changes in rating across time.

3. How many groups are being compared in this analysis?

   Answer: There are three groups. The "pre-" group, the "post-" group, and the "6 months later" group.

4. Is this a between-subjects or a within-subjects research design?

   Answer: This is a within-subjects research design because each participant completed the pre-workshop ratings, the post-workshop ratings, and the 6-month follow-up ratings. Because each participant provided data to each group mean, it is a within-subjects design.

5. What is (are) the dependent variable(s)/criterion variable(s)?

   Answer: The dependent variables are the ratings that participants provided of their willingness, optimism, enthusiasm, confidence, theoretical knowledge, and clinical skills in working with clients with borderline personality disorder.

6. Based on your answers to the first five questions, what statistical tool(s) do you suggest Krawitz (2004) use to make sense of these data?

   Answer: With one nominal predictor variable and a scale criterion variable, three groups in a within-subjects design, Krawitz (2004) needs to use the one-way, repeated-measures analysis of variance (ANOVA) that we described in Chapter 10.

Study 8: "Effects of Gender and Type of Praise on Task Performance Among Undergraduates"

1. Let's examine the type of data we have. Do we have any nominal variable(s)? Ordinal variable(s)? Scale variable(s)? Be sure to state explicitly the type of data we have for each variable in this research.

   Answer: We have two nominal variables: The type of feedback provided (person praise or process praise) and participant gender. There is a scale variable, that is, participant's performance on the Nina puzzle task.

2. How many independent/predictor variable(s) do we have in this study? What is (are) the independent/predictor variable(s)?

   Answer: There is one independent variable (type of feedback provided). It is an independent variable because the researchers randomly assigned participants to receive one of these two types of feedback.

There is one predictor variable (participant gender). It is considered a predictor variable and not a true independent variable because the researchers could not randomly assign participants to a gender.

3. How many groups are being compared in this analysis?

   Answer: There are a total of four groups in this experiment. Specifically, we have (1) females who received process praise; (2) females who received person praise; (3) males who received process praise; and (4) males who received person praise.

4. Is this a between-subjects or a within-subjects research design?

   Answer: This is a between-subjects design because participants were randomly assigned to one and only one of the four groups in this experiment.

5. What is (are) the dependent variable(s)/criterion variable(s)?

   Answer: The dependent variable is task performance, which was operationalized by the number of times they found the word *Nina* in six puzzles during a 3-minute time period.

6. Based on your answers to the first five questions, what statistical tool(s) do you suggest Lessard et al. (2015) use to make sense of these data?

   Answer: With nominal independent/predictor variables and a scale-dependent variable, Lessard et al. (2015) needs to use a factorial ANOVA, which we discussed in Chapter 11.

Study 9: "Please Respond ASAP: Workplace Telepressure and Employee Recovery"

1. Let's examine the type of data we have. Do we have any nominal variable(s)? Ordinal variable(s)? Scale variable(s)? Be sure to state explicitly the type of data we have for each variable in this research.

   Answer: There are four variables: conscientiousness, affective organizational commitment, job involvement, and workplace telepressure. All four of these variables are scale variables.

2. How many independent/predictor variable(s) do we have in this study? What is (are) the independent/predictor variable(s)?

   Answer: In the description of their research, Barber and Santuzzi (2015) were interested in learning how conscientiousness, affective organizational commitment, and job involvement were related to and predictive of workplace telepressure. Therefore, we have three predictor variables, those being conscientiousness, affective organizational commitment, and job involvement.

3. How many groups are being compared in this analysis?

   Answer: Our predictor variables were each scale variable; therefore, we have no groups being compared in this study.

4. What is (are) the dependent variable(s)/criterion variable(s)?

   Answer: Workplace telepressure is the criterion variable. It is the variable being predicted by conscientiousness, affective organizational commitment, and job involvement.

5. Based on your answers to the first five questions, what statistical tool(s) do you suggest Barber and Santuzzi (2015) use to make sense of these data?

   Answer: This study consists of only scale data. Because Barber and Santuzzi (2015) wanted to learn how these variables related to each other, they should consult Chapter 12 about correlations. Because they were also interested in how conscientiousness, affective organizational commitment, and job involvement predicted workplace telepressure, they should consult Chapter 13 about multiple regression.

NOTES

1. Researchers refer to checking this assumption as a manipulation check. That is, they check to see whether their experimental manipulation served the purpose they intended it to serve.
2. Of course, the computer could and did record participants' actual performance on the anagram task, so the researchers knew when someone inflated his or her performance.
3. If you're left-handed, it probably seems this is just one more way the world caters to right-handed people.
4. For the purposes of this chapter, I am including a discussion only of "left-handed" and "right-handed" people. However, McDowell et al. (2015) did examine "inconsistently-handed" people as well in a separate series of analyses. If you are interested in those results, please read the original article.

APPENDIX A

Statistical Tables

Table A.1 The Unit Normal Table

Column (A) lists *z*-score values. Column (B) lists the proportion of the area between the mean and the *z*-score value. Column (C) lists the proportion of the area beyond the *z* score in the tail of the distribution. (Note: Because the normal distribution is symmetrical, areas for negative *z* scores are the same as those for positive *z* scores.)

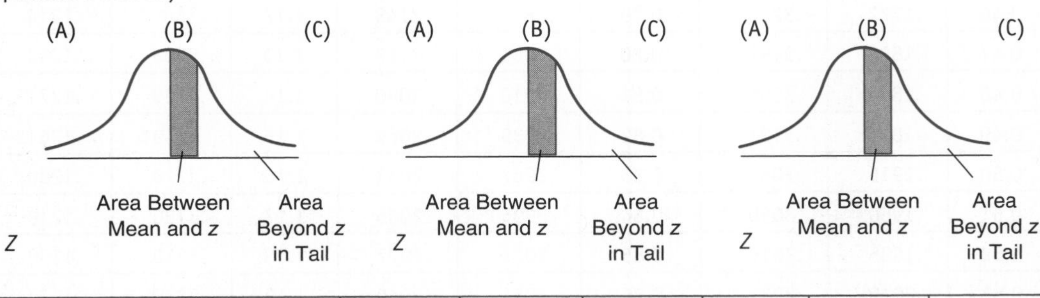

(A) z	(B) Area Between Mean and z	(C) Area Beyond z in Tail	(A) z	(B) Area Between Mean and z	(C) Area Beyond z in Tail	(A) z	(B) Area Between Mean and z	(C) Area Beyond z in Tail
0.00	.0000	.5000	0.15	.0596	.4404	0.30	.1179	.3821
0.01	.0040	.4960	0.16	.0636	.4364	0.31	.1217	.3783
0.02	.0080	.4920	0.17	.0675	.4325	0.32	.1255	.3745
0.03	.0120	.4880	0.18	.0714	.4286	0.33	.1293	.3707
0.04	.0160	.4840	0.19	.0753	.4247	0.34	.1331	.3669
0.05	.0199	.4801	0.20	.0793	.4207	0.35	.1368	.3632
0.06	.0239	.4761	0.21	.0832	.4168	0.36	.1406	.3594

(Continued)

Table A.1 (Continued)

(A) *z*	(B) Area Between Mean and *z*	(C) Area Beyond *z* in Tail	(A) *z*	(B) Area Between Mean and *z*	(C) Area Beyond *z* in Tail	(A) *z*	(B) Area Between Mean and *z*	(C) Area Beyond *z* in Tail
0.07	.0279	.4721	0.22	.0871	.4129	0.37	.1443	.3557
0.08	.0319	.4681	0.23	.0910	.4090	0.38	.1480	.3520
0.09	.0359	.4641	0.24	.0948	.4052	0.39	.1517	.3483
0.10	.0398	.4602	0.25	.0987	.4013	0.40	.1554	.3446
0.11	.0438	.4562	0.26	.1026	.3974	0.41	.1591	.3409
0.12	.0478	.4522	0.27	.1064	.3936	0.42	.1628	.3372
0.13	.0517	.4483	0.28	.1103	.3897	0.43	.1664	.3336
0.14	.0557	.4443	0.29	.1141	.3859	0.44	.1700	.3300
0.45	.1736	.3264	0.78	.2823	.2177	1.11	.3665	.1335
0.46	.1772	.3228	0.79	.2852	.2148	1.12	.3686	.1314
0.47	.1808	.3192	0.80	.2881	.2119	1.13	.3708	.1292
0.48	.1844	.3156	0.81	.2910	.2090	1.14	.3729	.1271
0.49	.1879	.3121	0.82	.2939	.2061	1.15	.3749	.1251
0.50	.1915	.3085	0.83	.2967	.2033	1.16	.3770	.1230
0.51	.1950	.3050	0.84	.2995	.2005	1.17	.3790	.1210
0.52	.1985	.3015	0.85	.3023	.1977	1.18	.3810	.1190
0.53	.2019	.2981	0.86	.3051	.1949	1.19	.3830	.1170
0.54	.2054	.2946	0.87	.3078	.1922	1.20	.3849	.1151
0.55	.2088	.2912	0.88	.3106	.1894	1.21	.3869	.1131
0.56	.2123	.2877	0.89	.3133	.1867	1.22	.3888	.1112
0.57	.2157	.2843	0.90	.3159	.1841	1.23	.3907	.1093
0.58	.2190	.2810	0.91	.3186	.1814	1.24	.3925	.1075
0.59	.2224	.2776	0.92	.3212	.1788	1.25	.3944	.1056
0.60	.2257	.2743	0.93	.3238	.1762	1.26	.3962	.1038
0.61	.2391	.2709	0.94	.3264	.1736	1.27	.3980	.1020
0.62	.2324	.2676	0.95	.3289	.1711	1.28	.3997	.1003
0.63	.2357	.2643	0.96	.3315	.1685	1.29	.4015	.0985
0.64	.2389	.2611	0.97	.3340	.1660	1.30	.4032	.0968

0.65	.2422	.2578	0.98	.3365	.1635	1.31	.4049	.0951
0.66	.2454	.2546	0.99	.3389	.1611	1.32	.4066	.0934
0.67	.2486	.2514	1.00	.3413	.1587	1.33	.4082	.0918
0.68	.2517	.2483	1.01	.3438	.1562	1.34	.4099	.0901
0.69	.2549	.2451	1.02	.3461	.1539	1.35	.4115	.0885
0.70	.2580	.2420	1.03	.3485	.1515	1.36	.4131	.0869
0.71	.2611	.2389	1.04	.3508	.1492	1.37	.4147	.0853
0.72	.2642	.2358	1.05	.3531	.1469	1.38	.4162	.0838
0.73	.2673	.2327	1.06	.3554	.1446	1.39	.4177	.0823
0.74	.2704	.2296	1.07	.3577	.1423	1.40	.4192	.0808
0.75	.2734	.2266	1.08	.3599	.1401	1.41	.4207	.0793
0.76	.2764	.2236	1.09	.3621	.1379	1.42	.4222	.0778
0.77	.2794	.2206	1.10	.3643	.1357	1.43	.4236	.0764
1.44	.4251	.0749	1.77	.4616	.0384	2.10	.4821	.0179
1.45	.4265	.0735	1.78	.4625	.0375	2.11	.4826	.0174
1.46	.4279	.0721	1.79	.4633	.0367	2.12	.4830	.0170
1.47	.4292	.0708	1.80	.4641	.0359	2.13	.4834	.0166
1.48	.4306	.0694	1.81	.4649	.0351	2.14	.4838	.0162
1.49	.4319	.0681	1.82	.4656	.0344	2.15	.4842	.0158
1.50	.4332	.0668	1.83	.4664	.0336	2.16	.4846	.0154
1.51	.4345	.0655	1.84	.4671	.0329	2.17	.4850	.0150
1.52	.4357	.0643	1.85	.4678	.0322	2.18	.4854	.0146
1.53	.4370	.0630	1.86	.4686	.0314	2.19	.4857	.0143
1.54	.4382	.0618	1.87	.4693	.0307	2.20	.4861	.0139
1.55	.4394	.0606	1.88	.4699	.0301	2.21	.4864	.0136
1.56	.4406	.0594	1.89	.4706	.0294	2.22	.4868	.0132
1.57	.4418	.0582	1.90	.4713	.0287	2.23	.4871	.0129
1.58	.4429	.0571	1.91	.4719	.0281	2.24	.4875	.0125
1.59	.4441	.0559	1.92	.4726	.0274	2.25	.4878	.0122
1.60	.4452	.0548	1.93	.4732	.0268	2.26	.4881	.0119
1.61	.4463	.0537	1.94	.4738	.0262	2.27	.4884	.0116
1.62	.4474	.0526	1.95	.4744	.0256	2.28	.4887	.0113
1.63	.4484	.0516	1.96	.4750	.0250	2.29	.4890	.0110

(Continued)

Table A.1 (Continued)

(A) z	(B) Area Between Mean and z	(C) Area Beyond z in Tail	(A) z	(B) Area Between Mean and z	(C) Area Beyond z in Tail	(A) z	(B) Area Between Mean and z	(C) Area Beyond z in Tail
1.64	.4495	.0505	1.97	.4756	.0244	2.30	.4893	.0107
1.65	.4505	.0495	1.98	.4761	.0239	2.31	.4896	.0104
1.66	.4515	.0485	1.99	.4767	.0233	2.32	.4898	.0102
1.67	.4525	.0475	2.00	.4772	.0228	2.33	.4901	.0099
1.68	.4535	.0465	2.01	.4778	.0222	2.34	.4904	.0096
1.69	.4545	.0455	2.02	.4783	.0217	2.35	.4906	.0094
1.70	.4554	.0446	2.03	.4788	.0212	2.36	.4909	.0091
1.71	.4564	.0436	2.04	.4793	.0207	2.37	.4911	.0089
1.72	.4573	.0427	2.05	.4798	.0202	2.38	.4913	.0087
1.73	.4582	.0418	2.06	.4803	.0197	2.39	.4916	.0084
1.74	.4591	.0409	2.07	.4808	.0192	2.40	.4918	.0082
1.75	.4599	.0401	2.08	.4812	.0188	2.41	.4920	.0080
1.76	.4608	.0392	2.09	.4817	.0183	2.42	.4922	.0078
2.43	.4925	.0075	2.74	.4969	.0031	3.05	.4989	.0011
2.44	.4927	.0073	2.75	.4970	.0030	3.06	.4989	.0011
2.45	.4929	.0071	2.76	.4971	.0029	3.07	.4989	.0011
2.46	.4931	.0069	2.77	.4972	.0028	3.08	.4990	.0010
2.47	.4932	.0068	2.78	.4973	.0027	3.09	.4990	.0010
2.48	.4934	.0066	2.79	.4974	.0026	3.10	.4990	.0010
2.49	.4936	.0064	2.80	.4974	.0026	3.11	.4991	.0009
2.50	.4938	.0062	2.81	.4975	.0025	3.12	.4991	.0009
2.51	.4940	.0060	2.82	.4976	.0024	3.13	.4991	.0009
2.52	.4941	.0059	2.83	.4977	.0023	3.14	.4992	.0008
2.53	.4943	.0057	2.84	.4977	.0023	3.15	.4992	.0008
2.54	.4945	.0055	2.85	.4978	.0022	3.16	.4992	.0008
2.55	.4946	.0054	2.86	.4979	.0021	3.17	.4992	.0008
2.56	.4948	.0052	2.87	.4979	.0021	3.18	.4993	.0007

2.57	.4949	.0051	2.88	.4980	.0020	3.19	.4993	.0007
2.58	.4951	.0049	2.89	.4981	.0019	3.20	.4993	.0007
2.59	.4952	.0048	2.90	.4981	.0019	3.21	.4993	.0007
2.60	.4953	.0047	2.91	.4982	.0018	3.22	.4994	.0006
2.61	.4955	.0045	2.92	.4982	.0018	3.23	.4994	.0006
2.62	.4956	.0044	2.93	.4983	.0017	3.24	.4994	.0006
2.63	.4957	.0043	2.94	.4984	.0016	3.25	.4994	.0006
2.64	.4959	.0041	2.95	.4984	.0016	3.30	.4995	.0005
2.65	.4960	.0040	2.96	.4985	.0015	3.35	.4996	.0004
2.66	.4961	.0039	2.97	.4985	.0015	3.40	.4997	.0003
2.67	.4962	.0038	2.98	.4986	.0014	3.45	.4997	.0003
2.68	.4963	.0037	2.99	.4986	.0014	3.50	.4998	.0002
2.69	.4964	.0036	3.00	.4987	.0013	3.60	.4998	.0002
2.70	.4965	.0035	3.01	.4987	.0013	3.70	.4999	.0001
2.71	.4966	.0034	3.02	.4987	.0013	3.80	.4999	.0001
2.72	.4967	.0033	3.03	.4988	.0012	3.90	.49995	.00005
2.73	.4968	.0032	3.04	.4988	.0012	4.00	.49997	.00003

Source: Based on J. E. Freund, *Modern Elementary Statistics* (11th edition). Pearson Prentice Hall, 2004.

APPENDIX B

Table B.1 The *t* Distribution

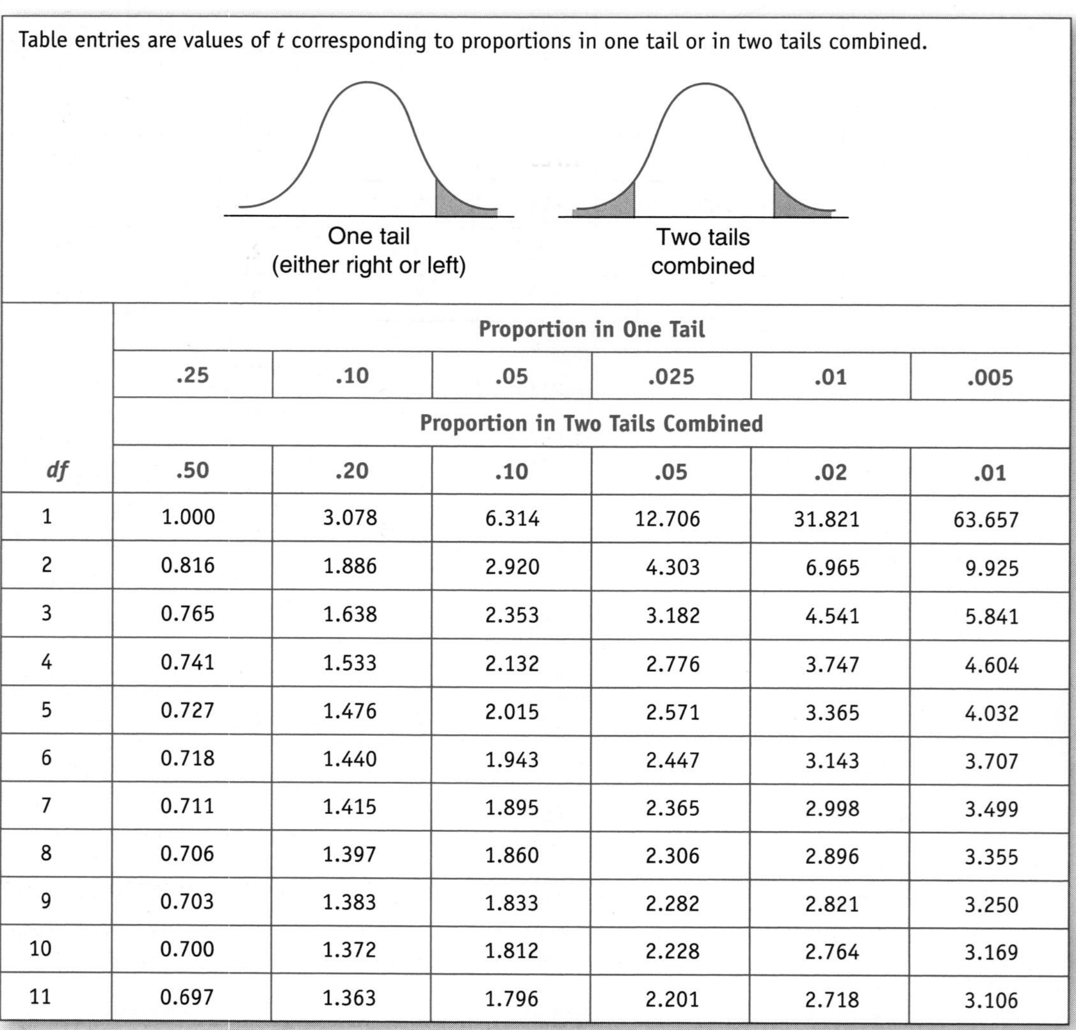

Table entries are values of t corresponding to proportions in one tail or in two tails combined.

	Proportion in One Tail					
	.25	.10	.05	.025	.01	.005
	Proportion in Two Tails Combined					
df	.50	.20	.10	.05	.02	.01
1	1.000	3.078	6.314	12.706	31.821	63.657
2	0.816	1.886	2.920	4.303	6.965	9.925
3	0.765	1.638	2.353	3.182	4.541	5.841
4	0.741	1.533	2.132	2.776	3.747	4.604
5	0.727	1.476	2.015	2.571	3.365	4.032
6	0.718	1.440	1.943	2.447	3.143	3.707
7	0.711	1.415	1.895	2.365	2.998	3.499
8	0.706	1.397	1.860	2.306	2.896	3.355
9	0.703	1.383	1.833	2.282	2.821	3.250
10	0.700	1.372	1.812	2.228	2.764	3.169
11	0.697	1.363	1.796	2.201	2.718	3.106

	Proportion in One Tail					
	.25	.10	.05	.025	.01	.005
	Proportion in Two Tails Combined					
df	.50	.20	.10	.05	.02	.01
12	0.695	1.356	1.782	2.179	2.681	3.055
13	0.694	1.350	1.771	2.160	2.650	3.012
14	0.692	1.345	1.761	2.145	2.624	2.977
15	0.691	1.341	1.753	2.131	2.602	2.947
16	0.690	1.337	1.746	2.120	2.583	2.921
17	0.689	1.333	1.740	2.110	2.567	2.898
18	0.688	1.330	1.734	2.101	2.552	2.878
19	0.688	1.328	1.729	2.093	2.539	2.861
20	0.687	1.325	1.725	2.086	2.528	2.845
21	0.686	1.323	1.721	2.080	2.518	2.831
22	0.686	1.321	1.717	2.074	2.508	2.819
23	0.685	1.319	1.714	2.069	2.500	2.807
24	0.685	1.318	1.711	2.064	2.492	2.797
25	0.684	1.316	1.708	2.060	2.485	2.787
26	0.684	1.315	1.706	2.056	2.479	2.779
27	0.684	1.314	1.703	2.052	2.473	2.771
28	0.683	1.313	1.701	2.048	2.467	2.763
29	0.683	1.311	1.699	2.045	2.462	2.756
30	0.683	1.310	1.697	2.042	2.457	2.750
40	0.681	1.303	1.684	2.021	2.423	2.704
60	0.679	1.296	1.671	2.000	2.390	2.660
120	0.677	1.289	1.658	1.980	2.358	2.617
∞	0.674	1.282	1.645	1.960	2.326	2.576

Source: Table III of R. A. Fisher and F. Yates, *Statistical Tables for Biological, Agricultural and Medical Research*, 6th ed. London: Longman Group Ltd., 1974 (previously published by Oliver and Boyd Ltd., Edinburgh). Adapted and reprinted with permission of Addison Wesley Longman.

APPENDIX C

Table C.1 Critical Values for the *F* Distribution

Critical values at a .05 level of significance are given in lightface type.
Critical values at a .01 level of significance are given in boldface type.

	Degrees of freedom numerator											
		1	2	3	4	5	6	7	8	9	10	20	∞
Degrees of freedom denominator	1	161 **4052**	200 **5000**	216 **5403**	225 **5625**	230 **5764**	234 **5859**	237 **5928**	239 **5928**	241 **6023**	242 **6056**	248 **6209**	254 **6366**
	2	18.51 **98.49**	19.00 **99.00**	19.16 **99.17**	19.25 **99.25**	19.30 **99.30**	19.33 **99.33**	19.36 **99.34**	19.37 **99.36**	19.38 **99.38**	19.39 **99.40**	19.44 **99.45**	19.5 **99.5**
	3	10.13 **34.12**	9.55 **30.92**	9.28 **29.46**	9.12 **28.71**	9.01 **28.24**	8.94 **27.91**	8.88 **27.67**	8.84 **27.49**	8.81 **27.34**	8.78 **27.23**	8.66 **26.69**	8.5 **26.1**
	4	7.71 **21.20**	6.94 **18.00**	6.59 **16.69**	6.39 **15.98**	6.26 **15.52**	6.16 **15.21**	6.09 **14.98**	6.04 **14.80**	6.00 **14.66**	5.96 **14.54**	5.80 **14.02**	5.6 **13.5**
	5	6.61 **16.26**	5.79 **13.27**	5.41 **12.06**	5.19 **11.39**	5.05 **10.97**	4.95 **10.67**	4.88 **10.45**	4.82 **10.27**	4.78 **10.15**	4.74 **10.05**	4.56 **9.55**	4.37 **9.02**
	6	5.99 **13.74**	5.14 **10.92**	4.76 **9.78**	4.53 **9.15**	4.39 **8.75**	4.28 **8.47**	4.21 **8.26**	4.15 **8.10**	4.10 **7.98**	4.06 **7.87**	3.87 **7.39**	3.67 **6.88**
	7	5.59 **13.74**	4.74 **9.55**	4.35 **8.45**	4.12 **7.85**	3.97 **7.46**	3.87 **7.19**	3.79 **7.00**	3.73 **6.84**	3.68 **6.71**	3.63 **6.62**	3.44 **6.15**	3.23 **5.65**
	8	5.32 **11.26**	4.46 **8.65**	4.07 **7.59**	3.84 **7.01**	3.69 **6.63**	3.58 **6.37**	3.50 **6.19**	3.44 **6.03**	3.39 **5.91**	3.34 **5.82**	3.15 **5.36**	2.93 **4.86**
	9	5.12 **10.56**	4.26 **8.02**	3.86 **6.99**	3.63 **6.42**	3.48 **6.06**	3.37 **5.80**	3.29 **5.62**	3.23 **5.47**	3.18 **5.35**	3.13 **5.26**	2.93 **4.80**	2.71 **4.31**
	10	4.96 **10.04**	4.10 **7.56**	3.71 **6.55**	3.48 **5.99**	3.33 **5.64**	3.22 **5.39**	3.14 **5.21**	3.07 **5.06**	3.02 **4.95**	2.97 **4.85**	2.77 **4.41**	2.54 **3.91**
	11	4.84 **9.65**	3.98 **7.20**	3.59 **6.22**	3.36 **5.67**	3.20 **5.32**	3.09 **5.07**	3.01 **4.88**	2.95 **4.74**	2.90 **4.63**	2.86 **4.54**	2.65 **4.10**	2.40 **3.60**

Degrees of freedom denominator	Degrees of freedom numerator											
	1	2	3	4	5	6	7	8	9	10	20	∞
12	4.75 **9.33**	3.89 **6.93**	3.49 **5.95**	3.26 **5.41**	3.11 **5.06**	3.00 **4.82**	2.92 **4.65**	2.85 **4.50**	2.80 **4.39**	2.76 **4.30**	2.54 **3.86**	2.30 **3.36**
13	4.67 **9.07**	3.80 **6.70**	3.41 **5.74**	3.18 **5.20**	3.02 **4.86**	2.92 **4.62**	2.84 **4.44**	2.77 **4.30**	2.72 **4.19**	2.67 **4.10**	2.46 **3.67**	2.21 **3.17**
14	4.60 **8.86**	3.74 **6.51**	3.34 **5.56**	3.11 **5.03**	2.96 **4.69**	2.85 **4.46**	2.77 **4.28**	2.70 **4.14**	2.65 **4.03**	2.60 **3.94**	2.39 **3.51**	2.13 **3.00**
15	4.54 **8.68**	3.68 **6.36**	3.29 **5.42**	3.06 **4.89**	2.90 **4.56**	2.79 **4.32**	2.70 **4.14**	2.64 **4.00**	2.59 **3.89**	2.55 **3.80**	2.33 **3.36**	2.07 **2.87**
16	4.49 **8.53**	3.63 **6.23**	3.24 **5.29**	3.01 **4.77**	2.85 **4.44**	2.74 **4.20**	2.66 **4.03**	2.59 **3.89**	2.54 **3.78**	2.49 **3.69**	2.28 **3.25**	2.01 **2.75**
17	4.45 **8.40**	3.59 **6.11**	3.20 **5.18**	2.96 **4.67**	2.81 **4.34**	2.70 **4.10**	2.62 **3.93**	2.55 **3.79**	2.50 **3.68**	2.45 **3.59**	2.23 **3.16**	1.96 **2.65**
18	4.41 **8.28**	3.55 **6.01**	3.16 **5.09**	2.93 **4.58**	2.77 **4.25**	2.66 **4.01**	2.58 **3.85**	2.51 **3.71**	2.46 **3.60**	2.41 **3.51**	2.19 **3.07**	1.92 **2.57**
19	4.38 **8.18**	3.52 **5.93**	3.13 **5.01**	2.90 **4.50**	2.74 **4.17**	2.63 **3.94**	2.55 **3.77**	2.48 **3.63**	2.43 **3.52**	2.38 **3.43**	2.15 **3.00**	1.88 **2.49**
20	4.35 **8.10**	3.49 **5.85**	3.10 **4.94**	2.87 **4.43**	2.71 **4.10**	2.60 **3.87**	2.52 **3.71**	2.45 **3.56**	2.40 **3.45**	2.35 **3.37**	2.12 **2.94**	1.84 **2.42**
21	4.32 **8.02**	3.47 **5.78**	3.07 **4.87**	2.84 **4.37**	2.68 **4.04**	2.57 **3.81**	2.49 **3.65**	2.42 **3.51**	2.37 **3.40**	2.32 **3.31**	2.09 **2.88**	1.81 **2.36**
22	4.30 **7.94**	3.44 **5.72**	3.05 **4.82**	2.82 **4.31**	2.66 **3.99**	2.55 **3.76**	2.47 **3.59**	2.40 **3.45**	2.35 **3.35**	2.30 **3.26**	2.07 **2.83**	1.78 **2.31**
23	4.28 **7.88**	3.42 **5.66**	3.03 **4.76**	2.80 **4.26**	2.64 **3.94**	2.53 **3.71**	2.45 **3.54**	2.38 **3.41**	2.32 **3.30**	2.28 **3.21**	2.04 **2.78**	1.76 **2.26**
24	4.26 **7.82**	3.40 **5.61**	3.01 **4.72**	2.78 **4.22**	2.62 **3.90**	2.51 **3.67**	2.43 **3.50**	2.36 **3.36**	2.30 **3.25**	2.26 **3.17**	2.02 **2.74**	1.73 **2.21**
25	4.24 **7.77**	3.38 **5.57**	2.99 **4.68**	2.76 **4.18**	2.60 **3.86**	2.49 **3.63**	2.41 **3.46**	2.34 **3.32**	2.28 **3.21**	2.24 **3.13**	2.00 **2.70**	1.71 **2.17**
26	4.22 **7.72**	3.37 **5.53**	2.98 **4.64**	2.74 **4.14**	2.59 **3.82**	2.47 **3.59**	2.39 **3.42**	2.32 **3.29**	2.27 **3.17**	2.22 **3.09**	1.99 **2.66**	1.69 **2.13**
27	4.21 **7.68**	3.35 **5.49**	2.96 **4.60**	2.73 **4.11**	2.57 **3.79**	2.46 **3.56**	2.37 **3.39**	2.30 **3.26**	2.25 **3.14**	2.20 **3.06**	1.97 **2.63**	1.67 **2.10**
28	4.20 **7.64**	3.34 **5.45**	2.95 **4.57**	2.71 **4.07**	2.56 **3.76**	2.44 **3.53**	2.36 **3.36**	2.29 **3.23**	2.24 **3.11**	2.19 **3.03**	1.96 **2.60**	1.65 **2.07**
29	4.18 **7.60**	3.33 **5.42**	2.93 **4.54**	2.70 **4.04**	2.54 **3.73**	2.43 **3.50**	2.35 **3.33**	2.28 **3.20**	2.22 **3.08**	2.18 **3.00**	1.94 **2.57**	1.63 **2.04**

(Continued)

Table C.1 (Continued)

Degrees of freedom denominator	Degrees of freedom numerator: 1	2	3	4	5	6	7	8	9	10	20	∞
30	4.17 **7.56**	3.32 **5.39**	2.92 **4.51**	2.69 **4.02**	2.53 **3.70**	2.42 **3.47**	2.34 **3.30**	2.27 **3.17**	2.21 **3.06**	2.16 **2.98**	1.93 **2.55**	1.61 **2.01**
31	4.16 **7.53**	3.30 **5.36**	2.91 **4.48**	2.68 **3.99**	2.52 **3.67**	2.41 **3.45**	2.32 **3.28**	2.25 **3.15**	2.20 **3.04**	2.15 **2.96**	1.92 **2.53**	1.60 **1.89**
32	4.15 **7.50**	3.29 **5.34**	2.90 **4.46**	2.67 **3.97**	2.51 **3.65**	2.40 **3.43**	2.31 **3.26**	2.24 **3.13**	2.19 **3.02**	2.14 **2.93**	1.91 **2.51**	1.59 **1.88**
33	4.14 **7.47**	3.28 **5.31**	2.89 **4.44**	2.66 **3.95**	2.50 **3.63**	2.39 **3.41**	2.30 **3.24**	2.23 **3.11**	2.18 **3.00**	2.13 **2.91**	1.90 **2.49**	1.58 **1.87**
34	4.13 **7.44**	3.28 **5.29**	2.88 **4.42**	2.65 **3.93**	2.49 **3.61**	2.38 **3.39**	2.29 **3.22**	2.23 **3.09**	2.17 **2.98**	2.12 **2.89**	1.89 **2.47**	1.57 **1.86**
35	4.12 **7.42**	3.27 **5.27**	2.87 **4.40**	2.64 **3.91**	2.49 **3.59**	2.37 **3.37**	2.29 **3.20**	2.22 **3.07**	2.16 **2.96**	2.11 **2.88**	1.88 **2.45**	1.56 **1.85**
36	4.11 **7.40**	3.26 **5.25**	2.87 **4.38**	2.63 **3.89**	2.48 **3.57**	2.36 **3.35**	2.28 **3.18**	2.21 **3.05**	2.15 **2.95**	2.11 **2.86**	1.87 **2.43**	1.55 **1.84**
37	4.11 **7.37**	3.25 **5.23**	2.86 **4.36**	2.63 **3.87**	2.47 **3.56**	2.36 **3.33**	2.27 **3.17**	2.20 **3.04**	2.14 **2.93**	2.10 **2.84**	1.86 **2.42**	1.54 **1.83**
38	4.10 **7.35**	3.24 **5.21**	2.85 **4.34**	2.62 **3.86**	2.46 **3.54**	2.35 **3.32**	2.26 **3.15**	2.19 **3.02**	2.14 **2.92**	2.09 **2.83**	1.85 **2.40**	1.53 **1.82**
39	4.09 **7.33**	3.24 **5.19**	2.85 **4.33**	2.61 **3.84**	2.46 **3.53**	2.34 **3.30**	2.26 **3.14**	2.19 **3.01**	2.13 **2.90**	2.08 **2.81**	1.84 **2.39**	1.52 **1.81**
40	4.08 **7.31**	3.23 **5.18**	2.84 **4.31**	2.61 **3.83**	2.45 **3.51**	2.34 **3.29**	2.25 **3.12**	2.18 **2.99**	2.12 **2.88**	2.07 **2.80**	1.84 **2.37**	1.51 **1.80**
42	4.07 **7.27**	3.22 **5.15**	2.83 **4.29**	2.59 **3.80**	2.44 **3.49**	2.32 **3.26**	2.24 **3.10**	2.17 **2.96**	2.11 **2.86**	2.06 **2.77**	1.82 **2.35**	1.50 **1.78**
44	4.06 **7.24**	3.21 **5.12**	2.82 **4.26**	2.58 **3.78**	2.43 **3.46**	2.31 **3.24**	2.23 **3.07**	2.16 **2.94**	2.10 **2.84**	2.05 **2.75**	1.81 **2.32**	1.49 **1.76**
60	4.00 **7.08**	3.15 **4.98**	2.76 **4.13**	2.53 **3.65**	2.37 **3.34**	2.25 **3.12**	2.17 **2.95**	2.10 **2.82**	2.04 **2.72**	1.99 **2.63**	1.75 **2.20**	1.39 **1.60**
120	3.92 **6.85**	3.07 **4.79**	2.68 **3.95**	2.45 **3.48**	2.29 **3.17**	2.18 **2.96**	2.09 **2.79**	2.02 **2.66**	1.96 **2.56**	1.91 **2.47**	1.66 **2.03**	1.25 **1.38**
∞	3.84 **6.63**	3.00 **4.61**	2.60 **3.78**	2.37 **3.32**	2.21 **3.02**	2.10 **2.80**	2.01 **2.64**	1.94 **2.51**	1.88 **2.41**	1.83 **2.32**	1.57 **1.88**	1.00 **1.00**

Source: The entries in this table were computed by the author.

APPENDIX D

Table D.1 The Studentized Range Statistic (q)

The critical values for q correspond to alpha = .05 (lightface type) and alpha = .01 (boldface type).

	Range								
df_E	2	3	4	5	6	7	8	9	10
6	3.46 **5.24**	4.34 **6.32**	4.90 **7.02**	5.30 **7.55**	5.63 **7.98**	5.91 **8.33**	6.13 **8.62**	6.32 **8.87**	6.50 **9.10**
7	3.34 **4.95**	4.17 **5.91**	4.68 **6.54**	5.06 **7.00**	5.36 **7.38**	5.60 **7.69**	5.82 **7.94**	5.99 **8.17**	6.15 **8.38**
8	3.26 **4.75**	4.05 **5.64**	4.53 **6.21**	4.89 **6.63**	5.17 **6.97**	5.41 **7.26**	5.60 **7.47**	5.78 **7.70**	5.93 **7.89**
9	3.20 **4.60**	3.95 **5.43**	4.42 **5.95**	4.76 **6.34**	5.03 **6.67**	5.24 **6.91**	5.43 **7.13**	5.60 **7.33**	5.74 **7.50**
10	3.15 **4.48**	3.88 **5.27**	4.33 **5.77**	4.66 **6.14**	4.92 **6.43**	5.12 **6.67**	5.30 **6.89**	5.46 **7.06**	5.60 **7.22**
11	3.11 **4.38**	3.82 **5.16**	4.27 **5.63**	4.59 **5.98**	4.83 **6.25**	5.03 **6.48**	5.21 **6.69**	5.36 **6.85**	5.49 **7.01**
12	3.08 **4.32**	3.78 **5.05**	4.20 **5.50**	4.51 **5.84**	4.75 **6.10**	4.96 **6.32**	5.12 **6.52**	5.26 **6.67**	5.39 **6.82**
13	3.05 **4.26**	3.73 **4.97**	4.15 **5.41**	4.47 **5.74**	4.69 **5.98**	4.88 **6.19**	5.06 **6.39**	5.21 **6.53**	5.33 **6.68**
14	3.03 **4.21**	3.70 **4.90**	4.11 **5.33**	4.41 **5.64**	4.64 **5.88**	4.83 **6.10**	4.99 **6.28**	5.13 **6.41**	5.25 **6.56**
15	3.01 **4.17**	3.68 **4.84**	4.09 **5.26**	4.38 **5.56**	4.59 **5.80**	4.79 **6.01**	4.95 **6.18**	5.09 **6.31**	5.21 **6.46**
16	2.99 **4.13**	3.65 **4.79**	4.05 **5.19**	4.33 **5.50**	4.56 **5.72**	4.74 **5.94**	4.89 **6.10**	5.03 **6.23**	5.15 **6.37**

(Continued)

Table D.1 (Continued)

	Range								
df_E	2	3	4	5	6	7	8	9	10
17	2.98 **4.10**	3.63 **4.75**	4.02 **5.15**	4.30 **5.44**	4.52 **5.66**	4.70 **5.86**	4.85 **6.02**	4.99 **6.14**	5.11 **6.28**
18	2.97 **4.07**	3.62 **4.71**	4.01 **5.10**	4.29 **5.39**	4.49 **5.60**	4.68 **5.80**	4.84 **5.95**	4.97 **6.08**	5.08 **6.21**
19	2.96 **4.05**	3.59 **4.68**	3.98 **5.05**	4.26 **5.35**	4.47 **5.56**	4.65 **5.75**	4.80 **5.91**	4.93 **6.03**	5.04 **6.15**
20	2.95 **4.02**	3.58 **4.64**	3.96 **5.02**	4.24 **5.31**	4.45 **5.51**	4.63 **5.71**	4.78 **5.86**	4.91 **5.98**	5.01 **6.09**
22	2.94 **3.99**	3.55 **4.59**	3.93 **4.96**	4.20 **5.27**	4.41 **5.44**	4.58 **5.62**	4.72 **5.76**	4.85 **5.87**	4.96 **6.00**
24	2.92 **3.96**	3.53 **4.55**	3.91 **4.92**	4.17 **5.17**	4.37 **5.37**	4.54 **5.55**	4.69 **5.70**	4.81 **5.81**	4.92 **5.93**
26	2.91 **3.94**	3.52 **4.51**	3.89 **4.87**	4.15 **5.13**	4.36 **5.33**	4.53 **5.49**	4.67 **5.63**	4.79 **5.74**	4.90 **5.86**
28	2.90 **3.91**	3.50 **4.48**	3.87 **4.83**	4.12 **5.09**	4.33 **5.28**	4.49 **5.45**	4.63 **5.58**	4.75 **5.69**	4.86 **5.81**
30	2.89 **3.89**	3.49 **4.45**	3.85 **4.80**	4.10 **5.05**	4.30 **5.24**	4.47 **5.40**	0.60 **5.54**	4.73 **5.64**	4.84 **5.76**
40	2.86 **3.82**	3.45 **4.37**	3.79 **4.70**	4.05 **4.93**	4.23 **5.11**	4.39 **5.26**	4.52 **5.39**	4.65 **5.49**	4.73 **5.60**
60	2.83 **3.76**	3.41 **4.28**	3.75 **4.60**	3.98 **4.82**	4.16 **4.99**	4.31 **5.13**	4.44 **5.25**	4.56 **5.36**	4.65 **5.45**
100	2.81 **3.72**	3.36 **4.22**	3.70 **4.52**	3.93 **4.74**	4.11 **4.90**	4.26 **5.04**	4.39 **5.15**	4.50 **5.23**	4.59 **5.34**
∞	2.77 **3.64**	3.31 **4.12**	3.63 **4.40**	3.86 **4.60**	4.03 **4.76**	4.17 **4.88**	4.28 **4.99**	4.39 **5.08**	4.47 **5.16**

Source: The entries in this table were computed by the author.

APPENDIX E

Table E.1 Critical Values for the Pearson Correlation*

*To be significant, the sample correlation, *r*, must be greater than or equal to the critical value in the table.

	Level of Significance for One-Tailed Test			
	.05	.025	.01	.005
	Level of Significance for Two-Tailed Test			
df = *n* − 2	.10	.05	.02	.01
1	.988	.997	.9995	.99999
2	.900	.950	.980	.990
3	.805	.878	.934	.959
4	.729	.811	.882	.917
5	.669	.754	.833	.874
6	.622	.707	.789	.834
7	.582	.666	.750	.798
8	.549	.632	.716	.765
9	.521	.602	.685	.735
10	.497	.576	.658	.708
11	.476	.553	.634	.684
12	.458	.532	.612	.661
13	.441	.514	.592	.641
14	.426	.497	.574	.623
15	.412	.482	.558	.606
16	.400	.468	.542	.590
17	.389	.456	.528	.575

(Continued)

Table E.1 (Continued)

	Level of Significance for One-Tailed Test			
	.05	.025	.01	.005
	Level of Significance for Two-Tailed Test			
df = *n* − 2	.10	.05	.02	.01
18	.378	.444	.516	.561
19	.369	.433	.503	.549
20	.360	.423	.492	.537
21	.352	.413	.482	.526
22	.344	.404	.472	.515
23	.337	.396	.462	.505
24	.330	.388	.453	.496
25	.323	.381	.445	.487
26	.317	.374	.437	.479
27	.311	.367	.430	.471
28	.306	.361	.423	.463
29	.301	.355	.416	.456
30	.296	.349	.409	.449
35	.275	.325	.381	.418
40	.257	.304	.358	.393
45	.243	.288	.338	.372
50	.231	.273	.322	.354
60	.211	.250	.295	.325
70	.195	.232	.274	.302
80	.183	.217	.256	.283
90	.173	.205	.242	.267
100	.164	.195	.230	.254

Source: Table VI of R. A. Fisher and F. Yates, *Statistical Tables for Biological, Agricultural and Medical Research*, 6th ed. London: Longman Group Ltd., 1974 (previously published by Oliver and Boyd Ltd., Edinburgh). Adapted and reprinted with permission of Addison Wesley Longman.

APPENDIX F

Table F.1 Critical Values of Chi-Square (χ^2)

Level of Significance		
df	.05	.01
1	3.84	6.64
2	5.99	9.21
3	7.81	11.34
4	9.49	13.28
5	11.07	15.09
6	12.59	16.81
7	14.07	18.48
8	15.51	20.09
9	16.92	21.67
10	18.31	23.21
11	19.68	24.72
12	21.03	26.22
13	22.36	27.69
14	23.68	29.14
15	25.00	30.58
16	26.30	32.00
17	27.59	33.41
18	28.87	34.80

(Continued)

Table F.1 (Continued)

Level of Significance		
df	**.05**	**.01**
19	30.14	36.19
20	31.41	37.47
21	32.67	38.93
22	33.92	40.29
23	35.17	41.64
24	36.42	42.98
25	37.65	44.31
26	38.88	45.64
27	40.11	46.96
28	41.34	48.28
29	42.56	49.59
30	43.77	50.89
40	55.76	63.69
50	67.50	76.15
60	79.08	88.38
70	90.53	100.42

Source: From Table IV of R. A. Fisher and F. Yates, *Statistical Tables for Biological, Agricultural and Medical Research*, 6th ed. London: Longman Group Ltd., 1974 (previously published by Oliver and Boyd Ltd., Edinburgh). Reprinted with permission of Addison Wesley Longman Ltd.

APPENDIX G

Table G.1 Critical Values for the Spearman Correlation*

*To be significant, the sample correlation, *r*, must be greater than or equal to the critical value in the table.

	Level of Significance for One-Tailed Test			
	.05	.025	.01	.005
	Level of Significance for Two-Tailed Test			
n	**.10**	**.05**	**.02**	**.01**
4	1.000			
5	.900	1.000	1.000	
6	.829	.886	.943	1.000
7	.714	.786	.893	.929
8	.643	.738	.833	.881
9	.600	.700	.783	.833
10	.564	.648	.745	.794
11	.536	.618	.709	.755
12	.503	.587	.671	.727
13	.484	.560	.648	.703
14	.464	.538	.622	.675
15	.443	.521	.604	.654
16	.429	.503	.582	.635
17	.414	.485	.566	.615

(Continued)

Table G.1 (Continued)

	Level of Significance for One-Tailed Test			
	.05	.025	.01	.005
	Level of Significance for Two-Tailed Test			
n	.10	.05	.02	.01
18	.401	.472	.550	.600
19	.391	.460	.535	.584
20	.380	.447	.520	.570
21	.370	.435	.508	.556
22	.361	.425	.496	.544
23	.353	.415	.486	.532
24	.344	.406	.476	.521
25	.337	.398	.466	.511
26	.331	.390	.457	.501
27	.324	.382	.448	.491
28	.317	.375	.440	.483
29	.312	.368	.433	.475
30	.306	.362	.425	.467
35	.283	.335	.394	.433
40	.264	.313	.368	.405
45	.248	.294	.347	.382
50	.235	.279	.329	.363
60	0.214	.255	.300	.331
70	.190	.235	.278	.307
80	.185	.220	.260	.287
90	.174	.207	.245	.271
100	.165	.197	.233	.257

Source: Reprinted with permission from the *Journal of the American Statistical Association*.

APPENDIX H

Table H.1a Critical Values of the Mann-Whitney U for $\alpha = .05$*

*Critical values are provided for a one-tailed test at $\alpha = .05$ (lightface type) and for a two-tailed test at $\alpha = .05$ (boldface type). To be significant for any given n_A and n_B, the obtained U must be equal to or less than the critical value in the table. Dashes (–) in the body of the table indicate that no decision is possible at the stated level of significance and values of n_A and n_B.

$n_B \backslash n_A$	1	2	3	4	5	6	7	8	9	10	11	12	13	14	15	16	17	18	19	20
1	–	–	–	–	–	–	–	–	–	–	–	–	–	–	–	–	–	–	0	0
	–	–	–	–	–	–	–	–	–	–	–	–	–	–	–	–	–	–	–	–
2	–	–	–	–	0	0	0	1	1	1	1	2	2	2	3	3	3	4	4	4
	–	–	–	–	–	–	–	**0**	**0**	**0**	**0**	**1**	**1**	**1**	1	1	**2**	**2**	2	2
3	–	–	0	0	1	2	2	3	3	4	5	5	6	7	7	8	9	9	10	11
	–	–	–	–	**0**	**1**	**1**	**2**	**2**	**3**	**3**	**4**	**4**	**5**	5	6	6	7	7	8
4	–	–	0	1	2	3	4	5	6	7	8	9	10	11	12	14	15	16	17	18
	–	–	–	**0**	**1**	**2**	**3**	**4**	**4**	**5**	**6**	**7**	**8**	**9**	**10**	**11**	**11**	**12**	**13**	**13**
5	–	0	1	2	4	5	6	8	9	11	12	13	15	16	18	19	20	22	23	25
	–	–	**0**	**1**	**2**	**3**	**5**	**6**	**7**	**8**	**9**	**11**	**12**	**13**	**14**	**15**	**17**	**18**	**19**	**20**
6	–	0	2	3	5	7	8	10	12	14	16	17	19	21	23	25	26	28	30	32
	–	–	**1**	**2**	**3**	**5**	**6**	**8**	**10**	**11**	**13**	**14**	**16**	**17**	**19**	**21**	**22**	**24**	**25**	**27**
7	–	0	2	4	6	8	11	13	15	17	19	21	24	26	28	30	33	35	37	39
	–	–	**1**	**3**	**5**	**6**	**8**	**10**	**12**	**14**	**16**	**18**	**20**	**22**	**24**	**26**	**28**	**30**	**32**	**34**
8	–	1	3	5	8	10	13	15	18	20	23	26	28	31	33	36	39	41	44	47
	–	**0**	**2**	**4**	**6**	**8**	**10**	**13**	**15**	**17**	**19**	**22**	**24**	**26**	**29**	**31**	**34**	**36**	**38**	**41**
9	–	1	3	6	9	12	15	18	21	24	27	30	33	36	39	42	45	48	51	54
	–	**0**	**2**	**4**	**7**	**10**	**12**	**15**	**17**	**20**	**23**	**26**	**28**	**31**	**34**	**37**	**39**	**42**	**45**	**48**
10	–	1	4	7	11	14	17	20	24	27	31	34	37	41	44	48	51	55	58	62
	–	**0**	**3**	**5**	**8**	**11**	**14**	**17**	**20**	**23**	**26**	**29**	**33**	**36**	**39**	**42**	**45**	**48**	**52**	**55**
11	–	1	5	8	12	16	19	23	27	31	34	38	42	46	50	54	57	61	65	69
	–	**0**	**3**	**6**	**9**	**13**	**16**	**19**	**23**	**26**	**30**	**33**	**37**	**40**	**44**	**47**	**51**	**55**	**58**	**62**
12	–	2	5	9	13	17	21	26	30	34	38	42	47	51	55	60	64	68	72	77
	–	**1**	**4**	**7**	**11**	**14**	**18**	**22**	**26**	**29**	**33**	**37**	**41**	**45**	**49**	**53**	**57**	**61**	**65**	**69**
13	–	2	6	10	15	19	24	28	33	37	42	47	51	56	61	65	79	75	80	84
	–	**1**	**4**	**8**	**12**	**16**	**20**	**24**	**28**	**33**	**37**	**41**	**45**	**50**	**54**	**59**	**63**	**67**	**72**	**76**

(Continued)

Table H.1a (Continued)

$n_B \backslash n_A$	1	2	3	4	5	6	7	8	9	10	11	12	13	14	15	16	17	18	19	20
14	–	2	7	11	16	21	26	31	36	41	46	51	56	61	66	71	77	82	87	92
	–	**1**	**5**	**9**	**13**	**17**	**22**	**26**	**31**	**36**	**40**	**45**	**50**	**55**	**59**	**64**	**67**	**74**	**78**	**83**
15	–	3	7	12	18	23	28	33	39	44	50	55	61	66	72	77	83	88	94	100
	–	**1**	**5**	**10**	**14**	**19**	**24**	**29**	**34**	**39**	**44**	**49**	**54**	**59**	**64**	**70**	**75**	**80**	**85**	**90**
16	–	3	8	14	19	25	30	36	42	48	54	60	65	71	77	83	89	95	101	107
	–	**1**	**6**	**11**	**15**	**21**	**26**	**31**	**37**	**42**	**47**	**53**	**59**	**64**	**70**	**75**	**81**	**86**	**92**	**98**
17	–	3	9	15	20	26	33	39	45	51	57	64	70	77	83	89	96	102	109	115
	–	**2**	**6**	**11**	**17**	**22**	**28**	**34**	**39**	**45**	**51**	**57**	**63**	**67**	**75**	**81**	**87**	**93**	**99**	**105**
18	–	4	9	16	22	28	35	41	48	55	61	68	75	82	88	95	102	109	116	123
	–	**2**	**7**	**12**	**18**	**24**	**30**	**36**	**42**	**48**	**55**	**61**	**67**	**74**	**80**	**86**	**93**	**99**	**106**	**112**
19	0	4	11	18	25	32	39	47	54	62	69	77	84	92	100	107	115	123	130	138
	–	**2**	**8**	**13**	**20**	**27**	**34**	**41**	**48**	**55**	**62**	**69**	**76**	**83**	**90**	**98**	**105**	**112**	**119**	**120**
20	0	4	11	18	25	32	39	47	54	62	69	77	84	92	100	107	115	123	130	138
	–	**2**	**8**	**13**	**20**	**27**	**34**	**41**	**48**	**55**	**62**	**69**	**76**	**83**	**90**	**98**	**105**	**112**	**119**	**127**

Source: From KIRK. *Statistics*, 5E. © 2008 Wadsworth, a part of Cengage Learning, Inc. Reproduced by permission. www.cengage.com/permissions.

Table H.1b Critical Values of the Mann-Whitney *U* for $\alpha = .01$*

*Critical values are provided for a one-tailed test at $\alpha = .01$ (lightface type) and for a two-tailed test at $\alpha = .01$ (boldface type). To be significant for any given n_A and n_B, the obtained *U* must be equal to or less than the critical value in the table. Dashes (–) in the body of the table indicate that no decision is possible at the stated level of significance and values of n_A and n_B.

$n_B \backslash n_A$	1	2	3	4	5	6	7	8	9	10	11	12	13	14	15	16	17	18	19	20
1	–	–	–	–	–	–	–	–	–	–	–	–	–	–	–	–	–	–	–	–
	–	–	–	–	–	–	–	–	–	–	–	–	–	–	–	–	–	–	–	–
2	–	–	–	–	–	–	–	–	–	–	–	–	0	0	0	0	0	0	1	1
	–	–	–	–	–	–	–	–	–	–	–	–	–	–	–	–	–	–	**0**	**0**
3	–	–	–	–	–	–	0	0	1	1	1	2	2	2	3	3	4	4	4	5
	–	–	–	–	–	–	–	–	**0**	**0**	**0**	**1**	**1**	**1**	**2**	**2**	**2**	**2**	**3**	**3**
4	–	–	–	–	0	1	1	2	3	3	4	5	5	6	7	7	8	9	9	10
	–	–	–	–	–	**0**	**0**	**1**	**1**	**2**	**2**	**3**	**3**	**4**	**5**	**5**	**6**	**6**	**7**	**8**
5	–	–	–	0	1	2	3	4	5	6	7	8	9	10	11	12	13	14	15	16
	–	–	–	–	**0**	**1**	**1**	**2**	**3**	**4**	**5**	**6**	**7**	**7**	**8**	**9**	**10**	**11**	**12**	**13**
6	–	–	–	1	2	3	4	6	7	8	9	11	12	13	15	16	18	19	20	22
	–	–	–	**0**	**1**	**2**	**3**	**4**	**5**	**6**	**7**	**9**	**10**	**11**	**12**	**13**	**15**	**16**	**17**	**18**
7	–	–	0	1	3	4	6	7	9	11	12	14	16	17	19	21	23	24	26	28
	–	–	–	**0**	**1**	**3**	**4**	**6**	**7**	**9**	**10**	**12**	**13**	**15**	**16**	**18**	**19**	**21**	**22**	**24**

8	–	–	0	2	4	6	7	9	11	13	15	17	20	22	24	26	28	30	32	34
	–	–	–	**1**	**2**	**4**	**6**	**7**	**9**	**11**	**13**	**15**	**17**	**18**	**20**	**22**	**24**	**26**	**28**	**30**
9	–	–	1	3	5	7	9	11	14	16	18	21	23	26	28	31	33	36	38	40
	–	–	**0**	**1**	**3**	**5**	**7**	**9**	**11**	**13**	**16**	**18**	**20**	**22**	**24**	**27**	**29**	**31**	**33**	**36**
10	–	–	1	3	6	8	11	13	16	19	22	24	27	30	33	36	38	41	44	47
	–	–	**0**	**2**	**4**	**6**	**9**	**11**	**13**	**16**	**18**	**21**	**24**	**26**	**29**	**31**	**34**	**37**	**39**	**42**
11	–	–	1	4	7	9	12	15	18	22	25	28	31	34	37	41	44	47	50	53
	–	–	**0**	**2**	**5**	**7**	**10**	**13**	**16**	**18**	**21**	**24**	**27**	**30**	**33**	**36**	**39**	**42**	**45**	**48**
12	–	–	2	5	8	11	14	17	21	24	28	31	35	38	42	46	49	53	56	60
	–	–	**1**	**3**	**6**	**9**	**12**	**15**	**18**	**21**	**24**	**27**	**31**	**34**	**37**	**41**	**44**	**47**	**51**	**54**
13	–	0	2	5	9	12	16	20	23	27	31	35	39	43	47	51	55	59	63	67
	–	–	**1**	**3**	**7**	**10**	**13**	**17**	**20**	**24**	**27**	**31**	**34**	**38**	**42**	**45**	**49**	**53**	**56**	**60**
14	–	0	2	6	10	13	17	21	24	28	31	35	38	43	47	51	55	59	63	67
	–	–	**1**	**4**	**7**	**11**	**15**	**18**	**21**	**24**	**27**	**31**	**34**	**38**	**42**	**45**	**49**	**53**	**56**	**60**
15	–	0	3	7	11	15	19	24	28	33	37	42	47	51	56	61	66	70	75	80
	–	–	**2**	**5**	**8**	**12**	**16**	**20**	**24**	**29**	**33**	**37**	**42**	**46**	**51**	**65**	**60**	**64**	**69**	**73**
16	–	0	3	7	12	16	21	26	31	36	41	46	51	56	61	66	71	76	82	87
	–	–	**2**	**5**	**9**	**13**	**18**	**22**	**27**	**31**	**36**	**41**	**45**	**50**	**55**	**60**	**65**	**70**	**74**	**79**
17	–	0	4	8	13	18	23	28	33	38	44	49	55	60	66	71	77	82	88	93
	–	–	**2**	**6**	**10**	**15**	**19**	**24**	**29**	**34**	**39**	**44**	**49**	**54**	**60**	**65**	**70**	**75**	**81**	**86**
18	–	0	4	9	14	19	24	30	36	41	47	53	59	65	70	76	82	88	94	100
	–	–	**2**	**6**	**11**	**16**	**21**	**26**	**31**	**37**	**42**	**47**	**53**	**58**	**64**	**70**	**75**	**81**	**87**	**92**
19	–	1	4	9	15	20	26	32	38	44	50	56	63	69	75	82	88	94	101	107
	–	**0**	**3**	**7**	**12**	**17**	**22**	**28**	**33**	**39**	**45**	**51**	**56**	**63**	**69**	**74**	**81**	**87**	**93**	**99**
20	–	1	5	10	16	22	28	34	40	47	53	60	67	73	80	87	93	100	107	114
	–	**0**	**3**	**8**	**13**	**18**	**24**	**30**	**36**	**42**	**48**	**54**	**60**	**67**	**73**	**79**	**86**	**92**	**99**	**105**

Glossary

Algorithm: step-by-step procedure that guarantees a correct solution to a problem.

Alpha level (or significance level): probability value that states the likelihood that a statistical result occurred by chance.

Analysis of variance (ANOVA): statistical tool used to compare means of three or more groups of data.

Applied research: uses descriptive, predictive, and explanatory research methods to answer specific research questions in specific contexts.

Availability heuristic: estimating the frequency of some event happening, based on how easily we can think of examples of that event.

Bar graph: graphical representation of the frequency of nominal data in which each category appears on the x-axis and the frequency of occurrence for a given score appears on the y-axis.

Base-rate fallacy: tendency to prefer information derived from one's experience and ignore information that is representative of most people or situations.

Between-groups variability: amount of variability *between scores across groups*; includes an estimate of the effect of the independent variable and error variance.

Between-subjects design: experimental design in which participants are randomly assigned to one and only one experimental group (condition).

Bonferroni adjustment: dividing the alpha level (normally .05) by the number of statistical comparisons being made; this controls the chance of making a Type I error across all statistical tests being conducted.

Case studies: studies that examine in depth one or more people with a certain characteristic.

Ceiling effect: lack of variability in a dataset that occurs because scores are clustered together at the top end of the range of possible scores.

Central Limit Theorem: (a) for a given sample size, the distribution of sample means will have a mean equal to the population mean; (b) the distribution will have a standard deviation calculated by taking the population standard deviation and dividing it by the square root of the sample size; and (c) as the sample size increases, the distribution will be a normal distribution.

Conditions: term used to denote the number of groups in an experiment.

Confidence interval: interval estimate that contains the population mean a certain percentage of time, based on repeated sampling of that population.

Construct validity: degree to which a variable is operationalized appropriately.

Constructs: variables that cannot be directly assessed but must be inferred in some way.

Continuous variable: variable that can have a fractional value.

Correlation matrix: visual display of correlation coefficients.

Correlational method: analysis tool that examines how and the extent to which two variables are related to each other.

Criterion validity: how well a measure predicts an outcome.

Critical value: marks the start of the region of null hypothesis rejection; if a test statistic exceeds the critical value, it falls in the region of null hypothesis rejection.

Cronbach's alpha: measure of internal reliability; it is the mean correlation of all correlations between different possible halves of a measurement tool.

Curvilinear relationship: results when the relationship between two variables is not a linear relationship.

Degrees of freedom: number of scores in a sample that can be changed.

Dependent variable: behavior that results from the independent variable.

Descriptive research: depicts variables as they exist in the world.

Descriptive statistics: quantitative procedures that are used to organize and summarize (describe) information about a sample.

Difference score: number that is the difference between a person's performance in one experimental condition and his or her performance in a second experimental condition.

Directional (one-tailed) hypothesis: research hypothesis that states the nature (i.e., direction) of the relationship between variables in the population.

Discrete variable: variable that can only have a whole number value.

Effect size: statistical measurement of how powerful the relationship is between variables (e.g., between an independent variable and a dependent variable).

Egocentrism: tendency to perceive the world from our individual, unique perspective.

Error variance: amount of variability between scores resulting from uncontrolled variables and random variation.

Estimated standard error of the mean: estimate of the standard deviation of the sampling distribution.

Explanatory research: draws cause-and-effect relationships between variables.

Factor: variable that is expected to influence behavior or cognitions; factor is another name for *independent variable.*

Factorial design: research design that examines two or more influences on behavior.

Factorial notation: shorthand that tells us how many independent variables (factors) and how many levels of each independent variable (factor) a research study has.

Family-wise Type I error: likelihood of detecting at least one statistically significant result when conducting multiple statistical tests. It is called "family-wise" because it is the error rate for a series (family) of statistical tests.

Floor effect: lack of variability in a dataset that occurs because scores are clustered together at the low end of the range of possible scores.

Framing effect: tendency to be persuaded by the way information is presented.

Frequency distribution: table that contains all scores in a dataset, along with each score's frequency of occurrence.

Frequency polygon: line graph that displays frequency of occurrence of scores; used for continuous data.

Gambler's fallacy: tendency to think that two mutually exclusive outcomes are somehow related.

Grand mean: mean obtained from averaging scores across all groups in an experiment.

Grouped frequency distribution table: table that contains all scores in a dataset, clustering the scores into categories, and presents the frequency of occurrence for each category rather than for individual scores.

Heuristic: mental shortcut that allows us to make decisions quickly.

Histogram: similar to a bar graph, except used for ordinal and scale data that are discrete; that is, each score is different from all other scores.

Homogeneity of variances: assumption of the independent samples t test that the variability of each group is approximately equal.

Hypothesis: specific, formal prediction about the outcome of a research study.

Illusory correlation: tendency to perceive a relationship when no relationship really exists.

Independent samples t test: statistical tool used to compare means of two mutually exclusive groups of people.

Independent variable: variable that a researcher manipulates (changes) to create experimental groups (conditions). It should affect subsequent behavior or mental processes.

Inferential statistics: quantitative procedures that are used to learn if we can draw conclusions (inferences) about a population based on a sample.

Interaction: occurs when the effect of one factor depends on the levels of a second factor.

Internal reliability: extent to which people tend to score similarly on different parts of a measurement that is completed only once.

Interval scale: one on which the distance (interval) between each number is of the same magnitude.

Kurtosis: how "flat" or "peaked" a normal distribution is; indicates how much variability there is in the distribution of scores.

Law of small numbers: results based on small amounts of data are likely to be a fluke and not representative of the true state of affairs in the world.

Levels: term used to denote the number of groups in an experiment.

Line graph: graph used to depict the relationship between two scale variables.

Linear relationship: relationship between two variables that is displayed with a straight line.

Main effect: effect of one factor on a dependent variable.

Mean: arithmetic average of a dataset.

Median: middle score in a dataset that divides the dataset in half so that an equal number of scores fall above and below that score.

Mediating variable: variable that helps explain the relationship between two other variables.

Mode: most frequently occurring score in a dataset.

Multiple regression: statistical tool in which we use two or more predictor variables to forecast scores on an outcome variable.

Negative correlation: increases in one variable tend to be accompanied by decreases in a second variable. In other words, the two variables tend to relate in the opposite direction.

Negatively skewed distribution: data distribution in which there are a few unusually low (skewed) scores; most scores tend to be toward the high end of the distribution.

Nominal scale: categorical data.

Nondirectional (two-tailed) hypothesis: research hypothesis that does not state the nature (i.e., does not state the direction) of the relationship between variables in the population.

Nonlinear relationship: relationship between two variables that is displayed by a curved line.

Normal distribution: dataset in which the measures of central tendency are approximately equal to each other, thus, creating a symmetrical, bell-shaped distribution of scores.

Null hypothesis: hypothesis that there is no relationship between variables in the population that are being studied in a sample.

Observational studies: consist of watching behaviors in naturalistic and laboratory settings.

One-sample *t* test: parametric statistical tool that allows us to learn whether a sample differs from the population from which it was drawn when the population standard deviation is not known.

One-way, between-subjects ANOVA: analysis in which there is one independent variable and each participant is assigned to one and only one experimental level.

One-way, repeated-measures ANOVA: analysis in which there is one independent variable and each participant contributes data to all levels of the experiment.

Operational definition: specification of precisely how a variable is measured in a research study.

Ordinal scale: rank-ordered data.

Outcome variable: variable that is measured as a function of the predictor variable; also called a *criterion* variable.

Outlier: score that is extremely high or extremely low compared with most other scores in a dataset.

Paired samples *t* test: statistical tool used to compare the difference between two means provided by the same sample of people.

Parameter: number that expresses a value in the population.

Partial eta squared: measure of effect size that can be reported in an ANOVA.

Pearson moment correlation coefficient: statistic that quantifies the linear relationship between two variables; often referred to simply as a correlation coefficient.

Percentile rank: percentage of scores that are at or below a particular score in a normal distribution.

Population: entire group of people you want to draw conclusions about.

Positive correlation: increases (or decreases) in one variable tend to be accompanied by increases (or decreases) in a second variable. In other words, the two variables tend to relate in the same direction.

Positively skewed distribution: data distribution in which there a few unusually high (skewed) scores; most scores tend to be toward the low end of the distribution.

Predictive research: makes forecasts about future events.

Predictor variable: nonmanipulated variable that is used to forecast an outcome variable.

***p* value (or significance level):** probability that a statistical outcome was obtained by chance and is a Type I error.

Quasi-experiment: compares naturally existing groups, such as socioeconomic groups.

Random assignment: uses a random process, such as flipping a coin, to put members of a sample in one of the groups (conditions) in an experiment. Its purpose is to minimize preexisting differences among members of the sample so that researchers can be confident of the effects of the independent variable.

Range: the difference between the highest and the lowest score in a dataset.

Ratio scale: interval data that has a meaningful zero point.

Region of null hypothesis rejection: extreme sample results that are unlikely (depending on alpha level) to be obtained if the null hypothesis is true in the population. When a sample result lies in the region of null hypothesis rejection, we "reject" the null hypothesis.

Regression line: straight line that best fits (summarizes) the datapoints in a scatterplot.

Reliability: extent to which a measure produces consistent results.

Representativeness heuristic: judging how likely something or someone is to the typical instance of a mental category that we hold; can lead us to ignore other relevant information.

Research hypothesis: hypothesis that there is a relationship between variables in the population that are being studied in a sample.

Sample: subset of people from the population that is intended to represent the characteristics of the larger population.

Sampling distribution: distribution of sample means for a fixed sample size drawn from a population.

Sampling error: discrepancy between characteristics of the population and characteristics of the sample.

Scale data: refers to interval and ratio data without making a distinction between them.

Scatterplot: graph that visually displays the relationship between two scale variables.

Spurious correlation: real relationship between two variables or events that exists because both variables are correlated to a third, unmeasured variable.

Standard deviation: measure of the extent to which scores in a dataset tend to vary around the mean.

Standard error of the difference between the means: standard deviation of a difference between two group means.

Standard error of the difference scores: standard deviation of a mean difference score within a sample.

Standard error of the mean: standard deviation of the sampling distribution.

Statistic: number that expresses a value in the sample.

Statistical power: probability of rejecting a null hypothesis that is false in the population.

Statistical significance: occurs when an inferential statistical tool suggests that the null hypothesis should be rejected.

Sum of squares: sum of each score's squared deviation from the mean.

Surveys: series of questions to which people respond via a questionnaire or an interview.

Test statistic: result of using an inferential statistical tool that is compared to a critical value.

Test–retest reliability: extent to which people tend to score similarly on a measurement that is completed at two different points in time.

Time plot: type of line graph that plots the value of a variable on the y-axis as it changes over time, which is displayed on the x-axis.

Tukey's HSD post hoc test: procedure used after (hence, "post hoc") an F ratio has been calculated. This procedure allows us to learn which group means are significantly different from one another.

Type I error: rejecting a null hypothesis when it is true.

Type II error: failing to reject the null hypothesis when it is false.

Univariate regression: statistical tool in which we use one predictor variable to forecast scores on an outcome variable.

Valid: extent to which a measure is appropriate to use in a given context.

Values: term used to denote the number of groups in an experiment.

Variability: extent to which scores are similar (or different) in a dataset.

Variable: characteristic that has different values or changes among individuals.

Variance: average squared deviation from the mean.

Within-groups variability: amount of variability between scores *within each experimental group*.

Within-subjects design: research design in which each participant provides at least two responses to be compared. Stated differently, each participant is in every group created by the independent variable.

***z* score:** number that indicates how many standard deviations away from the mean a given score is.

***z* test:** parametric statistical tool that allows us to compare a sample to the population from which it was drawn when the population parameters are known.

Zero correlation: no relationship exists between two variables.

References

Allen, N. J., & Meyer, J. P. (1990). The measurement and antecedents of affective, continuance, and normative commitment to the organization. *Journal of Occupational Psychology, 63,* 1–18.

Asparouhova, E., Hertzel, M., & Lemmon, M. (2009). Inference from streaks in random outcomes: Experimental evidence on beliefs in regime shifting and the law of small numbers. *Management Science, 55,* 1766–1782.

Ayduk, O., Downey, G., & Kim, M. (2001). Rejection sensitivity and depressive symptoms in women. *Personality and Social Psychology Bulletin, 27,* 868–877.

Barber, L. K., & Santuzzi, A. M. (2015). Please respond ASAP: Workplace telepressure and employee recovery. *Journal of Occupational Health Psychology, 20,* 172–189.

Bar-Hillel, M. (1980). The base-rate fallacy in probability judgments. *Acta Psychologica, 44,* 211–233.

Baron, R. A., & Richardson, D. R. (2004). *Human aggression* (2nd ed.). New York, NY: Plenum.

Barsalou, L. W. (1999). Perceptual symbol systems. *Behavioral & Brain Sciences, 22,* 577–609.

Bass, R. N., Brown, D. D., Laurson, K. R., & Coleman, M. M. (2013). Physical fitness and academic performance in middle school students. *Acta Paediatrcia, 102,* 832–837.

Bernard, D. L., McManus, J. L., & Saucier, D. A. (2014). Blacks in the red: Racial discrimination in funding allocations. *Psi Chi Journal of Psychological Research, 19,* 28–36.

Blanchflower, D. G., & Oswald, A. J. (2008). Is well-being U-shaped over the life cycle? *Social Science & Medicine, 66,* 1733–1749.

Box, J. F. (1978). *R. A. Fisher: The life of a scientist*. New York, NY: Wiley.

Brustein, J. (2014, July). Americans now spend more time on Facebook than they do on their pets. *Bloomberg Business.* Retrieved April 11, 2016, from http://www.bloomberg.com/bw/articles/2014-07-23/heres-how-much-time-people-spend-on-facebook-daily

Bushman, B. J., Wang, M. C., & Anderson, C. A. (2005). Is the curve relating temperature to aggression linear or curvilinear? Assaults and temperature in Minneapolis reexamined. *Journal of Personality and Social Psychology, 89,* 62–66.

Buss, A. H., & Perry, M. (1992). The aggression questionnaire. *Journal of Personality and Social Psychology, 63,* 452–459.

Buysse, D. J., Reynolds III, C. F., Monk, T. H., Berman, S. R., & Kupfer, D. J. (1989). The Pittsburgh Sleep Quality Index: A new instrument for psychiatric practice and research. *Psychiatry Research, 28,* 193–213.

Campbell, C. R., & White, K. R. G. (2015). Working it out: Examining the psychological effects of music on moderate-intensity exercise. *Psi Chi Journal of Psychological Research, 20,* 73–79.

Cherulnik, P. D., & Wilderman, S. K. (1986). Symbols of status in urban neighborhoods: Contemporary perceptions of nineteenth-century Boston. *Environment and Behavior, 18,* 604–622.

Christopher, A. N., & Wojda, M. R. (2008). Social dominance orientation, right-wing authoritarianism, sexism, and prejudice toward women in the workforce. *Psychology of Women Quarterly, 32,* 65–73.

Clayton, R. B., Osborne, R. E., Miller, B. K., & Oberle, C. D. (2013). Loneliness, anxiousness, and substance use as predictors of Facebook use. *Computers in Human Behavior, 29,* 687–693.

Cohen, J. (1988). *Statistical power analysis for the behavioral sciences* (2nd ed.). Hillsdale, NJ: Erlbaum.

Cohen, J. (1992). A power primer. *Psychological Bulletin, 112,* 115–159.

College Board. (2015). *Average scores*. Retrieved December 1, 2014, from http://professionals.collegeboard.com/testing/sat-reasoning/scores/averages

Comer, R. J. (2015). *Abnormal psychology* (2nd ed.). New York, NY: Worth.

Costa, P. T., & McCrae, R. R. (2008). The Revised NEO Personality Inventory (NEO-PI-R). *The SAGE Handbook of Personality Theory and Assessment, 2,* 179–198.

Cox, L. S., Tiffany, S. T., & Christen, A. G. (2001). Evaluation of the brief questionnaire of smoking urges (QSU-brief) in laboratory and clinical settings. *Nicotine & Tobacco Research, 3,* 7–16.

Crandall, C. S., & Eshleman, A. (2003). A justification-suppression model of the expression and experience of prejudice. *Psychological Bulletin, 129,* 414–446.

Davidson, C. L., Babson, K. A., Bonn-Miller, M. O., Soutter, T., & Vannoy, S. (2013). The impact of exercise on suicide risk: Examining pathways through depression, PTSD, and sleep in an inpatient sample of veterans. *Suicide and Life-Threatening Behavior, 43,* 279–289.

Duckworth, A. L., Peterson, C., Matthews, M. D., & Kelly, D. R. (2007). Grit: Perseverance and passion for long-term goals. *Journal of Personality and Social Psychology, 9,* 1087–1101.

Ellison, N. B., Steinfield, C., & Lampe, C. (2007). The benefits of Facebook "friends:" Social capital and college students' use of online social network sites. *Journal of Computer-Mediated Communication, 12,* 1143–1168.

Eskine, K. J. (2012). Wholesome foods and wholesome morals? Organic foods reduce prosocial behavior and harshen moral judgments. *Social Psychological and Personality Science, 4,* 251–254.

Eysenck, S. G., Pearson, P. R., Easting, G., & Allsopp, J. F. (1985). Age norms of impulsiveness, venturesomeness, and empathy in adults. *Personality and Individual Differences, 6,* 613–619.

Federal Bureau of Investigation. (2015). *Uniform Crime Reporting Statistics*. Retrieved July 3, 2015, from http://www.ucrdatatool.gov/Search/Crime/State/RunCrimeTrendsInOneVar.cfm

Fenigstein, A., Scheier, M., & Buss, A. (1975). The self consciousness scale. *Journal of Consulting and Clinical Psychology, 43,* 522–527.

Fiedler, K. (2000). Illusory correlations: A simple associative algorithm provides a convergent account of seemingly divergent paradigms. *Review of General Psychology, 4,* 25–58.

Fratkin, J. L., & Baker, S. C. (2013). The role of coat color and ear shape on the perception of personality in dogs. *Anthrozoos, 26,* 125–133.

Gazzaniga, M. S., & LeDoux, J. E. (1978). *The integrated mind.* New York, NY: Plenum Press.

Gilovich, T., & Savitsky, K. (2002). Like goes with like: The role of representativeness in erroneous and pseudoscientific beliefs. In T. Gilovich, D. W. Griffin, & D. Kahneman (Eds.), *Heuristics and biases: The psychology of intuitive judgment* (pp. 617–624). New York, NY: Cambridge University Press.

Gilovich, T., Vallone, R., & Tversky, A. (1985). The hot hand in basketball: On the misperception of random sequences. *Cognitive Psychology, 17,* 295–314.

Gino, F., & Wiltermuth, S. S. (2014). Evil genius? How dishonesty can lead to great creativity. *Psychological Science, 25,* 973–981.

Glick, P., & Fiske, S. T. (1996). The Ambivalent Sexism Inventory: Differentiating hostile and benevolent sexism. *Journal of Personality and Social Psychology, 70,* 491–512.

Glick, P., Larsen, S., Johnson, C., & Branstiter, H. (2005). Evaluations of sexy women in low- and high-status jobs. *Psychology of Women Quarterly, 29,* 389–395.

Goldberg, L. R., Johnson, L. A., Eber, H. W., Hogan, R., Ashton, M. C., Cloninger, C. R., & Gough, H. C. (2006). The International Personality Item Pool and the future of public-domain personality measures. *Journal of Research in Personality, 40,* 84–96.

Goodman, G., Edwards, K., & Chung, H. (2014). Interaction structures formed in the psychodynamic therapy of five patients with borderline personality disorder in crisis. *Psychology and Psychotherapy, 87,* 15–31.

Haig, B. (2003). Understanding spurious correlations. *Understanding Statistics, 2,* 125–132.

Hardisty, D. J., Johnson, E. J., & Weber, E. U. (2010). A dirty word or a dirty world? Attribute framing, political affiliation, and query theory. *Psychological Science, 21,* 86–92.

Hassandra, M., Theodorakis, Y., Kosmidou, E., Grammatikopoulos, V., & Hatzigeorgiadis, A. (2009). I do not smoke—I exercise: A pilot study of a new educational resource for secondary education students. *Scandinavian Journal of Public Health, 37,* 372–379.

Herrera, C., Grossman, J. B., Kauh, T. J., & McMaken, J. (2011). Mentoring in schools: An impact study of Big Brothers-Big Sisters school-based mentoring. *Child Development, 82,* 346–361.

Hinkel, D. E., Wiersma, W., & Jurs, S. G. (1988). *Applied statistics for the behavioral sciences* (2nd ed.). Boston, MA: Houghton Mifflin.

Hoelter, J. (1979). Multidimensional treatment of fear of death. *Journal of Consulting & Clinical Psychology, 47,* 996–999.

Hoffman, N. G., Hunt, D. E., Rhodes, W. M., & Riley, K. J. (2003). UNCOPE: A brief substance dependence screen for use with arrestees. *Journal of Drug Issues, 33,* 29–44.

Hoyle, R. H., Stephenson, M. T., Palmgreen, P., Lorch, E. P., & Donohew, R. L. (2002). Reliability and validity of a brief measure of sensation seeking. *Personality and Individual Differences, 32,* 401–414.

Index Fund Advisors. (2014). *Step 9—History: Understand the historical risks and returns of indexes*. Retrieved November 1, 2014, from https://www.ifa.com/12steps/step9/

Jones, J. R. (2001). *What's in a name? Big Five inferences from given names* (Unpublished senior thesis). Anderson College, Anderson, SC.

Kanungo, R. N. (1982). Measurement of job and work involvement. *Journal of Applied Psychology, 67,* 341–349.

Kasser, T., & Sheldon, K. M. (2000). Of wealth and death: Materialism, mortality salience, and consumption behavior. *Psychological Science, 11*, 348-351.

Khawaja, N. G., & Armstrong, K. A. (2005). Factor structure and psychometric properties of the frost multidimensional perfectionism scale: Developing shorter versions using an Australian sample. *Australian Journal of Psychology*, *57*, 129–138.

Krawitz, R. (2004). Borderline personality disorder: Attitudinal change following training. *Australian and New Zealand Journal of Psychiatry, 38,* 554–559.

Kumar, A., Killingsworth, M. A., & Gilovich, T. (2014). Waiting for Merlot: Anticipatory consumption of experiential and material purchases. *Psychological Science, 25,* 1924–1931.

Lambert, N. M., Stillman, T. F., Hicks, J. A., Kamble, S., Baumeister, R. F., & Fincham, F. D. (2013). To belong is to matter: Sense of belonging enhances meaning in life. *Personality and Social Psychology Bulletin, 39,* 1418–1427.

Lessard, L., Grossman, A., & Syme, M. L. (2015). Effects of gender and type of praise on task performance among undergraduates. *Psi Chi Journal of Psychological Research 20,* 11–17.

Lyle, K. B., Hanaver-Torrez, S. D., Hackl Hackländer, R. P., & Edlin, J. M. (2012). Consistency of handedness, regardless of direction, predicts baseline memory accuracy and potential for memory enhancement. *Journal of Experimental Psychology: Learning, Memory, and Cognition, 38*, 187–193.

MacDonald, G., & Leary, M. R. (2005). Why does social exclusion hurt? The relationship between social pain and physical pain. *Psychological Bulletin, 131,* 202–223.

Macmillan, N. A., & Creelman, C. D. (2005). *Detection theory: A user's guide*. Mahwah, NJ: Lawrence Erlbaum.

Maslach, C., & Jackson, S. E. (1981). The measurement of experienced burnout. *Journal of Occupational Behavior, 2,* 99–113.

Mayer, J. D., & Gaschke, Y. N. (1988). The experience and meta-mood. *Journal of Personality and Social Psychology, 55,* 102–111.

McDowell, A., Trammell, J., & Krumrei-Mancuso, E. J. (2015). How handedness direction and consistency relate to declarative memory task performance. *Psi Chi Journal of Psychological Research, 20,* 228–235.

Mednick, S. A. (1962). The associative basis of the creative process. *Psychological Review*, *69*, 220–232.

Mittelmark, M. B., Aarø, L. E., Henriksen, S. G., Siqveland, J., & Torsheim, T. (2004). Chronic social stress in the community and associations with psychological distress: A social psychological perspective. *International Journal of Mental Health Promotion, 6,* 5–17.

Mueller, P. A., & Oppenheimer, D. M. (2014). The pen is mightier than the keyboard: Advantages of longhand over laptop note taking. *Psychological Science, 25,* 1159–1168.

Murdock, K. K. (2013). Texting while stressed: Implications for students' burnout, sleep, and well-being. *Psychology of Popular Media Culture, 2,* 207–221.

Nair, U. S., Collins, B. N., & Napolitano, M. A. (2013). Differential effects of a body image exposure session on smoking urge between physically active and sedentary female smokers. *Psychology of Addictive Behaviors, 27,* 322–327.

National Center for Education Statistics. (2014). *Fast facts*. Retrieved October 2, 2014, from http://nces.ed.gov/fastfacts/display.asp?id = 372

National Safety Council. (2015). *Injury Facts 2015 is your source for safety data*. Retrieved July 11, 2015, from http://www.prnewswire.com/news-releases/national-safety-council-statistics-indicate-falls-in-the-home-a-growing-problem-71044832.html

Nickerson, R. S. (2002). The production and perception of randomness. *Psychological Review, 109,* 330–357.

O'Hara, R. E., Walter, M. I., & Christopher, A. N. (2009). Need for cognition and conscientiousness as predictors of political interest and voting. *Journal of Applied Social Psychology, 39,* 1397–1416.

Pelham, B. W. (2013). *Intermediate statistics: A conceptual course*. Thousand Oaks, CA: Sage.

Pratto, F., Sidanius, J., Stallworth, L. M., & Malle, B. F. (1994). Social dominance orientation: A personality variable predicting social and political attitudes. *Journal of Personality and Social Psychology, 67,* 741–763.

Raskin, R., & Terry, H. (1988). A principal-components analysis of the Narcissistic Personality Inventory and further evidence of its construct validity. *Journal of Personality and Social Psychology, 54,* 890–902.

Reifman, A. S., Larrick, R. P., & Fein, S. (1991). Temper and temperature on the diamond: The heat-aggression relationship in major league baseball. *Personality and Social Psychology Bulletin, 17,* 580–585.

Reilly, M. D. (1982). Working wives and convenience consumption. *Journal of Consumer Research, 8,* 407–418.

Reiter, A. (2015, January). How many slices of pizza does the average American eat in a lifetime? *The Food Network.* Retrieved April 11, 2016, from http://blog.foodnetwork.com/fn-dish/2015/01/how-many-slices-of-pizza-does-the-average-american-eat-in-a-lifetime/

Richins, M. L., & Dawson, S. (1992). A consumer values orientation for materialism and its measurement: Scale development and validation. *Journal of Consumer Research, 19,* 303–316.

Rosenberg, M. (1965). *Society and the adolescent self-image.* Princeton, NJ: Princeton University Press.

Rozin, P. (1999). The process of moralization. *Psychological Science, 10,* 218–221.

Russell, D. W. (1996). UCLA Loneliness Scale (Version 3): Reliability, validity, and factor structure. *Journal of Personality Assessment, 66,* 20–40.

Schaufeli, W. B., Martinez, I. M., Marques Pinto, A., Salanova, M., & Bakker, A. B. (2002). Burnout and engagement in university students: A cross-national study. *Journal of Cross-Cultural Psychology, 33,* 464–481.

Singleton, R. A., Jr., & Wolfson, A. R. (2009). Alcohol consumption, sleep, and academic performance among college students. *Journal of Studies on Alcohol and Drugs, 70,* 355–363.

Snyder, B. (2015, July). Donald Trump announces he's worth over $10 billion. *Fortune.* Retrieved April 11, 2016, from http://fortune.com/2015/07/15/donald-trump-sec-filing/

Stanovich, K. E. (2004). *How to think straight about psychology* (7th ed.). Boston, MA: Pearson.

Stirling, B. D., Greskovich, M. S., & Johnson, D. R. (2014). Response bias toward fearful stimuli increases as stimulus noise increases. *Psi Chi Journal of Psychological Research, 19,* 37–42.

Taleb, N. N. (2004). Bleed or blowup? Why do we prefer asymmetric payoffs? *Journal of Behavioral Finance, 5,* 2–7.

Terrell, H. K., Hill, E. D., & Nagoshi, C. T. (2008). Gender differences in aggression: The role of status and personality in competitive interactions. *Sex Roles, 59,* 814–826.

Troisi, J. D., & Gabriel, S. (2011). Chicken soup really is good for the soul: "Comfort food" fulfills the need to belong. *Psychological Science, 22,* 747–753.

Tversky, A., & Kahneman, D. (1974). Judgment under uncertainty: Heuristics and biases. *Science, 185,* 1124–1131.

U.S. Department of State. (2014). *Terrorism deaths, injuries and kidnappings of private U.S. citizens overseas in 2013.* Retrieved December 29, 2014, from http://www.state.gov/j/ct/rls/crt/2013/224833.htm

U.S. Geological Survey. (2015). *Water questions & answers: How much water does the average person use at home per day?* Retrieved April 11, 2016, from http://water.usgs.gov/edu/qa-home-percapita.html

Wendt, L. M. (2013). *Academic burnout over the course of a collegiate career: A cross-sectional analysis of first-year and senior students* (Unpublished honor's thesis, Albion College, Albion, MI).

West, M. A., Borrill, C. S., & Unsworth, K. L. (1998). Team effectiveness in organizations. In C. L. Cooper & I. T. Robertson (Eds.), *International review of industrial and organizational psychology: 1998* (pp. 1–48). Chichester, England: Wiley.

Wong, A. Y. S., Hsia, Y., Chan, E. W., Murphy, D. G. M., Simonoff, E., Buitelaar, J. K., & Wong, I. C. K. (2014). The variation of psychopharmacological prescription rates for people with Autism Spectrum Disorder (ASD) in 30 countries. *Autism Research, 7,* 543–554.

Woodmansee, J. J., & Cook, S. W. (1967). Dimensions of racial attitudes: Their identification and measurement. *Journal of Personality and Social Psychology, 7,* 240–250.

Woodward, L., Milliken, J., & Humy, S. (2014). Give a dog a bad name and hang him: Evaluating big, black dog syndrome. *Society, Animals, & Welfare, 20,* 236–253.

Yan, X., Su, J., Zhu, X., & He, D. (2013). Loneliness and subjective happiness as mediators of the effects of core self-evaluations on life satisfaction among Chinese college students. *Social Indictors Research, 114,* 757–766.

Yerkes, R. M., & Dodson, J. D. (1908). The relation of strength of stimulus to rapidity of habit formation. *Journal of Comparative Neurology & Psychology, 18,* 459–482.

Zabel, K. L., Christopher, A. N., Marek, P., Wieth, M., & Carlson, J. J. (2009). Mediational effects of sensation seeking on the age and financial risk-taking relationship. *Personality and Individual Differences, 47,* 917–921.

Index

Chapter 10: Comparing Three or More Repeated Group Means: The One-Way, Repeated-Measures Analysis of Variance (ANOVA)		
Statistical Concept	**Plain English Description**	**Mathematical Formula**
Sums of squares (SS)	Sum of the squared deviations from the group mean	$\Sigma(x - M)^2$
Total sums of squares (SS total)	Sum of the squared deviation of each score from the grand mean in a [dataset]	Σ(x – grand mean)^2
Between sums of squares (SS between)	Sum of the squared deviation of each group mean from the grand mean, multiplied by the number of people in the group	Σ(group mean – grand mean)^2 x number of people in the group
Within-group sums of squared (SS within-groups)	Sum of the squared deviation of each score within a group from its group mean	Σ(x – group mean)^2
Error sums of squares (SS error)	Within-groups sums of squares minus participant individual differences	SSwithin-groups – SS participant
Participant individual differences (SS participant)	Sum of each person's overall mean score's squared deviation from the grand mean, multiplied by the number of groups in the analysis	Σ(overall mean score – grand mean)^2 x number of groups
Total degrees of freedom (df total)	Total number of responses, minus 1	Total number responses – 1
Between degrees of freedom (df between)	Number of groups being analyzed, minus 1	Number of groups – 1
Within-groups degrees of freedom (df within-groups)	Number of responses, minus the number of groups being analyzed	Total number of responses – number of groups
Participant degrees of freedom (df participant)	Sample size minus 1	Sample size – 1
Error degrees of freedom (df error)	Within-groups df minus participant df	df within-groups – df participant
Mean Square (MS)	Sums of squares divided by degrees of freedom	SS/df
Mean Square between (MS between)	Between sums of squares divided by between df	SS between/df between
Mean Square error (MS error)	Error sums of squares divided by error df	SS error/ df error
F ratio test statistic	Mean square between divided by mean square error	MS between/MS error
Effect size (partial eta squared)	Between sums of squares divided by between sums of squares plus error sums of squares	$\eta_p^2 = \frac{SS_{between}}{SS_{between} + SS_{error}}$
Honestly Significant Difference (HSD)	Square root of mean square error divided by the number of participants in each group, all multiplied by a constant (Q)	$= Q \times \sqrt{\frac{MS_{error}}{\text{number of participants in each group}}}$

Chapter 11: Analyzing Two or More Influences on Behavior: Factorial Designs for Two Between-Subjects Factors		
Statistical Concept	**Plain English Description**	**Mathematical Formula**
Sums of squares (SS)	Sum of the squared deviations from the group mean	$\Sigma(x - M)^2$
Total sums of squares (SS_{total})	Sum of the squared deviation of each score in the entire dataset from the grand mean in a dataset	Σ(x – grand mean)^2
Within-groups sums of squares($SS_{within\text{-}groups}$)	Sum of the squared deviation of each score within a group from its group mean	Σ(x – group mean)^2
Total between-groups sums of squares ($SS_{between\text{-}groups}$)	Sum of the squared deviation of each group mean from the grand mean	Σ(group mean – grand mean)^2
Between-groups sums of squares for each main effect ($SS_{main\ effect}$)	Marginal mean minus the grand mean, squared, then multiplied by the numbers of people in each group	(Marginal mean – grand mean)^2 x number of people in each group
Between-groups sums of squares for the interaction($SS_{interaction}$)	Total between-groups sums of squares minus between groups sums of squares for each main effect	$SS_{total} - SS_{first\ main\ effect} - SS_{second\ main\ effect}$
Total degrees of freedom (df_{total})	Total sample size minus 1	Sample size – 1
Within-groups degrees of freedom ($df_{within\text{-}groups}$)	Total sample size minus the number of groups being compared	Sample size – number of groups in the ANOVA
Between-groups sums of squares for each main effect ($df_{main\ effect}$)	Number of groups being compared for that factor minus 1	Number of groups - 1
Between-groups sums of squares for the interaction ($df_{interaction}$)	Degrees of freedom for each main effect multiplied together	$df_{main\ effect}$ x $df_{main\ effect}$
Mean Square (MS)	Sums of squares divided by degrees of freedom	SS/df
Mean Square within-group ($MS_{within\text{-}groups}$)	Within-groups sums of squares divided by within-groups degrees of freedom	$SS_{within\text{-}groups}/df_{within\text{-}groups}$
Mean Square between-groups for each main effect and interaction	Respective between-groups sums of squares divided by between-groups sums of squares	$SS_{between\text{-}groups}/df_{between\text{-}groups}$
F ratio test statistic for each main effect and interaction	Respective mean square between-groups divided by mean square within-groups	$MS_{between\text{-}groups}/MS_{within\text{-}groups}$
Effect size (partial eta squared)	Respective between-groups sums of squares divided by total sums of squares	$SS_{between\text{-}groups}/SS_{total}$